CONTRACT

This is a new type of book. It provides a
important academic and other writings on
in articles or journal chapters, or as books. These writings, with their full citation, are gathered under familiar contract law subject-headings, and the most significant half of them are digested in a summary of a few lines each. The book aims to cover all writings published in the English language about the Common Law of contracts, and includes sections on contract theory and the history of contract law, as well as sections for the more traditional substantive topics (such as the interpretation of contracts, penalty clauses, remoteness of damage and anticipatory breach).

This work should prove an invaluable resource for practitioners, academics and students, increasing awareness of important writings, and saving readers time by familiarising them with the work that has already been done in their particular fields.

Contract Law

An Index and Digest of Published Writings

Adam Kramer

•HART•
PUBLISHING
OXFORD AND PORTLAND, OREGON
2010

Published in North America (US and Canada) by
Hart Publishing
c/o International Specialized Book Services
920 NE 58th Avenue, Suite 300
Portland, OR 97213-3786
USA
Tel: +1 503 287 3093 or toll-free: (1) 800 944 6190
Fax: +1 503 280 8832
E-mail: orders@isbs.com
Website: http://www.isbs.com

Hart Publishing Ltd, 16C Worcester Place, Oxford, OX1 2JW
Telephone: +44 (0)1865 517530 Fax: +44 (0)1865 510710
E-mail: mail@hartpub.co.uk
Website: http://www.hartpub.co.uk

British Library Cataloguing in Publication Data
Data Available

ISBN: 978-1-84113-574-8

Typeset by Forewords, Oxon
Printed and bound in Great Britain by
TJ International Ltd, Padstow, Cornwall

For Kathryn

FOREWORD

It is a rare event to be able to write a foreword for a new type of book. We are now thoroughly familiar with textbooks, monographs, practitioner works, text cases and materials books and journal articles on the law of contract. This book is different in that it indexes leading writings on the law of contract, and does much more than merely list all the significant writings: the author provides a succinct account of the major pieces.

In this electronic age one might be forgiven for asking whether there is a need for a book of this type. After all, it is possible to search electronically for much legal material. However, it is not possible to search electronically for everything with ease. In particular, it can be extremely difficult to find essays which are published as chapters in books. Further, search engines do not differentiate between publications in terms of their quality. Thus, in drawing together in one volume leading contributions to our understanding of the law of contract, this book provides an extremely valuable service.

This book will be of interest to students, academics and practitioners. Its relevance to students and academics is clear. Perhaps less clear is its significance for practitioners. If this book had been produced thirty years ago, its relevance to practitioners would have been questioned. But times have changed. Today the work of academics is cited to and by appellate courts in many of our leading contract cases. It is therefore necessary for counsel to be familiar with the leading academic contributions to the issue that is before the court.

A book of this nature ideally requires an interest in academic legal issues as well as an involvement in legal practice. Adam Kramer fits these requirements perfectly: he is a barrister with a busy practice in commercial chambers, he has spent time as an academic lawyer in a leading law faculty and he continues to produce impressive, scholarly articles on the law of contract. Indeed, one of his essays was recently cited by the House of Lords in *Transfield Shipping Inc v Mercator Shipping Inc* [2008] UKHL 48, a decision that is notable for its references to academic materials of the type to be found in this book.

This book will, I am sure, facilitate the further citation of academic articles in our courts and it will also assist students and academics in their research projects. I look forward to using it in my own research. I hope that it will be widely consulted and that in time it will provide a model that others working in different areas of the law will choose to follow.

Ewan McKendrick
University of Oxford
October 2009

PREFACE

Whether lawyers (and by this I include academics, practitioners and judges) are aware of a relevant article or chapter of commentary at the right time has more to do with accidents of location, good memory, and downright luck than with the merit of the piece. How often has a crucial article been found while looking for something else, or during an unfocused flick through journals, books of essays or the footnotes of another article? I have found it irritating as a barrister and academic writer to know that there is almost certainly a relevant and helpful article that, despite diligent efforts, I will only become aware of a few weeks after final submission of my skeleton argument or publication of my own article. It is equally unsatisfying as an author of law writings to know that your carefully crafted contribution may well not be as widely read and therefore influential as it deserves.

Of course, there are the electronic indices and the commercial legal information providers, but I have found these variously not comprehensive, unwieldy, insufficiently discerning, uninformative or (for those not in universities) expensive. It is hoped that this book is none of those things.

The purpose of this book, then, is simply to make research by all contract lawyers easier. I have not sought to create an exhaustive database, but rather to include important and well-spread examples of works in each particular topic, knowing that the footnotes within those works will lead to further useful works. I have covered contract law not because it is the area most in need of an index and digest, but because it is the area I know best. Other books on other areas (probably written by other authors) may follow.

Readers that way inclined may also find this book interesting as showing how academic debate and publishing operates. Reading for this book I observed the worst and best of academia. I saw the sometimes justified but sometimes shameful republishing of the same article under different titles on different continents, and the churning out of banal pieces with no apparent purpose. I also saw the writers returning to wrestle with a topic again and again, and insightful contributions to a debate being overlooked by other academics for no good reason, or insightful debates that have been ignored in the courts. It is not always the fittest meme that survives, and any writer in universities knows that the demands of funding and promotion can steer the topics and destinations of research as much as inspiration and genuine interest. However, although I saw a lot of writing that added nothing or (which is not the same thing) was for other academics and could have no useful application to any point that might arise in a court, I also saw a large body of clever and helpful analysis that might well contribute to a skeleton argument or appellate judgment if only it were known of.

I began this experiment in around 2002, and Richard Hart, always game for a "punt" (his word), contracted it for publication shortly afterwards. I was a lecturer then, building on the increasingly long bibliographies at the end of my lecture notes. I then moved to London, became a barrister, got married, and wrote a book about how to become a barrister (also published by Hart), in that order. This book has progressed, ever so slowly, throughout. However the Alexander Maxwell Scholarship that I was awarded in 2007 allowed me to justify taking time out of my practice to finish this book off, and without that scholarship this probably would never have been finished. The other patrons have been my wife, Kathryn, and our cat, Daisy, neither of whom miaowed when I spent evenings and weekends working through volumes 25–46 of a particular journal rather than spending them at home. Thanks also go to Jamie Edelman for putting me right on a few points, and various friends whose early input helped shape the book.

A final thought: I invite readers not to rage into the abyss at glaring omissions or misunderstandings I have made of their own or others' works, but to let me know about them (akramer@3vb.com). If this book works, there will be a second edition eventually, and I can correct the failings of the first and improve the usefulness of the endeavour. (There may also be a companion website to allow for more prompt updating and correcting, an e-book should come out shortly after the print version, and that may be later adapted into an online searchable electronic resource.)

Adam Kramer
Gray's Inn, London
May 2009

CONTENTS

USING THIS BOOK

THE SELECTION

The book aims to cover articles, chapters, monographs and other books published in English about contract law in the common law world. From these, I have selected writings on each particular contract law topic that I think are the most useful, original or important, aiming to provide a reasonable coverage of jurisdictions and subject areas. I have presumptively favoured the readily available over the inaccessible, and the recent (because often more useful) over the old.

THE TIERS

The writings that are included are divided into two tiers.

First tier writings

These are recommended as the most useful, original or important.

As well as being listed, most of these first tier writings have been digested in a summary of a few lines.

Where no summary has been provided, this is because the title is all the summary needed, or the text is general and not susceptible to useful summary.

Second tier writings

These writings are recommended as useful, original and important, but to a lesser extent than the first tier writings. None of these are digested; they are all merely listed.

Further, in both tiers, those writings that are helpful as a general reference, summary or first port of call (as opposed to writings on a specific point or with a particular thesis) are marked with this symbol: ○

ARRANGEMENT

The writings are arranged under topic headings, and listed in chronological order within each topic, and author surname order within a particular year.

CAVEAT

Although the noble dream is of even coverage of all writings about contract law wherever published and in whatever field, the reality is inevitably less even. I do not pretend to have read every contract law writing ever published, and do not profess to have understood every one that I have read. This digest is naturally biased towards England and Wales, if only because of what was readily accessible to me. It is also biased by my sympathies: I am an Oxford-educated, white, male practitioner (barrister) in commercial litigation and black-letter/mid-level theoretical academic. I have little practical experience of transactional contract law and little academic experience of (for example) economic analysis (which, as many readers will know, is the most popular form of contract law analysis in the US). I find some writings easier to understand and therefore value, since they fit more easily into the tradition and conversation in which my own thoughts and work sit. For all of these reasons, I earnestly entreat readers to write in with suggestions for inclusion, with improvements to digests, or with other comments and recommendations.

1

TEXTBOOKS

1.1 GENERAL

Australia

- JW Carter, *Carter on Contract*, 2 vols, loose leaf (Sydney, LexisNexis, 2002 updated)
- NC Seddon and MP Ellinghaus, *Cheshire & Fifoot's Law of Contract*, 8th Australian edn (LexisNexis, 2002)
- JW Carter, Elisabeth Peden and GJ Tolhurst, *Contract Law in Australia*, 2 vols, 5th edn (Sydney, LexisNexis, 2007)
- Lindy Willmott, Sharon Christensen, Des Butler and Bill Dixon, *Contract Law*, 3rd edn (Melbourne, Oxford University Press, 2008)
- Jeannie Paterson, Andrew Robertson and Arlen Duke, *Principles of Contract Law*, 3rd edn (Sydney, Law Book Co, 2009)

Canada

- John D McCamus, *The Law of Contracts* (Toronto, Irwin Law, 2005)
- SM Waddams, *The Law of Contracts*, 5th edn (Toronto, Canada Law Book Inc, 2005)
- GHL Fridman, *The Law of Contracts*, 5th edn (Toronto, Carswell, 2006)
- A Swan, *Canadian Contract Law*, 2nd edn (LexisNexis, 2009)

England and Wales

- J Beatson, *Anson's Law of Contract*, 28th edn (Oxford, Oxford University Press, 2002)

- Patrick S Atiyah and Stephen A Smith, *An Introduction to the Law of Contract*, 6th edn (Oxford, Clarendon Press, 2006)
- M Furmston, *Cheshire, Fifoot & Furmston's Law of Contract*, 15th edn (Oxford, Oxford University Press, 2006)
- Michael Furmston (ed), *The Law of Contract*, 3rd edn (London, Butterworths, 2007)
- Edwin Peel, *Treitel on the Law of Contract*, 12th edn (London, Sweet & Maxwell, 2007)
- Hugh Beale (ed), *Chitty on Contracts: Volume 1: General Principles*, 30th edn (London, Sweet & Maxwell, 2008 plus supplements)

  The pre-eminent contract law textbook, both for coverage (vol 1 is over 2,000 pages) and authority, first published in 1826 from Joseph Chitty's text.

Europe

- Conor Quigley, *European Community Contract Law: Volume 1: The Effect of EC Legislation on Contractual Rights, Obligations and Remedies* (London, Kluwer Law International, 1997)
- Martijn Hesselink, *An Introduction to European Contract Law* (Oxford, Hart Publishing, 2009)

Hong Kong

- Betty M Ho, *Hong Kong Contract Law*, 2nd edn (Butterworths, 1994)
- Michael J Fisher and Desmond G Greenwood, *Contract Law in Hong Kong* (Hong Kong University Press, 2007)

India

- RG Padia, *Mulla on Indian Contract and Specific Relief Acts*, 2 vols, 13th edn (LexisNexis, 2006)
- Avtar Singh, *Law of Contract and Specific Relief*, 5th edn (2009)

Ireland

- Robert Clark, *Contract Law in Ireland*, 6th edn (Dublin, Round Hall, 2008)

Malaysia

- Dato' Seri Visu Sinnadurai, *Law of Contract*, 2 vols, 3rd edn (Kuala Lumpur, LexisNexis, 2003)

New Zealand

- John Burrows, Jeremy Finn and Stephen Todd, *Burrows Finn & Todd's Law of Contract in New Zealand*, 2nd edn (Wellington, LexisNexis, 2002)
- Maree Chetwin, Stephen Graw, Raymond Tiong, *An Introduction to the Law of Contract in New Zealand*, 4th edn (Wellington, Brookers, 2006)

South Pacific

- Jennifer Corrin Care, *Contract Law in the South Pacific* (London, Cavendish, 2001)

USA

- Arthur L Corbin, Joseph M Perillo et al., *Corbin on Contracts: Revised Edn,* 15 vols (St Paul, MN, West Publishing, 1993 plus supplements)
- Richard A Lord, *Williston on Contracts,* 31 vols, 4th edn (New York, Lawyers' Cooperative Publishing, 1990–1999 plus supplements)
- EA Farnsworth, *Farnsworth on Contracts*, 3rd edn (New York, Aspen Law & Business, 2003 plus supplements)

1.2 SPECIFIC CONTRACT TYPES (ENGLAND ONLY)

Bills of Exchange and Letters of Credit

- Peter Ellinger and Dora Neo, *Law and Practice of Documentary Letters of Credit* (Oxford, Hart Publishing, 2009)
- Ali Malek and David Quest, *Jack on Documentary Credits: The Law and Practice*, 4th edn (London, Tottel, 2009)

Bills of Lading and Contracts of Carriage

- Guenter H Treitel and FMB Reynolds, *Carver of Bills of Lading*, 2nd edn (London, Sweet & Maxwell, 2005)
- John F Wilson, *Carriage of Goods by Sea*, 6th edn (Pearson, 2007)
- Richard Aikens, Michael Bools and Richard Lord, *Bills of Lading* (Informa, 2007)
- Hugh Beale (ed), *Chitty on Contracts: Volume 2: Specific Contracts*, 30th edn (London, Sweet & Maxwell, 2008) chs 35–36
- Stewart C Boyd, Steven Berry, Andrew S Burrows, Bernard Eder, David Foxton and Christopher F Smith, *Scrutton on Charterparties and Bills of Lading*, 21st edn (London, Sweet & Maxwell, 2008)
- Malcolm Clarke and David Yates, *Contracts of Carriage by Land and Air*, 2nd edn (Informa, 2008)

Charterparties

- Michael Wilford, Terence Coghlin and John D Kimball, *Time Charters*, 5th edn (London, Lloyd's, 2003)
- Stewart C Boyd, Steven Berry, Andrew S Burrows, Bernard Eder, David Foxton and Christopher F Smith, *Scrutton on Charterparties and Bills of Lading*, 21st edn (London, Sweet & Maxwell, 2008)

Commercial Law

- Roy Goode and Ewan McKendrick, *Commercial Law*, 4th edn (LexisNexis Butterworths, 2009)

Computer Contracts

- Richard Morgan and Kit Burden, *Morgan & Burden on Computer Contracts*, 8th edn (London, Sweet & Maxwell, 2009)

Construction Contracts

- Stephen Furst, Vivian Ramsey, Adrian Williamson and John Uff, *Keating on Building Contracts*, 8th edn (London, Sweet & Maxwell, 2006 plus supplements)
- Richard Wilmot-Smith, *Construction Contracts: Law and Practice* (Oxford, Oxford University Press, 2006)
- Hugh Beale (ed), *Chitty on Contracts: Volume 2: Specific Contracts*, 30th edn (London, Sweet & Maxwell, 2008) ch 37
- Atkin Chambers, *Hudson's Building and Engineering Contracts*, 2 vols, 12th edn (London, Sweet & Maxwell, 2009 plus supplements)
- *Emden's Construction Law*, 7 vols, loose leaf (London, Butterworths, updated)

Consumer Credit Contracts

- Fred Philpott, William Hibbert, Stephen Neville, Simon Popplewell, Bradley Say, Peter Sayer and Julia Smith, *The Law of Consumer Credit and Hire* (Oxford, Oxford University Press, 2009)
- Roy Goode, *Consumer Credit: Law and Practice*, loose leaf (LexisNexis Butterworths, updated)

Employment Contracts

- DK Dix, Douglas Crump and David Pugsley, *Contracts of Employment*, 7th edn (London, Butterworths, 1997)

- Janet Gaymer, *The Employment Relationship* (London, Sweet & Maxwell, 2000)
- Mark R Freedland, *The Personal Employment Contract* (Oxford, Oxford University Press, 2005)
- Douglas Brodie, *The Employment Contract: Legal Principles, Drafting and Interpretation* (Oxford, Oxford University Press, 2005)
- Hugh Beale (ed), *Chitty on Contracts: Volume 2: Specific Contracts*, 30th edn (London, Sweet & Maxwell, 2008) ch 39

Guarantees

- Geraldine Andrews and Richard Millett, *Law of Guarantees*, 5th edn (London, Sweet & Maxwell, 2007)
- Hugh Beale (ed), *Chitty on Contracts: Volume 2: Specific Contracts*, 30th edn (London, Sweet & Maxwell, 2008) ch 44
- Jim O'Donovan and John Phillips, *The Modern Law of Guarantee*, 2nd English edn (London, Sweet & Maxwell, forthcoming 2010)
- Richard Salter (ed), *The Modern Law of Guarantees* (LexisNexis Butterworths, 2009)

Insurance and Reinsurance Contracts

- Colin Edelman, *The Law of Reinsurance* (Oxford, Oxford University Press, 2005)
- Hugh Beale (ed), *Chitty on Contracts: Volume 2: Specific Contracts*, 30th edn (London, Sweet & Maxwell, 2008) ch 41
- Malcolm A Clarke, *The Law of Insurance Contracts*, 5th edn (London, LLP, 2006) and *Law of Insurance Contracts*, loose leaf (London, LLP, updated)
- Nicholas Leigh-Jones, John Birds and David Owen, *MacGillivray on Insurance Law*, 11th edn (London, Sweet & Maxwell, 2008)
- Robert Merkin, *Colinvaux and Merkin's Insurance Contract Law*, loose leaf (London, Sweet & Maxwell, updated)
- John S Butler and Robert M Merkin, *Reinsurance Law*, 2 vols, loose leaf (London, Sweet & Maxwell, updated)
- Terry O'Neill and Jan Woloniecki, *The Law of Reinsurance in England and Bermuda*, 3rd edn (London, Sweet & Maxwell, 2009)

Joint Venture Agreements

- Ian Hewitt, *Joint Ventures*, 4th edn (London, Sweet & Maxwell, 2008)

Loans

- James O'Donovan, *Lender Liability* (London, Sweet & Maxwell, 2005)

Music and Media Contracts

- Richard Bagehot and Nicholas Kanaar, *Music Business Agreements*, 3rd edn (London, Sweet & Maxwell, 2009)
- Deborah Fosbrook and Adrian C Laing, *Media and Business Contracts Handbook*, 4th edn (London, Sweet & Maxwell, 2009)

Partnership Agreements

- Mark Blackett-Ord, *Partnership Law*, 3rd edn (Tottel, 2007)
- Roderick I'Anson Banks, *Lindley and Banks on Partnership*, 18th edn (London, Sweet & Maxwell, 2002 plus supplements)

Sale and Supply Contracts

- Hugh Beale (ed), *Chitty on Contracts: Volume 2: Specific Contracts*, 30th edn (London, Sweet & Maxwell, 2008) ch 43
- Richard Christou, *Sale and Supply of Goods and Services* (London, Sweet & Maxwell, 2007)
- MG Bridge, *Sale of Goods*, 2nd edn (Oxford, Oxford University Press, 2009)
- AG Guest et al, *Benjamin's Sale of Goods*, 7th edn (London, Sweet & Maxwell, 2006 plus supplement)

Settlement Agreements

- David Foskett and others, *The Law and Practice of Compromise*, 7th edn (London, Sweet & Maxwell, 2009)

Shareholders' Agreements

- John Cadman, *Shareholders' Agreements*, 5th edn (London, Sweet & Maxwell, 2009)
- Katherine Reece Thomas and Chris Ryan, *The Law and Practice of Shareholders' Agreements*, 3rd edn (London, LexisNexis Butterworths, 2009)

Professional Services Contracts

- John L Powell and Roger Stewart, *Jackson and Powell on Professional Negligence*, 6th edn (London, Sweet & Maxwell, 2006 plus supplements)
- AM Dugdale, *Professional Negligence*, 4th edn (London, LexisNexis, 2007)
- Mark Simpson (ed), *Professional Negligence and Liability*, 2 vols, loose leaf (London, LLP, updated)

Wills

- John Ross Martyn, Stuart Bridge and Mika Oldham, *Theobald on Wills*, 16th edn (London, Sweet & Maxwell, 2001)
- Francis Barlow, Christopher Sherrin, Richard Wallington, Susannah Meadway and Michael Waterworth, *Williams on Wills*, 9th edn (London, LexisNexis Butterworths, 2008)

1.3 TORT AND RESTITUTION

Australia and New Zealand

- Ross Grantham and Charles Rickett, *Enrichment and Restitution in New Zealand* (Oxford, Hart Publishing, 2000)

- Francis Trinidade and Peter Cane, *The Law of Torts in Australia*, 4th edn (South Melbourne, Oxford University Press, 2007)
- Rosalie Balkin and Jim Davis, *Law of Torts*, 4th edn (Sydney, Butterworths, 2008)
- Keith Mason, J W Carter and GJ Tolhurst, *Restitution Law in Australia*, 2nd edn (Sydney, LexisNexis Butterworths, 2008)
- James Edelman and Elise Bant, *Unjust Enrichment in Australia* (Oxford University Press, 2006)

Canada

- Lewis N Klar, *Tort Law*, 4th edn (Toronto, Carswell, 2008)
- Peter D Maddaugh and John D McCamus, *The Law of Restitution*, 2nd edn (Toronto, Canada Law Book, 2004)

England and Wales

- S WH Rogers, *Winfield & Jolowicz on Tort*, 17th edn (London, Sweet & Maxwell, 2006)
- Gareth Jones, *Goff & Jones: The Law of Restitution*, 7th edn (London, Sweet & Maxwell, 2006 plus supplements)
- Anthony Dugdale (ed), *Clerk and Lindsell on Torts*, 18th edn (London, Sweet & Maxwell, 2004 plus supplements)
- Andrew Burrows, *The Law of Restitution*, 3rd edn (Oxford, Oxford University Press, 2010)

USA

- George E Palmer, *Law of Restitution*, 4 vols (New York, Aspen Publishers, 1978 plus supplements)

1.4 STUDENT TEXTS (ENGLAND ONLY)

University Texts and Casebooks

- HG Beale, WD Bishop and MP Furmston, *Contract: Cases and Materials*, 5th edn (Oxford, Oxford University Press, 2007)
- Mindy Chen-Wishart, *Contract Law*, 2nd edn (Oxford, Oxford University Press, 2008)
- Ewan McKendrick, *Contract Law: Text, Cases and Materials*, 3rd edn (Oxford, Oxford University Press, 2008)
- Andrew Burrows, *A Casebook on Contract*, 2nd edn (Oxford, Hart Publishing, 2009)

1.5 FOR CIVIL LAWYERS

Rainer Wörlen, *An Introduction to English Civil Law I*, 2nd edn (Alpmann und Schmidt, 2002) ch 6; Marcella Chartrand, Catherine Millar and Edward Wiltshire, *English for Contract and Company Law*, 2nd edn (London, Sweet & Maxwell, 2003); John Cartwright, *An Introduction to the English Law for Civil Lawyers* (Oxford, Hart Publishing, 2007)
In English.

Giovanni Criscuoli, *Il contratto nel diritto inglese* [*The Contract in English law*], 2nd edn (Padova, CEDAM, 2001); Guido Alpa and Rossella Delfino, *Il Contratto nel Common Law inglese* [*The Contract in English Common Law*], 2nd edn (Padova, CEDAM, 2005)
In Italian.

Pierre Lerat and Jean-Louis Sourioux, *Dictionnaire juridique: terminologie du contrat* [*Legal Dictionary: Contract Terminology*] (Paris, Conseil international de la langue française, 1994); Michael Jewell, *An Introduction to English Contract Law* [for German student, with German comparative materials, in English], 2nd edn (Baden-Baden, Nomos Verlagsgesellschaft, 2002)
In German.

E Farnsworth, *Introduccion Sistema Legal de los Estados Unidos* [*Introduction to the US Legal System*] (Buenos Aires, Zavalia, 1990) ch 11
In Spanish.

Pierre Lerat and Jean-Louis Sourioux, *Dictionnaire juridique: terminologie du contrat* [*Legal Dictionary: Contract Terminology*] (Paris, Conseil international de la langue française, 1994); J-C Montanier and G Samuel, *Le contrat en droit anglais* (Presses Universitaires de Grenoble, 1999); Olivier Moréteau, *Droit anglais des affaires* [*English Business Law*] (Dalloz, 2000)
In French.

2

PRE-CONTRACTUAL LIABILITY

2.1 GENERALLY

Ewoud H Hondius (ed), *Precontractual Liability: Reports to the XIIIth Congress International Academy of Comparative Law* (Boston, Kluwer, 1991)

SM Waddams, 'Pre-Contractual Duties of Disclosure' in Peter Cane and Jane Stapleton (eds), *Essays for Patrick Atiyah* (Oxford, Clarendon Press, 1991) 237–56

Nili Cohen, 'Pre-Contractual Duties: Two Freedoms and the Contract to Negotiate' in Jack Beatson and Daniel Friedmann (eds), *Good Faith and Fault in Contract Law* (Oxford, Clarendon Press, 1995) 25–56

Paula Giliker, *Pre-Contractual Liability in English and French Law* (London, Kluwer Law International, 2002)

Kit Barker, 'Coping with Failure—Reappraising Pre-Contractual Remuneration' (2003) 19 *Journal of Contract Law* 105–33

John Cartwright and Marijn Hesselink (eds), *Precontractual Liability in European Private Law* (Cambridge, Cambridge University Press, 2009)

2.2 PRELIMINARY AGREEMENTS

Generally

E Allan Farnsworth, 'Precontractual Liability and Preliminary Agreements: Fair Dealing and Failed Negotiations' (1987) 87 *Columbia Law Review* 217–94

By enforcing agreements with open terms, agreements to negotiate, and other preliminary agreements, the law adequately provides for negotiating parties who have not yet reached a detailed final agreement. In an appendix the author outlines six types of preliminary agreement and the legal issues they raise.

Alan Schwartz and Robert E Scott, 'Precontractual Liability and Preliminary Agreements' (2007) 120 *Harvard Law Review* 661–707

○ Michael Furmston and Jill Poole, *Contract Formation: Law and Practice* (Oxford, Oxford University Press, 2010)

Letters of Intent

SN Ball, 'Work Carried Out in Pursuance of Letters of Intent—Contract or Restitution?' (1983) 99 *Law Quarterly Review* 572–92

○ Ralph B Lake and Ugo Draetta, *Letters of Intent and Other Precontractual Documents*, 2nd edn (Stoneham Massachusetts, Butterworths, 1994)

Michael Furmston, 'Letters of Intent and Other Preliminary Agreements' (2009) 25 *Journal of Contract Law* 95–107

Contracts to Negotiate

Charles L Knapp, 'Enforcing the Contract to Bargain' (1969) 44 *New York University Law Review* 673–728

Ian Brown, 'The Contract to Negotiate: A Thing Writ in Water' [1992] *Journal of Business Law* 353–68

Jeannie Marie Paterson, 'The Contract to Negotiate in Good Faith: Recognition and Enforcement' (1996) 10 *Journal of Contract Law* 120–40

A contract to negotiate in good faith should be upheld where it is certain and intended to be binding.

D McLauchlan, 'Rethinking Agreements to Agree' (1998) 18 *New Zealand Universities Law Review* 77–98

Parties should be bound if they intended to bind themselves, even if material terms remain to be agreed later, although this latter fact is relevant evidence as to whether the parties did intend to bind themselves.

D McLauchlan, 'The Justiciability of An Agreement to Negotiate in Good Faith' (2003) 20 *New Zealand Universities Law Review* 265–98

Umbrella Contracts

Stefanos Mouzos and Michael Furmston, 'From Contract to Umbrella Agreement' [2008] *Cambridge Law Journal* 37–50

Firm/Irrevocable Offers

DO McGovney, 'Irrevocable Offers' (1914) 27 *Harvard Law Review* 644–63

Where a promise to keep an offer open for a certain period is binding (because made in a deed or for consideration), purported revocation is not a successful revocation that gives a right to damages, but rather is no revocation at all and merely a breach sounding in damages.

Franklin M Schultz, 'The Firm Offer Puzzle: A Study of Business Practice in the Construction Industry' (1952) 19 *University of Chicago Law Review* 237–85; Richard Lewis, 'Contracts Between Businessmen: Reform of the Law of Firm Offers and an Empirical Study of Tendering Practices in the Building Industry' (1982) 9 *Journal of Law and Society* 153–75

Schulz: Despite the law, construction sub-contractors in practice consider firm offers to be binding. Lewis: Empirical investigation of tendering by construction sub-contractors shows that firm bids are often not considered by either party to be binding, and that where they are so considered resort is made to non-legal rather than legal sanctions.

Samuel J Stoljar, 'The False Distinction between Bilateral and Unilateral Contracts' (1955) 64 *Yale Law Journal* 515–36

Firm offers should be binding when they are relied upon (eg by use of a subcontractor's offer in producing a tender): they are reliance-bargains and are enforceable to protect the reliance interest.

Law Commission, *Working Paper 60: Firm Offers* (1975)

Firm offers should be binding if made in the course of business.

Michael J Cozzillio, 'The Option Contract: Irrevocable, not Irrejectable' (1990) 39 *Catholic University Law Review* 491–556

Avery Katz, 'When Should an Offer Stick? The Economics of Promissory Estoppel in Preliminary Negotiations' (1996) 105 *Yale Law Journal* 1249–1309

The law need not only seek to reflect what reliance already exists in the market, but can also regulate, because sophisticated players will adjust their reliance to the then prevailing legal rules. The most efficient rule would hold parties with high bargaining power to their pre-contractual offers (encouraging them to choose the most efficient time to invite reliance and so contract), but not hold parties with low bargaining power to theirs.

Omri Ben-Shahar, 'Contracts Without Consent: Exploring a New Basis for Contractual Liability' (2004) 152 *University of Pennsylvania Law Review* 1829–72

Melvin A Eisenberg, 'The Revocation of Offers' [2004] *Wisconsin Law Review* 271–308

Firm offers should be irrevocable, in both bilateral and unilateral contract cases.

2.3 DUTIES TO BARGAIN IN GOOD FAITH

Friedrich Kessler and Edith Fine, 'Culpa in Contrahendo, Bargaining in Good Faith, and Freedom of Contract: A Comparative Study' (1964) 77 *Harvard Law Review* 401–49

Tariq Hassan, 'The Principle of Good Faith in the Formation of Contracts' (1980) 5 *Suffolk Transnational Law Journal* 1–52

John Spencer, 'A Call for a Common Law Culpa in Contrahendo Counterpart' (1981) 15 *University of San Francisco Law Review* 587–616

Yoav Ben-Dror, 'The Perennial Ambiguity of Culpa in Contrahendo' (1983) 27 *American Journal of Legal History* 142–98

Pierre Legrand Jr, 'Pre-contractual Disclosure and Information: English and French Law Compared' (1986) 6 *Oxford Journal of Legal Studies* 322–52 and Paula Giliker, 'Regulating Contracting Behaviour: The Duty to Disclose in English and French Law' (2005) 13 *European Review of Private Law* 621–40

JW Carter and MP Furmston, 'Good Faith and Fairness in the Negotiation of Contracts: Parts I and II' (1994) 8 *Journal of Contract Law* 1–15 and 93–119

Although there is no general duty of good faith in pre-contractual negotiations, ideas of good faith inform the court's approach to questions of certainty and to pre-contractual liability through tort, restitution and collateral contract.

2.4 TORTS

Textbooks on Misstatements and Misrepresentations

- George Spencer Bower, Alex Kincombe Turner and KR Handley, *Actionable Misrepresentation*, 4th edn (London, Butterworths, 2000) ch 22
- Christian Witting, *Liability for Negligent Misstatements* (Oxford, Oxford University Press, 2004)
- John Cartwright, *Misrepresentation, Mistake and Non-Disclosure*, 2nd edn (London, Sweet and Maxwell, 2007)
- AM Dugdale, 'Negligence' in his (as ed), *Clerk and Lindsell on Torts*, 19th edn (London, Sweet & Maxwell, 2008 plus supplements) ch 8

Generally

DW McLauchlan, 'Pre-contractual Negligent Misrepresentation' (1977–80) 4 *Otago Law Review* 23–55

Barry J Reiter, 'Contracts, Torts, Relations and Reliance' in Barry J Reiter and John Swan (eds), *Studies in Contract Law* (Toronto, Butterworths, 1980) 235–311

G Richard Shell, 'Opportunism and Trust in the Negotiation of Commercial Contracts: Towards a New Cause of Action' (1991) 44 *Vanderbilt Law Review* 221–82

A proposal of a new cause of action of 'opportunistic breach of the bargaining relationship' to protect, by means of a reliance-based award, those who rely during pre-contractual negotiations upon (usually tacit) invitations to trust by then carrying out high-risk investment in the negotiation process, which investment is then wasted/lost.

Sharon Christensen, 'Recovery for Work Performed in Anticipation of Contract: Is Reliance an Element of Benefit?' (1993) 11 *Australian Bar Review* 144–62

Joachim Dietrich, 'Classifying Precontractual Liability: A Comparative Analysis' (2001) 21 *Legal Studies* 153–90 and 'The "Other" Category in the Classification of Obligations' in Andrew Robertson (ed), *The Law of Obligations: Connections and Boundaries* (London, UCL Press, 2004) 111–26

Pre-contractual liability cases sit on a spectrum between tort and contract rather than belonging fully to either cause of action. [2001] All the cases could be consolidated into a single action as in the Civilian doctrine of *culpa in contrahendo*. [2004] They share common features (namely detrimental reliance by the claimant on a belief that a contract does or will exist, and conduct of the defendant that gives rise to an assumption or imposition of the risk of failure to contract) and the temptation towards clear classification should be resisted.

Ben McFarlane, 'Proprietary Estoppel and Failed Contractual Negotiations' (2005) 69 *Conveyancer and Property Lawyer* 501–23

Ruth Sefton-Green, *Mistake, Fraud and Duties to Perform in European Contract Law* (Cambridge, Cambridge University Press, 2005)

Section 2(1) of the (English) Misrepresentation Act 1967

See also Non-Reliance Clauses and Exclusion of Liability for Misrepresentation in 6.2

PS Atiyah and GH Treitel, 'Misrepresentation Act 1967' (1967) 30 *Modern Law Review* 369–88

Problems arising out of the Act, including the uncertain measure of damages under section 2(2) and the fiction of fraud in section 2(1).

Anne Ruff, 'Esso Petroleum Co Ltd. v Mardon: When Is a Misstatement not a Misrepresentation?' (1977) 11 *The Law Teacher* 100–14

RD Taylor, 'Expectation, Reliance and Misrepresentation' (1982) 45 *Modern Law Review* 139–58

Damages under section 2(1) (and damages for promissory estoppel) should be based upon the tortious, reliance measure.

DW McLauchlan, 'Assessment of Damages for Misrepresentations Inducing Contracts' (1986) 6 *Otago Law Review* 371–419

John Cartwright, 'Damages for Misrepresentation' (1987) 51 *Conveyancer and Property Lawyer* 423–33

Analysis of section 2(1) and its context shows that damages under it are to be calculated on the tort of deceit measure.

Ian Brown and Adrian Chandler, 'Deceit, Damages and the Misrepresentation Act 1967, s. 2(1)' [1992] *Lloyd's Maritime and Commercial Law Quarterly* 40–72

Manitoba Law Reform Commission, *Report 82: Pre-Contractual Misstatements* (1994)

The Commission propose legislation abolishing tort damages for pre-contractual misstatements and awarding damages primarily on the expectation (breach of warranty) measure.

Jill Poole and James Devenney, 'Reforming Damages for Misrepresentation: The Case for Coherent Aims and Principles' [2007] *Journal of Business Law* 269–305

Damages in fraud cases are not limited to compensation but extend to protection and victimisation, but this should not apply in section 2(1) cases, which should be limited to the losses resulting from the specific misrepresentation. The no transaction measure including compensation for all the losses resulting from making the contract, and generous application of the lost opportunity award, should not apply to non-fraudulent cases.

2.5 RESTITUTION

See also 3.9 Restitution and Void Contracts

Gareth Jones, 'Claims Arising Out of Anticipated Contracts Which Do Not Materialize' (1979) 18 *University of Western Ontario Law Review* 447–60

An investigation of the overlapping availability of restitution on the one hand, and reliance damages for estoppel on the other, when anticipated contracts do not materialise.

SN Ball, 'Work Carried Out in Pursuance of Letters of

Intent—Contract or Restitution?' (1983) 99 *Law Quarterly Review* 572–92

Courts are failing to give effect to the expectations of businessmen, and should be readier to find contracts between negotiating parties and to fill the gaps in such contracts. There is also a need for a form of liability that sits between contract and restitution.

William Howarth, 'Contract, Reliance and Business Transactions' [1987] *Journal of Business Law* 122–30

Ewan McKendrick, 'The Battle of the Forms and the Law of Restitution' (1988) 8 *Oxford Journal of Legal Studies* 197–221 and 'Work Done in Anticipation of a Contract Which Does Not Materialise' in WR Cornish, Richard Nolan, J O'Sullivan and G Virgo (eds), *Restitution Past, Present and Future: Essays in Honour of Gareth Jones* (Oxford, Hart Publishing, 1998) 163–94; Steve Hedley, 'A Response' in WR Cornish, Richard Nolan, J O'Sullivan and G Virgo (eds), *Restitution Past, Present and Future: Essays in Honour of Gareth Jones* (Oxford, Hart Publishing, 1998) 195–98

McKendrick examines the action for restitution for unjust enrichment in cases of contracts that have not materialised, identifying a legitimate role for such actions but also pointing to problems of analysis and under-protection. Hedley argues that unjust enrichment has little or no role to play in such situations because where payment is due under *quantum meruit* it is because there was an implied agreement to pay for the work, in other words a contract.

JW Carter, 'Ineffective Transactions' in PD Finn (ed), *Essays on Restitution* (Sydney, Law Book Co, 1990) 206–40

Sharon Christensen, 'Recovery for Work Performed in Anticipation of Contract: Is Reliance an Element of Benefit?' (1993) 11 *Australian Bar Review* 144–62

A Wyvill, 'Enrichment, Restitution and the Collapsed Negotiation Cases' (1993) 11 *Australian Bar Review* 93–130

In service cases, restitution for unjust enrichment will only be available when money has been made or expenditure avoided by the recipient of the service, since it is only in those cases that a benefit can be said to have been conferred. Other cases are explicable as cases of equitable estoppel arising in situations of unconscionability.

EP Pegoraro, 'Recovery of Benefits Conferred Pursuant to Failed Anticipated Contracts- Unjust Enrichment, Equitable Estoppel or Unjust Sacrifice' (1995) 23 *Australian Business Law Review* 117–44

In 'pure' service cases, unjust enrichment is unsuitable as no benefit has been conferred (and this cannot be cured by arguing free acceptance of a benefit), and equitable estoppel is unsuitable because of its need for unconscionable conduct and its award of expectation damages in such situations. Instead, the case law should be based on a principle of recompense for unjust sacrifice based either on free acceptance or a lack of good faith.

JW Carter, 'Restitution and Contract Risk' in Mitchell McInnes (ed), *Restitution: Developments and Unjust Enrichment* (North Ryde, NSW, Law Book Co, 1996) 137–61

DYK Fung, *Pre-contractual Rights and Remedies: Restitution and Promissory Estoppel* (Sweet & Maxwell Asia, 1999)

○ Gareth Jones, *Goff & Jones: The Law of Restitution*, 7th edn (London, Sweet & Maxwell, 2006 plus supplements) ch 26

2.6 OBLIGATIONS TO CONTRACT: THE COMMON CALLINGS

See also Human Rights and Anti-Discrimination in 16.4

Joseph H Beale Jr, 'The Carrier's Liability: Its History' (1898) 11 *Harvard Law Review* 158–68

Hugh Evander Willis, 'The Right of Bailees to Contract Against Liability for Negligence' (1907) 20 *Harvard Law Review* 297–312

George Jarvis Thompson, 'The Relation of Common Carrier of Goods and Shipper, and its Incidents of Liability' (1925) 38 *Harvard Law Review* 28–63

Chris Cashmore, 'The Nature of an Action Against a Common Carrier' (1990) 10 *Oxford Journal of Legal Studies* 579–85

Graham McBain, 'Time to Abolish the Common Carrier' [2005] *Journal of Business Law* 545–96

A survey of the history and modern manifestations of common (public) carriers and the special rules applicable to them, concluding that the rules are anomalous and should be abolished.

3

FORMATION

3.1 CAPACITY

Henry Goudy, 'Contracts by Lunatics' (1901) 17 *Law Quarterly Review* 147–54

Lunatics should not be bound, even if the other contractor was ignorant of the lunacy.

Rankine Wilson, 'Lunacy in Relation to Contract, Tort and Crime' (1902) 18 *Law Quarterly Review* 21–30

Mannie Brown, 'Can the Insane Contract?' (1933) 11 *Canadian Bar Review* 600–24

Paul Matthews, 'Contracts for Necessaries and Mental Incapacity' (1982) 33 *Northern Ireland Legal Quarterly* 148–68

It is not clear that the executed contracts rule, permitting payment of a reasonable price, applies to executory contracts for necessaries when the court has taken control of an incapable person.

AH Hudson, 'Mental Incapacity in Property and Contract Law' [1984] *Conveyancer and Property Lawyer* 32–42 and 'Mental Incapacity Revisited' [1986] *Conveyancer and Property Lawyer* 178–86

Law Commission, *Report 134: Minors' Contracts* (1984)

The Report led to the Minors' Contracts Act 1987.

JR Carby-Hall and I Boruta, 'The Contractual Position of Minors and the Prohibition on Employment in David Freestone (ed), *Children and the Law: Essays in Honour of Professor HK Bevan* (Hull, Hull University Press, 1990) 30–57

3.2 AUTHORITY

Companies

MP Furmston, 'Who Can Plead that a Contract is *Ultra Vires?*' (1961) 24 *Modern Law Review* 715–20

Andrew Griffiths, *Contracting with Companies* (Oxford, Hart Publishing, 2005)

Government and Public Body Contractors

Terence Daintith, 'Regulation by Contract: The New Prerogative' (1979) 32 *Current Legal Problems* 41–59

Sue Arrowsmith, 'Judicial Review and the Contractual Powers of Public Authorities' (1990) 106 *Law Quarterly Review* 277–92 and 'Government contracts and public law' (1990) 10 *Legal Studies* 231–44

Paul Craig, 'Contract, Government and Community Law' in FD Rose (ed), *Consensus Ad Idem—Essays in the Law of Contract in Honour of Guenter Treitel* (London, Sweet & Maxwell, 1996) 141–57

ACL Davies, 'Ultra Vires Problems in Government Contracts' (2006) 112 *Law Quarterly Review* 98–123

Legislation is needed to codify the government's contracting powers and to limit the right of a government to use *ultra vires* arguments, and to give contractors the rights to compensatory damages where a contract is found to be *ultra vires*.

ACL Davies, *Accountability: A Public Law Analysis of Government by Contract* (Oxford, Oxford University Press, 2001)

○ Sue Arrowsmith, *The Law of Public and Utilities Procurement*, 2nd edn (London, Sweet & Maxwell, 2005)

Peter Vincent-Jones, *The New Public Contracting: Regulation, Responsiveness, Relationality* (Oxford, Oxford University Press, 2006)

3.3 AGREEMENT

Offer and Acceptance

See also Firm/Irrevocable Offers in 2.2

Arthur L Corbin, 'Offer and Acceptance, and Some of the Resulting Legal Relations' (1917) 26 *Yale Law Journal* 169–206

KN Llewellyn, 'On Our Case Law of Contract: Offer and Acceptance: I and II' (1938) 48 *Yale Law Journal* 1–36 and 779–818

Rudolf B Schlesinger (general ed), *Formation of Contracts: A Study of the Common Core of Legal Systems* (London, Stevens & Sons, 1968)

John E Murray Jr, 'Contracts: A New Design for the Agreement Process' (1968) 53 *Cornell Law Review* 785–806

Peter Meijes Tiersma, 'The Language of Offer and Acceptance:

Speech Acts and the Question of Intent' (1986) 74 *University of California Law Review* 189–232

Speech act theory is used to identify when the illocutionary act of making an offer or an acceptance has taken place (either when the relevant performative phrase or an equivalent, even silence, has been used). Further, the necessary intent for a binding offer or acceptance is not mental assent or sincerity but rather illocutionary intent: the intention that the words or actions be understood as a commitment (even if the speaker did not intend to commit himself).

Avery Katz, 'The Strategic Structure of Offer and Acceptance: Game Theory and the Law of Contract Formation' (1990) 89 *Michigan Law Review* 215–95

Melvin Aron Eisenberg, 'Expression Rules in Contract Law and Problems of Offer and Acceptance' (1994) 82 *Californian Law Review* 1127–90

Standardised expression rules (such as that an advertisement is not an offer, a counter-offer terminates the offeree's power of acceptance, and an auctioneer does not make an offer to sell to the highest bidder unless the sale is 'without reserve') cannot, on the whole, be justified.

Richard Craswell, 'Offer, Acceptance, and Efficient Reliance' (1996) 48 *Stanford Law Review* 481–553

Mathias M Siems, '"Unevenly formed contracts": Ignoring the "Mirror of Offer and Acceptance"' (2004) 12 *European Review of Private Law* 771–88

Some contracts are not 'evenly formed' by offer and acceptance but 'unevenly formed', eg when there are more than two parties or contracts are made face to face, or when parties have otherwise just slid into a contract.

Omri Ben-Shahar, 'Contracts Without Consent: Exploring a New Basis for Contractual Liability' (2004) 152 *University of Pennsylvania Law Review* 1829–72

Proposals of a principle of 'no-retraction', by which an offeree has the option to enforce an offer (with gaps filled on terms most favourable to the offerors) and the offeror may not retract it, the manifestation of the offeror's single will being binding. As negotiating parties converge towards full agreement, the principle of no-retraction comes to have less effect than the usual mutual assent principle of contracting, since the quantity of terms on which a (non-retractable) proposal/offer has been made and yet a final agreement not reached decreases towards zero. In a case of cross-purposes mistake, the no-retraction principle would have the effect of the parties being able to enforce the other party's view of the term on which they were at cross-purposes (there then being, in effect, two binding contracts).

○ Michael Furmston and Jill Poole, *Contract Formation: Law and Practice* (Oxford, Oxford University Press, 2010)

Communication and Formation of Contracts Inter Absentes

Clarence D Ashley, 'Formation of Contract *Inter Absentes*' (1902) 2 *Columbia Law Review* 1–9

An acceptance does not need to be communicated to the offeror, save where such communication is required by the offeror.

Artur Nussbaum, 'Comparative Aspects of the Anglo-American Offer-and-Acceptance Doctrine' (1936) 36 *Columbia Law Review* 920–29

PH Winfield, 'Some Aspects of Offer and Acceptance' (1939) 55 *Law Quarterly Review* 499–520

David Marshall Evans, 'The Anglo-American Mailing Rule' (1966) 15 *International & Comparative Law Quarterly* 553–75

Ian R Macneil, 'Time of Acceptance: Too Many Problems for a Single Rule' (1964) 112 *University of Pennsylvania Law Review* 947–79

Beth A Eisler, 'Default Rules for Contract Formation by Promise and the Need for Revision of the Mailbox Rule' (1991) 79 *Kentucky Law Journal* 557–83

Simon Gardner, 'Trashing with Trollope: A Deconstruction of the Postal Rules of Contract' (1992) 12 *Oxford Journal of Legal Studies* 170–94

The postal rule can be explained by reference to the social perception of the postal service and the phenomenon of posting at the time of the rule's inception.

Simone WB Hill, 'Flogging a Dead Horse—The Postal Rule and Email' (2001) 17 *Journal of Contract Law* 151–62

The postal rule should not be applied to email communication.

Franco Ferrari, 'A Comparative Overview on Offer and Acceptance Inter Absentes' (1992) 10 *Boston University International Law Journal* 171–202; and 'Offer and Acceptance Inter Absentes' in Jan M Smits (ed), *Elgar Encylopedia of Comparative Law* (Edward Elgar, 2006) 497–516

Acceptance by Silence or Conduct

C Miller, 'Felthouse v Bindley Revisited' (1972) 35 *Modern Law Review* 489–93

Online Contracting

Tom Allen and Robin Widdison, 'Can Computers Make Contracts?' (1996) 9 *Harvard Journal of Law and Technology* 25–52

CC Nicoll, 'Can Computers Make Contracts?' [1998] *Journal of Business Law* 35–49

Dennis Campbell and Christian Campbell (eds), *Law of International On-line Business: A Global Perspective* (London, Sweet & Maxwell, 1998)

Donnie L Kidd Jr and William H Daughtrey Jr, 'Adapting Contract Law To Accommodate Electronic Contracts: Overview and Suggestions' (1999–2000) 26 *Rutgers Computer and Technology Law Journal* 215–76

Robert A Hillman and Jeffrey J Rachlinski, 'Standard-Form Contracts in the Electronic Age' (2002) 77 *New York University Law Review* 429–95

Stephan Kinsella and Andrew Simpson, *Online Contract Formation* (New York, Oceana, 2004)

The Battle of the Forms

AJC Hoggett, 'Changing a Bargain by Confirming It' (1970) 33 *Modern Law Review* 518–29

The legal effect of confirmation notes is unclear. Barring their effect through a course of dealing and the like, such notes should be legally ineffective, being post-contractual, however estoppel and the parol evidence rule are applied to uncertain effect to sometimes give legal effect to terms in such documents.

Edward J Jacobs, 'The Battle of the Forms: Standard Term Contracts in Comparative Perspective' (1985) 34 *International & Comparative Law Quarterly* 297–316

If a counter-offer does not differ as to the important terms then agreement has been reached.

Ewan McKendrick, 'The Battle of the Forms and the Law of Restitution' (1988) 8 *Oxford Journal of Legal Studies* 197–221

Victor P Goldberg, 'The "Battle of the Forms": Fairness, Efficiency, and the Best-Shot Rule' (1997) 76 *Oregon Law Review* 155–71

EH Hondius and Ch Mahé, 'The Battle of Forms: Towards a Unified Solution' (1997–98) 12 *Journal of Contract Law* 268–76

Rejection of an Offer

EA Farnsworth, 'Preclusion by Rejection' in his *Changing Your Mind: The Law of Regretted Decisions* (New Haven, Yale University Press, 1998) 174–80

Acceptance and Revocation of Unilateral Contracts

Clarence D Ashley, 'Offers Calling for a Consideration other than a Counter-Promise' (1910) 23 *Harvard Law Review* 159–68

Offers of a unilateral contract may give rise to an estoppel preventing the offeror from revoking the offer once the offeree has commenced (but not yet completed) performance of the requested act.

DO McGovney, 'Irrevocable Offers' (1914) 27 *Harvard Law Review* 644–63

An offer of a unilateral contract comprises two offers of a unilateral contract: the principal offer which is accepted by the completion of the requested act, and the implied collateral offer to keep the principal offer open, which collateral offer is accepted and so binding by the commencement of the requested act.

I Maurice Wormster, 'The True Conception of Unilateral Contracts' (1916) 26 *Yale Law Journal* 136–42

It is right that an offer of a unilateral contract can be revoked at any time prior to completion of the requested act.

Samuel J Stoljar, 'The False Distinction between Bilateral and Unilateral Contracts' (1955) 64 *Yale Law Journal* 515–36

The labelling of bilateral and unilateral contracts is misleading as all contracts are two-sided; a better distinction is between expectation-bargains (contracts protecting the expectation interest) and reliance-bargains (contracts protecting the reliance interest). Where a promise is made in exchange for a promisee's act it is a reliance-bargain, and becomes binding (the offer is accepted) upon the commencement of the reliance (the requested act).

AH Hudson, 'Gibbons v Proctor Revisited' (1968) 84 *Law Quarterly Review* 503–12

Mark Pettit Jr, 'Modern Unilateral Contracts' (1983) 63 *Boston University Law Review* 551–96

AWB Simpson, 'Quackery and Contract Law: The Case of the Carbolic Smoke Ball' (1985) 14 *Journal of Legal Studies* 345–89 also in his *Leading Cases in the Common Law* (Oxford, Clarendon Press, 1995) 259–91

An investigation of the historical context of the Carbolic Smoke Ball case.

Peter Meijes Tiersma, 'Reassessing Unilateral Contracts: The Role of Offer, Acceptance, and Promise' (1992) 26 *UC Davis Law Review* 1–86

Unilateral contracts are not contracts, but rather immediately conditional promises.

Paul Mitchell and John Phillips, 'The Contractual Nexus: Is Reliance Essential?' (2002) 22 *Oxford Journal of Legal Studies* 115–34

In reward cases, if the acceptor performs the requested act it is not an acceptance if the offeree doesn't know about the offer, but is an acceptance if the offeree did know but would have done the act anyway.

3.4 THE OBJECTIVE PRINCIPLE AND UNILATERAL AND CROSS-PURPOSES MISTAKE

General Texts

○ John Cartwright, *Misrepresentation, Mistake and Non-disclosure*, 2nd edn (London, Sweet and Maxwell, 2007)

Catherine MacMillan, *Mistakes in Contract Law* (Oxford, Hart Publishing, 2009)

Generally

See also 4.4 Interpretation and the Objective Principle

Edwin W Patterson, 'Equitable Relief for Unilateral Mistake' (1928) 28 *Columbia Law Review* 859–904

A discussion of rescission, the refusal of specific performance, and reformation (rectification) as remedies in unilateral mistake cases.

JDI Hughes, 'Consensus and Estoppel' (1938) 54 *Law Quarterly Review* 370–80

The objective test and doctrine of unilateral mistake are applications of the rules of estoppel to situations in which there is a lack of consensus. Cross-purposes mistake cases are those in which there is a lack of consensus but in which estoppel is inapplicable

JA Weir, 'Mistake in the Law of Contracts. Smith v Hughes' (1941) 19 *Canadian Bar Review* 391–437

GC Cheshire, 'Mistake as Affecting Contractual Consent' (1944) 60 *Law Quarterly Review* 175–89

As a harbinger for the first edition of Cheshire and Fifoot's *The Law of Contract*, this article provides an account of the law of mistake, outlining the three doctrines of 'common', 'mutual' (often known as 'cross-purposes') and 'unilateral' mistake. This remains one of the clearest and most accurate expositions of the subject available.

TH Tylor, 'General Theory of Mistake in the Formation of Contract' (1948) 11 *Modern Law Review* 257–68

C Grunfeld, 'Reflections on Some Aspects of Operative Mistake in Contract' (1950) 13 *Modern Law Review* 50–68

CJ Slade, 'The Myth of Mistake in the English Law of Contract' (1954) 70 *Law Quarterly Review* 385–408

There is no doctrine of unilateral mistake. Unilateral mistake cases turn on the terms of the agreement and depend upon the non-correspondence of the offer with the acceptance.

KO Shatwell, 'The Supposed Doctrine of Mistake in Contract: A Comedy of Errors' (1955) 33 *Canadian Bar Review* 164–93

PS Atiyah, 'Judicial Techniques and Contract Law' (1968) 2 *Ottawa Law Review* 337–362, a later version of which appears in his *Essays on Contract*, revised edn (Oxford, Clarendon Press, 1990) 244–74

Samuel Stoljar, 'A New Approach to Mistake in Contract' (1965) 28 *Modern Law Review* 265–85

JR Spencer, 'Signature, Consent and the Rule in L'Estrange v Graucob' [1973] *Cambridge Law Journal* 104–22; William Howarth 'The Meaning of Objectivity in Contract' (1984) 100 *Law Quarterly Review* 265–81; JP Vorster, 'A Comment on the Meaning of Objectivity in Contract' (1987) 103 *Law Quarterly Review* 274–87

Spencer and Howarth argue that objectivity is variable depending upon the perspective that is adopted: that of the promisor, the promisee, or a fly on the wall (detached objectivity). Spencer argues that objectivity must be viewed from the communicatee's point of view. Howarth argues that the law shows no clear and coherent preference for any one of the three perspectives, and advocates consideration of detached objectivity as a way of resolving the debate. Vorster argues that the distinction between promisor and promisee objectivity is misleading, and the law should and does look from both parties' points of view, since communications and terms emanate from both parties. According to Vorster, the contract is formed on the basis of the shared subjective understanding or, where there is not one, on the basis of the reasonable understanding subjectively held by one party. Otherwise there is no contract.

Anthony T Kronman, 'Mistake, Disclosure, Information, and the Law of Contracts' (1978) 7 *Journal of Legal Studies* 1–34

The unilateral mistake rule is efficient because the promisee, if he knows or should have known of the mistake, can more cheaply rectify the mistake before the contract is entered into because of his superior access to relevant information. This applies where (as in most unilateral mistake cases) the promisee has casually acquired the relevant information, for example by comparing the promisor's mistaken bid with other bids, since a rule requiring disclosure will not discourage investment in the expertise to detect such mistakes. However where the promisee has deliberately searched for the information, it is efficient for the law to protect this information by what is essentially a property right and so permit non-disclosure, in order to encourage the investment in the expertise that detects such information and mistakes. In such cases the costs of the investment and search mean that the promisee is not the cheaper mistake-preventer.

Joseph Raz, 'Promises in Morality and Law' (1982) 95 *Harvard Law Review* 916–38 also in Brian Bix (ed), *Contract Law: Second Series: Volume I* (Aldershot, Ashgate, 2000) 269–91

The objective principle is a form of estoppel by which non-voluntary obligations are enforced in order to protect the practice of undertaking voluntary obligations.

Robert L Birmingham, 'Holmes on "Peerless": Raffles v Wichelhaus and the Objective Theory of Contract' (1985) 47 *University of Pittsburgh Law Review* 183–204

Linguistic theory (notably Wittgenstein), and particularly the distinctions between syntactic and semantic content and between reference and meaning, are used to support Holmes's view that *Raffles* v *Wichelhaus* can be explained by an objective theory of interpretation.

David Goddard, 'The Myth of Subjectivity' (1987) 7 *Legal Studies* 263–78

Following a 'contract as promise' approach, contract law is and can only be concerned with what we say, not what we intend. The implications of this strict view, including recommendations for the virtual abolition of the doctrines of implied terms and common and unilateral mistake, are briefly discussed.

AW Brian Simpson, 'Contracts for Cotton to Arrive: The Case of the Two Ships Peerless' (1989) 11 *Cardozo Law Review* 287–334

Anne De Moor, 'Intention in the Law of Contract—Elusive or Illusory?' (1990) 106 *Law Quarterly Review* 632–55

For a contract to be formed, the parties must both actually intend to enter into the contract. The objective principle, by which the meaning is not dependent upon intention, applies only to the content (the terms) of the contract, not the prior formal commitment to enter it at all.

Andrew Kull, 'Unilateral Mistake: The Baseball Card Case' (1992) 70 *Washington University Law Quarterly* 57–84

Eric Rasmusen and Ian Ayres, 'Mutual and Unilateral Mistake in Contract Law' (1993) 22 *Journal of Legal Studies* 309–43

The efficiency of mistake rules, concluding that a distinction between mutual and unilateral mistake is not justified on efficiency grounds.

Esther Stern, 'Objectivity, Legal Doctrine and the Law of Mistaken Identity' (1995) 8 *Journal of Contract Law* 154–92

Timothy AO Endicott, 'Objectivity, Subjectivity, and Incomplete Agreements' in J Horder (ed) *Oxford Essays in Jurisprudence: Fourth Series* (Oxford, Oxford University Press, 2000) 151–71

An account of the law of agreement, arguing that subjective intention to act is required, but that the act (the agreement) is then interpreted objectively. The (subjective) knowledge and behaviour of the interpreter are taken into account because they affect what the interpreter had reason to think the promisor was committing herself to. Agreements are often incomplete (eg through vagueness), and where there are such unanswered questions the courts may, unless the incompleteness is severe, resolve them to uphold the facility of contracting.

Melvin A Eisenberg, 'Mistake in Contract Law' (2001) 91 *California Law Review* 1573–643

Employing principles of efficiency, morality and experience/administrability, and looking from behind a veil of ignorance: evaluative (preference-related) mistakes should not give rise to relief; significant mechanical errors should relieve parties from contracts, and relief should still be granted when the errors were not and could not have been expected to have been known to the other party, although in such cases the innocent party should be compensated for any loss suffered through reliance; cross-purposes mistakes prevent a contract arising but the parties should be required to share out their total reliance losses on a comparative fault basis. Where parties are mistaken as to interpretation but one interpretation is more reasonable, that interpretation should bind, although courts should not be overly astute to find one interpretation more reasonable (and therefore reject the explanation of a cross-purposes mistake) when the question is finally balanced. Where the non-mistaken/more reasonable party knows of the other's mistake, the mistaken interpretation should prevail.

Melvin A Eisenberg, 'Disclosure in Contract Law' (2001) 91 *California Law Review* 1645–92

Parties should be required to give pre-contractual disclosure of material facts (other than the party's own preferences, intentions and evaluations) to correct the other party's mistaken assumption save where the buyer acquired the knowledge other than adventitiously or the risk of a mistaken assumption was allocated.

Daniel Friedmann, 'The Objective Principle and Mistake and Involuntariness in Contract and Restitution' (2003) 119 *Law Quarterly Review* 68–93

Rescission should be available in more cases of unilateral mistake than at present, including in cases of unilateral mistake not as to the terms of the contract when the mistake is known to the other party, and also in cases of unilateral mistake not known to the other party (providing the rescinding party is liable for the other party's reliance losses). Only confusion can result from treating mistake in contract as governed by the same principles as mistake in unjust enrichment law.

James Gordley, 'Mistake in Contract Formation' (2004) 52 *American Journal of Comparative Law* 433–68

Gerard McMeel, 'Interpretation and mistake in contract law: "The fox knows many things..."' [2006] *Lloyd's Maritime and Law Quarterly* 49–81

Mindy Chen-Wishart, 'Contractual Mistake, Intention in Formation and Vitiation: the Oxymoron of *Smith v Hughes*' in Jason W Neyers, Richard Bronaugh and Stephen GA Pitel (eds), *Exploring Contract Law* (Oxford, Hart Publishing, 2009) 341–78

Unilateral mistake is about a lack of agreement (applying the objective principle from the point of view of 'observer contextual objectivity') as to a term or as to whom the agreement is with.

Mistaken Identity

AL Goodhart, 'Mistake as to Identity in the Law of Contract' (1941) 57 *Law Quarterly Review* 228–44

Cases of unilateral mistake as to identity are cases in which there was no agreement because the offer, objectively interpreted, was not open to the party who purported to accept it. This article was cited by the Court of Appeal in *Ingram* v *Little* as influential.

Glanville L Williams, 'Mistake as to Party in the Law of Contract: Parts I and II' (1945) 23 *Canadian Bar Review* 271–292 and 380–416

JF Wilson, 'Identity in Contract and the Pothier Fallacy' (1954) 17 *Modern Law Review* 515–29; J Unger, 'Identity in Contract and Mr Wilson's Fallacy' (1955) 18 *Modern Law Review* 259–67; JC Smith and JAC Thomas, 'Pothier and the Three Dots' (1957) 20 *Modern Law Review* 38–43

Wilson argues that an intention to contract with a specific third person is not necessary for voidability for unilateral mistake and is merely one way of satisfying the true test that the contractor did not intend to contract with the rogue, and that Pothier does not define the limits of the test and so cannot be used to support (or refute) the 'identifiable third person' test. Unger supports Wilson's interpretation of Pothier but criticises his general views. Smith and Thomas examine Pothier's views and conclude that Pothier has been misunderstood and in fact his views conflict with Wilson's.

RA Samek, 'Some Reflections on the Logical Basis of Mistake of Identity of Party' (1960) 38 *Canadian Bar Review* 479–508

Richard Bronaugh, 'The Place of Identity in Contract Formation' (1980) 18 *University of Western Ontario Law Review* 185–240

Christopher Hare, 'Identity Mistakes: A Missed Opportunity?' (2004) 67 *Modern Law Review* 993–1007

The confirmation in *Shogun Finance v Hudson* that unilateral mistakes are merely a question of offer and acceptance is to be welcomed, but the minority's rejection of the distinction between *inter praesentes* and *inter absentes* dealings and resulting restriction on the applicability of the doctrine is to be preferred.

Catharine MacMillan, 'Rogues, Swindlers and Cheats: The Development of Mistake of Identity in English Contract Law' [2005] *Cambridge Law Journal* 711–44

DW McLauchlan, 'Mistake of Identity and Contract Formation' (2005) 21 *Journal of Contract Law* 1–50

Robert Stevens, 'Objectivity, Mistake and the Parol Evidence Rule' in Andrew Burrows and Edwin Peel (eds), *Contract Terms* (Oxford, Oxford University Press, 2007) 101–21

The majority in *Shogun* were right that agreement depends upon the objective principle and whether identity is a term of the deal (as to which, it usually will be in arm's length transactions and usually won't be in face-to-face transactions). Mistakes as to identity will prevent title passing, as a matter of property law, by delivery, but mistakes as to liability will not.

Sean Thomas, 'Mistake of Identity: A Comparative Analysis' [2008] *Lloyd's Maritime and Commercial Law Quarterly* 188–213

The focus on contract in rogue cases is misplaced. It is better to analyse such situations in terms of whether the *title* is voidable (in the context of the *nemo dat quod non habet* rule).

The (New Zealand) Contractual Mistakes Act 1977

DW McLauchlan, 'Mistake of identity After the Contractual Mistakes Act 1977' (1983) 10 *New Zealand Universities Law Review* 199–231

The Act changes very little in relation to mistake of identity cases, and fails even to clarify whether a bona fide purchaser for value without notice gets good title from a rogue.

Mindy Chen-Wishart, 'The Contractual Mistakes Act 1977 and Contract Formation' (1986) 6 *Otago Law Review* 334–54

DW McLauchlan, 'Mistake as to Contractual Terms under the Contractual Mistakes Act 1977' (1986) 12 *New Zealand Universities Law Review* 123–59

Andrew Beck, 'The New Zealand Contractual Mistakes Act: A Lesson in Legislation' [1987] *Lloyd's Maritime and Law Quarterly* 325–39

A survey of the case-law on the 1977 Act, arguing that the Act should only be relevant after the objective principle has been given full application.

A Beck and R Sutton, 'The Contractual Mistakes Act 1977' in New Zealand Law Commission, *Report 25: Contract Statutes Review* (1993) 127–71

DW McLauchlan and CEF Rickett, 'Mistake and Ignorance under the New Zealand Contractual Mistakes Act 1977' (1995) 8 *Journal of Contract Law* 193–208

Richard Sutton, 'Keeping it Simple: New Zealand's Code of Contractual Mistake' in EJH Schrage (ed), *Unjust Enrichment and the Law of Contract* (London, Kluwer Law International, 2001) 381–95

Rectification for Unilateral Mistake

See also Rectification for Common Mistake in 5.2

Andrew Burrows, 'Construction and Rectification' in Andrew Burrows and Edwin Peel (eds), *Contract Terms* (Oxford, Oxford University Press, 2007) 77–99

Given the developments in construction, and particularly if pre-contractual negotiations are or become admissible in construction cases, rectification would largely be redundant, and the parties would be able to outflank the bars to rectification (such as laches) by relying upon construction. (The extent to which rectification for unilateral mistake would be redundant depends on whether construction moves to a 'promisee objectivity' approach.)

David McLauchlan, 'The "Drastic" Remedy of Rectification for Unilateral Mistake' (2008) 124 *Law Quarterly Review* 608–40

Rectification is not an exceptional response to an equitable wrong or sharp practice of some sort, but rather is the alteration of a document to reflect the parties' agreement, as construed in the ordinary way. The focus should, therefore, be on what terms one party led the other to believe had been agreed.

Mindy Chen-Wishart, 'Contractual Mistake, Intention in Formation and Vitiation: the Oxymoron of *Smith v Hughes*' in Jason W Neyers, Richard Bronaugh and Stephen GA Pitel (eds), *Exploring Contract Law* (Oxford, Hart Publishing, 2009) 341–78

Non Est Factum

John H Baker, 'Non Est Factum' (1970) 23 *Current Legal Problems* 53–70

The doctrine of *non est factum* has been taken out of its natural context of deeds, and has gone too far. Innocent third parties should be able to raise estoppel to counter arguments of *non est factum*.

Richard J Bragg, '"Fundamental or Radical" Changes in the Law of Non Est Factum' (1971) 35 *Conveyancer and Property Lawyer* 231–42

Julius Stone, 'The Limits of Non Est Factum after Gallie v Lee' (1972) 88 *Law Quarterly Review* 190–224

JR Spencer, 'Signature, Consent and the Rule in L'Estrange v Graucob' [1973] *Cambridge Law Journal* 104–22

Mindy Chen-Wishart, 'Contractual Mistake, Intention in Formation and Vitiation: the Oxymoron of *Smith v Hughes*' in Jason W Neyers, Richard Bronaugh and Stephen GA Pitel (eds), *Exploring Contract Law* (Oxford, Hart Publishing, 2009) 341–78

Non est factum applies 'actor objectivity': the mistake must be one a reasonable person with the promisor's disability would have made. It is justified by the need for sufficient autonomy before a party can be taken to have consented to a contract.

3.5 THE INTENTION TO CREATE LEGAL RELATIONS

Generally

BA Hepple, 'Intention to Create Legal Relations' [1970] *Cambridge Law Journal* 122–37

There is no separate requirement of an intention to create legal relations. Intention is relevant to consideration, which requires that a benefit was *intended* as the price for a promise, ie was part of a bargain.

S Hedley, 'Keeping Contract in its Place: *Balfour v Balfour* and the Enforceability of Informal Arrangements' (1985) 5 *Oxford Journal of Legal Studies* 391–415

A deconstruction of the requirement of an intention to create legal relations, arguing that it is a fiction. In arm's length agreements there is no such requirement, although parties can intentionally disavow the legal effects that their agreement would otherwise have. Agreements between those not at arm's length are unenforceable except when, and to the extent that, one party has already relied on an agreement by performing.

Wendell H Holmes, 'The Freedom Not To Contract' (1986) 60 *Tulane Law Review* 751–98

Brenda Cossman, 'A Matter of Difference: Domestic Contracts and Gender Equality' (1990) 28 *Osgoode Hall Law Journal* 303–80

Michael Freeman, 'Contracting in the Haven: *Balfour* v *Balfour* Revisited' in Roger Halson (ed), *Exploring the Boundaries of Contract* (Aldershot, Dartmouth, 1996) 68–82

Balfour v Balfour should be discarded: English law now gives those in family relationships the power to contract.

Melanie B Leslie, 'Enforcing Family Promises: Reliance, Reciprocity, and Relational Contracts' (1999) 77 *North Carolina Law Review* 551–636

Bernard Rudden, 'The Gentleman's Agreement in Legal Theory and Modern Practice' (1999) 7 *European Review of Private Law* 199–220

Debora L Threedy, 'Feminists & Contract Doctrine' (1999) 32 *Indiana Law Review* 1247–66

David Allen, 'The Gentleman's Agreement in Modern Legal Theory and in Modern Practice' (2000) 29 *Anglo-American Law Review* 204–27

Maria Keyes and Kylie Burns, 'Contract and the Family: Whither Intention' (2002) 26 *Melbourne University Law Review* 577–95

Contracts to Marry

J Dundas White, 'Breach of Promise of Marriage' (1894) 10 *Law Quarterly Review* 135–52

Ian FG Baxter, 'The Contract to Marry' (1963) 23 *Revue du Barreau de la Province de Québec* 44–51

Comfort Letters

Paula Giliker, 'Taking Comfort in Certainty: To Enforce or Not To Enforce the Letter of Comfort' [2004] *Lloyd's Maritime and Commercial Law Quarterly* 219–33

The English non-enforcement of comfort letters makes more commercial sense than, and should be preferred to, the opposite French approach.

3.6 CONSIDERATION

The History of Consideration

Robert L Henry, 'Consideration in Contracts (601 AD to 1520 AD)' (1917) 26 *Yale Law Journal* 664–98

WS Holdsworth, 'The Modern History of the Doctrine of Consideration' (1922) 2 *Boston University Law Review* 87–97

AWB Simpson, 'The Equitable Doctrine of Consideration and the Law of Uses' (1965) 16 *University of Toronto Law Journal* 1–36

The equitable doctrine of consideration in the law of uses up to the mid-sixteenth century, when consideration began to be linked to the action of *assumpsit*.

JL Barton, 'The Early History of Consideration' (1968) 85 *Law Quarterly Review* 372–91

Consideration did not arise out of any particular form of action but rather out of general principles as to promises and when they should be enforced.

JN Adams, 'Consideration for Requirements Contracts' (1978) 94 *Law Quarterly Review* 73–84

JH Baker, 'Origins of the "Doctrine" of Consideration, 1535–1585' in Morris S Arnold, Thomas A Green, Sally A Scully and Stephen D White (eds), *On the Laws and Customs of England: Essay in Honour of Samuel E Thorne* (Cambridge, MA, Harvard University Press, 1981) 336–58

Kevin Teeven, 'Mansfield's Reform of Consideration in Light of the Origins of the Doctrine' (1991) 21 *Memphis State University Law Review* 669–703

Val D Ricks, 'The Sophisticated Doctrine of Consideration' (2000) 9 *George Mason Law Review* 99–144

Consideration Generally

See also 9.2 Consideration for Contract Modifications

Arthur L Corbin, 'Does a Pre-existing Duty Defeat Consideration? Recent Noteworthy Decisions' (1918) 27 *Yale Law Journal* 362–81

Arthur L Corbin, 'The Effect of Options on Consideration' (1925) 34 *Yale Law Journal* 571–90

Arthur L Goodhart, 'Blackmail and Consideration in Contracts' (1928) 44 *Law Quarterly Review* 436–49 also in his *Essays in Jurisprudence and the Common Law* (Cambridge, Cambridge University Press, 1931) 175–89

Surrendering a liberty to do an immoral act is not valid consideration and so a contract to pay someone to surrender such a liberty is unenforceable.

John H Wigmore, 'The Scientific Rôle of Consideration in Contract' in Max Radin and AM Kidd (eds), *Legal Essays in Tribute to Orrin Kip McMurray* (Berkeley, CA, University of California Press, 1935) 641–56

Consideration is needed to keep contract distinct from deceit and estoppel.

Lord Wright, 'Ought the Doctrine of Consideration to be Abolished from the Common Law?' (1936) 49 *Harvard Law Review* 1225–53 also in his *Legal Essays and Addresses* (Cambridge, Cambridge University Press, 1939) 287–326

Yes. The requirement should be as to a deliberate or serious intention to contract, and consideration should merely be one possible source of extrinsic corroboratory evidence of that intention.

Law Revision Committee, *Sixth Interim Report of the Law Revision Committee: Statute of Frauds and the Doctrine of Consideration* (1937); CJ Hamson, 'The Reform of Consideration' (1938) 54 *Law Quarterly Review* 233–57

Lord Wright's committee recommended that a contract be enforceable if in writing *or* if supported by consideration *or* if giving rise to detrimental reliance; part payment of a debt should be good consideration; firm offers should remain open as promised whether or not there is consideration for them doing so; unilateral offers are accepted by the commencement of performance by the other party. Hamson criticises the report.

Malcolm P Sharp, 'Pacta Sunt Servanda' (1941) 41 *Columbia Law Review* 783–98

Roscoe Pound, 'Individual Interests of Substance—Promised Advantages' (1945) 59 *Harvard Law Review* 1–42

KO Shatwell, 'The Doctrine of Consideration in the Modern Law' (1954) 1 *Sydney Law Review* 289–331

Edwin W Patterson, 'An Apology for Consideration' (1958) 58 *Columbia Law Review* 929–63

The doctrine of consideration can be justified, with qualifications, as a test of enforceability that is workable for promises entered into by those not thinking of legal consequences. Parts of the doctrine, such as the pre-existing duty rule, cannot be justified.

PS Atiyah, *Consideration in Contracts: A Fundamental Restatement* (Canberra, Australian National University Press, 1971), a later version of which, including responses to Treitel's response, appears as 'Essay 8: Consideration: A Restatement' in his *Essays on Contract*, revised edn (Oxford, Clarendon Press, 1990) 179–243; GH Treitel, 'Consideration: A Critical Analysis of Professor Atiyah's Fundamental Restatement' (1976) 50 *Australian Law Journal* 439–49

In his inaugural lecture at Australia National University, Atiyah argues that the axioms that make up the orthodox explanation of the law of consideration do not accurately describe the law, and that consideration would be better understood as a broader determination that there is sufficient reason to enforce a promise. Such a formulation would bring promissory estoppel cases within the law of contract and would do away with the need for, among other things, invented consideration. Treitel criticises Atiyah's views as ignoring or misunderstanding aspects of the law and as not elaborating upon Atiyah's proposed basis for deciding when to enforce promises.

Stanley D Henderson, 'Promises Grounded in the Past: The Idea of Unjust Enrichment and the Law of Contracts' (1971) 57 *Virginia Law Review* 1115–84

KCT Sutton, *Consideration Reconsidered: Studies on the Doctrine of Consideration of the Law of Contract* (St Lucia, Queensland, University of Queensland Press, 1974) and 'Promises and Consideration' in PD Finn (ed), *Essays on Contract* (Sydney, Law Book Co, 1987) 35–80

PS Atiyah, 'When Is an Enforceable Agreement not a Contract? Answer: When it Is an Equity' (1976) 92 *Law Quarterly Review* 174–80; PJ Millett, 'Crabb v Arun DC—A Riposte' (1976) 92 *Law Quarterly Review* 342–46

Atiyah argues that *Crabb v Arun DC* was really a contract case and that if the representation was precise enough for an estoppel it was precise enough for a contract. Consideration can be found in possible future payment or action in reliance (even if unrequested). Millet points out that the point had been conceded by counsel and argues that in any case there was no firm agreement, consideration or authority.

Richard A Posner, 'Gratuitous Promises in Economics and Law' (1977) 6 *Journal of Legal Studies* 411–26

Gratuitous promises create utility over a mere gift by increasing the present value of an uncertain future stream of transfer. A general rule of non-enforceability of low value promises (whether gratuitous or not) is justified but a rule of non-enforceability of only gratuitous promises is not.

John Swan, 'Consideration and the Reasons for Enforcing Contracts' (1977) 15 *University of Western Ontario Law Review* 83–122 also in Barry J Reiter and John Swan (eds), *Studies in Contract Law* (Toronto, Butterworths, 1980) 23–59

The extent to which non-commercial promises should be enforced depends upon the interest justifying the enforcement, usually the reliance or unjust enrichment interest.

Brian Coote, 'Consideration and the Joint Promisee' [1978] *Cambridge Law Journal* 301–12

Even in cases of joint promises, consideration must move from each promisee.

Melvin Aron Eisenberg, 'Donative Promises' (1979) 47 *University of Chicago Law Review* 1–33 and 'The Principles of Consideration' (1982) 67 *Cornell Law Review* 640–65

Bargain should not be required for a contract to be enforceable, rather a broader range of considerations such as the likelihood of deliberativeness and the ease of administration should be considered. As a result, there should be an end to the blanket non-enforcement of promises given in exchange for performance of a pre-existing duty, and promises ancillary to bargains (such as firm offers).

Geoffrey MacCormack, '"Gift", "Exchange" and "Contract"' in Anthony Blackshield, *Legal Change: Essays in Honour of Julius Stone* (Sydney, Butterworths, 1983) 68–81

An analysis of anthropological and ethnographic data for the purposes of identifying and distinguishing gifts, exchanges and contracts. Exchanges overlap with gifts, which lack agreement, and contracts, which require agreement.

Daniel A Farber and John H Matheson, 'Beyond Promissory Estoppel: Contract Law and the "Invisible Handshake"' (1985) 52 *University of Chicago Law Review* 903–47

All promises should be enforceable, without reliance or consideration, if made in furtherance of economic activities.

James D Gordon III, 'A Dialogue About the Doctrine of Consideration' (1990) 75 *Cornell Law Review* 986–1005 and 'Consideration and the Commercial-Gift Dichotomy' (1991) 44 *Vanderbilt Law Review* 283–315

A critique of the doctrine of consideration in the form of a fictional (and humorous) dialogue between a businessman and his lawyer. It is proposed that the doctrine is replaced by a distinction between gifts and commercial transactions, the latter defined as promises related to an exchange.

Roy Goode, 'Abstract Payment Undertakings' in Peter Cane and Jane Stapleton (eds), *Essays for Patrick Atiyah* (Oxford, Clarendon Press, 1991) 209–36

Steven Shavell, 'An Economic Analysis of Altruism and Deferred Gifts' (1991) 20 *Journal of Legal Studies* 401–22

Andrew Kull, 'Reconsidering Gratuitous Promises' (1992) 21 *Journal of Legal Studies* 39–65

The rule against enforcement of gratuitous promises is unjustified as such promises are beneficial. Further, in practice in America a serious unequivocal gratuitous promise will almost always be enforced.

Steve Thel and Edward Yorio, 'The Promissory Basis of Past Consideration' (1992) 78 *Virginia Law Review* 1045–101

Melvin Aron Eisenberg, 'The World of Contract and the World of Gift' (1997) 85 *California Law Review* 821–66

The consideration requirement is justified because the emotional and relationship benefits of affective gifts would be undermined if they were legally enforceable, and donors should morally be allowed to change their mind if there has been no reliance by the done.

Eric A Posner, 'Altruism, Status, and Trust in the Law of Gifts and Gratuitous Promises' [1997] *Wisconsin Law Review* 567–09

Barry Hough and Ann Spowart-Taylor, 'The Doctrine of Consideration: Dead or Alive in English Employment Contracts?' (2001) 17 *Journal of Contract Law* 193–211

Andrew S Gold, 'Consideration and the Morality of Promising' in Jason W Neyers, Richard Bronaugh and Stephen GA Pitel (eds), *Exploring Contract Law* (Oxford, Hart Publishing, 2009) 115–37

The law of consideration makes moral sense because in cases of gratuitous promises it would be immoral to force performance by coercion.

Consideration and Bilateral Contracts

James Barr Ames, 'Two Theories of Consideration: Part 2' (1899) 13 *Harvard Law Review* 29–43; CC Langdell, 'Mutual Promises as a Consideration for Each Other' (1901) 14 *Harvard Law Review* 496–508; Samuel Williston, 'Consideration in Bilateral Contracts' (1914) 27 *Harvard Law Review* 503–29; Henry Winthrop Ballantine, 'Mutuality and Consideration' (1914) 28 *Harvard Law Review* 121–34

Ames: the consideration in bilateral contract cases is the fact of the promise itself and not its being a binding legal obligation. Any promise will do, including a promise to perform a pre-existing duty owed to the promisee or a third party is sufficient consideration. Langdell: the *binding* promise is the consideration. Williston: the consideration is the fact of the promise itself, but it must be a promise to do something that would itself amount to consideration. Ballantine: the consideration is not the present detriment of a promise but the future value of the promised performance.

Herman Oliphant, 'Mutuality of Obligation in Bilateral Contracts' (1925) 25 *Columbia Law Review* 705–23; Samuel Williston, 'The Effect of One Void Promise in a Bilateral Agreement' (1925) 25 *Columbia Law Review* 857–69; Arthur L Corbin, 'Non-Binding Promises as Consideration' (1926) 26 *Columbia Law Review* 550–58; Herman Oliphant, 'Mutuality of Obligation in Bilateral Contracts at Law' (1928) 25 *Columbia Law Review* 997–1013

Brian Coote, 'The Essence of Contract Parts 1 and 2' (1988–9) 1 *Journal of Contract Law* 91–112 and 183–204

In bilateral executory contracts, ie the exchange of promises, consideration can be found in the assumption of legal obligations, which is not merely a consequence of the promising but is what was bargained for.

Consideration and Unilateral Contracts

James Barr Ames, 'Two Theories of Consideration: Part 1' (1899) 12 *Harvard Law Review* 515–31

Any act or forbearance can amount to consideration in cases of unilateral contracts, including forbearance to prosecute a groundless claim and performance of pre-existing contractual duties to the other contracting party or a third party.

AL Goodhart, 'Unilateral Contracts' (1951) 67 *Law Quarterly Review* 456–60; JC Smith, 'Unilateral Contracts and Consideration' (1953) 69 *Law Quarterly Review* 99–106; AL Goodhart, 'Unilateral Contracts and Consideration: A Short Replication' (1953) 69 *Law Quarterly Review* 106–10

AT Denning, 'Developments in the Doctrine of Consideration' (1952) 15 *Modern Law Review* 1–10; Francis Bennion, 'Want of Consideration' (1953) 16 *Modern Law Review* 441–52

Comparisons with Civil Law Cause or Causa

Ernest G Lorenzen, 'Causa and Consideration in the Law of Contracts' (1919) 28 *Yale Law Journal* 621–46

Malcolm S Mason, 'The Utility of Consideration—A Comparative View' (1941) 41 *Columbia Law Review* 825–48

Arthur T von Mehren, 'Civil Law Analogues to Consideration: An Exercise in Comparative Analysis' (1959) 72 *Harvard Law Review* 1009–78

AG Chloros, 'The Doctrine of Consideration and the Reform of the Law of Contract: A Comparative Analysis' (1968) 17 *International & Comparative Law Quarterly* 137–57

BS Markesinis, 'Cause and Consideration: A Study in Parallel' [1978] *Cambridge Law Journal* 53–75 also in his *Foreign Law and Comparative Methodology: A Subject and a Thesis* (Oxford, Hart Publishing, 1997) 47–67

The results of and reasoning behind the two doctrines are similar. However, cause has been refined into a coherent theoretical concept operating from formation to the end of the contract, whereas consideration is overly technical and largely confined to formation.

3.7 FORM

James Barr Ames, 'Specialty Contracts and Equitable Defences' (1895) 9 *Harvard Law Review* 49–59

Samuel Williston, 'Discharge of Contracts by Alteration: Parts I and II' (1905) 18 *Harvard Law Review* 105–19, 165–81

Lon L Fuller, 'Consideration and Form' (1941) 41 *Columbia Law Review* 799–824

Joseph M Perillo, 'The Statute of Frauds in the Light of the Functions and Dysfunctions of Form' (1974) 43 *Fordham Law Review* 39–82

A survey of the functions of form, suggesting a relaxation of the requirements of the Statute of Frauds, it only being necessary to prove contracts by clear and convincing evidence.

John P Dawson, *Gifts and Promises: Continental and American Law Compared* (New Haven, CT, Yale University Press, 1980)

PS Atiyah, 'Form and Substance in Contract Law' in Peter Birks and Neil MacCormick, *The Legal Mind: Essays for Tony Honoré* (Oxford, Clarendon Press, 1986), a later version of which appears as 'Essay 5' in his *Essays on Contract*, revised edn (Oxford, Clarendon Press, 1990) 93–120

Law Commission, *Report 163: Deeds and Escrow* (1987)

Graham Virgo and Charles Harpum, 'Breaking the Seal: The New Law on Deeds' [1991] *Lloyd's Maritime and Commercial Law Quarterly* 209–30

Law Commission, *Consultation Paper 143: The Execution of Deeds and Documents on Behalf of Bodies Corporate* (1996) and *Report 253: Execution of Deeds and Documents by or on behalf of Bodies Corporate* (1998)

Eric A Posner, 'The Decline of Formality in Contract Law' in FH Buckley (ed), *The Fall and Rise of Freedom of Contract* (Durham, NC, Duke University Press, 1999) 61–77

Simon Whittaker, 'The Reformulation of Contractual Formality' in Peter Birks and Arianna Pretto (eds), *Themes in Comparative law In Honour of Bernard Rudden* (Oxford, Oxford University Press, 2002) 199–220

Requirements of form are growing in English law, and often have a substantive function.

Form and E-commerce

See also Online Contracting in 3.3

Hugh Beale and Lowri Griffiths, 'Electronic Commerce: Formal Requirements in Commercial Transactions' [2002] *Lloyd's Maritime and Commercial Law Quarterly* 467–84

Statutory requirements of writing and signature can be satisfied (without further legislation) by email and website trading, although not EDI.

Gerhard Dannemann, 'Formation of contracts on the Internet' in Peter Birks and Arianna Pretto (eds), *Themes in Comparative law In Honour of Bernard Rudden* (Oxford, Oxford University Press, 2002) 179–98

Stephen Mason, *Electronic Signatures in Law*, 2nd edn (Tottel, 2007)

3.8 CERTAINTY

Robert A Samek, 'The Requirement of Certainty of Terms in the Formation of Contract: A Quantitative Approach' (1970) 48 *Canadian Bar Review* 203–34

Parties make bargains, not contracts. Providing there is a relative, ie reasonable, quantum of certainty as to the bargain in the circumstances, it should be upheld, and open terms should be filled by the courts.

Michael Howard, 'Contracts Expressly Providing for Further Agreement' (1977–80) 4 *Otago Law Review* 14–22

Kenneth C Sutton, 'The Uncertainty of Certainty of Contracts' (1981) 5 *Otago Law Review* 11–34

WF Pratt, Junior, 'Afterword: Contracts and Uncertainty' (1983) 46 *Law and Contemporary Problems* 169–80

Mark P Gergen, 'The Use of Open Terms in Contract' (1992) 92 *Columbia Law Review* 997–1081

An analysis of the efficiency of open terms (those giving one party discretion).

3.9 RESTITUTION AND VOID CONTRACTS

See also 2.5 Restitution

JW Carter, 'Ineffective Transactions' in PD Finn (ed), *Essays on Restitution* (Sydney, Law Book Co, 1990) 206–40

JW Carter, 'Services Rendered Under Ineffective Contracts' [1990] *Lloyd's Maritime and Commercial Law Quarterly* 495–519

Peter Birks, 'No Consideration: Restitution after Void Contracts' (1992) 23 *University of Western Australia Law Review* 195–234

Despite comments in the swaps cases, restitution for a transfer under a void contract is only available where there has been a failure of consideration, ie where the contract is executory or the consideration received can be restored to bring about a total failure.

Sarah Worthington, 'The Proprietary Consequences of Contract Failure' and Janet Ulph, 'Comment' in Francis D Rose, *Failure of Contracts* (Oxford, Hart Publishing, 1997) 67–89, 91–100

AS Burrows, 'Free Acceptance and the Law of Restitution' (1988) 104 *Law Quarterly Review* 576–599, a later version of which appears in his *Understanding the Law of Obligations* (Oxford, Hart Publishing, 1998) 72–98

Restitution by *quantum meruit* or *quantum valebat* following transfers under a void, unenforceable, incomplete or anticipated contract is grounded on failure of consideration and not a principle of free acceptance.

Sonja Meier, 'Restitution after Executed Void Contracts' in P Birks and F Rose (eds), *Lessons of the Swaps Litigation* (London, Mansfield Press, 2000) 168–213

A survey of the law and discussion of the role and justifications of the failure of consideration requirement.

Ben Kremer, 'Recovering Money Paid Under Void Contracts: Absence of Consideration and Failure of Consideration' (2001) 17 *Journal of Contract Law* 37–68

William Swadling, 'Rescission, Property, and the Common Law' (2005) 121 *Law Quarterly Review* 123–53

Title to goods may be transferred by other ways than a contract, and even when the contract is void or voidable at law this does not mean that good title has not passed by means of delivery.

○ Gareth Jones, *Goff & Jones: The Law of Restitution*, 7th edn (London, Sweet & Maxwell, 2006 plus supplements) chs 21–23 and 25

4

THE TERMS OF THE CONTRACT

4.1 INCORPORATION

Signed Documents

JR Spencer, 'Signature, Consent, and the Rule in *L'Estrange* v *Graucob*' [1973] *Cambridge Law Journal* 104–22

The objective test requires that signature should only bind the signer to a term where the other party did not know or have good reason to know that the signer did not intend to agree to the relevant term: the rule in *L'Estrange v Graucob* is wrong.

RA Samek, 'The Objective Theory of Contract and the Rule in *L'Estrange v Graucob*' (1974) 52 *Canadian Bar Review* 351–71

Spencer's theory is at heart a subjective theory, and should be rejected in favour of the objective theory, which is used to secure minimum standards of business certainty and security.

Matthew Chapman, 'Common Law Contract and Consent: Signature and Objectivity' (1998) 49 *Northern Ireland Legal Quarterly* 363–84

The notice test for onerous terms should apply to signed contracts and only informed consent should give rise to a promisor being bound.

Elisabeth Peden and JW Carter, 'Incorporation of Terms by Signature: L'Estrange Rules!' (2005) 21 *Journal of Contract Law* 96–106

Incorporation by Notice

HB Sales, 'Standard Form Contracts' (1953) 16 *Modern Law Review* 318–42

There should be a commission with the power to prepare compulsory standard forms by means of statutory instrument.

RW Hodgin, 'The Fiction of the Ticket Cases' (1972) 23 *Northern Ireland Legal Quarterly* 174–89

Malcolm Clarke, 'Notice of Contractual Terms' [1976] *Cambridge Law Journal* 51–81

Elizabeth MacDonald, 'The Duty to Give Notice of Unusual Contract Terms' [1988] *Journal of Business Law* 375–85

The 'red hand rule' of incorporation is examined, with particular reference to its ancestry and the distinction between unusual terms on the one hand and unreasonable terms on the other.

Elizabeth MacDonald, *Exemption Clauses and Unfair Terms*, 2nd edn (Tottel, 2006) ch 1

Incorporation by a Course of Dealing

Elizabeth MacDonald, 'Incorporation of Contract Terms by a "Consistent Course of Dealing"' (1988) 8 *Legal Studies* 48–66

The 'course of dealing' rule is an application of the ordinary objective test and of the related principle of reasonable notice.

Jane Swanton, 'Incorporation of Contractual Terms by a Course of Dealing' (1988–9) 1 *Journal of Contract Law* 223–48

Shantanu Majumdar, 'The Incorporation of Terms and Conditions by a Course of Dealing—Is it Time to Reconsider an Old Chesnut?' (2001) *Commercial Liability Law Review* 12–20

4.2 ORDER OF PERFORMANCE

Contingent Conditions and Independent Obligations

Arthur L Corbin, 'Discharge of Contracts' (1913) 22 *Yale Law Journal* 513–30

Geo P Costigan Jr, 'Conditions in Contracts' (1907) 7 *Columbia Law Review* 151–71

Edwin W Patterson, 'Constructive Conditions in Contracts' (1942) 42 *Columbia Law Review* 903–54

Samuel J Stoljar, 'The Contractual Conception of Condition' (1953) 69 *Law Quarterly Review* 485–511

JW Carter, 'Conditions and Conditions Precedent' (1991) 4 *Journal of Contract Law* 90–106

Donald H Clark, 'Risk Allocation on Failure of Contingent Conditions. Part One: A No Fault Scheme' (2000) 19 *New Zealand Universities Law Review* 206–49

Entire Obligations and Part Performance

Arthur L Corbin, 'Conditions in the Law of Contract' (1919) 28 *Yale Law Journal* 739–68

The rule of substantial performance is not about the degree to which a condition must be satisfied, but rather about whether the condition precedent is that most of a particular task be performed (rather than that all of it be performed).

Glanville L Williams, 'Partial Performance of Entire Contracts: Parts I and II' (1941) 57 *Law Quarterly Review* 373–99, 490–511

Anthony Beck, 'The Doctrine of Substantial Performance: Conditions and Conditions Precedent' (1975) 38 *Modern Law Review* 413–27

Substantial performance is only a question of what performance was intended to be a condition precedent to payment or the other party's performance. *Quantum meruit* for part performance should be available unless the parties (unusually) intended it not to be.

SM Waddams, 'Restitution for the Part Performer' in Barry J Reiter and John Swan (eds), *Studies in Contract Law* (Toronto, Butterworths, 1980) 151–79

The harsh effects of the entire obligation rule, by which the breaching party is treated as forfeiting his right to payment, are frequently avoided in practice. Further, save where there is clear evidence that the performer contractually agreed to forfeit payment on non-completion, the part-performer should be granted restitution for unjust enrichment because the anticipated exchange has failed to materialise. The innocent party should pay the lower of the objective value of the work done, and the contract price less the cost of completing the work.

Law Commission, *Working Paper 65: Pecuniary Restitution on Breach of Contract* (1975) and *Report 121: Pecuniary Restitution on Breach of Contract* (1983)

A breaching part-performer of an entire obligation should be entitled to restitution of the value of his part performance.

AS Burrows, 'Law Commission Report on Pecuniary Restitution for Breach of Contract' (1984) 47 *Modern Law Review* 76–86

John Azzi, 'Restitution: Recovery of Benefits Conferred Under a Partly Performed Contract' (1990) 64 *Australian Law Journal* 630–49

Geoffrey Mead, 'Restitution Within Contract?' (1991) 11 *Legal Studies* 172–88

Restitution for unjust enrichment should be available even where the contract subsists where part performance has been freely accepted.

Martin Dockray, '*Cutter v Powell*: A Trip outside the Text' (2001) 117 *Law Quarterly Review* 664–82

Ben McFarlane and Robert Stevens, 'In Defence of Sumpter v Hedges' (2002) 118 *Law Quarterly Review* 569–99

A defence of the rule whereby part (even a substantial part) performance of an entire obligation does not give rise to a contractual right to any payment or (absent frustration) any right to restitution for unjust enrichment, and an investigation of when an obligation should be construed as being entire.

4.3 STANDARD FORMS

Karl N Llewellyn, 'What Price Contract?—An Essay in Perspective' (1931) 40 *Yale Law Journal* 704–51 also in Brian Bix (ed), *Contract Law: Second Series: Volume I* (Aldershot, Ashgate, 2000) 3–50

A sketch of the social roles of contracts and contract law, discussing standardisation of contracts and the dangers of systematisation of contract law.

Morris R Cohen, 'The Basis of Contract' (1933) 46 *Harvard Law Review* 553–92

Standardisation of contracts is beneficial for freedom and effectiveness, but standardised contracts must be overseen by public bodies and courts.

Karl N Llewellyn, 'Book Review: Prausnitz: The Standardization of Commercial Contracts in English and Continental Law' (1939) 52 *Harvard Law Review* 700–5

The problems of standard form contracts cannot be dealt with covertly by strained construction and other techniques, but require the moulding of the terms themselves (through mandatory terms and the like) according to the particular type of relation involved.

Friedrich Kessler, 'Contracts of Adhesion—Some Thoughts About Freedom of Contract' (1943) 43 *Columbia Law Review* 629–42

When freedom of contract is dogmatically asserted, standardised mass contracts of adhesion enable enterprises to legislate by contract and force the courts to bend rules or stretch tort into the sphere of contract.

Karl Llewellyn, 'The Form or Boiler Plate Agreement' in his *The Common Law Tradition—Deciding Appeals* (Boston, MA, Little Brown and Co, 1960) 362–71

A consumer agreeing to a standard form assents to the negotiated terms, the broad type of transaction, and all not unreasonable or indecent terms that do not alter the reasonable meaning of the negotiated terms.

C Grunfeld, 'Reform in the Law of Contract' (1961) 24 *Modern Law Review* 62–84

Nicholas S Wilson, 'Freedom of Contract and Adhesion Contracts' (1965) 14 *International & Comparative Law Quarterly* 172–93

Arthur Allen Leff, 'Contract as Thing' (1970) 19 *American University Law Review* 131–57

Contracts of adhesion should not be thought of as contracts, not being the product of a cooperative process. Instead, they are things, specifically unilaterally manufactured products, which are bought or not bought.

W David Slawson, 'Standard Form Contracts and the Democratic Control of Lawmaking Power' (1971) 84 *Harvard Law Review* 529–66 and 'The New Meaning of Contract: The Transformation of Contract Law By Standard Forms' (1984) 46 *University of Pittsburgh Law Review* 21–74

[1971] Because of the lack of manifested consent involved in their creation, standard forms are not contracts. In the standard form case, the parties have not (both) consented to the private law by which they are to be governed, and thus the private law of the form should be subjected to external control by reference to public standards (for example through the perfectly competitive market or through judicial scrutiny of the form's terms). [1984] Contract no longer means the manifestation of mutual assent but has come to mean the reasonable expectations of the parties from whatever sources they may derive.

JH Baker, 'From Sanctity of Contract to Reasonable Expectations' (1979) 32 *Current Legal Problems* 17–39

There is a movement within the law from contract to the enforcement of (often extra-contractual) reasonable expectations which can be seen in the development of promissory estoppel, the application of the Unfair Contract Terms Act 1977 and the implication of terms. This may even signal the replacement of rules with subjective principles of fairness.

George Gluck, 'Standard Form Contracts: The Contract Theory Reconsidered' (1979) 28 *International & Comparative Law Quarterly* 72–90

Todd D Rakoff, 'Contracts of Adhesion: An Essay in Reconstruction' (1983) 96 *Harvard Law Review* 1174–284 also in Larry Alexander (ed), *Contract Law: Volume II* (Aldershot, Dartmouth, 1991) 73–184

Contracts of adhesion are a different social practice from other contracts. Standard form terms should be presumptively unenforceable, and the courts should look at whether the purpose of the term is merely the augmentation of the power of the drafter, whether the term seeks to uphold the organisational structure of the standard form author, and whether the term goes beyond the practice of the drafter.

Steve Hedley, 'Contracts as Promises' (1993) 44 *Northern Ireland Legal Quarterly* 12–33

The modern orthodox view is back-to-front in holding that standard form contracts are agreed, but statutory implied terms are imposed in opposition to promises.

Michael I Meyerson, 'The Reunification of Contract Law: The

Objective Theory of Consumer Form Contracts' (1993) 47 *University of Miami Law Review* 1263–333

The objective theory requires courts to determine what the reasonable consumer would have assented to.

James J White, 'Autistic Contracts' (2000) 45 *Wayne Law Review* 1693–732

Randy Barnett, 'Consenting to Form Contracts' (2002) 71 *Fordham Law Review* 627–45

Form contracts, save to the extent that their terms are both radically unexpected and unlikely to have been read, are consensual.

Robert A Hillman, 'Rolling Contracts' (2002) 71 *Fordham Law Review* 743–59

Robert A Hillman and Jeffrey J Rachlinski, 'Standard-Form Contracts in the Electronic Age' (2002) 77 *New York University Law Review* 429–95

Russell Korobkin, 'Bounded Rationality, Standard Form Contracts, and Unconscionability' (2003) 70 *University of Chicago Law Review* 1203–95

Consumers normally price only a few product attributes as part of their decision, giving businesses an incentive to otherwise rely on inefficient terms that favour themselves.

Omri Ben-Shahar (ed), *Boilerplate: The Foundation of Market Contracts* (Cambridge, Cambridge University Press, 2007)

4.4 INTERPRETATION AND THE OBJECTIVE PRINCIPLE

See also 3.4 The Objective Principle and Unilateral and Cross-Purposes Mistakes

General texts

Nicole Kornet, *Contract Interpretation and Gap Filling: Comparative and Theoretical Perspectives* (Antwerp, Intersentia, 2006)

Catherine Mitchell, *Interpretation of Contracts* (London, Routledge, 2007)

○ Kim Lewison, *The Interpretation of Contracts*, 4th edn (London, Sweet & Maxwell, 2007)

○ Gerard McMeel, *The Construction of Contracts: Interpretation, Implication and Rectification* (Oxford, Oxford University Press, 2007)

○ Steven J Burton, *Elements of Contract Interpretation* (New York, Oxford University Press, 2009)

Generally

Oliver Wendell Holmes, 'The Theory of Legal Interpretation' (1898–1899) 12 *Harvard Law Review* 417–20

Zechariah Chafee Jr, 'The Disorderly Conduct of Words' (1942) 20 *Canadian Bar Review* 752–76

Glanville L Williams, 'The Doctrine of Repugnancy: 1. Conditions in Gifts and 2. In the Law of Arbitration and 3. Clogging the Equity and Miscellaneous Applications' (1943) 59 *Law Quarterly Review* 343–58 and (1944) 60 *Law Quarterly Review* 69–82 and 190–94

Glanville Williams, 'Language and the Law: Parts I to V' (1945) 61 *Law Quarterly Review* 71–86, 179–95, 293–303, 384–405 and (1946) 62 *Law Quarterly Review* 387–406

An investigation of the use of language in the law, applying linguistic philosophy among other tools, with parts II–IV being the most relevant to the contract lawyer.

GHL Fridman, 'Construing, Without Constructing a Contract' (1962) 76 *Law Quarterly Review* 521–36

William F Young Jr, 'Equivocation in the Making of Agreements' (1964) 64 *Columbia Law Review* 619–47

An examination, drawing on Wittgenstein and others, of vagueness and equivocation (noting their ubiquity), and of the use of custom, negotiations and context (ie parol evidence) to identify the most reasonable of the conflicting understandings in all but the hardest cases (of which *Raffles v Wichelhaus* is one).

Edwin W Patterson, 'The Interpretation and Construction of Contracts' (1964) 64 *Columbia Law Review* 833–65

E Allan Farnsworth, '"Meaning" in the Law of Contracts' (1967) 76 *Yale Law Journal* 939–65

An explanation, using linguistic theory, as to how an interpreter can find out what a contractual document or utterance 'means'.

AR Carnegie, 'Terminability of Contracts of Unspecified Duration' (1969) 85 *Law Quarterly Review* 392–414

Lord Denning, 'The construction of contracts' in *The Discipline of Law* (London, Butterworths, 1979) 32–50

Robert S Summers, 'Statutes and Contracts as Founts of Formal Reasoning' in Peter Cane and Jane Stapleton (eds), *Essays for Patrick Atiyah* (Oxford, Clarendon Press, 1991) 71–86

Amy H Kastely, 'Out of Whiteness: On Race Codes and White

Race Consciousness in Some Tort, Criminal, and Contract Law' (1994) 63 *University of Cincinatti Law Review* 269–315

The objective theory of contract interpretation imposes the norms of privileged white men.

Brian Langille and Arthur Ripstein, 'Strictly Speaking—It Went Without Saying' (1996) 2 *Legal Theory* 63–81

It is legitimate to imply into contracts what went without saying as part of the basic process of interpretation, even if the content being implied never crossed the mind of the contractors.

DW McLauchlan, 'The Plain Meaning Rule of Contract Interpretation' (1996) 2 *New Zealand Business Law Quarterly* 80–102, 'Common Assumptions and Contractual Interpretation' (1997) 113 *Law Quarterly Review* 237–45 and 'A Contract Contradiction' (1999) 30 *Victoria University of Wellington Law Review* 175–95

Actual intention is relevant to the interpretation of contracts just as it is relevant to the formation of contracts. Where there is a common intention, or an intention of one party of which the other party knew or should have known, that should displace any objective meaning. At most there should be a presumption that the plain meaning was intended, which would be rebuttable after examination of all relevant evidence including pre-contractual negotiations and subsequent conduct.

Lord Hoffmann, 'The Intolerable Wrestle with Words and Meanings' (1997) 114 *South African Law Journal* 656–74

Larry A DiMatteo, *Contract Theory: The Evolution of Contractual Intent* (Michigan, Michigan State University Press, 1998)

A sophisticated analysis of the law of contractual intent as a dialectic within which subjective approaches are in tension with (often illusory but seemingly easier to justify) objective approaches.

Gerard McMeel, 'The Rise of Commercial Construction in Contract Law' [1998] *Lloyd's Maritime and Commercial Law Quarterly* 382–93

SC Smith, 'Making Sense of Contracts' (1999) *Scots Law Times* 307–12

Karen Eggleston, Eric A Posner and Richard Zeckhauser, 'The Design and Interpretation of Contracts: Why Complexity Matters' (2000) 95 *Northwestern University Law Review* 91–132

The complexity or otherwise of contracts may provide indications as to the negotiating process, the parties' goals, and whether one party took advantage of the other.

DW McLauchlan, 'The New Law of Contract Interpretation' (2000) 19 *New Zealand Universities Law Review* 147–76

Joseph M Perillo, 'The Origins of the Objective Theory of Contract Formation and Interpretation' (2000) 69 *Fordham Law Review* 427–77

Contrary to received wisdom, the objective theory is not a nineteenth-century invention but rather has been the dominant theory since time immemorial.

Johan Steyn, 'Interpretation: Legal Texts and their Landscape' in Basil S Markesinis (ed), *The Clifford Chance Millennium Lectures* (Oxford, Hart Publishing, 2000) 79–90 and 'The Intractable Problem of Legal Texts' (2003) 25 *Sydney Law Review* 5–19 also in Sarah Worthington (ed), *Commercial Law and Commercial Practice* (Oxford, Hart Publishing, 2003) 123–38.

William C Whitford, 'The Role of the Jury (and the Fact/Law Distinction) in the Interpretation of Written Contracts' [2001] *Wisconsin Law Review* 931–64

Adam Kramer, 'Common Sense Principles of Contract Interpretation (And How We've Been Using Them All Along)' (2003) 23 *Oxford Journal of Legal Studies* 173–96

The principles of contractual interpretation are an application of the ordinary methods of interpretation that are used in everyday communication.

Stewart Macaulay, 'The Real and the Paper Deal: Empirical Pictures of Relationships, Complexity and the Urge for Transparent Simple Rules' (2003) 66 *Modern Law Review* 44–79 also in David Campbell, Hugh Collins and John Wightman, *Implicit Dimensions of Contract* (Oxford, Hart Publishing, 2003) 51–102

Ewan McKendrick, 'The Interpretation of Contracts: Lord Hoffmann's Re-Statement' in Sarah Worthington (ed), *Commercial Law and Commercial Practice* (Oxford, Hart Publishing, 2003) 139–62

A survey of the reception in the courts of Lord Hoffmann's decision and dicta in *ICS v West Bromwich*.

Michael Kirby, 'Towards a Grand Theory of Interpretation: The Case of Statutes and Contracts' (2003) 24 *Statute Law Review* 95–111

Jacques H Herbots, 'Interpretation of Contracts' in Jan M Smits (ed), *Elgar Encylopedia of Comparative Law* (Cheltenham, Edward Elgar, 2006) 325–47

Andrew Burrows, 'Construction and Rectification' in Andrew Burrows and Edwin Peel, *Contract Terms* (Oxford, Oxford University Press, 2007) 77–99

Gerard McMeel, 'Overview: the Principles and Policies of Contractual Construction' in Andrew Burrows and Edwin Peel, *Contract Terms* (Oxford, Oxford University Press, 2007) 27–51

Catherine Mitchell, 'Narrativising Contract Law' (2008) 29 *Legal Studies* 19–46

The Matrix of Fact and the Parol Evidence Rule

James B Thayer, 'The 'Parol Evidence' Rule: Parts I and II' (1893) 6 *Harvard Law Review* 325–48 and 418–40

Charles T McCormick, 'The Parol Evidence Rule as a Procedural Device for Control of the Jury' (1932) 41 *Yale Law Journal* 365–85

JP McBaine, 'The Rule Against Disturbing Plain Meaning of Writings' (1943) 31 *California Law Review* 145–66; E Allan Farnsworth, '"Meaning" in the Law of Contracts' (1967) 76 *Yale Law Journal* 939–65

The parol evidence rule should be abolished: it is based upon an unsound assumption that words can ever have an unambiguous, acontextual meaning.

AK Corbin, 'The Interpretation of Words and the Parol Evidence Rule' (1965) 50 *Cornell Law Quarterly* 161–90

Extrinsic evidence is always necessary to interpret a contract: where the words are said to have a plain meaning, the interpreter is still using the extrinsic evidence of linguistic experience.

John D Calamari and Joseph M Perillo, 'A Plea for a Uniform Parol Evidence Rule and Principles of Contract Interpretation' (1967) 42 *Indiana Law Journal* 333–54

Law Commission, *Working Paper 70: The Parol Evidence Rule* (1976) and *Report 154: The Parol Evidence Rule* (1986); Scottish Law Commission, *Discussion Paper 97: Contract Law: Extrinsic Evidence, Supersession, and the Actio Quanti Minoris* (1994) and *Report 162: Three Bad Rules in Contract Law* (1996)

The English Law Commission decided that there was no need to legislate to abolish the English parol evidence rule because the rule no longer has any content. The Scottish Law Commission concluded that the Scottish parol evidence rule was stricter than the English rule, and should be replaced by a rebuttable presumption that a written document contains all the express terms of the contractual agreement. The proposed Bill was enacted as the Contract (Scotland) Act 1997.

Lawrence A Cunningham, 'Toward a Prudential and Credibility-centred Parol Evidence Rule' (2000) 68 *University of Cincinnati Law Review* 269–321

SM Waddams, 'Do We Need a Parol Evidence Rule?' (1991) 19 *Canadian Business Law Journal* 385–96

When there is agreement that writing prevails, it should be allowed do so. Further, signature should raise a presumption that there is an agreement that writing is to prevail.

Christopher Staughton, 'Interpretation of Maritime Contracts' (1995) 26 *Journal of Maritime Law and Commerce* 259–71

Mark K Glasser and Keith A Rowley, 'On Parol: The Construction and Interpretation of Written Agreements and the Role of Extrinsic Evidence in Contract Litigation' (1997) 49 *Baylor Law Review* 657–62

Christopher Staughton, 'How Do the Courts Interpret Commercial Contracts?' [1999] *Cambridge Law Journal* 303–13

The use of the matrix of facts and the liberality of contractual interpretation have gone too far.

Hugh Collins, 'Objectivity and Committed Contextualism in Interpretation' in Sarah Worthington (ed), *Commercial Law and Commercial Practice* (Oxford, Hart Publishing, 2003) 189–209

For the committed contextualist, the context determines everything, including how much weight should be given to the words of the text (which is determined by the type of document being interpreted). Further, this reveals that contract interpretation is very different from statutory interpretation because they are involved with different language games: the former is about no more than the impression of the reasonable reader; the latter is about orders, prohibitions, and so the purpose and intention of the drafter (Parliament).

Alan Schwartz and Robert E Scott, 'Contract Theory and the Limits of Contract Law' (2003) 113 *Yale Law Journal* 541–620

In the case of commercial contracts, law should aim for efficiency, which requires adoption of a narrow textualist theory of contract interpretation, except where the parties so request.

Hon JJ Spigelman QC, 'From Text to Context: Contemporary Contractual Interpretation' (2007) 81 *Australian Law Journal* 322–37

Contextual interpretation often goes too far, particularly where, as is often the case in commercial transactions, third parties are involved.

Robert Stevens, 'Objectivity, Mistake and the Parol Evidence Rule' in Andrew Burrows and Edwin Peel, *Contract Terms* (Oxford, Oxford University Press, 2007) 101–21

The parol evidence rule is a rule of construction. Where a document is intended to be the entire embodiment of terms, or even the entire evidence as to terms, all other evidence is irrelevant to that extent.

Evidence of Pre-contractual Negotiations and Subsequent Conduct

Johan Steyn, 'Written Contracts: To What Extent May Evidence Control Language?' (1988) 41*Current Legal Problems* 23–32

A defence of the rules excluding evidence of pre-contractual negotiations and subsequent conduct.

Stephen Charles, 'Interpretation of Ambiguous Contracts by Reference to Subsequent Conduct' (1991) 4 *Journal of Contract law* 16–36

DW McLauchlan, 'Subsequent Conduct as an Aid to Interpretation' (1996) 2 *New Zealand Business Law Quarterly* 237–60

Evidence of subsequent conduct should be admissible when interpreting contracts.

Scottish Law Commission, *Discussion Paper 101: Interpretation in Private Law* (1996) and *Report 160: Interpretation in Private Law* (1997)

The Report proposes a Bill to codify the rules of interpretation, maintaining the rules rendering inadmissible evidence of pre-contractual negotiations and subsequent conduct.

David V Snyder, 'Language and Formalities in Commercial Contracts: A Defence of Custom and Conduct' (2001) 54 *SMU Law Review* 617–54

Gerard McMeel, 'Prior Negotiations and Subsequent Conduct—The Next Step Forward for Contractual Interpretation?' (2003) 119 *Law Quarterly Review* 272–97

The rules rendering inadmissible evidence of prior negotiations and subsequent conduct render the law incoherent and should be abolished, taking the modern approach to interpretation to its logical conclusion. Nevertheless, prior negotiations and subsequent conduct should only be admitted when they exhibit a consensus and are relevant, and should be regulated by means of assessments as to materiality and careful case-management.

Donald Nicholls, 'My Kingdom for a Horse: The Meaning of Words' (2005) 121 *Law Quarterly Review* 577–91

Although sometimes of limited usefulness, evidence of prior negotiations and subsequent conduct will often be relevant and should be admissible.

Custom

Lisa Bernstein, 'Merchant Law in a Merchant Court: Rethinking the Code's Search for Immanent Business Norms' (1996) 144 *University of Pennsylvania Law Review* 1765–822

Lisa Bernstein, 'The Questionable Empirical Basis of Article 2's Incorporation Strategy: A Preliminary Study' (1999) 66 *University of Chicago Law Review* 710–80

Richard Craswell, 'Do Trade Customs Exist?' in Jody S Kraus and Steven D Walt (eds), *The Jurisprudential Foundations of Corporate and Commercial Law* (Cambridge, Cambridge University Press, 2000) 118–48

Courts should beware simplistic identification of customs, which are patterns of behaviour arising out of case-by-case judgments that cannot be identified in isolation from normative and policy analyses.

Jody S Kraus and Steven D Walt, 'In Defence of the Incorporation Strategy' in their (as eds), *The Jurisprudential Foundations of*

Corporate and Commercial Law (Cambridge, Cambridge University Press, 2000) 193–237

Rules incorporating the norms of commercial practice reduce the cost of specifying contract terms, outweighing the disadvantage of higher interpretive costs (over plain-meaning regimes).

RA Epstein, 'Confusion about Custom: Disentangling Informal Customs from Standard Contractual Provisions' (1999) 66 *University of Chicago Law Review* 821–35

David V Snyder, 'Language and Formalities in Commercial Contracts: A Defense of Custom and Conduct' (2001) 54 *SMU Law Review* 617–54

John Wightman, 'Beyond Custom: Contract, Contexts, and the Recognition of Implicit Understandings' in David Campbell, Hugh Collins and John Wightman, *Implicit Dimensions of Contract* (Oxford, Hart Publishing, 2003) 143–86

Implicit understandings are made up of a society's 'general understandings', personal 'inter-party understandings' and particular trade sector 'customary understandings'. There will be more implicit understandings surrounding contracts within a contracting community (two repeat players) than surrounding contracts characteristic of personal consumption (experience or credence goods consumer contracts), and this can explain the problem of standard forms in the latter type of contract. Further, where the implicit understandings run out in the latter type of contract, there are good reasons for holding the parties to the consumer's unilateral expectations even when these do not reflect actual practice.

Entire Agreement Clauses

Elisabeth Peden and JW Carter, 'Entire Agreement—and Similar—Clauses' (2006) 22 *Journal of Contract Law* 1–15

Such clauses operate by making an attempt to prove additional terms a breach of contract, rather than by estoppel. Logically, they are principally about integrating the express terms into one document, and therefore implied terms and pre-contractual misrepresentations should be dealt with by a different clause.

Catherine Mitchell, 'Entire Agreement Clauses: Contracting Out of Contextualism' (2006) 22 *Journal of Contract Law* 222–45 and *Interpretation of Contracts* (London, Routledge, 2007) chs 4 and 5

An analysis of entire agreement clauses as a (in some cases) reasonable contracting out of contextual interpretation in favour of more formal interpretation (to avoid the costs of contextualism and the risk of judicial error).

John Cartwright, 'Excluding Liability for Misrepresentation' in Andrew Burrows and Edwin Peel (eds), *Contract Terms* (Oxford, Oxford University Press, 2007) 213–31

Reasonable Expectations

Barry Reiter and John Swan 'Contracts and the Protection of Reasonable Expectations' in their (as eds), *Studies in Contract Law* (Toronto, Butterworths, 1980) 1–22

Stephen Waddams, 'Good Faith, Unconscionability, and Reasonable Expectations' (1995) 9 *Journal of Contract Law* 55–68

Johan Steyn, 'Fulfilling the Reasonable Expectations of Honest Men' (1997) 113 *Law Quarterly Review* 433–42

Catherine Mitchell, 'Leading a Life of its Own? The Roles of Reasonable Expectations in Contract Law' (2003) 23 *Oxford Journal of Legal Studies* 639–65

Criticism of ritual appeals to reasonable expectations, observing that 'reasonable expectations' has different senses depending upon its different possible bases (institutional, empirical and normative), and an examination of the relationship between reasonable expectations and a contract's terms.

Roger Brownsword, 'After *Investors*: Interpretation, Expectation and the Implicit Dimension of the "New Contextualism"' in David Campbell, Hugh Collins and John Wightman (eds), *Implicit Dimensions of Contract* (Oxford, Hart Publishing, 2003) 103–41

In addition to expectations that are reasonable because of their basis in widespread practice, there may be expectations that are reasonable because they reflect a priori entitlements, and such entitlement-based reasonable expectations might plausibly start from a co-operative default position.

Cooperation and Good Faith

JF Burrows, 'Contractual Co-operation and the Implied Term' (1968) 31 *Modern Law Review* 390–407

English law contains an underlying principle or policy requiring co-operation within narrow limits; thus one must not interfere with the enjoyment of what one has contracted to provide, must not hinder the other party's performance, and occasionally must actively co-operate. A variety of implied terms are derived from this policy, as are a few legal rules such as that one must not derogate from one's grant.

John N Adams, 'The Economics of Good Faith in Contract' (1995) 8 *Journal of Contract Law* 126–37

Good faith is not only a matter of concern to consumer-welfarists. Market-individualists should also be concerned by the interference with the parties' risk exchange that bad faith in the performance of contracts may give rise to.

Roger Brownsword, '"Good Faith in Contract" Revisited' (1996) 49 *Current Legal Problems* 111–57, 'From Co-operative Contracting to a Contract of Co-operation' in David Campbell and Peter Vincent-Jones (eds), *Contract and Economic Organisation* (Aldershot, Dartmouth, 1996) 14–39 and 'After *Investors*: Interpretation, Expectation and the Implicit Dimension of the 'New Contextualism" in David Campbell, Hugh Collins and John Wightman (eds), *Implicit Dimensions of Contract* (Oxford, Hart Publishing, 2003) 103–41

(2003) One aspect of the context relevant to interpretation is the contractual culture: individualistic or co-operative or somewhere in between. It might be best to adopt a default presumption as to the ethic for situations in which the ethic cannot be identified within the practice surrounding the contract. (1996a) A good faith requirement is needed to recreate the normative setting in which contracts are made and so to better give effect to the parties' implicit understandings. (1996b) Co-operative contracting is centrally about the moral requirements arising out of the contractual community of interest.

Elisabeth Peden, '"Cooperation" in English Contract Law—To Construe or Imply?' (2000) 16 *Journal of Contract Law* 56–67 and *Good Faith in the Performance of Contracts* (Chatswood, NSW, Butterworths, 2003a); JW Carter and Elisabeth Peden, 'Good Faith in Australian Contract Law' (2003b) 19 *Journal of Contract Law* 155–72

[2000 and 2003a] Co-operation is not an implied term but rather is a general principle of contract law that takes effect as the main principle of construction, employed in discovering the parties' intentions. [2003b] An unpacking of the content of the concept of good faith, concluding that the principal elements are honesty, loyalty to the contract and a requirement to consider the other party's legitimate interests. These principles are immanent in the law and there is no need for an implied term of good faith.

Estoppel by Convention

Rory Derham, 'Estoppel by Convention—Parts I and II' (1997) 71 *Australian Law Journal* 860–881 and 976–96

Piers Feltham, Daniel Hochberg, Tom Leech and George Spencer Bower, *Spencer Bower on the Law Relating to Estoppel by Representation*, 4th edn (Tottel, 2004)

4.5 IMPLIED TERMS

Generally

E Allan Farnsworth, 'Disputes Over Omissions in Contracts (1968) 68 *Columbia Law Review* 860–91

Parties do not have expectations concerning all possible situations, and only some expectations that they do have are reduced to contract language. In gaps the courts 'infer', applying actual expectations were there are some, or fairness and justice, sometimes reasoning by analogy with what the parties agreed or deciding which party had the burden of expression.

Lord Denning, 'The Construction of Contracts' in *The Discipline of Law* (London, Butterworths, 1979) 32–50

Richard E Speidel, 'Restatement Second: Omitted Terms and Contract Method' (1982) 67 *Cornell Law Review* 785–809

Todd D Rakoff, 'The Implied Terms of Contracts: Of "Default Rules" and "Situation-Sense"' in Jack Beatson and Daniel Friedmann (eds), *Good Faith and Fault in Contract Law* (Oxford, Clarendon Press, 1995) 191–228

Taking Karl Llewellyn's idea of 'situation-sense' as his point of departure, there should be a greater role for transaction or relationship types (ie descriptive generalisations about the parties' situations) in the implication of terms and the design of default rules.

George M Cohen, 'Implied Terms and Interpretation in Contract Law' in Boudewijn Bouckaert and Gerrit De D Geest (eds), *Encyclopedia of Law and Economics, Volume III: The Regulation of Contracts* (Cheltenham, Elgar, 2000) 78–99

Terms Implied in Fact

S Stoljar, 'Prevention and Co-operation in the Law of Contract' (1953) 31 *Canadian Bar Review* 231–260

JF Burrows, 'Implied Terms and Presumptions' (1968–1969) 3 *New Zealand Universities Law Review* 121–41

The officious bystander test only makes sense in the frequent situations in which a presumption of one sort or another exists in favour of or against a particular term. Where the court has no pre-existing inclination it will have to select among several alternative terms, and the officious bystander test will rarely assist in so doing.

Lord Hoffmann, 'Anthropomorphic Justice: The Reasonable Man and His Friends' (1995) 29 *Law Teacher* 127–41

Jeannie Marie Paterson, 'Terms Implied in Fact: the Basis for Implication' (1998) 13 *Journal of Contract Law* 103–25

Terms are implied on the basis of what would have been intended had the parties considered the gap in question, ie on the parties' hypothetical intention. The process of implication can be improved by recognising that often parties will intend to allocate responsibilities in the most economically efficient manner (as between the two parties), and will favour co-operation, although there are dangers in implying terms based upon fairness.

Andrew Phang, 'Implied Terms, Business Efficacy and the Officious Bystander—A Modern History' [1998] *Journal of Business Law* 1–34

An investigation of the sources of the Bowen LJ's business efficacy test in *The Moorcock*, and MacKinnon LJ's officious bystander test of *Shirlaw v Southern Foundries*, using historical and biographical analysis to suggest ways of understanding and reconciling the tests, as well as suggesting that it is Scrutton LJ (through his earlier decision in *Reigate v Union Manufacturing Company (Ramsbottom) Ltd*) and not MacKinnon LJ who should be credited with inventing the officious bystander test.

Elisabeth Peden, '"Cooperation" in English Contract Law—To Construe or Imply?' (2000) 16 *Journal of Contract Law* 56–67 and *Good Faith in the Performance of Contracts* (Chatswood, NSW, Butterworths, 2003)

A survey of the rules governing the implication of terms and their history. There is no need for a doctrine of implication in fact and such cases should be determined on the ordinary principles of construction, with the business efficacy and obviousness tests operating as useful tests of construction. Co-operation is not an implied term but rather is a general principle of contract law that takes effect as the main principle of construction, employed in discovering the parties' intentions.

Adam Kramer, 'The Implication of Contract Terms as an Instance of Interpretation' [2004] *Cambridge Law Journal* 384–411

The implication of terms in fact is a special instance of contractual interpretation and the strictness of the implication tests, as compared with the basic test of supplementation by interpretation, is explained by the primariness of the information that is going without saying in implied term cases.

Trust and Confidence

Douglas Brodie, 'The Heart of the Matter: Mutual Trust and Confidence' (1996) 25 *Industrial Law Journal* 121–36, 'Beyond Exchange: The New Contract of Employment' (1998) *Industrial Law Journal* 79–102, 'Mutual Trust and the Values of the Employment Contract' (2001) 30 *Industrial Law Journal*

84–100, and 'Legal Coherence and the Employment Revolution' (2001) 117 *Law Quarterly Review* 604–25

The implications and impact of the implied duty of trust and confidence in employment contracts.

Lindsay J, 'The Implied Term of Trust and Confidence' (2001) 30 *Industrial Law Journal* 1–16

Manitoba Law Reform Commission, *Report 107: Good Faith and the Individual Contract of Employment* (2001)

Following the Supreme Court of Canada decision in *Wallace v United Grain Growers Ltd*, there is a need for legislation implying an obligation upon employers to act in good faith in the performance or termination of the employment contract, breach of which would give rise to compensatory, aggravated or punitive damages.

Kelly Godfrey, 'Contracts of Employment: Renaissance of the Implied Term of Trust and Confidence' (2003) 77 *Australian Law Journal* 764–76

David Cabrelli, 'The Implied Duty of Mutual Trust and Confidence: An Emerging Overarching Principle?' (2005) 34 *Industrial Law Journal* 284–307

Despite the evolution of the implied duty of trust and confidence, the law shows no signs of subsuming the employer's duty of care and other implied duties (and key differences, such as some being mandatory and others derogable, prevent this).

Matthew Boyle, 'The Relational Principle of Trust and Confidence' (2007) 27 *Oxford Journal of Legal Studies* 633–57

The duty of trust and confidence embodies the relational nature of the employment relationship, governing the content of both parties' duties within the relationship, the remedies for breach of those duties, and variations and termination of the relationship.

Jennie Marie Paterson, 'The Standard of Good Faith performance: Reasonable Expectations or Community Standards?' in Michael Bryan (ed), *Private Law in Theory and Practice* (2007, London, Routledge) 153–66

If there is a duty of good faith performance, it should be based upon reasonable expectations and not community standards.

Duties of Good Faith

See also 2.3 Duties to Bargain in Good Faith

Raphael Powell, 'Good Faith in Contracts' (1956) 9 *Current Legal Problems* 16–38

There is no overriding duty of good faith, but such duties operate most effectively elsewhere when they appeal to common usage for their standards.

E Allan Farnsworth, 'Good Faith Performance and Commercial Reasonableness Under the Uniform Commercial Code' (1963) 30 *University of Chicago Law Review* 666–79

Robert S Summers, '"Good Faith" in General Contract Law and the Sales Provisions of the Uniform Commercial Code' (1968) 54 *Virginia Law Review* 195–267

Good faith is best understood as an 'excluder', with no general meaning of its own but rather which excludes many forms of bad faith (principally where a party frustrates the justified expectations of the other).

Steven J Burton, 'Breach of Contract and the Common Law Duty to Perform in Good Faith', (1980) 94 *Harvard Law Review* 369–403; Robert S Summers, 'The General Duty of Good Faith—Its Recognition and Conceptualization' (1982) 67 *Cornell Law Review* 810–35; Steven J Burton, 'More on Good Faith Performance of a Contract: A Reply to Professor Summers' (1984) 69 *Iowa Law Review* 497–512

Eric G Anderson, 'Good Faith in the Enforcement of Contracts' (1988) 73 *Iowa Law Review* 299–350

BJ Reiter, 'Good Faith in Contracts' (1983) 17 *Valparaiso University Law Review* 705–34

HK Lücke, 'Good Faith and Contractual Performance' in PD Finn (ed), *Essays on Contract* (Sydney, Law Book Co, 1987) 155–82

Paul Finn, 'Commerce, the Common Law and Morality' (1989) 17 *Melbourne University Law Review* 87–99

J Steyn, 'The Role of Good Faith and Fair Dealing in Contract Law: A Hair-Shirt Philosophy?' [1991] *Denning Law Journal* 131–41 also (1992) 58 *Arbitration* 51–56

Malcolm Clarke, 'The Common Law of Contract in 1993: Is There a General Doctrine of Good Faith?' (1993) 23 *Hong Kong Law Journal* 318–41

Roger Brownsword, 'Two Concepts of Good Faith' (1994) 7 *Journal of Contract Law* 197–244, '"Good Faith in Contract" Revisited' (1996a) 49 *Current Legal Problems* 111–57, 'From Co-operative Contracting to a Contract of Co-operation' in David Campbell and Peter Vincent-Jones (eds), *Contract and Economic Organisation* (Aldershot, Dartmouth, 1996b) 14–39 and 'After *Investors*: Interpretation, Expectation and the Implicit Dimension of the 'New Contextualism'' in David Campbell, Hugh Collins and John Wightman (eds), *Implicit Dimensions of Contract* (Oxford, Hart Publishing, 2003) 103–41

[1994] A good faith requirement is needed, adopting a general non-adversarial ethic in commercial as well as consumer contracting rather than adopting good faith as an exception to the usual rule. (1996a) A good faith regime should be adopted, replacing the adversarial ethic with a co-operative one, either on moral grounds or on the grounds of rationality. (1996b) Co-operative contracting is guided by the contractual community of interest, restraining permissible regard for self-interest. (2003) Good faith might be justified by a theory of a prior entitlements, taking a Kantian approach.

Gillian K Hadfield, 'Judicial Competence and the Interpretation of Incomplete Contracts' (1994) 23 *Journal of Legal Studies* 159–84

Michael Bridge, 'Good Faith in Commercial Contracts' in Roger Brownsword, Norma J Hird and Geraint Howells (eds), *Good Faith in Contract: Concept and Context* (Aldershot, Dartmouth, 1999) 139–64

Ewan McKendrick, 'Good Faith: A Matter of Principle?' in ADM Forte (ed), *Good Faith in Contract and Property Law* (Oxford, Hart Publishing, 1999) 39–62

The dangers and advantages of introducing a general doctrine of good faith.

R Zimmermann and S Whittaker (eds), *Good Faith in European Contract Law* (Cambridge, Cambridge University Press, 2000)

Emily MS Houh, 'The Doctrine of Good Faith in Contract Law: A (Nearly) Empty Vessel?' [2005] *Utah Law Review* 1–56

Woo Pei Yee, 'Protection Parties' Reasonable Expectations: A General Principle of Good Faith' (2001) *Oxford University Commonwealth Law Journal* 195–229

Robert E Scott, 'The Death of Contract Law' (2004) 54 *University of Toronto Law Journal* 369–90

Contract law has become expensive, uncertain and so unfit for purpose. There is a need for a return to classical/minimalist contract law, leaving more to self-enforcement by the parties.

Terms Implied in Law

Edwin W Patterson, 'Compulsory Contracts in the Crystal Ball' (1943) 43 *Columbia Law Review* 731–49

The tort-like elements of the many contracts which, although voluntary in the sense that they or the social position giving rise to them were voluntarily undertaken in the first place, contain compulsory terms.

Andrew Boon Leong Phang, 'Implied Terms Revisited' [1990] *Journal of Business Law* 394–413

Criticism of the existence and operation of the rules by which contract terms are implied in law.

Elisabeth Peden, 'Policy Concerns Behind Implication of Terms in Law' (2001) 117 *Law Quarterly Review* 459–76

Policy concerns are rarely discussed by the courts but are nevertheless relevant to the implication of terms in law.

Implied and Collateral Contracts

KW Wedderburn, 'Collateral Contracts' [1959] *Cambridge Law Journal* 58–85

A defence of the use of collateral contracts where there are two stages of a transaction.

David W McLauchlan, 'The Inconsistent Collateral Contract' (1976) 3 *Dalhousie Law Journal* 136–77

Inconsistent collateral contracts should be enforceable either directly, or as part of the main agreement viewed as being partly in writing and partly oral.

GH Treitel, 'Bills of Lading and Third Parties' (1986) 10 *Lloyd's Maritime and Commercial Law Quarterly* 294–304 and 'Bills of Lading and Implied Contracts' [1989] *Lloyd's Maritime and Commercial Law Quarterly* 162–73

The law of implied contracts between bill of lading consignees and third party carriers.

John E Stannard, 'The Road to Shanklin Pier, or the Leading Case that Never Was' (2007) 57 *Northern Ireland Legal Quarterly* 375–90

4.6 EXCLUSION AND PENALTY CLAUSES AND UNFAIR TERMS

General Texts

- Elizabeth MacDonald, *Exemption Clauses and Unfair Terms*, 2nd edn (Tottel, 2006)
- Roger Brownsword and Christian Twigg-Flesner, *Exclusion Clauses* (London, Sweet & Maxwell, 2009)

Generally

See also 8.2 Third Part Rights to Rely on Exclusion Clauses, and the Effect of Breach on Exclusion Clauses, and the Doctrine of Fundamental Breach in 10.5

Emlin McClain, 'Contractual Limitation of Liability for Negligence' (1915) 28 *Harvard Law Review* 550–64

Brian Coote, *Exception Clauses* (London, Sweet & Maxwell, 1964)

Exception clauses are duty-defining or delimiting, not merely defensive.

Jan Hellner, 'Consequential Loss and Exemption Clauses' (1981) 1 *Oxford Journal of Legal Studies* 13–49

William Howarth, 'Some Common Law Limitations to the Construction of Exclusion Clauses' (1985) 36 *Northern Ireland Legal Quarterly* 101–21

Hugh Beale, 'Unfair Contracts in Britain and Europe' (1989) 42 *Current Legal Problems* 197–205

Why unfair clauses make it into contracts and possible approaches to challenging them, with the tentative conclusion that a clause is fair if it does not cause unfair surprise and represents a balance of risk and price that is acceptable to a sufficient margin of aware consumers.

John JA Burke, 'Reinventing Contract' (2003) 10(2) *Murdoch University Electronic Journal of Law*

Content controlling rules for standardised contracts should be looked at broadly, outside contract law.

Hugh Beale, 'Exclusion and Limitation Clauses in Business Contracts: Transparency' in Andrew Burrows and Edwin Peel (eds), *Contract Terms* (Oxford, Oxford University Press, 2007) 191–209

Construing Exclusion Clauses

Nyuk Chin, 'The Problem of Exception Clauses: A Theory of Performance-Related Risks' (1983) 15 *University of Western Australia Law Review* 347–97

There is a minimum standard of exchange preventing exclusion of certain breaches of contract, such as wilful breaches.

JW Carter, '"Commercial" Construction and the *Canada SS Rules*' (1995) 9 *Journal of Contract Law* 69–102

Even in an age of commercial construction, secondary construction rules are still useful in assisting the court construing exclusion clauses in determining the parties' presumed intention. Further, commercial construction should lead to a functional approach to exclusion clauses, sometimes treating them as defining the scope of a duty rather than excluding liability.

JW Carter and David Yates, 'Perspectives on Commercial Construction and the *Canada SS* Case' (2004) 20 *Journal of Contract Law* 233–64

Edwin Peel, 'Whither Contra Proferentem' in Andrew Burrows and Edwin Peel (eds), *Contract Terms* (Oxford, Oxford University Press, 2007) 53–75

The 'exemption rule' part of the *contra proferentem* principle is justified as an interpretative aid reminding the court to require to be convinced that a result was intended where that result contradicts or qualifies other basic obligations.

Discretionary Powers

Hugh Collins, 'Discretionary Powers in Contracts' in David Campbell, Hugh Collins and John Wightman (eds), *Implicit Dimensions of Contract* (Oxford, Hart Publishing, 2003) 219–54

Terence Daintith, 'Contractual Discretion and Administrative Discretion: A Unified Analysis' (2005) 68 *Modern Law Review* 554–93

UK Unfair Terms Legislation Generally

Elizabeth MacDonald, 'Mapping the Unfair Contract Terms Act 1977 and the Directive on Unfair Terms in Consumer Contracts' [1994] *Journal of Business Law* 441–62

An exploration of problems in establishing the scope of the two pieces of legislation.

Law Commission and Scottish Law Commission, *Consultation Paper 166: Unfair Terms in Contracts* (2002) and Report 292: *Unfair Terms in Contracts* (2005)

The Commissions recommend a unified regime (replacing UCTA and the UTCCR) for consumers, maintained protection for businesses and increased protection for small businesses.

○ Chris Willett, *Fairness in Consumer Contracts: The Case of Unfair Terms* (Aldershot, Ashgate, 2007)

The (English) Unfair Contract Terms 1977 Act

Law Commission and Scottish Law Commission, *Report 69: Exemption Clauses Second Report* (1975)

Peter KJ Thompson, *Unfair Contract Terms Act 1977* (London, Butterworths, 1978)

Norman Palmer and David Yates, 'The Future of the Unfair Contract Terms Act 1977' [1981] *Cambridge Law Journal* 108–34

The 1977 Act can be circumvented by using duty-defining, rather than liability-excluding, clauses.

Richard Kidner, 'The Unfair Contract Terms Act 1977 – Who Deals As Consumer?' (1987) 38 *Northern Ireland Legal Quarterly* 46–57

John N Adams and Roger Brownsword, 'The Unfair Contract Terms Act: A Decade of Discretion' (1988) 104 *Law Quarterly Review* 94–119

Robert A Pearce, 'Acting in the Course of a Business' [1989] *Lloyd's Maritime and Commercial Law Quarterly* 371–81

Elizabeth MacDonald, 'Exclusion Clauses: the Ambit of s 13(1) of the Unfair Contract Terms Act 1977' (1992) 12 *Legal Studies* 277–301

Steve Wilson and Sheila Bone, 'Businesses, Standard Terms and the Unfair Contract Terms Act 1977' (2002) *Journal of Obligations and Remedies* 29–39

An investigation of the meaning of the Act's requirement that contracting was on the 'other's written standard terms of business'.

Elizabeth MacDonald, 'UCTA Thirty Years On' in Andrew Burrows and Edwin Peel (eds), *Contract Terms* (Oxford, Oxford University Press, 2007) 154–72

The extent to which businesses are covered by UCTA when 'dealing as a consumer' or dealing on the 'other's written standard terms of business', and the underused potential of section 3(2)(b)(i) (which concerns clauses which allow the performance to differ from that reasonably expected by the other).

The (European) Unfair Terms in Consumer Contracts Directive

Hans Erich Brandner and Peter Ulmer, 'The Community Directive on Unfair Terms in Consumer Contracts: Some Critical Remarks on the Proposal Submitted by the EC Commission' (1991) 28 *Common Market Law Review* 647–62

The proposed directive and the extent to which it should apply to core or price terms.

Hugh Collins, 'Good Faith in European Contract Law' (1994) 14 *Oxford Journal of Legal Studies* 229–54

The likely effect of European harmonisation in general, and the 1993 EC Directive in particular, on UK contract law.

Susan Bright and Christopher Bright, 'Unfair Terms in Land Contracts: Copy Out or Cop Out?' (1995) 111 *Law Quarterly Review* 655–73

Roger Brownsword, Geraint Howells and Thomas Wilhelmsson, 'Between Market and Welfare: Some Reflections on Article 3 of the EC Directive on Unfair Terms in Consumer Contracts' in Chris Willett (ed), *Aspects of Fairness in Contract* (London, Blackstone, 1996) 25–58

An in-depth analysis of Article 3 and the good faith test.

Hugh Beale, 'Legislative Control of Fairness: The Directive on Unfair Terms in Consumer Contracts', in Jack Beatson and Daniel Friedmann (eds), *Good Faith and Fault in Contract Law* (Oxford, Clarendon Press, 1995) 231–61

Roger Brownsword and Geraint G Howells, 'The Implementation of the EC Directive on Unfair Terms in Consumer Contracts—Some Unresolved Questions' [1995] *Journal of Business Law* 243–63

Mário Tenreiro, 'The Community Directive on Unfair Terms and National Legal Systems: The Principle of Good Faith and Remedies for Unfair Terms' (1995) 3 *European Review of Private Law* 273–305

The drafting process of the Directive.

Anne de Moor, 'Common and Civil Law Conceptions of Contract: The Case of the Directive on Unfair Terms in Consumer Contracts' (1995) 3 *European Review of Private Law* 257–71

A national contract law is a product of a particular legal system and community and this raises problems when implementing the Directive, which aims for harmonisation.

Elizabeth MacDonald, 'The Emperor's Old Clauses: Unincorporated Clauses, Misleading Terms and the Unfair Terms in Consumer Contracts Regulations' [1999] *Cambridge Law Journal* 413–36

Unincorporated terms, although having no legal effect, affect consumers' perceptions of their rights, and the Regulations should be construed to cover such non-terms and their effects in creating an imbalance in usable rights, so that they fall within the Director General's authority.

Simon Whittaker, 'Unfair Contract Terms, Public Services and the Construction of a European Conception of Contract' (2000) 116 *Law Quarterly Review* 95–120

Susan Bright, 'Winning the Battle Against Unfair Contract Terms' (2000) 20 *Legal Studies* 331–52

The enforcement of the 1999 Regulations by the Office of Fair Trading through pre-emptive challenges, and a comparison of the 1999 Regulations with their 1994 predecessors.

Jeremy Simmonds, 'Bankers' Documents and the Unfair Terms in Consumer Contracts Regulations 1999' (2002) 17 *Journal of International Banking Law* 205–19

Law Commission and Scottish Law Commission, *Consultation Paper 166: Unfair Terms in Contracts* (2002) and *Report 292: Unfair Terms in Contracts* (2005)

UCTA and UTCCR should be consolidated, and a draft Unfair Contract Terms Bill is attached.

Jesse Elvin, 'The Application of the Unfair Terms in Consumer Contract Regulations 1999' (2003) 14 *Kings College Law Journal* 39–63

Elizabeth MacDonald, 'Unifying Unfair Terms Legislation' (2004) 67 *Modern Law Review* 69–93

John Vickers, 'Contracts and European Consumer Law: An OFT Perspective' and Ulf Bernitz 'The Commission's Communications and Standard Contract Terms' in Stefan Vogenauer and Stephen Weatherill (eds), *The Harmonisation of European Contract Law: Implications for European Private Laws, Business and Legal Practice* (Oxford, Hart Publishing, 2006) 171–84 and 185–95

Susan Bright, 'Unfairness and the Consumer Contract Regulations' in Andrew Burrows and Edwin Peel (eds), *Contract Terms* (Oxford, Oxford University Press, 2007) 173–90

The extent to which the unfairness test is interested in matters of procedure as compared with matters of policy, and discussion of the way the Directive is and can be applied in the more general arena of the OFT challenge (rather than individual litigation).

Paolisa Nebbia, *Unfair Contract Terms in European Law: A Study in Comparative and EC Law* (Oxford, Hart Publishing, 2007)

Florian Bruder, 'Burden of Proof and the Unfair Terms in Consumer Contracts Directive' (2007) 15 *European Review of Private Law* 205–31

Penalty Clauses

Alvin C Brightman, 'Liquidated Damages' (1925) 25 *Columbia Law Review* 277–304

Ian R Macneil, 'Power of Contract and Agreed Remedies' (1962) 47 *Cornell Law Review* 495–528

AH Hudson, 'Penalties Limiting Damages' (1974) 90 *Law Quarterly Review* 31–34; GH Gordon, 'Penalties limiting Damages' (1974) 90 *Law Quarterly Review* 296–97; AH Hudson, 'Penalties Limiting Damages' (1975) 91 *Law Quarterly Review* 25–26; JL Barton, 'Penalties and Damages' (1976) 92 *Law Quarterly Review* 20–26

Whether the claimant should be limited to the amount fixed in the penalty clause where loss exceeds the amount set down as payable by the clause (eg because the clause fixes the amount payable in a variety of different breaches).

Law Commission, *Working Paper No 61: Penalty Clauses and Forfeiture of Monies Paid* (1975)

These provisions should be subject to judicial control even where they take effect without a breach wherever the object of the provision is to secure an act which is the true purpose of the contract, and there should be a statutory percentage level that is permitted for deposits in sales of land.

Roger Brownsword, 'Remedy-Stipulation in the English Law of Contract: Freedom or Paternalism' (1977) 9 *Ottawa Law Review* 95–155

Charles J Goetz and Robert E Scott, 'Liquidated Damages, Penalties and the Just Compensation Principle: Some Notes on an Enforcement Model and a Theory of Efficient Breach' (1977) 77 *Columbia Law Review* 554–94 also in Larry Alexander (ed), *Contract Law: Volume II* (Aldershot, Dartmouth, 1991) 257–97; Kenneth W Clarkson, Roger LeRoy Miller and Timothy J Muris, 'Liquidated Damages vs Penalties: Sense or Nonsense?' [1978]

Wisconsin Law Review 351–90; SA Rea Jr, 'Efficiency Implications of Penalties and Liquidated Damages' (1984) 13 *Journal of Legal Studies* 147–67; Gerrit De Geest and Filip Wuyts, 'Penalty Clauses and Liquidated Damages in Contract Law' in Boudewijn Bouckaert and Gerrit De D Geest (eds), *Encyclopedia of Law and Economics, Volume III: The Regulation of Contracts* (Cheltenham, Elgar, 2000) 141–61

An economic analysis of liquidated damages/penalty clauses. Goetz and Scott argue that the penalty clause rules are inefficient in denying true compensation in cases of non-provable idiosyncratic losses, and in forcing review of other cases, and a general principle of unconscionability is preferable. Clarkson et al argue that the rules are efficient, only upholding the clauses where there is no opportunity or incentive to (wastefully) induce breach. Rea argues that the penalty rule is generally efficient, as clauses fixing damages at above the level of losses (ex ante) are usually evidence of mistake or unconscionability. De Geest and Wuyts survey the field.

Philip R Kaplan, 'A Critique of the Penalty Limitation on Liquidated Damages' (1977) 50 *Southern California Law Review* 1055–90

The harsh treatment by the law of liquidated damages clauses is unjustified and good faith attempts to liquidate damages should be enforced.

Alan Milner, 'Liquidated Damages: An Empirical Study in the Travel Industry' (1979) 42 *Modern Law Review* 508–32

Charles R Knoeber, 'An Alternative Mechanism to Assure Contractual Reliability' (1983) 12 *Journal of Legal Studies* 333–43

The most effective and efficient way to assure performance may be for the promisor to enter into a third party bond payable on default (which provides an incentive to perform but, unlike liquidated damages clauses, does not provide an incentive for the promisee to induce breach) and for the promisee to enter into a third party bond payable on upward renegotiation (to prevent the promisor holding the promisee to ransom). However this will be undesirable where efficient breach or renegotiation (eg due to unforeseen circumstances) are likely.

Garry A Muir, 'Stipulations for the Payment of Agreed Sums' (1982–85) 10 *Sydney Law Review* 503–27

A criticism of the penalty rules, proposing their abolition.

Hugh Beale, 'Penalties in Termination Provisions' (1988) 104 *Law Quarterly Review* 355–359

Stephen A Smith, 'Future Freedom and Freedom of Contract' (1995) 59 *Modern Law Review* 167–87

Stipulated damages clauses should not be enforced because the law should not facilitate parties unduly giving away their future freedom, although such clauses do have evidentiary value.

Mindy Chen-Wishart, 'Controlling the power to agree damages' in Peter Birks (ed), *Wrongs and Remedies of the Twenty-first Century* (Oxford, Clarendon Press, 1996) 271–99

The penalty test should be expanded beyond payments resulting from breach, and beyond disproportionality of the clause itself (to take in the totality of the contract).

Hugh Collins, 'Fairness in Agreed Remedies' in Chris Willett (ed), *Aspects of Fairness in Contract* (London, Blackstone, 1996) 97–121

TA Downes, 'Rethinking Penalty Clauses' in Peter Birks (ed), *Wrongs and Remedies of the Twenty-first Century* (Oxford, Clarendon Press, 1996) 249–69

The penalty rule should be replaced by an approach based upon unconscionability that asks whether the contract was freely negotiated.

Scottish Law Commission, *Report 171: Penalty Clauses* (1999)

Penalties should be struck out or modified (eg reduced) by the court if 'manifestly excessive' (the test for which should include consideration of events after inception) and extended to cases of payments or other events (eg forfeiture) following failure to perform (even without a breach).

Louise Gullifer, 'Agreed Remedies' in Andrew Burrows and Edwin Peel (eds), *Commercial Remedies: Current Issues and Problems* (Oxford, Oxford University Press, 2003) 191–219

Brian Eggleston, *Liquidated Damages and Extension of Time In Construction Contracts* (Oxford, Wiley–Blackwell, 2009)

Thomas Thompson, 'A Fresh Look at Liquidated Damages' (2006) 22 *Construction Law Journal* 259–306

JW Carter and Elisabeth Peden, 'A Good Faith Perspective on Liquidated Damages' (2007) 23 *Journal of Contract Law* 157–79 also in Charles EF Rickett (eds), *Justifying Remedies in Private Law* (Oxford, Hart Publishing, 2008) 149–74

Relief Against Forfeiture of Deposits or Property

Law Commission, *Working Paper No 61: Penalty Clauses and Forfeiture of Monies Paid* (1975)

Charles Harpum 'Relief Against Forfeiture and the Purchaser of Land' [1984] *Cambridge Law Journal* 134–76

Nyuk Y Chin, 'Relieving Against Forfeiture: Windfalls and Conscience' (1995) 25 *University of Western Australia Law Review* 110–26

Relief against forfeiture is based not upon unconscionability but on the fact that in the relevant situations the expectations of the defendant are not unduly violated by the parties' being compelled to continue the contract.

Hossein Abedian and Michael P Furmston, 'Relief Against Forfeiture after Breach of an Essential Time Stipulation in the Light of *Union Eagle Ltd v Golden Achievements Ltd*' (1997–98) 12 *Journal of Contract Law* 189–216

DW McLauchlan, 'Forfeiture of Deposits: Punishing the Contract Breaker' [2002] *New Zealand Law Review* 1–18; Peter Watts, 'Forfeiture of Deposits: Enforcing Agreements' [2002] *New Zealand Law* 19–31

Louise Gullifer, 'Agreed Remedies' in Andrew Burrows and Edwin Peel (eds), *Commercial Remedies: Current Issues and Problems* (Oxford, Oxford University Press, 2003) 191–219

Michael Bryan, 'Equitable Relief from Forfeiture: Performance or Restitution?' in Charles EF Rickett (eds), *Justifying Remedies in Private Law* (Oxford, Hart Publishing, 2008) 363–84

5

COMMON MISTAKE AND FRUSTRATION

5.1 THE BASES OF THE TWO DOCTRINES

Edwin W Patterson, 'The Apportionment of Business Risks Through Legal Devices' (1924) 24 *Columbia Law Review* 335–59

Lee B McTurnan, 'An Approach to Common Mistake in English Law' (1963) 41 *Canadian Bar Review* 1–53

John Swan, 'The Allocation of Risk in the Analysis of Mistake and Frustration' in Barry J Reiter and John Swan (eds), *Studies in Contract Law* (Toronto, Butterworths, 1980) 181–233

Common mistake and frustration are about the contractual allocation of risk between the parties, and most cases can be determined by looking to the reasonable expectations and understandings of the parties.

Jeffrey L Harrison, 'A Case for Loss Sharing' (1982–83) 56 *Southern California Law Review* 573–604

In frustration cases reliance losses should be shared evenly as contracts are common enterprises.

Robert A Hillman, 'An Analysis of the Cessation of Contractual Relations' (1983) 68 *Cornell Law Review* 617–59

Cessation in cases of termination, frustration and mistake are all about determining whether there is an express or implied right to cessation (ie an allocation of risk of the event) and, in the absence of such an express or implied right, filling the gap by the application of fairness.

Subha Narasimhan, 'Of Expectations, Incomplete Contracting, and the Bargain Principle' (1986) 74 *California Law Review* 1123–202

Andrew Kull, 'Mistake, Frustration, and the Windfall Principle of Contract Remedies' (1991) 43 *Hastings Law Journal* 1–55

Mistake and frustration are indistinguishable and both describe mutual mistakes as to value and, as such, are ubiquitous; the cases can be best explained by the windfall principle, by which courts let windfalls lie where they fall. This is justifiable on the basis that to redistribute in such unforeseen situations is costly but does not increase fairness or efficiency. Furthermore, although parties do not anticipate frustration or mistake, they do anticipate interruption in contractual performance, and, realising that they may have to walk away from the contract, set timing and conditions accordingly (eg set whether payment is to be made in advance, in instalments or on delivery). Thus to do nothing in the event of a mistake or frustration ending a contract does, in fact, give effect to the result chosen by the parties. When the courts do find that the risk has not been allocated by the parties they merely confirm the status quo, rescinding only if a contract is executory.

John C Smith, 'Contracts–Mistake, Frustration and Implied Terms' (1994) 110 *Law Quarterly Review* 400–19

Cases of common mistake are best explained as instances of implied terms (specifically, implied conditions precedent). The discussion is of common mistake but, as the author observes, it is equally applicable to frustration (which could be explained by implied conditions subsequent).

Andrew J Morris, 'Practical Reasoning and Contract as Promise: Extending Contract-Based Criteria to Decide Excuse Cases' [1997] *Cambridge Law Journal* 147–74

'Excuse cases' (cases of impossibility, frustration and mistake) are not cases of gaps in the usual sense since they are not cases in which the contract does not provide a complete answer. Rather they are cases in which the answer that the contract provides seems in some sense contrary to the intention of the parties or purpose of the contract—in other words internal reasons (the words of the contract) are defeated by other internal reasons (the purposes of the contract).

Michele De Gregario, 'Impossible Performance or Excused Performance? Common Mistake and Frustration After *Great Peace Shipping*' (2005) 16 *King's College Law Journal* 69–98

James Gordley, *Foundations of Private Law: Property, Tort, Contract, Unjust Enrichment* (Oxford, Oxford University Press, 2006) chs 15 and 16

5.2 COMMON MISTAKE

General Texts

○ John Cartwright, *Misrepresentation, Mistake and Non-Disclosure*, 2nd edn (London, Sweet and Maxwell, 2007) 15.13–15.31

Generally

CJ Slade, 'The Myth of Mistake in the English Law of Contract' (1954) 70 *Law Quarterly Review* 385–408

There is no doctrine of common mistake. Common mistake cases turn on the terms of the agreement (as indeed do unilateral mistake cases), and depend upon implied conditions precedent that have not been satisfied (just as unilateral mistake cases turn on the non-correspondence of the offer and acceptance).

KO Shatwell, 'The Supposed Doctrine of Mistake in Contract: A Comedy of Errors' (1955) 33 *Canadian Bar Review* 164–93

There is no doctrine of common mistake such as can render a contract void.

PS Atiyah, '*Couturier v Hastie* and the Sale of Non-Existent Goods' (1957) 73 *Law Quarterly Review* 340–49

Res extincta and *res sua* are questions of construction requiring selection between three possibilities: that the contract is void (the risk is shared), that the buyer has promised to pay whatever happens (so the risk falls on him), or that the seller has promised that the goods exist (so the risk falls on him). Prima facie, a seller promises that goods have at some time existed, but a contract is void if goods have existed but perish prior to the sale.

PS Atiyah and FAR Bennion, 'Mistake in the Construction of Contracts' (1961) 24 *Modern Law Review* 421–43

Mistake is a matter of construction of the total contract and thus of express or implied assumption of risk in the parties (be the risk assumed by one party, both parties or neither party).

Lee B McTurnan, 'An Approach to Common Mistake in English Law' (1963) 41 *Canadian Bar Review* 1–53

A contract must be intended to deal with matters of which parties are consciously ignorant, but not those matters parties have unquestioning faith in. In the latter case (more likely for future facts, ie frustration, than present facts, ie common mistake) a contract may need to be discharged if enforcement would unjustly impose on one party the risk of the non-existence of a factor.

Samuel Stoljar, 'A New Approach to Mistake in Contract' (1965) 28 *Modern Law Review* 265–85

Edward H Rabin, 'A Proposed Black-Letter Rule Concerning Mistaken Assumptions in Bargain Transactions' (1967) 45 *Texas Law Review* 1273–300

Andrew Phang, 'Common Mistake in English Law—The Proposed Merger of Common Law and Equity' (1989) 9 *Legal Studies* 291–306

NH Andrews, 'Mistaken Settlements of Disputed Claims' [1989] *Lloyd's Maritime and Commercial Law Quarterly* 432–49

Janet Kikolm Smith and Richard L Smith, 'Contract Law, Mutual Mistake, and Incentives to Produce and Disclose Information' (1990) 19 *Journal of Legal Studies* 467–88

Melvin A Eisenberg, 'Mistake in Contract Law' (2003) 91 *California Law Review* 1573–643

Mistranscriptions of a prior agreement should give rise to rectification. In cases of shared factual mistakes, relief should be granted where the mistaken fact was explicitly or tacitly assumed to be true by the parties (ie it formed part of the background that went without saying), although the risk should be borne by a party to whom it was allocated in the contract, or a party who knew or was reckless as to the risk of mistake or had superior information. Where the shared assumption gave rise to a windfall rather than a loss, the windfall should be borne by the party in possession at the time of discovery unless the risk of the windfall has been allocated by the contract.

Catherine MacMillan, 'How Temptation Led to Mistake: an Explanation of *Bell* v *Lever Bros Ltd*' (2003) 119 *Law Quarterly Review* 625–59

Gerard McMeel, 'Interpretation and Mistake in Contract Law: "The fox knows many things..."' [2006] *Lloyd's Maritime and Law Quarterly* 49–81

David Capper, 'Reconfiguring Mistake in Contract Formation' in Michael Bryan (ed), *Private Law in Theory and Practice* (2007, London, Routledge) 119–51

When it is impossible to make a contract, because for example the subject-matter property does not exist or it is impossible, a contract is void. Otherwise, a serious common mistake should only render a contract voidable.

Kelvin FK Low, 'Coming to Terms With the *Great Peace* in Common Mistake' in Jason W Neyers, Richard Bronaugh and Stephen GA Pitel (eds), *Exploring Contract Law* (Oxford, Hart Publishing, 2009) 319–39

Catherine MacMillan, *Mistakes in Contract Law* (Oxford, Hart Publishing, 2009)

Rectification for Common Mistake

Leonard Bromley, 'Rectification in Equity' (1971) 87 *Law Quarterly Review* 532–38; Marcus Smith, 'Rectification of Contracts for Common Mistake, *Joscelyne v Nissen* and Subjective States of Mind' (2007) 123 *Law Quarterly Review* 116–32

Bromley argues that rectification requires only a common subjectively held intention and no outward expression of accord. Smith disagrees, arguing that rectification of contracts is based upon the parties' objective intentions.

Scottish Law Commission, *Report 79: Obligations: Report on Rectification of Contractual and Other Documents* (1983)

○ ICF Spry, *The Principles of Equitable Remedies* (Law Book Co, 2007) ch 6

David McLauchlan, 'The "Drastic" Remedy of Rectification for Unilateral Mistake' (2008) 124 *Law Quarterly Review* 608–40

○ Gerard McMeel, *The Construction of Contracts: Interpretation, Implication and Rectification* (Oxford, Oxford University Press, 2007) ch 17

Restitution Upon Common Mistake

See also 3.9 Restitution and Void Contracts

5.3 FRUSTRATION

General Texts

- Roy Granville McElroy and Glanville Williams, *Impossibility of Performance* (Cambridge, Cambridge University Press, 1941)
- Guenter H Treitel, *Frustration and Force Majeure,* 2nd edn (London, Sweet & Maxwell, 2004)
- Christoph Brunner, *Force Majeure and Hardship Under General Contract Principles: Exemption for Non-performance in International Arbitration* (Austin, TX, Kluwer, 2009)

Generally

William Herbert Page, 'The Development of the Doctrine of Impossibility of Performance' (1920) 18 *Michigan Law Review* 589–614

It is necessary to distinguish the doctrines of frustration of the venture from the law of impossibility.

Lord Wright, 'Some Developments of Commercial Law in the Present Century' in his *Legal Essays and Addresses* (Cambridge, Cambridge University Press, 1939) 252–86

Frustration is about determining what is just, and supplementing the contract when the contract is silent.

WW Buckland, '*Casus* and Frustration in Roman and Common Law' (1933) 46 *Harvard Law Review* 1281–300

HWR Wade, 'The Principle of Impossibility in Contract' (1940) 56 *Law Quarterly Review* 519–56

Roy Granville McElroy and Glanville Williams, 'The Coronation Cases: Part I' (1941) 4 *Modern Law Review* 241–60

The key coronation cases are not in fact frustration cases but rather are cases of the total failure of consideration for the hirer's payment, in which the hirer has an option to perform or withhold and the other party a defence to an action for breach.

Edwin W Patterson, 'Constructive Conditions in Contracts' (1942) 42 *Columbia Law Review* 903–54

GJ Webber, 'Frustration of Contracts' (1951) 4 *Current Legal Problems* 283–304

Frustration is not a matter of the parties' intention but rather a matter of fairness.

John Henry Schlegel, 'Of Nuts, and Ships, and Sealing Wax, Suez, and Frustrating Things—Thc Doctrine of Impossibility of Performance' (1969) 23 *Rutgers Law Review* 445–48

A discussion of the Suez Canal cases, concluding that the doctrine of frustration should merely reflect the rule that courts should only enforce contracts when it is reasonable to do so. When an unusual situation arises the contract should be brought to an end and the expenses incurred split between the parties, save where the event is within a normal range of events incidental to an average broker or wholesaler's contract (slight delay and small market fluctuation).

Richard A Posner and Andrew M Rosenfield, 'Impossibility and Related Doctrines in Contract Law: An Economic Analysis' (1977) 6 *Journal of Legal Studies* 83–118; Christopher J Bruce, 'An Economic Analysis of the Impossibility Doctrine' (1982) 11 *Journal of Legal Studies* 311–33; A Mitchell Polinsky, 'Risk Sharing Through Breach of Contract Remedies' (1983) 12 *Journal of Legal Studies* 427–44; Robert L Birmingham, 'Why Is There Taylor v Caldwell? Three Propositions about Impracticability' (1989) 23 *University of San Francisco Law Review* 379–98; Alan O Sykes, 'The Doctrine of Commercial Impracticability in a Second-best World' (1990) 19 *Journal of Legal Studies* 43–94; George G Triantis, 'Contractual Allocations of Unknown Risks: A Critique of the Doctrine of Commercial Impracticability' (1992) 42 *University of Toronto Law Review* 450–83; Gerhard Wagner, 'In Defense of the Impossibility Defense' (1995) 27 *Loyola University of Chicago Law Journal* 55–96; John Elofson, 'The Dilemma of Changed Circumstances in Contract Law: An Economic Analysis of the Foreseeability and Superior Risk Bearer Tests' (1996) 30 *Columbia Journal of Law and Social Problems* 1–40

Economic analyses of the doctrines of frustration and impracticability. Posner and Rosenfield argue that, where the risk is not allocated and the unprovided-for event was not avoidable at reasonable cost, the contract should be (and in law generally is) discharged where the party on whom the loss will fall is the superior risk-bearer, being the party better able to self- or market-insure through having greater knowledge of the size and probability of the event and a lower transaction cost of insuring. Bruce develops Posner and Rosenfield's model to take more account of mitigation (which he argues the court should have done in *Taylor v Caldwell*) and applies this model to various British and American cases. Polinsky calculates the effects of remedies for breach on the allocation of risk of changes in circumstances. Birmingham argues that no rule can efficiently decide cases like *Taylor*, which sort of case is unrelated to the decidable *Krell v Henry* type of case. Sykes questions the court's ability to identify the efficient circumstances for discharge, especially if factors such as risk-bearing capacity and moral hazard are ignored. Triantis argues that even the risks of the unforeseeable can be and are rationally allocated by parties, typically as part of broader risks, albeit that such risks are often inaccurately assessed. The allocation should be left to the market, whose participants are becoming increasingly sophisticated. For Wagner, the doctrine is approximately efficient, and provides a necessary incentive for the promisee to curtail reliance. Elofson supports a foreseeability basis of frustration as economically optimal.

Marcia J Speziale, 'The Turn of the Twentieth Century as the Dawn of Contract "Interpretation": Reflections in Theories of Impossibility' (1978–79) 17 *Duquesne Law Review* 555–90

Richard E Speidel, 'The New Spirit of Contract' (1982) 2 *Journal of Law and Commerce* 193–210

Leon E Trakman, 'Frustrated Contracts and Legal Fictions' (1983) 46 *Modern Law Review* 39–55

Courts should restrain themselves from finding a commercial contract to be frustrated, and should avoid the implied terms doctrine so as not to undermine business conventions and the agreement of sophisticated parties.

Clifford G Hall, 'Frustration and the Question of Foresight' (1984) 4 *Legal Studies* 300–07

Foresight of an event as likely should preclude the argument by the foreseeing party that the event frustrated the contract. This is best explained by the doctrine of self-induced frustration rather than as a question of assumption of risk.

Leon E Trakman, 'Winner Takes Some: Loss Sharing and Commercial Impracticability' (1985) 69 *Minnesota Law Review* 471–520

Robert A Hillman, 'Court Adjustment of Long-term Contracts: An Analysis Under Modern Contract Law' [1987] *Duke Law Journal* 1–33

Andrew Phang, 'Frustration in English Law—A Reappraisal' (1992) 21 *Anglo-American Law Review* 278–309

There can be no frustration where the event was within the reasonable control of one party or was foreseeable.

GH Treitel, 'Alternatives and Frustration' in Jack Beatson and Daniel Friedmann (eds), *Good Faith and Fault in Contract Law* (Oxford, Clarendon Press, 1995) 377–96

The effect various provisions for alternative modes of performance have on the effect of supervening changes of circumstance.

Ewan McKendrick, 'Force Majeure and Frustration—Their Relationship and a Comparative Assessment' in his, *Force Majeure and Frustration of Contract*, 2nd edn (London, LLP, 1995) 33–54

Andrew Rogers, 'Frustration and Estoppel' in Ewan McKendrick (ed), *Force Majeure and Frustration of Contract*, 2nd edn (London, LLP, 1995) 245–253

Many frustration cases could be better dealt with as common assumption estoppel cases.

Jack Beatson, 'Increased Expense and Frustration' in FD Rose (ed), *Consensus Ad Idem—Essays in the Law of Contract in Honour of Guenter Treitel* (London, Sweet & Maxwell, 1996) 121–140

Increased expense and commercial impracticability may sometimes be enough to frustrate contracts.

DJ Ibbetson, 'Absolute Liability in Contract: The Antecedents of *Paradine v Jane*' in FD Rose (ed), *Consensus Ad Idem—Essays in the Law of Contract in Honour of Guenter Treitel* (London, Sweet & Maxwell, 1996) 3–37

Thomas Roberts, 'Commercial Impossibility and Frustration of Purpose: A Critical Analysis' (2003) 16 *Canadian Journal of Law and Jurisprudence* 129–45

James Gordley, 'Impossibility and Changed and Unforeseen Circumstances' (2004) 52 *American Journal of Comparative Law* 513–30

Martin Schmidt-Kessel and Katrin Mayer, 'Supervening Events and *Force Majeure*" in Jan M Smits (ed), *Elgar Encyclopedia of Comparative Law* (Cheltenham, Edward Elgar, 2006) 689–698

Leases

Roy Granville McElroy and Glanville Williams, 'The Coronation Cases: Part I' (1941) 4 *Modern Law Review* 241–60

Warren Barr, 'Frustration of Leases—The Hazards of Contractualisation' (2001) 52 *Northern Ireland Legal Quarterly* 82–97

There should be no doctrine of frustration in landlord and tenant law, and property law doctrines should be applied instead.

Self-induced Frustration

AH Hudson, 'Prorating in the English Law of Frustrated Contracts' (1968) 31 *Modern Law Review* 535–43

The possibility of prorating, ie apportioning, among several customers a supply limited by a frustrating event.

JP Swanton, 'The Concept of Self-induced Frustration' (1989–90) 2 *Journal of Contract Law* 206–26

War

E Merrick Dodd, 'Impossibility of Performance of Contracts due to War-time Regulations' (1919) 32 *Harvard Law Review* 789–805

Discussions of frustration by reason of government requisitioning of goods, orders for production of goods, interference with raw material availability, and priority orders.

Arnold D McNair, 'War-time Impossibility of Performance of Contract' (1919) 35 *Law Quarterly Review* 84–100 and 'Frustration of Contract by War' (1940) 56 *Law Quarterly Review* 173–207

Paxton Blair, 'Breach of Contract Due to War' (1920) 20 *Columbia Law Review* 413–37

○ Lord McNair and AD Watts, *Legal Effects of War* (Cambridge, Cambridge University Press, 1944) ch 5

○ George J Webber, *Effect of War on Contracts*, 2nd edn (London, Solicitors' Law Stationery Society, 1946) parts III and IV

Suspension of Obligations

Edwin W Patterson, 'Temporary Impossibility of Performance of Contract' (1961) 47 *Virginia Law Review* 798–810

Discharge

Arthur L Corbin, 'Discharge of Contracts' (1913) 22 *Yale Law Journal* 513–30

Restitution at Common Law

Roy Granville McElroy and Glanville Williams, 'The Coronation Cases: Part II' (1941) 5 *Modern Law Review* 1–20

Glanville L Williams, 'The End of Chandler v Webster' (1942) 6 *Modern Law Review* 46–57

The common law action for restitution for total failure of consideration following the House of Lords decision in *Fibrosa v Fairbairn*.

Andrew Stewart and JW Carter, 'Frustrated Contracts and Statutory Adjustment: The Case for a Reappraisal' [1992] *Cambridge Law Journal* 66–112

Paul Mitchell, '*Fibrosa Spolka Akcyjna v Fairbairn Lawson Combe Barbour Ltd* (1942)' in Charles Mitchell and Paul Mitchell, *Landmark Cases in the Law of Restitution* (Oxford, Hart Publishing, 2006) 247–84

Restitution under the (English) Law Reform (Frustrated Contracts) Act 1943

○ Glanville Williams, *The Law Reform (Frustrated Contracts) Act 1943* (London, Stevens, 1944)

Brice Dickson, 'An Action for Unjust Enrichment' (1983) 34 *Northern Ireland Legal Quarterly* 106–24; AM Haycroft and DM Waksman, 'Frustration and Restitution' [1984] *Journal of Business Law* 207–25

Analysis and criticism of the decision in *BP v Hunt (No. 2)*.

Ewan McKendrick 'Frustration, Restitution and Loss of Apportionment' in Andrew Burrows (ed), *Essays on the Law of Restitution* (Oxford, Clarendon Press, 1991) 147–70 and 'The Consequences of Frustration—The Law Reform (Frustrated Contracts) Act 1943' in his *Force Majeure and Frustration of Contract*, 2nd edn (London, LLP, 1995) 223–44

A survey of the history and application of the Act in the light of *BP v Hunt (No. 2)*, explaining it as a scheme of mutual restitution.

Andrew Stewart and JW Carter, 'Frustrated Contracts and Statutory Adjustment: The Case for a Reappraisal' [1992] *Cambridge Law Journal* 66–112

The 1943 Act and other such statutory schemes give too much unguided discretion, and the best approach is that of the common law (save that the requirement of a total failure of consideration must be overruled) where the retention of a benefit would amount to unjust enrichment.

○ Gareth Jones, *Goff & Jones: The Law of Restitution*, 7th edn (London, Sweet & Maxwell, 2006 plus supplements) 20-061 to 20-082

Other Frustration Statutes

Philip D Weiss, 'Apportioning Loss after Discharge of a Burdensome Contract: A Statutory Solution' (1960) 69 *Yale Law Journal* 1054–89

Law Reform Commission of British Columbia, *Project 8: Report on the Need for Frustrated Contracts Legislation in British Columbia* (1971)

New South Wales Law Reform Commission, *25: Report on Frustrated Contracts* (1976)

Pauline Moran, 'Restitutionary Principles and the Frustrated Contracts Act 1944' (1980–3) 4 *Auckland University Law Review* 56–65

Law Reform Commission of Saskatchewan, *Proposals for a Frustrated Contracts Act* (1988)

Cliona Kelly, 'Drafting an Irish Frustrated Contracts Act: Lessons from British Columbia' in Paula Giliker (ed), *Re-examining Contract and Unjust Enrichment: Anglo-Canadian Perspectives* (Leiden, Martinus Nijhoff, 2007) 109–32

5.4 FORCE MAJEURE CLAUSES

David Yates, 'Drafting Force Majeure and Related Clauses' (1991) 3 *Journal of Contract Law* 186–213; Michael Furmston, 'Drafting of Force Majeure Clauses—Some General Guidelines' in Ewan McKendrick (ed), *Force Majeure and Frustration of Contract*, 2nd edn (London, LLP, 1995) 57–62; Alan Berg, 'The Detailed Drafting of a Force Majeure Clause' in Ewan McKendrick (ed), *Force Majeure and Frustration of Contract*, 2nd edn (London, LLP, 1995) 63–120

William Swadling, 'The Judicial Construction of Force Majeure Clauses' in Ewan McKendrick (ed), *Force Majeure and Frustration of Contract*, 2nd edn (London, LLP, 1995) 3–19

Force majeure clauses are usually treated as clauses that define the parties' obligations rather than as exclusion clauses.

E McKendrick, 'Force Majeure and Frustration—Their Relationship and a Comparative Assessment' in Ewan McKendrick (ed), *Force Majeure and Frustration of Contract*, 2nd edn (London, LLP, 1995) 33–54 and 'Force Majeure Clauses: the Gap between Doctrine and Practice' in Andrew Burrows and Edwin Peel (eds), *Contract Terms* (Oxford, Oxford University Press, 2007) 233–51

PJM Declercq, 'Modern Analysis of the Legal Effect of Force Majeure Clauses in Situations of Commercial Impracticability' (1995) 15 *Journal of Law and Commerce* 213–56

○ Guenter H Treitel, *Frustration and Force Majeure*, 2nd edn (London, Sweet & Maxwell, 2004)

Donald Robertson, 'Force Majeure Clauses' (2009) 25 *Journal of Contract Law* 62–82

6

MISREPRESENTATION, DURESS, UNDUE INFLUENCE AND UNCONSCIONABILITY

6.1 DURESS, UNDUE INFLUENCE AND UNCONSCIONABILITY

General Texts

- John Cartwright, *Unequal Bargaining: A Study of Vitiating Factors in the Formation of Contracts* (Oxford, Clarendon Press,1991) chs 7–9
- Nelson Enonchong, *Duress, Undue Influence and Unconscionable Dealing* (London, Sweet & Maxwell, 2006)

Generally

Arthur Allen Leff, 'Unconscionability and the Code—The Emperor's New Clause' (1967) 115 *University of Pennsylvania Law Review* 485–559

The distinction between procedural and substantive unconscionability.

Richard A Epstein, 'Unconscionability: A Critical Reappraisal' (1975) 18 *Journal of Law & Economics* 293–315 also in Larry Alexander (ed), *Contract Law: Volume II* (Aldershot, Dartmouth, 1991) 185–207

Non-enforcement of contracts for unconscionability is justified within a freedom of contract framework only where there is a defect in formation (duress, fraud, undue influence) or, in limited circumstances, incompetence of one party, but is not justified by the substantive terms of the agreement.

Alan Schwartz, 'A Reexamination of Nonsubstantive Unconscionability' (1977) 63 *Virginia Law Review* 1053–83

Only a lack of information, and not poverty, incompetence or monopoly power, can justify (on economic grounds) invalidation of a contract for nonsubstantive unconscionability (ie unconscionability not related to the harshness of the bargain).

Hugh Beale, 'Inequality of Bargaining Power' (1986) 6 *Oxford Journal of Legal Studies* 123–36

Spencer Nathan Thal, 'The Inequality of Bargaining Power Doctrine: The Problem of Defining Contractual Unfairness' (1988) 8 *Oxford Journal of Legal Studies* 17–33

If there is procedurally unfair bargaining, then the substantive terms of a contract should be looked at. Procedurally unfair bargaining means weakness-based inequality of bargaining power (since strength-based inequality, ie monopoly, requires assessment of contestability in the market) and arises when one party has no information, a lack of bargaining alternatives, or is in a relationship of trust.

Megan Richardson, 'The Utilitarian-Economic Model of Contractual Obligation: Unconscionability at the Frontier' (1995) 20 *Melbourne University Law Review* 481–502

Andrew Phang and Hans Tjio, 'From Mythical Equities to Substantive Doctrines—Yerkey in the Shadow of Notice and Unconscionability' (1999) 14 *Journal of Contract Law* 72–107

The 'special wives' equity' principle should be assimilated within the doctrines of undue influence and third party notice.

Stephen Waddams, 'Unconscionable Contracts: Competing Perspectives' (1999) 62 *Saskatchewan Law Review* 1–17

Armin Hadjiani, 'Duress and Undue Influence in English and German Contract Law: A Comparative Study of Vitiating Factors in Common and Civil Law' (2002) *Oxford University Comparative Law Forum* 1

James Devenney and Adrian Chandler, 'Unconscionability and the Taxonomy of Undue Influence' [2007] *Journal of Business Law* 541–69

Stephen Smith, 'The Limits of Contract' in Jason W Neyers, Richard Bronaugh and Stephen GA Pitel (eds), *Exploring Contract Law* (Oxford, Hart Publishing, 2009) 1–24

Rules of incapacity, duress, undue influence and misrepresentation are not part of contract law but rather part of the general law of obligations applicable to all obligations.

Duress

See also 9.4 Duress and Contract Modifications

John Dalzell, 'Duress by Economic Pressure: I and II' (1942) 20 *North Carolina Law Review* 237–77 and 341–86

John P Dawson, 'Economic Duress, an Essay in Perspective' (1947) 45 *Michigan Law Review* 253–90

Jack Beatson, 'Duress as a Vitiating Factor in Contract' [1974] *Cambridge Law Journal* 97–115, a later version of which forms part of 'Duress, Restitution, Contract Renegotiation' in his *The Use and Abuse of Unjust Enrichment* (Oxford, Clarendon Press, 1991) 95–136

AJE Jaffey, 'Wrongful Pressure in Making Contracts' in D Lasok (ed), *Fundamental Duties* (Oxford, Pergamon Press, 1980) 187–200

PS Atiyah, 'Economic Duress and the Overborne Will' (1982) 98 *Law Quarterly Review* 197–202; David Tiplady, 'Concepts of Duress' (1983) 99 *Law Quarterly Review* 188–94; PS Atiyah, 'Duress and the Overborne Will Again' (1983) 99 *Law Quarterly Review* 353–56

Atiyah criticises the 'overborne will' theory of duress, arguing that even when under duress a person still has a choice and so their will still operates. Tiplady argues that Atiyah has misunderstood the theory.

MH Ogilvie, 'Wrongfulness, Rights and Economic Duress' (1984) 16 *Ottawa Law Review* 1–33

Pressure is wrongful where it deprives of the right to earn a living as one might wish, driving one into dire economic straits.

Michael Philips, 'Are Coerced Agreements Voluntary?' (1984) 3 *Law and Philosophy* 133–45; Joan McGregor, 'Philips on Coerced Agreements' (1988) 7 *Law and Philosophy* 225–36

Andrew Stewart, 'Economic Duress—Legal Regulation of Commercial Pressure' (1984) 14 *Melbourne University Law Review* 410–41

The unlawfulness of the threatened act should give rise to a rebuttable presumption of illegitimacy, and threats to do the lawful should be illegitimate if commercially unreasonable.

PA Chandler, 'Economic Duress: Clarity or Confusion?' [1989] *Lloyd's Maritime and Commercial Law Quarterly* 270–77

Andrew Phang, 'Economic Duress: Recent Difficulties and Possible Alternatives' [1997] *Restitution Law Review* 53–65

Legitimate and illegitimate economic duress are indistinguishable and hence the doctrine should be replaced with one of unconscionability.

Richard A Posner, 'Blackmail, Privacy and Freedom of Contract' (1993) 141 *University of Pennsylvania Law Review* 1817–48

Blackmail is generally inefficient because although ostensibly voluntary, it is likely to be wealth-reducing not wealth-maximising.

Rick Bigwood, 'Coercion in Contract: The Theoretical Constructs of Duress' (1996) 46 *University of Toronto Law Journal* 201–71 and *Exploitative Contracts* (Oxford, Oxford University Press, 2003)

Duress requires both a coercive proposal by the oppressor and the constraining of choice by the oppressed: the coercion must be unjustified and the succumbing to the coercion justified. A coercive proposal is a threat coupled with a demand, being a proposal to make the other party worse off than they would otherwise expect or be normatively entitled to be (whereas a non-coercive proposal, an offer coupled with a demand, proposes to make the other party better off). Further, either the threat must be illegitimate (unlawful) or the demand must be illegitimate (because it bears no proportionate relationship to the intrinsic purposes of the power used to obtain it). The constraining of choice requires that the proposal is a cause of the contracting and there was no reasonable legal or extra-legal alternative available to the choosing party.

Hamish Stewart, 'A Formal Approach to Contractual Duress' (1997) 47 *University of Toronto Law Journal* 175–262

Stephen A Smith, 'Contracting Under Pressure: A Theory of Duress' [1997] *Cambridge Law Journal* 343–73

Duress should give rise to contract avoidance in either of two situations: wrongdoing (wrongful threats) or loss of autonomy (having no real choice).

Oren Bar-Gill and Omri Ben-Shahar, 'The Law of Duress and the Economics of Credible Threats' (2004) *Journal of Legal Studies* 391–430 and 'Credible Coercion' (2004) 83 *Texas Law Review* 717–80

It is difficult to know when the law should provide relief in cases of credible threats, since the relief may induce the execution of the threat.

Ewan McKendrick, 'The Further Travails of Duress' in Andrew Burrows and Lord Rodger (eds), *Mapping the Law: Essays in Memory of Peter Birks* (Oxford, Oxford University Press, 2006) 181–99

Undue Influence

WHD Winder, 'Undue Influence and Coercion' (1939) 3 *Modern Law Review* 97–120

Herbert Fingarette, 'Victimization: A Legalist Analysis of Coercion, Deception, Undue Influence, and Excusable Prison Escape' (1985) 42 *Washington and Lee Law Review* 65–118

Peter Birks and Chin Nyuk Yin, 'On the Nature of Undue Influence' in Jack Beatson and Daniel Friedmann (eds), *Good Faith and Fault in Contract Law* (Oxford, Clarendon Press, 1995) 57–97

Once cases of pressure (the duress cases and some cases currently characterised as undue influence cases) are separated off, undue influence can and should be understood as based upon an impairment of the influencee's judgmental capacity in situations in which this impairment is relational in original, rather than on immoral exploitative conduct of the influencer. In other words, undue influence is plaintiff-sided and not defendant-sided, and is the relational comparator to other doctrines governing judgmental disability such as those of minority and intoxication.

Catherine Callaghan, 'Manifest Disadvantage in Undue Influence: An Analysis of its Role and Necessity' (1995) 25 *Victoria University of Wellington Law Review* 289–313

Belinda Fehlberg, 'The Husband, the Bank, the Wife and her Signature—The Sequel' (1996) 59 *Modern Law Review* 675–94 and *Sexually Transmitted Debt: Surety Experience and English Law* (Oxford, Clarendon Press, 1997)

An analysis, drawing on empirical evidence, of the social realities of the marriage relationship, and of the law seeking to (but failing to) protect sureties.

Rick Bigwood, 'Undue Influence: "Impaired Consent" or "Wicked Exploitation"?' (1996) 16 *Oxford Journal of Legal Studies* 503–15, *Exploitative Contracts* (Oxford, Oxford University Press, 2003) and 'Contracts by Exploitation: From Unfair Advantage to Transactional Neglect' (2005) 25 *Oxford Journal of Legal Studies* 65–96

[1996] Cases of involuntariness are not merely about power imbalances, but rather about unfairly taking advantage (either actively or passively) of such power imbalances, and both undue influence and unconscionable dealings fit this model. [2003] Contractual exploitation is processual not substantive. Unconscionable dealing is about exploiting (by failing to take neighbourly steps to eliminate or reduce) a special disadvantage. Undue influence is about exercising influence arising out of a relationship. [2005] Cases of unfairly taking advantage of pre-existing bargaining imbalances (the relational undue influence and unconscionable dealing cases) are not about exploitation but are rather founded upon 'transactional neglect', and hence the law requires only failure to take care not to derive advantage from the other contracter's weakness (and does not require actual advertence of the other party's weakness or disability).

Mindy Chen-Wishart, 'The O'Brien Principle and Substantive Unfairness' [1997] *Cambridge Law Journal* 60–70

Mark Pawlowki and Sarah Greer, 'Constructive Notice and Independent Legal Advice: A Study of Lending Institution Practice' (2001) 65 *Conveyancer and Property Lawyer* 229–48

Michael J Trebilcock and Steven Elliott, 'The Scope and Limits of Legal Paternalism: Altruism and Coercion in Family Financial Arrangements' in Peter Benson (ed), *The Theory of Contract Law: New Essays* (Cambridge, Cambridge University Press, 2001) 45–85

Efficiency requires a legal requirement that sureties are independently advised.

○ Mark Pawlowski and James Brown, *Undue Influence and the Family Home* (London, Cavendish, 2002)

Andrew Phang and Hans Tjio, 'The Uncertain Boundaries of Undue Influence' [2002] *Lloyd's Maritime and Commercial Law Quarterly* 231–45; Dominic O'Sullivan, 'Developing O'Brien' (2002) 118 *Law Quarterly Review* 337–59; M Thompson, 'Wives, Sureties and Banks' [2002] *Conveyancer and Property Lawyer* 174–92; Simone Wong, 'Revisiting *Barclays Bank v O'Brien* and Independent Legal Advice for Vulnerable Sureties' [2002] *Journal of Business Law* 439–56

Fiona R Burns, 'Undue Influence Inter Vivos and the Elderly' (2002) 26 *Melbourne Law Review* 499–536 and 'The Elderly and Undue Influence Inter Vivos' (2003) 23 *Legal Studies* 251–83

KN Scott, 'Evolving Equity and the Presumption of Undue Influence' (2002) 18 *Journal of Contract Law* 236–49

Pauline Ridge, 'Uncertainties Surrounding Undue Influence: Its Formation, Application, and Relationship to Other Doctrines' [2003] *New Zealand Law Review* 329–60

Rosemary Auchmuty, 'The Rhetoric of Equality and the Problem of Heterosexuality' in Linda Mulcahy and Sally Wheeler (eds), *Feminist Perspectives on Contract Law* (London, Cavendish, 2005) 51–74

The extension of the undue influence rules from wives to all intimate relationships obscures the basis of the rule in the gendered power dynamic in a heterosexual relationship.

Mindy Chen-Wishart, 'Undue Influence—*Beyond* Impaired Consent and Wrong-doing Towards a Relational Analysis' in AS Burrows and A Rodger (eds), *Mapping the Law: Essays in Memory of Peter Birks* (Oxford, Oxford University Press 2006) 201–22 and 'Undue Influence: Vindicating the Relationships of Influence' (2006) 59 *Current Legal Problems* 231–66

The polarised debate about whether the doctrine is based upon impaired consent or wrongdoing is misplaced. Undue influence is about the active (pressure) or passive (standing by) subversion of the implicit norms of the particular relationship of influence, which harms the relational autonomy of the party under influence, while failing to protect the influenced party's welfare interest. Independent legal advice rebuts undue influence if it renders the relationship arm's length, and passes on the obligation from the influential party to the advisor, and can also show that the welfare interest was in fact protected.

Jesse Elvin, 'The Purpose of the Doctrine of Presumed Undue Influence' in Paula Giliker (ed), *Re-examining Contract and Unjust Enrichment: Anglo-Canadian Perspectives* (Leiden, Martinus Nijhoff, 2007) 231–53

Rick Bigwood, 'From Morgan to Etridge: Tracing the (Dis)Integration of Undue Influence in the United Kingdom' in Jason W Neyers, Richard Bronaugh and Stephen GA Pitel (eds), *Exploring Contract Law* (Oxford, Hart Publishing, 2009) 379–430

Recent developments have unjustifiably removed the fiduciary underpinnings of relational undue influence and robbed the category of its purpose.

Unconscionability

MJ Trebilcock, 'The Doctrine of Inequality of Bargaining Power: Post-Benthamite Economics in the House of Lords' (1976) 26 *University of Toronto Law Journal* 359–85

Robert W Clark, 'The Unconscionability Doctrine Viewed from an Irish Perspective' (1980) 31 *Northern Ireland Legal Quarterly* 114–46

Michael J Trebilcock, 'An Economic Approach to the Doctrine of Unconscionability' in Barry J Reiter and John Swan (eds), *Studies in Contract Law* (Toronto, Butterworths, 1980) 379–421

Economically, a general judicial doctrine of unconscionability can be justified in situations of situational monopoly (lack of a realistic alternative supplier) or impaired information processing ability (weak or defective individuals) but should not be used to redress distributive inequality.

Malcolm Cope, "The Review of Unconscionable Bargains in Equity' (1983) 57 *Australian Law Journal* 279–95

AH Angelo and EP Ellinger, 'Unconscionability: A Comparative Study of the Approaches in England, France, Germany and the United States' (1993) 14 *Loyola of Los Angeles International and Comparative Law Journal* 439–506

Nicholas Bamforth, 'Unconscionability as a Vitiating Factor' [1995] *Lloyd's Maritime and Commercial Law Quarterly* 538–56

Unconscionability is based upon unjust enrichment, allowing restitution in cases of unconscientious receipt, defined as the dishonest exploitation of a special disadvantage to force a severely disadvantageous bargain on one with inadequate independent advice.

Peter Birks and Chin Nyuk Yin, 'On the Nature of Undue Influence', in Jack Beatson and Daniel Friedmann (eds), *Good Faith and Fault in Contract Law* (Oxford, Clarendon Press, 1995) 57–97; David Capper, 'Undue Influence and Unconscionability: A Rationalisation' (1998) 114 *Law Quarterly Review* 479–504

The Interrelationship of the Various Doctrines

SM Waddams, 'Unconscionability in Contracts' (1976) 39 *Modern Law Review* 369–93

The is need for a general principle by which relief is granted in cases of unconscionability, drawing on various features and doctrines of the existing law (such as the rules concerning penalty clauses, exclusion clauses and forfeiture) that, it is argued, would be better and more honestly explained by such a principle.

Andrew Boon Leong Phang, 'Undue Influence—Methodology, Sources and Linkages' [1995] *Journal of Business Law* 552–74

R Bigwood, 'Undue Influence: "Impaired Consent" or "Wicked Exploitation"?' (1996) 16 *Oxford Journal of Legal Studies* 503–15

Undue influence and unconscionable dealings should not be merged because although both concern exploitation and vulnerability, the source of the vulnerability is different in each case and so the two doctrines emphasise different situations.

David Capper, 'Undue Influence and Unconscionability: A Rationalisation' (1998) 114 *Law Quarterly Review* 479–504

The doctrines of undue influence and unconscionability stem from a common basis and should be combined into a single doctrine that applies when there is (plaintiff-sided) relational inequality and (defendant-sided) unconscionable conduct (which can consist of as little as the passive receipt of benefits), with transactional imbalance being a powerful indicator although not a requirement. The more relational inequality there is, the less unconscionable the defendant's conduct needs to be, and vice versa.

6.2 MISREPRESENTATION

In relation to tort damages claims, see 2.4 Torts

Generally

PS Atiyah, 'Misrepresentation, Warranty and Estoppel' (1971) 9 *Alberta Law Review* 347–385, later version of which appears in his *Essays on Contract,* revised edn (Oxford, Clarendon Press, 1990) 275–328

An investigation of the distinction between representations and warranties, questioning whether estoppel by representation is really distinct from contractual warranty.

SM Waddams, 'Pre-contractual Duties of Disclosure' in Peter Cane and Jane Stapleton (eds), *Essays for Patrick Atiyah* (Oxford, Clarendon Press, 1991) 237–56

○ George Spencer Bower, Alex Kincombe Turner and KR Handley, *Actionable Misrepresentation*, 4th edn (London, Butterworths, 2000)

Rick Bigwood, 'Pre-contractual Misrepresentation and the Limits of the Principle in *With* v *O'Flanagan*' [2005] *Cambridge Law Journal* 94–125

Supervening falsification prior to the contract being induced but after the making of a representation is not a misrepresentation if not known of by the representor, because the representor is not responsible (even innocently) for the misrepresentation.

○ John Cartwright, *Misrepresentation, Mistake and Non-disclosure*, 2nd edn (London, Sweet and Maxwell, 2007)

Non-Reliance Clauses and Exclusion of Liability for Misrepresentation

See also Entire Agreement Clauses in 4.4

Nick Seddon, 'Can Contract Trump Estoppel?' (2003) 77 *Australian Law Journal* 126–136

The extent to which entire agreement or other contractual clauses can exclude liability for equitable estoppel.

John Cartwright, 'Excluding Liability for Misrepresentation' in Andrew Burrows and Edwin Peel (eds), *Contract Terms* (Oxford, Oxford University Press, 2007) 213–31

○ John Cartwright, *Misrepresentation, Mistake and Non-disclosure*, 2nd edn (London, Sweet and Maxwell, 2007) ch 9

Mark P Gergen, 'Contracting Out of Liability for Deceit, Inadvertent Misrepresentation and Negligent Misstatement' in Jason W Neyers, Richard Bronaugh and Stephen GA Pitel (eds), *Exploring Contract Law* (Oxford, Hart Publishing, 2009) 237–66

6.3 RESCISSION FOR UNDUE INFLUENCE, MISREPRESENTATION, ETC

General Texts

○ George Spencer Bower, Alex Kincombe Turner and KR Handley, *Actionable Misrepresentation*, 4th edn (London, Butterworths, 2000) chs 14–17

○ Dominic O'Sullivan, Steven Elliot and Rafal Zakrzewski, *The Law of Rescission* (Oxford, Oxford University Press, 2007)

Generally

Nyuk Yin Nahan, 'Rescission: A Case for Rejecting the Classical Model?' (1997) 27 *University of Western Australia Law Review* 66–85

The present law should be replaced by a simple doctrine of pecuniary rescission (rather than proprietary restitution with various bars).

Janet O'Sullivan, 'Rescission as a Self-help Remedy: A Critical Analysis' [2000] *Cambridge Law Journal* 509–43

It is undesirable and a historical confusion to regard rescission as being effected merely by the exercise of an election by the relevant party, rather than by a court order (and that when a court order is effected it is backdated to the date of the election). If this self-help view is abolished, it will be understood that, in the absence of a court order, a party cannot by means of an election effect recaption of property which passed under the avoided contract, nor can he prevent good title subsequently passing to a third party (without notifying the third party).

Michael Bridge, 'Innocent Misrepresentation in Contract' (2004) 57 *Current Legal Problems* 277–304

Innocent and negligent misrepresentation should not give rise to a right to rescind (although a right to rescind for mistake or terminate for breach will sometimes be available when there has been such a misrepresentation.)

William Swadling, 'Rescission, Property, and the Common Law' (2005) 121 *Law Quarterly Review* 123–53; Birke Häcker, 'Rescission of Contract and Revesting of Title: A Reply to Mr Swadling' (2006) 14 *Restitution Law Review* 106–11

Swadling: Where a contract is legally (rather than equitably) voidable (ie for fraud or duress) and is rescinded, this does not mean that title to any property transferred pursuant to the contract also revests. Although in some cases of voidness (fraudulent misrepresentation as to the subject-matter of the contract or identity of the contractor) the delivery will itself by ineffective by reason of mistake, in other cases (duress or fraud as to other matters) the delivery will be effective in transferring property rights despite the contract being ineffective. Häcker: Contract and delivery are alternative methods of conveyance so if a contract is avoided delivery will not have taken place, and there is no reason why a deliveror should not be able to revest title in himself.

Sarah Worthington, 'The Proprietary Consequences of Rescission' (2002) 10 *Restitution Law Review* 28–68; Birke Häcker, 'Rescission and Third Party Rights' (2006) 14 *Restitution Law Review* 21–40

Third party rights should not bar rescission and unjust enrichment remedies should be available when property return is impossible.

Partial Rescission

DJ Meikle, 'Partial Rescission—Removing the Restitution from a Contractual Doctrine' (2003) 19 *Journal of Contract Law* 40–73

Rescission is contractual, with the restitution (leading to the status quo ante) being a separate step. Further, partial rescission (which must be distinguished from rescission on terms) is justifiable where the rescinding party has evidenced an unvitiated intention to enter into a contract on specific terms other than those ultimately made, the contractual obligation for which therefore subsists.

Andrew Robertson, 'Partial Rescission, Causation and Benefit' (2001) 17 *Journal of Contract Law* 163–80

Jill Poole and Andrew Keyser, 'Justifying Partial Rescission in English Law' (2005) 121 *Law Quarterly Review* 273–99

In addition to the jurisdiction to award rescission at the election of the fraudulent misrepresentee where *restitutio in integrum* is possible (with or without exercise of the concurrent jurisdiction to impose terms), partial rescission should also be available in cases of non-fraudulent misrepresentations at the court's (and not the misrepresentee's) discretion where it would be unconscionable not to hold the misrepresentee to a more limited contract.

Damages in Lieu of Rescission under section 2(2) of the (English) Misrepresentation Act 1967

PS Atiyah and GH Treitel, 'Misrepresentation Act 1967' (1967) 30 *Modern Law Review* 369–88

Hugh Beale, 'Damages in Lieu of Rescission for Misrepresentation' (1995) 111 *Law Quarterly Review* 60–65

Michael Bridge, 'Innocent Misrepresentation in Contract' (2004) 57 *Current Legal Problems* 277–304

The O'Brien *Doctrine of Notice: Misrepresentation and Undue Influence by a Third Party*

NY Chin, 'Undue Influence and Third Parties' (1992) 5 *Journal of Contract Law* 108–56

Martin Dixon and Charles Harpum, 'Fraud, Undue Influence and Mortgages of Registered Land' [1994] *Conveyancer and Property Lawyer* 421–24; Peter Sparkes, 'The Proprietary Effect of Undue Influence' [1995] *Conveyancer and Property Lawyer* 250–56; M Thompson, ''The Enforceability of Mortgages' [1994] *Conveyancer and Property Lawyer* 140–45

The application of the *O'Brien* principle to the unregistered and registered land systems, and whether notice is a proprietary concept to bind a purchaser to an equity, or a contractual or restitutionary concept defining a wrong by the purchaser bank.

Graham Battersby, 'Equitable Fraud Committed by Third Parties' (1995) 15 *Legal Studies* 35–46

John Mee, 'An Alternative Approach to Third Party Undue Influence and Misrepresentation' (1995) 46 *Northern Ireland Legal Quarterly* 147–62

Notice should not be required for *O'Brien* vitiation, although it should be relevant to the defence of change of position in good faith. Thus there should be no rescission in the case of guarantees for past debts, since the loan is not made by way of change of position in reliance.

Kit Barker, '*O'Brien*, Notice and the Onus of Proof' in Francis D Rose (ed), *Restitution and Banking Law* (Mansfield Press, 1998) 78–88

John Cartwright, 'Taking Stock of O'Brien' (1997) 7 *Restitution Law Review* 1–20

Whether *O'Brien* is a narrow doctrine relating to some or all guarantees, or a wide doctrine relating to the impairment of consent by a third party.

Eoin O'Dell, 'Restitution, Coercion by a Third Party, and the Proper Role of Notice' [1997] *Cambridge Law Journal* 71–79

The *O'Brien* principle is based on unjust enrichment and the presence or absence of notice of the recipient is only relevant to the defence of a *bona fide* purchaser for value without notice.

○ Nelson Enonchong, *Duress, Undue Influence and Unconscionable Dealing* (London, Sweet & Maxwell, 2006) chs 21–26

6.4 THE (NEW ZEALAND) CONTRACTUAL REMEDIES ACT 1979

See below in 10.5

7

ILLEGALITY AND RESTRAINT OF TRADE

7.1 GENERAL TEXTS

- Nelson Enonchong, *Illegal Transactions* (London, LLP, 1998)
- Richard A Buckley, *Illegality and Public Policy*, 2nd edn (London, Sweet & Maxwell, 2009)

7.2 GENERALLY

Walter Gellhorn, 'Contracts and Public Policy' (1935) 35 *Columbia Law Review* 679–96

It is not helpful to ask whether, when they passed criminal or other statutes, the legislature intended contracts to be treated as void. Instead the courts should have recourse to public policy as set down in legislative and administrative texts.

JK Grodecki, 'In pari causa potior est conditio possidentis' (1955) 71 *Law Quarterly Review* 254–74

Criticism of the doctrine of *in pari delicto*, preferring the courts to examine the transaction as a whole and grant relief as would best serve the public interest.

RA Buckley, 'Participation and Performance of Illegal Contracts' (1974) 25 *Northern Ireland Law Quarterly* 421–29

RA Buckley, 'Implied Statutory Prohibition of Contracts' (1975) 38 *Modern Law Review* 535–42

AH Hudson, 'Contractual Compromises of Criminal Liability' (1980) 43 *Modern Law Review* 532–42

GH Treitel, 'Contract and Crime' in CFG Tapper (ed), *Crime, Proof and Punishment (Essays in Memory of Rupert Cross)* (Butterworths, London, 1981) 81–108

Law Commission, *Consultation Paper 154, Illegal Transactions: The Effect of Illegality on Contracts and Trusts* (1999)

The rules on illegality and public policy should be subject to judicial discretion.

RA Buckley, 'Illegal Transactions: Chaos or Discretion?' (2000) 20 *Legal Studies* 155–80; Nelson Enonchong, 'Illegal Transactions: The Future? (*LCCP No 154*)' [2000] *Restitution Law Review* 82–104

Discussion of the Law Commission's 1999 consultation paper.

Law Commission, *Consultation Paper 189: The Illegality Defence* (2009)

Courts should consider the particular claim (not the contract as a whole) and conduct a balancing exercise of the legitimate expectation that contracts will be enforced against the underlying policies of the illegality defence, namely: the purpose of the rule rendering the conduct illegal, consistency, preventing profit from wrongdoing, deterrence and the integrity of the legal system.

7.3 RESTRAINT OF TRADE AND RESTRICTIVE COVENANTS

Robert S Stevens, 'Involuntary Servitude by Injunction: The Doctrine of *Lumley v Wagner* Considered' (1921) 6 *Cornell Law Review* 235–70

Harlan M Blake, 'Employee Agreements Not to Compete' (1960) 73 *Harvard Law Review* 625–91

AG Guest, 'The House of Lords and the Law of Contract' (1968) 2 *Journal of the Association of Law Teachers* 3–11

Michael J Trebilcock, *The Common Law of Restraint of Trade: A Legal and Economic Analysis* (London, Sweet and Maxwell, 1986)

Stephen A Smith, 'Of Remedies and Restrictive Covenants' (1994) 7 *Journal of Contract Law* 164–80

Linden Gardens and *Surrey v Bredero Homes* should have been decided on the basis that the key covenants were unenforceable as unwarranted restraints on trade, since they do not protect any legitimate interest and merely seek to allow the covenantee to extract money, and the restriction that land covenants are not susceptible to the doctrine of restraint of trade should be abolished.

Stephen A Smith, 'Reconstructing Restraint of Trade' (1995a) 15 *Oxford Journal of Legal Studies* 565–95 and 'Future Freedom and Freedom of Contract' (1995b) 59 *Modern Law Review* 167–87

[1995a] In determining whether a term illegally restricts freedom, bargaining power and procedural fairness are not important, although the commercial sophistication of the parties may be because it can indicate the absence of cognitive defects in framing the obligation, and substantive unfairness is also not important, although the consideration given by the covenantee may be

relevant to the interest of the covenantee purportedly being protected by the covenant. In addition, the public interest element of the test should be abandoned. [1995b] The rules on restraint of trade clauses can be justified by the need to prevent an individual giving away his autonomy.

○ Paul Goulding (ed), *Employee Competition: Covenants, Confidentiality, and Garden Leave* (Oxford, Oxford University Press, 2007)

○ Alexandra Kamerling and Christopher Osman, *Restrictive Covenants under Common and Competition Law*, 5th edn (London, Sweet & Maxwell, 2007)

7.4 WAR

J Dundas White, 'Trading with the Enemy' (1900) 16 *Law Quarterly Review* 397–413

Leslie Scott, 'Effects of War on Contracts' (1914) 30 *Law Quarterly Review* 77–90

○ Lord McNair and AD Watts, *Legal Effects of War* (Cambridge, Cambridge University Press, 1944) ch 4

7.5 CHAMPERTY

AH Dennis 'Law of Maintenance and Champerty' (1890) 6 *Law Quarterly Review* 169–88

Percy H Winfield, 'The History of Maintenance and Champerty' (1919) 35 *Law Quarterly Review* 50–72 and 'Assignment of Choses in Action in Relation to Maintenance and Champerty' (1919) 35 *Law Quarterly Review* 143–62

JH Baker, 'Solicitors and the Law of Maintenance 1590–1640' [1973] *Cambridge Law Journal* 56–80

YL Tan, 'Champertous Contracts and Assignments' (1990) 106 *Law Quarterly Review* 656–79

7.6 THE EFFECT OF ILLEGALITY

GH Treitel, 'Mutuality in Contract' (1961) 77 *Law Quarterly Review* 83–97

Leon E Trakman, 'The Effect of Illegality in the Law of Contract: Suggestions for Reform' (1977) 55 *Canadian Bar Review* 625–55

Judges should be given discretion in evaluating the effects of illegality.

Francis Rose, 'Restitutionary and Proprietary Consequences of Illegality' in FD Rose (ed), *Consensus Ad Idem—Essays in the Law of Contract in Honour of Guenter Treitel* (London, Sweet & Maxwell, 1996) 203–34

A survey of restitutionary and other effects of illegality.

Aleco Vrisakis and JW Carter, 'Restitution of Payments Made Under Contracts Prohibited by Statute' (2000) 15 *Journal of Contract Law* 228–41

Peter Birks, 'Recovering Value Transferred Under an Illegal Contract' (2000) 1 *Theoretical Inquiries in Law* 155–204

Illegality does not bar restitution, although stultification will do so where restitution would make nonsense of the law's refusal to enforce the contract, so restitution should be allowed in some cases, eg where to disallow restitution would be to inflict a disproportionate penalty for illegality.

○ Gareth Jones, *Goff & Jones: The Law of Restitution*, 7th edn (London, Sweet & Maxwell, 2006 plus supplements) ch 24

The New Zealand 'Illegal Contracts Act 1970'

Brian Coote, 'Illegal Contracts Act 1970' in New Zealand Law Commission, *Report 25: Contract Statutes Review* (1993) 173–86

8

PRIVITY AND THIRD PARTY RIGHTS

8.1 THIRD PARTY RIGHTS TO SUE

Samuel Williston, 'Contracts for the Benefit of a Third Person' (1902) 15 *Harvard Law Review* 767–809

Law Revision Committee, *Sixth Interim Report of the Law Revision Committee: Statute of Frauds and the Doctrine of Consideration* (1937)

Lord Wright's committee recommended that third parties be able to enforce terms that purport to confer directly a benefit on them, subject to cancellation by the first and second parties before the third party had adopted the right.

Glanville Williams, 'Contracts for the Benefit of Third Parties' (1944) 7 *Modern Law Review* 123–37

The extent to which trusts can be used to get around the privity rule.

Gabriela Shalev, 'Third Party Beneficiary: A Comparative Analysis' (1976) 11 *Israel Law Review* 315–38

Anthony Jon Waters, 'The Property In the Promise: A Study of the Third Party Beneficiary Rule' (1985) 98 *Harvard Law Review* 1109–210

The origins and American history of the rule allowing third parties to sue on contracts, and the 1859 case of *Lawrence v Fox*.

Robert Flannigan, 'Privity—The End of an Era (Error)' (1987) 103 *Law Quarterly Review* 564–93 also in in Peter Kincaid (ed), *Privity: Private Justice or Public Regulation* (Aldershot, Ashgate, 2001) 28–59

NH Andrews, 'Does a Third Party Beneficiary Have a Right in English Law?' (1988) 8 *Legal Studies* 14–34

Although they may not have active rights to sue directly, third parties do still have primary and secondary contractual rights, which justify the award of specific performance or substantial damages to the promisee.

Samuel Stoljar, 'Contracts for Third Parties: In Search of the Problems' (1988–89) 13 *New Zealand Universities Law Review* 68–96

Peter Kincaid, 'Third Parties: Rationalising a Right to Sue' [1989] *Cambridge Law Journal* 243–70

To justify giving a third party a right to sue it is necessary to demonstrate a link between that third party and the defendant (and his duty) sufficient to justify the correlative right to sue. Detrimental reliance, reliance or reasonable expectations might provide such a link, although it is weaker than the link between the promisor and the promisee (the bargain).

John N Adams and Roger Brownsword, 'Privity and the Concept of a Network Contract' (1990) 10 *Legal Studies* 12–37

There should be no privity rule as between contracts to any of a network of contracts for one objective (as defined). If a party is privy to one, they should be able to sue or be sued on any, subject to the allocation of obligations and the exclusions intended within the network.

Deryck Beyleveld and Roger Brownsword, 'Privity, Transitivity and Rationality' (1991) 54 *Modern Law Review* 48–71

Sub-contracting situations such as *Junior Books v Veitchi* are transitive. The organic relationship between the contract and the sub-contract means that the sub-contractor is involved in the main contract ('the subsumption principle') and so, at least when the customer's recourse against the contractor is barred ('the breakdown principle'), the customer should have a direct contractual action against the sub-contractor and the sub-contractor should be able to rely on any defences or limitations in his sub-contract.

John Fleming Powers, 'Expanded Liability and the Intent Requirement in Third Party Beneficiary Contracts' [1993] *Utah Law Review* 67–148

The intention that the third party benefit, a pre-condition in the US to third party rights.

Werner Lorenz, 'Contracts and Third-Party Rights in German and English Law' in BS Markesinis (ed), *The Gradual Convergence* (Oxford, Clarendon Press, 1994) 65–97

Louis Proksch, 'Restitution and Privity' (1994) 68 *Australian Law Journal* 188–92

A third party beneficiary under a contract may be able to sue a breaching promisor in unjust enrichment for restitution of the expense saved by the promisor as a result of the wrong to the third party of breaching the contract.

Simon Whittaker, 'Privity of Contract and the Law of Tort: The French Experience' (1995) 15 *Oxford Journal of Legal Studies* 327–70 and 'Privity of Contract and the Tort of Negligence: Future Directions' (1996) 16 *Oxford Journal of Legal Studies* 191–230

Stephen A Smith, 'Contracts for the Benefit of Third Parties: In Defence of the Third Party Rule' (1997) 17 *Oxford Journal of Legal Studies* 643–63 also in Peter Kincaid (ed), *Privity: Private Justice or Public Regulation* (Aldershot, Ashgate, 2001) 141–71

The privity rule is justified because promissory obligations are only owed to the promisee. The unsatisfactoriness of the present law results from the failure to fully compensate the promisee for the failure of the promisor to confer a benefit on the third party, the under-recognition of collateral contracts due to the strictures of the requirement of consideration, the failure to recognise (in appropriate circumstances) a tortious/promissory estoppel obligation to the third party, and the failure to grant the promisee restitution in the absence of a total failure of consideration.

Johan Steyn, 'Fulfilling the Reasonable Expectations of Honest Men' (1997) 113 *Law Quarterly Review* 433–42

Ian B Stewart, 'Why Place Trust in a Promise?: Privity of Contract and Enforcement of Contracts by Third Party Beneficiaries' (1999) 73 *Australian Law Journal* 354–78

Melvin Aron Eisenberg, ''The Thirty-Party Beneficial Principle' in Peter Kincaid (ed), *Privity: Private Justice or Public Regulation* (Aldershot, Ashgate, 2001) 172–98

Sir Guenter Treitel, 'The Battle Over Privity' in *Some Landmarks of Twentieth Century Contract Law* (Oxford, Clarendon Press, 2002) 47–105

The development of privity in the last 150 years of English law.

Vernon Valentine Palmer, 'Contracts in Favour of Third Persons in Europe: First Steps Towards Tomorrow's Harmonisation' (2003) 11 *European Review of Private Law* 8–27

Gunther Teubner, 'Expertise as Social Institution: Internalising Third parties into the Contract' in David Campbell, Hugh Collins and John Wightman (eds), *Implicit Dimensions of Contract* (Oxford, Hart Publishing, 2003) 333–63

Jann Hallebeek and Harry Dondorp (eds), *Contracts for a Third-Party Beneficiary. A Historical and Comparative Account* (Leiden, Martinus Nijhoff, 2008)

8.2 THIRD PARTY RIGHTS TO RELY ON EXCLUSION CLAUSES

Graham Battersby, 'Exemption Clauses and Third Parties' (1975) 25 *University of Toronto Law Journal* 371–405 and 'Exemption Clauses and Third Parties: Recent Decisions' (1978) 28 *University of Toronto Law Journal* 78–83

(Contrary to decisions such as *Scruttons v Midland Silicones*) privity should not prevent exemption clauses having effects on parties not privity to them, because such clauses often either limit the scope of the tortious duty that arises (between the third party and a party to the contract) or amount to a waiver of tortious liability. Further, there are many situations in which courts have already recognised vicarious immunity or other third party immunity.

Barry J Reiter, 'Contracts, Torts, Relations and Reliance' in Barry J Reiter and John Swan (eds), *Studies in Contract Law* (Toronto, Butterworths, 1980) 235–311

Deryck Beyleveld and Roger Brownsword, 'Privity, Transitivity and Rationality' (1991) 54 *Modern Law Review* 48–71

John N Adams and Roger Brownsword, 'Privity of Contract–That Pestilential Nuisance' (1993) 56 *Modern Law Review* 722–32

John G Fleming, 'Employee's Tort in a Contractual Matrix: New Approaches in Canada' (1993) 13 *Oxford Journal of Legal Studies* 430–39

The important Supreme Court of Canada decision in *London Drugs Ltd v Kuene & Nagel.*

Shane Nossal, 'Bailment on Terms, Himalaya Clauses, and Exclusive Jurisdiction Clauses: The Decision of the Privy Council in *The Makhutai*' (1996) 26 *Hong Kong Law Journal* 321–38

JLR Davis, 'Privity and Exclusion Clauses' in Peter Kincaid (ed), *Privity: Private Justice or Public Regulation* (Ashgate, 2001) 284–308

Michael O'Meara, 'From *Elder Dempster* to *London Drugs*: The Saga of Vicarious Immunity' (2005) 21 *Journal of Contract Law* 131–54

The courts should recognise a doctrine of vicarious immunity, fashioning tortious duties in the light of their contractual matrix.

8.3 BINDING THIRD PARTIES TO EXCLUSION CLAUSES

NE Palmer, 'Sub-bailment on terms [1988] *Lloyd's Maritime and Commercial Law Quarterly* 466–76

Deryck Beyleveld and Roger Brownsword, 'Privity, Transitivity and Rationality' (1991) 54 *Modern Law Review* 48–71

Peter Devonshire, 'Sub-bailment on Terms and the Efficacy of Contractual Defences Against a Non-contractual Bailor' [1996] *Journal of Business Law* 329–43

The case law indicates that whether an owner will be bound by the terms of the sub-bailment depends upon whether the owner expressly or impliedly consented to those terms, although ostensible authority of the bailee to bind the bailor may also suffice.

8.4 THE (US) RESTATEMENT (SECOND) OF CONTRACTS

Harry G Prince, 'Perfecting the Third Party Beneficiary Standing under Section 302 of the Restatement (Second) of Contracts' (1984) 25 *Boston College Law Review* 919–98

Melvin Aron Eisenberg, ''The Thirty-Party Beneficial Principle' in Peter Kincaid (ed), *Privity: Private Justice or Public Regulation* (Aldershot, Ashgate, 2001) 172–98

Anthony Jon Waters, 'Privity, Property, and Pragmatism: Can American Law Answer Kincaid's Questions?' in Peter Kincaid (ed), *Privity: Private Justice or Public Regulation* (Aldershot, Ashgate, 2001) 309–36

8.5 THE (NEW ZEALAND) CONTRACTS (PRIVITY) ACT 1982

Francis Dawson, 'New Zealand Privity of Contract Bill' (1982) 2 *Oxford Journal of Legal Studies* 448–54

Rodney Newman, 'The Doctrine of Privity of Contract: The Common Law and The Contracts (Privity) Act 1982' (1983) 4 *Auckland University Law Review* 339–60

S Todd, 'Contracts (Privity) Act 1982' in New Zealand Law Commission, *Report 25: Contract Statutes Review* (1993) 217–28

8.6 THE (ENGLISH) CONTRACTS (RIGHTS OF THIRD PARTIES) ACT 1999

Law Commission, *Consultation Paper 121: Privity of Contract: Contracts for the Benefit of Third Parties* (1991) and *Report 242: Privity of Contract: Contracts for the Benefit of Third Parties* (1996)

Jack Beatson, 'Reforming the Law of Contracts for the Benefit of Third Parties: A Second Bite at the Cherry' (1992) 45 *Current Legal Problems* 1–28

Peter Kinkaid, 'The UK Law Commission's Privity Proposals and Contract Theory' (1995) 8 *Journal of Contract Law* 51–66 and Peter Kincaid, 'Privity and Private Justice in Contract' (1997–98) 12 *Journal of Contract Law* 47–64 also in his (as ed) *Privity: Private Justice or Public Regulation* (London, Ashgate, 2001) at 60–81; John Adams, Deryck Beyleveld and Roger Brownsword, 'Privity of Contract—The Benefits and the Burdens of Law

Reform' (1997) 60 *Modern Law Review* 238–64; Stephen A Smith, 'Contracts for the Benefit of Third Parties: In Defence of the Third Party Rule' (1997) 17 *Oxford Journal of Legal Studies* 643–63 also in Peter Kincaid (ed), *Privity: Private Justice or Public Regulation* (Ashgate, 2001) 141–71; Catherine Mitchell, 'Privity Reform and the Nature of Contractual Obligations' (1999) 19 *Legal Studies* 229–44

The authors analyse the Law Commission's proposals and draft Bill. Kinkaid: The proposals are theoretically incoherent, undermining promise as the basis of contractual liability and removing the justifications for allowing the plaintiff to sue. If a general third party action is needed, it should be found in tort. Intention does not justify the giving of a right to a third party. Adams, Beyleveld and Brownsword: Legitimate expectation and not contractual intention should govern the conferral of rights on third parties. Smith: The proposals fail to clearly situate the third party's right in contract, tort or agency, but rather give it aspects of all those legal areas, leaving it confused. Mitchell: The Law Commission proposals may have wide-ranging effects on the nature of contractual obligations, particularly given that the crystallisation test suggests that it is reliance and not agreement that is founding the third party's right to sue.

Andrew Burrows, 'Reforming Privity of Contract: Law Commission Report 242' [1996] *Lloyd's Maritime and Commercial Law Quarterly* 467–86 and 'The Contracts (Rights of Third Parties) Act 1999 and its implications for Commercial Contracts' [2000] *Lloyd's Maritime and Commercial Law Quarterly* 540–54

The Law Commissioner discusses the proposals that led to the 1999 Act, and the Act itself.

Meryll Dean, 'Removing a Blot on the Landscape—The Reform of the Doctrine of Privity' [2000] *Journal of Business Law* 143–52; Catharine MacMillan, 'A Birthday Present for Lord Denning: The Contracts (Rights of Third Parties) Act 1999' (2000) 63 *Modern Law Review* 721–38; Neil Andrews, 'Strangers to Justice no Longer: The Reversal of the Privity Rule Under the Contracts (Rights of Third Parties) Act 1999' [2001] *Cambridge Law Journal* 353–81

The authors survey the 1999 Act and its implications.

Peter Kinkaid, 'Privity Reform in England' (2000) 116 *Law Quarterly Review* 43–47 also in his (as ed) *Privity: Private Justice or Public Regulation* (Aldershot, Ashgate, 2001) 82–87

The 1999 Act is regrettable as it undermines the basis of civil liability, which until now has been to permit the state's coercive force only to be used when there is a justifying relationship between the claimant and defendant based upon the nexus of fact and fault (in the case of contract, the invocation of trust through a bargained for promise and the wrongfulness of later breaking that promise).

○ Robert Merkin (ed), *Privity of Contract: The Impact of the Contracts (Rights of Third Parties) Act 1999* (London, LLP, 2000)

Clare Ambrose, 'When Can a Third Party Enforce an Arbitration Clause?' [2001] *Journal of Business Law* 415–32

Thomas Roe, 'Contractual Intention under Section 1(1)(b) and 1(2) of the Contracts (Rights of Third Parties) Act 1999' (2000) 65 *Modern Law Review* 887–94

Guenter Treitel, 'The Contracts (Rights of Third Parties) Act 1999 and the Law of Carriage of Goods by Sea' in Francis Rose (ed), *Lex Mercatoria: Essays on International Commercial Law in Honour of Francis Reynolds* (London, LLP, 2000) 345–80

Anthony Diamond, 'The Third Man: the 1999 Act Sets Back Separability?' (2001) 17 *Arbitration International* 211–18

Roger Brownsword and Dale Hutchinson, 'Beyond Promissory Principle and Protective Pragmatism' in Peter Kincaid (ed), *Privity: Private Justice or Public Regulation* (Aldershot, Ashgate, 2001) 126–46

The crystallisation test in section 2 does not fit well with the enforceability test of section 1, but sense can be made of this if both are understood as depending upon the parties' reasonable expectations.

Catherine Mitchell, 'Searching for the Principles Behind Privity Reform' in Peter Kincaid (ed), *Privity: Private Justice or Public Regulation* (Aldershot, Ashgate, 2001) 104–25

Andrew Phang, 'On Justification and Method in Law Reform—The Contracts (Rights of Third Parties) Act 1999' (2002) 18 *Journal of Contract Law* 32–51

Robert Stevens, 'The Contracts (Rights of Third Parties) Act 1999' (2004) 120 *Law Quarterly Review* 292–323

The author outlines various uncertainties in the 1999 Act and argues that the law was more coherent without it.

Chee Ho Tham, 'Trust, not Contract: Restoring Trust in the Contracts (Rights of Third Parties) Act' (2005) 21 *Journal of Contract Law* 107–30; Brian Coote, 'Contract not Trust: Questions About the Contracts (Rights of Third Parties) Act from Another Perspective' (2006) 22 *Journal of Contract Law* 72–80

Chee: The Act is best understood as a development of the trust of a promise doctrine. Coote: No it is not.

8.7 CONTRACTS WITH PROPRIETARY EFFECT

Simon Gardner, 'The Proprietary Effect of Contractual Obligations under *Tulk* v *Moxhay* and *De Mattos* v *Gibson*' (1982) 98 *Law Quarterly Review* 279–323; Andrew Tettenborn, 'Contracts, Privity of Contract and the Purchaser of Personal Property' [1982] *Cambridge Law Journal* 58–86

When a purchaser of property can be bound to observe covenants entered into by previous owners of the property.

William Swadling, 'The Proprietary Effect of Hire of Goods' in Norman Palmer and Ewan McKendrick (eds), *Interests in Goods*, 2nd edn (London, LLP, 1998) 491–526

8.8 ASSIGNMENT

Bob Allcock, 'Restrictions on the Assignment of Contractual Rights' [1983] *Cambridge Law Journal* 328–46

Non-assignment clauses do not affect the rights of the assignee as against the assignor, but may prevent the assignee acquiring rights against the obligor, although a declaration of trust by the assignor in favour of the assignee may improve the assignee's position.

MP Furmston, 'The Assignment of Contractual Burdens' (1998) 13 *Journal of Contract Law* 42–54

Situations in which, contrary to received wisdom, the burden of a contract may be assigned.

J Tolhurst, 'Equitable Assignment of Legal Rights: A Resolution to a Conundrum' (2002) 118 *Law Quarterly Review* 98–123

○ AS Burrows, 'Chapter 19: Assignment' in Hugh Beale (ed), *Chitty on Contracts: Volume I: General Principles*, 30th edn (London, Sweet & Maxwell, 2008 plus supplements)

Gerard McMeel, 'The Modern Law of Assignment: Public Policy and Contractual Restrictions on Transferability' [2004] *Lloyd's Maritime and Commercial Law Quarterly* 483–512

○ Greg Tolhurst, *The Assignment of Contractual Rights* (Oxford, Hart Publishing, 2006)

○ Marcus Smith, *The Law of Assignment: The Creation and Transfer of Choses in Action* (Oxford, Oxford University Press, 2007)

9

MODIFICATION

9.1 GENERALLY

JB Ames, 'Novation' (1893) 6 *Harvard Law Review* 184–94

Tony Dugdale and David Yates, 'Variation, Waiver and Estoppel—A Reappraisal' (1976) 37 *Modern Law Review* 686–97

DG Baird, 'Self-interest and Co-operation in Long-term Contracts' (1990) 19 *Journal of Legal Studies* 583–96

Roger Halson, 'The Modification of Contractual Obligations' (1991) 44 *Current Legal Problems* 111–33

Christine Jolls, 'Contracts as Bilateral Commitments: A New Perspective on Contract Modification' (1997) 26 *Journal of Legal Studies* 203–37

Allowing parties to bind themselves to non-modifiable contracts is more efficient in some circumstances than refusing to give effect to non-modification clauses, given the effect that knowing the contract cannot be modified has on the parties' behaviour.

Erich Schanze, 'Failure of Long-Term Contracts and the Duty to Re-negotiate' and Geoffrey Samuel, 'Failure of Long-Term Contracts and the Duty to Re-negotiate—A Comment' in Francis D Rose (ed), *Failure of Contracts* (Oxford, Hart Publishing, 1997) 155–65, 167–74

JW Carter, 'The Renegotiation of Contracts' (1998) 13 *Journal of Contract Law* 185–213

William T Allen and Glaya Levy, 'The Uses of Ambiguity in Commercial Contracts: On Facilitating Re-Bargaining' and Paul Lomas, 'Commentary' in Sarah Worthington (ed), *Commercial Law and Commercial Practice* (Oxford, Hart Publishing, 2003) 163–80 and 181–87

An implied duty of good faith may be efficient precisely because it is ambiguous and so facilitates re-negotiation when circumstances change.

Mark P Gergen, 'The Law's Response to Exit and Loyalty in Contract Disputes' in Nili Cohen and Ewan McKendrick (eds), *Comparative Remedies for Breach of Contract* (Oxford, Hart Publishing, 2004) 75–101

9.2 CONSIDERATION FOR CONTRACT MODIFICATIONS

Samuel Williston, 'Successive Promises of the Same Performance' (1895) 8 *Harvard Law Review* 27–38

CJ Hamson, 'The Reform of Consideration' (1938) 54 *Law Quarterly Review* 233–57

SJ Stoljar, 'The Modification of Contracts' (1957) 35 *Canadian Bar Review* 485–528

FMB Reynolds and GH Treitel, 'Consideration for the Modification of Contracts' (1965) 7 *Malaya Law Review* 1–23

Richard A Posner, 'Gratuitous Promises in Economics and Law' (1977) 6 *Journal of Legal Studies* 411–26

Gratuitous modifications should be enforceable (because efficient) where unexpected events prevent performance otherwise, or where the promisee can get a better price, but not where the promisee is merely exercising a monopoly position that has developed since the contract was signed.

BJ Reiter, 'Courts, Consideration and Common Sense' (1977) 27 *University of Toronto Law Journal* 439–512

John Swan, 'Consideration and the Reasons for Enforcing Contracts' (1977) 15 *University of Western Ontario Law Review* 83 122 also in Barry J Reiter and John Swan (eds), *Studies in Contract Law* (Toronto, Butterworths, 1980) 23–59

Commercial contract variations should be enforceable providing there is no duress or unconscionability, as in such cases there is no reason to doubt that due deliberation has been made by the promisor and business expectations require enforcement.

Varouj A Aivazian, Michael J Trebilcock and Michael Penny, 'The Law of Contractual Modifications: The Uncertain Quest for a Bench Mark of Enforceability' (1984) 22 *Osgoode Hall Law Journal* 173–212

An economic analysis of the enforcement of contractual modifications.

Brian Coote, 'Consideration and Benefit in Fact and in Law' (1990–91) 3 *Journal of Contract Law* 23–29

JW Carter, Andrew Phang and Jill Poole, 'Reactions to Williams v Roffey' (1995) 8 *Journal of Contract Law* 248–71

Mindy Chen-Wishart, 'Consideration: Practical Benefit and the Emperor's New Clothes' in Jack Beatson and Daniel Friedmann (eds), *Good Faith and Fault in Contract Law* (Oxford, Clarendon Press, 1995) 123–50

The *Williams v Roffey Bros* decision gives rise to an illusory and theoretically unbounded requirement of consideration, and it would be better for promissory estoppel to be extended to use as a sword. At the least, modifications made binding by performance of an existing obligation and practical benefit to the promisee should be interpreted as being conditional upon actual performance of the existing obligation, and revocable without it, for the purposes of damages assessments.

Janet O'Sullivan, 'In Defence of Foakes v Beer' [1996] *Cambridge Law Journal* 219–28

Debt cases can be distinguished from other variation cases because of the inherently commensurable nature of money and the absence of mitigation and remoteness rules limiting recovery in debt cases, and so the decision in *Re Selectmove* that the *Williams v Roffey Bros* ruling does not affect the strict rule from *Foakes v Beer* is correct.

Peter Luther, 'Campbell, Espinasse and the Sailors: Text and Context in the Common Law' (1999) 19 *Legal Studies* 526–51

An investigation of the texts and context of the *Stilk v Myrick* decision, arguing that it is neither simply about consideration nor simply about duress, and turns on the special policy concerns relating to merchant seamen at the time.

Elizabeth Cooke, 'Working Together? Contract, Estoppel and the Business Relationship' (2002) *Journal of Obligations and Remedies* 5–20

Sir Guenter Treitel, 'Agreements to Vary Contracts' in *Some Landmarks of Twentieth Century Contract Law* (Oxford, Clarendon Press: 2002) 11–46

Brian Coote, 'Consideration and the Variation of Contracts' [2003] *New Zealand Law Review* 361–80

Better to have no requirement of consideration for variations than to allow practical benefit of the performance of the contract to count as consideration.

9.3 WAIVER AND PROMISSORY ESTOPPEL

GC Cheshire and CHS Fifoot, 'Central London Property Trust Ltd v High Trees House Ltd' (1947) 63 *Law Quarterly Review* 283–301

The *High Trees* decision is a welcome development from common law waiver.

Benjamin F Boyer, 'Promissory Estoppel: Principle from Precedents (Parts I and II)' (1952) 50 *Michigan Law Review* 639–74 and 873–98

ID Campbell, 'Gratuitous Waiver of Contractual Obligations' (1963–65) 1 *New Zealand Universities Law Review* 232–55

Promissory estoppel should be abandoned in favour of waiver.

Tony Dugdale and David Yates, 'Variation, Waiver and Estoppel—A Re-appraisal' (1976) 39 *Modern Law Review* 680–97

Waivers prior to breach should bind if there is unambiguous agreement to vary, although they should be revocable if made in the absence of consideration.

Waivers after breach do not alter the terms of the contract, rather they bar a remedy, and should require reasonable reliance upon the representation.

Lord Denning, 'Developments in the Doctrine of Consideration' (1952) 15 *Modern Law Review* 1–10, 'The Way of an Iconoclast' (1966) 5 *Journal of the Society of Public Teachers of Law* 77–90 and 'High Trees' in his *The Discipline of the Law* (London, Butterworths, 1979) 197–223

The author describes the early development of the doctrine of promissory estoppel from his point of view at the centre of it.

Jay M Feinman, 'Promissory Estoppel and Judicial Method' (1984) 97 *Harvard Law Review* 678–718

GA Kennedy J, 'Equitable Estoppel' (1984) 58 *Australian Law Journal* 573–89

Samuel Stoljar, 'Estoppel and Contract Theory' (1990–91) 3 *Journal of Contract Law* 1–22

Estoppel operates to identify agreements varying, supplementing or clarifying contracts, and should be subsumed within contract principles.

○ Sean Wilken, *The Law of Waiver, Variation and Estoppel,* 2nd edn (Oxford, Oxford University Press, 2002)

AJ Phipps, 'Resurrecting the Doctrine of Common Law Forbearance' (2007) 123 *Law Quarterly Review* 286–313

There is still room for the common law doctrine of forbearance, binding a waiving party to a promised forbearance even if no consideration has been provided for a variation and there is no reliance on unconscionability such as would found an estoppel, although the forbearance (unlike the variation) is revocable on reasonable notice.

9.4 DURESS AND CONTRACT MODIFICATIONS

RJ Sutton, 'Duress by Threatened Breach of Contract' (1974) 20 *McGill Law Journal* 554–86

Subha Narasimhan, 'Modification: The Self-Help Specific Performance Remedy' (1987) 97 *Yale Law Journal* 61–95

Given the limited availability of specific performance, it will often make sense for a contractor to agree to an increase in price and then to contest the modification after the (originally) promised performance has been received. Such 'self-help specific performance' is not justified except where true specific performance would be available, or at least would be available but for problems in administering such a remedy. Further, these conclusions impact upon when duress should be found because, except where self-help specific performance is justified, the 'innocent' party is himself acting opportunistically in agreeing to the modification.

Elizabeth Macdonald, 'Duress by Threatened Breach of Contract' [1989] *Journal of Business Law* 460–73

A central element of a duress by threatened breach is the lack of a reasonable (legal or extra-legal) alternative to entering the transaction. This test is justifiable as providing a balance between the rights of individuals not to be coerced and the need to prevent compromises being reopened.

Jack Beatson, 'Duress as a Vitiating Factor In Contract' [1974] *Cambridge Law Journal* 97–115, a later version of which forms part of 'Duress, Restitution, and Contract Renegotiation' in his *The Use and Abuse of Unjust Enrichment* (Oxford, Clarendon Press, 1991) 95–136

Daniel A Graham and Ellen R Peirce, 'Contract Modification: An Economic Analysis of the Hold-Up Game' (1989) 52 *Law & Contemporary Problems* 9–32

Roger Halson, 'Opportunism, Economic Duress and Contractual Modifications' (1991) 107 *Law Quarterly Review* 649–78

The economic efficiency of law of duress as it relates to the modification of contracts. Generally it guards against opportunism, in other words does not enforce modifications that exploit through coercion contract-created vulnerability, although the law is inefficient, eg by refusing to enforce modifications even when they are responding to unanticipated changes in circumstances.

SM Waddams, 'Restitution As Part of Contract Law' in Andrew *Burrows* (ed), *Essays on the Law of Restitution* (Oxford, Clarendon Press, 1991) 197–213

Stephen A Smith, 'Contracting Under Pressure: A Theory of Duress' [199]) *Cambridge Law Journal* 343–73

9.5 AGREED TERMINATION

Samuel Williston, 'Rescission by Parol Agreement' (1904) 4 *Columbia Law Review* 455–69

The formality requirements of agreed rescission of formal contracts.

10

BREACH AND TERMINATION

10.1 GENERALLY

See also 4.2 Order of Performance

Allan Farnsworth, 'On Trying to Keep One's Promises: The Duty of Best Efforts in Contract Law' (1984–85) 46 *University of Pittsburgh Law Review* 1–20

GH Treitel, 'Fault in the Common Law of Contract' in Maarten Bos and Ian Brownlie (eds), *Liber amicorum for the Rt Hon Lord Wilberforce, PC, CMG, OBE, QC* (Oxford, Clarendon Press, 1987) 185–210

The common law's approach, to only sometimes require fault for breach (eg due diligence, reasonable care obligations) or sometimes allow fault to affect contract rules (eg in frustration cases), is preferable to the general civil law requirement of fault.

JW Carter, *Breach of Contract*, 2nd edn (London, Sweet & Maxwell, 1991)

Barry Nicholas, 'Fault and Breach of Contract' in Jack Beatson and Daniel Friedmann (eds), *Good Faith and Fault in Contract Law* (Oxford, Clarendon Press, 1995) 337–55

The civil law requirement of faulty breach is dealt with in the common law at the anterior stage of duty definition through implied terms and the allocation of the risk of unforeseen consequences.

○ John E Stannard, *Delay in the Performance of Contractual Obligations* (Oxford, Oxford University Press, 2007)

10.2 CURE AND RE-TENDER

Antonia Apps, 'The Right to Cure Defective Performance' [1994] *Lloyd's Maritime and Commercial Law Quarterly* 525–59

10.3 ANTICIPATORY BREACH AND RENUNCIATION

Samuel Williston, 'Repudiation of Contracts: Parts I and II' (1901) 14 *Harvard Law Review* 317–31 and 421–41

The law of repudiation in situations of anticipatory breach and manifestation of an intention not to perform. No action for breach can arise until the date for performance has arrived.

Joseph H Beale Jr, 'Damages Upon Repudiation of a Contract' (1908) 17 *Yale Law Journal* 443–56

Herbert R Limburg, 'Anticipatory Repudiation of Contracts' (1914) 10 *Cornell Law Quarterly* 135–80

Henry Winthrop Ballantine, 'Anticipatory Breach and the Enforcement of Contractual Duties' (1924) 22 *Michigan Law Review* 329–52

L Vold, 'Withdrawal of Repudiation after Anticipatory Breach of Contract' (1926) 5 *Texas Law Review* 9–17

PM Nienabar, 'The Effect of Anticipatory Repudiation: Principle and Policy' [1962] *Cambridge Law Journal* 213–33

WED Davies, 'Anticipatory Breach and Mitigation of Damages' (1963) 5 *University of Western Australia Law Review* 576–90

E Tabachnick, 'Anticipatory Breach of Contract' (1972) 25 *Current Legal Problems* 149–78

A defence of the doctrine of anticipatory breach and its requirement that repudiation be accepted for termination to occur.

Samuel Stoljar, 'Some Problems with Anticipatory Breach' (1974) 9 *Melbourne University Law Review* 355–69

Anticipatory breach is mainly of importance in relation to the duty to mitigate loss.

Francis Dawson, 'Metaphors and Anticipatory Breach of Contract' [1981] *Cambridge Law Journal* 83–107

Anticipatory breach (by renunciation) should be understood as an actual breach of an implied promise not to hinder or prevent compliance with the innocent party's obligations (especially conditions precedent to the promisor's obligations). The acceptance of the innocent party is necessary to perfect the breach since without that the performance of the conditions precedent by the innocent party cannot be said to been prevented. Accordingly there was no breach in *White & Carter v McGregor* as performance of the innocent party's obligations was not hindered and did not require the co-operation of the promisor.

Scottish Law Commission, *Discussion Paper 109: Remedies for Breach of Contract* (1999) and *Report 174: Report on Remedies for Breach of Contract* (1999)

There should be legislation clarifying the *White & Carter v McGregor* rule limiting the right to seek performance following anticipatory breach.

Jay Jie Ze, 'Anticipatory Breach of Contract—the PRC System and English Comparisons' [2005] *Lloyd's Maritime and Commercial Law Quarterly* 253–71

There should be no anticipatory breach by disablement or impossibility caused by the party's own act or default, and instead there should be a doctrine of suspension of performance until the other party has given an adequate assurance of performance, as exists under the UCC.

Qiao Liu, 'Inferring Future Breach: Towards a Unifying Test of Anticipatory Breach of Contract' [2007] *Cambridge Law Journal* 574–604

Anticipatory breach is not based upon intentional renunciation. Rather it is the giving, by words or conduct, of sufficient evidence (looked at retrospectively) that the party will actually commit a fundamental breach when the time for performance comes so as to justify the other party in inferring this and terminating the contract without waiting.

Michael Mustill, '*The Golden Victory*—Some Reflections' (2008) 124 *Law Quarterly Review* 569–85

The law of anticipatory breach cannot be rationalised with the remainder of the law but is a rule of its own.

10.4 REPUDIATORY/FUNDAMENTAL BREACH

SJ Stoljar, 'Untimely Performance in the Law of Contract' (1955) 71 *Law Quarterly Review* 527–61

FMB Reynolds, 'Warranty, Condition and Fundamental Term' (1963) 79 *Law Quarterly Review* 534–55

The categories of term (warranty, condition, fundamental term) should be abandoned leaving the question of repudiatory breach, which releases the innocent party where the other party has failed to a sufficient degree, to turn solely on the nature of the breach.

Francis Dawson, 'Waiver of Conditions Precedent on a Repudiation' (1980) 96 *Law Quarterly Review* 239–47

Robert A Hillman, 'An Analysis of the Cessation of Contractual Relations' (1983) 68 *Cornell Law Review* 617–59

Cessation in cases of termination, frustration and mistake are all about determining whether there is an express or implied right to cessation (ie an allocation of risk of the event) and, in the absence of such an express or implied right, filling the gap by the application of fairness.

Roger Brownsword, 'Retrieving Reasons, Retrieving Rationality? A New Look at the Right to Withdraw for Breach of Contract' (1992) 5 *Journal of Contract Law* 83–107

A repudiatory breach should perhaps only arise where the breach gives the innocent party a good reason for terminating rather than affirming, such as that the breach treats the obligation with disdain, is fundamental, or raises doubts about the competence of the breaching party, or that the breach puts the innocent party at risk if he has to prove loss.

Mark Pawlowski, 'Acceptance of Repudiatory Breach in Leases' (1995) 59 *Conveyancer and Property Lawyer* 379–90

Brian John Davenport, 'Some Thoughts on the Classification of Contract Terms' in Francis Rose (ed), *Lex Mercatoria: Essays on International Commercial Law in Honour of Francis Reynolds* (London, LLP, 2000) 1–12

Sir Guenter Treitel, 'Types of Contractual Terms' in *Some Landmarks of Twentieth Century Contract Law* (Oxford, Clarendon Press: 2002) 107–37

John E Stannard, 'In the Contractual Last Chances Saloon: Notices Making Time of the Essence' (2004) 120 *Law Quarterly Review* 137–62

The effects of a non-breaching party giving a notice that time is of the essence after the other party has breached. Failure to perform following such a notice gives a defence to an action for specific performance, disproves any allegation of waiver of breach, and operates as evidence of repudiation.

JW Carter, GJ Tolhurst and Elisabeth Peden, 'Developing the Intermediate Term Concept' (2006) 22 *Journal of Contract Law* 268–86

The intermediate term concept from *Hong Kong Fir* is about discovering whether performance of the breached obligation is a condition precedent to the other party's obligation to perform (although not necessarily to the entire remainder of the contract).

10.5 THE EFFECTS OF REPUDIATORY BREACH

Suspension of Performance

JW Carter, 'Suspending Performance for Breach' in Jack Beatson and Daniel Friedmann (eds), *Good Faith and Fault in Contract Law* (Oxford, Clarendon Press, 1995) 485–522

There is need of a default rule suspending the obligation to perform upon repudiatory (including anticipatory) breach by the other party, until such time as the contract is terminated or sufficient assurances of intention and ability to perform are given by the breaching party.

Election

L Vold, 'Anticipatory Breach of Contracts and Necessity of Election' (1927–28) 26 *Michigan Law Review* 502–30

JM Thomson, 'Repudiatory Breach, Illegality and Contracts of Employment' (1973) 38 *Modern Law Review* 346–49 and 'The Effect of Repudiatory Breach' (1978) 41 *Modern Law Review* 137–46

Contracts end automatically at the time of repudiatory breach unless there is evidence of a waiver of the repudiation.

FD Rose, 'The Effects of Repudiatory Breaches of Contract' (1981) 34 *Current Legal Problems* 235–57

Andrew Beech, 'Terminating a Contract: Dispensing with the Requirement of Readiness and Willingness' (1992) 5 *Journal of Contract Law* 47–59

It should not be a precondition to a right to terminate that an innocent party is ready and willing to perform.

JW Carter, Andrew Phang and Sock-Yong Phang, 'Performance Following Repudiation: Legal and Economic Interests' (1999) 15 *Journal of Contract Law* 97–132

A non-breaching party's right to affirm a contract in the face of a repudiation should be limited by a mitigation principle to avoid waste.

Qiao Liu, 'Claiming Damages upon an Anticipatory Breach: Why Should an Acceptance Be Necessary?' (2005) 25 *Legal Studies* 559–77

Damages should be available upon anticipatory breach without an acceptance in case of disablement leading to impossibility or injury distinct from loss of bargain.

Aleka Mandaraka Sheppard, 'Demystifying the Right of Election in Contract Law' (2006) 18 *Singapore Academy of Law Journal* 60–95, also published in [2007] *Journal of Business Law* 442–70

Waiver and election and their requirements.

Termination

Arthur L Corbin, 'Discharge of Contracts' (1913) 22 *Yale Law Journal* 513–30

CB Morison, 'Rescission of Executory Contracts for Partial Failure in Performance: Parts I and II' (1912) 28 *Law Quarterly Review* 398–412 and (1913) 29 *Law Quarterly Review* 61–75

AM Shea, 'Discharge from Performance by Failure of Condition' (1979) 42 *Modern Law Review* 623–45

Repudiatory breach does not give rise to rescission or the end of any contractual obligations. Rather a repudiatory breach is a breach when the performance that has been withheld is, according to the implied intention of the parties, a condition precedent of the other party's obligation to perform obligations, and those obligations of which it is a condition are then no longer enforceable. The doctrine of acceptance is merely a reflection of the innocent party's one chance to waive the breach.

Robin Evans-Jones and Kathryn Kruse, 'Failure of Consideration' in David Johnston and Reinhard Zimmermann (eds), *Unjustified Enrichment: Key Issues a Comparative Perspective* (Cambridge, Cambridge University Press, 2002) 128–56

The separation of contractual and restitutionary meanings of (failure of) consideration in the *Fibrosa* decision, and the background to that separation.

Mark P Gergen, 'Restitution as a Bridge Over Troubled Contractual Waters' (2002) 71 *Fordham Law Review* 709–41

Restitution should not generally be available upon breach (only in limited cases of opportunistic breach, and the deprivation of a windfall).

Steven Lurie, 'Towards and Unified Theory of Breach: Tracing the History of the Rule that Rescission Ab Initio Is Not a Remedy for Breach of Contract' (2003) 19 *Journal of Contract Law* 250–79

Simon Honeyball and David Pearce, 'Contract, Employment and the Contract of Employment' (2006) 35 *Industrial Law Journal* 30–55

The contractual basis for the survival of restrictive covenants after the termination of employment.

JW Carter, 'Partial Termination of Contracts' (2008) 24 *Journal of Contract Law* 1–27

The Effect of Breach on Exclusion Clauses, and the Doctrine of Fundamental Breach

AG Guest, 'Fundamental Breach of Contract' (1961) 77 *Law Quarterly Review* 98–118; FMB Reynolds, 'Warranty, Condition and Fundamental Term' (1963) 79 *Law Quarterly Review* 534–55; Lord Devlin, 'The Treatment of Breach of Contract' [1966] *Cambridge Law Journal* 192–215

Brian Coote, 'The Effect of Discharge by Breach on Exception Clauses' [1970] *Cambridge Law Journal* 221–40, 'Discharge for Breach and Exception Clauses

Since Harbutt's Plasticine' (1977) 40 *Modern Law Review* 31–46 and 'The Second Rise and Fall of Fundamental Breach' (1981) 55 *Australian Law Journal* 788–803

Francis Dawson, 'Fundamental Breach of Contract' (1975) 91 *Law Quarterly Review* 380–405

A doctrine of fundamental breach, at least in effect, may operate when, as a matter of proper construction, the exclusion clauses is a promise and full performance is a condition precedent to the operation of that promise.

Nyuk Chin, 'The Problem of Exception Clauses: A Theory of Performance-related Risks' (1983) 15 *University of Western Australia Law Review* 347–97

There is a minimum standard of exchange preventing exclusion of certain breaches of contract, such as wilful breaches. To this extent, the doctrine of fundamental breach is correct.

Charles Debattista, 'Fundamental Breach and Deviation in the Carriage of Goods by Sea' [1989] *Journal of Business Law* 22–36; John Livermore, 'Deviation, Deck Cargo and Fundamental Breach' (1989–90) 2 *Journal of Contract Law* 241–65; Simon Baughen, 'Does Deviation Still Matter?' [1991] *Lloyd's Maritime and Commercial Law Quarterly* 70–96; Brian Coote, 'Deviation and the Ordinary Law' in Francis Rose (ed), *Lex Mercatoria: Essays on International Commercial Law in Honour of Francis Reynolds* (London, LLP, 2000) 13–37; Martin Dockray, 'Deviation: A Doctrine All at Sea?' [2000] *Lloyd's Maritime and Commercial Law Quarterly* 76–98

The abolition of the doctrine of fundamental breach casts serious doubts upon the surviving rules governing the effects of deviation on sea carriage contracts, although Coote warns that some of the special effects may survive.

Damages Following Termination

AL Goodhart, 'Measure of Damages When a Contract is Repudiated' (1962) 78 *Law Quarterly Review* 263–70

Contrary to *White & Carter v McGregor*, there should be a duty to minimise loss following an unaccepted repudiation.

Samuel Stoljar, 'Some Problems with Anticipatory Breach' (1974) 9 *Melbourne University Law Review* 355–69

Thomas H Jackson, '"Anticipatory Repudiation" and the Temporal Element of Contract Law: An Economic Inquiry into Contract Damages in Cases of Prospective Nonperformance' (1978) 31 *Stanford Law Review* 69–119

JW Carter, 'The Effect of Discharge of a Contract on the Assessment of Damages for Breach on Repudiation: Parts I and II' (1988) 1 *Journal of Contract Law* 113–33 and 249–64

The effects termination (and the events before and after termination) have on the assessment of damages.

Restitution

See also 4.2 Order of Performance and 14.2 Contract and Unjust Enrichment

George E Palmer, 'The Contract Price as a Limit on Restitution for Defendant's Breach' (1959) 20 *Ohio State Law Journal* 264–88

Law Commission, *Working Paper 65: Pecuniary Restitution on Breach of Contract* (1975)

Michael Albery, 'Mr Cyprian Williams' Great Heresy' (1975) 91 *Law Quarterly Review* 337–56

Only damages, and not restitution, are available upon termination for repudiatory breach.

J Beatson, 'Discharge for Breach: The Position of Instalments, Deposits and Other Payments Due Before Completion' (1981) 97 *Law Quarterly Review* 389–419 a later version of which appears in his *The Use and Abuse of Unjust Enrichment* (Oxford, Clarendon Press, 1991) 45–77

A rationalisation of the complex rules of recovery of part payments and deposits after termination.

Andrew Burrows, 'Free Acceptance and the Law of Restitution' (1988) 104 *Law Quarterly Review* 576–99, a later version of which appears in his *Understanding the Law of Obligations* (Oxford, Hart Publishing, 1998) 72–98

Restitution by *quantum meruit* or *quantum valebat* following discharge of a contract is grounded on failure of consideration not a principle of free acceptance. *Planché v Colburn* is a case of expectation damages for breach of contract and not a restitution case.

Andrew Kull, 'Restitution as a Remedy for Breach of Contract' (1994) 67 *Southern California Law Review* 1465–518

A Burrows, 'Solving the Problem of Concurrent Liability' (1995) 48 *Current Legal Problems* 103–24, a later version of which appears in his *Understanding the Law of Obligations* (Oxford, Hart Publishing, 1998) 16–44

When a contract is discharged the innocent party should be able to claim restitution even where this gives a better remedy than contractual damages, unless this option is expressly or impliedly excluded by what was agreed in the contract.

Ewan McKendrick, 'Total Failure of Consideration and Counter-Restitution: Two Issues or One?' in Peter Birks (ed), *Laundering and Tracing* (Oxford, Oxford University Press, 1995) 217–42

Peter Birks, 'Failure of Consideration' in FD Rose (ed), *Consensus Ad Idem—Essays in the Law of Contract in Honour of Guenter Treitel* (London, Sweet & Maxwell, 1996) 179–202

The requirement that a failure of consideration be 'total' should be abolished, and counter-restitution (whether *in specie* or in money) should be regularly available.

JW Carter, 'Discharged Contracts: Claims for Restitution' (1997) 11 *Journal of Contract Law* 130–47

Restitution following discharge of a contract must be developed on proper principles of unjust enrichment including requiring genuine acceptance of real benefit (difficult to prove where the benefit was provided pursuant to contractual obligations) before a *quantum meruit* claim is awarded.

J Beatson, 'The Temptation of Elegance: Concurrence of Restitutionary and Contractual Claims' in William Swadling and Gareth Jones, *The Search for Principle Essays in Honour of Lord Goff of Chieveley* (Oxford, Oxford University Press, 1999) 143–70

Even after discharge of the contract the contract may still expressly or impliedly exclude the right to restitution.

Peter Jaffey, 'Restitutionary Claims Arising on Contractual Termination' in EJH Schrage (ed), *Unjust Enrichment and the Law of Contract* (London, Kluwer Law International, 2001) 243–55

Claims for recovery of prepayments or *quantum meruit* are not restitutionary but are actually contractual reliance claims, although not requiring a breach of contract: they are claims for payments or work done in reliance upon the agreement.

Julian Bailey, 'Reputation, Terms and Quantum Meruit' (2006) 22 *Construction Law Journal* 217–40

The impact of the contract price on the amount of recovery under *quantum meruit*.

Gerard McMeel, 'Unjust Enrichment, Discharge for Breach, and the Primacy of Contract' in Andrew Burrows and Lord Rodger, *Mapping the Law: Essays in Memory of Peter Birks* (Oxford, Oxford University Press, 2006) 181–99

Unlike where a contract is rescinded due to a vice in negotiations, in which case it would be unjust to allow one party to retain the benefit of the contract, contracts discharged for breach should not necessarily lead to full restitution.

In some cases the parties' intentions may oust restitution on the proper construction of the contract (eg as shown by staged payments) or the contractual setting (eg where the sub-contractor cannot sue the customer in unjust enrichment).

Peter Butler, 'Advance Contractual Payments: Enforcement and Restitution for Failure of Basis' in Charles Rickett and Ross Grantham (eds), *Structure and Justification in Private Law: Essays for Peter Birks* (Oxford, Hart Publishing, 2008) 225–244

○ Gareth Jones, *Goff & Jones: The Law of Restitution*, 7th edn (London, Sweet & Maxwell, 2006 plus supplements) 20-001 to 20-057

John Tarrant, 'Total Failure of Consideration' (2006) 33 *University of Western Australia Law Review* 132–52

Restitution on failure of consideration following termination is really the payment of debts arising where the right to retain monies paid conditionally upon performance has accrued, which is a question of construction of the contract.

The (New Zealand) Contractual Remedies Act 1979

JF Burrows, 'The Contractual Remedies Act 1979—Six Years On' (1985–88) 6 *Otago Law Review* 220–44

JF Burrows, 'The Contractual Remedies Act 1979' and F Dawson, 'Contractual Remedies Act 1979: Commentary' in New Zealand Law Commission, *Report 25: Contract Statutes Review* (1993) 61–110

DW McLauchlan, 'Contract Law Reform in New Zealand: the Contractual Remedies Act 1979' (1981) 1 *Oxford Journal of Legal Studies* 284–95

Francis Dawson and David W McLauchlan, *The Contractual Remedies Act 1979* (Auckland, Sweet & Maxwell, 1981)

Francis Dawson, 'The New Zealand Contract Statutes' [1985] *Lloyd's Maritime and Commercial Law Quarterly* 42–57

10.6 TERMINATION PURSUANT TO EXPRESS CONTRACT CLAUSES

Brian R Opeskin, 'Damages for Breach of a Contract Terminated Under Express Terms' (1990) 106 *Law Quarterly Review* 293–326

When a contract is terminated for breach in exercise of an express contractual power, loss of bargain damages for loss of future performance should be recoverable.

JW Carter, 'Termination Clauses' (1990–91) 3 *Journal of Contract Law* 90–125

Simon Whittaker, 'Termination Clauses' in Andrew Burrows and Edwin Peel (eds), *Contract Terms* (Oxford, Oxford University Press, 2007) 253–84

JW Carter, 'Partial Termination of Contracts' (2008) 24 *Journal of Contract Law* 1–27

11

REMEDIES

11.1 GENERAL TEXTS

- GH Treitel, *Remedies for Breach of Contract: A Comparative Account* (Oxford, Clarendon Press, 1988)
- Donald R Harris, David Campbell and Roger Halson, *Remedies in Contract and Tort*, 2nd edn (London, Butterworths, 2000)
- Andrew Burrows, *Remedies for Torts and Breach of Contract*, 3rd edn (Oxford, Oxford University Press, 2004)

11.2 GENERALLY

E Allan Farnsworth, 'Legal Remedies for Breach of Contract' (1970) 70 *Columbia Law Review* 1145–216

Hugh Beale and Tony Dugdale, 'Contracts Between Businessmen: Planning and the Use of Contractual Remedies' (1975) 2 *British Journal of Law and Society* 45–60

Empirical evidence shows that extra-contractual devices are preferred to legal remedies, although contractors will expend costs in negotiating in detail where the risk justified it.

Patricia H Marschall, 'Wilfulness: A Crucial Factor in Choosing Remedies for Breach of Contract' (1982) 24 *Arizona Law Review* 733–62

Daniel Friedmann, 'Good Faith and Remedies for Breach of Contract' in Jack Beatson and Daniel Friedmann (eds), *Good Faith and Fault in Contract Law* (Oxford, Clarendon Press, 1995) 399–425

JW Carter and MJ Tilbury, 'Remedial Choice and Contract Drafting' (1998) 13 *Journal of Contract Law* 5–34

Stephen Waddams, 'Breach of Contract and the Concept of Wrongdoing' (2000) 12 *Supreme Court Law Review* 1–29 also in Lionel Smith (ed), *Ruled by Law: Essays in Memory of Mr Justice John Sopinka* (Toronto, Butterworths, 2000)

A survey of specific performance, the tort of wrongfully inducing breach and disgorgement damages shows that in limited situations it is right to characterise a breach of contract as a wrong.

Marco Torsello, 'Remedies for Breach of Contract' in Jan M Smits (ed), *Elgar Encylopedia of Comparative Law* (Cheltenham, Edward Elgar, 2006) 610–29

11.3 THEORY

Generally

Donald Harris, 'Incentives to Perform, or Break Contracts' (1992) 45 *Current Legal Problems* 29–47

If viewed as a series of incentives to perform or breach, the legal rules concerning contract remedies are inconsistent.

Roy Kreitner, 'Multiplicity in Contract Remedies' in Nili Cohen and Ewan McKendrick (eds), *Comparative Remedies for Breach of Contract* (Oxford, Hart Publishing, 2004) 19–49

There is no unified theory that can successfully explain contract remedies. Instead, remedies should be understood by reference to their appropriateness (regarding fairness, social utility and administrative concerns) to the particular type of contract and contractual relationship at issue.

Barak Medina, 'Renegotiation, "Efficient Breach" and Adjustment: The Choice of Remedy for Breach of Contract as a Choice of Contract-Modification Theory' in Nili Cohen and Ewan McKendrick (eds), *Comparative Remedies for Breach of Contract* (Oxford, Hart Publishing, 2004) 51–72

Underlying most accounts of remedies is the formalist premise that remedies are extra-contractual, but this premise is not always justified. If it is accepted that contracts are incomplete, it makes sense, at least in some circumstances, to see remedies as modification mechanisms by which the courts exercise a delegated authority to modify the incomplete agreement by drafting *ex post* terms that deal with a change of circumstances.

The Relationship Between Contract Rights and Remedies

Peter Birks, 'Obligations: One Tier or Two?' in JAC Thomas, Peter Stein and ADE Lewis (eds), *Studies in Justinian's Institutes: In Memory of JAC Thomas* (London, Sweet & Maxwell, 1983) 18–38, 'The Concept of a Civil Wrong' in David G Owen (ed), *Philosophical Foundations of Tort Law* (Oxford, Clarendon press,

1985) 29–51, 'Definition and Division: A Meditation on Institutes 3.13' in *The Classification of Obligations* (1997, Clarendon Press, Oxford) 1–35

Richard Craswell, 'Contract Law, Default Rules and the Philosophy of Promising' (1989) 88 *Michigan Law Review* 489–529

Theories of promising such as autonomy-based and transfer theories are content-neutral as to the rules governing remedies, which rules must be determined by further independent values.

EL Sherman, 'An Essay on Private Remedies' (1993) 6 *Canadian Journal of Law and Jurisprudence* 89–112

The theory behind remedies has no intrinsic moral value and undermines the security of rights by encouraging their judicial modification ex post facto.

Nicholas J McBride, 'A Fifth Common Law Obligation' (1994) 14 *Legal Studies* 35–69

Peter Birks, 'Equity in the Modern Law: An Exercise in Taxonomy' (1996) 26 *University of Western Australia Law Review* 1–99, and 'Rights, Wrongs and Remedies' (2000) 20 *Oxford Journal of Legal Studies* 1–37

[1996] The contractual right to performance is one of the primary rights and correlative obligations arising from the category of causative events called 'manifestations of consent' (a category of 'not-wrongs'). This right may be vindicated by specific relief (or possibly the monetary equivalent of specific relief), but breach of the obligation is a wrong, a type of causative event that itself gives rise to a secondary (remedial) right to whatever remedy the law deems suitable (since wrongs have a wide-open remedial potential). The law of contract has settled on compensatory damages as the chosen remedy, but the choice to allow restitutionary damages in some circumstances is in principle available. The right to set aside contracts for duress or undue influence arises from the causative event (not-wrong) of unjust enrichment. [2000] Where the choice arises, the language of rights should be preferred to the language of remedies, not least because of the varied meanings of the latter and its inapplicability to causative events other than wrongs.

Stephen A Smith, '"The Reliance Interest in Contract Damages" and the Morality of Contract Law' in *Issues in Legal Scholarship, Symposium: Fuller and Perdue* (Berkeley Electronic Press, 2001) Art 1, 1–38

If the creation of contract rights is explicable by a property-like theory, then only the rules of contract creation are properly the domain of contract law. The rules of breach and remedies are a part of tort law, which governs the infringement of property and property-like rights.

David Wright, 'Wrong and Remedy: A Sticky Relationship' [2001] *Singapore Journal of Legal Studies* 300–24

Dori Kimel, *From Promise to Contract: Towards a Liberal Theory of Contract* (Oxford, Hart Publishing, 2003) ch 4, a revised version of which appears as 'Remedial Rights and Substantive Rights in Contract Law' (2002) 8 *Legal Theory* 313–38

Aurelien Jolly, 'Is it Useful—or Even Possible—to Distinguish Primary from Secondary Liabilities Arising from Contractual Obligation?' (2003) 14 *European Business Law Review* 57–68

Daniel Friedmann, 'Rights and Remedies' in Nili Cohen and Ewan McKendrick (eds), *Comparative Remedies for Breach of Contract* (Oxford, Hart Publishing, 2004) 3–17

It is simplistic to suggest either that rights are fully determinative of remedies or vice versa; the interaction between the two is more complicated. Contract rights do have a role in guiding conduct even beyond the ambit of the remedies available for their infringement due to acoustic separation, whereby the remedy is to some extent unpredictable at the time of contracting and breach, and so cannot operate merely as a price to be paid for the right not to perform.

Michael Tilbury, 'Remedies and the Classification of Obligations' in Andrew Robertson (ed), *The Law of Obligations: Connections and Boundaries* (London, UCL Press, 2004) 11–30

Monist views of perfect congruency between right and remedy are unsustainable, but there is still an unbreakable relationship between the two. While there is a remedial discretion arising directly (in the case of equitable remedies) or indirectly (through flexible tests), the right provides the first and most important point in determining the appropriate remedy. It is, therefore, misleading to hive off specific remedies, as Birks does, as vindications of primary rights and so not remedies generally; they share many features with other remedies and include their own remedial discretions.

Ernest J Weinrib, 'Two Conceptions of Remedies' in Charles EF Rickett (ed), *Justifying Remedies in Private Law* (Oxford, Hart Publishing, 2008) 3–32

Stephen Smith, 'The Limits of Contract' in Jason W Neyers, Richard Bronaugh and Stephen GA Pitel, *Exploring Contract Law* (Oxford, Hart Publishing, 2009) 1–24

Rules of remedies are not part of contract law but rather part of the general law of obligations applicable to all obligations.

Charlie Webb, 'Justifying Damages' in Jason W Neyers, Richard Bronaugh and Stephen GA Pitel (eds), *Exploring Contract Law* (Oxford, Hart Publishing, 2009) 139–170

Compensatory awards (save where cost of cure damages to purchase alternative performance) cannot be justified by the contractual right to performance, but must be justified by a separate right.

12

SPECIFIC RELIEF

12.1 ACTION FOR DEBT/ACTION FOR AN AGREED SUM

See also 10.3 Anticipatory Breach and Renunciation

Rafal Zakrzewski, 'The Nature of a Claim on an Indemnity' (2006) 22 *Journal of Contract law* 54–71

An indemnity clause may give a primary right to prevent loss, breach of which would give a right to compensation (a 'prevent loss indemnity') and/or may give rise to a primary right to compensation (a 'redress loss indemnity'). It may be that the latter type of debt claim should nevertheless be subject to mitigation and remoteness rules, unless excluded by the parties.

12.2 SPECIFIC PERFORMANCE AND INJUNCTIONS

General Texts

- Gareth Jones and William Goodhart, *Specific Performance*, 2nd edn (London, Butterworths, 1996)
- ICF Spry, *The Principles of Equitable Remedies*, 7th edn (Pyrmont, NSW, Law Book Co, 2007) chs 3–5
- Robert J Sharpe, *Injunctions and Specific Performance*, loose leaf (Aurora, Ontario, Canada Law Book, updated)

Generally

George L Clark, 'Some Problems in Specific Performance' (1918) 31 *Harvard Law Review* 271–87

Ralph E Clark, 'Specific Performance in Connection with Receiverships' (1920) 33 *Harvard Law Review* 64–84

Anthony T Kronman, 'Specific Performance' (1978) 45 *University of Chicago Law Review* 351–82; Alan Schwartz, 'The Case for Specific Performance' (1979) 89 *Yale Law Journal* 271–306 also in Larry Alexander (ed), *Contract Law: Volume II* (Aldershot, Dartmouth, 1991) 353–88; Peter Linzer, 'On the Amorality of Contract Remedies—Efficiency, Equity, and the Second Restatement' (1981) 81 *Columbia Law Review* 111–39 also in Larry Alexander (ed), *Contract Law: Volume II* (Aldershot, Dartmouth, 1991) 299–327; Timothy J Muris, 'The Costs of Freely Granting Specific Performance' [1982] *Duke Law Journal* 1053–69; Edward Yorio, 'In Defense of Money Damages for Breach of Contract' (1982) 82 *Columbia Law Review* 1365–424; Steven Shavell, 'The Design of Contracts and Remedies for Breach' (1984) 99 *Quarterly Journal of Economics* 121–48; Thomas S Ulen, 'The Efficiency of Specific Performance: Toward a Unified Theory of Contract Remedies' (1984–85) 83 *Michigan Law Review* 341–401; William Bishop, 'The Choice of Remedy for Breach of Contract' (1985) 14 *Journal of Legal Studies* 299–320 also in Larry Alexander (ed), *Contract Law: Volume II* (Aldershot, Dartmouth, 1991) 389–410; Paul G Mahoney, 'Contract Remedies and Options Pricing' (1995) 24 *Journal of Legal Studies* 139–63

Economic analyses of specific performance.

Marion Hetherington, 'Keeping the Plaintiff out of his Contractual Remedies: The Heresies that Survive Johnson v Agnew' (1980) 96 *Law Quarterly Review* 403–12

AS Burrows, 'Specific Performance at the Crossroads' (1984) 4 *Legal Studies* 102–15

Elizabeth Macdonald, 'The Inadequacy of Adequacy: The Granting of Specific Performance' (1987) 38 *Northern Ireland Legal Quarterly* 244–56

Randy E Barnett, 'Rights and Remedies in a Consent Theory of Contract' in RG Frey and Christopher W Morris (eds), *Liability and Responsibility* (Cambridge, Cambridge University Press, 1991) 135–72

A consent theory of contract supports a presumption in favour of specific performance, although this does not apply to contracts for personal services because rights to control the future use of one's person are inalienable (although rights to damages upon not using one's person in a particular way are alienable). The inalienability does not apply to contracts for corporate services.

Donald H Clark, 'Rethinking the Role of Specific Performance in the Contractual Setting' in J Beryman (ed), *Remedies: Issues and Perspectives* (Toronto, Carswell, 1991) 139–73

SM Waddams, 'The Choice of Remedy for Breach of Contract' in Jack Beatson and Daniel Friedmann (eds), *Good Faith and Fault in Contract Law* (Oxford, Clarendon Press, 1995) 471–84

Stephen A Smith, 'Performance, Punishment and the Nature of Contractual Obligation' (1997) 60 *Modern Law Review* 360–77; Dori Kimel, *From Promise to Contract: Towards a Liberal Theory of Contract* (Oxford, Hart Publishing, 2003) ch 4, a revised version of which appears as 'Remedial Rights and Substantive Rights in Contract Law' (2002) 8 *Legal Theory* 313–38

Smith argues that if they were generally available, the threat of specific performance and punitive damages for deliberate breach would obscure parties' motives for performance and would thus deprive the performance of contracts of much of its bond-creating potential. For this reason, specific performance should only be awarded when damages cannot adequately compensate for tangible harms suffered upon breach (either because something is priceless or its value cannot be assessed). Kimel counters that contracts displace the bond-creation that a promise would otherwise have and in fact contracts support personal detachment. There is little bond-creating potential to be obscured by the general availability of specific performance. However, the law's preference for the less intrusive damages remedy over an order for specific performance is justified by the harm principle.

Douglas Brodie, 'Specific Performance and Employment Contracts' (1998) 27 *Industrial Law Journal* 37–48

Richard Austen-Baker, 'Difficulties with Damages as a Ground for Specific Performance' (1999) 10 *Kings College Law Journal* 1–11

Damages will be an inadequate remedy and so specific performance will be required where there are intrinsic difficulties with quantifying damages, but this will not necessarily be the case where the difficulties of quantification are only extrinsic (forensic, evidential). Further, the uniqueness of property is really one example of damages being unquantifiable (because there being no market).

Darryn M Jensen, 'The Rights and Wrongs of Discretionary Remedialism' [2003] *Singapore Journal of Legal Studies* 178–208

Lionel Smith, 'Understanding Specific Performance' in Nili Cohen and Ewan McKendrick (eds), *Comparative Remedies for Breach of Contract* (Oxford, Hart Publishing, 2004) 221–33

Specific performance, and damages in lieu of it that accurately mirror it, over-compensate by bypassing the duty to mitigate, but in doing so prevent expropriation of the claimant's patrimonial right to performance. Specific performance thus shares similarities with disgorgement, the tort of wrongful interference and the rule in *White & Carter v McGregor.*

Melvin A Eisenberg, 'Actual and Virtual Specific Performance, the Theory of Efficient Breach, and the Indifference Principle in Contract Law' (2005) 93 *California Law Review* 975–1050

Where a satisfactory replacement is not available in the market (ie virtual specific performance), specific performance should usually be awarded in preference to ordinary expectation damages.

J Smits, D Haas and G Hesen, *Specific Performance in Contract Law: National and Other Perspectives* (Intersentia, 2008)

Ralph Cunnington, 'The Inadequacy of Damages as a Remedy for Breach of Contract' in Charles EF Rickett (ed), *Justifying Remedies in Private Law* (Oxford, Hart Publishing, 2008) 115–45

Injunctions

Robert S Stevens, 'Involuntary Servitude by Injunction: The Doctrine of Lumley v Wagner Considered' (1921) 6 *Cornell Law Review* 235–70

Damages in Lieu of Specific Performance or Injunctions

See also Wrotham Park Damages for the Hypothetical Price of a Release in 13.2

Barry J Reiter and Robert J Sharpe, '*Wroth v Tyler*: Must Equity Remedy Contract Damages?' (1979) 3 *Canadian Business Law Journal* 146–60

Terence Ingman, 'Damages in Equity—A Step in the Wrong Direction?' (1994) 58 *Conveyancer and Property Lawyer* 110–21

Damages in lieu cannot extend beyond the amount that would be awarded at common law.

○ Peter M McDermott, *Equitable Damages* (Sydney, Butterworths, 1994)

David Halpern, 'Damages in Lieu of an Injunction: How Much?' (2001) 65 *Conveyancer and Property Lawyer* 453–61

13

DAMAGES

13.1 GENERAL TEXTS

- ○ Andrew Tettenborn (ed), *The Law of Damages* (London, Butterworths, 2003)
- ○ Andrew Burrows, *Remedies for Torts and Breach of Contract*, 3rd edn (Oxford, Oxford University Press, 2004)
- ○ Harvin D Pitch and Ronald Snyder, *Damages for Breach of Contract*, 2nd edn, loose leaf (Toronto, Carswell, 1989 updated)
- ○ Stephen M Waddams, *The Law of Damages*, loose leaf (Toronto, Canada Law Book Inc, updated)
- ○ Harvey McGregor, *McGregor on Damages*, 18th edn (London, Sweet & Maxwell, 2009 plus supplements)

13.2 COMPENSATORY/EXPECTATION DAMAGES

Generally

George T Washington, 'Damages in Contract at Common Law: Parts I and II' (1931) 47 *Law Quarterly Review* 345–79 and (1932) 48 *Law Quarterly Review* 90–108
An historical study of the action for damages.

Samuel Stoljar, 'Normal, Elective and Preparatory Damages in Contract' (1975) 91 *Law Quarterly Review* 68–85
The relationship between difference in value and lost profits in an expectation damages award.

Horst Lücke, 'Two Types of Expectation Interest in Contract Damages' (1989) 12 *University of New South Wales Law Journal* 98–113

Adrian Chandler, 'Defective Performance of Building Contracts: Expectations in a Straitjacket' (1996) 13 *International Construction Law Review* 255–75

The Expectation Measure: Difference in Value v Cost of Cure

Elizabeth Macdonald, 'Breach of a Contractual Obligation: Cost of Work or Market Value?' (1988) 52 *Conveyancer and Property Lawyer* 421–29; Alexander FH Loke, 'Cost of Cure or Difference in Market Value? Toward a Sound Choice in the Basis for Quantifying Expectation Damages' (1996) 10 *Journal of Contract Law* 189–211

The award of cost of cure is necessary to give effect to the consumer surplus (where there is one, and where no substitute performance is available in the market), and the requirement of an intention to carry out remedial works both demonstrates and gives effect to this consumer surplus.

Timothy J Muris, 'Cost of Completion or Diminution in Market Value: The Relevance of Subjective Value' (1992) 12 *Journal of Legal Studies* 379–400

Brian Coote, 'Contract Damages, *Ruxley* and the Performance Interest' [1997] *Cambridge Law Journal* 537–70

Contract remedies are concerned with the protection of the right to performance and not merely the protection of the right to the economic benefits of performance. All legal benefits under the contract, including loss of enjoyment/consumer surplus and the non-conferment of a benefit on a third party, should be compensated by the cost of cure/alternative performance measure. The difference in value should only be awarded where cost of cure is objectively unreasonable as the objectively reasonable person would retain the imperfect performance and the damages and so be 'double dipping'. (How the particular claimant will use the damages, and *res inter alios acta*, should thus be irrelevant.) General damages for loss of amenity would only be required to compensate for the period of time up until a cure can be effected through cost of cure damages, or in the fairly rare cases where cost of cure damages are not awarded.

Rosalind MM McInnes, 'The Yellow Brick Road: *Ruxley* Revisited' (1998) 14 *Construction Law Journal* 33–43

Ewan McKendrick, 'Breach of Contract and the Meaning of Loss' (1999) 48 *Current Legal Problems* 37–73

Cost of cure damages should be awarded when the claimant's interest is in literal performance rather than economic return.

Melvin A Eisenberg, 'Actual and Virtual Specific Performance, the Theory of Efficient Breach, and the Indifference Principle in Contract Law' (2005) 93 *California Law Review* 975–1050

Where available, virtual specific performance (the obtaining of a good faith replacement in the market) is preferable to both specific performance and ordinary expectation damages.

James Edelman, 'Gain-based Damages and Compensation' in Andrew Burrows and Lord Rodger (eds), *Mapping the Law: Essays in Memory of Peter Birks* (Oxford, Oxford University Press, 2006) 141–60 and 'The Meaning of Loss and

Enrichment' in Robert Chambers, Charles Mitchell and James Penner (eds), *Philosophical Foundations of the Law of Unjust Enrichment* (Oxford, Oxford University Press, 2009) 211–41

Charlie Webb, 'Performance and Compensation: An Analysis of Contract Damages and Contractual Obligation' (2006) 26 *Oxford Journal of Legal Studies* 41–71; Stephen A Smith, 'Substitutionary Damages' in Charles EF Rickett (ed), *Justifying Remedies in Private Law* (Oxford, Hart Publishing, 2008) 93–114

The performance and compensation interests are distinct, and the award of damages on the cost of cure basis is (in most circumstances) a performance remedy like specific performance and not a compensatory remedy. Consequently, the duty to mitigate should not apply and the claimant should always have to provide an undertaking to apply the damages awarded to paying for the cure.

David Pearce and Roger Halson, 'Damages for Breach of Contract: Compensation, Restitution and Vindication' (2008) 28 *Oxford Journal of Legal Studies* 73–98

Some damages awards cannot be explained as being compensatory (or restitutionary), but rather are 'vindicatory', ie concerned with vindicating the right to performance.

Robert Stevens, 'Damages and the Right to Performance: A *Golden Victory* or Not?' in Jason W Neyers, Richard Bronaugh and Stephen GA Pitel (eds), *Exploring Contract Law* (Oxford, Hart Publishing, 2009) 171–98

Contract breach is actionable *per se* and so damages are awarded not for compensation, but as vindication or substitution for the contract right that has been infringed. Damages therefore primarily value the right infringed.

Charlie Webb, 'Justifying Damages' in Jason W Neyers, Richard Bronaugh and Stephen GA Pitel (eds), *Exploring Contract Law* (Oxford, Hart Publishing, 2009) 139–70

The substitutive damages theory does not work.

Wrotham Park Damages for the Hypothetical Price of a Release

See also Disgorgement and Restitutionary Damages in 13.5

Peter Jaffey, 'Disgorgement and "Licence Fee Damages" in Contract' (2004) 20 *Journal of Contract Law* 57–73

Licence fee damages are appropriate where the contract was intended to create a licensing power by means of eg a negative covenant.

Craig Smith, 'Recognising a Valuable Lost Opportunity to Bargain when a Contract Is Breached' (2005) 21 *Journal of Contract Law* 250–76

Francesco Giglio, *The Foundations of Restitution for Wrongs* (Oxford, Hart Publishing, 2007)

Craig Rotherham, '"Wrotham Park Damages" and Accounts of Profits: Compensation or Restitution?' [2008] *Lloyd's Maritime and Commercial Law Quarterly* 24–55

Only a gain-based account explains the law in this area.

Graham Virgo, 'Restitutionary Remedies for Wrongs: Causation and Remoteness' in Charles EF Rickett (ed), *Justifying Remedies in Private Law* (Oxford, Hart Publishing, 2008) 301–31

Damages Measured by Reliance/Wasted Expenditure

See also Reliance Theories in 16.3

Lon L Fuller and William R Perdue Jr, 'The Reliance Interest in Contract Damages (Parts 1 and 2)' (1936–37) 46 *Yale Law Journal* 52–96, 373–420 also in Larry Alexander (ed), *Contract Law: Volume II* (Aldershot, Dartmouth, 1991) 211–55 and in *Issues in Legal Scholarship, Symposium: Fuller and Perdue* (Berkeley, CA, Berkeley Electronic Press, 2001)

Damages are mainly about protecting the reliance interest, although damages for 'essential reliance' (the price, loosely termed) should not exceed the expectation measure as that would allow escape from a bad bargain, whereas damages for 'incidental reliance' should not be so limited (although the latter should be subject to remoteness rules).

DW McLauchlan, 'Damages for Pre-contractual Expenditure' (1984–85) 11 *New Zealand Universities Law Review* 346–61

Marc Owen, 'Some Aspects of the Recovery of Reliance Damages in the Law of Contract' (1984) 4 *Oxford Journal of Legal Studies* 393–420; Michael B Kelly, 'The Phantom Reliance Interest in Contract Damages' [1992] *Wisconsin Law Review* 1755–846; Michael G Bridge, 'Expectation Damages and Uncertain Future Losses' in Jack Beatson and Daniel Friedmann (eds), *Good Faith and Fault in Contract Law* (Oxford, Clarendon Press, 1995) 427–69

The authors seek to reconceptualise reliance damages not as a separate measure seeking to put the claimant in the position he was in before contracting, but rather as compensation for wasted expenditure in situations in which it cannot be proved that the innocent party would have made either a profit or a loss and so it is presumed that he would have broken even.

Gregory S Crespi, 'Recovering Pre-contractual Expenditure as an Element of Reliance Damages' (1995) 49 *Southern Methodist University Law Review* 43–72

SM Waddams, 'Damages: Assessment of Uncertainties' (1998) 13 *Journal of Contract Law* 55–72

Gerald Ng, 'The Onus of Proof in a Claim for Reliance Damages for Breach of Contract' (2006) 22 *Journal of Contract Law* 139–55

David McLauchlan, 'Reliance Damages for Breach of Contract' [2007] *New Zealand Law Review* 417–457

Although damages for wasted expenditure may be recoverable as a measure of the expectation interest (where it is too difficult to estimate the profits lost, and there is a presumption that the claimant would have broken even), there are no such things as 'reliance damages' or the 'reliance interest' (ie the right to damages to put one in the pre-contract position) in contract law. Further, pre-contractual expenditure may sometimes be recoverable under the ordinary rules.

Transferred Loss and Damages on Behalf of a Third Party

John Hodgson, 'Jackson v Horizon Holidays—A Case of Mistaken Identity?' (1992) 1 *Nottingham Law Journal* 27–35

The *Jackson* case is best understood as a tort of negligence case.

John Cartwright, 'Remedies in Respect of Defective Buildings after *Linden Gardens*' (1993) 9 *Construction Law Journal* 281–96

Stephen A Smith, 'Of Remedies and Restrictive Covenants' (1994) 7 *Journal of Contract Law* 164–80

Linden Gardens should have been decided on the basis that the key covenant was unenforceable as unwarranted restraints on trade.

John Cartwright, 'Damages, Third Parties and Common Sense' (1996) 10 *Journal of Contract Law* 244–58

The *Linden Gardens* narrow ground might be extended into a generally applicable principle allowing recovery of all foreseeable losses, regardless of who suffers them.

Norman Palmer and Gregory Tolhurst, 'Compensatory and Extra-compensatory Damages: The Role of "The Albazero" in Modern Damages Claims: Parts I and II' (1997) 12 *Journal of Contract Law* 1–20 continued at 97–113

The origins and development of the *Albazero* rule (also known as the 'narrow ground').

Brian Coote, 'Dunlop v Lambert: The Search for a Rationale' (1998) 13 *Journal of Contract Law* 92–102 and 'The Performance Interest, Panatown and the Problem of Loss' (2001) 117 *Law Quarterly Review* 81–95

Support for the 'broad ground' of Lord Griffiths (in the *St Martins* case) and criticism of the orthodox interpretation of *Dunlop v Lambert*, although consequential losses might be best recovered for the benefit of the third party rather than for the promisee himself, or on the narrow ground.

Norman Palmer and Gregory Tolhurst, 'Compensatory and Extra-compensatory Damages: Linden Gardens and the "Lord Griffiths" Principle' (1998) 13 *Journal of Contract Law* 143–55

IN Duncan Wallace, 'Third Party Damage: No Legal Black Hole?' (1999) 115 *Law Quarterly Review* 394–410

Support for the 'broad ground' provided that it is limited to defective or incomplete work cases and that there is sufficient affinity of interest between the promisee and third party to make recovery reasonable. The 'narrow ground' should be used only restrictedly, eg in cases of delay.

Hannes Unberath, 'Third Party Losses and Black Holes: Another View' (1999) 115 *Law Quarterly Review* 535–46 and *Transferred Loss: Claiming Third Party Loss in Contract Law* (Oxford, Hart Publishing, 2003)

The 'narrow ground' and *Albazero*-principle cases (as well as other areas of the law such as bailee recovery for bailors, agent recovery for undisclosed principals, and trustee recovery for beneficiary) are best understood not as recovery where transfer is contemplated by the contracting parties but as cases subject to a legal rule of transferred loss: the promisee can sue on behalf of the third party where the third party suffers loss instead of the promisee by reason of a special relationship between the two (irrespective of whether the promisor foresaw or contemplated such a transfer and relationship).

Andrew Burrows, 'No Damages for a Third Party's Loss' (2001) *Oxford University Commonwealth Law Journal* 107–13

The broad ground is wrong and gives rise to double-liability problems, and the proper rule should be that recovery is possible only when the claimant has or will expend the money on repairs. A third party's direct contractual right should not prevent the claimant recovering unless the third party gets all that was promised or the direct conferral indicates an intention that claimant have no right to damages.

Ewan McKendrick, 'The Common Law at Work: The Saga of Alfred McAlpine Construction Ltd v Panatown Ltd' (2003) 3 *Oxford University Commonwealth Law Journal* 145–80

An examination of the *Alfred McAlpine v Panatown* case against its factual, transactional and taxation background, supporting the narrow ground/transferred loss basis when this reflects the bargain (and questioning the House of Lords' interpretation of Panatown's bargain as reflected by the duty of care deed), and concluding that Panatown was rightly refused damages on the broad ground as its lack of intention to spend such damages on repairs indicated a lack of interest in performance.

David Friedman QC, 'Black Hole Cases' (2008) 24 *Construction Law Journal* 10–21

Interest and Compound Interest

FA Mann, "On Interest, Compound Interest and Damages" (1985) 101 *Law Quarterly Review* 30–47

Esther Martin-Pelegrin, 'Compound Interest as Damages and Upon Damages for Breach of Contract' (1999) 16 *International Construction Law Review* 453–82

Law Commission, *Report 287: Pre-Judgment Interest on Debts and Damages* (2004)

Scottish Law Commission, *Report 203: Report on Interest on Debts and Damages* (2006)

John Barber, 'Late Payment of Commercial Debts (Interest) Act 1998—No Laughing Matter' (2007) 23 *Construction Law Journal* 331–43

Inflation

IN Duncan Wallace, 'Cost of Repair and Inflation' (1980) 96 *Law Quarterly Review* 101–09 and 'Inflation and Assessment of Construction Cost Damages' (1982) 98 *Law Quarterly Review* 406–12

Andrew Burgess, 'Avoiding Inflation Loss in Contract Damages Awards: The Equitable Damages Solution' (1985) 34 *International & Comparative Law Quarterly* 317–41

Equitable damages should be awarded to compensate for losses due to the inflation between the date of damage and the date of payment or judgment.

13.3 NON-PECUNIARY LOSSES

Generally

Donald Harris, Anthony Ogus and Jenny Phillips, 'Contract Remedies and the Consumer Surplus' (1979) 95 *Law Quarterly Review* 581–610

Consumers are not solely concerned with profit and value but also with the 'consumer surplus' (the subjective value of a state of affairs or good based upon pleasure or utility, which often exceeds the market value), and the pursuit of efficiency requires that the courts take account of this in awarding damages for breach. The authors then survey the extent to which the law of contract remedies already recognises and protects the consumer surplus.

Francis Dawson, 'General Damages in Contract for Non-Pecuniary Loss' (1982–83) 10 *New Zealand Universities Law Review* 232–60

Samuel A Rea Jr, 'Nonpecuniary Loss and Breach of Contract' (1982) 11 *Journal of Legal Studies* 35–53

Economic analysis shows that full compensation for non-pecuniary loss is inefficient.

Andrew Phang, 'Subjectivity, Objectivity and Policy—Contractual Damages in the House of Lords' [1996] *Journal of Business Law* 362–81

Brian Coote, 'Contract Damages, *Ruxley* and the Performance Interest' [1997] *Cambridge Law Journal* 537–70

Contract remedies are concerned with the protection of the right to performance and not merely the protection of the right to the economic benefits of performance. All legal benefits under the contract, including loss of enjoyment/consumer surplus and the non-conferment of a benefit on a third party, should be compensated by the cost of cure/alternative performance measure.

Janet O'Sullivan, 'Loss and Gain at Greater Depth: The Implications of the *Ruxley* Decision' and Edwin Peel, 'Loss and Gain at Greater Depth: The Implications of the *Ruxley* Decision—A Comment' in Francis D Rose (ed), *Failure of Contracts* (Oxford, Hart Publishing, 1997) 1–25, 27–34

Ewan McKendrick 'Breach of Contract and the Meaning of Loss' (1999) 48 *Current Legal Problems* 37–73, and 'The Common Law at Work: The Saga of Alfred McAlpine Construction Ltd v Panatown Ltd' (2003) 3 *Oxford University Commonwealth Law Journal* 145–80

[1999] The protection of the expectation interest should extend beyond protection of the financial position of the claimant as people do not only enter contracts to make money. [2003] The aim of damages is best understood not as putting the claimant in the financial position he would have been in, but rather as providing an appropriate substitute for the performance to which the claimant was entitled.

Margaret F Brinig, '"Money Can't Buy Me Love": A Contrast between Damages in Family Law and Contract' (2002) 27 *Journal of Corporation Law* 567–602

Catherine Mitchell, 'Promise, Performance and Damages for Breach of Contract' (2003) 2 *Journal of Obligations and Remedies* 67–86

A Tettenborn, 'Non-pecuniary Loss: The Right Answer but Bad Reasoning' (2003) 2 *Journal of Obligations and Remedies* 94–107

Ewan McKendrick and Katherine Worthington, 'Damages for Non-pecuniary Loss' in Nili Cohen and Ewan McKendrick, *Comparative Remedies for Breach of Contract* (Oxford, Hart Publishing, 2004) 287–322

A classification of non-pecuniary loss, broadly as follows: (i) positive loss by non-conferral of a promised non-pecuniary benefit, including: express conferral, implied conferral, objective added value, no intrinsic financial value;

and (ii) consequential loss, including: physical harm, psychiatric injury, embarrassment or injury to reputation, physical inconvenience and distress or loss of enjoyment. The application of principles limiting liability (such as remoteness and mitigation) to such cases is also considered.

David Pearce and Roger Halson, 'Damages for Breach of Contract: Compensation, Restitution and Vindication' (2008) 28 *Oxford Journal of Legal Studies* 73–98

Wrotham Park damages, subjective/loss of amenity damages and third-party loss damages are best understood as vindicatory of the right to performance.

Charlie Webb, 'Justifying Damages' in Jason W Neyers, Richard Bronaugh and Stephen GA Pitel (eds), *Exploring Contract Law* (Oxford, Hart Publishing, 2009) 139–70

Loss is about how a promisee values the performance the promisee did not receive.

Mental Distress, Disappointment and Physical Inconvenience

Bernard S Jackson, 'Injured Feelings Resulting from Breach of Contract' (1977) 26 *International & Comparative Law Quarterly* 502–15

Recovery of damages for injured feelings can be based solely upon remoteness providing remoteness is understood as based upon an implied term. Where an interest is protected by the law of tort (such as freedom from financial loss and nervous shock), there should be a presumption that foreseeable losses within that interest are recoverable under the contract; where an interest is not protected by the law of tort (such as freedom from mental distress), there should be a presumption that the interest is not protected by the contract.

Edward Veitch, 'Sentimental Damages in Contract' (1977) 16 *University of Western Ontario Law Review* 227–42

AS Burrows, 'Mental Distress Damages in Contract—A Decade of Change' [1984] *Lloyd's Maritime and Commercial Law Quarterly* 119–34

Mental distress damages should be recoverable whether or not mental satisfaction was a predominant object of the contract, providing they were not too remote. Recovery of damages for mental injury resulting from breach of contract should be subject to the broader tort test of remoteness.

Charlotte K Goldberg, 'Emotional Distress Damages and Breach of Contract: A New Approach' (1986) 20 *University of California Davis Law Review* 57–104

Distress damages should be available where one or both parties are not contracting for profit, and where emotional distress is foreseeable (because the contract has an emotional aspect).

John A Sebert Jr, 'Punitive and Non-pecuniary Damages in Actions Based upon Contract: Towards Achieving the Objective of Full Compensation' (1986) 33 *UCLA Law Review* 1565–678

Kim Franklin, 'Damages for Heartache: The Award of General Damages For Inconvenience and Distress in Building Cases' (1988) 4 *Construction Law Journal* 265–74

Douglas J Whaley, 'Paying for the Agony: The Recovery of Emotional Distress Damages in Contract Actions' (1992) 26 *Suffolk University Law Review* 935–58

Elizabeth Macdonald, 'Contractual Damages for Mental Distress' (1994) 7 *Journal of Contract Law* 134–55

The 'main purpose' test should be abandoned in favour of a test asking whether a mental benefit was *a* purpose of the contract.

Francis Dawson, 'Reflections on Certain Aspects of the Law of Damages for Breach of Contract' (1995) 9 *Journal of Contract Law* 20–87

Nelson Enonchong, 'Breach of Contract and Damages for Mental Distress' (1996) 16 *Oxford Journal of Legal Studies* 617–40

There is no justification for a rule against damages for mental distress damages and the cases show that, providing the court is satisfied that the distress is real and significant and passes other hurdles (such as causation and remoteness), it should be compensated.

Law Commission, *Consultation Paper 132: Aggravated, Exemplary and Restitutionary Damages* (1993) and *Report 247: Aggravated, Exemplary and Restitutionary Damages* (1997)

Aggravated damages are compensatory damages for mental distress and as such should not be distinguished from contract damages for mental distress.

Scottish Law Commission, *Discussion Paper 109: Remedies for Breach of Contract* (1999) and *Report 174: Report on Remedies for Breach of Contract* (1999)

Eugene Kontorovich, 'The Mitigation of Emotional Distress Damages' (2001) 68 *University of Chicago Law Review* 491–520

Mara Kent, 'The Common-law History of Non-economic Damages in Breach of Contract Actions versus Wilful Breach of Contract Actions' (2004) 11 *Texas Wesleyan Law Review* 481–504

Adam Kramer, 'An Agreement-centred Approach to Remoteness and Contract Damages' in Nili Cohen and Ewan McKendrick (eds), *Comparative Remedies for Breach of Contract* (Oxford, Hart Publishing, 2005) 249–86; Adrian Chandler and James Devenney, 'Breach of Contract and the Expectation Deficit: Inconvenience and Disappointment' (2007) 27 *Legal Studies* 126–54

Recovery of damages for mental distress turns on the scope of responsibility assumed and should be subsumed within a re-understood doctrine of remoteness.

John Hartshorne, 'Damages for Contractual Mental Distress after Farley v Skinner' (2006) 22 *Journal of Contract Law* 118–38

Tony Dugdale, 'Beyond Measurable Loss' (2007) 23 *Professional Negligence* 213–17

The recovery of personal preference damages in commercial contract cases.

Jill Poole, 'Awarding Damages for Distress and Loss of Reputation in England and Canada' in Paula Giliker (ed), *Re-examining Contract and Unjust Enrichment: Anglo-Canadian Perspectives* (Leiden, Martinus Nijhoff, 2007) 255–78

Distress damages should be recoverable only where there has been an express or implied assumption of responsibility, the latter only arising in cases of one-off losses where substitute performance is unavailable and the loss cannot be avoided.

Damages for Wrongful Dismissal

Douglas Brodie, 'A Fair Deal at Work' (1999) 19 *Oxford Journal of Legal Studies* 83–98

Damages for breach of the employer's duty of trust and confidence should include damages for injury to the employee's feelings.

Judy Fudge, 'The Spectre of *Addis* in Contracts of Employment in Canada and the UK' (2007) 36 *Industrial Law Journal* 51–67

Injury to Reputation

Nelson Enonchong, 'Contract Damages for Injury to Reputation' (1996) 59 *Modern Law Review* 592–602

The rule against such damages derives from *Withers v General Theatre Corp Ltd* and not *Addis v Gramophone Ltd*, and should be abolished.

Failure to Confer a Benefit upon a Third Party and Lord Griffiths' Broad Ground

See Transferred Loss and Damages on Behalf of a Third Party in 13.2

13.4 LIMITING PRINCIPLES AND QUANTIFICATION

Causation and What Would Have Happened: Hypotheticals Involving the Claimant or Defendant

Michael Gordon Lloyd, 'Ready and Willing to Perform: The Problem of Prospective Inability in the Law of Contracts' (1974) 36 *Modern Law Review* 121–33

The relevance of possible future breach by the claimant, had the contract continued, to the proof of causation of loss in relation to the damages payable for repudiatory breach by the defendant.

Douglas Brodie, 'A Fair Deal at Work' (1999) 19 *Oxford Journal of Legal Studies* 83–98

When assessing damages for wrongful dismissal, a more realistic look should be taken at how long the employment would have continued but for the wrongful dismissal, rather than automatically assuming that the employer would have done the best for itself (the *Lavarack* rule).

Causation and What Would Have Happened: Third Party Hypotheticals and Loss of a Chance

Ken Cooper, 'The Loss of a Chance or the Chance of a Loss?' (1972–73) 37 *Saskatchewan Law Review* 193–249

Helen Reece, 'Losses of Chances in the Law' (1996) 59 *Modern Law Review* 188–206

Loss of chance cases arise where the situation is (quasi)-indeterministic (not merely where it concerns a future hypothetical), because in such cases it is not possible for the claimant to provide his loss as he is required to bear the risk of uncertainty in evidence but not the risk of uncertainty in the world.

Graham Reid, 'The Hypothetical Outcome in Professional Negligence Claims: Parts I and II' (2001) 17 *Professional Negligence* 129–37 and 262–69

Jill Poole, 'Loss of Chance and the Evaluation of Hypotheticals in Contractual Claims' [2007] *Lloyd's Maritime and Commercial Law Quarterly* 63–82

Andrew Burrows, 'Uncertainty about Uncertainty: Damages for Loss of a Chance' [2008] *Journal of Personal Injury Law* 31–43

The author surveys the law of loss of a chance in contract and tort, concluding that there is no real distinction between the two causes of action, and that there may be a justification for awarding loss of a chance in economic cases, where it is normal to give a present financial value, and not personal injury cases, where it is perhaps better to wait and see.

Quantification, Time of Assessment and Events Occurring after Breach

David Simon and Gerald A Novack, 'Limiting the Buyer's Market Damages to Lost Profits: A Challenge to the Enforceability of Market Contracts' (1979) 92 *Harvard Law Review* 1395–438

For reasons of efficiency and deterrence, damages for failure to deliver (or late delivery of) a market commodity should be the difference in market value, whether or not the purchaser would or could in fact have realised the market value and sold the goods (such as where the buyer would have resold at a contracted price but is not obliged to do so, or would have held the goods as a long-term investment).

SM Waddams, 'The Date for the Assessment of Damages' (1981) 97 *Law Quarterly Review* 445–61

When the date of assessment is later than the date of breach.

Francis Reynolds, 'The Golden Victory—A Misguided Decision' (1998) 38 *Hong Kong Law Journal* 333–45

Robert Stevens, 'Damages and the Right to Performance: A *Golden Victory* or Not?' in Jason W Neyers, Richard Bronaugh and Stephen GA Pitel (eds), *Exploring Contract Law* (Oxford, Hart Publishing, 2009) 171–98

Sub-sales reducing loss should be ignored and the difference in value should be awarded (although sub-sales increasing loss are recoverable unless too remote) and *Bence Graphics* is wrong. The *Golden Victory* is correct because damages in respect of obligations that had not yet accrued, like consequential losses and damages in lieu of a specific remedy, must be assessed at the date of judgment (whereas substitutive damages for breach of accrued rights are assessed at the date performance was due).

JW Carter and Elisabeth Peden, 'Damages Following Termination for Repudiation: Taking Account of Later Events' (2008) 24 *Journal of Contract Law* 145–75

Mitigation

Robert A Hillman, 'Keeping the Deal Together After Material Breach—Common Law Mitigation Rules, the UCC, and the Restatement (Second) of Contracts' (1976) 47 *University of Colorado Law Review* 553–616

When an innocent party should mitigate its loss by accepting an offer by the breaching party.

David Feldman and DF Libling, 'Inflation and the Duty to Mitigate' (1979) 95 *Law Quarterly Review* 270–86

Charles J Goetz and Robert E Scott, 'The Mitigation Principle:

Toward a General Theory of Contractual Obligation (1983) 69 *Virginia Law Review* 967–1024

An economic analysis of the mitigation rules.

Anne Michaud, 'Mitigation of Damage in the Context of Remedies for Breach of Contract' (1984) 15 *Revue Générale de Droit* 293–340

Andrew Burgess, 'Avoiding Inflation Loss in Contract Damages Awards: The Equitable Damages Solution' (1985) 34 *International & Comparative Law Quarterly* 317–41

For full compensation, damages awards must allow for inflation between the date of damage and the date of the award. Equitable damages may provide an answer to this problem.

Michael G Bridge, 'Mitigation of Damages in Contract and the Meaning of Avoidable Loss' (1989) 105 *Law Quarterly Review* 398–423

No one factor or principle can fully explain the duty to mitigate. Further, the author criticises the cases treating failure to enter into fresh contracts with the breaching party as a failure to mitigate.

Michael B Kelly, 'Defendant's Responsibility to Minimize Plaintiff's Loss: A Curious Exception to the Avoidable Consequences Doctrine' (1996) 47 *South Carolina Law Review* 391–429

Melvin A Eisenberg, 'The Duty to Rescue in Contract Law' (2002) 71 *Fordham Law Review* 647–94

Dori Kimel, *From Promise to Contract: Towards a Liberal Theory of Contract* (Oxford, Hart Publishing, 2003) ch 4, a revised version of which appears as 'Remedial Rights and Substantive Rights in Contract Law' (2002) 8 *Legal Theory* 313–38

The harm principle explains the mitigation rule.

David Campbell, 'The Relational Constitution of Remedy: Co-operation as the Implicit Second Principle of Remedies for Breach of Contract' (2004) 11 *Texas Wesleyan Law Review* 455–80

Stephen A Smith, 'Substitutionary Damages' in Charles EF Rickett (eds), *Justifying Remedies in Private Law* (Oxford, Hart Publishing, 2008) 93–114

Contributory Negligence

NE Palmer and PJ Davies, 'Contributory Negligence and Breach of Contract—English & Australasian Attitudes Compared' (1980) 29 *International & Comparative Law Quarterly* 415–51

Damages should not be reduced for contributory under the 1945 Act in cases of contractual breach.

J Swanton, 'Contributory Negligence as a Defence to Actions for Breach of Contract' (1981) 55 *Australian Law Journal* 278–89

PA Chandler, 'Contributory Negligence and Contract: Some Underlying Disparities' (1989) 40 *Northern Ireland Legal Quarterly* 152–81

Contributory negligence should not give rise to a reduction of damages in any case of contractual breach, whether negligent and concurrent or otherwise.

Law Commission, *Report 219: Contributory Negligence as a Defence in Contract* (1993)

There should be legislation allowing for a reduction for contributory negligence in cases of contractual duties of care save where the parties had excluded such a rule.

Gehan N Gunasekara, 'Judicial Reasoning by Analogy with Statutes: The Case of Contributory Negligence and the Law of Contract in New Zealand' (1993) 14 *Statute Law Review* 84–110

Scottish Law Commission, *Discussion Paper 109: Remedies for Breach of Contract* (1999) and *Report 174: Report on Remedies for Breach of Contract* (1999)

There should be a reduction of damages for contributory fault in all cases of breach.

Nick Seddon, 'Contract Damages where Both Parties Are at Fault' (2000) 15 *Journal of Contract Law* 207–27

Michael Tilbury and JW Carter, 'Converging Liabilities and Security of Contract: Contributory Negligence in Australian Law' (2000) 16 *Journal of Contract Law* 78–101

Contributory negligence should be applicable to contract claims in concurrent liability situations.

Timothy Michael FitzPatrick, 'Contributory Negligence and Contract—A Critical Reassessment: Parts I and II' (2001) 30 *Common Law World Law Review* 255–71 and 412–33

Contributory negligence should apply to all contract claims.

Andrew Burrows, 'The Bracton Law Society Lecture: Damages for Breach of Contract: A Developing Hierarchy?' (2003) 35 *Bracton Law Journal* 28–44

Remoteness

FE Smith, 'The Rule in Hadley v Baxendale' (1900) 16 *Law Quarterly Review* 275–87

A criticism of the (then) prevailing view, as supported by Justice Willes and by Mayne, that knowledge of special circumstances rendering loss foreseeable is insufficient for liability and that an assumption of responsibility for the loss is required. The author also consolidates the rules in *Hadley v Baxendale* in a way that foreshadows the simplification made in the *Victoria Laundry* case.

Leon Green, *Rationale of Proximate Cause* (Kansas City, MO, Vernon Law Book Co, 1927) ch 2

Questions of legal causation and remoteness should be understood as questions as to whether the interest infringed was protected under the terms of the agreement, properly interpreted; in other words, whether the risk was one that falls within the scope of the contract.

SL Porter, 'The Measure of Damages in Contract and Tort' [1934] *Cambridge Law Journal* 176–91

JF Wilson and CJ Slade, 'A Re-examination of Remoteness' (1952) 15 *Modern Law Review* 458–71

GA Mulligan, 'Damages for Breach: Quantum, Remoteness and Causality: Part IV: Special Damages in South African Law' (1956) 73 *South African Law Journal* 27–46

The development of the English law remoteness rule, from Roman law through Molinaeus and Pothier to the modern day, and the remoteness rule in South Africa. The author concludes by disagreeing with Judge Wessel's tacit agreement view of remoteness (still good law in South Africa).

RA Samek, 'The Relevant Time of Foreseeability of Damage in Contract' (1964) 38 *Australian Law Journal* 125–30

Where there has been a wilful or reckless breach, the relevant time for determining whether losses are foreseeable and so recoverable should be the time of breach and not the time of contracting.

PN Todd, 'Rules of Contract and Tort: A Cause of Action Classification?' (1979) 13 *The Law Teacher* 151–61

Richard Danzig, 'Hadley v Baxendale: A Study in the Industrialization of the Law' (1975) 4 *Journal of Legal Studies* 249–84 also in (1977) *Ius Commune* VI 234–73 and in his *The Capability Problem in Contract Law: Further Readings on Well-known Cases* (West Publishing, 1978)

A fascinating investigation of the decision in and rise to prominence of *Hadley v Baxendale,* by reference to its historical context and the connections and influences of the counsel and judges in the case, raising questions as to whether the decision should continue to apply in the modern context.

Sir Robin Cooke, 'Remoteness of Damages and Judicial Discretion' [1978] *Cambridge Law Journal* 288–300; Rex Ahdar, 'Remoteness, "Ritual Incantation" and the Future of Hadley v Baxendale: Reflections from New Zealand' (1994) 7 *Journal of Contract Law* 53–75

Cooke criticises the law on remoteness of damages in contract and tort, arguing that courts should openly admit to a discretionary approach weighing up various factors of which directness and foreseeability are only two. Ahdar criticises Cooke's proposed approach.

Katherine Swinton, 'Foreseeability: Where Should the Award of Contract Damages Cease?' in Barry J Reiter and John Swan (eds), *Studies in Contract Law* (Toronto, Butterworths, 1980) 61–91

The foreseeability limitation on contract damages is policy-driven, and there should be explicit recognition of the relevant policies and interests that the courts seek to protect in order that the rule may become more predictable and consistent in application.

William Bishop, 'The Contract–Tort Boundary and the Economics of Insurance' (1983) 12 *Journal of Legal Studies* 241–66; Ian Ayres and Robert Gertner, 'Filling Gaps in Incomplete Contracts: An Economic Theory of Default Rules' (1989) 99 *Yale Law Journal* 87–130; Jeffrey M Perloff, 'Breach of Contract and the Foreseeability Doctrine of *Hadley v Baxendale*' (1981) 10 *Journal of Legal Studies* 39–63; Gwyn D Quillen, 'Contract Remedies and Cross-subsidization' (1988) 61 *Southern California Law Review* 1125–142; Richard A Epstein, 'Beyond Foreseeability: Consequential Damages in the Law of Contract' (1989) 18 *Journal of Legal Studies* 105–38; Jason Scott Johnston, 'Strategic Bargaining and the Economic Theory of Contract Default Rules' (1990) 100 *Yale Law Journal* 615–55; Lucian Arye Bebchuk and Steven Shavell, 'Information and the Scope of Liability for Breach of Contract: The Rule of Hadley v Baxendale' (1991) 7 *Journal of Law, Economics and Organization* 284–312; Melvin Aron Eisenberg, 'The Principle of *Hadley v Baxendale*' (1992) 80 *California Law Review* 563–613 and 'The Emergence of Dynamic Contract Law' (2000) 88 *California Law Review* 1743–814 also in (2001) 2 *Theoretical Inquiries in Law* 1–78; Barry E Adler, 'The Questionable Ascent of Hadley v Baxendale' (1999) 51 *Stanford Law Review* 1547–89; George S Geis, 'Empirically Assessing Hadley v Baxendale' (2005) 32 *Florida State University Law Review* 897–956

Economic analysis of the rule of remoteness, viewing it as a default (as opposed to immutable) rule and arguing about whether it is an efficient one. Bishop argues that the remoteness rule is only justified in cases of information asymmetry (usually cases of strict contractual obligations) where useful information could be cheaply communicated and so prevent adverse selection; the foreseeability (ie tort) test should apply in situations of information symmetry (typically cases of contractual or tortious duties of care and contractual warranties of quality). Ayres and Gertner explain the remoteness rule as a penalty default, discouraging strategic information withholding. Adler argues the penalty default analysis requires caution because the rule does not necessarily operate efficiently when information asymmetry exists between the parties. Perloff argues that the rule is efficient although other rules are also efficient, and Bebchuk and Shavell argue that the rule will often save transaction costs by encouraging high-value buyers to communicate information to sellers. For Quillen, the remoteness rule can be used to avoid inefficient cross-subsidisation of buyers by limiting recovery to losses that all buyers will suffer. Johnston argues that the information-forcing explanation is unrealistic because of the strategic incentives not to disclose information (the promisor trying to convince the promisee that the chances of breach are low, and the promisee trying to convince the promisor that the contract is of low value); instead the efficiency of the remoteness rule comes from its being an expansive default rule. Epstein argues that, when it comes to consequential damages, the expectation measure is inefficient and that fixed damages set below the actual loss suffered are far preferable. To this end, as a default rule, the tacit agreement test of remoteness is more efficient than the foreseeability test. Eisenberg [1992] argues that the foreseeability test is inefficient and that, when matters are not determined by a contractual allocation of loss or the requirements of fair disclosure, the foreseeability test should be replaced by a more expansive regime of proximate cause, as has already begun in the practice of large modern companies. Eisenberg [2000] argues that the rule does not work in the case of high-volume homogenous commodities suppliers because they do not amend the terms, price or precautions for any individual contract even where they are exposed to supranormal damages, and in such situations the rule of proximate cause would be more efficient. Geis conducts empirical analysis suggesting that the efficiency of the rule very much depends upon the type of buyer and market.

HLA Hart and Tony Honoré, *Causation in the Law*, 2nd edn (Oxford, Clarendon Press, 1985) esp ch 11

Irrespective of whether a claim is formulated in tort or contract, two very different rules are at play: causation rules governing physical harm and incidental expense, which are mainly concerned with interventions in the chain between the breach and the harm; and remoteness rules governing failure to provide opportunities for gain. Further, the contractual concept of risk, where applicable, bypasses the need to prove causation.

MN Kniffin, 'A Newly Identified Contract Unconscionability: Unconscionability of Remedy' (1988) 63 *Notre Dame Law Review* 247–76

Section 351(3) of the Restatement (Second) of Contracts, by which US courts have a discretion to refuse to award damages for foreseeable loss where such damages would be disproportionate, is the natural successor to earlier decisions on contract damages based upon the assumption of risk and the relationship between price and the loss claimed.

Clayton P Gillette, 'Commercial Relationships and the Selection of Default Rules for Remote Risks' (1990) 19 *Journal of Legal Studies* 535–81

DA Ipp, 'Problems and Progress in the Remoteness of Damage' in PD Finn (ed), *Essays on Damages* (Sydney, Law Book Co, 1992) 14–41

Franco Ferrari, 'Comparative Ruminations on the Foreseeability of Damages in Contract Law' (1993) 53 *Louisiana Law Review* 1257–70

Thomas A Diamond and Howard Foss, 'Consequential Damages for Commercial Loss: An Alternative to Hadley v Baxendale' (1994) 63 *Fordham Law Review* 665–714

The current remoteness rules should be replaced by a situational approach to liability so as to encourage increased efficiency, notably by imposing more expansive liability than at present in cases of intentionally or wilfully inefficient breaches, and less expansive liability than at present in cases in which the innocent party has failed to disclose special circumstances relating to potential losses.

Florian Faust, 'Hadley v Baxendale: An Understandable Miscarriage of Justice' (1994) 15 *Journal of Legal History* 41–72

An historical analysis of the *Hadley* case, arguing that it was a decision on the (then) tortious liability of a common carrier (the contractual assumpsit cause of action having been discontinued), in part responding to Danzig's historical analysis (digested above in this section), and arguing that the contemplation rule was established in order to restrict the jury's discretionary power over contract damages.

Francis Dawson, 'Reflections on Certain Aspects of the Law of Damages for Breach of Contract' (1995) 9 *Journal of Contract Law* 20–87

A fictitious dialogue between a tutor and pupil presenting and probing the argument that remoteness rules measure the scope of a tacitly assumed secondary obligation to pay damages in the event of breach.

John Cartwright, 'Remoteness of Damage in Contract and Tort: A Reconsideration' [1996] *Cambridge Law Journal* 488–514

Comparison of the tortious and contractual rules of remoteness, finding the test of remoteness to follow from the reason for the imposition of the duty that has been breached. Consequently, in cases of an assumption of responsibility leading to a tortious duty of care, the stricter contractual remoteness test based on the scope of the risk undertaken should be applied.

James Gordley, 'Responsibility in Crime, Tort, and Contract for the Unforeseeable Consequences of an Intentional Wrong: A Once and Future Rule?' in Peter Cane and Jane Stapleton (eds), *The Law of Obligations: Essays in Celebration of John Fleming* (Oxford, Clarendon Press, 1998) 175–208

In cases of wrongful intentional breach, in which the perpetrator knows he is appropriating or harming that which belongs to the other party, the breaching party should be liable for unforeseeable losses. A brief comparative and historical account is given in support of the author's argument.

John Cartwright, 'Compensatory Damages: Some Central Issues of Assessment' in Andrew Burrows and Edwin Peel (eds), *Commercial Remedies: Current Issues and Problems* (Oxford, Oxford University Press, 2003) 3–19

Hugh Conway-Jones, 'The Historical Setting for *Hadley v Baxendale*' (2004) 11 *Texas Wesleyan Law Review* 243–48; James J Fishman, 'Joseph Baxendale' (2004) 11 *Texas Wesleyan Law Review* 249–52

Andrew Tettenborn, '*Hadley v Baxendale:* Contract Doctrine or Compensation Rule?' (2004) 11 *Texas Wesleyan Law Review* 505–21

The *Hadley v Baxendale* rule should apply as a common standard to both contract and torts (at least torts not requiring deliberate wrongdoing).

Adam Kramer, 'An Agreement-centred Approach to Remoteness and Contract Damages' in Nili Cohen and Ewan McKendrick (eds), *Comparative Remedies for Breach of Contract* (Oxford, Hart, 2005) 249–86, 'Remoteness: New Problems with the Old Text' in Djakhongir Saidov and Ralph Cunnington (eds), *Contract Damages: Domestic and International Perspectives* (Oxford, Hart Publishing, 2008) 277–304, and 'The New Test of Remoteness in Contract' (2009) 125 *Law Quarterly Review* 408–15

The rules of remoteness, along with rules governing mental distress and the *South Australia Asset Management* scope of duty test, are all best understood as giving effect to the allocation of risk implicitly agreed and assumed by the parties and contained in the contractual agreement.

James Gordley, *Foundations of Private Law: Property, Tort, Contract, Unjust Enrichment* (Oxford, Oxford University Press, 2006) 395–407

Foreseeability is only relevant because lack of foreseeability indicates an unfair (applying commutative justice) disproportion between the amount of damages and price charged.

Andrew Tettenborn, 'Hadley v Baxendale Foreseeability: A Principle Beyond its Sell-by Date' (2007) 23 *Journal of Contract Law* 120–47

The principle of foreseeability should be abandoned as a basis for remoteness, which should be based upon the agreement, the purpose of the relevant obligation and the interests it was intended to protect.

Hon Mr Justice Anselmo Reyes, 'On Two Suggested Alternatives to the Rule in *Hadley v Baxendale*' (2008) 38 *Hong Kong Law Journal* 347–58

Andrew Robertson, 'The Basis of the Remoteness Rule in Contract' (2008) 28 *Legal Studies* 172–96

Tacit assumptions do not extend to the allocation of risk for the consequences of breach and so remoteness cannot be justified by the implicit allocation of risk. Instead, remoteness is a doctrine by which gaps in the parties' agreement are filled by rules of fairness, and should reflect the degree of fault of the defendant (deliberateness of the breach), the degree of disproportion between the loss and the price or other benefit to the defendant, commercial practice and the availability of insurance, and whether the defendant had a reasonable opportunity to limit his liability.

Lord Hoffmann, 'The *Achilleas*' (2010) 14 *Edinburgh Law Review* 47–61

The Scope of Duty

DW McLauchlan, 'A Damages Dilemma' (1997–98) 12 *Journal of Contract Law* 114–44; Jane Stapleton, 'Negligent Valuers and Falls in the Property Market' (1997) 117 *Law Quarterly Review* 1–7

Criticism of the *SAAMCO* decision on scope of duty.

Edwin Peel, 'SAAMCO Revisited' and R Butler, 'SAAMCO in Practice', both in A Burrows and E Peel (eds), *Commercial Remedies: Current Issues and Problems* (Oxford, Oxford University Press, 2003) 55–70 and 71–87

Leonard Hoffmann, 'Causation' (2005) 121 *Law Quarterly Review* 592–603

Adam Kramer, 'An Agreement-centred Approach to Remoteness and Contract Damages' in Nili Cohen and Ewan McKendrick (eds), *Comparative Remedies for Breach of Contract* (Oxford, Hart Publishing, 2005) 249–86

13.5 NON-COMPENSATORY DAMAGES

Generally

Hugh Beale, 'Exceptional Measures of Damages in Contract' in Peter Birks (ed), *Wrongs and Remedies in the Twenty-first Century* (Oxford, Clarendon Press, 1996) 217–47

Ralph Cunnington, 'The Inadequacy of Damages as a Remedy for Breach of Contract' in Charles EF Rickett (ed), *Justifying Remedies in Private Law* (Oxford, Hart Publishing, 2008) 115–45

Disgorgement and Restitutionary Damages

AM Tettenborn, 'Damages for Breach of Positive Covenants' (1978) 42 *Conveyancer and Property Lawyer* 366–74

Daniel Friedmann, 'Restitution of Benefits Obtained through the Appropriation of Property or Commission of a Wrong' (1980) 80 *Columbia Law Review* 504–58

Gareth Jones, 'The Recovery of Benefits Gained from Breach of Contract' (1983) 99 *Law Quarterly Review* 443–60

The remedy of account of profits should be generally available for breach of contract (although the requirement of causation in particular will often restrict its applicability).

EA Farnsworth, 'Your Loss or My gain? The Dilemma of the Disgorgement Principle in Breach of Contract' (1985) 94 *Yale Law Journal* 1339–93

Applying a strict requirement of causation, disgorgement should be measured by the savings made by the breaching party, and not their profit broadly conceived. Once this is understood, it is possible to more accurately assess when disgorgement is needed and justified. In addition to where it is already available, disgorgement should be available in cases in which the expectation measure does not enable the innocent party to obtain a substitute, typically because the cost of cure measure is too high or cure has become impossible.

P Birks, 'Restitutionary Damages for Breach of Contract: Contract: Snepp and the Fusion of Law and Equity ' [1987] *Lloyd's Maritime and Commercial Law Quarterly* 421–42

Restitutionary damages should be available in cases of cynical breach.

Elizabeth Macdonald, 'Breach of a Contractual Obligation—Cost of Work or Market Value?' [1988] *Conveyancer* 421–29

J Beatson, 'What Can Restitution Do for You?' (1989) 2 *Journal of Contract Law* 65–77

Sidney W Delong, 'The Efficiency of Disgorgement as a Remedy for Breach of Contract' (1989) 22 *Indiana Law Review* 737–76

M Jackman, 'Restitution for Wrongs' [1989] *Cambridge Law Journal* 302–21

Restitutionary damages should not be available in contract cases.

Samuel Stoljar, 'Restitutionary Relief for Breach of Contract' (1989–90) 2 *Journal of Contract Law* 1–12

Restitutionary damages operate as compensation where compensation is not readily calculable (because there is no market or the loss is subjective), although may be excluded where, for example, the cost of cure would be disproportionate and there has therefore been no loss.

Richard O'Dair, 'Restitutionary Damages for Breach of Contract and the Theory of Efficient Breach' (1993) 46 *Current Legal Problems* 113–34

Eric G Andersen, 'The Restoration Interest and Damages for Breach of Contract' (1994) 53 *Maryland Law Review* 1–106

Andrew Kull, 'Disgorgement for Breach, the "Restitution Interest," and the Restatement of Contracts' (2001) 79 *Texas Law Review* 2021–53

Lionel D Smith, 'Disgorgement of Profits for Breach of Contract: Property, Contract and "Efficient Breach"' (1994–95) *Canadian Business Law Journal* 121–40

Disgorgement should be available to prevent breaching parties expropriating innocent parties rights.

Stephen A Smith, 'Of Remedies and Restrictive Covenants' (1994) 7 *Journal of Contract Law* 164–80

Surrey v Bredero Homes should have been decided on the basis that the key covenant was unenforceable as unwarranted restraints on trade.

William Goodhart, 'Restitutionary Damages for Breach of Contract: the Remedy that Dare Not Speak Its Name' [1995] *Restitution Law Review* 3–14

Petter Jaffey, 'Restitutionary Damages and Disgorgement' [1995] *Restitution Law Review* 30–48

Restitutionary damages are punitive (but preferable to exemplary damages since in disgorgement cases the quantum is not at the discretion of the court). As a result, if they are to be allowed further safeguards must be considered (evidential, prevention of oppression, etc)

Harvey McGregor, 'Restitutionary Damages' in Peter Birks (ed), *Wrongs and Remedies in the Twenty-first Century* (Oxford, Clarendon Press, 1996) 203–16

Enrichment resulting from breach of contract, at least where deliberate or cynical, is unjust and should give rise to restitution (whether or not the obligation was specifically enforceable).

Richard Nolan, 'Remedies for Breach of Contract: Specific Enforcement and Restitution' and Peter Watts, 'Comment' in Francis D Rose (ed), *Failure of Contracts* (Oxford, Hart Publishing, 1997) 35–59

Restitutionary damages should only be available when the contract is a specifically performable contract to convey property.

Law Commission, *Consultation Paper 132: Aggravated, Exemplary and Restitutionary Damages* (1993) and *Report 247: Aggravated, Exemplary and Restitutionary Damages* (1997)

[1993] Restitutionary damages should be available for breach of a specifically enforceable contract or a contract between fiduciaries. [1997] Development of restitutionary damages for breach of contract should be left to the common law.

Catherine Mitchell, 'Remedial Inadequacy in Contract and the Role of Restitutionary Damages' (1999) 15 *Journal of Contract Law* 33–155

Hanoch Dagan, 'Restitutionary Damages for Breach of Contract: An Exercise in Private Law Theory' (2000) 1 *Theoretical Inqui-*

ries in Law 115–54, and his *The Law and Ethics of Restitution* (Cambridge, Cambridge University Press, 2004) ch 8

Restitutionary damages for breach cannot be justified as upholding the value of promise-keeping, which is neutral as to remedies for breach, or by the principle of unjust enrichment, which provides no guidance and instead depends upon other normative considerations. Neither the imperfect analogy with property nor the quest for efficiency can justify such damages. If, however, the law seeks to enforce a more co-operative conception of contract, this would entail a regime by which profits are divided amongst the parties (rather than all going to one or the other party).

J Edelman, 'Restitutionary Damages and Disgorgement Damages for Breach of Contract' [2000] *Restitution Law Review* 129–51, 'Gain-based Remedies for Wrongdoing' (2000) 74 *Australian Law Journal* 231–47, *Gain-based Damages: Contract, Tort, Equity and Intellectual Property* (Oxford, Hart Publishing, 2002) especially ch 5, 'Non-compensatory Damages for Breach of Contract and Torts' (2002) 75 *Australian Law Journal* 328–39 and 'Gain-based Damages and Compensation' in Andrew Burrows and Lord Rodger (eds), *Mapping the Law: Essays in Memory of Peter Birks* (Oxford, Oxford University Press, 2006) 141–60

Damages are an award of money and need not be compensatory to deserve the name. 'Restitutionary damages' should be distinguished from 'disgorgement damages'. Restitutionary damages for breach of contract (which must be distinguished from the similar remedy of restitution for unjust enrichment) should be awarded in order to reverse a transfer when the breaching party deprives the innocent party of a contractual right, such damages reflecting the market value of the contractual right transferred. Disgorgement damages strip a gain where it results from deliberate breach of contract to make a profit and (therefore) compensatory damages are inadequate to deter the breach, and the legitimate interest limitation from *Blake* should be refined and better expressed.

Ralph Cunnington, 'Equitable Damages: A Model for Restitutionary Damages' (2001) 17 *Journal of Contract Law* 212–39

Equitable damages such as in *Wrotham Park* are restitutionary and provide a framework for restitutionary damages.

Mitchell McInnes, 'Disgorgement for Breach of Contract: The Search for a Principled Relationship' in EJH Schrage (ed), *Unjust Enrichment and the Law of Contract* (London, Kluwer Law International, 2001) 225–42

Restitutionary damages are more likely to be justifiable in cases of breach of specifically enforceable contracts.

Daniel Friedmann, 'Restitution for Wrongs: The Measure of Recovery' (2001) 79 *Texas Law Review* 1879–926

Francesco Giglio, 'Restitution for Wrongs: A Comparative Study' (2001) *Oxford University Comparative Law Forum* 6

Andrew Phang and Lee Pey Woan, 'Rationalising Restitutionary Damages in Contract Law—An Elusive or Illusory Quest?' (2001) 17 *Journal of Contract Law* 240–73

Sam Doyle and David Wright, 'Restitutionary Damages—The Unnecessary Remedy?' (2001) 25 *Melbourne University Law Review* 1

Restitutionary damages, when available, are best understood not as a part of common law damages but as awards made under the equitable account for profits when common law damages are inadequate, and the label 'restitutionary damages' should be abandoned.

David Campbell, 'The Treatment of *Teacher* v *Calder* in *A-G* v *Blake*' (2002) 65 *Modern Law Review* 256–69 and David Campbell and Donald Harris, 'In Defence of Breach: A Critique of Restitution and the Performance Interest' (2002) 22 *Legal Studies* 208–37

In the absence of compelling empirical evidence, restitutionary damages should not generally be available in commercial cases as they will lead to inefficiency and frustrate the contracting parties' intentions.

Maree C Chetwin and David K Round, 'Breach of Contract and the New Remedy of Account of Profits' (2002) 38 *Abacus* 406

Janet O'Sullivan, 'Reflections on the Role of Restitutionary Damages to Protect Contractual Expectations' in David Johnston and Reinhard Zimmermann (eds), *Unjustified Enrichment: Key Issues in Comparative Perspective* (Cambridge, Cambridge University Press, 2002) 327–47

Filling gaps in compensatory awards is not a sufficient justification for awards of restitutionary damages, not least because such gaps can and should be filled by development of the principles of compensatory damages themselves (such as through recognition of the consumer surplus and awards in skimped performance cases).

Ewan McKendrick, 'Breach of Contract, Restitution for Wrongs, and Punishment' in Andrew Burrows and Edwin Peel (eds), *Commercial Remedies: Current Issues and Problems* (Oxford, Oxford University Press, 2003) 93–123.

The decision in *Attorney General v Blake* and its aftermath. Disgorgement damages and punitive damages are likely to play a small but significant role in remedial awards for breach of contract.

Andrew Phang and Lee Pey Woan, 'Restitutionary and Exemplary Damages Revisited' (2003) 19 *Journal of Contract Law* 1–39

An account for profits may sometimes be justified as a measure of compensatory damages (when the loss is difficult to quantify), and at other times may be justified on deterrence grounds where a breach of contract is wrongful.

P Benson, 'Disgorgement for Breach of Contract and Corrective Justice: An Analysis in Outline' in Jason W Neyers, Mitchell McInnes and Stephen GA Pitel (eds), *Understanding Unjust Enrichment* (Oxford, Hart Publishing, 2004) 311–30

The transfer of rights theory of contract formation justifies disgorgement damages in cases of contracts for unique property and other sorts of case in which specific performance is, in principle, available.

Ralph Cunnington, 'Contract Rights as Property Rights' in Andrew Robertson (ed), *The Law of Obligations: Connections and Boundaries* (London, UCL Press, 2004) 169–95

Peter Jaffey, 'Disgorgement and "Licence Fee Damages" in Contract' (2004) 20 *Journal of Contract Law* 57–73

Specific performance or disgorgement are justified where the breaching party knows that the other party has become dependent on performance because he cannot obtain the contractual benefit elsewhere, and so damages would be inadequate.

Justin Gleeson SC and James Watson, 'Account of Profits, Contracts and Equity' (2005) 79 *Australian Law Journal* 676–708

The account for profits, as awarded in *Attorney General v Blake*, should be available as a fair equivalent of what was bargained for where a party has undertaken to be an accounting party by entering into an important (eg non-negotiable) covenant the breach of which might lead to profit for the promisor but not to loss for the promise, and has breached without notice to the promisee.

James Edelman, 'Gain-based Damages and Compensation' in Andrew Burrows and Lord Rodger (eds), *Mapping the Law: Essays in Memory of Peter Birks* (Oxford, Oxford University Press, 2006) 141–60 and 'The Meaning of Loss and Enrichment' in Robert Chambers, Charles Mitchell and James Penner (eds), *Philosophical Foundations of the Law of Unjust Enrichment* (Oxford, Oxford University Press, 2009) 211–41

[2006] Edelman agrees with a rights-based approach to compensation (which subsumes restitutionary damages) in the case of contract rights held for non-commercial purposes, but not in commercial cases. [2009] Edelman recants from this view.

Lord Scott of Foscote, 'Damages' [2007] *Lloyd's Maritime and Commercial Law Quarterly* 465–73

Graham Virgo, 'Restitutionary Remedies for Wrongs: Causation and Remoteness' in Charles EF Rickett (ed), *Justifying Remedies in Private Law* (Oxford, Hart Publishing, 2008) 301–31

Punitive Damages

Charles M Louderback and Thomas W Jurika, 'Standards for Limiting the Tort of Bad Faith Breach of Contract' (1982) 16 *University of San Francisco Law Review* 187–228

A tort of bad faith breach should be applied outside insurance cases if one party is able to dictate terms, the weaker party is not seeking profit but rather an essential service or peace of mind, there is trust and confidence, and conduct frustrating the weaker party's enjoyment of its contract rights.

Thomas A Diamond, 'The Tort of Bad Faith Breach of Contract: When, If At All, Should It Be Extended Beyond Insurance Transactions' (1981) 64 *Marquette Law Review* 425–54

John A Sebert Jr, 'Punitive and Non-pecuniary Damages in Actions Based Upon Contract: Towards Achieving the Objective of Full Compensation' (1986) 33 *UCLA Law Review* 1565–678

P Birks, 'Restitutionary Damages for Breach of Contract, Snepp and the Fusion of Laws and Equity' (1987) *Lloyd's Maritime and Commercial Law Quarterly* 421–42

Punitive damages are unjustified in commercial contract cases because it is important that damage awards be predictable in order that efficient breach is facilitated. Where this is not the case, such as in employment and insurance contract cases, punitive damages may be justified by the effect in deterring undesirable breaches (damaging the employee or the insured party's dignity) that allowing such awards may have.

David ER Venour, 'Punitive Damages in Contract' (1988) 1 *Canadian Journal of Law and Jurisprudence* 87–104

David G Owen, 'The Moral Foundations of Punitive Damages' (1989) 40 *Alabama Law Review* 705–39

Leon E Trakman, 'Breach, Compensation and the Magic Carpet' in J Beryman (ed), *Remedies: Issues and Perspectives* (Toronto, Carswell, 1991) 373–94

Nicholas J McBride, 'A Case for Awarding Punitive Damages in Response to Deliberate Breaches of Contract' (1995) 24 *Anglo-American Law Review* 369–90 and 'Punitive Damages', in *Wrongs and Remedies in the Twenty-first Century* (Oxford, Oxford University Press, 1996) 175–202

Punitive damages should be awarded, at the least, if it can be clearly proven that the defendant's breach was willing (broadly: knowing), the defendant has not already been adequately punished by the criminal law, and the damages do not bankrupt or otherwise over punish the defendant.

Alan O Sykes, '"Bad Faith" Breach of Contract by First-Party Insurers' (1996) 25 *Journal of Legal Studies* 405–44; William S Dodge, 'The Case for Punitive Damages in Contracts' (1999) 48 *Duke Law Journal* 629–99

Sykes: Punitive damages may in principle be efficient but in practice the courts are unable to accurately identify opportunistic behaviour. Dodge: Punitive damages are efficient when the breach was opportunistic (such as bad faith refusal to pay and stonewalling denial of liability) and indeed beyond.

Law Commission, *Consultation Paper 132: Aggravated, Exemplary and Restitutionary Damages* (1993) and *Report 247: Aggravated, Exemplary and Restitutionary Damages* (1997)

Punitive damages should never be available for breach of contract.

Stephen A Smith, 'Performance, Punishment and the Nature of Contractual Obligation' (1997) 60 *Modern Law Review* 360–77

Punitive damages should only be awarded where the breaching party is seeking to avoid the obligation to pay damages or where specific performance should be ordered by for one reason or another cannot be ordered.

E Weinrib, 'Punishment and Disgorgement as Contract Remedies' (2002) 78 *Chicago-Kent Law Review* 101; Curtis Bridgeman, 'Corrective Justice in Contract Law: Is There a Case for Punitive Damages?' (2003) 56 *Vanderbilt Law Journal* 237–76; Pey-Woan Lee, 'Contract Damages, Corrective Justice and Punishment' (2007) 70 *Modern Law Review* 887–907

The authors debate whether punitive damages can be justified under a corrective justice framework. (See Corrective Justice in 13.6.)

Andrew Phang and Lee Pey Woan, 'Restitutionary and Exemplary Damages Revisited' (2003) 19 *Journal of Contract Law* 1–38

John Swan, 'Punitive Damages for Breach of Contract: A Remedy in Search of a Justification' (2004) 29 *Queens Law Journal* 596–646

Punitive damages are inconsistent with contract law and its compensatory thrust.

Ralph Cunnington, 'Should Punitive Damages be Part of the Judicial Arsenal in Contract Cases?' (2006) 26 *Legal Studies* 369–93

Punitive damages should be available to deter outrageous breaches where, and only where, the private and public interest in performance is not adequately protected by other remedies.

Lord Scott of Foscote, 'Damages' [2007] *Lloyd's Maritime and Commercial Law Quarterly* 465–73

James Edelman, 'In Defence of Exemplary Damages' in Charles EF Rickett (ed), *Justifying Remedies in Private Law* (Oxford, Hart Publishing, 2008) 225

None of the criticisms of exemplary damages justify their abolition.

13.6 THEORY

Generally

Bernhard Grossfeld, 'Money Sanctions for Breach of Contract in a Communist Economy' (1963) 72 *Yale Law Journal* 1326–46

James Edelman, 'The Meaning of "Damages" at Common Law and Equity' in Andrew Robertson (ed), *Law of Obligations: Connections and Boundaries* (London, UCL Press, 2004) 31–58

'Damages' should be understood to denote any monetary award given for a wrong, not merely a compensatory one. This will reveal, for example, that equitable compensation is merely one form of compensatory damages, and the equitable account for profits is one form of disgorgement damages, and it will facilitate the development of rules of causation or remoteness for equitable damages.

Ralph Cunnington, 'The Inadequacy of Damages as a Remedy for Breach of Contract' in Charles EF Rickett (ed), *Justifying Remedies in Private Law* (Oxford, Hart Publishing, 2008) 115–45

Corrective Justice

See also Corrective Justice in 16.3

E Weinrib, 'Punishment and Disgorgement as Contract Remedies' (2002) 78 *Chicago-Kent Law Review* 101; Curtis Bridgeman, 'Corrective Justice in Contract Law: Is There a Case for Punitive Damages?' (2003) 56 *Vanderbilt Law Journal* 237–76; Pey-Woan Lee, 'Contract Damages, Corrective Justice and Punishment' (2007) 70 *Modern Law Review* 887–907

Weinrib argues that, following Kant and disagreeing with Fuller and Perdue, a contract can be seen as the creation of an entitlement to the performance of a contract (not to its subject-matter or to the situation that would result from performance): the future performance by one party becomes the property of the other party. In this light, damages on the expectation measure, being the value of the promised performance (or the thing promised), are a just (by corrective justice) remedy for the infringement of the entitlement. Disgorgement damages, however, are not justifiable by the requirements of corrective justice, since the breaching party's gain does not fall within the innocent party's infringed entitlement. Breach of contract is not tantamount to alienation of a property right (since the breach of contract does not amount to an alienation of the right to performance of the contract), and the availability of specific performance does not change this. Punitive damages are not justifiable under principles of corrective justice (although more astute recognition of harm requiring compensatory damages is needed). Bridgeman agrees that the expectation measure of damages is justified as representing the normative loss to the promisor, since the promisor was entitled to performance, adding that the normative loss will sometimes require the award of the cost of cure and not merely the difference in value, will require subjective (idiosyncratic) and not merely objective valuation of the expectation, and will require punitive damages in cases of wilful breach when it is clear that a breach has not been contemplated with Holmesian equanimity by the promisee. Lee argues that punitive damages may not only be state punishment and may be understood as a retributive response to the moral injury inflicted by the breaching party, and therefore are not one-sided but correlative and can be justified within a corrective justice framework.

The Reliance Interest versus the Expectation Interest

Joseph Raz, 'Voluntary Obligations and Normative Powers' in (1972) Supp Vol 46 *Proceedings of the Aristotelian Society*, 'Promises and Obligations' in PMS Hacker and J Raz (eds), *Law, Morality, and Society: Essays in Honour of HLA Hart* (1977) 210 and 'Promises in Morality and Law' (1982) 95 *Harvard Law Review* 916–38; JE Penner, 'Voluntary Obligations and the Scope of the Law of Contract' (1996) 2 *Legal Theory* 325–57; Dori Kimel, *From Promise to Contract: Towards a Liberal Theory of Contract* (Oxford, Hart Publishing, 2003) ch 4, a revised version of which appears as 'Remedial Rights and Substantive Rights in Contract Law' (2002) 8 *Legal Theory* 313–38

Raz argues that the harm principle may indicate that reliance damages should often be preferred to expectation damages. Penner argues that expectation damages do not infringe the harm principle in any serious way, and are justified by the interest in performance arising out of the duty to perform, at least in the case of bargain agreements (and not mutual agreements such as employment contracts) which create a special new bond that they create (with little in the way of underlying constitutive obligations). Kimel argues that breach is inconsistent with the core contractual right to performance, from which it follows that non-performance is harmful and so reliance damages are inadequate.

Charles J Goetz and Robert E Scott, 'Enforcing Promises: An Examination of the Basis of Contract' (1980) 89 *Yale Law Journal* 52–96, 373–420 also in Larry Alexander (ed), *Contract Law: Volume II* (Aldershot, Dartmouth, 1991) 211–55 and in *Issues in Legal Scholarship, Symposium: Fuller and Perdue* (Berkeley, CA, Berkeley Electronic Press, 2001)

A hugely influential article arguing that contract law is about the protection of 'reliance interest'.

Daniel Friedmann, 'The Performance Interest in Contract Damages' (1995) 111 *Law Quarterly Review* 628–54; J Stapleton 'The Normal Expectancies Measure in Tort Damages' (1997) 113 *Law Quarterly Review* 628; J Stapleton, 'A New "Seascape" for Obligations: Reclassification on the Basis of Measure of Damages' in P Birks (ed), *The Classification of Obligations* (Oxford, Oxford University Press, 1997); Daniel Friedmann, 'Rights and Remedies' (1997) 113 *Law Quarterly Review* 424–26; Stephen A Smith, 'Rights, Remedies, and Normal Expectancies in Tort and Contract' (1997) 113 *Law Quarterly Review* 426–432; Daniel Friedmann, 'A Comment on Fuller and Perdue, the Reliance Interest in Contract Damages' in *Issues in Legal Scholarship, Symposium: Fuller and Perdue* (Berkeley, CA, Berkeley Electronic Press, 2001) art 3

Stapleton defends the view that the measure of damages is a useful tool in analysing the law of obligations, and distinguishes between 'normal expectancies' (usual in tort cases) and 'entitled result' damages (usual in contract cases). Friedmann, supported by Smith, argues that different damages measures result from differences in the rights that have been infringed, since damages put the innocent party in the position they would have been in but for the infringement.

Daniel Friedmann, 'A Comment on Fuller and Perdue, the Reliance Interest in Contract Damages' in *Issues in Legal Scholarship, Symposium: Fuller and Perdue* (Berkeley, CA, Berkeley Electronic Press, 2001) art 3

Fuller and Perdue's article introduced inappropriate terminology (the 'expectation interest' should be the 'performance interest'), is wrong, and has had very little effect on the law.

Richard Craswell, 'Against Fuller and Purdue' (2000) 67 *University of Chicago Law Review* 99–161

Fuller and Perdue's three-way classification of the expectation, restitution and reliance interests is no longer a useful analytical tool. Instead the starting point should be the true measure of expectation damages, separately categorising rules that award less than that measure (mitigation, remoteness etc) and those that award more (punitive damages, some awards of restitutionary and reliance damages).

Richard Craswell, 'How We Got This Way: Further Thoughts on Fuller and Perdue', *Issues in Legal Scholarship, Symposium: Fuller and Perdue* (Berkeley, CA, Berkeley Electronic Press, 2001) art 2

James Gordley, 'A Perennial Misstep: From Cajetan to Fuller and Perdue to "Efficient Breach"' in *Issues in Legal Scholarship, Symposium: Fuller and Perdue* (Berkeley, CA, Berkeley Electronic Press, 2001) art 4

Peter Benson, 'The Expectation and Reliance Interests in Contract Theory: A

Reply to Fuller and Perdue' in *Issues in Legal Scholarship, Symposium: Fuller and Perdue* (Berkeley, CA, Berkeley Electronic Press, 2001) art 5

W David Slawson, 'Why Expectation Damages for Breach of Contract Must Be the Norm: A Refutation of the Fuller and Perdue "Three Interests" Thesis' (2003) 81 *Nebraska Law Review* 839–67

Only the expectation interest meets the needs of the principal institutions in a modern market economy, providing a remedy for every breach, making contracts enforceable as soon as made, compensating for loss as properly valued, and providing the right incentives as to whether to breach.

The Duty to Perform and the Theory of Efficient Breach

OW Holmes Jr, *The Common Law* (1881) 301ff and 'The Path of the Law' (1897) 10 *Harvard Law Review* 457–78

A right is only as good as its remedies and a duty to keep a contract is merely a prediction that one must pay damages if the contract is not kept, so a contractual obligation is an obligation either to do or to pay damages.

WW Buckland, 'The Nature of Contractual Obligation' [1944] *Cambridge Law Journal* 247–51

JB Gebhardt, 'Pacta Sunt Servanda' (1947) 10 *Modern Law Review* 159–70

Under English Law, where specific performance is not awarded in situations in which it could be awarded, there is no moral or legal duty to perform. *Pacta sunt servanda* is a rule of English law only in that promises are understood by all to be binding at a pre-legal, subconscious level.

Peter Linzer, 'On the Amorality of Contract Remedies—Efficiency, Equity, and the Second Restatement' (1981) 81 *Columbia Law Review* 111–39 also in Larry Alexander (ed), *Contract Law: Volume II* (Aldershot, Dartmouth, 1991) 299–327

Ian R Macneil, 'Efficient Breach of Contract: Circles in the Sky' (1982) 68 *Virginia Law Review* 947–69 also in Larry Alexander (ed), *Contract Law: Volume II* (Aldershot, Dartmouth, 1991) 329–51

The general efficient breach analysis is fallacious because the efficient result can be reached without breach, eg through a negotiated release. Only if the transaction costs of a specific performance rule are proved to be higher than those obtaining from an expectation damages rule does efficiency point to the adoption of the latter rule. Further, the efficient breach theory is biased towards unco-operative behaviour and ignores the realities of relationships.

Daniel Friedmann, 'The Efficient Breach Fallacy' (1989) 18 *Journal of Legal Studies* 1–24

As an account of the law, the theory of efficient breach is descriptively inaccurate, normatively undesirable, and internally incoherent, as it provides inadequate protection and most so-called efficient breaches are not in fact efficient.

Lionel D Smith, 'Disgorgement of the profits of Breach of Contract: Property, Contract and "Efficient Breach"' (1995) 24 *Canadian Business Law Journal* 121–40

Disgorgement should be awarded in contract cases, as in property cases (which are not different in any relevant sense), to avoid the need to resort to fictitious compensation. The gain must have been caused (factually and legally) by the breach and not be too remote.

David W Barnes, 'The Anatomy of Contract Damages and Efficient Breach Theory' (1998) 6 *Southern California Interdisciplinary Law Journal* 397–490

Joseph M Perillo, 'Misreading Oliver Wendell Holmes on Efficient Breach and Tortious Interference' (2000) 68 *Fordham Law Review* 1085–106

James Gordley, 'A Perennial Misstep: From Cajetan to Fuller and Perdue to "Efficient Breach"' in *Issues in Legal Scholarship, Symposium: Fuller and Perdue* (Berkeley, CA, Berkeley Electronic Press, 2001) art 4

David Campbell and Donald Harris, 'In Defence of Breach: A Critique of Restitution and the Performance Interest' (2002) 22 *Legal Studies* 208–37

Commercial contracts do not entail a total commitment to perform. Breach is a legitimate legal institution and it is a function of compensatory damages to allow breach and so maximise the efficiency of commerce. The current default rule whereby specific performance is rare, and restitutionary damages can be expressly opted-into, leads to lower prices (since prices are fixed according to the cost of expected remedies). In the absence of persuasive empirical evidence, this default rule is preferable to the alternative.

Economic Theories

Robert L Birmingham, 'Breach of Contract, Damages Measures and Economic Efficiency' (1970) 24 *Rutgers Law Review* 273–92

The general damages remedy promotes economic efficiency.

John H Barton, 'The Economic Basis of Damages for Breach of Contract' (1972) 1 *Journal of Legal Studies* 277–304

In commercial contract cases, where the risks have not been allocated by the parties or custom, the party most able to manipulate the risk and allocate in response to it should bear that risk. If the risk-bearer would normally have access to data on the size of the risk when contracting, he should pay reliance costs plus a proportion of profit; if not, then he should pay total losses resulting from the risks.

Daniel A Farber, 'Reassessing the Economic Efficiency of Compensatory Damages for Breach of Contract' (1980) 66 *Virginia Law Review* 1443–84

Steven Shavell, 'Damage Measures for Breach of Contract' (1980) 11 *Bell Journal of Economics* 466–90

Robert Cooter and Melvin Aron Eisenberg, 'Damages for Breach of Contract' (1985) 73 *California Law Review* 1432–81

Expectation damages are generally preferable to reliance damages because they protect reliance but are cheaper to administer, better facilitate planning and are often the measure the parties would have chosen.

Richard Craswell, 'Contract Remedies, Renegotiation, and the Theory of Efficient Breach' (1989) 61 *Southern California Law Review* 629–70 also in Brian Bix (ed), *Contract Law: Second Series: Volume I* (Aldershot, Ashgate, 2000) 339–80

George M Cohen, 'The Fault Lines in Contract Damages' (1994) 80 *Virginia Law Review* 1225–349

From an economic perspective, only a fault-based approach to contract law can explain contract damages.

David W Barnes, 'The Meaning of Value in Contract Damages and Contract Theory' (1996) 46 *American University Law Review* 1–38

Omri Ben-Shahar and Lisa Bernstein, 'The Secrecy Interest in Contract Law' (2000) 109 *Yale Law Journal* 1885–925

When considering the efficiency of expectation damages, it is necessary to consider the costs to the innocent party of revealing the information necessary to establish the magnitude of expectation losses (eg lost profits).

Paul G Mahoney, 'Contract Remedies: General' in Boudewijn Bouckaert and Gerrit De D Geest (eds), *Encyclopedia of Law and Economics, Volume III: The Regulation of Contracts* (Cheltenham, Elgar, 2000) 117–40

Robert Cooter and Ariel Porat, 'Should Courts Deduct Nonlegal Sanctions from Damages?' (2001) 30 *Journal of Legal Studies* 401–22

Yes, where practicable.

David Gilo, 'The Deterrent Factor of Damages where Pricing is Affected' in Nili Cohen and Ewan McKendrick (eds), *Comparative Remedies for Breach of Contract* (Oxford, Hart Publishing, 2004) 235–47

Where contractors operate as firms in the marketplace, courts should be astute to detect when part of damages awards are likely to be passed on through pricing to customers. In such cases, damages at a higher level than the expectation measure should be awarded, in order to ensure that optimal incentives against breach are provided.

Relational Theory

JE Penner, 'Voluntary Obligations and the Scope of the Law of Contract' (1996) 2 *Legal Theory* 325–57

The harm principle cannot justify expectation damages in the case of breach of mutual, rather than bargain, agreements, ie relational contracts such as those of employment, where the only harm resulted from relying on the practice of making agreements rather than the mutual interest itself, and reliance or restitutionary awards are likely to be more appropriate.

14

CONCURRENT LIABILITY

14.1 CONTRACT AND TORT

Generally

G Fridman, 'The Interaction of Tort and Contract' (1977) 93 *Law Quarterly Review* 422–49

There should be a more relaxed concurrence of and cross-fertilisation between contract and tort, leading, at least in practice, to the distinctions between the two falling away.

John L Dwyer, 'Solicitor's Negligence—Tort or Contract?' (1982) 56 *Australian Law Journal* 524–41

FMB Reynolds, 'Tort Actions in Contractual Situations' (1984–1985) 11 *New Zealand Universities Law Review* 215–32

AJE Jaffey, 'Contract in Tort's Clothing' (1985) 5 *Legal Studies* 77–103

Tortious liability for negligent failure in providing a service (following an assumption of responsibility) is liability upon a gratuitous promise, and generally sounds in expectation damages, ie is contractual in all but name.

Peter Cane, *Tort Law and Economic Interests*, 2nd edn (London, Sweet & Maxwell, 1996) 129–49 and 307–43

Peter Cane, 'Contract, Tort and the Lloyd's Debâcle' in FD Rose (ed), *Consensus Ad Idem—Essays in the Law of Contract in Honour of Guenter Treitel* (London, Sweet & Maxwell, 1996) 96–120

Deryck Beyleveld and Roger Brownsword, 'Privity, Transitivity and Rationality' (1991) 54 *Modern Law Review* 48–71

Joost Blom, 'Fictions and Frictions on the Interface Between Contract and Tort' in Peter T Burns (ed), *Donoghue v Stevenson and the Modern Law of Negligence* (Paisley Papers) (Continuing Legal Education Society of British Columbia, 1991) 139–89

Madeleine van Rossum, 'Concurrency of Contractual and Delictual Liability in a European Perspective' (1995) 3 *European Review of Private Law* 539–66

Andrew Burrows, 'Solving the Problem of Concurrent Liability' (1995) 48 *Current Legal Problems* 103–24, a later version of which, with postscript, appears in his *Understanding the Law of Obligations* (Oxford, Hart Publishing, 1998) 16–44

A claimant should be able to freely choose causes of action that are independent unless the contract expressly or impliedly excludes the tortious cause of action. This leads to a free choice in cases of negligently caused physical damage or negligent misstatement. In cases of negligent performance of services leading to economic loss, the necessary assumption of responsibility is not independent of any contract and so as a matter of principle there should be no concurrent tort liability. However concurrent liability is necessary as a matter of practice until tortious remoteness and limitation rules cease to be more generous than their contractual equivalents.

Jane Swanton, 'Concurrent Liability in Tort and Contract: the Problem of Defining the Limits' (1996) 10 *Journal of Contract Law* 21–52

Nicholas J McBride, 'Classification and Legal Education' in Peter Birks (ed), *The Classification of Obligations* (Oxford, Clarendon Press, 1997) 71–89

Diane Skapinker and JW Carter, 'Breach of Contract and Misleading or Deceptive Conduct in Australia' (1997) 113 *Law Quarterly Review* 294–320

Simon Whittaker, 'The Application of the "Broad Principle of Hedley Byrne" as between Parties to a Contract' (1997) 17 *Legal Studies* 169–91

Ian Pease, 'The Extent of Concurrent Duties in Contract and Tort: Past Developments and Current Law' in Anthony Thornton and William Godwin (eds), *Construction Law: Themes and Practice: Essays in Honour of IN Duncan Wallace QC* (London, Sweet & Maxwell, 1998) 289–306

Robby Bernstein, *Economic Loss*, 2nd edn (London, Sweet & Maxwell, 1998) 777–808

Janet O'Sullivan, 'Suing in Tort where No Contractual Claim Will Lie—A Bird's Eye View' (2007) 23 *Professional Negligence* 165–92

The situations in which the lack of a contract prevents a *Hedley Byrne* duty of care arising.

Damages Rules

Barry J Reiter, 'Contracts, Torts, Relations and Reliance' in Barry J Reiter and John Swan (eds), *Studies in Contract Law* (Toronto, Butterworths, 1980) 235–311

Nothing should follow from the conceptual labels 'contract' and 'tort'. Whenever one party reasonably relies upon the other party to satisfy his reasonable expectations (such situations including promises, bailments, assumptions of responsibility, positions of expertise, etc) the courts should have a discretion to grant the disappointed party the suitable remedy (including damages on either the reliance or expectation measure, with the most appropriate remoteness test). Contractual provisions may well alter the scope of responsibility that would otherwise lie. Further, only where a promise is bought for consideration is the expectation measure likely to be appropriate.

Joost Blom, 'Remedies in Tort and Contract: Where Is the Difference?' in J Berryman (ed), *Remedies: Issues and Perspectives* (Toronto, Carswell, 1991) 395–422

A comparison of the rules governing damages in contract and tort cases, including argument that the test of remoteness should depend not on whether the action is in tort or in contract but on whether there was an opportunity for the claimant and defendant to bargain.

MJ Tilbury, 'Two Models of Concurrent Tort/Contract Liability and Their Application to Remoteness and the Measure of Damages' in J Berryman (ed), *Remedies: Issues and Perspectives* (Toronto, Carswell, 1991) 423–41

John Cartwright, 'Remoteness of Damage in Contract and Tort: A Reconsideration' [1996] *Cambridge Law Journal* 488–514

Comparison of the tortious and contractual rules of remoteness, finding the test of remoteness to follow from the reason for the imposition of the duty that has been breached. Consequently, in cases of an assumption of responsibility leading to a tortious duty of care, the stricter contractual remoteness test based on the scope of the risk undertaken should be applied.

Andrew Burrows, *Remedies for Torts and Breach of Contract*, 3rd edn (Oxford, Oxford University Press, 2004) 4–11

Adam Kramer, 'Remoteness: New Problems with the Old Text' in Djakhongir Saidov and Ralph Cunnington (eds), *Contract Damages: Domestic and International Perspectives* (Oxford, Hart Publishing, 2008) 277–304

14.2 CONTRACT AND UNJUST ENRICHMENT

See also 3.9 Restitution and Void Contracts, and Restitution in 10.5

Joseph M Perillo, 'Restitution in a Contractual Context' (1973) 73 *Columbia Law Review* 1208–26

J Beatson, 'Gap-filling and Risk-reversal' in his *The Use and Abuse of Unjust Enrichment* (Oxford, Clarendon Press, 1991) 78–94, 'The Temptation of Elegance: Concurrence of Restitutionary and Contractual Claims' in William Swadling and Gareth Jones (eds), *The Search for Principle Essays in Honour of Lord Goff of Chieveley* (Oxford, Oxford University Press, 1999) 143–70 and 'Restitution and Contract: Non-Cumul?' (2000) 1 *Theoretical Inquiries in Law* 83–114

[1991] Unjust enrichment should only apply when there is no contractual allocation of risk or, exceptionally, when the contractual allocation of risk is unfair. [1999 and 2000] There may be cases, particularly in long-term contracts, in which there is a gap in the contractual allocation of risk and unjust enrichment can then be applied without conflicting with contract rules even though a contract subsists. Further, even after discharge of the contract the contract may still expressly or impliedly exclude the right to restitution.

A Burrows, 'Solving the Problem of Concurrent Liability' (1995) 48 *Current Legal Problems* 103–24, a later version of which appears in his *Understanding the Law of Obligations* (Oxford, Hart Publishing, 1998) 16–44

Restitution is independent of contract but while a contract is live all restitutionary claims should be barred by the need to avoid circularity (eg a contractual obligation requiring the conferral of something that the restitutionary obligation would require to be returned). When a contract is discharged the innocent party should be able to claim restitution even where this gives a better remedy than contractual damages, unless this option is expressly or impliedly included by what was agreed in the contract.

JW Carter, 'Restitution and Contract Risk' in Mitchell McInnes (ed), *Restitution: Developments and Unjust Enrichment* (Sydney, LBC Information Services, 1996) 137–61

Andrew Skelton, *Restitution and Contract* (London, LLP, 1998)

Stephen A Smith, 'Concurrent Liability in Contract and Unjust Enrichment: The Fundamental Breach Requirement' (1999) 115 *Law Quarterly Review* 245–64

Unjust enrichment should give rise to an action for restitution even when a contract is valid and even when there has not been a fundamental breach or termination of the contract. When there has been a fundamental breach (whether or not the breach has been accepted and the contract terminated) the obligation is likely to be non-severable and so an unjust enrichment action would give rise to restitution of all the benefits conferred; where the breach is non-fundamental the obligation is likely to be severable and so an unjust enrichment action would give rise to restitution for the benefits conferred pursuant to that obligation only.

Andrew Tettenborn, 'Subsisting Contracts and Failure of Consideration: A Little Scepticism' [2002] *Restitution Law Review* 1–8

A contract should not bar restitution unless the terms of the contract are inconsistent with the existence of a claim for restitution for failure of consideration.

Michael Bryan, 'Rescission, Restitution and Contractual Ordering: The Role of Plaintiff Election' in Andrew Robertson (ed), *The Law of Obligations: Connections and Boundaries* (London, UCL Press, 2004) 59–74

Ralph Cunnington, 'Failure of Basis' [2004] *Lloyd's Maritime and Commercial Law Quarterly* 234–53

Restitution should be available even where a contract subsists if there is a gap in the contractual allocation of risk.

Steve Hedley, 'Implied Contract and Restitution' [2004] *Cambridge Law Journal* 435–55

The reliance upon the implied contract, or quasi-contract, should not be rejected out of hand, and indeed is useful in many cases of failed or non-contracts.

Gerard McMeel, 'Unjust Enrichment, Discharge for Breach, and the Primacy of Contract' in Andrew Burrows and Lord Rodger (eds), *Mapping the Law: Essays in Memory of Peter Birks* (Oxford, Oxford University Press, 2006) 181–99

Tang Hang Wu, 'Unjust Enrichment within a Valid Contract: A Close Look at Roxborough v Rothmans of Pall Mall Australia Ltd' (2007) *Journal of Contract Law* 201–27

Even where a gap in contractual allocation of risk can be shown, which is rare, unjust enrichment is not necessarily the right normative theory for the filling of that gap.

Stephen Waddams, 'Contract and Unjust Enrichment: Competing Categories, or Complementary Concepts?' in Charles Rickett and Ross Grantham (eds), *Structure and Justification in Private Law: Essays for Peter Birks* (Oxford, Hart Publishing, 2008) 167–83

Tariq A Baloch, *Unjust Enrichment and Contract* (Oxford, Hart Publishing, 2009)

Unjust enrichment should be available whenever there is a failure of the condition upon which the benefit was conferred. Where a contract is apportioned, unjust enrichment should be available even if the contract is subsisting and has not been terminated.

14.3 PROMISSORY ESTOPPEL AS A CAUSE OF ACTION

See also 9.3 Waiver and Promissory Estoppel

Warren L Shattuck, 'Gratuitous Promises—A New Writ?' (1937) 35 *Michigan Law Review* 908–45

Gratuitous promises should not give rise to specific performance or to damages on the contractual measure.

Orvill C Snyder, 'Promissory Estoppel as Tort' (1949) 35 *Iowa Law Review* 28–48

Warren A Seavey, 'Reliance upon Gratuitous Promises or Other Conduct' (1951) 64 *Harvard Law Review* 913–28

Estoppel is basically a tort doctrine.

David Jackson, 'Estoppel as a Sword: Parts 1 and 2' (1965) 81 *Law Quarterly Review* 84–105, 223–47

Estoppel can be used to establish the consideration, promise or negligence which then fulfils the cause of action in negligence or contract, and can in that sense be used as a sword. The limitation from *Combe v Combe* is therefore without foundation.

MP Thompson, 'From Representation to Expectation: Estoppel as a Cause of Action' [1983] *Cambridge Law Journal* 257–78

Daniel A Farber and John H Matheson, 'Beyond Promissory Estoppel: Contract Law and the "Invisible Handshake"' (1985) 52 *University of Chicago Law Review* 903–47

Promissory estoppel in the US is moving from a tort doctrine protecting reliance to a means of enforcing contracts whether or not there is detrimental reliance. All promises should be enforceable, without reliance or consideration, if made in furtherance of economic activities.

Randy E Barnett and Mary E Becker, 'Beyond Reliance: Promissory Estoppel, Contract Formalities, and Misrepresentations' (1987) 15 *Hofstra Law Review* 443–98; Mary E Becker, 'Promissory Estoppel Damages' (1987) 16 *Hofstra Law Review* 131–64

[1986] Promissory estoppel is a development of traditional contractual and tortious (misrepresentation) principles, providing a remedy in cases not caught by either doctrine. Judges applying this doctrine should not overly focus on reliance avoiding proper discussion of the formal requirements for contract liability and the standard for promissory misrepresentation (and why and when they should be relaxed). [1987] Whether an estoppel cases is a near-contract case or near-tort case generally affects the remedies awarded.

Juliet P Kostritsky, 'A New Theory of Assent-based Liability Emerging Under the Guise of Promissory Estoppel: An Explanation and Defense' (1987) 33 *Wayne Law Review* 895–964

W David Slawson, 'The Role of Reliance in Contract Damages' (1990) 76 *Cornell Law Review* 197–237

P Birks, 'Equity in the Modern Law: An Exercise in Taxonomy' (1996) 26 *University of Western Australia Law Review* 1–99

Estoppel describes the causative event (not-wrong) of a 'promise binding upon detrimental reliance' ('a detrimental reliance promise') and as such is part of contract. There is thus no need for a requirement of unconscionability within estoppel. As with other contracts, specific relief should generally be available to enforce the primary right, and the secondary right arising from the wrong of breach of a detrimental reliance promise should give rise to damages on the normal contractual measure.

Margaret Halliwell, 'Estoppel: Unconscionability as a Cause of Action' (1994) 14 *Legal Studies* 15–34

Nicholas J McBride, 'A Fifth Common Law Obligation' (1994) 14 *Legal Studies* 35–69 and 'Classification and Legal Education' in Peter Birks (ed), *The Classification of Obligations* (Oxford, Clarendon Press, 1997) 71–89

The duty protected by promissory estoppel is neither contractual nor tortious (the latter encompassing duties constraining conduct) but is a duty to ensure that others are not made worse off by reliance on one's promises. This duty is part of a more general duty not to knowingly employ another's goods without consent.

Andrew Robertson, 'Satisfying the Minimum Equity: Equitable Estoppel Remedies after *Verwayen*' (1996) 20 *Melbourne University Law Review* 805–47, 'Situating Equitable Estoppel within the Law of Obligations' (1997) 19 *Sydney Law Review* 32–64 and 'Reliance and Expectation in Estoppel Remedies' (1998) 18 *Legal Studies* 360–68

Estoppel is a civil wrong protecting reliance. Those cases in which an award seemingly goes beyond reliance damages are explicable on the basis that, even on the reliance-based approach, in many cases the minimum equity required to do justice will still fulfil the promisee's expectations.

Elizabeth Cooke, 'Estoppel and the Protection of Expectations' (1997) 17 *Legal Studies* 258–85 and *The Modern Law of Estoppel* (Oxford, Oxford University Press, 2000)

The primary function of the law of estoppel is to protect expectations and the Australian reliance-based approach should be rejected.

Roger Halson, 'The Offensive Limits of Promissory Estoppel' [1999] *Lloyd's Maritime and Commercial Law Quarterly* 256–77

Promissory estoppel should not create a cause of action, and its role in the modification of contracts and its distinction from estoppel by convention and proprietary estoppel should be maintained.

Michael Spence, 'Australian Estoppel and the Protection of Reliance' (1997) 11 *Journal of Contract Law* 203–21 and *Protecting Reliance: The Emergent Doctrine of Equitable Estoppel* (Oxford, Hart Publishing, 1999)

The Australian developments of an estoppel cause of action since *Walton Stores v Maher* are best seen as recognition of a tort-like obligation to make good losses resulting from induced assumptions.

James Edelman, 'Remedial Certainty or Remedial Discretion after Giumelli?' (1999) 15 *Journal of Contract Law* 179–99

Estoppel is about enforcing promises and its remedies (expectation damages and specific relief) should reflect this.

Donal Nolan, 'Following in the Their Footsteps: Equitable Estoppel in Australia and the United States' (2000) 11 *King's College Law Journal* 201–23

Stephen A Smith, '"The Reliance Interest in Contract Damages" and the Morality of Contract Law' in *Issues in Legal Scholarship, Symposium: Fuller and Perdue* (Berkeley, CA, Berkeley Electronic Press, 2001) art 1, 1–38

John Cartwright, 'Formality and Informality in Property and Contract' in Joshua Getzler (ed), *Rationalizing Property, Equity and Trusts: Essays in honour of Edward Burn* (London, Lexis Nexis UK, 2003) 36–52

- Sean Wilken, *The Law of Waiver, Variation and Estoppel*, 2nd edn (Oxford, Oxford University Press, 2002)

Stephen Waddams, 'Reliance' in his *Dimensions of Private Law: Categories and Concepts in Anglo-American Legal Reasoning* (Cambridge, Cambridge University Press, 2003) 57–79

- KR Handley, *Estoppel by Conduct and Election* (London, Sweet & Maxwell, 2006)

Andrew Robertson, 'Estoppels and Rights-creating Events: Beyond Wrongs and Promises' in Jason W Neyers, Richard Bronaugh and Stephen GA Pitel (eds), *Exploring Contract Law* (Oxford, Hart Publishing, 2009) 199–224

Estoppel is about the obligation not to cause harm through inconsistent conduct.

15

PROCEDURE, LITIGATION AND DRAFTING

15.1 LIMITATION

J Beatson, 'Limitation Periods and Specific Performance' in EZ Lomnicka and CJG Morse (eds), *Contemporary Issues in Commercial Law: Essays in Honour of AG Guest* (London, Sweet & Maxwell, 1997) 9–23

○ David W Oughton, John P Lowry and Robert M Merkin, *Limitation of Actions* (London, LLP, 1998) chs 8–17

Law Commission, *Consultation Paper 151: Limitation of Actions* (1998) and *Report 270: Limitation of Actions* (2001)

Contractual limitation should be governed by the same rules as most other actions: there should be a three-year limitation period from the date of knowledge, with a ten-year longstop.

○ Andrew McGee, *Limitation Periods,* 5th edn (London, Sweet & Maxwell, 2006 plus supplements) ch 10

15.2 CONTRIBUTION

Ernest J Weinrib, 'Contribution in a Contractual Setting' (1976) 54 *Canadian Bar Review* 338–50

Contribution should generally be available in a contractual setting.

Daniel J Bussel, 'Liability for Concurrent Breach of Contract' (1995) 73 *Washington University Law Quarterly* 97–143

PG Turner, 'Death of the "Rule" in Merryweather v Nixan' (2002) 18 *Journal of Contract Law* 196–223

○ Charles Mitchell, *The Law of Contribution and Reimbursement* (Oxford, Oxford University Press, 2003) chs 2B, 8B and 10B

15.3 DRAFTING

- Richard Christou, *Drafting Commercial Agreements*, 3rd edn (London, Sweet & Maxwell, 2004)

Marcel Fontaine and Filip De Ley, *Drafting International Contracts: An Analysis of Contract Clauses* (Ardsley, NY, Transnational Publishers, 2005)

- Mark Anderson and Victor Warner, *Drafting and Negotiating Commercial Contracts*, 2nd edn (Tottel, 2007)
- Deborah Fosbrook and Adrian C Laing, *The A–Z of Contract Clauses*, 4th edn (London, Sweet & Maxwell, 2007)

Richard Christou, *Boilerplate: Practical Clauses*, 5th edn (London, Sweet & Maxwell, 2009)

16

CONTRACT THEORY

16.1 GENERAL TEXTS

Jody S Kraus, 'Philosophy of Contract Law' in Jules Coleman and Scott J Shapiro (eds), *The Oxford Handbook of Jurisprudence and Philosophy of Law* (Oxford, Oxford University Press, 2002) 687–751

Eric A Posner, 'Contract Theory' in Martin Golding and William Edmunson (eds), *The Blackwell Guide to the Philosophy of Law and Legal Theory* (Oxford, Blackwell, 2005) 138–47

○ Stephen A Smith, *Contract Theory* (Oxford, Oxford University Press, 2004)

16.2 ABOUT THEORISING

KN Llewellyn, 'The Rule of Law in Our Case-law of Contract' (1939) 47 *Yale Law Journal* 1243–71

Contract law is the cases and not principles.

Jay M Feinman, 'The Significance of Contract Theory' (1990) 58 *University of Cincinnati Law Review* 1283–318

Melvin Eisenberg, 'The Theory of Contracts' in Peter Benson (ed), *The Theory of Contract Law: New Essays* (Cambridge, Cambridge University Press, 2001) 86–117

The theory of contracts can be descriptive or prescriptive, and either metric (about variables to be applied in the rules of law) or generative (about the method for generating rules of law), containing either doctrinal or social propositions, and can be axiomatic, deductive, interpretive or normative. Axiomatic and deductive theories cannot be sustained, interpretative theories are useful but inadequate in contract theorising, and normative theories should be pursued. The author then puts forward a multi-value generative theory of contract law, in preference to metric theories relying only on the moral value of autonomy or welfare value of giving effect to revealed preferences.

Andrew Tettenborn, 'From Chaos to Cosmos—Or Is it Confusion?' [2002] 2 *Web Journal of Current Legal Issues*

Warnings to those tempted to generalise principles of English obligations law, discussing among other examples unconscionability and frustration of contracts.

16.3 THEORIES

Promissory and Will Theories

Lon L Fuller, 'Consideration and Form' (1941) 41 *Columbia Law Review* 799–824; Duncan Kennedy, 'From the Will Theory to the Principle of Private Autonomy: Lon Fuller's "Consideration and Form"' (2000) 100 *Columbia Law Review* 94–175

Roscoe Pound, 'The Role of the Will in Law' (1954) 68 *Harvard Law Review* 1–19; Roscoe Pound, 'Promise or Bargain?' (1959) 33 *Tulane Law Review* 455–72

Joseph Raz, 'Promises and Obligations' in PMS Hacker and J Raz (eds), *Law, Morality, and Society: Essays in Honour of HLA Hart* (Oxford, Clarendon Press, 1977) 210–28

Charles Fried, *Contract as Promise: A Theory of Contractual Obligations* (Cambridge, MA, Harvard University Press, 1981); PS Atiyah, 'Review of Fried, Contract as Promise' (1981) 95 *Harvard Law Review* 509–28, a later version of which appears as 'Essay 6: The Liberal Theory of Contract' in his *Essays on Contract,* revised edn (Oxford, Clarendon Press, 1990) 121–49.

In this seminal work, Fried defends the classical will theory of contract law, providing a justificatory account of the law of contract as based upon the enforcement of promises intended by the parties, although qualified by external principles of fairness (such as duress), which principles are brought in to supplement the parties' promises where those promises have gaps. Atiyah subjects the liberal and classical theories of contract in general, and Fried's theory in particular, to root and branch criticism on both normative and descriptive grounds.

Joseph Raz, 'Promises in Morality and Law' (1982) 95 *Harvard Law Review* 916–38

Contract law should aim not to enforce promises per se but to protect the practice of undertaking voluntary obligations (obligations requiring and being justified by voluntariness), of which promises are an extreme form. Such protection requires compensation and prevention of erosion, and requires that people be held to what they appear to have promised. Implied terms are the normative consequences of the contract arising from the moral practices in which the contract is embedded.

PS Atiyah, *Promises, Morals and Law* (Oxford, Clarendon Press,

1982); Joseph Raz, 'Promises in Morality and Law' (1982) 95 *Harvard Law Review* 916–38

Atiyah puts forward the view that promising is a form of consent and does not create obligations but rather usually amounts to conclusive admissions of previous/external moral obligations. Raz criticises this view as internally inconsistent and unable to explain the binding force of promises.

AS Burrows, 'The Will Theory of Contract Revived—Fried's "Contract as Promise"' (1985) 38 *Current Legal Problems* 141–51

FH Buckley, 'Paradox Lost' (1988) 77 *Minnesota Law Review* 775–827 also in Larry Alexander (ed), *Contract Law Volume I* (1991, Aldershot, Dartmouth) 57–109

Brian Coote, 'The Essence of Contract Parts 1 and 2' (1988–9) 1 *Journal of Contract Law* 91–112 and 183–204

After surveying contract theories, it is concluded that the essence of contract is the assumption not merely of obligation but of legal obligation (by a means recognised by law).

Samuel Stoljar, 'Keeping Promises: The Moral and Legal Obligation' (1988) 8 *Legal Studies* 258–76

Steve Hedley, 'Contracts as Promises' (1993) 44 *Northern Ireland Legal Quarterly* 12–33

The modern orthodox view is back-to-front in holding that standard form contracts are agreed but statutory implied terms are imposed in opposition to promises.

Thomas Scanlon, 'Promises and Practices' (1990) 19 *Philosophy and Public Affairs* 199–226 and 'Promises and Contracts', in Peter Benson (ed), *The Theory of Contract Law: New Essays* (Cambridge, Cambridge University Press, 2001) 86–117

The morality of promises does not depend upon a social practice of promising but rather upon wrongs that arise out of engendering expectations, and only where promises are voluntary (because of the value choice).

Melvin Eisenberg, 'The Limits of Cognition and the Limits of Contract' (1995) 47 *Stanford Law Review* 211–59 also in Brian Bix (ed), *Contract Law: Second Series: Volume I* (Aldershot, Ashgate, 2000) 51–99

Cognitive limits, namely limits on rationality, dispositions such as optimism, and defective capability, justify the rules on liquidated damages and the approach to certain types of contracts (such as form contracts).

JE Penner, 'Voluntary Obligations and the Scope of the Law of Contract' (1996) 2 *Legal Theory* 325–57

Developing Raz's argument, of all voluntary undertakings, it is particularly (bilateral) agreements and not (unilateral) promises that underline contract law, and particularly bargain agreements rather than mutual agreements. Not all voluntary undertakings should be treated the same, and it may be that contract law should not concern itself with covenants (unilateral) and unincorporated associations or common intention constructive trusts (mutual agreements not bargains).

Anne de Moor, 'Are Contracts Promises?' in John Eekelar and John Bell (eds), *Oxford Essays in Jurisprudence: Third Series* (Oxford, Clarendon Press, 1997) 102–24

EA Farnsworth, *Changing Your Mind: The Law of Regretted Decisions* (New Haven, CT, Yale University Press, 1998)

An investigation of promises and their breach in the context of commitments and regrets generally.

Gillian K Hadfield, 'An Expressive Theory of Contract: From Feminist Dilemmas to a Reconceptualization of Rational Choice in Contract Law' (1998) 146 *University of Pennsylvania Law Review* 1235–86

Promising is sometimes done expressively as an articulation of present values, rather than instrumentally as a commitment to a future position. Refusing to enforce agreements in such cases (such as surrogacy agreements) is not, thus, a denial of the promisor's autonomy but rather a recognition that enforcement is not justified as there has been no commitment to the future (promised) position.

Hanoch Sheinman, 'Contractual Liability and Voluntary Undertakings' (2000) 20 *Oxford Journal of Legal Studies* 205–22

Whilst contracts are not always voluntarily undertaken, and their content is not always voluntarily selected, they are enforced (even when not intended to be voluntary undertakings, through the objective test) in order to uphold the practice of voluntary undertakings, which requires that legitimate expectations arising from credible misrepresentations (as well as representations) of voluntary undertaking be protected.

Dori Kimel, *From Promise to Contract: Towards a Liberal Theory of Contract* (Oxford, Hart Publishing, 2003) chs 1–3; Hanoch Sheinman, 'Are Normal Contracts Normal Promises?' [2004] 24 *Oxford Journal of Legal Studies* 517–37; Curtis Bridgeman, 'Liberalism and Freedom from the Promise Theory of Contract' (2004) 67 *Modern Law Review* 684–99

Kimel seeks to distinguish contracts from promises, arguing that while the latter facilitate personal relations through trust and respect, the former facilitate co-operation without the need for personal relations, and thus undermine personal relations, trivialise trust and facilitate personal detachment, essentially replacing promises. Sheinman criticises Kimel on the grounds that he is wrong that promises are about facilitating personal relations, since many take place in the market transaction context. Further, argues Sheinman, contracts may provide good opportunities for personal relations and may facilitate personal relations that otherwise would not have taken place. Bridgeman criticises the type of liberalism that Kimel uses to justify contract law, arguing that Rawlsian rights-based liberalism cannot justify forcing the particular morality of promising on everybody and that only a slightly more limited scope of contracting can be justified.

Andrew Robertson, 'The Limits of Voluntariness in Contract' (2005) 29 *Melbourne University Law Review* 179–217

Where, as is often the case, the decision not to read a standard form contract is not voluntary, the unread obligations are not voluntarily assumed. Similarly, developing the views of Barnett, default rules are often not voluntarily assumed because the costs of discovering the rules and the difficulty of avoiding them rob the silence of its ability to signal unambiguous assent to the rules.

Seana Valentine Shiffrin, 'The Divergence of Contract and Promise' (2007) 120 *Harvard Law Review* 708–53

Corrective Justice

See also Corrective Justice in 13.6

Jules L Coleman, *Risks and Wrongs* (Cambridge, Cambridge University Press, 1992)

E Weinrib, *The Idea of Private Law* (Cambridge, MA, Harvard University Press, 1995)

Distributive Justice

Anthony T Kronman, 'Contract Law and Distributive Justice' (1980) 89 *Yale Law Journal* 472–511 and 'A New Champion for the Will Theory: Review of Charles Fried, *Contract as Promise*' (1981) 91 *Yale Law Journal* 404–23

Kronman argues that the regulation of private transactions is (in addition to taxation) a legitimate means for redistribution of wealth, and various rules rendering advantage-taking impermissible (such as rules of duress) should be designed and evaluated with distributive justice in mind.

James Gordley, 'Equality in Exchange' (1981) 69 *California Law Review* 1587–676 also in Larry Alexander (ed), *Contract Law Volume II* (1991, Aldershot, Dartmouth) 3–72 and 'Contract Law in the Aristotelian Tradition' in Peter Benson (ed), *The Theory of Contract Law: New Essays* (Cambridge, Cambridge University Press, 2001) 265–334

Duncan Kennedy, 'Distributive and Paternalist Motives in Contract and Tort Law, with Special Reference to Compulsory Terms and Unequal Bargaining Power' (1982) 41 *Maryland Law Review* 563–658 also in Larry Alexander (ed), *Contract Law Volume II* (1991, Aldershot, Dartmouth) 471–566

Anthony T Kronman, 'Paternalism and the Law of Contracts' (1983) 92 *Yale Law Journal* 763–98 also in Larry Alexander (ed), *Contract Law Volume II* (1991, Aldershot, Dartmouth) 567–602

Paternalistic rules (illegality, mandatory consumer terms, incapacity, etc) are based upon at least three different principles of paternalism: economic efficiency and distributive justice, the protection of personal integrity, and protection in cases of defect of judgment and moral imagination

Peter Benson, 'Abstract Right and the Possibility of a Nondistributive Conception of Contract: Hegel and Contemporary Contract Theory' (1989) 10 *Cardozo Law Review* 1077–198

Larry Alexander and William Wang, 'Natural Advantages and Contractual Justice' (1984) 3 *Law and Philosophy* 281–97 also in Larry Alexander (ed), *Contract Law Volume II* (1991, Aldershot, Dartmouth) 453–69

WNR Lucy, 'Contract as a Mechanism of Distributive Justice' (1989) 9 *Oxford Journal of Legal Studies* 132–47

Contract should not be used for distributive justice in preference to taxation.

Megan Richardson, 'Contract Law and Distributive Justice Revisited' (1990) 10 *Legal Studies* 258–70

Hugh Collins, 'Distributive Justice Through Contracts' (1992) 45 *Current Legal Problems* 49–67

Martín Hevia, 'Kronman on Contract Law and Distributive Justice' (2007) 23 *Journal of Contract Law* 105–19

Consent and Transfer Theories

Randy E Barnett, 'A Consent Theory of Contract' (1986) 86 *Columbia Law Review* 269–21, also in Larry Alexander (ed), *Contract Law: Volume I* (Aldershot, Dartmouth, 1991) 3–55, and 'Rights and Remedies in a Consent Theory of Contract' in RG Frey and Christopher W Morris (eds), *Liability and Responsibility* (Cambridge, Cambridge University Press, 1991) 135–72 (a revised version of the 1986 and 1988 pieces)

[1986] Both will- and reliance-based theories fail to explain the interrelational quality of contracting and standards-based theories (efficiency, fairness) also cannot explain why contracts should be enforced. [1986, 1991] Contracts are based upon consent, defined as a manifested intention to alienate rights/transfer entitlements; contract liability stems from the wrongful interference with a valid rights transfer. A consent theory (and its requirement that intention be manifested) explains the objective approach to contract and the limits of that approach. Consent can be evidenced by a bargain or silence in the face of reliance, but they are not necessary. Contract defences describe situations in which the manifestation of consent is robbed of its normal moral significance because obtained improperly (duress, misrepresentation), obtained from one lacking in ability to assert meaningful consent (incapacity), or voluntary but failing to govern all contingencies (mistake, frustration).

Richard A Epstein, 'Inducement of Breach of Contract as a Problem of Ostensible Ownership' (1987) 16 *Journal of Legal Studies* 1–42

Randy E Barnett, 'Some Problems with Contract as Promise' (1992) 77 *Cornell Law Review* 1022–33

Peter Benson, 'The Idea of a Public Basis of Justification for Contract' (1995) 33 *Osgoode Hall Law Journal* 273–336, 'Contract Law' in Dennis Patterson, *A Companion to the Philosophy of Law and Legal Theory* (Oxford, Blackwell, 1996), 'The Unity of Contract Law' in his, as ed, *The Theory of Contract Law: New Essays* (Cambridge, Cambridge University Press, 2001) 118–205 and 'Contract as a Transfer of Ownership' (2007) 48 *William and Mary Law Review* 1673–731

[1995 and 1996] After criticising other theories of contract law, the author concludes that a justification of contract law should be public, ie consider contracts and people in the light of norms present in the public legal culture. Such a public justification builds on the normative principle of no liability for nonfeasance, the conception of a person and the idea of a transaction, and involves the transfer of possession of (a personal right to) performance. [2001 and 2007] The mutual assent of the parties transfers ownership in contract rights (which are personal rights, and a different type of ownership right to property rights), ie the exclusive authority to exercise control over the object or service promised.

Fred S McChesney, 'Tortious Interference with Contract versus "Efficient" Breach: Theory and Empirical Evidence' (1999) 28 *Journal of Legal Studies* 131–86

Stephen A Smith, 'Towards a Theory of Contract' in Jeremy Horder (ed), *Oxford Essays in Jurisprudence: Fourth Series* (Oxford, Oxford University Press, 2000) 106–29 and '"The Reliance Interest in Contract Damages" and the Morality of Contract Law' in *Issues in Legal Scholarship, Symposium: Fuller and Perdue* (Berkeley, CA, Berkeley Electronic Press, 2001) art 1, 1–38

[2000, 2001] Although not vulnerable to the harm-principle objection in the way that promissory theories are, the transfer theory does not explain contractual obligations because it is susceptible to the conceptual objection that in the contractual situation there is no pre-existing right to performance that can be transferred upon contracting. Contracts create new rights, and so the best theory to explain such rights may well resemble the intention-based theories that explain the creation of property rights (rather than theories of tortious obligations). [2001] It may be that the power of contracts to create new rights that give exclusionary reasons for action is explicable by the intrinsic (rather than instrumental) justification that contracts create special relationships. The transfer theory may, however, offer the best explanation of so-called contracts of simultaneous exchange. Here, transfer is not creating contractual obligations but rather acts as a free-standing legal category on the same level as tort, contract and property, and may include much that is currently found within property and unjust enrichment law.

Ralph Cunnington, 'Contract Rights as Property Rights' in Andrew Robertson (ed), *The Law of Obligations: Connections and Boundaries* (London, UCL Press, 2004) 169–95

A Gold, 'A Property Theory of Contract' (2009) 103 *Northwestern University Law Review* 1–62

The Death of (Classical) Contract

Grant Gilmore, *The Death of Contract*, 2nd edn (Columbus, OH, Ohio State University Press, 1974); Richard E Speidel, 'An Essay on the Reported Death and Continued Vitality of Contract' (1975) 27 *Stanford Law Review* 1161–83; JC Smith, 'The Law of Contract—Alive or Dead?' (1979) 13 *The Law Teacher* 73–82; Kerry L Macintosh, 'Gilmore Spoke Too Soon: Contract Rises from the Ashes of the Bad Faith Tort' (1994) 27 *Loyola of Los Angeles Law Review* 483–540; Symposium: Reconsidering Grant Gilmore's Death of Contract (1995) 90 *Northwestern University Law Review* 1–266; Richard Austen-Baker, 'Gilmore and the Strange Case of the Failure of Contract to Die After All' (2002) 18 *Journal of Contract Law* 1–31

Gilmore famously reports the death of contract (at the hands of tort law). Various authors criticise Gilmore's work and conclusions.

Robert A Hillman, 'The Crisis in Modern Contract Theory' (1988) 67 *Texas Law Review* 103–36

David Campbell, 'The Undeath of Contract: A Study in the Degeneration of a Research Programme' (1992) 22 *Hong Kong Law Journal* 20–47

Donal Nolan, 'The Classical Legacy and Modern English Contract Law' (1996) 59 *Modern Law Review* 603–19

Whilst classical contract law lives on in commercial contract law, a post-classical model is now applicable in consumer contract law.

Holmes

See also The Duty to Perform and the Theory of Efficient Breach in 13.6

Malcolm Sharp, 'Mr Justice Holmes: Contracts' (1964) 31 *University of Chicago Law Review* 268–78

Patrick J Kelley, 'A Critical Analysis of Holmes's Theory of Contract' (2000) 75 *Notre Dame Law Review* 1681–773

Oliver Wendell Holmes Junior's theory of contract in its historical context, concluding that Holmes's theory is flawed because of its positivist character.

PS Atiyah, 'Essay 3: Holmes and the Theory of Contract' in his *Essays on Contract* (Oxford, Clarendon Press, 1990) 57–72

Reliance Theories

See also Damages Measured by Reliance/Wasted Expenditure in 13.2

Lon L Fuller and William R Perdue Jr, 'The Reliance Interest in Contract Damages (Parts 1 & 2)' (1936–37) 46 *Yale Law Journal* 52–96, 373–420 also in Larry Alexander (ed), *Contract Law: Volume II* (Aldershot, Dartmouth, 1991) 211–55 and in *Issues in Legal Scholarship, Symposium: Fuller and Perdue* (Berkeley, CA, Berkeley Electronic Press, 2001)

A hugely influential article arguing that contract law is about the protection of the 'reliance interest'.

PS Atiyah, 'Contracts, Promises and the Law of Obligations' (1978) 94 *Law Quarterly Review* 193–223 also in Larry Alexander (ed), *Contract Law Volume I* (1991, Aldershot, Dartmouth) 291–321 and, with an added reply to critics, as 'Essay 2' in PS Atiyah, *Essays on Contract,* revised edn (Oxford, Clarendon Press, 1990) 10–56

The author's characteristic theory criticising classical contract law's unrealistic paradigm of the executory commercial contract entered into by voluntary agreements. Executory promises have little claim to binding legal obligation, and contract law obligations are created by reliance and payment in situations characteristic of obligation, with promises playing a role anterior to the creation of the obligation, the promise serving as evidence of the fairness of the obligation. Further, professed divisions between tort, contract and restitution are largely illusory and of only pedagogic value.

PS Atiyah, 'Fuller and the Theory of Contract' [1983] *Duke Law Journal* 669–94, a later version of which appears as 'Essay 4' in his *Essays on Contract*, revised edn (Oxford, Clarendon Press, 1990) 73–92

Robert Birmingham, 'Notes on the Reliance Interest' (1985) 60 *Washington Law Review* 217–65

Samuel Stoljar, 'Promise, Expectation and Agreement' [1988] *Cambridge Law Journal* 193–212

Randy E Barnett, 'The Death of Reliance' (1996) 46 *Journal of Legal Education* 518–36

The new orthodoxy (primarily under the US Second Restatement) accepts that even under promissory estoppel, promises are not in fact being enforced to protect detrimental reliance.

David W Barnes, 'The Net Expectation Interest in Contract Damages' (1999) 48 *Emory Law Journal* 1143–208

Stephen A Smith, '"The Reliance Interest in Contract Damages" and the Morality of Contract Law' in *Issues in Legal Scholarship, Symposium: Fuller and Perdue* (Berkeley, CA, Berkeley Electronic Press, 2001) art 1, 1–38

The reliance theory of contract cannot dispose of the idea of promises as without the concept of the promise it would not be reasonable to rely on a party not changing his mind. Reliance-based liability cannot explain why judges speak of a duty to perform and sometimes award specific performance, but it might justify an anterior obligation to compensate if one does not do what one said one would do. Reliance theory has difficulties explaining the law of offer and acceptance, but it is possible that an accepted promise might be a practical proxy for reliance-inducing statements (which, as a category, is much broader than contract). If it is legitimate to protect reliance, the reliance theory is not a theory of contract. Rather reliance-based liability, and the wrong of inducing reliance then failing to compensate, is a separate category sits somewhere between contract and tort.

Economic Theories and the Economics of Contracts

RH Coase, 'The Problem of Social Cost' (1960) 3 *Journal of Law & Economics* 1–69

The Coase Theorem: If there are no transaction costs, negotiations will always lead to efficient resource allocation.

S Todd Lowry, 'Bargain and Contract Theory in Law and Economics' (1976) 10 *Journal of Economic Issues* 1–22

Anthony Kronman and Richard Posner, *Economics of Contract Law* (Boston, MA, Little Brown, 1979)

Extracts from leading articles on the economics of contract law.

Oliver E Williamson, 'Transaction-Cost Economics: The Governance of Contractual Relations' (1979) 22 *Journal of Law & Economics* 233–62

Charles J Goetz and Robert E Scott, 'Enforcing Promises: An Examination of the Basis of Contract' (1980) 89 *Yale Law Journal* 1261–322 also in Larry Alexander (ed), *Contract Law: Volume I* (Aldershot, Dartmouth, 1991) 111–72

From the point of view of maximising the net beneficial reliance derived from the promise, the law as it stands (in terms of which promises it enforces and which promises it doesn't) is largely justifiable if expectation damages are viewed as a proxy for the reliance measure.

Duncan Kennedy and Frank Michelman, 'Are Property and Contract Efficient?' (1980) 8 *Hofstra Law Review* 711–70

LG Telser, 'A Theory of Self-Enforcing Contracts' (1980) 53 *Journal of Business* 27–44

PS Atiyah, 'The Theoretical Basis of Contract Law-An English Perspective' (1981) 1 *International Review of Law and Economics* 183–205, a later version of which appears as 'Essay 7' in his *Essays on Contract,* revised edn (Oxford, Clarendon Press, 1990) 150–78

FH Buckley, 'Paradox Lost' (1988) 72 *Minnesota Law Review* 775–827 also in Larry Alexander (ed), *Contract Law: Volume I* (Aldershot, Dartmouth, 1991) 57–109

A utilitarian theory of promising.

Daniel A Farber, 'Contract Law and Modern Economic Theory' (1983) 78 *Northwestern University Law Review* 303–39 also in Larry Alexander (ed), *Contract Law: Volume I* (Aldershot, Dartmouth, 1991) 173–209

The implications of major economic theories for contract law.

Richard Craswell, 'Efficiency and Rational Bargaining in Contractual Settings' (1992) 15 *Harvard Journal of Law & Public Policy* 805–38

Michael J Trebilcock, *The Limits of Freedom of Contract* (Cambridge, MA, Harvard University Press, 1993)

Richard Craswell, 'Two Economic Theories of Enforcing Promises' in Peter Benson (ed), *The Theory of Contract Law: New Essays* (Cambridge, Cambridge University Press, 2001) 19–44

Distinguishing economic theories treating enforcement as equivalent to performance and those treating enforcement as altering incentives.

David D Friedman, *Law's Order: What Economics Has to do with Law and Why it Matters* (Princeton, NJ, Princeton University Press, 2001) 145–70

EA Posner, 'Economic Analysis of Contract Law After Three Decades: Success or Failure?' (2003) 112 *Yale Law Journal* 829–80; Richard Craswell, 'In That Case, What is the Question? Economic Theory and the Demands of Contract Theory' (2003) 112 *Yale Law Journal* 903–24

Posner surveys economic analyses of contract law and concludes that they have largely failed (either through oversimplicity or lack of empirical grounding) to explain contract law rules, to predict contracting behaviour and to make clear normative recommendations for legal rules. Craswell argues that economic analysis is successful by more modestly but realistically making partial normative evaluations and recommendations as to incentives provided by particular rules in particular situations.

Alan Schwartz and Robert E Scott, 'Contract Theory and the Limits of Contract Law' (2003) 113 *Yale Law Journal* 541–620

Contract law, when applied to commercial contracts, should aim only for efficiency. This leads to the prescription of a narrow textualist theory of contract interpretation, except where the parties so request; the removal of most of the currently existing default rules (which are out of touch with commercial parties' wants); and the removal of most mandatory rules (which are grounded in paternalism and thus have no place in commercial contract law).

○ Richard Posner, *Economic Analysis of Law*, 7th edn (Chicago, Wolters Kluwer, 2007) ch 4

Scandinavian Legal Realism

Jan Hellner, 'Scandinavian Legal Realism in the Law of Contract' in Peter Cane and Jane Stapleton (eds), *Essays for Patrick Atiyah* (Oxford, Clarendon Press, 1991) 53–70

Welfarism, Critical Legal Studies and the Limits of Freedom of Contract

Samuel Williston, 'Freedom of Contract' (1921) 6 *Cornell Law Quarterly* 365–80

Arthur Lenhoff, 'The Scope of Compulsory Contracts Proper' (1943) 43 *Columbia Law Review* 586–602

Duncan Kennedy, 'Form & Substance in Private Law Adjudication' (1976) 89 *Harvard Law Review* 1685–778

In private law adjudication, form (rigid rules or open-textured standards) cannot be separated from substantive objectives, because individualism leads to the rigid application of rules, whereas altruism leads to the application of standards of administration.

James Gordley, 'Equality in Exchange' (1981) 69 *California Law Review* 1587–656 also in Larry Alexander (ed), *Contract Law: Volume II* (Aldershot, Dartmouth, 1991) 3–72

Barry J Reiter, 'The Control of Contract Power' (1981) 1 *Oxford Journal of Legal Studies* 347–74

The free market and private contracting power historically have not (despite what classical contract theorists say) been, and should not be, free from fetters imposed by statute and, importantly, by the judiciary.

Melvin Aron Eisenberg, 'The Bargain Principle and Its Limits' (1982) 95 *Harvard Law Review* 741–801 also in Larry Alexander (ed), *Contract Law: Volume I* (Aldershot, Dartmouth, 1991) 323–83

The paradigm understanding of unconscionability needs to be shifted from unfair surprise (procedural unfairness) to substantive unfairness. Where there is not a perfectly competitive market, the bargain should not be enforced to its full *extent* (and such enforcement would not be efficient).

Jay M Feinman, 'Critical Approaches to Contract Law' (1983) 30 *UCLA Law Review* 829–60

Contract law is contradictory and artificial.

Roberto Mangabeira Unger, 'The Critical Legal Studies Movement' (1983) 96 *Harvard Law Review* 561–675

In part IVB of this article the author applies critical legal studies to contract law, arguing that contract law is best understood as the product of tensions between two pairs of principles and counter-principles, namely: freedom to contract (principle) and community (counter-principle), and freedom of contract terms (principle) and fairness (counter-principle).

Clare Dalton, 'An Essay in the Deconstruction of Contract Doctrine' (1985) 94 *Yale Law Journal* 997–1114, also as 'Deconstructing contract doctrine' in Katherine T Bartlett and Rosanne Kennedy (eds), *Feminist legal theory: readings in law and gender* (Oxford, Westview Press, 1991) 287–304

Alan Schwartz, 'Justice and the Law of Contract: A Case for the Traditional Approach' (1986) 9 *Harvard Journal of Law & Public Policy* 107–16

John Adams and Roger Brownsword, 'The Ideologies of Contract Law' (1987) 7 *Legal Studies* 205–23

Contract law doctrines and cases are the fruits of a clash of market-individualist and consumer-welfarist ideologies, as applied by formalist or realist judges.

Patrick Atiyah, 'Contract and Fair Exchange' (1985) 35 *University of Toronto Law Journal* 1–24, a later version of which appears in his *Essays on Contract*, revised edn (Oxford, Clarendon Press, 1990) 329–54

Jean Braucher, 'Contract versus Contractarianism: The Regulatory Role of Contract Law' (1990) 47 *Washington and Lee Law Review* 697–739 also in Brian Bix (ed), *Contract Law: Second Series: Volume I* (Aldershot, Ashgate, 2000) 193–235

FH Buckley, 'Three Theories of Substantive Fairness' (1990) 19 *Hofstra Law Review* 33–66

Sylviane Colombo, 'Good Faith: The Law and Morality' [1993] *Denning Law Journal* 23–59

The law should guard against over-adherence to a free-market individualist ideology, and there should be a stronger role for good faith in contract law to correct inequalities.

Hugh Collins, 'The Transformation Thesis and the Ascription of Contractual Liability' in Thomas Wilhelmsson (ed), *Perspectives of Critical Contract Law* (Aldershot, Dartmouth, 1993) 293–310

Eric A Posner, 'Contract Law in the Welfare State: A Defense of the Unconscionability Doctrine, Usury Laws, and Related Limitations on the Freedom to Contract' (1995) 24 *Journal of Legal Studies* 283–320

Unconscionability and usury laws are efficient because they deter excessive credit risks which are inefficient and otherwise encouraged by the provision of welfare.

Stephen A Smith, 'In Defence of Substantive Unfairness' (1996) 112 *Law Quarterly Review* 138–58 and 'Future Freedom and Freedom of Contract' (1995) 59 *Modern Law Review* 167–87

[1995] As contract is a facility, the law should not provide the power to exercise autonomy by making contracts when such contracts themselves unduly limit autonomy, unless the contracter's self-interest provides a sufficiently strong safeguard against the unnecessary abdication of future freedom. As a result, the law should not enforce self-enslavement contracts, unnecessary restrictive covenants, clauses stipulating that equitable relief will be available and stipulated damages clauses. [1996] Similarly, substantively unfair contracts should not be enforced because, in relevant cases, an abnormally high price thwarts the prediction of purchasing power and so is an obstacle to planning and thus the achievement of an autonomous life.

Hugh Collins, 'The Sanctimony of Contract' in Richard Rawlings (ed), *Law, Society, and Economy: Centenary Essays for the London School of Economics and Political Science, 1895–1995* (Oxford, Clarendon Press, 1997) 63–90

Blake D Morant, 'The Teachings of Dr. Martin Luther King, Jr and Contract Theory: An Intriguing Comparison' (1998) 50 *Alabama Law Review* 63–114

Larry A DiMatteo, 'Equity's Modification of Contract: an Analysis of the Twentieth Century's Equitable Reformation of Contract Law' (1999) 33 *New England Law Review* 265–357

R Bigwood, 'Conscience and the Liberal Conception of Contract: Observing Basic Distinctions—Parts I and II' (2000) 16 *Journal of Contract* Law 1–36 and 191–222; P Watts, 'The Role of Conscience—A Commentary on "Conscience and the Liberal Conception of Contract"' (2000) 16 *Journal of Contract Law* 223–27

Andrew Phang, 'Security of Contract and the Pursuit of Fairness' (2000) 16 *Journal of Contract Law* 158–89

Duncan Kennedy, 'The Political Stakes in "Merely Technical" Issues of Contract Law' (2001) 1 *European Review of Private Law* 7–28

Dori Kimel, *From Promise to Contract: Towards a Liberal Theory of Contract* (Oxford, Hart Publishing, 2003) ch 5, a later version of which appears as 'Neutrality, Autonomy, and Freedom of Contract' (2001) 21 *Oxford Journal of Legal Studies* 473–94

Liberalism does not require as extreme a conception of freedom of contract as is usually supposed.

William C Whitford, 'A Comparison of British and American Attitudes Towards the Exercise of Judicial Discretion in Contract Law' in David Campbell, Hugh Collins and John Wightman, *Implicit Dimensions of Contract* (Oxford, Hart Publishing, 2003) 187–205

Roger Brownsword, *Contract Law: Themes for the Twenty-first Century*, 2nd edn (Oxford, Oxford University Press, 2006)

Relational Theories and Long-term Contracts

Ian R Macneil, 'The Many Futures of Contracts' (1974) 47 *Southern California Law Review* 691, 'Contracts: Adjustment of Long-term Economic Relations Under Classical. Neoclassical, and Relational Contract Law' (1978) 72 *Northwestern University Law Review* 854, *The New Social Contract: An Inquiry into Modern Contractual Relations* (1980), 'Economic Analysis of Contractual Relations: Its Shortfalls and the Need for a "Rich Classificatory Apparatus"' (1981) 75 *Northwestern University Law Review* 1018–63, 'Values in Contract: Internal and External' (1983) 78 *Northwestern University Law Review* 340–418 also in Larry Alexander (ed), *Contract Law Volume I* (1991, Aldershot, Dartmouth) 211–89, 'Barriers to the Idea of Relational Contracts' in F Nicklisch (ed), *The Complex Long-term Contract: Structures and International Arbitration* (Heidelberg, CF Müller, 1987) 31–46 and 'Relational Contract Theory: Challenges and Queries' (2000) 94 *Northwestern University Law Review* 877–908

The author's distinctive theory of contracting according to which contracts are embedded in complex relations and lie on a spectrum from contract relations to discrete transactions. Common contract norms apply to all contracts, whereas discrete and relational norms apply only to the extent that a contract is discrete and relational. Relational norms are geared towards the preservation and application of the relation itself.

Victor P Goldberg, 'Towards an Expanded Economic Theory of Contract' (1976) 10 *Journal of Economic Issues* 45–61

Charles J Goetz and Richard E Scott, 'Principles of Relational Contracts' (1981) 67 *Virginia Law Review* 1089–150

Steven NS Cheung, 'The Contractual Nature of the Firm' (1983) 26 *Journal of Law & Economics* 1–22

Clayton P Gillette, 'Commercial Rationality and the Duty to Adjust Long-term Contracts' (1985) 69 *Minnesota Law Review* 521–86

Although parties may not predict events, they can often rationally contract on the basis of such uncertainty and should be held to their agreement. The court should rarely allow adjustment.

Robert W Gordon, 'Macaulay, Macneil and the Discovery of Solidarity and Power in Contract Law' [1985] *Wisconsin Law Review* 565–80

B Yngvesson, 'Re-examining Continuing Relationships and the Law' [1985] *Wisconsin Law Review* 623–46

Hugh Collins, 'Contract and Legal Theory' in W Twining (ed), *Legal Theory and Common Law* (Oxford, Blackwell, 1986) 136–54

Robert E Scott, 'Conflict and Cooperation in Long-term Contracts' (1987) 75 *California Law Review* 2005–56

Vincent P Crawford, 'Long-term Relationships Governed by Short-term Contracts' (1988) 78 *American Economic Review* 485–99

David Campbell, 'The Social Theory of Relational Contract: Macneil as the Modern Proudhon' (1990) 18 *International Journal of the Sociology of Law* 75–95

Steven N Wiggins, 'The Comparative Advantage of Long-term Contracts and Firms' (1990) 6 *Journal of Law Economics and Organization* 155–70

Randy E Barnett, 'Conflicting Visions: A Critique of Ian Macneil's Relational Theory of Contract' (1992) 78 *Virginia Law Review* 1175–206

Macneil fails to appreciate the importance of contractual consent and the compatibility of consent with relational theory.

David Campbell and Donald Harris, 'Flexibility in Long-term Contracting: The Role of Cooperation' (1993) 20 *Journal of Law and Society* 166–91

Donald B King, 'Reshaping Contract Theory and Law: Death of Contracts II: Part One: Generalised Consent with Lawmade Obligations' (1994) 7 *Journal of Contract Law* 245–72 and 'Part Two: Ending Consideration and Beginning New Performance and Remedies' (1995) 8 *Journal of Contract Law* 16–36

Contracts are based on generalised but not specific consent, with many terms deriving from law-made or relationship-derived standards. Consideration can largely be abolished and there should be more emphasis on the relationship and its fairness.

David Campbell and Susan Clay, *Long-term Contracting: A Bibliography and Review of the Literature* (Oxford, Centre for Socio-legal Studies, 1995)

The first half of this work consists of a 40-page introduction/literature review in which Campbell presents a frank introduction to the field of long-term contracting, with critical discussion of comprehensively footnoted writings in that field. The second half of this work is a 40-page bibliography of the (pre-1995) writings in this field by lawyers, economists, management theorists and others.

Melvin A Eisenberg, 'Relational Contracts' in Jack Beatson and Daniel Friedmann (eds), *Good Faith and Fault in Contract Law* (Oxford, Clarendon Press, 1995) 291–304 and 'Why There Is

No Law of Relational Contract' (2000) 94 *Northwestern University Law Review* 805–22

There is no need for special rules or a law for relational contracts. Rather, as most or all contracts are relational (broadly conceived), the lessons of relational contract study should be learned by contract law as a whole.

Ewan McKendrick, 'The Regulation of Long-term Contracts in English Law' in Jack Beatson and Daniel Friedmann (eds), *Good Faith and Fault in Contract Law* (Oxford, Clarendon Press, 1995) 305–33

Jay M Feinman, 'Relational Contract Theory in Context' (2000) 94 *Northwestern University Law Review* 737–48

Robert E Scott, 'The Case for Formalism in Relational Contract' (2000) 94 *Northwestern University Law Review* 847–76

Matthew Lees, 'Contract, Conscience, Communitarian Conspiracies and Confucius: Normativism through the Looking Glass of Relational Contract Theory' (2001) 25 *Melbourne University Law Review* 82–121

Richard Austen-Baker, 'A Relational Law of Contract?' (2004) 20 *Journal of Contract Law* 125–44

Conventional contract law already gives effect to Macneil's contract norms

Dori Kimel, 'The Choice of Paradigm for Theory of Contract: Reflections on the Relational Model' (2007) 27 *Oxford Journal of Legal Studies* 233–55

Recent developments do not signal a shift to a relational paradigm for contract law, so much as an increase in the sophistication of the law's support for personal autonomy. Nor is it clear that further incorporation of relational norms into the law would support rather than undermine or inhibit the relations. Social relationships overlay and compete with the institutions of contract and promise and need not and should not be incorporated into those institutions.

Socio-legal and Empirical Analysis of Contracts

Stewart Macaulay, 'Non-contractual Relations in Business: A Preliminary Study' (1963) 28 *American Sociological Review* 55–67 also in Brian Bix (ed), *Contract Law: Second Series: Volume I* (Aldershot, Ashgate, 2000) 253–65

Empirical research into Wisconsin manufacturers and purchasing agents showed that businessmen often have minimal reliance upon law in planning, adjusting and enforcing their relationships and disputes, relying instead on non-legal sanctions, although there are useful purposes of drafted contracts (other than within contract law).

Stewart Macaulay, 'An Empirical View of Contract' [1985] *Wisconsin Law Review* 465–82

Hugh Beale and Tony Dugdale, 'Contracts between Businessmen: Planning and the Use of Contractual Remedies' (1975) 2 *British Journal of Law & Society* 45–60

On the basis of empirical research of engineering sellers and buyers, the authors concluded that lawyers, legal planning and legal remedies are often avoided by contracting parties, who prefer non-contractual negotiations and mechanisms, although specific legal planning may be employed on a particular issue if the risk justifies it.

James J White, 'Contract Law in Modern Commercial Transactions, An Artifact of Twentieth Century Business Life' (1982) 22 *Washburn Law Journal* 1–22

Peter Vincent-Jones, 'Contract and Business Transactions: A Socio-legal Analysis' (1989) 16 *Journal of Law and Society* 166–86

David Charny, 'Nonlegal Sanctions in Commercial Relationships' (1990) 104 *Harvard Law Review* 373–467

There are various forms of non-legal sanction (which include losses of opportunity, reputation and self-esteem) and in many situations they are likely to be preferred to legal sanctions by transacting parties. To enforce legally all non-legal commitments would be inefficient, would go against the parties' intentions and would stifle trust, but in certain situations (when the parties mistake the likelihood of breach or would want legal sanctions but cannot afford to draft the proper contract term) legal sanctions should be provided through promissory estoppel, implied terms or the duty of good faith.

David Campbell, 'Socio-legal Analysis of the Law of Contract' in PA Thomas (ed) *Socio-legal Studies* (Aldershot, Dartmouth Publishing, 1997) 239–78

Marrianne M Jennings, 'The True Meaning of Relational Contracts: We Don't Care About the Mailbox Rule, Mirror Images, or Consideration Anymore—Are We Safe?' (1995) 73 *Denver University Law Review* 3–22

Russell B Korobkin, 'Empirical Scholarship in Contract Law: Possibilities and Pitfalls' (2002) *University of Illinois Law Review* 1033–66

Discussion and a bibliography of (US) empirical contract scholarship.

Dori Kimel, *From Promise to Contract: Towards a Liberal Theory of Contract* (Oxford, Hart Publishing, 2003)

Mark C Suchman, 'The Contract as Social Artifact' (2003) 37 *Law and Society Review* 91–142

○ Hugh Collins, *Law of Contract: Law in Context*, 4th edn (Cambridge, Cambridge University Press, 2008)

Feminist and Critical Race Perspectives

Mary Joe Frug, 'Re-Reading Contracts: A Feminist Analysis of a

Casebook' (1985) 34 *American University Law Review* 1065–140

Anthony R Chase, 'Race, Culture and Contract Law: From the Cottonfield to the Classroom' (1995) 28 *Connecticut Law Review* 1–66

Beverley Brown, 'Contracting Out/Contracting In: Some Feminist Considerations' in Anne Bottomley (ed), *Feminist Perspectives on the Foundational Subjects of Law* (London, Cavendish, 1996) 5–15

Peter Goodrich, 'Gender and contracts' in Anne Bottomley (ed), *Feminist Perspectives on the Foundational Subjects of Law* (London, Cavendish, 1996) 17–46

Gillian K Hadfield, 'An Expressive Theory of Contract: From Feminist Dilemmas to a Reconceptualization of Rational Choice in Contract Law' (1998) 146 *University of Pennsylvania Law Review* 1235–86

Debora L Threedy, 'Feminists & Contract Doctrine' (1999) 32 *Indiana Law Review* 1247–66

John Wightman, 'Intimate Relationships, Relational Contract Theory, and the Reach of Contract' (2000) 8 *Feminist Legal Theory* 93–131

Linda Mulcahy, 'The Limitations of Love and Altruism—Feminist Perspectives on Contract Law' in Linda Mulcahy and Sandra Wheeler, *Feminist Perspectives on Contract Law* (London, Cavendish, 2005) 1–19; David Campbell, 'Afterword: Feminism, Liberalism and Utopianism in the Analysis of Contracting' in Linda Mulcahy and Sally Wheeler (eds), *Feminist Perspectives on Contract Law* (London, Cavendish, 2005) 161–73

Miscellaneous Theories

Morris R Cohen, 'The Basis of Contract' (1933) 46 *Harvard Law Review* 553–92

Contract law is based upon the sovereign power of the state being put at the disposal of one party over another party (by putting the state's forces at the disposal of the promisee), although this power cannot be used for purposes that are contrary to public policy, and the will need not be upheld to the exclusion of all other factors.

16.4 MANDATORY AND DEFAULT RULES

Default Rules

Charles J Goetz and Robert E Scott, 'The Limits of Expanded Choice: An Analysis of the Interactions Between Express and Implied Contract Terms' (1985) 73 *California Law Review* 261–322

Ian Ayres and Robert Gertner, 'Filling Gaps in Incomplete Contracts: An Economic Theory of Default Rules' (1989) 99 *Yale Law Journal* 87–130

An examination of default rules, as contrasted with immutable rules. Not all default rules should aim for what the parties would have wanted: the content of the default rule should depend upon the usual reason for the gap. In some situations, it is more efficient to impose a penalty default rule to discourage strategic information withholding.

Jules L Coleman, Douglas D Heckathorn and Steven M Maser, 'A Bargaining Theory Approach to Default Provisions and Disclosure Rules in Contract Law' (1989) 12 *Harvard Journal of Law and Public Policy* 639–709 also in Larry Alexander (ed), *Contract Law: Volume I* (Aldershot, Dartmouth, 1991) 429–99

Without looking to context, and when merely seeking to apply joint wealth maximisation, the law will fail to apply a rational rule to the parties, who are also concerned with rational division and other matters.

Richard Craswell, 'Contract Law, Default Rules and the Philosophy of Promising' (1989) 88 *Michigan Law Review* 489–529 also in Larry Alexander (ed), *Contract Law: Volume I* (Aldershot, Dartmouth, 1991) 387–427

Many theories of promising, such as Fried's autonomy-based theory and Barnett's transfer theory, have little to say about (they are 'content-neutral' as to) the background rules (mandatory and default rules) that govern matters such as the remedies for breach and excuses from performance. Short of coupling sophisticated analysis of intention and custom with extensive sociological data on expectations, there will always (ie even if Fried or Barnett's theories are accepted) be a need for further work on which values (economic, ethical or other) should govern background rules.

Jason Scott Johnston, 'Strategic Bargaining and the Economic Theory of Contract Default Rules' (1990) 100 *Yale Law Journal* 615–55

As a result of strategic bargaining incentives, expansive default rules (which often eliminate the strategic impediments to bargaining around the default) are the most efficient.

Robert E Scott, 'A Relational Theory of Default Rules for Commercial Contracts' (1990) 19 *Journal of Legal Studies* 597–616

The rational actor will always want an allocation of risks leading to joint maximisation of expected benefits and so will prefer co-operative strategies. However, binary winner-take-all, rather than co-operative, default rules (in mistake, excuse and breach cases) will often be justified as setting the stage for co-operative extra-legal adjustment, since to judicialise these rules would be to destroy their effectiveness.

David Charny, 'Hypothetical Bargains: The Normative Structure of Contract Interpretation' (1991) 89 *Michigan Law Review* 1815–79

Default rules should be (within limits) determined on instrumental terms (ie with a view to minimising prospective bargaining costs). This does not lead to a search for the hypothetical bargain that the parties would have entered into, but rather the result that will induce the parties to expend the least effort in bargaining around it. Where contractors would not bargain around a rule, the enquiry is broader.

Ian Ayres and Robert Gertner, 'Strategic Contractual Inefficiency and the Optimal Choice of Legal Rules' (1992) 101 *Yale Law Journal* 729–73

Randy Barnett, 'The Sound of Silence: Default Rules and Contractual Consent' (1992) 78 *Virginia Law Review* 821–911 also in Brian Bix (ed), *Contract Law: Second Series: Volume I* (Aldershot, Ashgate, 2000) 101–91, 'Rational Bargaining Theory and Contract: Default Rules, Hypothetical Consent, the Duty to Disclose, and Fraud' (1992) 15 *Harvard Journal of Law and Public Policy* 783–803 and '…And Contractual Consent' (1993) 3 *Southern California Interdisciplinary Law Journal* 421–44

Implied assent to courts filling contractual gaps (through default rules) can be realistically presumed in the light of a manifested intention to be legally bound (one of the requirements of Barnett's consent theory). However, consent to particular default rules can only be inferred if the parties had reason to know of the rule and could have afforded to contract around it if they had wanted to. Further, conventionalist defaults are preferable as they are better than other rules when, as is usually the case, there is tacit subjective agreement (since they are likely to reflect that agreement), they are better than other rules when one party is rationally ignorant (since they conform to what he would expect), and they are no worse than other rules in other situations. Such defaults can be determined by market choices, empirical research and a rational bargaining approach.

Steven J Burton, 'Default Principles, Legitimacy, and the Authority of a Contract' (1993) 3 *Southern California Interdisciplinary Law Journal* 115–66

Default rules cannot be justified by efficiency, communicatorian values, relational contract norms or consent, but rather upon the co-ordination principle of fairness (akin to but different from consent) requiring parties to seek to avoid contractual breakdown.

Jay M Feinman, 'Relational Contract and Default Rules' (1993) 3 *Southern California Interdisciplinary Law Journal* 43–58

W David Slawson, 'The Futile Search for Principles for Default Rules' (1993) 3 *Southern California Interdisciplinary Law Journal* 29–41

No principles governing default rules can be found because default rules include the whole of tort law and other laws besides, and such rules require no more legitimacy than they already have for their other purposes. Default rules theory could only usefully be applied to laws of meaning, narrowly defined, of which there are very few.

Dennis Patterson, 'The Pseudo-Debate Over Default Rules in Contract Law' (1993) 3 *Southern California Interdisciplinary Law Journal* 235–87

The debate about default rules largely misses the mark as the debate is about law from outside the law but does not make propositions as to the law that judges must in fact apply in interpreting a contract. Prudential arguments from economists and others can play a part in arguments as to what the law is, but only if they dovetail with textual and contextual arguments and do not prove too much.

Russell Korobkin, 'The Status Quo Bias and Contract Default Rules' (1998) 83 *Cornell Law Review* 608–87

CA Riley, 'Designing Default Rules in Contract Law: Consent, Conventionalism and Efficiency" (2000) 20 *Oxford Journal of Legal Studies* 367–90

Richard Craswell, 'Contract Law: General Theories' in Boudewijn Baouckaert and Gerrit De D Geest (eds), *Encyclopedia of Law and Economics, Volume III: The Regulation of Contracts* (Cheltenham, Elgar, 2000) 1–24

Mikko Wennberg, 'On Barnett's Theory of Default Rules' (2003) 16 *Canadian Journal of Law and Jurisprudence* 147–58

Martijn W Hesselink, 'Non Mandatory Rules in European Contract Law' (2005) 1 *European Review of Contract Law* 44–86

Andrew Robertson, 'The Limits of Voluntariness in Contract' (2005) 29 *Melbourne University Law Review* 179–217

Human Rights and Anti-Discrimination

JA Weir, 'Discrimination in Private Law' [1966] *Cambridge Law Journal* 165–69

Hugh Beale and Nicola Pittam, 'The Impact of the Human Rights Act 1998 on English Tort and Contract Law' in Daniel Friedmann and Daphne Barak-Erez, *Human Rights in Private Law* (Oxford, Hart Publishing, 2001) 131–59

There is likely to be almost no impact of the Human Rights Act 1998 on general contract law.

Peter Benson, 'Equality of Opportunity and Private Law' in Daniel Friedmann and Daphne Barak-Erez, *Human Rights in Private Law* (Oxford, Hart Publishing, 2001) 201–43

In cases of quasi-public persons and bodies (modern analogues of those in common callings), a right to non-discrimination can be justified.

Roger Brownsword, 'Freedom of Contract, Human Rights and Human Dignity' in Daniel Friedmann and Daphne Barak-Erez, *Human Rights in Private Law* (Oxford, Hart Publishing, 2001) 181–99

Respect for human dignity may lead to limits on freedom of contract (particularly in discrimination cases).

Amnon Reichman, 'Professional Status and the Freedom to Contract: Toward a Common Law Duty of Non-Discrimination' (2001) 14 *Canadian Journal of Law and Jurisprudence* 79–132

Emily MS Houh, 'Critical Race Realism: Re-claiming the Antidiscrimination Principle through the Doctrine of Good Faith in Contract Law' (2005) 66 *University of Pittsburgh Law Review* 455–520

Chantal Mak, *Fundamental Rights in European Contract Law: A Comparison of the Impact of Fundamental Rights on Contractual Relationships in Germany, the Netherlands, Italy and England* (Austin, TX, Wolters Kluwer, 2008)

Legislation

Edward P Belobaba, 'The Resolution of Common Law Contract Doctrinal Problems Through Legislative and Administrative Intervention' in Barry J Reiter and John Swan (eds), *Studies in Contract Law* (Toronto, Butterworths, 1980) 423–61

While the common law is up to the task of commercial law reform, reform of the law of consumer contracts requires legislation, ideally of an administrative rather than judicial bent.

JF Burrows, 'Contract Statutes: The New Zealand Experience' (1983) 4 *Statute Law Review* 76–97

Andrew Burrows, 'Improving Contract and Tort: The View from the Law Commission' in *Understanding the Law of Obligations* (Oxford, Hart Publishing, 1998) 164–217

17

CODIFICATION AND INTERNATIONAL HARMONISATION

17.1 NATIONAL

Arthur L Corbin, 'The Restatement of the Common Law by the American Law Institute' (1929) 15 *Iowa Law Review* 19–41

Aubrey L Diamond, 'Codification of the Law of Contract' (1968) 31 *Modern Law Review* 361–89

American Law Institute, *Restatement (Second) of Contracts* (1981 plus appendices)

The highly-influential American academic codification of contract law.

Harvey McGregor, *Contract Code Drawn Up on Behalf of the English Law Commission* (Milan, Giuffre, 1993)

A first attempt at a modern contract code for England and Wales.

American Law Institute and National Conference of Commissioners on Uniform State Laws, *Uniform Commercial Code* (1999)

The American commercial contract code (first drafted in 1952), enacted in one or other form in all US states (and at http://www.law.cornell.edu/ucc/).

17.2 EUROPEAN

○ Ole Lando and HG Beale (eds), *Principles of European Contract Law: Part 1* (Kluwer Law International, 1995), *Part 2* (Kluwer Law International, 2000) and *Part 3* (Kluwer Law International, 2003)

A suggested codification of European contract law.

Ole Lando, 'Eight Principles of European Contract Law' in Ross Cranston (ed), *Making Commercial Law: Essays in Honour of Roy Goode* (Oxford, Clarendon Press, 1997) 103–29

Pierre Legrand, 'Against a European Civil Code' (1997) 60 *Modern Law Review* 44–62

Jürgen Basedow, 'A Common Contract Law for the Common Market' (1996) 33 *Common Market Law Review* 1169–95

Argument in favour of the harmonisation of contract law throughout the Common Market by means of European directives.

Ole Lando, 'Optional or Mandatory Europeanisation of Contract Law' (2000) 8 *European Review of Private Law* 59–69

Klaus Peter Berger, 'Harmonisation of European Contract law and the Influence of Comparative Law' (2001) 50 *International & Comparative Law Quarterly* 877–900

Jan Smits, *The Making of European Private Law: Toward a Ius Commune Europaeum as a Mixed Legal System* (Antwerp, Intersentia, 2002) ch 6

Stefan Grundman and Jules Stuyck (eds), *An Academic Green Paper on European Contract law* (The Hague, Kluwer Law International, 2002)

Stephen Weatherill, 'The Commission's Options for Developing EC Consumer Protection and Contract Law: Assessing the Constitutional Basis' (2002) 13 *European Business Law Review* 497–514, 'European Contract Law: Taking the Heat Out of Questions of Competence' (2004) 15 *European Business Law Review* 23–32, 'Constitutional Issues—How Much Is Best Left Unsaid?' in Stefan Vogenauer and Stephen Weatherill (eds), *The Harmonisation of European Contract Law: Implications for European Private Laws, Business and Legal Practice* (Oxford, Hart Publishing, 2006) 89–103 and Stefan Vogenauer and Stephen Weatherill, 'The European Community's Competence to Pursue the Harmonisation of Contract Law—An Empirical Contribution to the Debate' in their (as eds), *The Harmonisation of European Contract Law: Implications for European Private Laws, Business and Legal Practice* (Oxford, Hart Publishing, 2006) 105–48; Jacques Ziller, 'The Legitimacy of the Codification of Contract Law in View of the Allocation of Competences between the European Union and its Member States' in Martijn W Hesselink (ed), *The Politics of a European Civil Code* (The Hague, Kluwer Law International, 2006) 89–113

The constitutional competence of the EC to harmonise contract law.

Eve Truilhé-Marengo, 'Towards a European Law of Contracts' (2004) 10 *European Law Journal* 463–78

Walter van Gerven, 'Harmonization of private law: do we need it?' (2004) 41 *Common Market Law Review* 505–32

Jan Smits (ed), *The Need for a European Contract Law: Empirical and Legal Perspectives* (Groningen, Europa, 2005)

Stefan Vogenauer and Stephen Weatherill (eds), *The Harmonisation of European Contract Law: Implications for European Private Laws, Business and Legal Practice* (Oxford, Hart Publishing, 2006)

Katharina Boelle-Woelki and Willem Grosheide (eds), *The Future of European Contract Law* (Kluwer, 2007)

Hugh Collins, *The European Civil Code: The Way Forward* (Cambridge, Cambridge University Press, 2008)

Christian Twigg-Flesner, *The Europeanisation of Contract Law* (Oxford, Routledge, 2008)

17.3 GLOBAL

Michael Joachim Bonell, *An International Restatement of Contract Law: The UNIDROIT Principles for International Commercial Contracts*, 3rd edn (Ardsley, NY, Transnational, 2005)

Arthur S Hartkamp, 'The UNIDROIT Principles for International Commercial Contracts and the Principles of European Contract Law' (1994) 2 *European Review of Private Law* 341–57

Michael Joachim Bonell, 'The UNIDROIT Principles for International Commercial Contracts and the Principles of European Contract Law: Similar Rules for the Same Purpose?' (1996) 26 *Uniform Law Review* 229–46 and 'The UNIDROIT Principles for International Commercial Contracts and the Principles of European Contract Law: a Comparison' in Ross Cranston (ed), *Making Commercial Law: Essays in Honour of Roy Goode* (Oxford, Clarendon Press, 1997) 91–101

Roy Goode, 'International Restatements of Contract and English Contract Law' in EZ Lomnicka and CJG Morse (eds), *Contemporary Issues in Commercial Law: Essays in Honour of AG Guest* (London, Sweet & Maxwell, 1997) 63–78

Grace Xavier, '"Global Harmonisation" of Contract Laws—Fact or Fiction?' (2004) 20 *Construction Law Journal* 3–18

Stefan Vogenhauer and Jan Kleinheisterkamp, *Commentary on the UNIDROIT Principles for International Commercial Contracts (PICC)* (Oxford, Oxford University Press, 2009)

18

COMPARATIVE CONTRACT LAW

18.1 GENERAL

A von Mehren (chief ed), *International Encyclopedia of Comparative Law: Volume VII: Contracts In General* and *Volume VIII: Specific Contracts* (Tübingen, Mohr, 1972-)

Hugh Collins, 'Methods and Aims of Comparative Contract Law' (1991) 11 *Oxford Journal of Legal Studies* 396–406

Parviz Owsia, *Formation of Contract: A Comparative Study under English, French, Islamic and Iranian Law* (London, Graham & Trotman, 1994)

Konrad Zweigert and Heinz Kötz, Tony Weir (trans), *An Introduction to Comparative Law*, 3rd edn (Oxford, Oxford University Press, 1998) part IIA

James Gordley, *Foundations of Private Law: Property, Tort, Contract, Unjust Enrichment* (Oxford, Oxford University Press, 2006) chs 13–18

Tadas Klimas, *Comparative Contract Law: A Transystemic Approach with an Emphasis on Continental Law: Cases, Text and Materials* (Durham, NC, Carolina Academic Press, 2006)

Jan M Smits (ed), *Elgar Encyclopedia of Comparative Law* (Cheltenham, Edward Elgar, 2006) chs 16, 30, 42, 46, 55 and 62

18.2 EUROPEAN

Anne de Moor, 'Contract and Agreement in English and French Law' (1986) 6 *Oxford Journal of Legal Studies* 275–87

D Harris and D Tallon (eds), *Contract Law Today: Anglo-French Comparisons* (Oxford, Clarendon Press, 1989)

Barry Nicholas, *The French Law of Contract*, 2nd edn (Oxford, Clarendon Press, 1992)

Jac Rinkes and Geoffrey Samuel, *Contractual and Non-Contractual Obligations in English Law: Systematic Analysis of the English law of Obligations in the Comparative Context of the Netherlands Civil Code* (Nijmegen, Ars Aequi Libri, 1992)

PDV Marsh, *Comparative Contract Law: England, France, Germany* (Aldershot, Gower, 1994)

Heinz Kötz and Axel Flessner, Tony Weir (trans), *European Contract Law: Volume One: Formation, Validity, and Content of Contracts; Contract and Third Parties* (Oxford, Clarendon Press, 1997)

R Zimmermann and S Whittaker (eds), *Good Faith in European Contract Law* (Cambridge, Cambridge University Press, 2000)

James Gordley, *The Enforceability of Promises in European Contract Law* (Cambridge, Cambridge University Press, 2001)

Ruth Sefton-Green, *Mistake, Fraud and Duties to Perform in European Contract Law* (Cambridge, Cambridge University Press, 2005)

Basil Markesinis, Hannes Unberath and Angus Johnston, *German Law of Contract: A Comparative Treatise* (Oxford, Hart Publishing, 2006)

Michael A Whincup, *Contract Law and Practice: The English Legal System and Continental Comparisons*, 5th edn (London, Kluwer Law International, 2006)

John Cartwright and Marijn Hesselink (eds), *Precontractual Liability in European Private Law* (Cambridge, Cambridge University Press, 2009)

Hugh Beale, Dennis Tallon, Stefan Vogenauer and Jacobien Rutgers, *Contract Law: Ius Commune Casebooks for the Common Law of Europe*, 2nd edn (Oxford, Hart Publishing, 2010)

19

CONTRACT AND OTHER AREAS OF LAW

19.1 CONTRACT AND AGENCY

Gerard McMeel, 'The Philosophical Foundations of the Law of Agency' (2000) 116 *Law Quarterly Review* 387–411

19.2 CONTRACT AND BAILMENT

Sir Joseph H Beale Jr, 'Gratuitous Undertakings' (1891) 5 *Harvard Law Review* 222–31

Gratuitous undertakings give rise to consent-founded liability, and the standard of care required should not depend upon the gratuitous nature of the undertaking.

Alice Erh-Soon Tay, 'The Essence of a Bailment: Contract, Agreement or Possession?' (1966) 5 *Sydney Law Review* 239–53

Andrew Bell, 'The Place of Bailment in the Modern Law of Obligations' in Norman Palmer and Ewan McKendrick (eds), *Interests in Goods*, 2nd edn (London, LLP, 1998) 461–89

Although much of bailment is a matter of contract, tort and other rules, there is a *sui generis* law of bailment.

○ Norman Palmer, 'Bailment' in Andrew Burrows (ed), *English Private Law*, 2nd edn (Oxford, Oxford University Press, 2000 plus supplements) ch 16

Gerard McMeel, 'The Redundancy of Bailment' [2003] *Lloyd's Maritime and Commercial Law Quarterly* 169–200 also Alistair Hudson (ed), *New Perspectives on Property law, Obligations and Restitution* (London, Cavendish, 2003) 247–77

Bailment is redundant and merely the application of contractual, tortious and proprietary principles.

○ EG McKendrick, 'Bailment' in Hugh Beale (ed), *Chitty on Contracts: Volume 2: Specific Contracts*, 30th edn (London, Sweet & Maxwell, 2008 plus supplements) ch 33

- ○ Norman Palmer (ed), *Palmer on Bailment*, 3rd edn (London, Sweet & Maxwell, 2009)

19.3 CONTRACT AND COMPANY LAW

William W Bratton Jr, 'The "Nexus of Contracts" Corporation: A Critical Appraisal' (1989) 74 *Cornell Law Review* 407–65

Henry N Butler and Larry E Ribstein, *The Corporation and the Constitution* (Washington DC, AEI Press, 1995)

Melvin Aron Eisenberg, 'The Structure of Corporation Law' (1989) 89 *Columbia Law Review* 1461–525; Fred S McChesney, 'Economics, Law, and Science in the Corporate Field: A Critique of Eisenberg' (1989) 89 *Columbia Law Review* 1530–48; Melvin Eisenberg, 'Contractariansim without Contracts: A Response to Professor McChesney' (1990) 90 *Columbia Law Review* 1321–31; Fred S McChesney, 'Contractariansim without Contracts? Yet Another Critique of Eisenberg' (1990) 90 *Columbia Law Review* 1332–39; Paddy Ireland, 'Recontractualising the Corporation: Implicit Contract as Ideology' in David Campbell, Hugh Collins and John Wightman, *Implicit Dimensions of Contract* (Oxford, Hart Publishing, 2003) 255–288 and 'Property and Contract in Contemporary Corporate Theory' (2003) 23 *Legal Studies* 453–509

Whether corporations are essentially contractual.

19.4 CONTRACT AND CRIME

Tom Hadden, 'Contract, Tort & Crime: The Forms of Legal Thought' (1971) 87 *Law Quarterly Review* 240–60

GH Treitel, 'Contract and Crime' in CFG Tapper (ed), *Crime, Proof and Punishment (Essays in Memory of Rupert Cross)* (Butterworths, London, 1981) 81–108

Although rare, there are cases of concurrent contractual and criminal liability where the public interest requires and/or the defendant has been dishonest, and contract law occasionally pursues the same purposes (such as deterrence) as the criminal law.

19.5 CONTRACT AND EMPLOYMENT

IT Smith, 'Is Employment Properly Analysed in Terms of a Contract?' (1975) 6 *New Zealand Universities Law Review* 341–66
The contractual basis of employment law is overstated.

Tony Kerr, 'Contract Doesn't Live Here Any More?' (1984) 47 *Modern Law Review* 30–46

Simon Honeyball, 'Employment Law and the Primacy of Contract' (1988) 18 *Industrial Law Journal* 97–108

19.6 CONTRACT AND FAMILY

PM Bromley, 'The Legal Aspects of Surrogacy Agreements' in David Freestone (ed), *Children and the Law: Essays in Honour of Professor HK Bevan* (Hull, Hull University Press, 1990) 1–29

Stephen Cretney, 'From Status to Contract?' in FD Rose (ed), *Consensus Ad Idem—Essays in the Law of Contract in Honour of Guenter Treitel* (London, Sweet & Maxwell, 1996) 251–81
The increasing importance of the parties' agreement in adoption and spousal support decisions.

Elizabeth S Scott and Robert E Scott, 'Marriage as Relational Contract' (1998) 84 *Virginia Law Review* 1225–334, a later version of which appears as 'A Contract Theory of Marriage' in FH Buckley (ed), *The Fall and Rise of Freedom of Contract* (Durham, NC, Duke University Press, 1999) 201–44
Marriage as a relational contract.

Margaret F Brinig, 'Contracting Around No-fault Divorce' in FH Buckley (ed), *The Fall and Rise of Freedom of Contract* (Durham, NC, Duke University Press, 1999) 275–80

19.7 CONTRACT AND FIDUCIARY DUTIES

Deborah Demott, 'Beyond Metaphor: An Analysis of Fiduciary Obligation' [1988] *Duke Law Journal* 879–924

Paul Finn, 'Contract and the Fiduciary Principle' (1989) 12 *University of New South Wales Law Journal* 76–97
Fiduciary law applies when there exist expectations of certain standards of conduct that are unusual between contracting parties, and should not be

applied more broadly where issues of good faith or unconscionability arise in the course of the ordinary contractual relationship.

Leonard I Rotman, 'The Fiduciary Concept, Contract Law, and Unjust Enrichment: A Functional Comparison' in Paula Giliker (ed), *Re-examining Contract and Unjust Enrichment: Anglo-Canadian Perspectives* (Leiden, Martinus Nijhoff, 2007) 87–108

19.8 CONTRACT AND THE LAW OF OBLIGATIONS

Peter Birks, 'Obligations: One Tier or Two?' in JAC Thomas, Peter Stein and ADE Lewis (eds), *Studies in Justinian's Institutes: In Memory of JAC Thomas* (London, Sweet & Maxwell, 1983) 18–38

Peter Birks, 'The Concept of a Civil Wrong' in David G Owen (ed), *Philosophical Foundations of Tort Law* (Oxford, Clarendon Press, 1985) 29–51, 'Equity in the Modern Law: An Exercise in Taxonomy' (1996) 26 *University of Western Australia Law Review* 1–99

Taking the impetus from Roman law and a desire for clear terminology and taxonomy, the author sets out a map of the whole of private law. The contractual right to performance is one of the primary rights and correlative obligations arising from the category of causative events called 'manifestations of consent' (a category of 'not-wrongs'). This right may be vindicated by specific relief (or possibly the monetary equivalent of specific relief), but breach of the obligation is a wrong, a type of causative event that itself gives rise to a secondary (remedial) right to whatever remedy the law deems suitable (since wrongs have a wide-open remedial potential). The right to set aside contracts for duress or undue influence arises from the causative event (not-wrong) of unjust enrichment.

John Carter, 'Contract, Restitution and Promissory Estoppel' (1989) 12 *University of New South Wales Law Journal* 30–58

J Swanton, 'The Convergence of Tort and Contract' (1989) 12 *Sydney Law Review* 40–75

AS Burrows, 'Contract Tort and Restitution—A Satisfactory Division of the Law of Obligations or Not?' (1993) 99 *Law Quarterly Review* 216–67, a later version of which appears as 'Dividing the Law of Obligations' in his *Understanding the Law of Obligations* (Oxford, Hart Publishing, 1998) 1–15

Contract is based on what is by convention treated as a voluntarily undertaken obligation; torts are imposed when there is wrongful interference (and the strict liability, damages measure, and availability of punitive damages follow from this).

Steve Hedley, 'Contract, Tort and Restitution: Or, On Cutting the Legal System Down to Size' (1988) 8 *Legal Studies* 137–71

The division between contract, tort and restitution/unjust enrichment is unworkable. A more workable framework would be to see obligations as the protection and transfer of types of asset (property, money, labour, confidence, etc), leading (among other things) to damages for infringement of an interest by conduct or receipt (with contract often falling into the receipt category).

Peter Linzer, 'Rough Justice: A Theory of Restitution and Reliance, Contracts and Torts' [2001] *Wisconsin Law Review* 695–775

19.9 CONTRACT AND PROPERTY

See also 8.7 Contracts with Proprietary Effect and 19.2 Contract and Bailment

Norman Palmer and Ewan McKendrick (eds), *Interests in Goods*, 2nd edn (London, Lloyd's Commercial Law Library, 1998)

Thomas W Merrill and Henry E Smith, 'The Property/Contract Interface' (2001) 101 *Columbia Law Review* 773–852

David Pearce, 'Property and Contract: Where Are We?' in Alistair Hudson (ed), *New Perspectives on Property Law, Obligations and Restitution* (London, Cavendish, 2003) 87–116

Robert Chambers, 'Integrating Property and Obligations' in Michael Bryan and Andrew Robertson (eds), *The Law of Obligations: Connections and Boundaries* (London, UCL Press, 2004) 127–44

Property, trusts and obligations should be integrated into the same taxonomy.

William Swadling, 'Rescission, Property, and the Common Law' (2005) 121 *Law Quarterly Review* 123–53

Title to goods may be transferred by other ways than a contract and so even when the contract is void or voidable at law this does not mean that good title has not passed by means of delivery.

19.10 CONTRACT AND TORT

See also 14.1 Contract and Tort

Sir Joseph H Beale Jr, 'Gratuitous Undertakings' (1891) 5 *Harvard Law Review* 222–31

Gratuitous undertakings give rise to consent-founded liability, and the standard of care required should not depend upon the gratuitous nature of the undertaking.

WDC Poulton, 'Tort or Contract' (1966) 82 *Law Quarterly Review* 346–70

Tom Hadden, 'Contract, Tort & Crime: The Forms of Legal Thought' (1971) 87 *Law Quarterly Review* 240–60

G Fridman, 'The Interaction of Tort and Contract' (1977) 93 *Law Quarterly Review* 422–49

There should be a more relaxed concurrence of and cross-fertilisation between contract and tort, leading, at least in practice, to the distinctions between the two falling away.

Jeffrey O'Connell, 'The Interlocking Death & Rebirth of Contract and Tort' (1977) 75 *Michigan Law Review* 659–85

Brian Morgan, 'The Negligent Contract-Breaker' (1980) 58 *Canadian Bar Review* 299–318

Christine French, 'The Contract/Tort Dilemma' (1983) 5 *Otago Law Review* 236–315

John Holyoak, 'Tort and Contract After *Junior Books*' (1983) 99 *Law Quarterly Review* 591–604

William Bishop, 'The Contract–Tort Boundary and the Economics of Insurance' (1983) 12 *Journal of Legal Studies* 241–66

Basil S Markesinis, 'An Expanding Tort Law—The Price of a Rigid Contract Law' (1987) 103 *Law Quarterly Review* 354–97

Israel Gilead, 'Non-consensual Liability of a Contractual Party: Contract, Negligence, Both, or In-between?' (2003) 3 *Theoretical Inquiries in Law* 511–44

Mauro Bussani and Vernon Valentine Palmer, *Pure Economic Loss in Europe* (Cambridge, Cambridge University Press, 2003) and 'Between Contract and Tort: Pure Economic Loss in Europe' in Nili Cohen and Ewan McKendrick (eds), *Comparative Remedies for Breach of Contract* (Oxford, Hart Publishing, 2004) 189–217

Andrew Robertson, 'On the Distinction Between Contract and Tort' in his (as ed), *Law of Obligations: Connections and Boundaries* (London, UCL Press, 2004) 87–109

No sharp distinction can be drawn between contract and tort as the content of both contractual and tortious obligations are partly voluntarily assumed, partly shaped by one party's actions, and partly imposed. The claim that contracts are voluntarily assumed is simplistic in the face of, among other things, the objective principle, the implication of terms in law, and gap-filling through the default rules of the remedial regime.

19.11 CONTRACT AND TRUSTS

John H Langbein, 'The Contractarian Basis of the Law of Trusts' (1995) 105 *Yale Law Journal* 625–75

19.12 CONTRACT AND UNJUST ENRICHMENT/RESTITUTION

See also Disgorgement and Restitutionary Damages in 13.5, and 14.2 Contract and Unjust Enrichment

Robert Childres and Jack Garamella, 'The Law of Restitution and the Reliance Interest in Contract' (1969) 64 *Northwestern University Law Review* 433–58

Peter BH Birks, 'Restitution and the Freedom of Contract' (1983) 36 *Current Legal Problems* 141–62

Geoffrey Mead, 'Restitution within Contract?' (1991) 11 *Legal Studies* 172–88

SM Waddams, 'Restitution as Part of Contract Law' in Andrew Burrows (ed), *Essays on the Law of Restitution* (Oxford, Clarendon Press, 1991) 197–213

Most defences to contractual liability derive from or are intimately associated with the law of restitution.

IM Jackman, 'Promissory Obligations in the Law of Restitution' (1995) 69 *Australian Law Journal* 614–30

Restitution for unjust enrichment in cases of non-monetary benefits voluntarily conferred (especially where a contract is unenforceable or an anticipated contract does not materialise) is based upon a non-contractual promise or agreement.

Steve Hedley, 'Contract, Restitution and Exchange' in his *Restitution: Its Division and Ordering* (London, Sweet & Maxwell, 2001)

20

LEGAL HISTORY

See also The History of Consideration in 3.6

20.1 GENERAL AND MISCELLANEOUS

Frederick Pollock, 'Contracts in Early English Law' (1893) 6 *Harvard Law Review* 389–404

JB Ames, 'The History of Assumpsit: Parts I and II' (1888) 2 *Harvard Law Review* 1–19, 58–69

George F Deiser, 'The Origin of Assumpsit' (1912) 25 *Harvard Law Review* 429–442

Sir William Serle Holdsworth, *A History of English Law* (London, Sweet & Maxwell, 1936–72)

E Allan Farnsworth, 'The Past of Promise: An Historical Introduction to Contract' (1969) 69 *Columbia Law Review* 576–607

AWB Simpson, *A History of the Common Law of Contract: The Rise of the Action of Assumpsit* (Oxford, Clarendon Press, 1975)

Grant Gilmore, *The Death of Contract*, 2nd edn (Columbus, OH, Ohio State University Press, 1974)

SJ Stoljar, *A History of Contract at Common Law* (Canberra, Australian National University Press, 1975)

Harold J Berman, 'The Religious Sources of General Contract Law: An Historical Perspective' (1986) 4 *Journal of Law and Religion* 103–24

James Gordley, *The Philosophical Origins of Modern Contract Doctrine* (Oxford, Clarendon Press, 1991)

John V Orth, 'Contract and the Common Law' in Harry N Schreiber (ed), *The State and Freedom of Contract* (Stanford, Stanford University Press, 1998) 44–65

DJ Ibbetson, *A Historical Introduction to the Law of Obligations* (Oxford, Oxford University Press, 1999)

20.2 FOURTEENTH–SIXTEENTH CENTURIES

JB Ames, 'Parol Contracts Prior to Assumpsit' (1895) 8 *Harvard Law Review* 252–64

Gilbert Stone, 'Concerning the Action of Debt at the Time of the Year Books' (1920) 36 *Law Quarterly Review* 61–76

AWB Simpson, 'The Place of Slade's Case in the History of Contract' (1958) 74 *Law Quarterly Review* 381–96; HK Lücke, 'Slade's Case and the Origin of the Common Counts: Parts I, II and III' (1965) 81 *Law Quarterly Review* 422–45, 539–61 and (1966) *Law Quarterly Review* 81–96

JH Baker, 'New Light on Slade's Case: Parts I and II' (1971) 29 *Cambridge Law Journal* 51–67, 213–36

RH Helmholz, 'Assumpsit and Fidei Laesio' (1975) 91 *Law Quarterly Review* 406–31

Morris S Arnold, 'Fourteenth-century Promises' (1976) 35 *Cambridge Law Journal* 321–34

David Ibbetson, 'Assumpsit and Debt in the Early Sixteenth Century: The Origins of the Indebitatus Count' (1982) 41 *Cambridge Law Journal* 142–61

David Ibbetson, 'Sixteenth Century Contract Law: *Slade's Case* in Context' (1984) 4 *Oxford Journal of Legal Studies* 295–317

20.3 SEVENTEENTH–EIGHTEENTH CENTURIES

FD Mackinnon, 'The Origins of Commercial Law' (1936) 52 *Law Quarterly Review* 30–45

Clinton W Francis, 'The Structure of Judicial Administration and the Development of Contract Law in Seventeenth-Century England' (1983) 83 *Columbia Law Review* 35–137

James Oldham, 'Reinterpretation of 18th Century English Contract Theory: The View from Lord Mansfield's Trial Notes' (1988) 76 *Georgetown Law Journal* 1949–92

Michael Lobban, 'Contractual Fraud in Law and Equity, c1750–c1850' (1997) 17 *Oxford Journal of Legal Studies* 441–76

David Lieberman, 'Contract Before "Freedom of Contract"' in Harry N Schreiber (ed), *The State and Freedom of Contract* (Stanford, Stanford University Press, 1998) 89–121

David Ibbetson, 'English Law before 1900' in Jann Hallebeek and Harry Dondorp (eds), *Contracts for a Third-party Beneficiary. A Historical and Comparative Account* (Leiden, Martinus Nijhoff, 2008) 93–113

20.4 NINETEENTH CENTURY

RM Jackson, 'The Scope of the Term "Contract"' (1937) 53 *Law Quarterly Review* 535–36

Morton J Horwitz, 'The Historical Foundations of Modern Contract Law' (1974) 87 *Harvard Law Review* 917–56

The modern will-based law of contract emerged in the nineteenth century out of the rise of the market economy, replacing the far more equitable and paternalistic view of contracts that had thrived until the end of the eighteenth century.

AWB Simpson, 'Innovation in Nineteenth Century Contract Law' (1975) 91 *Law Quarterly Review* 247–78 also in Brian Bix (ed), *Contract Law: Second Series: Volume I* (Aldershot, Ashgate, 2000) 305–36

A survey of the significance of nineteenth-century innovations in contract law (such as agreement, frustration and remoteness), concluding that they were largely imported from civil law and spurred on by the rise of the treatise.

AWB Simpson, 'The Horwitz Thesis and the History of Contracts' (1979) 46 *University of Chicago Law Review* 533–601

PS Atiyah, *The Rise and Fall of Freedom of Contract* (Oxford, Oxford University Press, 1979)

Through examination of the development of contract law in its social and economic context, the author argues that the will-based paradigm of the contract only really began in the late eighteenth century and took firm hold in the nineteenth century, as a result of the forces then at play. Forces have changed, and from the latter half of the nineteenth century onwards, individual control of transactions was replaced by collective control, rendering the will theory an inaccurate anachronism.

Charles Fried, 'Review of Atiyah, The Rise and Fall of Freedom of Contract' (1980) 93 *Harvard Law Review* 1858–68

20.5 TWENTIETH CENTURY

EA Farnsworth, 'Contracts Scholarship in the Age of the Anthology' (1987) 85 *Michigan Law Review* 1406–62

E Allan Farnsworth, 'Developments in Contract Law During the

1980s: The Top Ten' (1990) 41 *Case Western Reserve Law Review* 203–30

The top ten are: bad faith breach, the employment-at-will doctrine, precontractual negotiations and preliminary agreements, long-term contracts, intimate contracts, formalities versus reliance, relationship of contract and tort, unconscionability and related doctrines, contract theory, internationalisation.

Mark Pettit Jr, 'Freedom, Freedom of Contract, and the "Rise and Fall"' (1999) 79 *Boston University Law Review* 263–354

Leone Niglia, *The Transformation of Contract in Europe* (The Hague, Kluwer Law International, 2003)

David Ibbetson, 'English Law: Twentieth Century' in Jann Hallebeek and Harry Dondorp (eds), *Contracts for a Third-party Beneficiary. A Historical and Comparative Account* (Leiden, Martinus Nijhoff, 2008) 115–35

21

INFLUENCES AND DEVELOPMENT

21.1 PARTICULAR INDIVIDUALS

Arthur L Corbin, 'Mr Justice Cardozo and the Law of Contracts' (1939) 52 *Harvard Law Review* 408–39 and (1939) 48 *Yale Law Review* 426–57; Lawrence A Cunningham, 'Cardozo and Posner: A Study in Contracts' (1995) 36 *William & Mary Law Review* 1379–466

Lord Denning, 'The Way of the Iconoclast' (1959) *Journal of the Society of Public Teachers of Law* 77–90; PS Atiyah, 'Contract and Tort' in JL Jowell and JPWB McAuslan (eds), *Lord Denning: The Judge and the Law* (London, Sweet & Maxwell, 1984) 29–77; PS Atiyah, 'Lord Denning's Contribution to Contract Law' [1999] *Denning Law Journal* 1–12

Brice Dickson, 'The Contribution of Lord Diplock to the Law of Contract' (1989) 9 *Oxford Journal of Legal Studies* 441–62

Alan Schwartz, 'Karl Llewellyn and the Origins of Contract Theory' in Jody S Kraus and Steven D Walt (eds), *The Jurisprudential Foundations of Corporate and Commercial Law* (Cambridge, Cambridge University Press, 2000) 12–41

Joseph M Perillo, 'Pothier's Influence on the Common Law of Contract' (2004) 11 *Texas Wesleyan Law Review* 267–90

21.2 THE ROLE OF COMMERCE

Patrick Devlin, 'The Relation Between Commercial Law and Commercial Practice' (1951) 14 *Modern Law Review* 249–66

The author argues that the standard form contract has replaced custom as the principal mechanism keeping contract law in tune with commerce, and discusses the different ways lawyers and commercial people treat contracts and disputes.

Lord Irvine, 'The Law: An Engine for Trade' (2001) 64 *Modern Law Review* 337

Robert Bradgate, 'Contracts, Contract Law and Reasonable Expectations' in Sarah Worthington (ed), *Commercial Law and Commercial Practice* (Oxford, Hart Publishing, 2003) 651–90

21.3 THE ROLE OF MORALITY

Patrick Devlin, 'Morals and the Law of Contract' in his *The Enforcement of Morals* (London, Oxford University Press, 1965) 43–60

Andrew Phang, 'Positivism in the English Law of Contract' (1992) 55 *Modern Law Review* 102–11

21.4 THE ROLE OF EQUITY

Sir Anthony Mason, 'The Impact of Equitable Doctrine on the Law of Contract' (1998) 27 *Anglo-American Law Review* 1–28

The contributions that equity has made to the law of contract, in particular the law of undue influence and unconscionability, the law of fiduciaries, and the law of promissory estoppel.

Larry A DiMatteo, 'Equity's Modification of Contract: An Analysis of the Twentieth Century's Equitable Reformation of Contract Law' (1999) 33 *New England Law Review* 265–357

Andrew Burrows, 'We Do This at Common Law But That in Equity' (2002) 22 *Oxford Journal of Legal Studies* 1–16

In the first half, the author discusses the differences between law and equity and explains that the distinction should be removed with regard to some areas (such as mistake). The second half contains a discussion of equitable wrongs (breach of fiduciary duty, breach of confidence, proprietary estoppel) and how they could be assimilated into common law wrongs (torts and breach of contract).

Joachim Dietrich, 'Attempting Fusion: Professor Worthington's "Equity" and Its Integration with the Common Law' (2005) 34 *Common Law World Review* 62–84

Keith Mason, 'Fusion: Fallacy, Future or Finished?' in Simone Degeling and James Edelman (eds) *Equity in Commercial Law* (Sydney, Law Book Co, 2005) 41–76

21.5 THE ROLE OF PUBLIC LAW

Jack Beatson, 'Public Law Influences in Contract Law' in Jack Beatson and Daniel Friedmann (eds), *Good Faith and Fault in Contract Law* (Oxford, Clarendon Press, 1995) 263–88

Public law and statutory regimes have had little influence on the law of contract but this is to be regretted, eg contractual discretions might be subjected to controls taken from public law, and the doctrine of legitimate expectations and non-discrimination may assist in regulating the pre-contractual tendering process.

Sue Arrowsmith, 'The Impact of Public law on the Private Law of Contract' in Roger Halson (ed), *Exploring the Boundaries of Contract* (Aldershot, Dartmouth, 1996) 3–22

22

MISCELLANEOUS

22.1 NOVELTY

Douglass G Boshkoff, 'Selected Poems on the Law of Contracts', (1991) 66 New York University Law Review 1533–44

Twenty-nine limericks based on famous contract law cases and arranged by topic (eg "There once was a young man named Hadley/ Whose contract of transport went badly./ "My mill shaft is gone,/ All my goods are in pawn,/ And my business is closed," he said sadly.")

Louis E Wolcher, 'Annotated Contracts Haiku' (1992) 42 *Journal of Legal Education* 141

Franklin G Snyder, 'The Shaft: The *Hadley v Baxendale* Song' (2004) 11 *Texas Wesleyan Law Review* 239–42

22.2 CONTRACT LAW AND LITERATURE

Geoffrey P Miller, 'Contracts of Genesis' (1993) 22 *Journal of Legal Studies* 15–45

A survey of the stories of contracts in the Book of Genesis, arguing that they are intended to convey contract rules and that these rules make sense in the Canaan community of the time.

Mark Edwin Andrews, *Law Versus Equity in the 'Merchant of Venice': A Legalization of Act IV, Scene I* (Boulder, University of Colorado Press, 1965); Daniel J Kornstien, 'Fie Upon Your Law!' (1993) 5 *Cardozo Studies in Law and Literature* 35–56; Charles Spinosa, 'Shylock and Debt and Contract in The Merchant of Venice' (1993) 5 *Cardozo Studies in Law and Literature* 65–85; Daniel J Kornstein, *Kill All the Lawyers? Shakespeare's Legal Appeal* (Princeton, NJ, Princeton University Press, 1994); AG Harmon, *Eternal Bonds, True Contracts: Law and Nature in Shakespeare's Problem Plays* (New York, State University of New York Press, 2004)

The contractual legal themes in *A Merchant of Venice*.

Luke Wilson, 'Ben Jonson and the Law of Contract' (1993) 5 *Cardozo Studies in Law and Literature* 281–306

Lenora Ledwon, 'Common Sense, Contracts, and Law and Literature: Why Lawyers Should Read Henry James' (2000) 16 *Touro Law Review* 1065–90

Nishan Swais, 'Putting It in Writing: Drafting Faust's Contract with the Devil' (2001) 14 *Canadian Journal of Law and Jurisprudence* 227–47

22.3 TEACHING CONTRACT LAW

Lawrence M Friedman and Stewart Macaulay, 'Contract Law and Contract Teaching: Past, Present and Future' [1967] *Wisconsin Law Review* 805–21

John Tillotson, 'A Diagramatic Approach to Contract Law' (1969) 3 *Journal of Association of Law Teachers* 104–11

How diagrams can be used to elucidate contract cases and concepts.

John Tillotson, 'Anyone for Contracts?' (1976) 10 *The Law Teacher* 135–45

Contracts should not be taught abstractly but rather realistically and with reference to contract's setting in business and society.

Kenney Hegland, 'Fun and Games in the First Year: Contracts by Roleplay' (1981) 31 *Journal of Legal Education* 534–43

Kurt A Strasser, 'Teaching Contracts—Present Criticisms and a Modest Proposal for Reform' (1981) 31 *Journal of Legal Education* 63–86

Richard Lewis, 'Criticism of the Traditional Contract Course' (1982) 16 *The Law Teacher* 111–21

Jonathan M Hyman, 'Discovery and Invention: The NITA Method in the Contracts Classroom' (1991) 66 *Notre Dame Law Review* 759–84

Phyllis G Coleman and Robert M Jarvis, 'Using Skills Training to Teach First Year Contracts' (1996) 44 *Drake Law Review* 725–42

Simulated contract negotiation and advice tasks.

William J Woodward Jr, 'Contracts for Grownups' (1997) 47 *Journal of Legal Education* 139–48

Various, Teaching Contracts Issue (2000) 44 *Saint Louis University Law Journal* 1193–560

Aspects of and approaches to teaching contract law, and specific examples of such teaching.

Edith R Warkentine, 'Kingsfield Doesn't Teach My Contracts Class: Using Contracts to Teach Contracts' (2000) 50 *Journal of Legal Education* 112–33

Studying and drafting real contracts improves student-learning of contract law.

INDEX

INDEX TO AUTHORS

NARRATORI MODERNI

Di Andrea Vitali in edizione Garzanti:

Una finestra vistalago
La signorina Tecla Manzi
Un amore di zitella
La figlia del podestà
Il procuratore
Olive comprese
Il segreto di Ortelia
La modista
Dopo lunga e penosa malattia
Almeno il cappello
Pianoforte vendesi
La mamma del sole
Il meccanico Landru
La leggenda del morto contento
Zia Antonia sapeva di menta
Galeotto fu il collier
Regalo di nozze
Un bel sogno d'amore
Di Ilde ce n'è una sola
Quattro sberle benedette
Biglietto, signorina
La ruga del cretino (con Massimo Picozzi)
Le belle Cece
La verità della suora storta
Le mele di Kafka
Furto di luna (solo ebook)
Parola di cadavere (solo ebook)
Il rumore del Natale (solo ebook)
Seguendo la stella (solo ebook)
Addio bocce (solo ebook)
Il sapore del Natale (solo ebook)

ANDREA VITALI

VIVA PIÙ CHE MAI

Garzanti

Prima edizione: novembre 2016

Per essere informato sulle novità del Gruppo editoriale Mauri Spagnol visita:
www.illibraio.it

Pubblicato in accordo con Factotum Agency, Milano

ISBN 978-88-11-68767-2

Printed in Italy

www.garzantilibri.it

VIVA PIÙ CHE MAI

I personaggi e le situazioni raccontati in questo romanzo sono frutto di fantasia. I luoghi, invece, sono reali o solo in minima parte adattati alle esigenze della trama.

La luce della croce di Camaggiore.

Più sotto quella del campanile di Noceno.

Più sotto ancora quella del santuario della Madonna di Lezzeno.

Infine quelle di Bellano.

Le finestre del cotonificio, i lampioni del lungolago, quella lampeggiante del molo, poi…

Poi basta.

Ernesto Livera, detto Dubbio, finalmente svuotò la vescica. Erano due ore buone che gli scappava e aveva dovuto tenerla.

Scrollò, espirò, guardò il lago.

Lì da dove aveva pisciato, dalla riva, era calmo.

Non così da circa metà fino alla sponda opposta. Vedeva crestine bianche andare e venire. C'era vento, tivano che tagliava in diagonale, risparmiandolo per metà. Il cielo tuttavia era bello, sereno, stelle dappertutto, sembrava il cielo dei presepi.

L'aria…

Il Dubbio ne inspirò un bel po'. L'aria era quella dei giorni di luglio. Saporita, tiepida per quell'ora di notte, quasi densa. Spinse la barca in acqua, ci saltò dentro e si attaccò ai remi. Quando fu a un centinaio di metri dalla riva che aveva appena lasciato si fermò per guardarsi intorno. La notte faceva un rumore che conosceva bene. Una specie di suono cupo, chissà da dove veniva. Poi solo i rintocchi delle campanelle che segnalavano le reti dei pescatori. Udì un campanile. Se non s'era sbagliato erano le due. Ritirò i remi e mise in acqua il motorino da tre cavalli.

Bep-bep-bep...

Al minimo, non faceva più rumore del vento, dell'onda.

«Lavora tu per me», gli disse dandogli una pacca e continuando a guardarsi in giro.

Era stato dopo un po' che la barca era andata a sbattere contro qualcosa.

Qualcosa di grosso di sicuro, preso di punta, che l'aveva fatta sterzare bruscamente. Per rimetterla subito in linea il Dubbio spinse il timone verso la sua destra.

«Che cazzo...» mormorò.

E, bep-bep, il motore si spense.

Guardando oltre il bordo della barca, tra le onde, vide la cosa contro la quale era andato a sbattere.

Una massa scura.

Che, nel frattempo, era scivolata di lato all'imbarcazione.

Un tronco, forse la carogna di qualche animale.

Capitava, quando c'era stato qualche temporale i fiumi portavano a lago di tutto.

Gli mancava solo di danneggiare la barca...

Si mise in piedi, a gambe larghe, un remo in mano, lo puntò sulla cosa per allontanarla.

Allora cominciò ad avere un sospetto.

Tra le dotazioni della barca aveva anche una torcia. Gli serviva per segnalare la sua presenza se qualcuno lo aspettava su una riva per una consegna. La usava raramente. C'era il pericolo che i suoi segnali avvisassero le persone sbagliate. Frugò nel cassone a poppa, sperando che funzionasse, che le pile non si fossero ossidate, scaricate o quel diavolo che fosse.

La massa nel frattempo era scivolata a qualche metro di distanza dalla barca, portata dalla corrente. Il fascio della torcia la cercò per qualche secondo. Emetteva una luce giallognola, lo stesso colore di certe lune basse, ammalate di stanchezza. Un fascio grazie al quale il Dubbio riuscì infine a stabilire che non era né un tronco né la carogna di un animale.

Per un istante fu incapace di reagire. Quindi, i remi in acqua, si avvicinò a quella cosa, al cadavere che aveva incrociato la rotta della sua barca.

Girato, a faccia in giù.

Guardava il fondo del lago.

La corrente intanto, aiutata dal vento che rinfrescava, stava spostando in giù, verso Varenna, lui, la barca e il cadavere che si era appoggiato di nuovo al fianco dell'imbarcazione.

Che cazzo doveva fare?

Era come se un altro glielo domandasse e un altro ancora rispondesse: «Non lo so».

Perdeva tempo.

Scarrocciava sempre di più, ormai era all'altezza della punta di Morcate. L'onda era più alta, il tivanello stava diventando vento. Forse phon, era caldo.

Col remo tentò di spingere via il cadavere o di cacciarlo sott'acqua. Niente da fare. L'unico risultato fu quello di lacerarne il vestito, capire che era una donna, indossava il reggiseno.

Tentò un'ultima volta di spingerlo via, fissandosi bene, a gambe larghe, sul fondo della barca. Nel momento in cui diede il colpo un'onda lo fece traballare. Per non cadere in acqua si piegò in avanti spingendo sul remo. La pala perse l'appoggio.

Al Dubbio scappò un grido.

Pure il remo.

Lo mollò mentre si dava una spinta all'indietro per non cadere in acqua.

Si accucciò sul fondo della barca, si prese il viso tra le mani.

Il remo, vallo a prendere, il cadavere sempre lì.

La punta di Morcate era ormai superata. La corrente continuava a portarlo in giù e più verso il centro, quasi a metà tra Varenna e Bellagio.

Tornando a guardarsi in giro vide una luce che aveva appena doppiato il promontorio di Bellagio. Ballava, seguendo il ritmo delle onde.

Dirigeva verso di lui, veloce. Rapida come solo le imbarcazioni della Finanza della caserma di Nobiallo.

Di aspettare un miracolo non era più il caso, ragionò il Dubbio, e nemmeno di farsi beccare in piena notte, in mezzo al lago con un cadavere al fianco, di grane ne aveva già abbastanza.

Dal cassone della barca prese una rete piccola, a maglie fini, di quelle che usava per bracconare le arbole e la gettò sul cadavere. Con una cima la fissò allo scalmo del remo che aveva perduto.

Il phon adesso soffiava, soprattutto fischiava.

Meglio così.

Avviò il motorino.

Bep-bep-bep...

Quasi faticava anche lui a sentirlo.

Virò e, controcorrente, puntò verso la riva di Morcate.

Un'occhiata alle spalle, la luce non si vedeva. Ma mica era un bel segno.

Voleva solo dire che quelli l'avevano spenta e stavano risalendo la riva a motore al minimo. Finanza e guardapesca, stessa tattica, stesse rogne.

Doppiata la punta di Morcate puntò decisamente verso la riva. A venti metri da quella spense il motore, si mise in prua, manovrando con il solo remo che aveva finché sentì grattare la barca contro i sassi del fondo. Le gambe in acqua, tirò a sé la barca, slegò la cima che assicurava la rete, portò il corpo a riva. Solo allora si accorse che durante il tragitto il corpo si era girato, guardava in su, verso il cielo luminoso di stelle.

Verso di lui.

Il Dubbio non riuscì a resistere, accese un istante la torcia, illuminò quel viso di morta e tutto ciò che era accaduto dal giorno prima e che l'aveva portato lì, adesso, a pensare di essere finito dentro un macabro scherzo, a non voler credere a ciò che invece stava vedendo, gli passò rapidamente nella mente.

«E adesso che cazzo faccio?» mormorò.

1.

Se Biagio Trùfa Riffa avesse potuto scegliere che mestiere fare da grande, avrebbe scelto il dolce far niente.

Invece aveva ereditato il lavoro di Stefano Borrazza, l'ambulante che l'aveva preso con sé all'età di tredici anni, educandolo alla disciplina con pochi consigli e molti calci nel didietro.

E visto che il Borrazza non era il padrone della Fiat, adesso andava in giro anche lui a fare il mercato.

Vendeva scarpe, roba di cartone, prezzi stracciati.

Nato per quel mestiere, aveva la faccia come il culo, gran lappa e oltretutto era anche un bel giovanotto.

Quando apriva la bocca incantava.

Disponeva di un repertorio di allusioni erotiche da fare invidia e lo usava con dovizia senza badare troppo all'età e all'avvenenza dei bersagli.

Di bocca buona insomma.

Quando qualcuna abboccava ai suoi ami, se le circostanze lo permettevano il Riffa tendeva a concludere rapidamente l'affare. A volte anche al riparo del camioncino con il quale portava in giro la sua merce.

Quel giorno al mercato di Acquaseria, di cui aveva conquistato una piazza dopo ben tre anni di tentativi, aveva fatto caccia.

Grossa.

Due in un colpo solo.

Una delle due, non molto alta, bionda, bella piena davanti e con un culo che sembrava abitato da un serpente, l'aveva già vista un paio di volte. Era passata via dal suo banchetto senza però mai fermarsi. Le aveva anche fischiato dietro, ma quella niente.

Così a stima, aveva giudicato il Riffa, non apparteneva alla fauna locale.

Forse straniera, più che probabile visto che era tempo di vacanze.

Quel giorno invece si era fermata. Era insieme con un'amica che doveva fare acquisti. Carina di viso, l'amica, ma bassa, come un po' schiacciata.

Com'è che si diceva, tarchia, no?

E poi indossava pantaloni, brutto segno.

«In cosa posso esservi utile?» aveva chiesto il Riffa guardando la bionda.

Un paio di scarponcini, aveva risposto la tarchia.

«Che numero?» s'era informato il Riffa sempre guardando l'altra.

«Perché lo chiede a me?» aveva ribattuto quella, rivelando di essere italiana, italianissima e di avere un tono di voce capace di segarti sul posto.

«Trentasei», aveva intanto risposto la tarchia attirando l'attenzione del Riffa.

«Piedino da fata», aveva commentato lui.

«Piantala e fammi vedere i modelli», aveva detto la tarchia.

I modelli...

«Certo», aveva risposto il Riffa con una faccia da maître.

Però...

Ecco, non che ci fosse 'sto grande assortimento.

Uno che però era piaciuto alla tarchia il Riffa l'aveva trovato.

«Modello unico!»

Nel senso che stava in un angolo del camioncino, solitario come un cinghiale, da chissà quanto tempo: scarponcino scamosciato con il disegno di una bella stella alpina sul lato.

«Vi faccio un prezzo speciale», aveva detto poi.

Era ora di passare all'attacco. Aveva schiacciato l'occhio alla bionda che gli aveva risposto corrugando la fronte e con l'azzurro ghiacciato degli occhi.

«Che prezzo?» aveva chiesto la tarchia.

«Te lo dico domani sera», aveva rilanciato il Riffa.

La tarchia aveva fatto per dire qualcosa ma il Riffa l'aveva bruciata sul tempo.

«Ci vediamo alla festa dei crotti, su a Maso?»

Cominciava proprio la sera dopo, venerdì.

La tarchia aveva guardato la bionda, il Riffa aveva creduto di comprendere al volo.

Proprio vero che a volte le parole non servivano.

«Porto anche un mio amico», aveva detto, sicuro di aver centrato il bersaglio.

Si sarebbero divertiti un po', no?

La tarchia non aveva ancora fatto la mossa per parlare che la sua amica l'aveva preceduta.

«Se non ci vediamo, fa' che sia per colpa tua.»

L'invisibile calcolatrice del Riffa aveva preso nota del messaggio in codice: prima di tutto la bionda gli aveva detto sì anche se aveva voluto parlare da strafiga, e poi era passata dal lei al tu. Il Riffa aveva succhiato per qualche istante un'immaginaria caramella.

«Io mi chiamo Biagio», aveva detto poi.

Il nome del nonno. Nome del cazzo, vecchio. Non gli era mai piaciuto. D'altronde, se voleva che qualcuno facesse altrettanto, non poteva esimersi dal declinarlo.

«E tu?»

«Valeria», aveva risposto la bionda.

La tarchia non si era fatta sorprendere.

«Io Tina», si era accodata, mentre il Riffa stava dicendo quanto gli fosse sempre piaciuto quel nome e pensava al serpente che agitava il culo della bionda. Nella fantasia stava già raccontando a chi sapeva lui come aveva tenuto tra le mani con ferrea presa quelle chiappe sode mentre...

Aveva spezzato l'idillio una voce che reclamava ciabatte. Sciavàt!

«Lasciamolo lavorare», aveva detto la bionda con un tono che al Riffa era sembrato già denso di doppi sensi.

«Allora, domani sera», aveva canticchiato, consegnando la scatola con gli scarponcini alla... Tina?, Gina?, Pina? e beandosi della visione posteriore della Va-le-ria!, cui l'amica stava già chiedendo se davvero avesse intenzione di andare alla festa dei crotti.

«Perché no?» aveva risposto la Valeria.

La sera seguente sarebbe stata l'ultima che passava in paese prima di partire e starsene lontana da lì, e finalmente!, per un mese intero.

Inghilterra, Londra!

«Direi che è proprio il caso di festeggiare», aveva aggiunto giusto pcr rimarcare quanto desiderasse lasciarsi alle spalle per un po' la vita che aveva fatto sino ad allora, famiglia compresa.

«E se ci ritroviamo quello?» aveva chiesto la Tina.

«Ci divertiamo di più, no?» aveva sorriso la Valeria.

Perché, se credeva di aver fatto colpo...

Il Riffa ci credeva eccome, ma aveva quasi subito mollato le fantasie perché quella delle ciabatte insisteva.

«Ciabatte, va bene, arrivo.»

Cazzo di ciabatte, non vendeva quasi altro in quel paese.

Gli era venuta la tentazione di chiedere alla donna che aveva davanti, quattro denti e un viso di rughe che sembrava la rete di un letto, cosa diavolo se ne facessero delle ciabatte da quelle parti.

Le mangiavano forse?

Ma non aveva tempo da perdere in chiacchiere.

Doveva pensare al socio da portarsi dietro, quello che si sarebbe accollato la tarchia.

Perché su quello non c'era bisogno di discutere, la Valeria era roba sua, patti chiari eccetera.

Ma a chi poteva dirlo, chi poteva tirarsi dietro?, aveva

pensato il Riffa mentre buttava sotto gli occhi di Miss sorriso una ciabatta dietro l'altra.

Non che gli mancassero gli amici, i donda come lui che al massimo, poi, si sarebbero fatti quattro risate se le cose non andavano per il verso giusto. Ma è che lavoravano tutti, chi al cotonificio, chi sotto altri padroni. Gente che non voleva tirar tardi, che alla mattina doveva star su presto.

I quattro denti si erano offerti alla vista del Riffa.

La vecchiaccia aveva chiesto qualcosa.

«Cosa?» aveva domandato lui con malgarbo.

«Ho detto se di questo modello qui», aveva ripetuto la donna, «non ne ha di due numeri in più.»

L'aveva provato, erano un po' corte.

«Ma come provato?» era sbottato il Riffa.

Ci aveva messo dentro i piedi?

Che schifo!

Ma che sistema era?

«Il sistema che se lei c'ha la testa nelle nuvole io non c'ho tempo da perdere», aveva risposto la donna.

Se non dava retta a quello che i clienti gli chiedevano...

Il Riffa aveva afferrato la ciabatta.

«Guardi che non c'ho la rogna», aveva poi osservato la donna.

«No, macché», aveva replicato il Riffa.

Ma sottovoce.

Perché quello che aveva detto la donna gli aveva fatto balenare l'idea giusta. Tra i soci ce ne voleva uno che avesse tempo da perdere, che si potesse accontentare della tarchia senza rognare e che come lui non doveva rendere conto a nessuno o quasi.

Quello giusto c'era, si chiamava Ernesto Livera, detto Dubbio.

2.

I

Se avessero chiesto a Ernesto Livera, detto Dubbio, che lavoro gli sarebbe piaciuto fare, avrebbe risposto: «Boh!».

Un classico tra le risposte che il Dubbio dava spesso quando gli si domandava qualcosa.

La stessa che aveva dato, all'età di tredici anni, a un cliente che era tornato per la terza volta nell'arco della mattina nella falegnameria di suo padre per chiedergli dove diavolo si fosse cacciato il genitore. Da un anno circa il giovane Ernesto lo seguiva in bottega facendogli compagnia, eseguendo piccole commissioni e soprattutto, secondo il disegno del genitore, prendendo confidenza con l'ambiente che lui gli aveva destinato dopo che ne avesse pian piano appresa l'arte e il comandamento di fare le cose una per volta se le voleva fare bene.

«Boh», aveva risposto.

«E vallo a cercare no?» gli aveva consigliato il cliente con modi tutt'altro che gentili.

Se non era in falegnameria, aveva ragionato l'Ernesto, e considerato che il genitore non era uomo di carte e di osteria, non poteva che essere sulla riva del lago dove aveva posto fisso per la pesca degli agoni che si sarebbe aperta di lì a pochi giorni.

Lì infatti l'aveva trovato.

Ma morto stecchito, metà in acqua e metà sui sassi della riva, di lato alla passerella dalla quale per anni e anni aveva cribbiato l'acqua del lago.

Così, a sua volta, li aveva trovati lo spazientito cliente una mezz'ora più tardi: l'uno, come detto, morto, l'altro, l'Ernesto, con l'occhio perso e fisso verso qualcosa che non era di questo mondo. L'uomo gli aveva passato la mano davanti al viso ma il ragazzo non aveva battuto ciglio.

Nel giro di un paio d'ore in paese aveva cominciato a circolare la notizia di quel singolare dramma familiare, padre e figlio morti insieme sulla riva del lago.

Un altro paio d'ore e l'informazione si era precisata.

Padre morto di sicuro, figlio in gravi condizioni.

Gravissime anzi, quando non lo si era visto comparire al funerale del vecchio.

Quando infine, passata una quindicina di giorni, l'Ernesto era tornato tra i vivi, ormai era cosa nota che l'esperienza vissuta aveva scioccato il giovane al punto da trasportarlo per un certo periodo in una specie di limbo, un dormiveglia dentro il quale sembrava non sentire e non vedere e che a tratti veniva visitato dall'incubo di corpi che, secondo la descrizione fatta dal ragazzo alla madre e da questa trasferita al dottore, se ne stavano per metà in acqua e per metà stesi sui sassi della riva, senza dar modo di capire se venissero dal lago o nel lago ci volessero andare del tutto. Il dottore aveva tranquillizzato per quanto poteva la donna spiegando che l'immagine traumatica del padre approfittava del sonno, dell'abbassarsi delle difese del ragazzo per ripresentarsi. E andava bene che ciò non succedesse anche quando era sveglio, perché poteva capitare!

Poi, non avendo altri mezzi, aveva disposto un rigido ricovero domestico dell'Ernesto, alla larga da curiosi e compagnia bella e, quale terapia, s'era affidato al tempo senza poter escludere che, stante la giovane età, il carattere dell'Ernesto potesse patire conseguenze dall'esperienza vissuta.

Ragione per la quale, nonostante il ragazzo fosse poi uscito dallo stallo, aveva raccomandato a sua madre, Canterina Sbaffi, di tenerlo d'occhio e mai dimenticare, davanti a eventuali stranezze, ciò che gli era successo.

II

Della disgrazia, oltre ai debitori che si erano volatilizzati come uccelli di passo, aveva approfittato soprattutto tal Farfatti che si era avventato sulla Canterina, avanzando proposte di acquisto della falegnameria, serrandola in una sorta di assedio verbale cui la donna aveva infine ceduto poiché oltre al Farfatti nessuno aveva fatto altre proposte e quell'unico, anziché aumentare l'offerta, aveva continuato a ridurla e anche minacciato di desistere. Quale condizione la Canterina aveva posto che il neoproprietario si tenesse in bottega il figlio, così da completare l'apprendistato. Il Farfatti non aveva avuto niente in contrario, in fin dei conti un bocia tuttofare gli serviva.

Il Dubbio era rimasto alle dipendenze del Farfatti per qualche mese.

Nell'arco di quel tempo era capitato più di una volta che il subentrato padrone lo chiamasse per un bisogno senza ottenere risposta.

Si guardava in giro, lo cercava, niente da fare. L'Ernesto non era più in bottega.

Dopo parecchi episodi di questo genere, il Farfatti aveva voluto parlarne con la Canterina la quale, piangendo, gli aveva confessato che il ragazzo soffriva ancora la perdita del padre. Con la promessa che non l'avrebbe rivelato a nessuno, nemmeno al dottore, una sera gli aveva raccontato che l'Ernesto di tanto in tanto sognava suo padre ancora lì, sulla riva del lago, metà dentro e metà fuori, ma vivo e come se parlasse per chiedere aiuto. Il sogno era talmente pregnante che per convincersi che non fosse vero il giovane si doveva spingere a controllare.

Così ogni volta, dopo ogni notte in cui gli capitava.

«Capisco», aveva detto il Farfatti.

Ma capiva anche che una falegnameria, con tutto quel maneggiare tenaglie, sgorbie, scalpelli, morsetti, punteruoli, trapani, presse e seghe circolari era il posto ideale per perdere qualche dito, una mano o anche un braccio se uno correva dietro ai sogni.

«È un rischio», aveva sottolineato il Farfatti.

Per l'Ernesto e anche per lui che non voleva trovarsi in mezzo a qualche guaio, ispettorato del lavoro o quelle balle lì.

La Canterina s'era dichiarata d'accordo. E poiché nel frattempo aveva trovato un posto come cuciniera presso l'asilo infantile Tommaso Grossi, s'era decisa a togliere l'Ernesto dalla falegnameria, pregando il Farfatti di tenere per sé il segreto delle stravaganti allucinazioni del figlio, onde evitare che venisse bollato come «strano» e nessuno più lo volesse intorno.

Il Dubbio andava allora verso i quattordici anni e una bella sera, candido come un giglio, aveva dichiarato a sua madre di aver visto, giusto quella mattina, suo padre in carne e ossa.

All'uscita del figlio la donna s'era dapprima spaventata, mani sul viso e un grido represso.

Ma si era ricomposta immediatamente ripensando ai consigli che il dottor Lonati le aveva dato mesi prima: blandire le fantasie del ragazzo tenendo conto dell'età e della perdita subita, mai deriderle o contestarle, accompagnarle piuttosto con grazia materna verso la loro naturale estinzione poiché erano solo immagini di un dolore che si stava componendo.

Reagendo con autocontrollo, senza fare domande, aveva ottenuto il risultato di contenere le conseguenze della straordinaria rivelazione del figlio e, pur macerandosi da quella sera in una diuturna inquietudine, di non sentirlo più dire simili cose.

Per una quindicina di giorni però, dopodiché l'Ernesto, con una incomparabile tranquillità, era tornato sull'argomento affermando non solo che aveva rivisto il genitore ma, anche, che l'avrebbe fermato per parlargli se quello non fosse scomparso alla sua vista.

III

In quel periodo l'Ernesto aveva cominciato a consegnare a domicilio il pane per conto del forno dei fratelli Scaccola. Nessuna paga, qualche eventuale mancetta: tanto era bastato alla Canterina pur di non lasciare il figlio a casa da solo a guardare il soffitto o a bighellonare per il paese col rischio di ricadere in quelle che lei riteneva fossero pure fantasie nonostante le spiegazioni, il più delle volte oscure, del dottore.

Per qualche tempo le cose erano filate lisce tranne un paio di occasioni in cui l'Ernesto le era parso più distante e silenzioso del solito, facendole temere che stesse per uscirsene con qualche altra bella rivelazione circa il genitore. Ma le settimane trascorrevano quiete e così lo stato di all'erta della Canterina era scemato e di concerto era aumentata la fiducia nelle parole che il Lonati le aveva sempre detto: avere pazienza, dare tempo al tempo, l'unico, grande medico per quel tipo di ferite.

Ma era stato proprio lui, il dottor Lonati, a farsi ambasciatore della notizia che quella guarigione che ormai nella mente della Canterina era cosa quasi fatta era invece ancora lontana.

Un giovedì mattina, mentre lei stava spadellando nelle cucine dell'asilo, la superiora suor Guerriera l'aveva avvisata che il medico l'attendeva nell'atrio per dirle una cosa.

Quella mattina l'Ernesto s'era presentato come suo solito presso il forno Scaccola e aveva caricato la bicicletta con cui consegnava il pane. Nemmeno un'ora più tardi però alcuni clienti s'erano presentati al forno protestando per non aver ricevuto la quotidiana consegna. Poco dopo costoro, lo straccivendolo Càmola aveva avvisato i fratelli Scaccola di aver reperito la bici del negozio carica di sacchetti pieni di pane fresco abbandonata a sé stessa, appoggiata al muro del magazzino delle ferrovie mentre in contemporanea al dottor Lonati veniva richiesto un intervento presso la pretura bellanese dove s'era trovato faccia a faccia con l'Ernesto. Alla domanda su cosa ci facesse lì, il ragazzo aveva ripetuto ciò che aveva già detto al brigadiere Mellito su richiesta del pretore Mirmino Delpasso, incuriosito dalla presenza di un ragazzetto in aula.

«Sono venuto da mio papà», aveva risposto l'Ernesto indicando lo stesso pretore.

Solo allora il Lonati aveva notato come, a uno sguardo superficiale, ammantato di fantasia e rimpianto, il pretore Delpasso potesse somigliare al defunto Livera. Gli era stato chiaro come il ragazzo potesse averlo visto più di una volta, ma di sfuggita, nei giorni in cui il Delpasso giungeva a Bellano per dare corso alle udienze. Quella volta infine l'aveva visto bene, e l'allontanarlo dalla pretura aveva creato non poco trambusto poiché l'Ernesto s'era impuntato e aveva gridato di non voler più lasciare il padre adesso che l'aveva ritrovato.

Sedato e guardato a vista dalla sua infermiera, il giovane adesso era presso il suo ambulatorio. Ma era evidente, aveva infine detto il Lonati alla Canterina, che la desiderata guarigione era ancora una speranza e nulla più.

Bisognava pensare in fretta e bene a cosa fare, onde evitare che il ragazzo restasse segnato a vita da quei fenomeni.

L'optimum, aveva detto il dottore, sarebbe stato allontanarlo per un po' dall'ambiente dove aveva vissuto il trauma.

«Un po', quanto?» aveva chiesto la Canterina.

Per tutta risposta il Lonati aveva allargato le braccia, nemmeno lui era in grado di dirlo.
«Un po'», aveva ribadito, fin quanto fosse bastato.

IV

La Canterina poteva contare su una sorella che abitava a Concorezzo e su un fratello del defunto marito che allevava bestiame in un alpeggio dalle parti di Somaggia, in Val Chiavenna.
Il primo tentativo era stato presso la sorella.
Un fallimento.
A Concorezzo infatti l'Ernesto non aveva fatto altro che raccontare le sue visioni ai due cuginetti col risultato di spaventarli a furia di morti che non lo erano del tutto, che ogni tanto tornavano a farsi vivi e che chiedevano aiuto stando per metà a mollo nelle acque del lago e per l'altra metà sui sassi della riva.
Lo zio mandriano invece aveva tentato di raddrizzare l'Ernesto col codice della fatica dei campi. Il risultato era stato che dopo un po' l'Ernesto aveva imparato a nascondersi negli anfratti più inaccessibili dell'alpeggio onde evitare il lavoro, facendo ammattire l'uomo e convincendolo infine che fosse inutile perdere dell'altro tempo.
Una volta tornato a casa, la Canterina aveva seguito il consiglio della superiora dell'asilo suor Guerriera di rivolgersi al signor prevosto, e questi aveva proposto alla donna di fare del figlio una sorta di aiuto sacrista, visto che quello in carica da qualche tempo era spesso in bambola e più di una volta si era reso necessario andarlo a cercare in questa o quella osteria e strapparlo alle carte.
Era una possibilità tra l'altro, aveva sottolineato il prevosto, di farlo crescere in un ambiente sano e prepararlo a un lavoro di tutto rispetto, dando così all'Ernesto un futuro.

I primi tempi tutto era filato liscio. Il sacrista titolare, intuendo nella mossa del prevosto un ben preciso messaggio, s'era dato una raddrizzata maiuscola. Poi però, man mano che la confidenza tra i due s'era andata consolidando, l'Ernesto s'era fatto traviare divenendo complice passivo delle scappatelle dello scaccino, coprendolo e sostituendosi a lui. Poi, da un certo punto in avanti, attivo, nel senso che aveva cominciato a seguirlo nelle osterie e a imitarne i vizi.

A complicare la situazione, anche se in fondo aveva aiutato a risolverla allontanandolo dal cattivo maestro, era intervenuta un'epidemia di epatite, o itterizia, che tra i tanti aveva beccato anche il giovanotto e pareva essersi affezionata perniciosamente a lui. Passata la fase acuta e il lungo isolamento presso l'ospedale Umberto I, l'Ernesto era dovuto restare per un tempo altrettanto lungo a casa, debole, inappetente e inabile a qualunque lavoro.

Di buono c'era che dalla sua bocca non erano mai più uscite fantasie riguardanti il genitore, risultato che già di per sé la Canterina giudicava con soddisfazione.

«Sta diventando un uomo», le aveva risposto il dottor Lonati una volta, rispondendo a una sua confidenza circa lo stato dell'Ernesto.

Se n'era accorta anche lei.

Passata la malattia, l'Ernesto aveva cambiato un po' la voce, qualche pelo aveva cominciato a crescergli in faccia. Le aveva chiesto di non dargli più il bacetto della buonanotte. E poi, da uomo, aveva cominciato a darsi certi atteggiamenti, la sigaretta, qualche parolaccia di tanto in tanto.

Una cosa sola gli mancava perché potesse definirsi tale, entrare nella categoria: un bel lavoro che avrebbe spazzato via eventuali residui di sogni o fantasie.

Non era un problema, quello.

In paese non mancavano certo le occasioni per trovarlo: cotonificio, filanda, officine, artigiani, imprese edili...

Il problema vero era che nella testa dell'Ernesto l'idea che si dovesse lavorare per campare non aveva ancora preso piede.

Certo, gli era mancato l'esempio forte di un padre.

Ci voleva ancora un po' di tempo?

La Canterina glielo aveva dato.

Aveva temporeggiato per un po', illudendosi che prima o poi la sorprendesse con la lieta novella di aver trovato l'impiego che faceva per lui.

Infine, verificato che sul fronte del lavoro non si muoveva nulla, nemmeno in conseguenza della grazia che chiedeva ogni mattina prima di recarsi all'asilo pregando davanti al quadro di santa Rita da Cascia presso la chiesetta di Santa Marta, aveva preso lei l'iniziativa.

I diciotto anni si avvicinavano al galoppo, i suoi coetanei, chi di qua chi di là, lavoravano tutti.

E lui?

Che intenzioni aveva?

«Non ti piacerebbe avere un bel lavoro come tutti quelli della tua età?» aveva cominciato a chiedere, elencando una serie di impieghi alla portata di chiunque.

«Boh», era la risposta del Dubbio.

Come faceva a sapere se gli piaceva una cosa prima ancora di farla?

La logica dell'Ernesto era stringente, ma altrettanto lo era quella di sua madre.

«È anche vero che se prima non provi non potrai mai saperlo.»

Passati un sei mesi in schermaglie siffatte, la Canterina aveva deciso di rompere gli indugi e passare alle maniere forti.

Così non si poteva andare avanti.

O si trovava un lavoro oppure lei smetteva di fare il proprio, cioè lavare, stirare, fare da mangiare per lui.

In quell'occasione aveva solo minacciato, sperando di provocare una reazione.

Ma una sera di giugno, appurato che il figlio non l'aveva presa sul serio, era passata all'azione.

Oltre alle sigarette e a qualche bicchiere di vino all'osteria, l'Ernesto, visto che di anni ne aveva quasi diciannove, aveva cominciato a uscire dopo cena, e a fare tardi.

Quella sera, rientrando in casa verso l'una di notte, il Dubbio aveva trovato la porta chiusa e a nulla era servito tempestarla di pugni e gridare, se non a svegliare il vicino di casa, Agordo Scamozzi detto Schedina, che aveva minacciato di chiamare i carabinieri e, già che c'era, gli aveva consigliato di smettere di tormentare sua madre e di trovarsi invece un lavoro.

Tutti problemi, aveva riflettuto il Dubbio, che non poteva certo affrontare in quel momento.

La priorità era trovare un posto dove dormire visto che sua madre aveva deciso per la linea dura.

Ma dove?

Era stato lì per rispondersi il solito «Boh» quando gli era venuta un'idea.

Giù al molo, in una barca, coperto dai teli coi quali i pescatori proteggevano i loro legni dalle intemperie e dall'umidità notturna.

La notte era limpida, l'aria gradevole e così aveva fatto.

V

Così, raggomitolato, addormentato come un angioletto, l'aveva scoperto qualche ora più tardi, e non senza un certo spavento, il pescatore Remègola. Sulle prime aveva pensato di dargli una palata col remo, credendo che fosse un vagabondo. Dopo averlo ben guardato e visto che era il figlio del povero Livera, l'aveva lasciato in pace e s'era avviato.

Il Remègola, nel trattare la barca e nel remare, aveva la delicatezza di un filetto di persico. Così, quando il Dubbio s'era svegliato, anziché nel molo s'era trovato a mezzo chilometro dalla riva, appena visibile per la foschia, e davanti all'impassibile viso del pescatore che dopo avergli dato il buongiorno gli aveva chiesto cosa diavolo ci facesse sulla sua barca.

Mentre il Dubbio si confessava, la Canterina si era svegliata. Più che svegliata, aveva deciso che non riusciva più a stare nel letto.

Il suo cuore di mamma l'aveva tenuta in un dormiveglia per tutta la notte, col passare delle ore la decisione di lasciare l'Ernesto fuori di casa le era sembrata sempre più crudele benché non fosse priva di ragioni. L'aveva sentito picchiare pugni sulla porta e gridare, aveva resistito, aveva ascoltato il silenzio che era calato dopo le proteste del figlio e del Schedina, aveva sperato che ritornasse a bussare, nel qual caso gli avrebbe aperto...

Non era successo, si era consolata pensando che gli sarebbe servito da lezione ma adesso...

Si era vestita ed era uscita a cercarlo.

Aveva girato tutto il paese, Calchera, molo, lungolago, giardini di Puncia, lido, Bogino, piazza della chiesa, Pradegiana, niente.

Del giovanotto non c'era traccia.

Le previsioni più nere avevano cominciato a farsi largo nella sua fantasia quando, dopo essere stata anche al cimitero per chiedere la grazia di farglielo trovare dicendo due preghiere sulla tomba del marito, aveva avuto l'impressione che la fotografia del Livera senior la guardasse male, come a volerla rimproverare di essere stata tanto sconsiderata.

A quel punto era tornata a casa per riflettere su come comportarsi.

Era il caso di recarsi dai carabinieri per raccontare l'accaduto?

Mentre saliva le scale un inusitato odore di pesce le era entrato nel naso.

Si era fermata, il fiato mozzo, l'immagine netta dell'Ernesto che si buttava nel lago per farla finita, il corpo recuperato da qualche pescatore, adagiato adesso sul letto in attesa che lei comparisse.

Aveva raggiunto la porta di casa, che aveva dimenticato di chiudere a chiave, e l'aveva aperta, sicura di vedere l'imponente figura del prevosto che le andava incontro e cominciava a dirle parole atte a prepararla alla disgrazia.

Invece s'era trovata sotto gli occhi l'Ernesto sul cui volto brillavano come stelline alcune scaglie di pesce.

«Persici», aveva detto lui, senza notare neanche di striscio l'espressione del viso di sua madre, un guazzo di gioia e incredulità.

Li avevano presi quella mattina lui e il Remègola.

Li stava sfilettando, un po' per loro due e gli altri per il vicino di casa, il Schedina, quello che l'aveva insultato poche ore prima e al quale aveva appena venduto l'eccedenza.

3.

Alle due del pomeriggio il Riffa aveva deciso di chiudere bottega.

L'incasso era l'equivalente di quattro paia di ciabatte, un paio di scarpe con la suola di para e i famosi scarponcini scamosciati che non aveva riscosso, e non avrebbe riscosso mai più.

Perché lui era un signore!

Aveva ragionato così mentre inscatolava le scarpe che aveva esposto nel banchetto buttandole poi come capitava dentro il camioncino sotto gli occhi degli altri colleghi del mercato che lo guardavano stupiti.

Cazzo, alle due chiudeva già la baracca?

Con ancora tutto un pomeriggio davanti?

«E se arriva il vigile e ci chiede come mai sei già andato via?» gli aveva chiesto il pollivendolo che stava due piazze oltre la sua.

«Te digli che ho finito le ciabatte», aveva risposto il Riffa con in mano il sacco pieno di quell'articolo, che era stata l'ultima cosa che aveva buttato nel retro del camioncino.

Il pollivendolo si era grattato il cranio da cui spuntavano timidi capelli, tale e quale alla pelle dei polli non ancora strinati.

«Per me sei matto», aveva commentato tornando al suo posto.

«Sì, sono matto», aveva approvato sottovoce il Riffa.

Ma, per come la vedeva lui, era roba da matti stare ancora lì fino alle sette o alle otto di sera a guardare il panorama che aveva sotto gli occhi, quello del banchetto di formaggi sudati per via del caldo, a respirare l'aria satura di pollo arrosto, ad ascoltare le grida di un paio che stavano quasi in fondo alla fila dei banchi e che, a scadenza regolare, gridavano «Regalo tutto!» e «Donne, tutto per la vostra casa!».

E gridavano anche se non c'era in giro nessuno.

Chi era matto, lui o loro?

Il Riffa aveva chiuso il camioncino e si era pulito le mani fregandole sui pantaloni. Coi soldi che aveva fatto quella mattina s'era giusto ripagato la benzina per andata e ritorno, ma era partito senza pensieri alla prospettiva di arrivare a Bellano per le tre, tre e mezza al massimo e passare il pomeriggio al lido, steso al sole, ingannando il resto della giornata con gli occhi chiusi e un paio di birrette che, a quanto gli avevano detto, aiutavano a farsi l'abbronzatura.

Dal finestrino mezzo abbassato entrava un intenso profumo di catrame, asfalto steso di fresco e già cotto dal sole, che si mischiava con quello di sudore che impregnava la cabina del camioncino. Un misto che esaltava l'entusiasmo del Riffa: l'odore d'asfalto gli dava un'imprecisata idea di libertà, quello di sudore la conferma di essere un vero uomo, per di più libero di fare quello che più gli piaceva e non un servo come i suoi colleghi del mercato, pitocchi che sprecavano il meglio della vita pur di non perdere l'occasione di vendere una crosta di formaggio o uno scartozzello di ali di pollo.

E nemmeno... come si diceva?, sincope?

Sì, nemmeno sincope di una donna che non aveva altra idea se non quella di farsi sposare e farsi mantenere per tutta la vita.

Trombarle tutte e non sposarne nessuna, quella era la sua regola.

S'era già lasciato alle spalle Santa Maria, Rezzonico,

Pianello del Lario. Entrato in Dongo gli venne in mente quello che gli aveva detto uno del mercato, forse uno dei pochi normali, che la pensava un po' come lui, infatti aveva un banchetto di biancheria intima. Proprio lì a Dongo c'era un campeggio frequentato da olandesine e tedesche di passo. Facevano il bagno nude, giravano con le tette al vento, e che tette!

«Cosa credi che vengano qui sul lago a fare?» aveva detto.

«A prendere il sole», aveva risposto lui.

Ma schiacciando l'occhio.

«Proprio quello», aveva confermato l'altro.

Bisognava vedere alla sera, le macchine che arrivavano da tutte le parti e convergevano sulla piazzetta del baretto del campeggio. Tempo un paio d'ore, quando cominciava a far bello buio, una dopo l'altra partivano per i recessi più nascosti con sopra una, a volte due di quelle sgnacchere.

Il Riffa ci aveva pensato spesso, s'era immaginato la scena.

Docciato...

Non aveva la doccia in casa ma non è che ce l'avesse scritto in fronte. E comunque si lavava.

Quindi, docciato, deodorato, vestito come un cantante.

Arrivava con la sua bella macchina nello spiazzo davanti al baretto e scendeva. A quel punto, proprio nel momento in cui gli occhi delle olandesine e delle tedesche si puntavano su di lui, la fantasia si esauriva repentinamente perché non aveva la macchina.

E se non poteva recitare il suo ingresso trionfale col suo camioncino, men che meno poteva ospitare un'olandesina o una tedesca in quella cabina dove stagnava senza rimedio un odore di caserma.

«La macchina, figa!» aveva gridato quando era ormai a metà del ponte del passo.

Gli ci voleva una macchina per approfittare di tutte le occasioni che l'estate, la vita!, gli offriva.

Anche di seconda mano.

Ma anche per quelle di seconda mano ci volevano soldi per pagarle e per averli avrebbe dovuto arrendersi a fare due cose che non gli riuscivano per niente bene: lavorare un po' di più, con più impegno, più determinazione, e risparmiare.

Va be'!, si era detto.

Ormai per quell'anno era andata così, l'estate era in corso, doveva arrangiarsi come poteva.

Ci avrebbe pensato con l'inverno.

Attraversando Colico aveva rallentato, non voleva lasciare tra le mani del vigile l'incasso delle ciabatte e si era concentrato sul programma del pomeriggio, lido, sole, e il Dubbio da allertare per l'appuntamento della sera seguente.

Entrato in paese si era fermato in piazza Boldoni, davanti alla drogheria Coloniali.

Non aveva spento il motore, era sceso, traversato la strada e dato un'occhiata alle barche che stavano dentro il molo.

Il posto della *Canterina* era vuoto, sulla murata spiccava il cartello, vergato a mano, di un rosso ormai un po' scolorito su fondo bianco, con la scritta NOLLEGGIO BARCA.

Il proprietario del ristorante Cavallo Bianco con ingresso che dava sulla piazza si era fatto sulla porta per gridargli di spegnere il motore, la puzza dello scarico gli stava invadendo il locale.

«Hai visto il Dubbio?» gli aveva chiesto il Riffa ritornando verso il camioncino.

Era uscito un'oretta prima, aveva risposto il ristoratore.

Portava a fare un giro due che avevano mangiato lì da lui.

«Bon, se lo vedi digli che ho bisogno di lui.»

Che non si dimenticasse, era urgente.

4.

NOLLEGGIO era stata un'idea della Canterina che era al contempo mamma e barca.

Nolleggio, con due elle.

Impossibile contraddirla, anche perché l'Ernesto ne sapeva ancora meno di lei. E poi perché la donna aveva trasfuso in quella doppia elle fuori luogo tutto l'entusiasmo che le idee del figlio le avevano provocato: nolcggiare la barca ai turisti e fare domanda di assunzione alla Navigazione Lariana.

«Nolleggiare!» l'aveva corretto lei.

«Sì, va bene. Ma ti sembra una bella idea?»

Talmente bella che il cartello, NOLLEGGIO BARCA, l'aveva dipinto lei, dopodiché aveva esaudito due impegni che s'era presa come fossero voti: dapprima era filata alla chiesetta dedicata a Santa Marta e aveva ringraziato santa Rita da Cascia per la grazia ricevuta, subito dopo aveva fatto lo stesso con quello che lei considerava il braccio secolare della grazia stessa, il Remègola, perché se il Dubbio adesso andava verso i ventuno anni e viaggiava via abbastanza dritto era tutto sommato merito suo.

Il pescatore infatti, dopo che se l'era trovato in barca, un po' per scherzo e un po' no, visto che era solo al mondo e l'idea di avere un allievo cui insegnare tutte le magate che sapeva in fatto di pesci non gli dispiaceva, gli aveva proposto di seguirlo: prima di tutto imparava un mestiere che in fin dei conti gli dava da campare, bastava guardare lui che remava dall'età di quindici anni!

«E poi l'unico padrone che c'hai sei te.»

Il Dubbio s'era lasciato affascinare da quell'idea di libertà senza padroni.

Sua madre, manco a dirlo, aveva dato l'assenso.

«Qualunque lavoro va bene, purché sia onesto», aveva sentenziato.

A circa un anno di distanza il Dubbio aveva ragionato tra sé che il Remègola gli aveva raccontato un sacco di balle.

Sul campare di quel mestiere, va be', forse i suoi erano stati altri tempi e c'era in giro più pesce nel lago...

Ma c'erano state giornate in cui tutti e due non avevano fatto altro che guardare attraverso la rete, vuota come le loro tasche, i paesi della sponda opposta. E riguardo al non aver padroni, che cos'altro era il Remègola, che gli diceva a che ora doveva trovarsi al molo per uscire, quando buttare la rete e quando ritirarla, come remare, dove stare, quando parlare e quando stare zitto?

E allora un bel giorno gli aveva detto che si sentiva pronto per cominciare a fare il pescatore da solo.

«Ne devi così imparare di cose!» aveva esclamato il Remègola.

Il Dubbio lo sapeva ma ormai aveva deciso e gli aveva risposto con una scrollata di spalle.

«E poi non c'hai la barca», aveva osservato il pescatore.

«Invece sì», aveva risposto il Dubbio.

La *Canterina*!

«Ma non è tua mamma?» s'era stupito il Remègola.

5.

La *Canterina* era anche una barca.

Un barcarozzo già predisposto per un motore che suo padre, pescatore per diletto, aveva acquistato da uno di Onno, usato sì e no una decina di volte e che stava giù in deposito nel magazzino della falegnameria: tanto, aveva detto il Farfatti, fastidio non gli dava e semmai ne avessero avuto bisogno sapevano dove trovarla.

Era stato suo padre a volerla battezzare col nome della moglie.

E pensare che lei non ci aveva messo mai piede sopra.

Così aveva iniziato l'attività in proprio ed erano stati quasi subito cazzi amari.

Finché era durata la bella stagione il Dubbio non se l'era cavata male. Pesce ce n'era un po' per tutti anche se la maggior parte degli acquirenti del paese aveva già i suoi fornitori e il più delle volte il giovanotto doveva ricorrere a un sistema di vendita porta a porta per smaltire il pescato, metodo che si mangiava tutto il resto del tempo che non passava in barca.

Le difficoltà vere erano cominciate con la brutta stagione.

Combattere contro il freddo, il vento, il ghiaccio, la neve, la pioggia.

Non solo, ma anche contro quei pesci di merda che sembravano sentire il suo odore quando si avvicinava e gli sfuggivano giusto per andare a infilarsi nelle reti degli altri o disdegnando le sue esche.

La Canterina, la madre, aveva cominciato a intuire che la situazione si stava deteriorando quando per più di una volta aveva trovato l'Ernesto ancora a letto, addormentato, all'ora in cui invece avrebbe dovuto essere fuori in barca a combattere contro gli elementi naturali e le astuzie dei pesci. E s'era convinta che avrebbe dovuto ricominciare a usare il pugno di ferro quando, sempre più di una volta, tornata a casa dall'asilo infantile Tommaso Grossi dopo aver terminato il suo turno di cuciniera, l'aveva ribeccato sempre a letto, sempre addormentato.

Intuendo che la pazienza della madre si stava esaurendo, il Dubbio aveva tentato di prendere tempo, giurando e spergiurando che si sarebbe messo a cercare un lavoro diverso, magari un po' più comodo.

Per fortuna l'inverno era ormai agli sgoccioli e una mattina aveva deciso di ritentare la sorte.

Era uscito presto ed era rientrato senza aver rubato alle acque del lago nemmeno un'arborella.

Sul molo, intento a sistemare la sua barca, aveva visto il Remègola e gli si era avvicinato con in testa la precisa intenzione di comprargli un po' del pesce che lui invece aveva pescato, in modo da tenere a freno la rabbia di sua madre, almeno per quel giorno.

«Il pesce te lo regalo», aveva risposto il Remègola.

A patto però che lui si convincesse di non avere la stoffa per fare il pescatore.

«Sei un fighetta», gli aveva spiegato il Remègola senza alcuna intenzione di offendere.

Un pescatore della domenica, come ce n'erano in giro tanti, che magari affittavano una barchetta per farsi un giretto e tornare a casa con un paio di cavedani...

A quell'uscita il Dubbio s'era sentito folgorare da un'idea.

«Ma per il resto, se vuoi un mio parere, lascia perdere 'sto lavoro e magari fa' domanda di assunzione alla Navigazione, ho sentito che sono in cerca di personale.»

Il Dubbio era volato a casa senza nemmeno prendere il pesce che il Remègola, per compassione, alla fine gli voleva regalare.

Cazzo, quella sì che era un'idea!

Noleggiare una barca ai turisti e ai pescatorelli, gente che non si svegliava alle due del mattino e che d'inverno se ne stava al caldo sotto le coperte.

Circa la domanda alla Navigazione, va be', forse il Remègola non aveva tutti i torti e poi, per quanto constava a lui, quella non era gente che si ammazzava di lavoro.

Nell'apprendere le novità, la madre del Dubbio s'era sentita lievitare per la felicità e, dopo aver insistito sulla doppia elle di noleggio e averla eseguita di persona sul cartello, aveva esaudito i voti fatti.

Infine, pur non volendo ammettere che aveva ancora qualche riserva sulla buona volontà del figlio, aveva provveduto da sé, con l'aiuto del battellotto Circina, a redigere la domanda di assunzione alla Navigazione Lariana consegnandola brevi manu a Severo Pontida, comandante del battello *Nibbio*, che si era offerto di portarla presso gli uffici di direzione di Como, garantendo che grazie alla sua benevola intercessione l'Ernesto poteva ritenersi già arruolato.

6.

Due piedi che andavano in giro infilati in un paio di peduli macchiati e con su le calze anche nel mese di luglio potevano essere solo quelli del Dubbio.

Infatti.

Le due birre il Riffa le aveva bevute e poi si era addormentato a pancia sotto nonostante la spiaggia del lido fosse tutt'altro che comoda: un letto di ciottoli più che altro e chi voleva starsene un po' comodo si portava da casa sedie, sdraio o materassini.

Aveva aperto l'occhio sinistro, il Dubbio gli faceva ombra da quella parte.

«Uei», aveva salutato con la bocca mezzo schiacciata sulla riva.

«Cosa c'è di urgente?» aveva chiesto il Dubbio.

Il Riffa si era messo a sedere, abbracciandosi le gambe, aveva guardato il lago e si era grattato la testa. Poi aveva fatto cenno al Dubbio di sedersi.

«Domani pomeriggio tieniti libero», gli aveva detto sottovoce.

«Perché?» aveva chiesto il Dubbio.

Per tutta risposta il Riffa gli aveva messo sotto gli occhi indice e medio, il segno della vittoria.

Il Dubbio però non era in vena di risolvere enigmi.

«Cioè?» aveva chiesto.

Il Riffa allora aveva riunito in punta pollice e indice, il segno di quella cosa là.

«Ne ho beccate due», aveva chiarito.

«E allora?» aveva chiesto il Dubbio.

Il Riffa aveva ritirato le dita.

«Ma sei scemo?» aveva chiesto.

O faceva finta di non capire?

Il Dubbio l'aveva guardato senza rispondere.

«Sveglia!» gli aveva detto il Riffa.

L'Ernesto aveva sputacchiato di lato, stava sudando, tutto quel sole gli dava fastidio.

«'Scolta Riffa, non sono nello spirito giusto, te lo sai...»

Ma sì, lo sapeva, acconsentì il Riffa.

Lo sapeva bene che era un periodo di merda.

E proprio per questo, appena agganciate quelle due, aveva pensato a lui.

Per tirarlo un po' fuori.

«Tanto, guarda», aveva detto il Riffa, «i periodi di merda così come arrivano passano.»

«Se lo dici te...» aveva sospirato il Dubbio.

«Io lo dico ma tu dovresti saperlo», aveva ribattuto il Riffa.

Bastava, aveva aggiunto, che pensasse a quello che andava dicendo, attaccarsi su, buttarsi nel lago con un bel sasso al collo e tutte quelle storie lì, dopo la faccenda delle duecento stecche.

7.

I

Duecento stecche di sigarette precise precise.

Marlboro, Muratti, Astor, Peer, Parisienne con e senza filtro, Chesterfield e Turmac.

Proprio nel momento in cui, superate le iniziali incertezze ma senza aver compiuto nemmeno un commercio, il Dubbio aveva cominciato a sentirsi un contrabbandiere coi fiocchi ed era entrato nella parte, assumendo anche certi atteggiamenti da navigato: camminare con le mani in tasca e parlare con gli altri guardandosi sempre un po' intorno...

Era successo a poco più di un mese da quando era diventato un noleggiatore di barca.

Tutto era partito sotto i migliori auspici.

Prima di trovarsi qualche sorpresa, infatti, tipo la *Canterina* con due bei buchi adagiata sul fondo del molo, il Dubbio era andato a consigliarsi con il custode. Si chiamava Girgetta e anche lui all'occasione affittava barche o conduceva turisti in giro.

Il Girgetta non solo gli aveva detto che la sua concorrenza non gli avrebbe dato il minimo fastidio ma, anzi, era ben contento che un giovane di buona volontà si facesse avanti: lui era già in pensione di suo, quel lavoro lo faceva per diletto e per riempire la giornata ma ormai, fra artriti e artrosi, era sempre più frequente la voglia di mollare.

«Chissà mai che ti venga voglia di pigliartelo te 'sto molo», gli aveva detto il Girgetta.

«Boh», aveva risposto il Dubbio e il giorno seguente aveva attaccato il cartello NOLLEGGIO BARCA sedendosi poi sulla panchina di lato al monumento a Sigismondo Boldoni ad aspettare clienti.

Qualcosina aveva cominciato a muoversi verso la fine di giugno, quando, finite le scuole, parecchie famiglie venivano sul lago per passare l'estate. La maggior parte del merito però era stata del Girgetta: al Dubbio infatti indirizzava le richieste che non aveva voglia di soddisfare, soprattutto quando, anziché la sola barca, i clienti gli chiedevano anche un rematore. Il più del lavoro gli era capitato nel corso dei mesi di luglio e agosto, quattro, cinque, a volte anche sei uscite giornaliere che, alla tariffa oraria di lire millecinquecento, gli avevano permesso di arrivare a sfiorare l'incredibile quota di quasi duecentomila lire mensili.

«Ma adesso?»

La domanda gliel'aveva fatta proprio il Riffa, una sera di fine agosto.

«Cioè?» aveva chiesto il Dubbio.

Erano seduti sulla panchina che era ormai diventata quasi proprietà esclusiva dell'Ernesto.

Bella sera, ancora calda, ma...

«Non lo senti l'odore del fumo?» aveva chiesto ancora il Riffa.

«Che fumo?» aveva ribattuto il Dubbio.

Quello dei camini delle fabbriche che riaprivano, no?

La pacchia stava per finire, era così difficile da capire?

«Tutti quelli che lavorano in trafila, in fabbrica, in ditta sono tornati a casina e agli altri manca poco perché poi cominciano anche le scuole.»

Dopodiché, aveva aggiunto il Riffa, gli dicesse un po' lui chi avrebbe portato in giro in barchetta.

Il Dubbio s'era grattato la testa.

«Ci avevo pensato», aveva detto a bassa voce.
«Soluzioni?» aveva chiesto il Riffa.
Rimettersi a fare il pescatore di Chiaravalle?, aveva aggiunto con un ghignetto.
«Magari la Navigazione mi chiama», aveva mormorato il Dubbio.
Ormai però la domanda era partita da un bel po', ma da Como nisba.
«E se invece non ti chiama?» aveva insistito il Riffa.
Al Dubbio era scappata un po' la pazienza.
«Va be', allora dimmelo tu cosa fare visto che sai tutto!»
«Io», aveva risposto il Riffa, «con una barca sotto il culo come te, una mezza idea ce l'avrei.»
«Sarebbe?» aveva chiesto il Dubbio.
Lui conosceva, sulla sponda di là, uno che faceva deposito.
«Di roba di sfroso», aveva spiegato.
Perlopiù sigarette.
Si chiamava Franciscia, era una specie di capetto di una squadra di spalloni che gli portava la roba. Poi ci pensava lui a smistarla.
«Sì, va bene, e allora?» aveva chiesto il Dubbio.
«Allora lo sai quanto costa un pacchetto di sigarette, mettiamo le Alfa?»
«Col filtro?» aveva chiesto il Dubbio.
«Quale filtro?»
«Le Alfa, dico, col filtro o senza?»
«Ma cosa cazzo te ne frega del filtro! Rispondimi invece.»
Il Dubbio non lo sapeva.
Nemmeno il Riffa di preciso.
«Occhio e croce... duecento lire.»
E il Franciscia gliele vendeva a cento lire al pacchetto.
«Le Alfa?»
«Ma sei scemo?»
Muratti, Marlboro e tutte quelle altre marche fatte col tabacco vero, mica con la merda secca!

«Le paghi cento e le rivendi a duecento», aveva continuato il Riffa.

Il cioccolato a metà prezzo della merda, capiva?

«Sì», aveva risposto il Dubbio.

«Bene», aveva approvato il Riffa.

Perché, se aveva capito e sapeva fare i conti, non aveva bisogno di dirgli altro.

Certo che no, aveva risposto il Dubbio: comprava una stecca da dieci o da venti, la pagava mille o duemila lire, la rivendeva a duemila o quattromila e il resto era tutto guadagno!

«Allora non hai capito un cazzo!» aveva sussurrato il Riffa sconsolato.

Non aveva capito un cazzo, perché se si presentava dal Franciscia e gli chiedeva una o due stecche di sigarette se le ritrovava su per quel posto.

«Non è una tabaccheria, lui smercia all'ingrosso», aveva spiegato il Riffa.

Doveva prendere almeno cento, duecento stecche!

«E non fare quella faccia lì», aveva esclamato il Riffa stoppando l'obiezione che stava salendo alle labbra del Dubbio. Perché se sapeva fare bene i conti...

«Metti duecento stecche, che sulla *Canterina* ci stanno comode comode...»

... duecento stecche erano duemila pacchetti di sigarette a cento lire l'uno.

«Le paghi duecentomila lire», si era fermato il Riffa per vedere se il Dubbio aveva capito bene.

Bon, avanti allora.

«Se le rivendi a duecento lire al pacchetto, quanto fa?»

Il Dubbio aveva cominciato a fare i conti ma il Riffa ce li aveva già belli e pronti.

«Te lo dico io.»

Quattrocentomila lire belle tonde!

E se tirava via il prezzo d'acquisto, quanto gli restava in tasca?

«Duecentomila lire!»

Cioè, con una sola notte di lavoro, quello che lui aveva guadagnato in un mese.

Poteva così metterne in fila di bauscia e smortone da portare in giro per il lago prima di arrivare a quelle cifre in così poco tempo!

Il Dubbio si era immerso in un lungo, interminabile minuto di silenzio.

«Sì, ma io 'sto Franciscia non so nemmeno chi sia», aveva infine detto.

«Lo so io», aveva risposto il Riffa.

Non era un problema prendere contatti con lui.

«Quando vuoi», aveva concluso il Riffa, «se vuoi.»

II

Un paio di settimane.

Tanto c'era voluto al Dubbio per decidersi all'impresa e per mettere insieme il capitale necessario, obiettivo che aveva raggiunto investendo i risparmi della stagione estiva, vendendo sulla fiducia una cinquantina di stecche e infine intascando i soldi che la Canterina gli aveva dato per pagare in anticipo al Bombola tre mesi di fornitura di cherosene, visto che l'autunno era alle porte e conveniva portarsi avanti.

Quella di saldare in anticipo le uscite più onerose, come appunto il cherosene per la stufetta domestica, era un'abitudine consolidata per la donna.

«Non si sa mai cosa può capitare», diceva.

E debiti in giro non ne voleva lasciare.

Più o meno il Bombola aveva posto la stessa domanda al Dubbio quando questi l'aveva pregato di non fare cenno a sua madre del fatto di non essere stato pagato in anticipo come al solito.

«È capitato qualcosa?»

Cioè una spesa straordinaria, non voluta e tuttavia necessaria, come una malattia?
Il Dubbio se l'era cavata borbottando che gli avrebbe spiegato.
«Mi raccomando però, non dire niente», aveva aggiunto.
«Tranquillo», aveva assicurato il Bombola, certo di aver compreso ogni cosa.
C'era di sicuro una malattia di mezzo.
Della Canterina forse, per via dell'età.
Oppure dello stesso Dubbio, che a detta di tanti dalla morte del padre scoperta in quel modo non si era mai ripreso del tutto.
E tra i due, nel novero della clientela cui aveva confessato i suoi pensieri e ascoltato le risposte, era stato proprio il giovanotto a riscuotere il successo maggiore: d'altronde, poveretto, lo si poteva capire se dopo un fatto del genere non era più maturato come si doveva, se aveva paura della sua stessa ombra, se non era ancora né carne né pesce eccetera eccetera.
Il Dubbio invece, il capitale ormai in tasca, non viveva altro che per la sua prima, grande impresa da contrabbandiere e aveva dato il via al colpaccio avvisando il Riffa che era pronto.
«Io non c'entro niente eh!» l'aveva avvisato quello.
Faceva solo da intermediario, e nel caso di guai non aveva visto, sentito o detto niente.
Quale intermediario, secondo gli usi e costumi del Franciscia, s'era fatto consegnare la somma per l'acquisto delle duecento stecche.
Il Dubbio aveva accettato la consuetudine non senza un certo tremore.
«Ma siamo sicuri?»
Il Riffa gli aveva risposto con gli occhi.
Bastava lo sguardo?
Era bastato.

La sera del 14 settembre – la data si sarebbe impressa con lettere di sangue nella mente del Dubbio –, il novello contrabbandiere era partito dal molo di Bellano attorno alle nove e trenta per approdare circa tre ore più tardi su quello di Acquaseria.

L'appuntamento era con uno...

«Uno chi?» aveva chiesto il Dubbio al Riffa che gli aveva riferito quello che doveva fare.

«Uno e basta», era stata la risposta.

... uno che lo avrebbe aspettato tra mezzanotte e l'una e che, senza dire una parola, l'aveva portato un po' fuori dall'abitato e condotto fino a una stalletta abbandonata. Dopodiché gli aveva aperto la porta, aveva acceso l'accendino giusto il tempo di illuminare due sacchi.

«Sono lì», aveva detto.

Il tempo di dire grazie e il Dubbio non l'aveva più visto, sparito. Allora s'era caricato i sacchi in spalla ed era filato senza intoppi fino alla barca. Per la prima ora aveva remato come se fosse inseguito da qualcuno. Una volta verificato che le luci di entrambe le rive erano piccole piccole si era dato una calmata e in quel preciso istante erano cominciati i guai. Da babordo aveva visto nascere una prima luce poi una seconda in rapido avvicinamento e come se entrambe fossero sorte dalle acque del lago. La stessa cosa subito dopo l'aveva vista a tribordo. Una luce sola ma, come le altre due, in rapido avvicinamento. E poi aveva sentito il rumore di spari.

La velocità con la quale le luci si stavano avvicinando non gli aveva consentito di perdere tempo. Aveva preso i due sacchi e li aveva gettati nel lago, il più possibile lontano dalla barca. Lui invece si era steso, lungo e tirato quant'era, sul fondo della *Canterina,* augurandosi che i proiettili che gli stavano sparando addosso non riuscissero a bucare il legno della barca e a centrarlo in qualche modo. Era rimasto accucciato così fino a che lo spavento che gli aveva ottuso i sensi si era ridotto. Allora aveva cominciato a non percepire più il rumore degli spari e invece bello distinto quello di motori di motoscafo che stavano rallentando e con tutta evidenza avvicinandosi, stante la luce che aveva illuminato quasi a giorno intorno alla *Canterina*.

Poi, una volta spentosi del tutto il ruggire dei motori, aveva sentito una voce.

«Che cazzo ci fa quella barca?»

Subito dopo: «Ma chi cazzo sei?».

Il Dubbio, comunque sdraiato ancora sul fondo della barca, aveva girato il viso verso quella voce.

La luce intensa di una torcia che gli puntava contro gli aveva impedito di vedere chi l'avesse in mano ma non di capire che quello che gli si era accostato era un fuoribordo.

La prima voce s'era di nuovo levata forte per chiedere che cazzo ci facesse lì quella barca. La seconda voce stava parlottando col Dubbio, spiegandogli che bisognava avere una testa piena di sabbia per andarsene in giro per il lago in piena notte senza nemmeno una luce di segnalazione.

Per fortuna loro s'erano accorti della sua presenza.

Loro chi?, aveva chiesto il Dubbio.

Ma loro, no?

Quelli della produzione italo-svizzera che in quei giorni stava girando le riprese di un film, *Una donna non fa primavera*, che comprendeva anche scene di una specie di duello tra due bande rivali a bordo di motoscafi.

«Era su tutti i giornali», gli aveva detto la seconda voce.

Quella notte stavano appunto provando una di quelle scene. Lo sapevano tutti, Carabinieri, Guardia di Finanza, Navigazione Lariana, questura, pretura, municipi interessati, anche perché avevano dovuto chiedere fior di permessi.

E lui stava per mandare a puttane tutto quanto.

«Allora?» aveva chiesto gridando la prima voce.

«Attaccati ai remi e va' fuori dai coglioni più in fretta che puoi prima che al produttore venga in mente di chiederti i danni», gli aveva consigliato la seconda voce.

Il Dubbio non se l'era mica fatto ripetere.

Poi lenta, quando l'irrealtà della situazione appena vissuta era andata svanendo, s'era fatta largo la realtà.

Triste e dura realtà.

Aveva buttato nel lago i risparmi di tutta l'estate e tornava nel molo carico dei debiti che aveva nei confronti di coloro cui aveva già venduto le sigarette, senza dimenticare il Bombola e il suo cherosene.

Per prima cosa, il giorno dopo era andato dal Riffa a confessarsi e a chiedere consiglio.

«Cosa cazzo posso farci io?» gli aveva risposto quello.

Glielo aveva ben detto, no?, che lui faceva solo da intermediario, non vedeva, non sentiva, non parlava.

Il Dubbio s'era messo quasi a piangere, dicendo che allora non gli restava che appendersi da qualche parte o buttarsi nel lago con un sasso al collo.

«Aspetta una settimana, però, prima di farlo», gli aveva suggerito il Riffa.

Profetico senza saperlo.

Quello stesso giorno la moglie del Girgetta l'aveva chiamato per chiedergli se poteva sostituire in tutto e per tutto suo marito al molo, visto che lui era steso a letto per colpa della sciatica.

«Una settimanetta», gli aveva chiesto la donna.

La sciatica del Girgetta invece era andata avanti fino alla fine di ottobre, di pari passo con un'estate gentile che aveva favorito un regolare afflusso di affezionati amanti del lago.

Con i servizi che gli erano toccati il Dubbio era riuscito a tacitare i suoi creditori e a saldare quasi per intero il Bombola cui aveva comunque ripetuto di non far parola con nessuno del loro accordo.

8.

I

«O te o nessuno», aveva detto il Riffa cominciando a lanciare qualche ciottolo nel lago.

Piuttosto mandava a monte l'affare.

«Un peccato, perché la tua c'ha un culo che parla», aveva aggiunto tralasciando il serpente della bionda.

Il Dubbio aveva disegnato qualche ghirigoro sulla riva con la punta del piede.

«Va bene, dai», aveva poi detto a bassa voce.

«Sì, ma... con un po' di entusiasmo», gli aveva suggerito il Riffa.

Il Dubbio non gli aveva nemmeno risposto. Aveva girato i tacchi e s'era avviato lentamente per tornare alla sua postazione, sulla panchina di lato al monumento a Sigismondo Boldoni. Era sudato e doveva riflettere.

Niente di che.

Ma doveva inventare la balla giusta da raccontare alla Canterina, intesa quale madre. Mica poteva dirle, con quello che c'era in ballo, che andava in giro di notte a fare il donda col Riffa. Capace che la donna si decidesse a mettere in atto la minaccia, fin troppe volte sentita, di chiuderlo fuori casa una volta per tutte, e che s'arrangiasse. E lui sapeva, per esperienza, che sua madre era capace di farlo davvero.

Raggiunta la panchina, il Dubbio aveva pensato che forse avrebbe fatto bene a dire no al Riffa.

Tutto sommato era ancora in tempo.

Però...

Cos'aveva detto quello, del culetto della sua?

Parlava!

E lui era da un po' che non faceva discorsi del genere.

Se solo non avesse avuto una madre che lo curava come se avesse ancora dieci anni!

All'ombra degli ippocastani il Dubbio aveva passato il resto del pomeriggio cercando, senza riuscire, di decidere il da fare.

«Vedremo», aveva detto a mezza voce quando ormai erano le sette, ora di cena.

Una volta a casa, oltre al mangiare, s'era trovato bella e pronta la soluzione.

La Canterina gli aveva detto che aveva accettato di assistere un'anziana che stava morendo su all'ospizio.

«Faccio notte oggi, domani e dopo», gli aveva detto.

Poi, se quella non schiattava, arrivavano i parenti.

«Te, mi raccomando», aveva aggiunto.

«Cosa vuoi che faccia», aveva risposto lui.

Aveva già un viaggio prenotato, aveva mentito all'istante: uno che voleva uscire a metà pomeriggio e poi tirar notte per provare la pesca alla fiocina.

La Canterina gli aveva risposto solo con una smorfia.

Il giorno dopo una smorfia quasi identica era comparsa sul volto del Riffa.

II

Era metà pomeriggio, erano a metà strada tra Dervio e Corenno Plinio.

Sul volto del Riffa era comparsa quella smorfia, poi aveva fermato il camioncino e l'aveva guardato.

«E adesso che cazzo facciamo?» gli aveva chiesto poi.

Cosa facciamo?, aveva detto il silenzio del Dubbio.

«Perché», gli aveva spiegato il Riffa, «se non ti sei accorto abbiamo bucato!»

E ruote di scorta nisba.

Il Dubbio aveva guardato dal finestrino, l'ombra del camioncino per metà proiettata sul muro grezzo della casa di lato. C'era un'anziana alla finestra che sembrava indifferente a ciò che le passava sotto gli occhi. Alle sue spalle la penombra di una cucina, un'idea di frescura.

«Allora?» aveva ripreso il Riffa.

Il Dubbio aveva esitato un po' prima di rispondere.

«Possiamo usare la barca», aveva infine proposto.

«È vero!» aveva esultato il socio.

Allora via, senza perdere tempo!

Cosa che invece sembrava dovesse accadere perché il camioncino pareva non aver più alcuna intenzione di ripartire, come si fosse anche ingolfato o magari non ci fosse più benza.

Ma il Riffa era uomo dalle mille risorse!

Era sceso e aveva chiamato un gruppetto di bocia che stavano giocando vicino alla fontana della piazza di Corenno, dalla quale si diceva uscisse acqua quasi miracolosa. Il miracolo vero era stato che quelli non l'avessero mandato a quel paese o si fossero volatilizzati al richiamo. Invece li avevano aiutati a tirar via dalla strada il mezzo, spingendolo nella piazza e parcheggiandolo sul lato della chiesa dove c'era l'ingresso della sagrestia.

«Poi ci penso», aveva detto il Riffa.

S'erano avviati, lui davanti il Dubbio dietro, sotto il sole canaglia delle cinque del pomeriggio, tornando a piedi verso Bellano, destinazione molo, per saltare sulla barca e riprendere il viaggio verso la sponda di là, dove le due aspettavano.

Man mano che si avvicinavano alla riva e poi dopo, salendo a piedi verso il crotto, il Riffa s'era infoiato sempre di più, non aveva fatto altro che parlare di serpenti e culi che cantavano. Alla fine anche il Dubbio era entrato nella parte e quando finalmente avevano trovato le due ragazze aveva schiacciato l'occhio al Riffa, un vero amico.

Fin verso le dieci erano rimasti tutti assieme, seduti al tavolino del crotto del Buco dell'Orso, a bere, mangiare pane e salame, raccontarsi cose e ridere.

Già divisi in coppie.

Lui e la Tina da un lato, il Riffa e la Valeria dall'altro, di fronte a loro.

Al Dubbio non era sfuggito che col passare dei minuti il socio stava cominciando ad allungare le mani sotto il tavolo mentre la ragazza rispondeva con colpetti di spalla per dirgli di smetterla e ogni tanto, chissà perché, schiacciava l'occhio, ma non al Riffa, alla sua amica piuttosto, come se le volesse dire «Aspetta e vedrai».

Per conto suo aveva verificato che la Tina non parlava tanto. Peraltro contava che, come aveva detto il Riffa, parlasse il suo culetto. A un certo punto il Riffa aveva detto qualcosa all'orecchio della bionda e poi aveva comunicato che loro si allontanavano un momento, dovevano vedere una cosa. La bionda si era alzata con lui, aveva schiacciato ancora l'occhio alla Tina e salutato, ciao ciao.

A quel punto il Dubbio era piombato nell'imbarazzo.

E adesso?

Fino a quel momento la conversazione, le cazzate erano state prerogativa del Riffa, maestro di lappa. Lui invece non è che avesse 'ste gran cose da raccontare. Infine, prima che venisse in mente alla Tina di entrare in argomento, eventualità che l'avrebbe obbligato ad arrampicarsi sugli specchi, aveva sparato la domanda più banale.

«E voi cosa fate di bello?» aveva chiesto come se l'altra fosse stata ancora presente.

La ragazza non s'era fatta pregare.

La Tina gli aveva spiegato innanzitutto che loro due erano amiche, mica sorelle.

La Valeria per intanto, aveva poi spiegato, non faceva niente.

«Mica male», aveva commentato lui.

«Ha studiato», l'aveva ripreso lei con tono da rimprovero.

Gli sembrava niente?

Aveva studiato perché suo padre aveva un albergo giù ad Acquaseria e lei per intanto stava riflettendo su cosa fare in futuro. Le piacevano le lingue straniere e la mattina seguente sarebbe partita per l'Inghilterra, un mese intero, per migliorare l'inglese.

«Io, invece...»

E l'aveva presa un po' larga per spiegare che assisteva un certo Alessio Dalamonti, mobiliere brianzolo, fondatore di una delle tante case del mobile di Lissone il quale, una volta rimasto vedovo, aveva ceduto ai figli, un maschio e una femmina, l'attività per tornarsene sul lago di Como a vivere nella casetta dov'era nato.

«Aveva intenzione di godere i suoi ultimi anni contornato dalle bellezze del lago», aveva raccontato la ragazza, «ma venire qui e ammalarsi quasi subito di cataratta per colpa di un diabete mica tanto curato è stato un tutt'uno.»

Una fortuna per lei, aveva detto la ragazza, se si poteva chiamare fortuna una malattia. Una fortuna comunque perché fino a quando il commenda era stato in grado di cavarsela da solo, a dargli un'occhiata di tanto in tanto aveva provveduto un'ex infermiera, zitella, che abitava proprio di fronte a lui. Poi però, quando la situazione era precipitata, quella aveva detto ai figli che non se la sentiva di mantenere un impegno così gravoso. E loro avevano messo in giro la voce che cercavano una persona affidabile per badare al padre. A quel punto lei non aveva perso l'occasione.

Aveva solo la terza media, cosa poteva sperare di meglio?

Un bello stipendio, l'avevano messa anche a libri, l'ex infermiera le aveva insegnato quello che doveva fare e inoltre, nel caso di un bisogno improvviso, era pur sempre lì, bastava chiamarla: anzi, a volte non era nemmeno necessario farlo, passava lei di sua volontà.

«Lo fa anche per curiosare un po', chiacchierare», aveva spiegato la Tina. «D'altronde è sola, in paese non ha molte amicizie. Anzi, forse non ne ha nemmeno una.»

Per il resto, mestieri di casa e far da mangiare, non aveva bisogno di maestre. Così poteva anche stare vicino a sua madre, vedova, non proprio anziana ma che ogni tanto aveva botte di pressione alta che la obbligavano a stare a letto.

Alla fine della spiegazione la Tina era quasi senza fiato.

Le era rimasto giusto quel poco per fare la domanda che l'Ernesto temeva.

«E tu cosa fai di bello?»

«Chi, io?» aveva chiesto il Dubbio, come se lei avesse parlato a chissà chi.

E adesso cosa rispondo?, aveva poi domandato a sé stesso.

9.

E adesso cosa faccio?, si chiese il Dubbio.

A mezza voce, dopo che per quasi un minuto aveva pressoché smesso di respirare.

Si era allontanato dalla riva dove aveva lasciato il cadavere.

Non si era più girato a guardarlo.

Gli era bastato il rapido sguardo che gli aveva lanciato poco prima per rendersi conto che l'aveva lasciato per metà in acqua, proprio come quando aveva trovato suo padre, proprio come nei sogni che aveva avuto decine di volte.

Cristo, perché gli stava ancora capitando la stessa cosa?

Si era concentrato sull'unico remo che aveva, palettando un po' di qua e un po' di là per mantenere in rotta la barca.

L'altro remo, chissà dov'era, da qualche parte.

E per fortuna anonimo.

Sì, perché una volta gli era venuto in mente di dipingere il nome della barca anche sui remi. Poi aveva lasciato perdere, e meno male.

Un colpo di qua, un colpo di là, aveva impiegato almeno un'ora per raggiungere il molo. Una volta dentro, due colpi ancora e fu al suo posto barca. Un gruppetto di folaghe si spostò, emettendo il caratteristico richiamo.

E adesso?

Non poteva più rinviare la decisione.

Facile a dire.

Si sedette nella barca, le folaghe continuavano a richiamarsi.
Andare a casa, infilarsi nel letto, dormire, se ci riusciva.
Fare finta di niente.
Negare a sé stesso quello che aveva visto… anzi, quella che aveva visto, e poi quello che aveva fatto.
Ma un cadavere era un cadavere, mica un cavedano.
Di lì a poche ore qualcuno l'avrebbe visto, scoperto.
Poi…
Al Dubbio venne un brivido di freddo nonostante fosse ancora sudato.
Poi identificato.
Poi ci sarebbero state domande.
Chi l'aveva visto… vista, anzi.
Quando, dove, come, con chi.
E se alla fine fossero risaliti a lui, non poteva rispondere con delle balle così come aveva fatto con la Tina.

10.

E tu cosa fai di bello?

Alla domanda della Tina, il Dubbio s'era un po' incartato e mentre cercava di uscire dal ghetto dei suoi pensieri per trovare una risposta plausibile, a uno dei tavoli del crotto era scoppiato un litigio. Avevano cominciato a volare insulti del dio e piatti. Nessuno aveva osato intervenire poiché quasi tutti conoscevano i due litiganti e sapevano bene quanto fossero pesanti le loro mani.

Invece delle solite storie di caccia o pesca, l'alterco era scoppiato per una questione di precedenze. A contendersi il diritto a essere servito per primo erano stati Mistico Bertazza, un mandriano noto perché mangiava le noci con tanto di guscio, e un altro campione di idiozia, Guerino Finali detto Ciurcill perché menava vanto di aver stretto la mano al noto politico inglese la volta in cui l'aveva incontrato in giro per Bellagio: il Ciurcill doveva la sua fama al fatto di aver già tentato più volte di attraversare il lago a nuoto e d'inverno, impresa che l'avrebbe già ammazzato se non fossero intervenuti in tempo alcuni pescatori previdenti. Tuttavia, niente e nessuno l'aveva ancora convinto che era il caso di lasciar perdere e lui seguitava ad annunciare un prossimo tentativo.

Mentre i due si scaldavano continuando a insultarsi senza risparmiare madri e mogli, qualcuno aveva addirittura cominciato a fare il tifo, nella speranza che iniziassero a volare sganassoni per godersi la scena, fino a quando dalla cucina era uscita la Speranza, la figlia del padrone del crotto.

Capelli neri come le piume del corvo e occhi azzurri da matta.

Matta davvero come un cavallo, la Speranza s'era presentata con in mano la mannaia che usava per tagliare le costine e aveva chiesto chi volesse assaggiarla per primo.

Nel giro di un minuto le voci s'erano zittite, i litiganti s'erano dispersi ai quattro punti cardinali: se volevano spaccarsi la testa, andassero a farlo lontano da lì.

Il Dubbio aveva approfittato del litigio per evitare di rispondere. La Tina forse s'era dimenticata e aveva raccontato qualche aneddoto sulla particolare conduzione del crotto da parte di padre e figlia. Il conto che presentavano ai clienti risultava perlopiù singolare perché nel totale pesava non tanto quello che avevano mangiato e bevuto quanto la simpatia che avevano suscitato.

«Ci sono milanesi che questo crotto se lo ricorderanno finché campano», aveva ridacchiato la Tina.

Poi tra i due era sceso il silenzio.

Erano quasi le undici.

Il Riffa era via da un'oraccia.

La Tina aveva cominciato a sbadigliare.

Poi, in tutta franchezza, gli aveva detto che per lei s'era fatta l'ora di andare. Non che il commenda le misurasse il tempo delle uscite. Però non voleva nemmeno approfittare dell'ex infermiera che in occasioni come quella si prestava a sostituirla senza pretendere soldi. Si pagava da sé però, sfruttando quei favori che le faceva per passare a trovarla, assumendo talora arie da supervisore, cosa che a volte le risultava parecchio fastidiosa.

D'altronde, era comunque meglio tenersela buona.

In ogni caso: «Tu cosa vuoi fare?» aveva chiesto.

Il Dubbio s'era stretto nelle spalle.

Di stare lì ne aveva piene un po' le balle anche lui e oltretutto gli era sembrato evidente che almeno per quella sera non gli sarebbe riuscito di chiacchierare col culetto parlante della ragazza.

«Vieni o stai?» aveva insistito la ragazza.

«Ma sì, vengo anch'io», aveva risposto.

«E il tuo amico?» aveva chiesto lei con un sorrisetto.

«S'arrangia», aveva risposto il Dubbio.

Un'altra volta imparava a non approfittare. E poi, chissà dov'era infrattato.

«Non sono il suo tassista», aveva aggiunto per dare forza alla decisione.

E s'erano avviati.

In silenzio dapprima.

Poi, circa a metà discesa verso Acquaseria, la Tina aveva aperto bocca.

«Non mi hai ancora detto che mestiere fai.»

Un po' pensando al commenda della Tina e al suo mobilificio e un po' pensando alla falegnameria di suo padre, al Dubbio la risposta era venuta.

«Faccio tipo il falegname.»

La Tina aveva soppesato la risposta.

«Bello», aveva poi commentato.

E ce l'aveva un negozio, insomma...

«No, non proprio», aveva balbettato il Dubbio.

Non ancora.

Aveva messo su una specie di laboratorio a casa sua, in uno scantinato.

«È un bel mestiere», aveva detto la Tina.

«E be'», aveva cincischiato il Dubbio.

«Non mi sembri convinto.»

«Ma no», si era opposto il giovanotto.

Convinto era convinto.

«Si guadagna poco?» aveva chiesto la ragazza.

«Il fatto è che sono all'inizio», aveva risposto il Dubbio.

«Ma sistemi anche mobili?» aveva insistito la Tina.

«Certo», aveva affermato il Dubbio.

«E per un tavolino da sistemare quanto vorresti?» era

ritornata alla carica la ragazza pensando a un tavolino della bisnonna, di quelli che si tenevano in camera da letto con sopra uno specchio basculante e sotto la bacinella per l'acqua.

«Senza vederlo come faccio a dirtelo», aveva risposto il Dubbio.

Poi finalmente erano arrivati in paese.

«Io vado di qui», aveva detto la Tina indicando la direzione per la casa del commenda.

«Bon, ciao allora», aveva salutato il Dubbio.

E grazie per la compagnia.

Poi aveva deciso che in riva al lago, prima di partire, avrebbe fatto una bella pisciata guardando una dopo l'altra tutte le luci che gli stavano di fronte.

La luce della croce di Camaggiore.

Più sotto quella del campanile di Noceno.

Più sotto ancora quella del santuario della Madonna di Lezzeno.

Infine quelle di Bellano.

11.

Se non lui, chi?, si chiese il Dubbio.

La sua casa era lì, di fronte.

Ultimo piano del condominio sopra il ristorante Cavallo Bianco.

Lui.

Chi altri?

A chi altri poteva andare a raccontare quello che era successo, quello che aveva visto, quello che...

Tenerlo per sé, impensabile, impossibile.

Ci voleva qualcuno cui dirlo e da cui avere consigli sul da fare.

Lui solo.

Ma dormiva, la finestra di casa sua era buia.

Per forza, così a occhio saranno state le tre, tre e mezza.

Tuttavia il Dubbio sentì che non poteva fare altrimenti. Oltretutto doveva essere anche abbastanza abituato a essere svegliato a ogni ora della notte.

Pensarci oltre significava soltanto perdere tempo.

Si avviò, lasciandosi alle spalle il mezzobusto di Sigismondo Boldoni insensibile alle sue tribolazioni, attraversò la strada e raggiunse il portone del condominio.

Scrutò per bene la fila dei campanelli, ci mancava solo di sbagliare e svegliare chissà chi.

Poi, presa la mira, calcò l'indice destro sul bottone e udì in sottofondo il dlin dlon del citofono che avrebbe svegliato il dottor Lonati.

12.

Il Riffa invece dormiva della grossa.

Per sua fortuna era fatto così, comunque andassero le cose, il sonno non glielo toglieva neanche il Padreterno.

Nemmeno se andavano malissimo, come quella sera quando la Valeria non solo non gliel'aveva mollata ma gli aveva anche dato una girata coi fiocchi.

Una volta allontanatisi dal crotto, la ragazza gli aveva detto che aveva voglia di fare due passi e, con un tono di voce dolce come l'aria di luglio, che le sembrava buona cosa lasciare un po' soli la sua amica e il Dubbio. Gli aveva indicato un sentierino panoramico che aveva fatto venire l'acquolina in bocca al Riffa tanto sembrava fatto apposta per coloro che volevano andare in camporella. Per una buona mezz'ora, forse di più, lei non aveva fatto altro che fermarsi ogni due passi, indicargli le luci che c'erano sulla sponda opposta, chiedergli a che paese o frazione corrispondessero, se c'era un sentiero che portava a quella tal chiesetta o rifugio, se lui c'era mai stato, se la passeggiata era bella e se era faticosa, se lei ce l'avrebbe fatta, se ci volevano delle scarpe apposta e se lui ce le aveva e quanto costavano e di qui e di là e di su e di giù.

Una menata che il Riffa aveva sopportato, rispondendo sempre e più di una volta inventandosi le cose di sana pianta, in vista del premio finale. A un certo punto gli era sembrato che il momento di riscuotere fosse arrivato: era stato quando erano giunti nei pressi di uno slargo del sentiero, una specie di piccolo terrazzo naturale, e lei s'era appoggiata a una pianta per ammirare il lago sottostante mentre lui s'era perduto in analoga ammirazione per il sedere di lei, spinto in fuori stante la posizione o forse apposta per la sua vista. S'era avvicinato stretto stretto e poi le aveva cinto i fianchi con un braccio lasciando che la mano cadesse su una metà di quella mela del peccato.

Com'è come non è, gli era arrivato uno sganassone che sembrava essere uscito dal buio della notte ma senza che potesse capire da che parte.

E due domande a seguire.

Come si permetteva e cosa s'era messo in testa?

Il Riffa era rimasto sorpreso dalla reazione della ragazza e aveva borbottato qualche scusa.

«Forse ho esagerato», aveva ribattuto lei, ma riferendosi solo alla potenza della sberla.

Però doveva capire che non era abituata a essere trattata così.

«Anzi», aveva aggiunto, «credo che a nessuna ragazza piaccia essere trattata in questa maniera. A meno di essere una di quelle.»

Il Riffa, la mano sulla guancia che scottava, aveva ripetuto le scuse.

«Ma è che te mi piaci davvero», aveva confessato.

«Trova un altro modo di farmelo capire allora», aveva concluso lei, comunicando poi, visto che lui a lei piaceva per niente, che s'era fatta l'ora di ritornare al crotto.

Dove però non avevano più trovato né la Tina né il Dubbio.

Il primo pensiero del Riffa era stato che al Dubbio era andata meglio di lui e che al momento si stesse godendo la tarchia da qualche parte. La bionda, a una sua richiesta, aveva risposto di non avere fretta. Inoltre la passeggiata le aveva fatto venire un po' di fame, quindi nell'attesa erano tornati ad accomodarsi e avevano mangiato e bevuto qualcosa mentre il Riffa, tra un boccone e l'altro, s'era spremuto in frasi eleganti di corteggiamento. A un certo punto però, non comparendo nessuno, lo stesso Riffa era andato a chiedere notizie alla Speranza, se per caso avesse visto il suo socio e gli avesse lasciato detto qualcosa.

C'era mancato poco che la matta lo prendesse a padellate. Col bordello che c'era stato quella sera come poteva pretendere da lei di sapere dove fosse quello e cosa avesse detto quell'altra!

«Per me siete tutti uguali!» gli aveva sputato in faccia.

Ma non era finita lì. Perché dopo un po' la stessa Speranza era andata al loro tavolo. Continuava ad arrivare gente nonostante l'ora, e loro due se ne stavano lì come allocchi occupando due posti. O si decidevano a consumare sennò via, lasà lìber el pòst!

In quel momento, se il Riffa avesse avuto tra le mani il Dubbio l'avrebbe strozzato. Però del Dubbio continuava a non vedersi nemmeno l'ombra ed era ormai notte inoltrata.

Dove cazzo era finito?

Come faceva a tornare a Bellano senza la barca?

Dove diavolo andava a dormire?

«Ci penso io», gli aveva detto la Valeria mossa a compassione.

Al Riffa era passata subito la rabbia, sostituita da un brivido.

Ma la bionda aveva capito al volo.

«Non metterti in testa idee», gli aveva detto, «deve ancora nascere quello.»

Se voleva passare la notte al coperto, il posto glielo avrebbe trovato lei.

Dalla Tina, la sua amica. Nella casetta del commenda. Cioè, non proprio in casa, piuttosto in una specie di legnaia che c'era di lato alla casa e che il commenda aveva voluto far trasformare in una taverna quasi mai usata.

Lì dentro c'era tutto quello che gli serviva per passare la notte.

13.

Il Lonati fumava Turmac col filtro.

Nonostante i quotidiani richiami della moglie Vittoria, arrivava anche a due pacchetti al giorno.

Il Dubbio non gliele doveva mai far mancare. Era il suo principale cliente e al tempo stesso benefattore, perché grazie ai suoi buoni uffici l'Ernesto aveva messo insieme una lista di una dozzina di fedelissimi che come il Lonati si rifornivano solo e sempre da lui.

«Ma, alle tre di notte?» esordì il dottore davanti al viso sudato e stravolto del Dubbio.

Quasi le quattro ormai.

«Non è per le sigarette», rispose il Dubbio.

«Lo sospettavo», commentò il dottore.

Erano entrambi sulla soglia dell'appartamento. Il dottore in pigiama, un bel pigiama bordeaux coi bordi bianchi. Il Dubbio stava cercando le parole per dire ciò che doveva.

Ho trovato un cadavere nel lago?

Oppure, c'era un cadavere nel lago?

O sennò...

«Allora, Ernesto!» cercò di smuoverlo il Lonati.

Era uno dei pochi, tranne sua madre e qualche altro, che lo chiamava col suo vero nome. Il resto dei bellanesi forse non se lo ricordava nemmeno.

Il Dubbio ruppe gli indugi.

«È successa una cosa», disse.

«E fino a qui ci siamo», commentò il dottore.

Adesso però era arrivato il momento di dire cosa.

La signora Vittoria fece la sua comparsa in quel momento. Anche lei con una bella vestaglia addosso, beige, lunga fino ai piedi. Andò verso i due sistemandosi i capelli.

«Ma cosa fate lì sulla porta?» chiese.

«Niente», rispose il marito, «l'Ernesto mi deve dire una cosa, tu torna pure a letto.»

Poi cominciò a frugare nella tasca del pigiama. Gesto automatico, alla ricerca delle sigarette. Le aveva appoggiate sul tavolino della sala la sera prima dopo quel po' di televisione che aveva guardato insieme con la moglie.

Adesso il pensiero di fumare voleva soddisfazione.

«Dai, vieni dentro», disse all'Ernesto.

Sua moglie era ancora lì, nel corridoio. Il Lonati si girò per avviarsi alla volta della sala. Vedendolo di spalle il Dubbio trovò il coraggio di parlare.

«Ho appena visto un morto.»

«Che cosa?»

A chiedere fu la signora Vittoria.

Il dottore si girò di scatto.

Il Dubbio aveva fatto un paio di passi in corridoio, non aveva ancora chiuso la porta.

«Come hai detto?» chiese il dottore.

«Un morto», ripeté il Dubbio.

Anzi, corresse subito, una morta.

14.

Morti tutti in caserma?

Uno, due, tre, quattro, cinque squilli...

Sei, sette...

Infine: «Carabinieri Bellano».

Ma la voce era da oltretomba.

Il Lonati si qualificò.

«Buongiorno, dottore.»

Be', ragionò il Lonati, tutto sommato ci stava, ormai erano le quattro del mattino.

«Vorrei parlare col maresciallo», spiegò, «è urgente.»

«Vado a svegliarlo», rispose il carabiniere.

Sulla risposta il tono s'era incrinato. Il Lonati immaginò quanto poco piacesse a quel poveretto andare a svegliare il suo comandante.

«Attendo in linea?» chiese.

«Forse è meglio di no», rispose il carabiniere.

«Mi faccia richiamare allora», disse il Lonati e depose la cornetta. Poi tornò in sala e si sedette di fronte al Dubbio. L'aveva tenuto lì dopo che quello gli aveva raccontato la disavventura notturna.

Durante il resoconto aveva schiacciato tre cicche di Turmac nel posacenere. Anche sua moglie, via via sempre più sconcertata, aveva ascoltato. Aveva fatto un caffè.

«Tu sei sicuro di quello che mi hai detto?» chiese il Lonati una volta che si fu seduto, in attesa che il maresciallo chiamasse.

Il Dubbio aprì la bocca e fece per dire qualcosa. Parlò

per lui Vittoria, che aveva intuito dove suo marito volesse andare a parare visto che anche lei conosceva i trascorsi del giovanotto.

«Ma dai», esclamò rivolta al marito, «c'è un limite a tutto. Come puoi pensare che uno si inventi una cosa del genere!»

«Va bene, d'accordo», si arrese il Lonati.

Aveva parlato tanto per dire qualcosa, per essere sicuro al cento per cento.

Perché di lì a un po', quando il maresciallo Massimino Pezzati avrebbe richiamato, la faccia ce l'avrebbe messa lui, come stabilito col Dubbio. Storia che, a rigor di logica, l'Ernesto avrebbe fatto meglio a raccontare ai carabinieri anziché a lui.

«O no?» aveva chiesto il Lonati quando, terminato il resoconto dell'Ernesto, nella sala era sceso il silenzio.

«Dico bene o dico male?» aveva insistito il dottore.

Era stata la moglie a rispondere.

«Sì e no», aveva sentenziato.

Sì perché non si poteva discutere che quella fosse materia per carabinieri.

No perché, considerati proprio quei trascorsi che nessuno aveva nominato ma aleggiavano nell'aria del salotto e soprattutto dopo la faccenda del motore e del quadro, con un processo ancora in ballo, il Dubbio non aveva certo bisogno di inguaiarsi ancora di più.

Se mai gli serviva qualcuno che stesse dalla sua parte, che lo sostenesse.

Che lo consigliasse.

«E già», aveva sospirato il Lonati.

Il motore, il quadro, il processo...

15.

Il motore.

Un po' di colpa ce l'aveva il Riffa, anche se in sostanza non c'entrava niente.

Però glielo aveva messo in testa lui che sarebbe andata in un altro modo con quelli del cinema di notte se avesse avuto una barca a motore.

«Con sotto un bel tre cavalli li lasciavi lì a giocare a zero zero sette e tu andavi a letto bello tranquillo a sognare gli angioletti.»

Bella idea.

Si era piantata subito nella testa del Dubbio insieme con la consapevolezza che per farla crescere ci sarebbe voluto un concime che non aveva, cioè i soldi per comperare il tre cavalli.

«Datti da fare», era stato il gran consiglio del Riffa.

Magari, aveva aggiunto, uno di seconda mano gli veniva via per poco.

Chiedesse al Girgetta del molo: se c'era uno che ne poteva sapere qualcosa, quello era lui.

Il Dubbio aveva attuato il consiglio.

Il Girgetta gli aveva detto che poteva far girare la voce però gli aveva anche consigliato di andarlo a chiedere a quelli che come lui lavoravano con le barche o avevano un cantiere, magari il Gormetti a Varenna, che aveva più giro, o il Sciusciòt su a Dervio. Di sua iniziativa poi l'aveva detto al battellotto di Bellano, che per piacere informasse quelli della Navigazione che facevano scalo lì e che potevano a loro volta chiedere in tutti i porti del lago.

Alla fine tutto quel cercare aveva portato i suoi frutti. Era stato il Sciusciòt di Dervio a dirgli che se voleva aveva sottomano un motore da tre cavalli.

Il costo?

Gratis!

«Gratis?» s'era stupito il Dubbio.

C'era forse sotto qualche gabola?

«No», aveva assicurato il Sciusciòt.

Solo che il motore era un po' vecchio, non veniva usato da tempo e stava tra i piedi, tutto lì.

Quando il Girgetta l'aveva visto aveva detto che, più che vecchio, quel tre cavalli era antico, quasi un pezzo da museo: era un Bolynders Trim del '33, peraltro tenuto bene. E la fortuna del Dubbio era stata che il Girgetta conosceva a fondo quel modello per averne posseduto uno prima della guerra. Con invidiabile perizia l'aveva smontato, controllato in ogni sua parte e poi rimontato, consegnandolo al Dubbio dopo un paio di settimane.

«Pronto all'uso», gli aveva detto.

Purché, aveva aggiunto, non esagerasse, pretendendo da quel motore chissà quali prestazioni.

Il Dubbio aveva seguito le varie fasi di rimessa a nuovo del tre cavalli con la trepidazione di un padre che aspetta la nascita del suo primo figlio: non aveva fatto altro che tampinare il Girgetta per sapere quando sarebbe stato pronto e, in casa, non aveva avuto altro argomento di conversazione oltre a quello, sproloquiando su come la sua attività sarebbe finalmente cambiata grazie al tre cavalli e a come sarebbe evoluta in virtù dei guadagni che quel motorino d'anteguerra gli avrebbe permesso.

La Canterina aveva condiviso l'entusiasmo del figlio ma aveva anche considerato la possibilità che un colpo di sfortuna potesse in qualche maniera ostacolare i luminosi progetti dell'Ernesto e allora aveva ripreso l'abitudine di affidarsi a santa Rita affinché proteggesse il figlio e magari spingesse la Navigazione Lariana ad accettare la domanda di assunzione che ormai da tempo era stata presentata. Usciva di casa prima del solito così da potersi concedere, prima di raggiungere le cucine dell'asilo infantile, tutto il tempo necessario per pregare presso la chiesetta di Santa Marta davanti al quadro che raffigurava la santa degli impossibili.

Così non aveva visto l'individuo che si era presentato alla porta di casa sua, bussando e ribussando fino a quando era riuscito a buttare giù dal letto il Dubbio.

«Sei te quello che affitta la barca giù al molo?» gli aveva chiesto.

Il Dubbio l'aveva guardato mentre cercava di snebbiarsi del tutto. Era un biondino che non aveva mai visto con un accento che dava un po' sul bergamasco.

«Sei te o no?» aveva insistito quello.

«Perché?» aveva infine chiesto il Dubbio.

Perché, gli aveva spiegato il biondino continuando a saltellare da un piede all'altro, se era lui il noleggiatore era lì per prenotare: quel pomeriggio aveva bisogno di andare dall'altra parte del lago.

Il Dubbio ci aveva pensato un momento. Era una settimana che aveva montato il tre cavalli sulla *Canterina*, andava bene, l'aveva provato, anche se aveva fatto un giretto delle rive, niente di più.

«Allora?» era insorto il biondino.

Si voleva decidere a dirgli sì o no?

«Per che ora?» aveva chiesto il Dubbio.

«Per le tre lì al molo», aveva risposto il biondino.

Alle tre in punto il biondino s'era presentato, zainetto in spalla, ed erano partiti.

«Dove vado?» aveva chiesto il Dubbio.

«Te comincia ad andare, poi ti dico», era stata la risposta.

Dopo dieci minuti di silenzio, il biondino aveva aperto la bocca.

«Ma non si può andare un po' più veloci?»

Il Dubbio infatti teneva un'andatura turistica.

«Sì, si può», aveva risposto.

Ma a forzare più di tanto non aveva mai provato.

«E allora se si può, dai!» aveva detto il biondino.

Gli sarebbe piaciuto andare e tornare in giornata, aveva aggiunto sorridendo.

Il Dubbio aveva dato gas, il tre cavalli aveva risposto bene fino a che, più o meno quando erano stati a metà lago, bep-bep-bep, aveva esalato un rumore simile a un grugnito e poi s'era fermato.

«Cos'è successo?» aveva chiesto il biondino.

Niente di che, finita la benza.

La bestemmia del biondo s'era sentita sin nel profondo del lago.

«E adesso?»

C'erano i remi, no?

Altra bestemmia.

«Io non sono capace», aveva ringhiato.

Aveva bestemmiato il Dubbio allora. S'era guardato in giro.

«Cosa cazzo fai?» aveva chiesto il biondo.

Cercava di capire qual era la sponda più vicina. Il biondino l'aveva guardato male. Poi, senza dire altro, gli aveva indicato quella di là.

«E senza discussioni», aveva aggiunto.

Al Dubbio non era rimasto altro da fare che prendere in mano i remi e cominciare a remare mentre il biondino, approfittando di un sole tutto sommato tiepido, si era stravaccato a poppa e aveva chiuso gli occhi.

Passata una mezz'ora, dormiva francamente.

A svegliarlo ci aveva pensato il lacerante suono di una trombetta da stadio che il Dubbio aveva acquistato in occasione della festa dei Re Magi e che aveva messo nel cassetto di poppa, buona per ogni evenienza.

Come quella.

Richiamare l'attenzione di una vedetta della Guardia di Finanza che lo aveva visto mentre remava e farsi soccorrere dalla stessa.

«Che cazzo hai fatto?» aveva chiesto il biondino bruscamente risvegliato.

Il Dubbio, sorridendo, glielo aveva spiegato.

«Ma sei scemo?» era stata la conclusione.

16.

In attesa che il maresciallo Pezzati richiamasse, il dottor Lonati, fumando una sigaretta dopo l'altra, stava scegliendo quasi una per una le parole che di lì a poco avrebbe detto al carabiniere.

Poi, all'improvviso, come se solo allora si ricordasse di non averglielo chiesto, sbottò, rivolgendosi al Dubbio.

«Ma tu cosa ci facevi in mezzo al lago a quest'ora di notte?» chiese, visto che di sigarette non gliene aveva portato nemmeno un pacchetto.

Il Dubbio impallidì ancora di più.

Era la stessa domanda che gli aveva rivolto uno dei finanzieri che erano a bordo della vedetta.

«Ma cosa ci fate qui in mezzo al lago?»

Per una volta il Dubbio non aveva avuto esitazioni.

«Stavamo pescando.»

Allora era intervenuto uno che forse era maresciallo.

«Ah sì?» aveva chiesto.

E le canne, le reti, uno qualunque di quegli aggeggi che notoriamente si usano per pescare dov'erano?

Il biondino aveva aperto la bocca per dire qualcosa ma non gli era uscito niente. Aveva parlato ancora il maresciallo, o quel che l'èra.

«Seguiteci», e aveva fatto cenno a un suo sottoposto di tirare una cima ai due affinché l'assicurassero alla *Canterina.*

Poi erano partiti, direzione caserma della Guardia di Finanza di Nobiallo dove lo stesso sottufficiale aveva ordinato di dare un'occhiata ai documenti dei due e alla barca.

«Erano in giro a pescare ma si sono dimenticati le canne a casa», aveva ironizzato.

I documenti, niente di che.

Ernesto Livera, residente a Bellano, professione pescatore.

L'altro, Ermidio Moscarini, residente a San Paolo d'Argon, professione rappresentante di commercio.

La barca, invece...

«Guardi un po' cosa ho trovato», aveva detto il finanziere che aveva controllato la *Canterina* e frugato nello zaino del biondino.

«Oilà!» era sbottato il maresciallo.

Non gli pareva che fosse pesce.

«D'accordo con lei maresciallo», aveva detto il finanziere.

S'era fatto consegnare zaino e contenuto quindi s'era fatto portare il Dubbio e il biondo.

«Di chi è questo?» aveva chiesto esibendo il dipinto che il finanziere aveva trovato nello zaino.

«Mio, no», aveva risposto immediatamente il Dubbio.

«Allora vuol dire che è tuo», aveva concluso il maresciallo rivolgendosi al biondino.

«E allora?» era stata l'obiezione di quello.

Uno non poteva andare in giro con un quadro?

Il maresciallo s'era rilassato sulla sedia, le braccia conserte, e aveva sospirato.

«E magari l'hai dipinto tu?» aveva chiesto.

Il biondino aveva esitato un po' prima di rispondere.

«Se anche fosse?» aveva poi detto.

«Fosse così», aveva risposto il maresciallo, «direi che te ne vai in giro con un documento falso.»

Lui non era un esperto, aveva puntualizzato. Ma così, a stima, il quadro che aveva sotto gli occhi doveva avere un paio di secoli.

«Ma magari è tuo», era andato avanti il maresciallo, «e te lo stavi portando a spasso così, per fargli prendere un po' di aria.»

Il biondino aveva fatto per parlare. Il finanziere l'aveva fermato con un gesto della mano.

«Però sai com'è», aveva concluso, «a noi finanzieri la gente che pesca senza canne e porta a spasso per il lago quadri antichi non ci convince. Quindi, se non ti spiace, farei accomodare te e il tuo compare nel nostro salotto mentre io faccio un paio di telefonate. Dopodiché ne riparliamo e magari tutti e due mi dite la verità su cosa facevate in giro per il lago.»

17.

Be', ma cosa gli andava a dire al maresciallo?, era appena sbottato il dottor Lonati.

«Che durante la mia solita gita in barchetta tra mezzanotte e le due del mattino sono andato a sbattere...»

«No», lo interruppe la moglie Vittoria.

Sempre che il maresciallo richiamasse, osservò la donna visto che era già passata una decina di minuti, gli doveva dire di aver ricevuto una telefonata anonima che l'avvisava di quel fatto e che di conseguenza aveva ritenuto necessario, anzi, doveroso avvisare le forze dell'ordine onde procedere alle verifiche del caso.

Il Lonati la guardò.

La moglie gli rispose sgranando gli occhi, espressione che le era usuale quando riteneva inutile spiegare a parole quanto fosse ovvia una cosa.

«Se si decidesse a chiamare...» sospirò il Lonati.

La moglie aveva bella e pronta una soluzione anche in quel caso.

«Aspettiamo ancora qualche minuto e casomai richiamiamo noi», disse.

Poi si corresse: «Tu, cioè».

Il Lonati si sistemò sulla poltrona e poi sbuffò.

Non era convinto.

Guardò dapprima il Dubbio, che fissava un punto del tappeto che ricopriva quasi per intero il soggiorno.

«Ma non sarebbe più semplice...» disse, fermandosi subito.

«Cosa?» chiese la moglie.

«Voglio dire, non è che facendo così complichiamo le cose?»

«Le complichiamo, certo. Ma è per il bene dell'Ernesto», rispose.

Non ci si doveva dimenticare del processo che aveva in ballo per la storia del quadro.

18.

Un falso, una copia neanche tanto ben eseguita.

Sufficiente però a mettere nei guai il biondino e il Dubbio, creando un caso che al momento era ancora in attesa di essere chiarito. Allora, con un paio di telefonate, il maresciallo della Finanza aveva appurato che il quadro proveniva dalla chiesa di Taceno dalla quale era sparito all'incirca un mesetto prima: rappresentava un Cristo in croce ed era opera del pittore Giacomo Bellani, nato in Premana il 13 agosto 1745, artista di una certa notorietà, premiato dall'Accademia di Parma e noto per i soggetti sacri che ritraeva come appunto il crocifisso che lui stesso aveva donato alla parrocchia di Taceno. Pure il parroco del luogo, don Olindo Mezzi, si dilettava di pittura mostrando anche un certo virtuosismo e si teneva al corrente sulle novità del mondo artistico. Al suo ingresso in parrocchia, un paio d'anni prima, aveva ben valutato il dipinto del Bellani e giustamente temendo che prima o poi, visto che non era per niente protetto, sarebbe finito nelle mani di qualche collezionista privo di scrupoli, l'aveva sostituito con una copia fatta da lui stesso, senza che nessuno dei suoi parrocchiani si fosse mai accorto della differenza.

Del furto invece sì.

Di fronte alla nicchia orbata del crocifisso, il sagrestano Degregoli aveva strepitato come se avesse visto il diavolo. La notizia aveva fatto il giro della comunità in un batter d'occhio e, come c'era da aspettarsi, era finita anche tra le cronache del quotidiano locale. Ciò che nessuno sapeva, tranne il parroco copista e i carabinieri cui era stata presentata la denuncia, era che il quadro sparito era solo un falso mentre l'originale se ne stava al sicuro dentro un cassettone dell'armadio di camera del sacerdote. L'idea di continuare a tenere segreta la cosa era stata del maggiore dei carabinieri Marinai, allora comandante della tenenza di Lecco: a suo dire, era meglio che anche i ladri credessero di avere tra le mani il Bellani originale, se si voleva che prima o poi commettessero qualche passo falso e venissero allo scoperto. Al contrario, se ne sarebbero forse disfatti e addio fichi.

La segnalazione del furto, che si andava ad aggiungere ad altri analoghi avvenuti in quell'arco di tempo, era stata inviata a tutte del caserme del lago e proprio dalla voce del maresciallo Pezzati il collega della Guardia di Finanza aveva appreso con sorpresa di avere per le mani due ladri veri e un quadro falso. Il finanziere aveva peraltro restituito subito la sorpresa al collega bellanese, rivelandogli che uno dei due ladri era tal Ernesto Livera.

Il Dubbio?, era sfuggito al Pezzati.

Il finanziere aveva frainteso l'uscita del maresciallo.

Anche a lui, aveva infatti risposto, era venuto qualche dubbio.

Su come procedere, aveva chiarito.

Per la maggior parte dei casi aveva a che fare con contrabbandieri, sapeva come trattarli.

Con due ladri... insomma, se il Pezzati aveva qualche buon consiglio per incastrarli in fretta...

«Tu intanto evita di dire che quella che hai in mano è una crosta», aveva suggerito il Pezzati, così da permettergli di assumere informazioni precise sul biondino.

E, sempre per tenerli un po' sulla corda, chiedesse ai due dove l'avevano preso oppure chi l'avesse consegnato loro, cosa dovevano farne... quelle cose lì insomma, tutte domande che, il Pezzati ne era certo, avrebbero indotto nel biondino e nel Dubbio la certezza che lui ne sapesse molto di più di ciò che lasciava intendere.

Il finanziere aveva accettato il consiglio e una mezz'ora più tardi il telefono del maresciallo Pezzati era tornato a suonare, portando sconvolgenti novità.

19.

«Maresciallo.»
«Dottore.»
Il Pezzati alla fine s'era fatto vivo.
Due squilli prima che Vittoria Lonati guardasse il marito e lo invitasse.
«Rispondi, su, chi vuoi che sia?» aveva detto.
La voce del Pezzati, diagnosticò tra sé il Lonati, era così così. Sospesa tra la necessità di adeguare il tono perché stava parlando con lui e quella di contenere l'irritazione per la brusca sveglia, sebbene per una cosa urgente come doveva avergli riferito il suo carabiniere.
Tuttavia c'era urgenza e urgenza, aveva sottilizzato il Pezzati.
Di quale si trattava?
Furto, incidente, ferimento, rissa?
Omicidio?
«Non lo so», aveva risposto il carabiniere – carabiniere semplice Augusto Fantarini –, il primo che s'era sentito rivolgere le domande.
«Non lo so», rispose anche il dottor Lonati.
Ciò che sapeva glielo aveva appena detto: una mezz'ora prima, circa!, aveva ricevuto una telefonata anonima che l'aveva avvisato della presenza di un cadavere su una riva in località punta di Morcate.
«E c'è davvero?» chiese il Pezzati.
Il Lonati si strinse nelle spalle, guardò la moglie, sgranò gli occhi.

Ma che domanda era?

«Non lo so», rispose ancora.

Prima di ogni altra cosa aveva pensato che fosse bene avvisare lui senza indugi.

«Be'», bofonchiò il maresciallo ma abbastanza netto perché il dottore sentisse, «proprio senza indugi non direi visto che è passata mezz'ora dalla telefonata.»

All'osservazione del Pezzati, il Lonati riunì le dita a carciofo e mosse la mano su e giù, sotto gli occhi interrogativi della moglie.

Il gesto si spiegava da sé.

Il maresciallo stava mettendo in dubbio ciò che suo marito gli aveva appena detto?

«Maresciallo, mi permetta», obiettò il Lonati.

Forse non era passata proprio mezz'ora, forse si trattava solo di una ventina di minuti. Ma a parte quello, bisognava considerare lo sconcerto che provocava ricevere una telefonata di quel contenuto, a quell'ora di notte e per di più anonima.

«D'accordo, d'accordo», interloquì il Pezzati forse rendendosi conto di avere un po' esagerato.

Ma il Lonati no, voleva andare fino in fondo a quel punto, avere soddisfazione di spiegarsi per bene.

«Oltre a ciò», proseguì, «deve tener presente che prima di disturbarla ho considerato la possibilità che potesse trattarsi di uno scherzo.»

«Un po' pesante come scherzo», commentò il maresciallo.

Vittoria Lonati a quel punto fece due passi decisi verso il marito come volesse prendere in mano la situazione, cioè la cornetta del telefono, e sostituirsi a lui nel condurre il dialogo.

Il Lonati intanto stava finendo la sua perorazione.

«Infine», disse, «bisogna considerare il tempo tecnico.»

Intendendo con ciò il tempo che lui aveva impiegato per svegliarsi e scendere in caserma per richiamarlo.

Considerato tutto...

«Lei maresciallo cosa avrebbe fatto?» chiese il Lonati.

Mossa indovinata, il Pezzati tacque.

Poi deviò il discorso.

«La voce», chiese, «maschile o femminile?»

Cambiava qualcosa?

«Maschile», rispose comunque il dottore.

«Nota?»

Nel senso, specificò il maresciallo, che poteva avergli ricordato qualcuno di sua conoscenza?

Al Lonati scappò l'occhio sul Dubbio che continuava a mantenere la stessa identica posizione, le mani tra le gambe, lo sguardo fisso sul pavimento.

«No», mentì sereno.

«E...» riprese il Pezzati.

Il Lonati lo interruppe.

«Maresciallo mi permetta, le faccio osservare che in tutto la telefonata non sarà durata più di dieci secondi.»

Più o meno, aggiunse subito, onde evitare altre disquisizioni sul tempo.

Dall'altra parte del filo ci fu un sospiro di resa.

«A questo punto non resta altro da fare che andare a verificare», concluse il Pezzati.

Il dottore approvò senza parole, solo muovendo il capo.

«Lei è pronto?» chiese il maresciallo.

D'istinto il Lonati si guardò il pigiama.

«In che senso?» chiese.

«Voglio dire, è già pronto, vestito per uscire?»

«Mi sta dicendo che devo venire con lei?»

«Certo, mi sembra logico», rispose il Pezzati.

«Non pensavo...»

«Dottore», lo interruppe il maresciallo, «lo sa meglio di me, se c'è un cadavere la presenza di un medico è necessaria.»

Il Lonati stava per dire qualcosa quando il Dubbio mollò un formidabile starnuto.

«Salute», fece il Pezzati. «Sarò sotto casa sua fra cinque minuti.»

Dopodiché abbassò la cornetta.

«Devo andare», disse il Lonati con la cornetta ancora in mano.

«Qualche problema?» chiese la moglie.

«No», rispose lui.

Tranne il fatto che aveva avuto l'impressione che il maresciallo non gli credesse fino in fondo.

«Come se gli avessi raccontato delle frottole.»

«Perché, non è così?» ragionò la signora Vittoria.

20.

«Le cose stanno così», aveva detto il finanziere quando aveva richiamato il maresciallo Pezzati.

E con un tono di voce tutto sommato divertito.

Le cose, insomma, stavano che quel quadro o crosta che fosse non era di nessuno, stando alle risposte dei due.

Se ne erano rilanciata la proprietà come se giocassero a ping pong.

«Sarà suo», aveva risposto il biondino.

«Mio no», aveva ribattuto il Dubbio.

Secondo il Dubbio il biondino aveva lo zaino in spalla quando era salito sulla *Canterina* mentre secondo il biondino lo zaino con relativo contenuto era già sulla barca.

Pure il maresciallo Pezzati però aveva le sue belle novità da comunicare e per fare il paio con il collega finanziere aveva tenuto anche lui un tono ironico.

«Forse oltre a un quadro falso hai per le mani un fantasma», aveva scherzato.

«Sarebbe a dire?» aveva chiesto il finanziere.

Era semplice.

«Che lo smarrimento della carta d'identità di Ermidio Moscarini è stato denunciato circa un mese fa ai colleghi di Merate. Quindi dovresti chiedere al tuo ospite di declinare il suo vero nome e cognome e avvisarlo che si beccherà una denuncia per falsa identità oltre che per furto.»

«Ottimo», aveva pensato di concludere il finanziere.

«Però...» aveva interloquito il maresciallo Pezzati.

Se fosse stato in lui... senza volergli insegnare il mestiere... giusto perché aveva una certa esperienza di situazioni simili... insomma, li avrebbe separati per un po', senza dar loro spiegazioni di sorta.

«Magari facendo intendere che stai verificando certe cose sul loro conto ma senza dire quali cose. E vediamo quello che succede.»

In ogni caso, anche se quel trucchetto non avesse portato a niente, al momento di rilasciarli, perché era ovvio che non poteva trattenerli oltre quando avesse espletate le formalità relative alla comunicazione al magistrato, avrebbe dovuto lasciarli partire uno alla volta, e a distanza di tempo.

«Però fammi una cortesia», aveva chiesto il Pezzati.

L'avvisasse quando mollava il Dubbio perché gli sorrideva l'idea di starlo ad aspettare al molo, al rientro con la *Canterina*, per chiedergli qual buon vento lo portasse in giro per il lago.

21.

Il vento adesso era teso.

Il Lonati, in attesa in piazza Boldoni, aveva tentato un paio di volte, senza riuscire, di accendersi la quinta o sesta sigaretta della giornata. Resistette alla voglia di fare un ulteriore tentativo e anche a quella di girarsi per guardare la finestra della sala.

Uscendo aveva detto al Dubbio di aspettare fino a che non l'avesse visto partire col maresciallo prima di tornare a casa, e a Vittoria di rimettersi a letto.

Se il primo gli avrebbe ubbidito senz'altro, la seconda invece, ne era certo, sarebbe stata in piedi dietro la finestra, la luce dell'appartamento opportunamente spenta apposta per non farsi notare.

Si aspettava di veder giungere la camionetta dei carabinieri di fronte, invece il maresciallo lo sorprese alle spalle.

Alla guida c'era il Pezzati, solo.

«Solo?» si stupì il dottore.

«È soltanto nelle barzellette che i carabinieri vanno in giro in coppia.»

«Non intendevo...» fece il Lonati.

«Lo so», lo interruppe il maresciallo ripartendo. «Ma con la poca forza che ho a disposizione, per intanto andiamo a vedere noi due. Poi deciderò il da fare. Tanto se è un cadavere non può scappare. O no?»

Il Lonati abbozzò.

Forse era un effetto della telefonata di poco prima, ma

gli sembrava di continuare a intuire una vena di ironia, un po' di incredulità nel tono del maresciallo. Non sapendo cos'altro dire, girò lo sguardo verso il finestrino. Osservò per un po' il disordine che il vento stava creando.

Sul lago, per la strada dove volteggiavano foglie, rami secchi, cartacce.

Anche in cielo.

Le poche nuvole presenti correvano veloci verso il basso lago. Il phon non voleva ostacoli sul suo cammino. Se ne trovava, provvedeva a spazzarli.

«Sciò, via...» mormorò il Lonati.

«Come dice?» chiese il Pezzati.

Avevano appena imboccato la galleria delle Tre Madonne.

«Niente di che, stavo pensando», rispose il dottore.

«Anch'io stavo riflettendo», affermò il maresciallo.

Il Lonati si astenne dal chiedere su cosa.

«Vuole sapere cosa stavo pensando?» fece però il maresciallo.

«Mi dica», rispose il Lonati riflettendo a sua volta che non poteva fare altro.

«Mi stavo facendo una domanda.»

«E ha trovato la risposta?»

«No», rispose il maresciallo.

Perché non era una domanda semplice. Forse, anzi, era destinata a rimanere tale, senza risposta.

Chi infatti avrebbe potuto spiegare perché l'anonimo aveva telefonato a lui anziché ai carabinieri?

Il Lonati tacque.

Il maresciallo lasciò scorrere qualche istante, poi riprese.

«Oddio, uno che potrebbe rispondere ci sarebbe», disse.

Il dottore perseverò nel silenzio.

«E sa chi sarebbe?» chiese il maresciallo.

L'anonimo, si rispose ridacchiando.

Ma finché l'anonimo restava tale, la sua domanda sarebbe restata senza risposta.

«Non crede dottore?»

«Il ragionamento non fa una piega», sentenziò il Lonati.

«Già», timbrò il maresciallo mentre scalava un paio di marce e metteva la freccia a sinistra.

«Converrà parcheggiare qui, alla cava», disse.

Era uno spiazzo che si era pian piano creato dopo che per anni la montagna era stata fatta a fette. Spazio buio, protetto, luogo eletto per coppie fedifraghe o meno alle prese con necessità non rinviabili.

Prima di scendere il Pezzati prese dal sedile posteriore due torce. Verificò la prima, funzionava, la passò al Lonati.

Poi accese la sua, funzionava pure quella. Diresse il fascio di luce sui piedi del dottore.

«Cosa c'è?» chiese il Lonati.

«Le scarpe», osservò il Pezzati.

Scarpette da ambulatorio, tutt'altro che ideali per camminare su una riva di sassi, infida, scivolosa e al buio.

22.

Il Dubbio l'aveva riconosciuto da lontano, nonostante ormai cominciasse a calare la sera.

Il maresciallo, appoggiato alla murata del molo.

Era convinto di averla scampata, perché lui con quel quadro non c'entrava niente davvero.

Per sua fortuna, quando il finanziere l'aveva lasciato andare, s'era frugato in tasca e aveva trovato quelle poche lire che gli erano servite per pagarsi un paio di litri di miscela. Nonostante tutto, la sua preoccupazione maggiore era stata quella di arrivare a casa prima di sua madre, alla quale altrimenti avrebbe dovuto dare spiegazioni che non riusciva nemmeno a immaginare. Se avesse dovuto farsi la traversata tutta a remi, col piffero che sarebbe stato in tempo utile per evitare le immancabili domande della madre.

Ma, quando aveva visto la figura del Pezzati stagliata sul molo, con l'atteggiamento di chi sta a vedere se ci sono arbole, aveva capito che una spiegazione avrebbe dovuto darla comunque.

«In che guaio ti sei cacciato?» gli aveva infatti chiesto il maresciallo.

Il Dubbio era ancora sulla *Canterina*, stava assicurando la barca all'anello.

«Io non ho fatto niente», aveva risposto d'istinto.

«Ne sono convinto», aveva risposto il Pezzati con un sorriso beffardo.

Tuttavia, sebbene per mestiere fosse portato a non credere mai a ciò che usciva dalla bocca di individui come il Dubbio, in quel caso specifico aveva la netta sensazione che l'Ernesto non gli aveva mentito.

O, perlomeno, non era stato del tutto insincero.

«Sta di fatto che sei in un bel guaio», aveva insistito.

Il Dubbio era pallido.

Il Pezzati gli aveva allungato una mano per aiutarlo a salire dalla scaletta e poi l'aveva trattenuta.

«Me la devi raccontare tutta», gli aveva detto a bassa voce.

«Io...» aveva tentato di rispondere il Dubbio.

«Non qui», l'aveva interrotto il maresciallo.

In caserma.

E tenesse presente che voleva sentirsi raccontare le cose così com'erano accadute.

La verità, i fatti, mica balle.

«Perché sennò», aveva aggiunto il maresciallo Pezzati facendosi comprendere al volo dal Dubbio, «c'è il caso che un bel guaio te lo passi davvero questa volta.»

23.

Più di una volta il dottor Lonati ebbe l'impressione che il vento fosse così forte da deviare il fascio di luce della torcia.

Un'impressione, appunto. Perché era lui piuttosto che, con quelle scarpe da fighetta, scivolava sui sassi della riva rischiando di cadere a ogni passo.

Il Pezzati invece procedeva tranquillo, con metodo, di sasso in sasso, lungo tutta la riva che non misurava più di un centinaio di metri e da un lato era limitata dal muro di cinta di una villa al momento disabitata.

Una volta terminata l'ispezione della riva, il maresciallo disse al dottore di non muoversi e si avviò verso il promontorio della punta di Morcate.

Ormai albeggiava.

Entrambi avevano i pantaloni bagnati fin quasi alle ginocchia.

Il Pezzati si avventurò su quella roccia liscia, pressoché priva di appigli, che andava a finire come uno scivolo naturale dentro il lago.

Camminava di sbieco, puntando i piedi su alcuni spuntoni o piantandoli in alcune fessurazioni della roccia. Si spinse anche a dare un'occhiata oltre il promontorio, dove la massa della roccia continuava senza soluzione di continuità e liscia come uno specchio.

Non vide niente di particolare.

Onde, onde che andavano a sbattere contro i sassi e si rompevano in effimeri zampilli.

Mentre il Pezzati eseguiva l'ispezione, il Lonati s'era acceso due sigarette che più che altro s'era fumato il vento. Ciò non aveva fatto altro che aumentare il suo nervosismo. Man mano che il tempo era passato, via via che la luce del giorno era avanzata, gli era diventato sempre più evidente che su quella riva di cadaveri non c'era nemmeno l'ombra.

La riva però era quella, il Dubbio l'aveva indicata con estrema chiarezza. E non voleva nemmeno pensare che l'Ernesto gli avesse raccontato una balla del genere.

Tuttavia la realtà era quella.

Dipinta sul viso del maresciallo Pezzati che tornò al cospetto del dottore, il cappello in mano per evitare che il vento se lo portasse via e i capelli, ancora neri nonostante la mezza età, scompigliati.

«Come ha visto anche lei dottore, qui non c'è niente.»

Il Lonati abbozzò.

«Mi dispiace.»

«Le dispiace che non ci sia davvero un cadavere?»

«Non intendevo quello», chiarì il Lonati sorpreso dalla propria gaffe.

«Capisco», conciliò il maresciallo.

«Eppure...» lasciò cadere il dottore mentre si avviava per risalire verso la strada e tornare alla camionetta.

«Mi dica», lo stimolò il Pezzati.

Il Lonati si fermò.

Guardò verso la sponda occidentale del lago. Un battello ballonzolava tra un'onda e l'altra, puntava su Bellano.

«Le pare possibile che qualcuno si inventi una cosa del genere, per scherzo?»

Il Pezzati si era fermato pure lui a guardare il lago.

«Lei mi insegna dottore che il mondo è pieno di gente strana. Anche cattiva.»

O semplicemente fessa.

24.

Come il Dubbio.

Un fessacchiotto.

Il maresciallo Pezzati ne era convinto come di essere al mondo. Per quella ragione, una volta entrato in caserma con il giovanotto che gli camminava davanti, aveva deciso che se voleva sapere cosa avesse portato l'Ernesto ad andare in giro con un quadro falso e con uno che di falso aveva l'identità, doveva trattarlo come se non lo conoscesse.

A cominciare dall'uso del lei.

«Lei si sieda qui e aspetti che la chiami», aveva detto al Dubbio indicandogli una sedia della assai poco accogliente saletta d'attesa della caserma.

L'Ernesto non aveva avuto nemmeno il tempo per domandare se il maresciallo stesse parlando con lui. Il Pezzati infatti aveva imboccato subito la scala che portava al suo ufficio e per dieci minuti s'era sentito soltanto il gorgogliare delle tubature dell'acqua.

In quell'arco di tempo il maresciallo aveva istruito uno dei suoi carabinieri, quello che l'avrebbe assistito durante l'interrogatorio del Dubbio.

«Devo verbalizzare?» aveva chiesto il carabiniere.

«No», gli aveva detto il Pezzati.

Doveva mettersi alla scrivania e fare solo finta. Un po' di rumore insomma, picchiando sui tasti della macchina per scrivere.

«E di quello che senti ti dimentichi subito», aveva aggiunto.

Poi, una volta giudicato che il momento era arrivato, aveva mandato a chiamare il Dubbio.

«Mi raccomando, usa il lei.»

Disorientato dall'atteggiamento di maresciallo e carabiniere, il Dubbio era entrato nell'ufficio del Pezzati come se stesse camminando su un tappeto di uova o temesse buche nascoste dentro le quali cadere per non uscire mai più. S'era seduto davanti al comandante, serio in viso come non l'aveva mai visto, e aveva ascoltato attento attento ciò che era uscito dalle sue labbra.

«Mi capisca bene, signor Livera.»

Tutto ciò che avrebbe detto rispondendo alle sue domande sarebbe stato verbalizzato dal suo carabiniere che fungeva anche da testimone.

«Le conviene dunque pensare bene prima di rispondere, mi ha capito?»

All'Ernesto era uscito di gola un sì rugginoso.

«Cominciamo allora», aveva esordito il maresciallo dopo aver fatto un cenno al carabiniere.

Quindi era partito con la prima, e unica in verità, domanda di tutto l'interrogatorio.

«Voglio sapere per filo e per segno cos'è successo.»

Il Dubbio, di tanto in tanto incarcagliandosi, aveva raccontato ogni cosa. Si era perso anche in particolari del tutto irrilevanti, come il costo della trombetta da stadio che aveva usato per richiamare l'attenzione dei finanzieri e cose del genere.

Alla fine della deposizione il maresciallo si era alzato.

«Bene», aveva detto stando in piedi dietro la scrivania, «lei può andare, ma si tenga a disposizione. Avrò bisogno ancora di lei per farle firmare la confessione.»

Il carabiniere l'aveva guardato con stupore, il Pezzati, con un'occhiata, lo aveva pregato di non uscirsene con qualche battuta che gli rovinasse il gioco.

Poi, una volta soli, lo stesso carabiniere aveva avanzato la domanda.

«Lei maresciallo gli crede?»
«Assolutamente sì», aveva risposto il Pezzati.
Ciò non toglieva che il Dubbio fosse in un mezzo guaio.

25.

«Lei cosa ne pensa maresciallo?» chiese il dottor Lonati staccando gli occhi dal lago e fissandoli sul Pezzati. Sui suoi capelli soprattutto, che il vento gli aveva modellato come se avesse in testa un ventaglio.

«Niente, per il momento», fu la risposta del carabiniere.

Cos'aveva in mano allo stato per poter pensare a qualcosa? Lui piuttosto, il dottore. Aveva ricevuto la telefonata, quindi...

«Magari, nel frattempo le è venuto in mente qualcosa che poco fa non ricordava.»

Da quanto tempo il dottor Lonati non arrossiva?

Il Pezzati lo tolse dall'imbarazzo.

«Ma ci pensi con comodo, senza fretta», disse.

Attraversarono la strada. La roccia viva della cava era scura, sembrava che trasudasse umidità. Il sole stava prendendo possesso della cima del Bregagno sulla riva occidentale. Il Pezzati si fermò a un passo dalla camionetta.

«Intanto sono contento per lei», disse.

«Ah sì?» fece il Lonati all'erta.

«Anche lei dovrebbe esserlo», insisté il maresciallo.

Pur temendo la spiegazione, il Lonati cedette alla curiosità.

«E perché mai?»

«Be', le è passato il raffreddore», spiegò il maresciallo. «Non s'è accorto che non ha più starnutito?»

Poi si girò per nascondere un sorriso e salì sulla camionetta.

26.

Il Riffa aveva dormito della grossa.

Si svegliò che era ancora mezzo buio. Così, a occhio, non ancora le sei.

Fece largo al programma della giornata.

Per il mercato di quel giorno, a Lierna, amen.

Doveva sistemare due cose soprattutto: il camioncino e quel coglione del Dubbio che l'aveva piantato lì, sparito senza dirgli niente.

Aprì gli occhi sempre stando sdraiato sul divano dove aveva dormito.

Comodo tutto sommato.

Girando appena la testa diede un'occhiata all'ambiente. Distingueva poco di quello che aveva intorno. Aveva giusto un ricordo sgranato di ciò che la Tina qualche ora prima gli aveva permesso di vedere accendendo e spegnendo la luce nel giro di un minuto, forse meno.

E di quello che gli aveva detto.

Non toccare niente, non accendere la luce.

Pensare a dormire e basta.

Della sveglia si sarebbe occupata lei, la mattina dopo, alle sei, in tempo per filare a prendere il battello delle sei e mezza, così da sfuggire alla curiosità sempre all'erta della sua dirimpettaia, l'ex infermiera Maria Teresa Supposta, che per fortuna alla sera prendeva un sonnifero e quindi non si svegliava mai prima delle otto e mezza, nove del mattino.

Poi se n'era andata e aveva chiuso a chiave la porta.

27.

Maria Teresa Supposta era figlia del professor Amedeo Modesto Supposta che nel 1934, all'età di cinquantanove anni, era diventato primario ostetrico-ginecologo dell'ospedale Sant'Anna di Como e aveva fatto della figlia la sua prima infermiera dopo un corso da lui stesso diretto, volto a formare il personale che avrebbe lavorato dentro la nuova struttura.

Maria Teresa era risultata la migliore, e senza bisogno che il genitore influenzasse le sorti dell'esito finale. E questo perché da oltre dieci anni, e ormai andava verso i trentadue, seguiva la pratica paterna nell'ambulatorio privato che il professore aveva tenuto a Monza, in via dell'Oca, sino a poco prima di essere nominato primario presso il nosocomio comasco.

Nel decennio che aveva preceduto il suo arrivo a Como al seguito del genitore, la Maria Teresa aveva dovuto convivere con la consapevolezza che i suoi genitori stavano assieme per pura convenienza e, tiranneggiata dall'affetto per l'uno e per l'altra, s'era lasciata scappare il tempo tra le mani senza quasi accorgersi di quei pochi ma comunque papabili giovanotti che non avrebbero disdegnato di conoscerla più a fondo, scopo matrimonio.

A quasi trentadue anni certi ardori avevano ritrovato la lingua della gioventù. Ma solo quella ormai, nonostante le condizioni fossero mutate a suo favore con quel trasferimento a Como che l'aveva sganciata dalla madre dichiaratasi tetragona al trasloco e a qualsivoglia mutamento delle sue abitudini.

L'età non la poneva ancora del tutto nel fuorigioco di un possibile matrimonio. Ma il diavolo ci aveva messo lo zampino quando, a circa un anno dal suo insediamento al Sant'Anna, avevano cominciato a circolare voci, in parte vere in parte infondate, circa una tresca avviata con un aiuto chirurgo, tal Wermer Palanzati, metà svizzero tedesco e metà varesotto.

Sposato, e padre di due figli.

L'intervento deciso della madre superiora delle suore di Maria bambina, che sin dal 1855 per volontà del vescovo Romanò costituivano parte integrante del personale, aveva troncato ogni voce e salvato la Maria Teresa dalle grinfie del Wermer. Era vero infatti che lei se ne fosse incapricciata, ignorando però il suo stato civile e abboccando piuttosto a certe sue vaghe promesse il cui fine sarebbe stato quello di farne una donna perduta.

L'aiuto chirurgo era stato allontanato, la Maria Teresa s'era presa un mese di convalescenza che il genitore le aveva imposto di trascorrere lontano da Como, consigliandole una vacanza presso il Grand Hotel Royal di Cadenabbia.

Per il professor Supposta era stata quella l'occasione di scoprire il lago, le sue bellezze, le sue opportunità: era stato come se qualcuno l'avesse avvisato che appena fuori dai confini dell'ospedale c'era un lago con un mondo che non aspettava altro che lui lo visitasse e se ne innamorasse. E così era stato perché l'amore era scoccato insieme con una esplosiva passionaccia per l'acqua e gli sport che grazie a essa si praticavano, la navigazione a vela soprattutto. Da quel momento il professore, dapprima in solitudine e poi insieme con la figlia ormai guarita dal mal d'amore, aveva dedicato molta parte del tempo che il lavoro gli lasciava libero a gite che avevano finito per occupare addirittura interi fine settimana. Le sorprese di quelle escursioni erano stati alberghi e ristoranti, cibi, sagre e feste, spiagge e panorami.

Da lì ad affittare – prima per un solo mese d'estate, poi per tutta la stagione e infine per l'intero anno – un appartamento, e in un paio di occasioni una casetta singola, il passo era stato breve. Il risultato era stato che infine padre e figlia si erano trovati d'accordo nell'aver scoperto una seconda patria su quelle rive e che dunque era giunta l'ora di acquistare una casa che sancisse una volta per tutte il loro innamoramento per quelle sponde.

La scelta era caduta su un villino ad Acquaseria, paese nel quale padre e figlia avevano spesso fatto tappa, fermandosi anche più di una volta a pranzo presso l'unico ristorante del paese, fresco di inaugurazione e dal singolare nome di Alla Ruota che Gira.

La popolazione locale, di solito restia a manifestare entusiasmo nei confronti dei foresti, li aveva accolti con rispetto, quasi timore reverenziale.

Figurarsi, un esimio professore e la figlia che aveva sacrificato la propria vita ad assisterlo e ad assistere i malati che si affidavano alle loro cure. In quel bagno rassicurante di ossequiosa compiacenza, la natura della Maria Teresa si era adeguata al suo stato, consolandosi col pensiero che il destino aveva deciso così per lei, tanto era inutile rammaricarsene. Mentre suo padre, grazie alle novità del luogo che andava scoprendo di volta in volta e a un dinghy che aveva imparato a pilotare dopo qualche lezione, aveva scoperto la libertà di navigare, perlopiù solitario, andando di porto in porto a conoscere gli angoli più remoti del lago.

Nell'arco dei successivi vent'anni, tre cose avevano segnato in modo definitivo il destino della Maria Teresa.

La prima era stata la morte della madre, vittima di un bombardamento su Milano, in conseguenza della quale il padre aveva deciso di vendere la casa di proprietà a Monza. Nel 1950 l'altro importante avvenimento era stato la definitiva messa a riposo del professore, che l'aveva decisa a seguirne le sorti: aveva lasciato anche lei il Sant'Anna e da infermiera si era trasformata in casalinga di paese poiché quella di Acquaseria, da dimora per le vacanze e i fine settimana, era stata eletta a prima e unica casa. Nel 1952 infine, la Maria Teresa aveva dovuto fare i conti con la cocciutaggine del genitore che, fidandosi del suo intuito fatto esperto da lunghe ore di navigazione sul lago, non aveva tenuto conto di certe nuvolette foriere di cattive notizie, ed era uscito comunque per un giro scontrandosi poi con un improvviso menaggino dal quale era uscito sconfitto. I soccorsi scattati dalla riva di Acquaseria erano arrivati giusto in tempo per recuperare il corpo ormai privo di vita e la barca che non aveva patito danni.

Maria Teresa Supposta si era così trovata sola al mondo, proprietaria di una bella casa vistalago, di una barca che non sapeva pilotare e titolare di un invidiabile conto in banca: tutti elementi che avrebbero fatto la punta a più di un pretendente se non fosse stato che ormai aveva superato i cinquant'anni e quando apriva gli occhi ogni mattina doveva concentrarsi per capire bene dove fosse, cosa fosse diventata, e soprattutto cosa fosse stata, poiché il passato si allontanava, sfocandosi sempre di più.

28.

Più che vedere, il Riffa aveva intravisto l'arredamento che gli aveva fatto pensare ai rifugi di montagna.

Legno da tutte le parti.

Anche l'odore, notò adesso.

Inconfondibile.

Richiuse gli occhi, immaginando di essere davvero in un rifugio.

Le scuffie di vento che percuotevano il mondo di fuori erano quelle di una tormenta di neve. Bello essere lì con la Valeria che gli si stringeva addosso. Si riaddormentò con un sorriso da scemo stampato in viso e si risvegliò con un filo di luce che entrava da una finestrella e la Tina in piedi davanti a lui.

Erano le sei passate da qualche minuto.

«È ora di menare le tolle.»

Come folgore, nella mente del Riffa passò l'idea di afferrarla e tirarla a sé per dare corpo al sogno appena abbandonato. La ragazza però aveva un'espressione tutt'altro che invitante, meglio lasciar perdere.

Il Riffa buttò fuori le gambe dall'improvvisato letto.

«Niente caffè?» chiese tanto per fare lo spiritoso.

«Come no!» rispose la Tina. «E una brioche calda di forno?»

«Manca solo il giornale a questo punto», ribatté soddisfatto il Riffa.

«Perché, quelli non ti bastano?» osservò la ragazza accennando alla parete di fondo.

Poco oltre il divano, addossate alla parete, ce n'erano tre pile.

«Corriere della Sera».

Il Riffa ne prese una copia. Era del giorno prima.

Intonsa, era evidente che nessuno l'aveva sfogliata. L'indirizzo stampigliato era quello del commenda, il padrone di casa. Per curiosità diede un'occhiata anche alle altre copie, la maggior parte come quella che aveva preso: nessuno le aveva mai aperte.

«Perché sono qui?» chiese.

«Ogni tanto passa uno a prenderli, uno che rivende la carta», rispose la Tina.

«Sì, ma», fece il Riffa, «che gusto c'è a prendere il giornale senza nemmeno dargli un'occhiata?»

«Lascia perdere, non sono affari tuoi», fece la ragazza. «Piuttosto sbrigati, che il battello non ti aspetta.»

Il Riffa si passò le mani sul viso, lavaggio a secco.

«Grazie, neh», disse avviandosi.

La Tina gli lasciò fare qualche passo.

«Salutami il tuo amico», disse poi.

Il Riffa rispose con un gesto della mano, senza voltarsi.

Ci poteva scommettere che glielo avrebbe salutato.

29.

Non era così sicuro da farci una scommessa.

Però il maresciallo Pezzati aveva il sospetto che il dottore non gliela contasse giusta. Neanche da pensare che si fosse inventato tutto. Ma c'era qualcosa che...

Insomma, non gliela contava giusta.

Era rientrato in caserma, con quel pensiero fisso in testa, si era fermato nell'atrio sotto gli occhi del carabiniere Fantarini, che gli aveva aperto e fischiettava sottotono come, il maresciallo ci aveva già fatto caso, gli capitava spesso. Non sembravano canzonette o arie d'opera.

Al Pezzati sarebbe piaciuto sapere perché fischiettasse così spesso e soprattutto cosa. Prima o poi glielo avrebbe chiesto. Non era quello, però, il momento giusto.

Aveva levato lo sguardo verso di lui.

«Cosa c'è?» aveva chiesto.

«Niente maresciallo», aveva risposto il Fantarini interrompendo il fischio.

«Successo niente?»

Il carabiniere si era stretto nelle spalle. Se era successo qualcosa, aveva ragionato, l'unico che poteva saperlo era il signor maresciallo, visto che era uscito prima delle cinque e per via di una cosa urgente. Aveva taciuto però, e risposto alla domanda.

«Niente.»

Senza dire altro il Pezzati s'era avviato verso il suo ufficio. Ormai, dati l'ora e l'accaduto, la sua giornata poteva considerarsi già avviata. Poi s'era fermato e girato.

«Una cosa da fare te la do io», aveva detto rivolgendosi al Fantarini.

Forse, aveva appena pensato, il dottor Lonati gliela contava giusta ma non gliela diceva tutta.

Sì, era molto più probabile che fosse così.

«Pigliati l'elenco delle caserme dell'alto lago e comincia a chiedere se hanno notizie di persone disperse.»

«Disperse?» era sbottato il Fantarini.

«Disperse, esatto», aveva confermato il Pezzati. «Ti suona oscuro il termine?»

«No», aveva risposto con tranquillità il carabiniere.

Aveva solo fatto due più due.

«E quanto fa?» aveva chiesto il Pezzati.

Il Fantarini era arrossito. Ciononostante si era spiegato.

«Intendevo dire che stavo mettendo assieme le due cose, la telefonata del dottore e la sua uscita, maresciallo.»

«Bravo. E in conclusione?»

«Non ci sono ancora arrivato.»

«D'accordo. Allora, mentre aspetti, fa' quello che ti ho detto.»

Ma il Fantarini non era scattato.

«Devo anche chiedere, nel caso, di inviarci i dati anagrafici, un'eventuale fotografia...»

«Ma di chi?» aveva chiesto il maresciallo.

«Del disperso», aveva risposto il Fantarini.

O dispersa che fosse, aveva aggiunto subito.

«Ma chi diavolo ti ha detto che esiste un disperso!»

«Nessuno, ma...»

«Basta così, adesso!» si era indurito il Pezzati.

Come maresciallo era ben felice di avere al suo comando un carabiniere come quello: giovane, volenteroso, intuitivo. Solo che per il momento di tutte quelle belle qualità non sapeva che farsene.

Ubbidienza, solo quella.

«Vola», aveva detto, riprendendo subito la via del suo ufficio.

30.

La Tina intanto s'era incantata a guardare il panorama dalla finestra della cucina, gli alberi del lungolago sbattuti dalla forza del vento.

Aveva pensieri che si erano pian piano sostituiti a quello con il quale era rientrata in casa dopo aver liquidato il Riffa.

Un pensiero, anzi, che non avrebbe confessato a nessuno poiché ai più sarebbe risultato banale mentre ormai, da giorni, era per lei una sorta di incubo: cosa preparare per pranzo?

Solo un mesetto prima le sarebbe venuto da ridere se qualcuno le avesse detto che si sarebbe preoccupata come stava facendo adesso per una cosa banale come il mangiare.

Invece era proprio così.

E non perché le mancasse la fantasia davanti ai fornelli o perché non fosse capace: nell'un caso come nell'altro aveva appreso con diligenza le ricette, con tutte le relative astuzie, che prima sua nonna e poi sua madre le avevano insegnato diventando così una cuoca provetta che non avrebbe fatto sfigurare una trattoria o un ristorante.

Il commenda però da qualche tempo era diventato strano, inappetente, assaggiava appena, sbocconcellava, a differenza di come s'era sempre comportato davanti ai suoi stufati, alle cotolette col manico, agli agoni in carpione o ai lavarelli burro e salvia, quando dimenticava volentieri le raccomandazioni del dottore circa il diabete e toccava a lei dire basta davanti alle sue insistenze per averne ancora un zicchinino.

Nel giro di poche settimane l'uomo s'era smagrito, magri anche il suo spirito e l'allegria che lei gli aveva sempre conosciuto.

Il dottore, al quale la Tina aveva una volta esternato la sua preoccupazione, le aveva detto di stare tranquilla. Certe volte la magrezza accompagnava l'invecchiamento e non era segnale di malattia e circa l'appetito, se quello del commenda si era dato una regolata, il diabete non poteva che trarne vantaggio.

Della situazione aveva parlato anche con i due figli, i quali per tutta risposta avevano allargato le braccia, accodandosi e accontentandosi delle spiegazioni del dottore, la malattia, l'età...

Ma la Tina non era convinta, anzi.

Per tutto quello che stava accadendo al commenda aveva una sua spiegazione.

Tutt'altro che scientifica, se ne rendeva ben conto ed era stato proprio in virtù di quella considerazione se si era astenuta dal farne cenno al dottore, onde evitare il rischio di farsi ridere in faccia.

Però da un certo giorno...

Da un giorno, un giorno preciso, il commenda aveva iniziato a cambiare.

Silenzioso, a volte davvero triste, e inappetente tant'è che aveva cominciato a essere un vero problema per lei inventare qualcosa che lo stimolasse a mangiare.

Come adesso, divisa tra un bel risottino giallo o due fette di fegato alla veneziana con tanta cipolla. Doveva decidere e allo stesso tempo non dare ascolto a una vocina che le diceva che sarebbe stata fatica sprecata perché, come tante altre volte ormai, anche quel cibo sarebbe finito nella spazzatura.

Così, pensando, s'era incantata a guardare dalla finestra della cucina quel vento che faceva ciò che voleva sul lago e tra gli alberi e il pensiero del mangiare sembrava essere volato via insieme con una delle sue scuffie.

A riportarla alla realtà ci pensò il suono del campanello.

Dalla finestra della cucina non riusciva a vedere l'ingresso, il cancelletto che dava accesso al piccolo giardino che stava davanti alla casa del commenda.

Si spostò in sala per dare un'occhiata, immaginando chi potesse essere.

Considerata l'ora non poteva essere la Supposta né, tantomeno, il postino col quale, dopo averne scoperto il gioco, aveva troncato ogni genere di rapporto.

Vedendo chi c'era al cancelletto, sorrise e si affrettò ad aprire.

31.

Il Riffa stava in prua al battello, guardava fisso il pontile di Bellano che si avvicinava.

Fregava niente del vento, anzi.

Gli piaceva.

Si stava immaginando come se fosse in un fotoromanzo, meglio ancora in un film.

L'eroe che andava dritto alla meta per consumare la sua vendetta.

Se ne sarebbe ricordato per un pezzo il Dubbio, ci avrebbe pensato sette volte prima di tirargli ancora un pacco di quel genere.

Aveva la scena già pronta in mente: scendere dal battello, fare un salto al bar dell'Imbarcadero per bersi un cognac, che non gli serviva certo per darsi coraggio ma per cacciarsi di dosso il freddo che stava accumulando, presentarsi a casa del Dubbio, suonare e piantarsi a gambe larghe davanti alla porta.

Guardarlo in silenzio, diritto negli occhi.

Non poteva sbagliare, visto che in casa, oltre alla Canterina che usciva per andare alla prima messa e poi filava all'asilo, non c'era altri che lui.

Poi...

Il Riffa rifletté.

Gli mancava il seguito, il secondo tempo del film.

Poteva insultarlo.

Al Dubbio non avrebbe fatto né caldo né freddo.

Menarsi...?

Menarsi no... menarsi perché?

Oltretutto...

Ecco, mentre l'attracco si avvicinava sempre più, al Riffa venne in mente che, oltre a vendicarsi, quella mattina doveva pensare anche a portarsi a casa il camioncino. E, se non voleva farsela a piedi da Bellano a Corenno, doveva scroccargli un passaggio in barca per prendere la ruota bucata il giorno prima e portarla dal Ciba Pompista, l'unico su tutto il lago di Como che avrebbe tentato di rimetterla in sesto anziché consigliargli di buttarla nel cesso e comperarne una nuova.

Forse, rifletté il Riffa, la miglior vendetta era tenere al suo servizio il Dubbio tutta la giornata.

Una volta sceso dal battello, il Riffa era convinto che quella fosse la cosa migliore.

E se non era la migliore era senz'altro quella che, vista la situazione, gli conveniva di più.

Per le vendette c'era sempre tempo.

32.

Il maresciallo Pezzati stava alla finestra del suo ufficio, piazzato lì come se fosse di guardia a qualcosa.

Guardava.

Vedeva anche?

Vedeva il ventaccio che strapazzava gli ippocastani della piazza, la gente che gli passava sotto gli occhi rattrappita, come riassunta in sé onde offrire la minor superficie possibile a quell'ariaccia che spingeva o frenava secondo gli si camminasse davanti o contro?

Aveva visto il battello su cui viaggiava il Riffa avvicinarsi ballonzolando e poi attraccare al molo con la cautela di una vergine e il Riffa stesso che era sceso e aveva salutato il battellotto con una pacca sulle spalle?

Che guardasse era fuor di dubbio.

Se anche vedesse, lo sapeva solo lui.

Senz'altro pensava alle parole del dottor Lonati.

E aspettava.

Notizie, novità mentre il carabiniere semplice Fantarini aveva già chiamato un paio di caserme dell'alto lago senza che gliene avessero data mezza.

33.

Su quel nuovo postino, giunto in paese un paio di mesi prima, la Tina s'era illusa, s'era fatta una mezza idea.

Era bello, simpatico, gentile e spiritoso.

Aveva il ciuffo.

Soprattutto aveva cominciato a farle la corte.

Cioè, le era sembrato che fosse così.

Aveva attaccato bottone con la scusa del giornale, il «Corriere della Sera».

Spesso, per via dei disguidi postali, il «Corriere» giungeva a destinazione il giorno dopo, a volte anche più tardi.

Non conveniva andarlo a comperare all'edicola anziché insistere ad abbonarsi?

«Lo dico per lei eh!» le aveva detto il postino con un sorriso che sembrava quello di un attore.

La Tina gli aveva spiegato il perché e il percome, solo per il gusto di tenerlo un po' lì, al cancelletto della villetta, e guardarselo.

«Il commenda vuole così.»

Era una tradizione della sua famiglia.

Vero o no che fosse, le aveva detto una volta che la sua famiglia era abbonata al «Corriere» sin da quando era stato fondato.

«Tanto non ci sono testimoni», aveva riso la Tina, e lui con lei.

Per un po' era andata avanti così, la Tina ad aspettare con una certa ansia il passaggio del postino, Eugenio le aveva detto di chiamarsi, pronta ad abboccare a ogni amo che lui le gettava: come stava, se le piaceva il lavoro, che tipo era il commenda...

Senza contare la volta che l'aveva fatta ridere con la battuta sulla targa posta sul cancelletto della sua dirimpettaia, l'ex infermiera.

«Professor Amedeo Modesto Supposta e figlia.»

Da che era lì non l'aveva mai vista in faccia.

Forse aveva paura di lui e si nascondeva quando lo vedeva arrivare.

Ma dove poteva nascondersi una con quel cognome?, aveva commentato schiacciandole l'occhio per sottolineare il senso della battuta.

Alla Tina sarebbe piaciuto invitarlo dentro, offrirgli un caffè. Pensava che, seduto in cucina e lontano da occhi indiscreti e orecchie curiose, soprattutto da quelle della sua dirimpettaia, il bell'Eugenio avrebbe lasciato da parte le frasi convenzionali per passare ad altro.

Un invito magari.

Ci aveva pensato lei, una mattina di metà maggio, quando l'Eugenio era passato un po' più tardi del solito e sudato per colpa del caldo eccezionale che era scoppiato.

L'invito a entrare per bere qualcosa di fresco era uscito spontaneo dalle labbra della Tina.

Una volta dentro le erano bastati dieci minuti per capire che il postino tirava alla sua amica, la Valeria, e non a lei.

Non l'aveva presa nemmeno tanto larga per arrivare al punto, raccontandole che le aveva viste insieme poco dopo essere arrivato in quel paese: una sera, durante una specie di festa in piazza, con la gente che ballava.

La bionda, l'aveva battezzata tra sé.

L'aveva cercata dopo quella sera, senza mai più ritrovarla. Però, grazie al giro che gli avevano assegnato e al «Corriere della Sera», aveva ritrovato lei, quella che la sera della festa sembrava avesse il culo attaccato alla sedia con il Vinavil visto che aveva rifiutato i rari inviti ad alzarsi per ballare.

«Com'è che si chiama?» le aveva chiesto dopo aver bevuto mezzo bicchiere di acqua fresca di rubinetto.

La Tina aveva finto di niente, aveva risposto, la delusione mascherata con dignità.

Il postino non aveva nemmeno intuito quanto ci fosse rimasta male. Tanto che, a partire da quella mattina, non aveva più smesso di chiederle informazioni sull'amica.

Se aveva già un moroso, dove abitava, quanti anni aveva, se le piaceva solo ballare o anche andare al cinema...

La Tina aveva sempre cercato di evitare risposte precise.

Non erano così tanto amiche, aveva mentito, si vedevano poco.

Oppure, che la scusasse, ma non aveva tempo, aveva qualcosa sul fuoco o il commenda l'aveva appena chiamata.

Fino al giorno in cui era arrivata quella lettera e le cose avevano preso una piega diversa.

La Tina non aveva avuto più bisogno di mentire, il commenda aveva cominciato a non stare bene, come se avesse i pensieri altrove, la testa tra le nuvole.

34.

Distratto.

Inusina Colletti, uscendo dall'ambulatorio del dottor Lonati, comunicò la sua diagnosi ai sei presenti in sala d'attesa.

Sottovoce, disse che il dottore era lì ma la testa l'aveva da un'altra parte. Nonostante tutti i mali che gli aveva raccontato le aveva detto che doveva portare pazienza, era l'età, c'era poco da fare. E non le aveva prescritto neanche un po' di vitamine!

Peraltro il Lonati non aveva bisogno delle diagnosi dell'Inusina per capire in che stato fosse.

Distratto, appunto, con la testa da un'altra parte.

Per la precisione dalle parti del maresciallo Pezzati.

Lo vedeva come se fosse ancora insieme con lui. Sentiva su di sé lo sguardo dubbioso del carabiniere, nelle orecchie la battuta sul raffreddore.

E man mano che l'Inusina gli aveva raccontato tutti i suoi mali (dolorrri!, dolori dappertutto!, uno poi che cominciava lì e andava a finire là!), mentre lui si era limitato a fare sì col capo senza darle ascolto, i sospetti che il maresciallo gli aveva appena fatto intuire erano diventati i suoi.

Così aveva cominciato a pensare le stesse cose che il Pezzati aveva pensato di lui, mettendo però il Dubbio al posto suo quale soggetto.

L'Ernesto quindi gliela contava giusta, ma non gliela diceva tutta.

Nell'attesa che entrasse il secondo malato o bisognoso che fosse tamburellò le dita sul piano della scrivania, meditando di fare una visitina al Dubbio non appena terminata la mattina d'ambulatorio. Tuttavia si rese conto che non avrebbe resistito a palleggiare con le domande che gli nascevano in testa e facendo finta di ascoltare chi andava e veniva.

Si alzò allora e si fece alla soglia della sala d'attesa.

«Dovete avere pazienza», disse ai presenti, «ma devo correre per un'urgenza.»

Fuori l'aria era già calda, in sottofondo udì il rumore dell'acqua che il vento sbatteva con forza contro la riva.

Si infilò in contrada diretto a casa del Dubbio pressoché nello stesso momento in cui il Riffa, che era appena uscito dal caffè dell'Imbarcadero dopo averci passato una mezz'ora abbondante, faceva altrettanto.

35.

Come da programma, Biagio Trùfa Riffa era entrato al caffè dell'Imbarcadero e aveva ordinato il cognac.

Ma anziché buttarlo giù d'un fiato l'aveva centellinato come un signor contino per due ragioni: la prima era l'aver rinunciato ai propositi di vendetta, perlomeno nell'immediato, visto che il Dubbio gli serviva per l'operazione di recupero del camioncino. La seconda ragione era che a servirlo non era stato, come ci si poteva aspettare data l'ora, il taciturno Prestoni, proprietario del caffè, ma una sgarzolina nuova di zecca.

Nuova davvero, anche del mestiere.

Aveva perduto un paio di minuti per cercare la bottiglia del cognac tra le decine che esibivano le etichette nella tripla fila che le stava alle spalle.

Le era corso in aiuto il Riffa, indicandogliela, e dopo averle squadrato con comodo il posteriore, alto e sodo almeno quanto quello che il lato anteriore offriva.

Non c'era proprio niente da buttare via nella ragazza, tranne il pesante accento con il quale parlava e che la segnava come proveniente da un paesino di qualche valle lì intorno.

Ma su ciò il Riffa poteva sorvolare.

Una volta completati interrogatorio e cognac, all'ingresso di un assonnato ragioniere di banca, tal Fisichetti, il Riffa aveva salutato promettendo, non richiesto, di farsi vivo al più presto, ed era partito.

La vita era così, pensava imboccando la via che portava

a casa del Dubbio: perdi un'occasione e subito se ne presenta un'altra.

Certo, bisognava essere svelti a coglierla e in quanto a ciò Biagio Trùfa Riffa aveva su di sé la più alta delle opinioni.

Alla porta del Dubbio, nell'inconsapevole gara che stava correndo contro il dottor Lonati, giunse per primo, così che il dottore, anziché sul legno di casa Livera, quasi bussò sulla schiena del Riffa.

I due amici si stavano guardando negli occhi da pochi secondi.

Chi dei due avrebbe rotto il silenzio per primo?

Fu il terzo incomodo.

«Ho bisogno di te Ernesto», disse il Lonati guardando il Riffa che, al sentire il tocco sulla schiena, s'era girato pronto a scatenarsi ma si era subito sedato vedendo il dottore. Tra l'altro il tono che il Lonati aveva usato era grave, serio, faceva pensare a qualche malattia, di quelle che non perdonano.

Aveva un sapore di guai, insomma.

Il Riffa esitò appena.

«Passo più tardi», disse, e pur se continuava a guardare il Lonati era evidente che si rivolgeva al Dubbio.

Il quale non si era ancora mosso dalla posizione che aveva, piantato sulla soglia di casa.

Fece un solo passo quando il Riffa era già sparito, un passo indietro, giusto per far entrare il dottore che, una volta chiusasi la porta alle spalle: «Adesso mi racconti tutto», disse.

L'Ernesto allargò le braccia e boccheggiò.

«Non sono sicuro», gli uscì a bocconi.

Il Lonati spianò il viso in un'espressione di sorpresa.

«Sicuro?»

Sicuro di cosa?

Non era sicuro... borbottò tra sé il Lonati.

«Di cosa?»

36.

«Giusto per un saluto», disse la Valeria.

Era lei che aveva suonato al campanello di casa del commenda.

«Ieri sera non abbiamo avuto tempo...» aggiunse con un sorriso ammiccante. Era curiosa di sapere come fosse andata.

La Tina la guardò a sua volta forzando un sorriso che voleva nascondere un fondo di malinconia: era bella la Valeria, appena un po' truccata e anche elegante adesso che stava per partire, bella ed elegante come a lei non sarebbe mai riuscito essere. Con un colpo di spalle si riscosse dalla contemplazione dell'amica.

«Come vuoi che sia andata?» fece. «E tu?»

La Valeria assunse un'espressione divertita.

«Ma ti pare, con quell'imbecille?» rispose ridendo.

Chissà cosa si era messo in testa! Si era divertita però, a farlo sognare un po', a fargli credere che... per poi metterlo a posto.

Un clacson suonò.

La ragazza si girò verso una macchina, un 1100 blu, che stava davanti alla villetta, il motore acceso. Sulla fiancata spiccava, in lettere d'oro, la scritta Ristorante Alla Ruota che Gira.

«Arrivo!» gridò agitando la mano. «Mio padre ha paura che perda l'aereo», disse tornando a rivolgersi all'amica.

«Ma se parte alle due», osservò la Tina, e non erano ancora le nove.

«Lo so. Però secondo lui siamo già in ritardo.»

Un nuovo colpo di clacson fece sollevare al cielo gli occhi della Valeria.

«Che pizza!»

Suo padre, aggiunse ridendo, credeva di essere ancora ai suoi tempi. Meno male che per un mese non avrebbe dovuto rendergli conto di cosa faceva e dove andava.

«Beata te!» sospirò la Tina.

«Puoi dirlo», ribatté l'amica.

E per fortuna, aggiunse la Valeria, la sera prima era dovuto uscire anche lui per andare chissà dove ed era tornato a casa dopo di lei, così aveva evitato il solito interrogatorio, dov'era stata, con chi, cosa aveva fatto.

Se non avessero avuto quella fortuna, alle dieci di sera avrebbero visto i carabinieri arrivare su al crotto, a cercarla per riportarla a casa!

Alla Tina scappò un sorriso perché conosceva bene la mania di quell'uomo che non dava tregua a sua figlia, le imponeva orari di uscita e ritorno come se quella in cui abitava non fosse una casa ma una caserma. Continuava a trattarla come se avesse ancora dieci anni o come se temesse chissà quali pericoli.

Poi fece per dire qualcosa ma tacque perché le parve stupido raccomandarle di tornare, confessarle che avvertiva l'immotivata paura di non rivederla più.

La Valeria intuì che la sua amica cercava di contenere l'emozione, il magone per quel distacco.

Sfoderò il miglior sorriso di cui disponeva, e ne aveva una gamma da fare invidia.

«Su col morale!» disse.

In fin dei conti si trattava solo di un mesetto, sarebbe passato in un amen. Poi le sarebbe toccato ritornare lì e farsi rimettere al collo il guinzaglio.

«Il tempo vola!» sospirò la Valeria certa come non mai di ciò che aveva appena detto, convinta che quella parentesi di libertà sarebbe stata fin troppo breve.

37.

Alessandro Vergonese era giunto a Menaggio, fresco arruolato nella milizia confinaria, alla fine dell'estate del 1936. Vi giungeva direttamente, come aveva avuto subito cura di dire ai suoi colleghi, dalla «campagna d'Africa». Il tono voleva essere quello di chi aveva compiuto chissà quali imprese in quelle terre lontane. Il tono e anche una discreta facondia grazie alla quale il Vergonese farciva i suoi discorsi seminando nomi di luoghi e battaglie (Macallè, Ogaden, lago Ascianghi, ambe di qua, ambe di là) che i suoi commilitoni ricordavano sì e no per averne letto su qualche cronaca di giornale.

In verità il Vergonese in Africa c'era stato, ma non aveva mai sentito fischiare una pallottola, se non da lontano o durante qualche esercitazione, in quanto inquadrato nel Regio corpo delle truppe coloniali della Libia e, assegnato al secondo Reggimento della fanteria d'Africa, vi aveva svolto solo funzioni di sorveglianza al deposito dello stesso. Così aveva avuto il comodo di seguire le tappe della conquista grazie alla semplice lettura dei resoconti degli inviati di guerra.

Al tempo del suo arrivo, al comando del presidio di Menaggio c'era il console Assirto Tedeschetti che non vedeva l'ora di essere promosso console generale e di passare ad altro incarico in quel di Roma per continuare una brillante scalata nel cui curriculum per forza di cose non poteva mancare un periodo di comando territoriale.

Di ben altra tempra era stato il successore del Tedeschetti, il primo seniore Virgilio D'Argò, sorta di duce in miniatura.

Insediatosi nei primi mesi del 1938, aveva subito fatto intendere di che pasta fosse fatto e di che pasta voleva fossero gli uomini ai suoi ordini. Per qualche giorno se n'era stato chiuso nel suo ufficio a studiare la geografia del luogo e a immaginare trappole e appostamenti grazie ai quali avrebbe fatto vedere i sorci verdi agli oppositori del regime e a chiunque pensasse di poter attraversare la frontiera tra Italia e Svizzera come se stesse facendo una scampagnata. Parte di quel tempo poi l'aveva impiegata a passare in rassegna gli stati di servizio degli uomini che avrebbe comandato. Una volta chiarite le idee, li aveva fatti mettere tutti sull'attenti davanti alla scrivania del suo ufficio e aveva indicato coloro che non meritavano di stare sotto il suo comando, ragione per la quale si sarebbe adoperato per farli trasferire e sostituire da altri più atti allo scopo di difendere i patri confini.

Tra costoro, tre in totale, compariva anche il Vergonese i cui motivi di indegnità erano stati spiattellati senza sconti davanti ai presenti, suscitando non poca ilarità: a parte l'essere figlio di una donna che adesso recitava ruoli di secondo piano nelle commediole portate in giro col Carro di Tespi, era stato il suo «sedentario eroismo» durante la campagna d'Africa a sputtanarlo.

Il Vergonese però non si era scomposto più di tanto.

A differenza degli altri due destinati al trasferimento e che temevano di finire in qualche buco di culo di posto ai confini del regno, l'aveva presa con filosofia.

A ogni accenno sul destino che l'attendeva, rispondeva con una scrollatina di spalle. Molta filosofia, troppa.

Qui gatta ci cova, pensavano i suoi commilitoni, intuendo che il Vergonese stava preparando un colpo di mano di quelli che, militarmente pensando, qualunque corpo d'assalto gli avrebbe invidiato per astuzia e risultato finale.

38.

Dal 1100 adesso a ritmo regolare partivano colpi di acceleratore a vuoto per dare forza al richiamo.

Le due amiche erano ancora sulla porta di casa del commenda, una di fronte all'altra, con mezzo sorriso ciascuna sulle labbra. La metà della Tina era di partecipazione alla felicità dell'amica. Quella della Valeria derivava più dalla possibilità di potersi liberare per un mese intero dalla possessiva ossessione del genitore che ormai non sopportava più. Una volta, anni prima, la Valeria le aveva confessato con candore che la invidiava per essere orfana di padre.

«Piuttosto che averne uno così», aveva detto.

La Tina non aveva saputo cosa rispondere e quando, giorni dopo, aveva chiesto a sua madre Brigida che tipo fosse l'uomo che aveva sposato, lei si era limitata a rispondere: «Una brava persona», ed era finita lì.

Inutile insistere, sua madre era fatta così, parlava poco e chiedeva ancora meno, al punto che se non decideva lei di raccontare qualcosa delle sue giornate a casa del Dalamonti, sua madre non avrebbe manco saputo che cosa facesse tutto il giorno fuori di casa.

«Va' adesso», disse la Tina sentendo l'ennesima sgasata del 1100.

«E mi raccomando», aggiunse, immaginando di parlare un po' come fosse una vecchia zia.

D'altronde la Valeria in quell'ultimo periodo non aveva fatto altro che ripeterglielo in tutti i modi possibili: un mese intero in Inghilterra avrebbe di sicuro migliorato il suo inglese.

«Ma non solo quello!»

Perché era proprio lì che la Valeria stava andando.

Inghilterra, Londra!

Era un'idea nata l'anno precedente quando una famiglia di inglesi, padre, madre e due figli tutti bianchi come rape e che dopo due giorni di sole di lago avevano fatto chiamare il dottor Buzzini per farsi curare le scottature, aveva soggiornato un paio di settimane presso l'albergo Alla Ruota che Gira di proprietà di Alessandro Vergonese e della moglie Gerlina Visignola sposata nell'autunno del 1938, anno in cui, giocando d'anticipo, il Vergonese s'era dimesso dalla milizia lasciando di merda il neopromosso primo console D'Argò che invece, informato dalle spie che aveva tra i sottoposti di quanto poco il milite si preoccupasse della minaccia che gli pendeva sopra il capo, stava studiando il modo di dargli una lezione coi fiocchi.

L'aveva presa e incassata lui invece, la lezione, fingendo anche che non gli importasse e comprimendo l'invidia per il colpo che il Vergonese aveva fatto e che l'avrebbe sistemato per la vita, cioè il fidanzamento con la ricca figlia di Gino e Verdella Visignola, titolari della omonima e rinomata ditta di cappelli.

Per il divertimento, il più delle volte forzoso, della sua truppa, il D'Argò aveva fatto girare la battuta secondo la quale l'ex milite, da quell'inetto che era, aveva trovato il modo di «attaccare il cappello»: tra i carristi dov'era stato e, adesso, nella vita, dimostrando di essere, senza offesa, una cimice, niente altro che l'ultima ruota.

Quando un ex collega gliel'aveva riferito, il Vergonese si era limitato a rispondere di riferire al D'Argò che le ruote erano fatte per girare, permettendo, a chi lo sapeva, di cambiare la vista di panorami e prospettive.

39.

Il panorama sempre quello, la prospettiva un po' diversa.

Basta cappelli insomma.

Gli eleganti copricapo della ditta Visignola cominciavano ad avere il fiato corto: costi di produzione e distribuzione sempre più alti, la concorrenza, la moda in perenne evoluzione...

Era ora di arrendersi con onore ai tempi moderni e con un solido capitale alle spalle pensare al futuro.

Possibile, aveva detto ai futuri suoceri il Vergonese, che Acquaseria non avesse un albergo degno di questo nome, e proprio su quella riva di lago che era famosa per essere stata visitata dalle menti più brillanti d'Europa?

Sposava la loro figlia senza alcun bisogno di dote, era stata la sua proposta. Ma proponeva di finanziare l'apertura di un albergo che non avesse nulla da invidiare a tanti altri, garantendo un futuro a sé, alla prossima moglie, alla famiglia e ai figli che sarebbero venuti.

«Restituirò tutto, fino all'ultimo centesimo», aveva promesso.

L'albergo Alla Ruota che Gira era stato inaugurato a poco più di un anno dalle nozze e con l'Italia appena entrata in guerra, una guerra che peraltro sembrava lontana e che soprattutto pareva dovesse riguardare altri. Tant'è che proprio in quei primi mesi d'estate, fatti di scaramucce e facili vittorie, i turisti avevano cominciato a firmare i registri dell'albergo. Tra i primi c'erano stati degli svizzeri dell'interno che i coniugi Vergonese avevano accolto con particolare cortesia, manco fossero messaggeri inviati dal cielo per predire loro un futuro radioso. Era stato poi verso la fine del 1940 che presso l'albergo dei Vergonese aveva soggiornato per quasi due mesi e a spese della municipalità, in attesa che la casa cui aveva diritto fosse pronta per essere abitata, la nuova levatrice consorziale. Aveva trentacinque anni e si chiamava Maria Dominetti.

40.

Svizzeri, tedeschi o francesi.

Svizzeri e basta.

Tedeschi, olandesi.

Qualche austriaco.

Col passare degli anni l'albergo dei Vergonese era entrato nel novero delle piccole eccellenze del lago di Como, ospitando, oltre chc indigeni, stranieri provenienti dalle più varie parti del mondo.

Inglesi pochi.

Quando arrivavano destavano meraviglia e curiosità, manco provenissero da un altro pianeta.

Com'era l'Inghilterra?

Se ne leggevano di cose strane a volte sui giornali...

E Londra?

Così era maturata e aveva preso forma l'idea della Valeria di un soggiorno in Inghilterra.

Quegli inglesi, i cui due figli bianchi come rape avevano fatto chiamare il dottor Buzzini per farsi curare le scottature, erano capitati per caso Alla Ruota che Gira ma ci si erano trovati subito bene e s'erano fermati un paio di settimane.

La consuetudine a ricevere ospiti stranieri col tempo aveva dotato il Vergonese di un vocabolario stringato ma essenziale, sufficiente a intendersi con tutti nelle cose pratiche. A volte a sostegno interveniva anche il cuoco che aveva un passato di lavoro in Svizzera e se la cavava soprattutto coi crucchi.

Francese e tedesco perlopiù, le lingue con le quali si intendevano.

L'inglese scanchignava un po' stante la scarsità della clientela d'Oltremanica.

La Valeria aveva sopperito a quel bisogno. Aveva cominciato quando frequentava il terzo anno del liceo scientifico. Studiare non le piaceva, aveva già chiarito in famiglia che non sarebbe andata oltre la maturità, cosa che di fatto era accaduta. Ma, rispetto alle altre materie che aveva portato a casa con penose sufficienze, con l'inglese e le lingue in generale aveva dimostrato di saperci fare.

Parlarle più che scriverle, intendersi senza troppo badare alla forma.

Con quella famiglia di anglosassoni aveva stabilito una simpatica confidenza, con la madre soprattutto che aveva pochi anni più di lei e le aveva scaldato la fantasia con il racconto delle cose meravigliose, impensabili nel piccolo borgo di lago, che accadevano e maturavano in quel di Londra: la musica, certi locali, la moda... un sacco di cose insomma che avevano deciso la Valeria ad accettare con entusiasmo l'invito a passare un mese da loro.

Il Vergonese non aveva preso sul serio la faccenda. Alla fine della vacanza aveva salutato i pallidi inglesi con la certezza che non ne avrebbe avuta più notizia ma non aveva fatto i conti con la determinazione della figlia. La Valeria infatti aveva mantenuto un costante contatto epistolare con l'inglese e quando infine questa le aveva scritto di decidersi ad andarla a trovare, la ragazza aveva messo il padre di fronte a un ultimatum: se accettava di lasciarla partire prometteva di impegnarsi a lavorare nell'albergo al suo ritorno. Nel caso contrario, avrebbe approfittato della prima occasione per andare a lavorare da un'altra parte, mettendo a frutto la sua conoscenza delle lingue, e lasciando a lui solo l'albergo e il suo futuro.

Chi tra i due l'avesse spuntata stava lì adesso, sotto gli occhi della Tina, nel ripetuto richiamo del clacson, nell'ineffabile felicità del volto della Valeria cui infine l'amica diede tre bacetti alla moda svizzera chiedendole, dopo averla salutata per l'ennesima volta, di tenerla informata sulle novità del suo soggiorno londinese.

41.

«Novità», disse il carabiniere Fantarini.

Il maresciallo Pezzati levò il viso da certe carte che aspettavano da un paio di giorni.

«Abbiamo il disperso?» chiese.

«Non proprio», rispose con serietà il Fantarini.

Danneggiamenti piuttosto, forse atti di vandalismo su proprietà privata.

E furto, probabilmente con scasso.

Il tutto a Corenno Plinio.

L'aveva appena comunicato il vigile urbano Oltramonti, dipendente del comune di Dervio entro i cui confini cadeva il territorio di Corenno. Di competenza della stazione di Colico, è vero. Ma i colleghi di lassù, altrimenti impegnati, avevano detto al vigile di rivolgersi ai carabinieri di Bellano.

«D'accordo», fece il Pezzati.

E passiamo ai fatti.

«Eccoli», si preparò a esporre il Fantarini.

Poco meno di un'ora prima l'Oltramonti, visionata la cosa e giudicando che fosse materia per carabinieri, dopo essersi consultato col segretario comunale, aveva preso in mano la cornetta e chiamato, riferendo per bene ciò che aveva visto.

Il camioncino del Riffa aveva tutte e quattro le gomme a terra e soprattutto presentava evidenti segni di scasso: il portellone posteriore era stato forzato allo scopo di accedere all'interno e asportare l'intero carico di scarpacce. Sul fatto che lo stesso mezzo fosse parcheggiato al di fuori degli spazi consentiti l'Oltramonti aveva deciso di sorvolare. Conosceva il Riffa, al mercato di Dervio gli faceva ottimi sconti, e si rendeva conto che i danni subiti erano più che sufficienti senza bisogno di aggravarli con una multa e la spesa di un'eventuale rimozione forzata.

«Il Riffa hai detto?» chiese il Pezzati.

Così aveva detto l'Oltramonti: sulla fiancata del camioncino c'era la scritta RIFFA-SCARPE E ACCESSORI.

«È di qua?» chiese il Fantarini.

«Certo, chi non lo conosce», rispose il Pezzati.

Vendeva le migliori scarpe di cartone dell'intera Lombardia!

Be', rifletté il Pezzati, se non altro aveva un'ottima scusa per rimandare ad altro momento la lettura delle carte: disposizioni di servizio, poco importanti e soprattutto noiose.

«Si va?» scappò detto al Fantarini che non vedeva l'ora di entrare in azione.

«Calma leone», gli rispose il Pezzati.

Ma alzandosi dalla sedia e facendogli cenno col capo di seguirlo.

42.

«Calmati e raccontami bene tutto», disse il dottor Lonati.

Una volta entrato in casa e chiusa la porta, il Lonati aveva seguito il Dubbio lungo il corridoio ed era entrato in cucina. Un locale piccolo che faceva pensare a un'economia domestica sempre giocata sul filo del rasoio. Un calendario di «Bolero» alla parete. Chiazze di umidità, pentolini e mestoli che pendevano da una fila di chiodi e sedie spaiate. Sul tavolo una cerata con più di un buco di sigaretta. L'aria però odorava di pulito.

«Guarda che non puoi scappare», disse ancora il dottore spostando una sedia e poi decidendo di rimanere in piedi.

Il Dubbio infatti continuava a camminare avanti e indietro nello spazio tra la cucina a gas e il tavolo, di fronte al Lonati.

«Ma gliel'ho già detto», disse infine.

«Mi hai detto che non sei sicuro», ribadì il dottore.

Ma voleva sapere di cosa non si sentiva sicuro.

Di aver visto davvero un cadavere quella notte?

Se l'era forse sognato come...

«Perché, giusto affinché tu lo sappia, sulla riva che mi hai indicato non c'era alcun cadavere», disse il Lonati.

Il Dubbio ebbe un involontario scatto con la testa.

«C'era?» chiese il Lonati.

Ce l'aveva portato lui, come gli aveva confessato qualche ora prima?

«Sì o no?» insisté il Lonati.

«Sì», confermò il Dubbio.

«E allora di cosa non sei sicuro?»

Il Dubbio deviò lo sguardo verso la cerata. Ripensava a ciò che gli era successo poche ore prima sul lago, a come avesse agito di fretta, in automatico, spinto da chissà cosa...

Se invece avesse finto di niente non si sarebbe trovato nella situazione attuale a dover dire che...

«Ernesto», lo richiamò il Lonati, «o lo dici a me o lo dici al maresciallo.»

Il Dubbio alzò gli occhi, guardò il dottore.

«Che...» mormorò.

«Che?»

«Che fosse morta da poco», sussurrò poi.

Il Lonati soppesò la risposta.

«Ma avevi detto stanotte», disse infine chinando un po' il capo e guardando da sotto in su il giovanotto.

«Sì, ma...»

«Perché l'hai detto?»

«Non so...»

«Perché!» lo interruppe il Lonati.

Come faceva ad affermare con certezza una cosa del genere?

«Perché...»

«Perché?»

«Perché era... era bella», rispose il Dubbio.

«Bella?» sbottò il dottor Lonati. «Vorresti dire...»

Ma il Dubbio si sovrappose alla sua voce.

Bella, sì.

Bella nel senso che era ancora ben conservata, senza segni particolari per quanto aveva potuto vedere e... e non era gonfia, aveva un colore normale, insomma, pallida ma pallida come... come una che avesse freddo e non che fosse morta.

Il Lonati l'aveva lasciato parlare.

Alla fine incrociò le braccia.
«L'hai guardata bene», disse.
Il Dubbio incrociò lo sguardo del Lonati.
Gli era sfuggito il tono della sua voce: aveva voluto affermare una cosa oppure era un'altra domanda?

43.

Un altro cognacchino.

Perché no?

Un altro cognacchino e un'altra chiacchieratina con la nuova sgarzolina del caffè dell'Imbarcadero.

L'idea aveva preso subito possesso della mente del Riffa una volta lasciato il Dubbio alle prese col dottor Lonati.

Maresciallo Pezzati permettendo, però.

Il quale, vedendolo sul punto di attraversare la strada per fare vela verso il bar mentre lui, in piedi davanti al portone della caserma, stava in attesa della camionetta col Fantarini alla guida, lo chiamò al volo.

«Riffa, giusto te!»

«Io?» fece il Riffa.

«Proprio», confermò il maresciallo facendogli cenno di avvicinarsi.

«Mi dica.»

«Dimmi una cosa. Dove hai lasciato il camioncino questa notte?»

Il Riffa si grattò la testa.

Fu lì per chiedere perché ma si trattenne.

«Lo so», disse invece, con una vena di pentimento non richiesto nel tono della voce. «Comunque stavo proprio andando a recuperarlo.»

«Bene», approvò il Pezzati, «perché allora facciamo la stessa strada.»

«In che senso?» chiese il Riffa.

Qualcosa stava cominciando a non quadrargli.

«Nel senso che anch'io vado da quelle parti. Non lo vuoi un passaggio?»

Era chiaro che il maresciallo sapeva dove aveva lasciato il mezzo e voleva divertirsi un po'.

«Be'...» fece il Riffa.

Difficile dire no a un maresciallo dei carabinieri.

Il Fantarini con la camionetta intanto stava arrivando.

«Allora?» fece il Pezzati.

«Va bene, grazie», rispose il Riffa.

Ma poco convinto.

Gli sembrava di sentire odore di bruciato.

Lungo la strada nessuno parlò.

Il Fantarini attento alla guida. Il Pezzati fischiettava. Il Riffa invece, seduto dietro, l'occhio fisso in avanti e ogni tanto a scrutare lo specchietto retrovisore per vedere se lo sguardo del maresciallo lo cercasse.

Era tranquillo in coscienza ma, come dire?, allo stesso tempo non si sentiva del tutto sereno.

Forse, rifletté, era quello stare lì così, sulla camionetta dei carabinieri... non gli sembrava una cosa normale.

E va be'!, concluse quando ormai Dervio era alle spalle.

Tanto mancava poco all'arrivo, dopodiché saluti e grazie per il passaggio.

Il Riffa stava per dire che ormai era arrivato, la piazza di Corenno alle viste, quando il maresciallo: «Eccoci giunti», lo anticipò.

«Anch'io», fece il Riffa.

«Non ne dubito», disse il Pezzati senza guardarlo.

«Come dice?» chiese il Riffa.

La risposta arrivò dal carabiniere Fantarini che, messa la freccia, svoltò a sinistra ed entrò ballonzolando sull'acciottolato della piazza per parcheggiare dietro al camioncino di Biagio Trùfa Riffa dove, quale piantone, stava il vigile urbano Oltramonti.

Al Riffa bastò un'occhiata per rendersi conto del disastro.

E bestemmiò.

«Per favore!» lo riprese il maresciallo.

I due carabinieri scesero, il Riffa invece sembrava incollato al sedile.

«Ti serve un invito?» chiese il Pezzati.

Il vigile Oltramonti intanto stava facendo segno di seguirlo.

«Me ne sono accorto solo dopo», disse raggiungendo il lato di sinistra del camioncino sulla cui fiancata una mano incerta munita di pennello intinto nel minio aveva aggiunto a completamento della scritta RIFFA-SCARPE E ACCESSORI: DI MERDA.

«Qualcuno ti vuole proprio bene eh?» commentò il maresciallo.

Il Riffa taceva.

«Non dici niente?» chiese il Pezzati.

44.

Nel silenzio della cucina, rotto di tanto in tanto dal tremare dei vetri scossi dalle scuffie del vento, la Tina non aveva ancora trovato niente di nuovo che potesse risvegliare l'appetito del commenda.

Ormai aveva dato fondo al suo personale ricettario.

Carni e pesci cucinati in tutti i modi che conosceva. Verdure, crude, cotte, fritte.

Non s'era risparmiata nemmeno coi dolci, anche se, col diabete...

Dalle sue mani uscivano certe crostate che il commenda aveva sempre definito «spaziali» e che ormai erano diventate un ricordo da quando il dottore le aveva proibite.

Eppure la Tina, fregandosene del divieto, aveva tentato anche con quelle pur di avere una ripresa del commenda.

Del suo appetito, certo.

Ma soprattutto del suo sorriso, della sua allegria, del suo stile di vita. Delle chiacchiere con le quali avevano spesso riempito le lunghe ore del pomeriggio, lui raccontando della sua gioventù, delle fatiche fatte per mettere in piedi l'azienda, della soddisfazione di aver cresciuto due figli con la testa sulle spalle, lei rispondendo alle curiosità del commenda circa la sua vita in quel paese e soprattutto riguardo ai suoi sogni, a ciò che si aspettava dal futuro.

Era una parola, futuro, che al commenda piaceva, la ripeteva spesso.

Ma dal giorno in cui era arrivata quella lettera la Tina non gliel'aveva più sentita pronunciare. Da quel giorno il commenda era cambiato di punto in bianco, come se gli avessero comunicato chissà quale disgrazia. O, peggio, avesse avuto una rivelazione.

Più volte la ragazza era stata tentata di parlarne col dottore. Un po' per timidezza, un po' per non passare per sciocca aveva sempre taciuto l'idea che quel banale evento avesse fatto precipitare il commenda dentro pensieri che non avevano più niente a che fare con la vita, con quella parola, futuro, che era fuggita dal gruppo di quelle che ormai sempre più rare gli uscivano dalle labbra.

S'era limitata a chiedere cosa si poteva fare affinché il commenda riprendesse un poco dello smalto che aveva sempre avuto, nonostante la malattia.

Ma anche il dottore le aveva risposto che c'era poco da fare. Poco da fare contro il declino, il declino della vita.

Poteva solo dire che non era la prima volta che assisteva a viraggi del genere nel carattere, nel comportamento di una persona anziana.

E spesso, purtroppo...

La Tina aveva capito che il dottore si stava arrampicando sui vetri, non gliene aveva fatta una colpa.

Aveva ben presente che nessuno campava in eterno e nessuno poteva fare miracoli.

Ma dentro di sé non riusciva a perdonare il postino.

Quell'imbecille!

Se avesse curato meno il ciuffo di capelli di cui andava tanto fiero e si fosse occupato di più del suo lavoro, di controllare gli indirizzi cui consegnava la posta, facile che quella lettera non sarebbe giunta in casa e il commenda avrebbe potuto godere ancora un po' di serenità.

45.

Pensaci, gli aveva detto il Lonati.

«Lo dico per il tuo bene.»

Gli aveva anche suggerito di non dire niente a sua madre di quello che era capitato. E di tenere presente che l'unica cosa giusta da fare era dire la verità, e dirla soprattutto all'unica persona che doveva conoscerla, il Pezzati.

Poi se n'era andato, l'ambulatorio aspettava.

Il Dubbio adesso ci stava pensando.

Alle parole del dottore.

Ma soprattutto a quello che aveva visto.

O che credeva di aver visto e alle conseguenze che aveva tirato.

In fin dei conti, però...

In fin dei conti s'era trattato di uno sguardo, un paio di secondi, sotto la luce falsa della torcia, sulla barca che ballava per via del vento e delle onde.

Poteva descriverlo?

Il Dubbio, l'occhio fisso su un disegno della cerata, un fagiano che si involava, se lo chiese ad alta voce.

«Potrei descriverlo?»

No, si rispose.

Si mise nei panni del maresciallo che di certo gli avrebbe chiesto di fare uno sforzo.

«No, cazzo!» rispose.

Forse era meglio se evitava le parolacce.

«No!» picchiando un pugno sul fagiano che non fece una piega.

Avrebbe mollato, il Pezzati?
Difficile.
Avrebbe insistito.
E lui, avrebbe fatto altrettanto?
«Sì», disse ad alta voce il Dubbio.
No, no, no, non poteva descriverlo perché...
«Perché magari ci siamo inventati tutto?»
Al Dubbio parve di sentire la voce del maresciallo Pezzati.
Lo vide, come già l'aveva visto una volta e anche allora c'era di mezzo il Riffa. Il Pezzati stava seduto al suo posto, un po' inclinato di lato, una mano che batteva il tempo sulla pancia, lo sguardo affilato.
Chiuse gli occhi per scacciare dalla mente l'immagine del carabiniere.
«Cazzo!» gridò.
Avrebbe dovuto fare finta di niente, starsene zitto anziché andare a svegliare il Lonati.
«Cazzo!» gridò di nuovo.
«Cosa c'è?» chiese la Canterina che stava rientrando in quel momento.
L'Ernesto non se l'aspettava.
Guardò sua madre come se fosse un'apparizione.
«Ho chiesto, cosa c'è?» ripeté la madre.
L'aveva sentito gridare, aveva trovato la porta mezza aperta...
Qualcosa, rifletté il Dubbio, doveva inventarsi per rispondere, e doveva farlo in fretta e bene.
«Perché?» chiese tanto per prendere tempo.

46.

«Perché?» chiese Biagio Trùfa Riffa.

Il maresciallo Pezzati gli aveva appena detto di risalire con loro sulla camionetta.

«Perché il furto è con scasso e, che tu lo voglia o meno, parte la denuncia d'ufficio. Devi venire in caserma per firmare le carte.»

La spiegazione al Riffa era suonata zifola, fessa.

Ma non aveva osato obiettare.

Saltare su allora, op!, sulla camionetta e partire per tornare a Bellano sotto lo sguardo umido del vigile Oltramonti che si stava preparando a giocarsi per un po' di tempo la generosità del Riffa e magari di qualche altro collega del mercato.

E già, perché adesso toccava a lui predisporre la rimozione del camioncino prima che cominciasse la catena di santantonio delle lamentele, sacrista, prevosto, sindaco. E per farlo avrebbe dovuto interpellare il soccorso stradale del Viatico che aveva prezzi come se commerciasse diamanti. In sostanza, il conto che sarebbe arrivato al Riffa l'avrebbe pagato anche lui in termini di scarpe e scarpette, polli arrosto, braghe eccetera venute via a gratis, perché quelli del mercato si passavano la voce e si vendicavano così.

Se invece il Riffa fosse rimasto lì, anziché andar via coi caramba... insomma, in qualche modo si sarebbero arrangiati senza spendere soldi e lui avrebbe mantenuto il credito aperto con quelli del mercato.

D'altronde l'Oltramonti non aveva potuto fare altro che ubbidire, lui come il Biagio.

Che adesso, sempre seduto dietro sulla camionetta, evitava con cura di incrociare nello specchietto retrovisore lo sguardo del Pezzati e guardava invece fuori il panorama che passava alla velocità di quaranta chilometri orari. D'altronde gli occhi doveva pur piazzarli da qualche parte, evitando con cura di esibire lo sguardo basso, afflitto, quello del colpevole reo confesso, perché stavolta la vittima era proprio lui, anche se era chiaro come il sole che il maresciallo aveva pensato alla storia di due anni prima.

47.

«Perché», aveva appena finito di spiegare la Canterina, «ti sembra normale che uno si metta a gridare come un dannato, da solo, in casa?»

Cosa potevano pensare i vicini?

«Di quello che pensano loro non me ne frega niente», rispose il Dubbio.

«Nemmeno se pensano che stai gridando con me, che mi tratti così?»

L'Ernesto scrollò le spalle, senza parole, evitando lo sguardo di sua madre che invece nel frattempo aveva appena fatto una rapida ispezione della cucina.

Tutto in ordine, così come l'aveva lasciata la sera prima.

Strano, quantomeno.

«Non hai ancora fatto colazione?» investigò.

Colazione?, rifletté il Dubbio.

Ma se non s'era nemmeno svestito, buttato sul letto così com'era dopo essere uscito dalla casa del Lonati.

Lo fulminò l'idea che quella era la balla giusta.

«Colazione?» ripeté. «E chi ne ha voglia!»

Fino alle tre in giro per fiocina...

«È andata bene?» chiese la Canterina tanto per mantenere viva la conversazione e senza riuscire a frenare un certo tremolante sospetto nel tono della voce.

«Così», rispose l'Ernesto.

Risposta tutt'altro che convincente. E che spinse la Canterina a valutare meglio l'aspetto del figlio, il suo atteggiamento, lo sguardo.

«Be', adesso allora va' a riposarti un po'», propose.

«Riposare?» grugnì il Dubbio. «Magari», aggiunse picchiando un pugno sul tavolo.

«Dico», sbottò allora la Canterina fissando in viso il figlio, «si può sapere cosa ti prende? Sembri un leone in gabbia!»

48.

Ruggiva come un trattore l'850, ed era targata Viterbo. Venuta via per quattro lire da un rivenditore sfasciacarrozze di Berbenno, era stata il mezzo con il quale il Riffa aveva cominciato a girare per i mercati prima del camioncino.

Una bella notte, quella tra il 1° e il 2 novembre di due anni prima, aveva preso fuoco. Quando i pompieri erano giunti sul posto, non avevano potuto fare altro che spegnere le fiamme, che tra l'altro s'erano già attaccate all'edera secca che ricopriva il muro accanto al quale la macchina era stata parcheggiata, perché per salvare qualcosa era troppo tardi. Alla fine l'850 non c'era più, ridotta a uno scheletro di metallo.

Dell'incendio il Pezzati aveva sentito parlare al bar. E lì avrebbe lasciato morire la faccenda se quel giorno non si fosse presentato in caserma l'assicuratore Gaspare Nano il quale, con una cert'aria di superiorità, gli aveva chiesto se per caso non avesse notato niente di strano in quell'incidente.

Dopo avergli chiesto a cosa si riferisse, sentita la spiegazione del Nano, aveva risposto: «No. E lei?».

«Io sì», aveva dichiarato l'assicuratore con un sorriso furbetto.

«Sono tutto orecchie», aveva detto il maresciallo allargando le braccia in un gesto di accoglienza.

Prima di tutto, aveva ripreso il Nano, bisognava sapere che l'auto era assicurata da pochi mesi.

«Colpa mia», aveva aggiunto l'assicuratore provocando la reazione del maresciallo.

Di che colpa parlava, visto che assicurare anche automobili era il suo lavoro?

Il Nano aveva scosso il capo.

«Un altro al mio posto non l'avrebbe fatto», aveva risposto.

Lui s'era lasciato impietosire dalle balle del Riffa. Era l'unico suo bene, ci lavorava, ci portava in giro la merce, a volte ci dormiva anche, quando doveva raggiungere piazze libere un po' lontane.

Così dopo sei mesi aveva preso fuoco.

«Sfortuna?» aveva insinuato il Pezzati.

«Forse no», aveva risposto l'assicuratore.

Forse no perché la macchina del Riffa era parcheggiata lungo la stradina chc portava al cimitcro.

«Buia, vuota e senza case intorno.»

E poi perché gli stessi vigili del fuoco gli avevano detto che non avevano trovato nemmeno l'ombra di una scarpa, per quanto bruciata.

«Il che significa che non c'erano scarpe a bordo», aveva concluso il maresciallo.

«No, se mi permette. A mio giudizio significa che il Riffa le aveva preventivamente scaricate onde evitare che bruciassero insieme con la macchina.»

Quando tornava da mercati lontani, Chiavenna o Verceia, o da qualche fiera che lo teneva impegnato tutto il giorno, il Riffa non scaricava e parcheggiava davanti al municipio o in piazza della chiesa, lo sapeva dalla guardia notturna Bellematti che per amicizia gliela teneva d'occhio.

E il giorno prima il Riffa era stato alla fiera di Tutti i Santi a Grosotto!

«D'accordo, ho capito, può andare», aveva concluso il Pezzati.

E, una volta partito il Nano, era partito lui, direzione

casa Riffa dove s'era trovato sotto gli occhi il giovanotto steso a letto, le coperte tirate fin sotto il naso, febbricitante, a suo dire.

Quasi trentanove dal pomeriggio del giorno prima!

Forse aveva preso freddo su in Valtellina...

Così, arrivato a Bellano, aveva deciso di saltare il mercato di Mandello per starsene a letto e si era fatto aiutare dal Dubbio per scaricare la macchina e mettere la merce al sicuro in casa.

Poi, per sdebitarsi del piacere, aveva lasciato le chiavi della macchina al socio, così, se voleva farsi un giro...

Ma il socio, no.

Sentito mezz'ora più tardi, il Dubbio aveva detto al Pezzati che, pur avendo avuto una mezza idea di fare un giro, aveva desistito quando, a circa metà strada verso Vendrogno, quasi all'altezza della frazione di Pradello, aveva visto che nella macchina non c'era quasi più benza, quindi aveva fatto dietro front e cara grazia se era riuscito ad arrivare all'altezza del cimitero.

Si era infilato in quella stradina e basta.

Le chiavi, l'unica cosa che adesso restava della macchina, le aveva ancora in tasca.

«Le devo dare a lei?» aveva chiesto il Dubbio.

«Grazie. Le tengo per ricordo», aveva risposto il Pezzati. «E di' al tuo socio che è difficile fare due volte tredici al totocalcio.»

Quel ricordo il maresciallo l'aveva custodito con cura nel cassetto della sua scrivania e adesso lo mostrò al Riffa, poco prima di chiedergli cosa avesse fatto di bello il pomeriggio precedente.

49.

Il Riffa aveva assunto modi e toni di un bambino intento a recitare la poesia di Natale.

Innocenza allo stato puro.

No, il pomeriggio precedente non stava andando a nessun mercato.

Di pomeriggio?

Ma quando mai!

Stava andando al crotto del Buco dell'Orso.

Sopra Acquaseria.

Aveva un appuntamento.

Una gnoc...

Cioè, una ragazza.

Però aveva bucato.

E il motore faceva le bizze.

E, no, non aveva la ruota di scorta.

Lo sapeva che bisognava averla, però...

Va be', avrebbe provveduto.

In ogni caso, aveva fatto dietro front.

Come?

A piedi.

Da Corenno a Bellano, sotto quel sole canaglia.

Come dice maresciallo?

Addio crotto?

Ma scherza!

Per quella gnoc... cioè ragazza, anche a nuoto.

Ma no, dicevo tanto per dire.

In barca.

No, non mia.
Quella del...
Era stato a quel punto che il Riffa aveva perso la memoria della poesia che stava recitando.
La storia del tredici al totocalcio gli era tornata in mente.
«La barca del...?» chiese il Pezzati.
Il Riffa rimase un attimo in apnea prima di rispondere.
Tuttavia rifletté che ormai s'era infilato in un vicolo cieco, balle al maresciallo non ne poteva contare, l'avrebbe scoperto in quattro e quattr'otto.
«La barca del Dubbio», disse.
«Ma guarda che bella coincidenza», sorrise il Pezzati.
Coincidenza o no, era proprio così, sorrise il Riffa.
«È venuto con me e siamo stati insieme tutta la sera», aggiunse.
«Be', vediamo subito se è vero», rispose il Pezzati risoluto.
Fantarini!
E sul viso del Riffa si dipinse un'espressione come se fosse l'uomo più sereno del mondo.

50.

Sul viso del commenda adesso c'era quasi sempre un'espressione attonita, come se qualcuno gli avesse prelevato dal sangue le misteriose molecole che riescono a far ridere o anche solo sorridere.

Pure il rito del giornale aveva perduto ogni fascino, tant'è che da giorni ormai le copie del «Corriere della Sera» andavano a finire intonse nella tavernetta dove il Riffa aveva dormito.

Nei giorni in cui il postino col ciuffo aveva continuato a farle domande, illudendola che si stesse interessando a lei, le aveva chiesto anche di quel fatto: cosa se ne faceva il commenda del giornale?

Era evidente che aveva preso informazioni, era venuto a sapere che l'uomo non era più in grado di leggere.

Lei, stupida, gli aveva anche risposto, rivelando una cosa che sino ad allora aveva tenuto per sé, temendo altrimenti di violare l'intimità del commenda e della sua vita.

«Glielo leggo io», aveva risposto.

Dopo pranzo, per un'oretta.

Politica, economia, qualcosa di cronaca.

Per fortuna niente sport, non gliene fregava niente.

A lei, poi...

Ma, prima...

Di ciò la Tina non aveva detto niente, non avrebbe detto niente a nessuno, nemmeno a sua madre.

Prima che lei leggesse, il commenda si teneva il giornale tra le mani, lo accarezzava, lo annusava.

«Per me l'amore ha questo profumo», le aveva detto una volta.

La Tina aveva provato, aveva annusato.

Come odore, niente male.

Ma da lì a definirlo profumo...

Cosa c'entrasse l'amore però, per quale motivo il commenda collegasse l'odore della carta stampata al profumo dell'amore, non era riuscita a immaginarlo e s'era ben guardata dal chiederlo. Aveva sorriso tra sé, riflettendo che, in attesa di conoscere di persona il profumo dell'amore, per intanto aveva fatto esperienza di quello della carta stampata. Al momento giusto avrebbe fatto il paragone e forse compreso ciò che il commenda aveva voluto dire.

Di una cosa era certa, che a fargli scoprire quel profumo per il momento sconosciuto non sarebbe stato di certo il postino col ciuffo, che faceva lo stupido con lei ma invece puntava alla Valeria. Allora niente, e circolare.

51.

Niente, aveva risposto il Dubbio alla domanda di sua madre. Non aveva niente di particolare. Solo che era un po' stanco. Figurarsi, dopo una notte così... E inoltre doveva andare.

«Andare?» sbottò la Canterina.

«Sì», confermò il Dubbio.

«Ma dove?»

«A fare un servizio», la risposta più semplice.

«A che ora torni?» chiese la Canterina.

«Quanto torno te lo dico.»

E in un amen il Dubbio fu fuori casa, lasciando la Canterina in mezzo al corridoio con ancora nel naso l'odore di incenso e alcol denaturato dell'ospizio e un pensiero.

Temeva quel figlio.

Beninteso, non ne aveva paura.

Temeva per lui.

Era un timore materno, il risultato di troppe paure. Su tutte quella che l'assenza di un padre si stesse facendo sentire sempre di più, aggiunta a quella di aver fallito nel tentativo di non fargli pesare troppo la sua mancanza.

Aveva paura che ciò che gli era successo gli avesse un po' indebolito...

«Che cosa?» le aveva chiesto il dottor Lonati la volta in cui aveva vinto la ritrosia e gli aveva esposto i suoi timori.

Nemmeno davanti a lui aveva avuto il coraggio di pronunciare quella parola, misteriosa e spaventosa insieme.

«La mente?»

Era stato il Lonati a completare la frase.
Lei aveva confermato con un cenno del capo.
Lui aveva allargato le braccia.
«Chi può dirlo.»
Non si era sentita per nulla consolata da quelle parole, s'era tenuta per sé le paure che di tanto in tanto assumevano i contorni di fantasmi veri e propri. Se li sentiva intorno nei momenti in cui intuiva che qualcosa non stava girando per il verso giusto. Non l'aiutavano a placarsi certi atteggiamenti del figlio, quel po' di barba, le sigarette, le parolacce, le porte sbattute, le rispostacce...
Artifizi che nascondevano l'insicurezza di un bambino che aveva più di vent'anni e che proprio per quello prima o poi si sarebbe ficcato in un guaio di quelli grossi.
«Perché i giudici valutano in relazione ai reati e all'età in cui vengono commessi, del resto a loro importa poco», le aveva detto lo stesso maresciallo Pezzati quando lei aveva voluto consultarlo per chiedere un aiuto dopo la faccenda del quadro.
«Bisogna che suo figlio stia attento ai compagni che si sceglie», aveva aggiunto.
Come il sedicente Ermidio Moscarini la cui parola, per il momento, valeva quanto quella del Dubbio.
Ma anche altri, meno sospetti.
Non proprio criminali, furbetti piuttosto.
Tipo il Riffa.
Proprio quello che l'Ernesto, una volta uscito di casa, aveva intenzione di andare a beccare per chiedergli...
Però...
Il Dubbio si arrestò a metà via Manzoni, proprio all'altezza dell'incrocio di questa con via Porta, sotto il cui arco i piccioni avevano stabilito il proprio cagatoio.
Perché, se davvero... ragionò il Dubbio.
Ma allora, che cazzo doveva fare?
Dare retta al Lonati e andare dal maresciallo?
Oppure...

52.

Scattante il Fantarini.

Al comando del Pezzati uscì fischiettando e sempre fischiettando rientrò, portando la notizia che il Dubbio non era in casa e almeno per il momento, secondo quanto detto da sua madre, irreperibile.

Il maresciallo Pezzati ebbe appena il tempo di aprire mezza bocca per dire qualcosa che il Fantarini lo anticipò.

«Però potrei sapere dove trovarlo», disse.

«Ah sì?» chiese il Pezzati.

«Sì, cioè...» rispose il Fantarini.

Con precisione assoluta non avrebbe potuto dirlo.

Poiché però mentre si recava verso l'abitazione della di lui madre aveva buttato l'occhio nel molo e aveva intravisto la barca del soggetto, la *Canterina*, posizionata nell'apposito alaggio e poi, ritornando verso la caserma dopo aver appurato che non era in casa, aveva notato l'assenza della barca di cui sopra, aveva supposto che il Livera si fosse allontanato con la stessa e quindi...

«E quindi ce ne andiamo a cercarlo su e giù per il lago?» chiese il Pezzati.

«Non intendevo dire questo, anche perché non siamo dotati degli idonei mezzi», rispose il carabiniere.

Tuttavia giudicava che fosse sufficiente attenderne il ritorno per intercettarlo e portarlo in caserma.

«Un comitato di benvenuto», sorrise il Pezzati.

«Come dice maresciallo?» chiese il Fantarini.

«Dicevo di occupartene tu. Me lo tieni d'occhio e non appena arriva me lo porti qui.»

Anche se... pensò il Pezzati rientrando nell'ufficio dove aveva lasciato il Riffa che continuava a dimostrare un'olimpica serenità. Insomma, aveva fatto il conto di tenersi lì il Biagio per un confronto diretto col Dubbio, sentire se le due campane suonavano lo stesso ritornello. Ma se quello non c'era, il giochetto saltava e non aveva motivi per trattenere oltre Biagio Trùfa Riffa.

«Te puoi andare», gli disse quindi. «Ma tieniti a disposizione oggi, non allontanarti dal paese, potrei avere ancora bisogno», aggiunse.

Doveva pur mettergli un po' di pepe al culo, fargli intuire che sospettava qualcosa dietro lo scempio del camioncino.

«Dove vuole che vada?» fu la candida risposta del Riffa.

Uscito il Riffa toccò al carabiniere.

«Tu invece tieni gli occhi aperti e appena trovi il Dubbio lo porti qui, evitando che parli con altri se non con te, e men che meno con quello che è appena uscito.»

«Agli ordini», rispose il Fantarini che, appena oltrepassata la soglia dell'ufficio del Pezzati, riattaccò la solfa del fischio. A piena gola, addirittura con entusiasmo.

Cosa diavolo avrà da fischiare sempre?, si chiese per l'ennesima volta il Pezzati.

E soprattutto cosa fischiava? Era ormai certo che non fossero canzonette né arie d'opera. Ma, cosa?

Si stava perdendo dietro a quel pensiero quando, pochi minuti più tardi, suonò il telefono.

Era il derviese vigile urbano Oltramonti.

Aveva notizie delle scarpe del Riffa.

E lui cosa c'entrava?, pensò il maresciallo.

Una cosa strana, aggiunse il vigile.

«Ho preferito avvisare prima lei, caso mai ci sia sotto qualcosa», concluse l'Oltramonti, anticipando l'obiezione del Pezzati.

53.

Fischi alle orecchie, sensazione di camminare sulle uova, nausea.

Cominciava sempre così e per un paio di giorni, anche tre o quattro nei casi peggiori, la mamma della Tina doveva stare sempre a letto, o quasi.

La pressione, aveva detto il dottor Buzzini.

Anche l'artrosi cervicale.

Mettiamoci pure il tempo umido, il caldo oppure il cambio di stagione.

La menopausa, no?

Magari, ma l'aveva superata da un po'.

In ogni caso, fosse una sola la causa oppure la somma di questo e di quella, il risultato era che la signora Brigida si ritrovava «mezza invalida» come diceva lei e non poteva fare a meno di ricorrere all'aiuto della figlia che, quando capitava, doveva dividersi a metà tra il commenda e la genitrice.

Erano all'incirca le undici quando la Tina ricevette la telefonata di sua madre.

Si sentiva un po' «così».

Poteva fare una scappata da lei?

«Subito», rispose la ragazza.

Il commenda non si era svegliato da molto, era ancora in camera sua, al secondo piano della villetta.

La Tina gli disse che si doveva allontanare per un'oretta. Niente di nuovo, era già capitato. Si raccomandò che l'aspettasse lì, non si muovesse, e soprattutto non cercasse di scendere da solo al piano di sotto, col rischio di rotolare giù per le scale.

«Ti aspetto qui», la tranquillizzò il commenda.

Prima di avviarsi alla volta di casa la Tina mise però in atto la solita misura di controllo.

Traversò la strada e suonò al campanello dell'ex infermiera, la zitella Maria Teresa Supposta.

«Gli dà un'occhiata per favore?» chiese la Tina parlando dalla strada.

Strano a dirsi, ma nonostante la confidenza che tra le due s'era ormai stabilita, la Tina non aveva mai varcato la soglia di casa Supposta.

Non che ne avesse desiderio, non era curiosa.

E poi, in verità, avrebbe potuto muovercisi con sicurezza e forse anche a occhi chiusi, perché l'ex infermiera gliel'aveva descritta quasi per intero nelle occasioni in cui, con una scusa o con l'altra, si presentava dal commenda e in un certo senso si faceva invitare per un caffè.

Rompeva la solitudine, la Tina l'aveva capito, ma rompeva pure un po' le balle con le chiacchiere con le quali si intratteneva facendo durare anche per mezz'ora una tazzina di caffè.

Perché a lei importava poco che quel giorno la Supposta avesse fatto le pulizie di fondo dello studio, pieno di attestati, diplomi e medaglie, che più lei che l'esimio genitore aveva voluto mettere in mostra. O che avesse spolverato uno per uno tutti i libri, quelli di medicina e gli altri, i romanzetti, che tra tutti erano più di trecento.

O che le fosse venuta l'idea di cambiare la disposizione dei mobili del salotto, cosa che lei da sola non avrebbe potuto fare stante l'età, per la qual ragione avrebbe dovuto cercare qualcuno che l'aiutasse, ma qualcuno di fidato che magari proprio lei, la Tina, le poteva indicare visto che, per quanto abitasse ormai da tanti anni lì, non conosceva quasi nessuno, e l'idea che degli estranei le entrassero in casa, insomma, la capiva, no?

Sopportare.

Alla Tina non restava altro da fare, lasciarsi scivolare addosso quelle inutili chiacchiere per poter contare poi sul prezioso aiuto della Supposta nei momenti di necessità.

Come quello.

«Certo», rispose l'ex infermiera che non aveva fretta di chiedere cosa fosse successo, l'avrebbe fatto di lì a poco o solo più tardi.

Il tempo di asciugarsi i capelli che aveva appena finito di lavare, disse, e si sarebbe piazzata nel salotto di casa del commenda pronta a rispondere a eventuali chiamate e in attesa del ritorno della Tina.

Col fon in mano, impugnato come se fosse un'arma da fuoco, la Supposta partì ad asciugare proprio mentre il Dubbio tirava in secco la *Canterina* sulla riva di Acquaseria, discretamente umido stante gli schizzi d'acqua che l'avevano investito durante la traversata del lago.

54.

A notarlo era stata certa Biagina Bologna, spiegò l'Oltramonti al maresciallo Pezzati.

Era una un po' suonata che tutte le mattine, estate o inverno che fosse, partiva all'alba e faceva il giro delle rive raccogliendo ogni sorta di cose.

«Lenze, ami, barattoli, tappi... non so che cosa ne faccia, in ogni caso non dà fastidio a nessuno. Contenta lei...»

Un paio d'ore prima s'era presentata in municipio dicendo che sulla riva proprio di lato allo sbocco del torrente Varrone c'era un sacco enorme e le era sembrato che dentro ci fosse qualcosa che si muoveva.

«Ovviamente io sono partito al volo», disse l'Oltramonti.

Individuato il sacco, che si era incastrato tra due massi della riva, l'aveva aperto verificando dapprima che non conteneva niente di vivo. Facile che la Bologna si fosse lasciata suggestionare dal movimento impresso al sacco dal moto ondoso.

Però s'era trovato di fronte a quella bella sorpresa.

«Scarpe», disse l'Oltramonti.

«Mmm...» commentò il Pezzati.

«È ben strano, no?» sbottò il vigile.

«Siamo sicuri che siano le scarpe del Riffa?» chiese il maresciallo.

L'Oltramonti si strinse nelle spalle.

«La qualità è quella», rispose raccogliendone una in mano e verificando in un attimo come, dopo essere stata a mollo in acqua, si stava già sformando, decomponendo, come se fosse fatta di cartone.

«E poi, maresciallo», aggiunse il vigile, «sono tutte sinistre!»

55.

Lo notò mentre si stava dando gli ultimi colpi di fon.

Andò avanti, fonfon, continuando a guardare.

Da escludere che fosse il figlio maschio del commenda, il bel Vittorio: malvestito questo, sempre elegante l'altro. E non era neanche del paese, mai visto prima.

Due colpi ancora di fon mentre quello aveva suonato al campanello del cancelletto.

Fu tentata di aprire la finestra del bagno, che dava proprio sulla villetta del commenda, per dirgli che non c'era nessuno in casa, se aveva bisogno dicesse a lei.

Ma quello, visto che non otteneva risposta, aveva già spinto il cancelletto e s'era avviato verso la porta di casa.

Allora spense il fon, anche se sulla coppa i capelli non erano ancora del tutto asciutti, e si mise alla finestra del bagno.

Be', ma... mormorò tra sé indecisa sul da fare.

Gridare oppure...

Insomma, quello, chiunque fosse, dopo aver bussato alla porta di casa, benché nessuno lo avesse ricevuto, aveva tentato la maniglia e, trovato aperto, stava entrando.

Gridare.

E poi?

Se le si fosse rivoltato contro?

Tuttavia non poteva lasciare che entrasse in casa col rischio di far prendere un colpo al povero commenda.

Nemmeno se la sentiva di affrontarlo di persona.

Con cosa?

Col fon?
Maria Teresa Supposta decise.
Carabinieri!
E, mollato il fon, volò al telefono.
Un estraneo, forse un ladro, si stava introducendo in casa del povero Dalamonti.

56.

Era talmente raro che sua moglie lo chiamasse al telefono quando era in ambulatorio...

Sulle prime il Lonati non ne riconobbe la voce.

«Cosa c'è?» chiese poi, subito in ansia.

«Niente», rispose Vittoria.

Niente di grave intendeva.

Però una cosa c'era, le ballava in testa dalla notte prima.

«Magari ti faccio solo perdere tempo, ma...»

Ma si trattava di un pensiero talmente strano, forse talmente stupido che se l'avesse tenuto per sé ancora un po' avrebbe finito per non dire niente.

«Va bene, Vittoria, dimmelo», disse il Lonati facendo segno all'anziano che gli stava davanti di dargli un paio di minuti per parlare liberamente al telefono tornando ad accomodarsi in sala d'aspetto.

«Stanotte...» disse la donna.

Il Dubbio non era tornato a casa subito dopo la sua partenza col maresciallo, destinazione riva di Morcate.

«Colpa mia.»

L'aveva trattenuto lei con qualche chiacchiera. Cioè, più che chiacchiere, domande. Lei aveva chiesto, lui aveva risposto: come se la stavano cavando lui e sua madre, se la Canterina stava bene di salute, cose così.

Non l'aveva fatto per ficcare il naso negli affari altrui però. La ragione era un'altra.

«E magari ti verrà da ridere se te la dico», si premunì la donna.

«Basta che tu lo faccia», fu la lapidaria risposta del Lonati.

«Subito.»

Perché sin da quando l'Ernesto aveva raccontato ciò che gli era capitato, prima ancora che lui si decidesse a chiamare il Pezzati, nella sua mente s'erano proiettate due immagini, due precise immagini sovrapposte una all'altra fino a diventare una sola: quella della posizione in cui l'Ernesto aveva trovato suo padre, morto sulla riva del lago per metà in acqua, e quella del cadavere che lui aveva detto di aver trascinato a riva e lasciato nella medesima posizione.

Il Lonati aggrottò la fronte.

Stava pensando alla possibilità che fosse vero ciò che sua moglie non aveva voluto, o non aveva osato dire.

Era possibile che il Dubbio si fosse inventato... ma no, nemmeno inventato... che avesse avuto... che avesse vissuto una specie di sogno, un'allucinazione... una di quelle fantasie che aveva avuto quand'era più giovane e che sembravano essere sparite?

«Ci sei?» chiese la moglie.

Il Lonati rispose: «Ci sono».

«Mi sono spiegata?»

Alla perfezione, le assicurò il marito.

Poi salutò, restando con la cornetta del telefono stretta nella mano, in sottofondo il segnale di occupato, lo sguardo a fissare la parete di fronte, rispondendo con piccoli scatti della testa alle domande che gli stavano nascendo nei pensieri.

57.

Il Viatico se la prese comoda.

Il vigile Oltramonti l'aveva avvisato che c'era un camioncino da rimuovere.

«Da dove e di chi?» aveva chiesto.

Poi aveva valutato le risposte.

Da Corenno, ed era un buon affare.

Del Riffa di Bellano, e da buono l'affare diventava incerto, quando non una fregatura bella e buona.

Quindi, prima di mettersi in marcia, uscì in bicicletta dalla sua carrozzeria alla ricerca del Riffa.

Lo trovò che sbucava da via Porta dopo essere andato a cercare per la seconda volta il Dubbio senza trovare nessuno in casa.

Un'occhiata al molo e, vista l'assenza della *Canterina*, comprese anche lui come il carabiniere Fantarini che il Dubbio era in giro per il lago.

A fare cosa, lo sapeva il demonio.

Però considerato che era lui al momento che non aveva altro da fare, oltre a pensare al guaio del camioncino e del furto di scarpe, aveva deciso di posizionarsi in piazza, aspettando che rientrasse.

Il Viatico invece gli rovinò il programma.

«Se vuoi che ti porti giù il camioncino», gli disse senza preamboli quando lo trovò, «pagamento anticipato.»

«Sarebbe a dire?» chiese il Riffa.

«Sarebbe a dire che ti conosco bene», rispose il Viatico.

Ergo, pagamento anticipato.

«E te allora lascialo lì dov'è», sganassò il Riffa facendo la mossa di andarsene per raggiungere la piazza.

«No, eh», lo bloccò il Viatico.

Perché lui aveva l'ordine del vigile Oltramonti di spostarlo dalla piazza, e l'avrebbe eseguito.

Con la differenza che, se lui non avesse pagato, oltre al costo della rimozione avrebbe dovuto aggiungere quello della multa, obbligatoria, per occupazione abusiva di suolo pubblico.

«Vedi te», concluse il Viatico.

Il Riffa cercò di individuare una scappatoia per prendere tempo.

Ma per il Viatico il tempo era denaro.

«Io te l'ho detto», disse girando la bicicletta dalla quale non era nemmeno sceso. «Alle due vado su a prenderlo. Se ti fai trovare qui in piazza, e coi soldi in mano, bene, sennò cazzi tuoi.»

Cos'altro poteva fare il Riffa se non accettare, pur controvoglia?

58.

Cosa poteva rispondere il Dubbio al carabiniere che, entrato in casa del commenda dopo la segnalazione della signora Supposta, gli chiese: «Cosa ci fa qui?».

Rispondere con sincerità?

Dire che era lì a cercare una ragazza che si chiamava Tina per chiederle...

Rispose la prima cosa che gli venne in mente, la più stupida.

«Niente», facendo sorridere il carabiniere che rispose: «Bene, adesso però venga con me, così lo spiega al signor maresciallo».

E lo seguì sotto lo sguardo della signora Maria Teresa Supposta la quale, i capelli ancora non del tutto asciutti, aveva assunto l'espressione con cui redarguiva le infermiere più giovani ai bei tempi del primariato di suo padre.

Espressione severa, con cui aveva imparato a mascherare ogni tipo di delusione come quella di non poter assistere all'interrogatorio e capire cosa diavolo cercasse quel giovanotto nella casa del commenda.

59.

La Tina, non altro.

Per quello il Dubbio, presa la via del molo e saltato sulla *Canterina*, aveva fatto prua verso la sponda di là.

Per un po' aveva forzato il tre cavalli al limite delle sue possibilità, non vedeva l'ora di arrivare e chiarirsi i pensieri.

Poi aveva dato giù di gas, all'improvviso.

Un pensiero l'aveva frenato.

Non sapeva dove abitava la Tina.

Be', bastava chiedere.

Forse, meglio chiedere dove abitava il suo datore di lavoro.

E il nome?

Il commenda, poteva andare.

La casa del commenda dove c'era una ragazza che si chiamava Tina, ecco la frase giusta.

Poi il tono della voce, aveva pensato il Dubbio.

Doveva essere privo di fretta, di ansia. Doveva essere quello di uno che non conosceva il paese, che era lì per un motivo preciso e che si era dimenticato l'indirizzo.

«Cazzo!» aveva gridato ormai nella solitudine del centro lago e riducendo ancora la velocità peraltro già ridicola.

Ma non poteva arrivare di là e balbettare a rischio che lo prendessero per un vagabondo o peggio.

Si guardò in giro notando alcune vele che già filavano al soffio della prima breva.

Doveva, doveva...

Era stato quando aveva fissato lo sguardo sul fondo della barca per evitare di perdersi in vaghi pensieri che l'idea buona gli era venuta.

La cassetta con gli attrezzi della pesca!

Ecco, con quella in mano, e vestito concio com'era, poteva passare per un operaio che doveva fare un lavoretto qualunque in casa del commenda.

«Quella dove abita una ragazza che si chiama Tina, è lei che mi ha chiamato», aveva detto a un salumiere dai baffi umbertini che aveva evitato di rispondergli perché in sua vece l'avevano fatto almeno tre voci di donna che stavano in fila per la spesa.

Tutto liscio.

Fino a quando il carabiniere l'aveva fatto saltare per aria con quella domanda.

«Cosa ci fa qui?»

60.

Ormai il danno era fatto.

I danni, anzi.

Un, due, tre, pollice, indice, medio.

Quattro gomme a terra, scarpe rubate e il conto del Viatico. L'ultimo era quello che gli rugava di più.

Non che gli mancassero i soldi per pagare, pensava il Riffa, ma avrebbe preferito spenderli in troie piuttosto che darli a quello lì. Peraltro, con quattro gomme bucate, non sarebbe stato semplice riportare a casa il camioncino senza un carro attrezzi.

Fosse stata una sola...

Una sola, con l'aiuto del Dubbio e una gommaccia presa in prestito, ce l'avrebbero fatta.

Ma sembrava che quel giorno tutti fossero d'accordo a sparare contro di lui, visto che anche il socio era sparito, da casa e dal molo.

Il Riffa aveva pizzicato una cosa all'osteria del Ponte tanto per mangiare e poi all'una era già seduto su una panchina di piazza in attesa che quel ladro del Viatico passasse a prenderlo.

«Non hai fame?» gli aveva chiesto la Rispola, cameriera varicosa che serviva a tavola con una sigaretta perennemente accesa all'angolo destro della bocca.

«C'ho i pensieri», aveva risposto lui.

Un sospetto.

Un dubbio, appunto.

Che di lì a poco si sarebbe chiarito, divenendo certezza.

61.

Per il carabiniere scelto Dangolo e il carabiniere semplice Firrìa, in forza presso la caserma di Menaggio, fu una mezza delusione giungere a destinazione col Dubbio e non trovarvi altro che il collega Inverighi, così da non poter dimostrare al maresciallo Alborati di avere eseguito l'ordine alla perfezione.

«Mi raccomando, non mi fate casini», aveva detto loro l'Alborati dopo aver ricevuto la segnalazione di Maria Teresa Supposta.

Avesse potuto ci sarebbe andato lui, se non avesse dovuto attendere una telefonata del colonnello Spaventa dal comando provinciale. In alternativa avrebbe mandato il brigadiere Sparagna, se in quel momento non si fosse trovato a colloquio col responsabile dell'ufficio tecnico del comune di Menaggio. In ogni caso, quando il Dangolo e il Firrìa entrarono in caserma si trovarono faccia a faccia col solo Inverighi il quale, prima di ogni altra cosa, disse loro che il maresciallo aveva ordinato di aspettare che lui ritornasse prima di fare alcunché.

«Ritornare da dove?» chiese il Firrìa.

«Dall'ospedale», rispose il collega.

Presso il cui pronto soccorso, accompagnato con la macchina dallo Sparagna, s'era recato dopo essersi preso una storta alla caviglia scivolando su un gradino.

Nonostante il dolore e le imprecazioni, prima di salire sull'auto del brigadiere l'Alborati aveva tenuto a chiarire di trattenere l'eventuale fermato fino al suo ritorno.

«Quindi?» chiese il Dangolo.

L'Inverighi aveva già la risposta in mano, le chiavi della camera di sicurezza.

«Lo mettiamo lì dentro e aspettiamo», disse, facendo tintinnare il mazzo.

Il Dubbio a quel punto tentò di dire la sua.

Durante il tragitto tra la casa del commenda e la caserma aveva riflettuto su cosa rispondere alle inevitabili domande che gli sarebbero toccate.

S'era deciso, infine.

Avrebbe dichiarato che era lì a cercare la Tina, chiamandola in causa quale testimone e ottenendo così la conferma che si conoscevano. Non aveva alcuna intenzione di rubare. Il fatto di non avere refurtiva addosso e di non avere manomesso nemmeno un cassetto nell'abitazione avrebbe deposto a suo favore.

Aveva violato una proprietà privata, d'accordo. Non aveva forzato porte o finestre però, aveva trovato tutto aperto e ciò aveva indotto in lui la convinzione che la ragazza fosse in casa, da qualche parte. Tant'è che era entrato chiamandola e usando un tono urbano: forse il commenda l'aveva anche sentito e avrebbe potuto confermare.

Aveva ripassato più volte la linea difensiva e adesso, dentro la caserma, gli era sembrato il momento giusto per dichiararla.

«Veramente...» cominciò quindi a dire approfittando di un istante in cui anche il tintinnio delle chiavi s'era smorzato.

Ma il carabiniere Dangolo, allo stato il più alto in grado essendo scelto, gli intimò di tacere.

«Hai sentito cos'ha detto il maresciallo?»

E, come se fosse una scenetta più volte provata, l'Inverighi gli mise sotto gli occhi il mazzo delle chiavi mentre il Firrìa, allungando il braccio sinistro con un gesto da tavoleggiante, gli indicò la porta della camera di sicurezza.

62.

Sulle prime non ci aveva creduto.

Severino Giubbiani, settantaduenne, pensionato, pescatore di trote.

Bevitore anche.

Sulle prime pensò di aver esagerato con i bianchini mattutini e che adesso, lì sulla riva del torrente Varrone, il sole di luglio gliela stesse facendo pagare. Quindi, lasciate passare le prime tre o quattro scarpe fino a che, raggiunta a pelo d'acqua la foce del torrente, si persero nell'orizzonte del lago, continuò a pescare come se niente fosse.

Poi però, quando l'insolita visione non solo riprese, ma assunse il corpo di una specie di processione visto che sotto i suoi occhi passavano scarpe una via l'altra, decise di piantar lì di pescare, tanto l'ultima trota che gli era riuscito di portare a casa risaliva alla bellezza di diciotto mesi prima, e rifletté sul da fare.

Dirlo alla moglie Vivarina era da escludere, gli avrebbe risposto la solita solfa sul bere di meno.

Comunicarlo al Bernacchi, proprietario dell'omonima osteria dove ogni mattina si macerava di vino, era non tanto da escludere ma da evitare, almeno per il momento: il Bernacchi gli avrebbe anche creduto ma lui non avrebbe resistito alla tentazione di entrare lì e raccontare senza consumare, col rischio di farci notte e costringendo la Vivarina a venirlo a cercare.

L'altra via possibile era quella di avvisare dello strano

fenomeno il vigile urbano Oltramonti, al quale lo univa una lontana parentela in quanto il padre dell'Oltramonti era fratello di un cugino del nonno eccetera eccetera.

Severino Giubbiani non aveva alcuna certezza che il vigile lo avrebbe preso sul serio. Prima di partire quindi, a mo' di prova della sua sincerità, cercò di tirare a riva una di quelle scarpe che gli stavano passando sotto gli occhi.

Dai e dai, alla fine riuscì a farne abboccare una.

La tirò a sé con lentezza, come se fosse una trota da record, di quelle che poi il corrispondente del giornale pubblicava con tanto di fotografia, predatore e preda.

Durante tutta l'operazione di recupero trattenne il fiato e riprese a respirare solo quando ebbe in mano il pescato.

Un mocassino scamosciato, beige, dalla suola che si stava già scollando, numero quarantadue.

Destro.

63.

La Canterina aveva ormai perso la speranza di pranzare in compagnia di suo figlio.

Aveva anche perso l'appetito in verità e spento il fuoco sotto l'acqua per la pasta.

Erano quasi le due, l'aveva già portata a bollitura un paio di volte in attesa che l'Ernesto comparisse.

Si sedette al tavolo di cucina, le mani, intrecciate una nell'altra, posate sul fagiano che poche ore prima s'era beccato senza dare segno di averli patiti i cazzotti del Dubbio.

Si era accorta che mentre se ne stava così aveva cominciato a scuotere lenta lenta la testa, di qua e di là, come se seguisse il movimento di un invisibile metronomo.

Annusava l'aria, l'odore di cucina che i suoi vestiti emanavano.

Il riso, il purè, i piselli...

Il misto odore di tutto quello che preparava per alimentare bambine e bambini dell'asilo, roba che li avrebbe aiutati a diventare grandi e a imboccare strade diverse una dall'altra.

Buone o cattive strade.

Che, quale che fosse la scelta, avrebbero portato i mostriciattoli a lasciare soli coloro che li avevano messi al mondo.

Giusto così, era la vita.

Ma c'era modo e modo di farlo.

Forse per questo stava dondolando senza rendersene

conto la testa. Perché, pensava la Canterina, c'era solitudine e solitudine. In altre parole, se in alcuni momenti ci si poteva sentire soli, in altri invece si poteva avere la certezza di esserlo.

64.

Uno scherzo?

Un sogno?

Un'allucinazione?

Il dottor Lonati pensava e fumava.

Sua moglie Vittoria inalava l'odore delle Turmac.

Buono il profumo, pessimo il sapore, le aveva provate.

Gli servì il caffè.

«Cosa pensi?» gli chiese.

L'avesse saputo con precisione... Navigava a vista.

Però si stava convincendo che le possibilità erano due sole, proprio come le rive del lago.

O davvero il Dubbio, come aveva raccontato, aveva incrociato un cadavere e l'aveva trascinato a riva e poi il lago se l'era ripreso grazie al ventaccio che c'era quella notte e alle onde che picchiavano sulla riva...

«Nel qual caso non ce l'ha raccontata per intero...»

«Perché?» chiese la moglie.

«Non lo so», rispose il Lonati, «ma mi sento che manca qualcosa.»

Oppure sua moglie aveva ragione.

Allora, in quel caso, la faccenda diventava se possibile ancora più seria. Perché un conto era un cervello ancora bambino che restava impressionato da una certa esperienza e ne pativa le conseguenze in forma di sogni o incubi cui si poteva anche credere che fossero realtà. Ben altro se tutto ciò accadeva dentro una zucca che ormai doveva essere matura, adulta.

Se questa seconda ipotesi si fosse rivelata vera, l'Ernesto non poteva più essere considerato normale, bisognava prendere provvedimenti. Per il bene suo innanzitutto, e anche degli altri. A quel punto non era nemmeno possibile escludere che fenomeni del genere, non certo così clamorosi, anticipatori, fossero già accaduti e il Dubbio non ne avesse parlato mai con nessuno, neanche con la Canterina, il che comunque sarebbe stato lo stesso, visto il timore che quella donna aveva di affrontare certi discorsi, evitandoli con cura, negando, sottraendosi.

C'erano un sacco di domande in ballo, rifletté il dottor Lonati.

E per avere le risposte, bisognava essere stati in compagnia del Dubbio per vedere cosa fosse capitato la notte prima su quella barca.

65.

E la barca tornò sooola...

Il maresciallo Pezzati questa volta ci prese.

Renato Carosone, Gegè Di Giacomo, mare crudele, mare crudele...

Sua madre era una fanatica di Carosone e delle sue canzoni.

Tu vò fà l'americano, Torero...

Nonostante avesse ottant'anni suonati, non passava giorno che non prendesse uno dei suoi vinili e se lo ascoltasse sorridendo beata e a occhi chiusi, seduta sulla poltroncina di lato all'altrettanto âgée mobile radio. Gli capitava spesso di sentire gli echi di quelle canzoni che conosceva a memoria quando la chiamava al telefono per chiederle come stava, finendo quasi sempre a essere lui a dare conto della propria salute e di quella della moglie.

E il carabiniere Fantarini era entrato in caserma fischiettando proprio quel motivo, stavolta non c'era alcuna possibilità di errore: troppe volte il Pezzati l'aveva sentito.

Come mai fischiettava quel genere di musica invece delle canzonette da jukebox più adatte alla sua giovane età?

Innocente e in un certo senso anche schietta, empatica curiosità.

L'avrebbe chiesto subito al Fantarini se questi, entrato nell'ufficio, con addosso la fregola della notizia che stava riportando, non gli avesse tolto il tempo di domandare alcunché. Riferì concitato che la *Canterina*, la barca del Dubbio cioè, era appena rientrata al molo, ma priva di conducente.

In sostanza, la barca era tornata *sooola*, come nella canzone.

«Cioè?» chiese il maresciallo, tralasciando per il momento Carosone e il suo sestetto.

In sostanza era successo che Giordano Pinza, bagnino tuttofare del lido Perla del lago, in quel di Bellagio, mentre svolgeva le sue funzioni consistenti perlopiù nel controllare con tanto di binocolo che i grassi turisti tedeschi non abbandonassero i confini del tratto di lago destinato ai loro bagni, aveva notato un'imbarcazione del tipo di quelle usate dai pescatori locali che vagava per le acque del lago come se fosse priva di guida.

Dopo averla tenuta d'occhio per un po', si era convinto che non ci fosse nessuno a bordo e quindi aveva avvisato il comando della Guardia di Finanza di Nobiallo che aveva mandato un mezzo a recuperarla, verificando e confermando prima di tutto che la barca era alla deriva e poi, grazie all'intervento del pescatore bellagino Ivano Saliva, indicato ai militari dallo stesso Pinza, appurando che la barca era di tal Ernesto Livera, detto Dubbio, di Bellano.

«La barca è la sua perché si chiama come sua madre», aveva affermato il Saliva scuotendo la testa.

Circa il proprietario, non aveva notizie da dare. Ma s'era impegnato ad agganciare la *Canterina* per riportarla a Bellano.

Il Saliva era stata la fonte delle notizie che il carabiniere Fantarini stava snocciolando al maresciallo: ligio all'ordine ricevuto, non aveva perduto d'occhio il molo e quando aveva visto la barca del Dubbio rientrare al traino s'era fatto raccontare tutta la storia e poi si era precipitato in caserma a riferirla.

Allo stato quindi la situazione era che il Dubbio non si

sapeva che fine avesse fatto e che la Guardia di Finanza stava perlustrando le rive del lago, chiedendo a velisti e navigatori di diporto se per caso avessero notato qualcosa che potesse aiutare a risolvere il mistero.

Il Fantarini non lo disse per evitare di accentuare il malumore che stava crescendo sul viso del suo maresciallo.

Ma, allo stato, i dispersi erano saliti al numero di due.

66.

Alle due spaccate il Viatico si era fermato all'imbocco di via Cavour.

Non aveva nemmeno spento il motore.

Non aveva nemmeno tirato giù il finestrino.

Aveva fatto un gesto col mento al Riffa che era seduto sulla panchina.

Vieni o non vieni?

Il Riffa s'era alzato facendo in modo che si capisse che lo faceva controvoglia.

Salito sul camioncino, il Viatico aveva allungato la mano destra, aperta, sul cui palmo il Riffa aveva depositato i soldi del servizio.

Non una parola era volata tra i due durante il tragitto da Bellano a Corenno e ciò, stante i finestrini chiusi della cabina, aveva incrementato nel Riffa la convinzione che si stesse andando incontro a uno dei giorni più caldi di quel mese di luglio.

Quindi, aveva pensato tra sé mentre guardava fisso la strada, il camioncino e le scarpe potevano aspettare.

Una volta ritornato a Bellano si sarebbe concesso un bel bagno.

Sennonché, una volta arrivati nella piazza del paese, Biagio Trùfa Riffa notò un certo movimento, incompatibile a suo giudizio con la temperatura dell'ora, cosa che gli aveva fatto nascere il sospetto che il vagheggiato pomeriggio al lido fosse in pericolo.

Dal gruppetto di uomini e donne che stazionava a

stretto contatto col suo camioncino emerse il vigile Oltramonti.

«Era ora», disse.

«Eravamo d'accordo per le due, due e un quarto, no?» ribatté il Viatico.

«Parlavo con lui», chiarì il vigile accennando al Riffa.

«Che cazzo c'entro io?» soffiò stanco il Riffa.

«Come che cazzo c'entri?» chiese l'Oltramonti.

Aveva la camicia di servizio sudata fino a metà torace e l'alito sapeva di vino.

«Ma il maresciallo non ti ha detto niente?»

67.

Il maresciallo Alborati aveva avuto un trattamento di favore. Un po' perché maresciallo, un po' perché aveva avvisato che in caserma lo aspettava un presunto ladro in attesa di essere interrogato.

Peraltro, favore o no, tra visita, lastra, per fortuna non c'era niente di rotto, applicazione di una doccia gessata, c'erano volute un paio d'ore.

Il Dubbio le aveva trascorse cercando di consolidare, ripetendola tra sé più volte, la linea di difesa che dimostrava come fosse entrato in quella casa senza alcuna intenzione di delinquere. Quando l'Alborati lo mandò a prendere per iniziare l'interrogatorio, si sentiva sicuro di sé. Quasi.

Il maresciallo, volto marezzato e baffo grigio, lo aspettava seduto, il gambone ingessato steso su una sedia di lato alla scrivania. Sulla stessa, aperta, la cassetta con gli attrezzi per la pesca con la quale il Dubbio aveva tentato di farsi passare per operaio.

«Che ci volevi fare con questa?» fu la prima domanda del maresciallo.

Non era così che l'Ernesto s'era immaginato l'avvio dell'interrogatorio.

«Niente...»

«Fermo lì», lo stoppò l'Alborati.

Poi gli indicò il gambone.

Gli faceva male, e non poteva fare altro che stringere i denti.

«Portare pazienza», spiegò.

Lo capiva?

«Sì», fece il Dubbio.

«Bene», approvò il maresciallo.

Perché allora avrebbe anche capito che tutta la pazienza di cui disponeva era al servizio del dolore per la sua caviglia.

Altra non ne aveva, per niente e per nessuno.

«Continui a capirmi?» chiese ancora il maresciallo.

«Sì», di nuovo il Dubbio.

«Allora siamo amici», sorrise l'Alborati.

E visto che erano amici lui gli avrebbe fatto una sola domanda alla quale lui avrebbe risposto, dopodiché, proprio a dimostrazione del fatto che erano amici, gli avrebbe fatto mettere la firma sul gesso.

«D'accordo?» chiese il maresciallo.

Al Dubbio non restò altro da fare che sorridere per dovere e rispondere ancora di sì, in attesa della domanda dell'Alborati che non si fece aspettare.

«Dimmi cosa cazzo sei entrato a fare in casa d'altri con in mano una cassetta piena di ami, fili e galleggianti.»

Al Dubbio non parve vero.

Gli sembrò facile, fin troppo.

Cazzo, sembrava che lui e quel maresciallo lì si fossero messi d'accordo prima per recitare una specie di commedia in due battute.

«Niente...» cominciò a dire, e il maresciallo non obiettò alla sua uscita poiché, visto che ormai erano amici, sapeva che dopo quell'ennesimo «Niente» il Dubbio gli avrebbe spiegato il perché e il percome si era introdotto nella casa del Dalamonti.

68.

«E cosa mi doveva dire il maresciallo?» aveva chiesto il Riffa mentre il Viatico aveva cominciato le manovre per agganciare il camioncino.

«Del sacco pieno di scarpe», aveva risposto il vigile Oltramonti. Del sacco pieno di scarpe sinistre.

«Sinistre?» era sbottato il Riffa.

«Tutte», aveva confermato il vigile.

«E le destre?»

E, le destre... Purtroppo la voce era corsa.

«Ma che cazzo dici, che voce, cos'è che correva?» s'era inalberato il Riffa.

Sentendo il suo tono in rapida ascesa, parte degli spettatori schierati in cerchio intorno al Viatico che manovrava la gru s'era spostata di qualche passo mettendosi a tiro d'orecchio. L'Oltramonti non aveva voluto correre il rischio che il Riffa, in preda alla rabbia, si lasciasse scappare qualcosa di compromettente.

«Spostiamoci un po'», aveva suggerito, incamminandosi.

Il Viatico li aveva visti allontanarsi.

Un fischio, diretto al Riffa.

«Dove vai?»

«Torno subito», aveva risposto il Riffa.

«Vedi te. Io due minuti e ho finito», e non aveva aggiunto altro.

Voleva dire che se c'era bene, se no per tornare a Bellano si doveva arrangiare.

«Allora, cos'è 'sta storia?» aveva ripreso il Riffa.

L'Oltramonti, più tranquillo, aveva spiegato. Purtroppo, come già aveva detto, la voce era corsa e lui non aveva potuto farci niente. Sennò qualche paio di scarpe avrebbe potuto recuperarlo, quelle che non s'erano troppo rovinate stando a mollo nell'acqua.

«Purtroppo però il Giubbiani...»

«E chi cazzo è 'sto Giubbiani?» aveva ringhiato il Riffa.

Ma quello, aveva spiegato il vigile, che l'aveva avvisato che dal fiume venivano giù scarpe, le sue, quelle che sino al giorno prima lui teneva nel camioncino e che erano sparite!

Purtroppo il Giubbiani non era riuscito a tenere la bocca chiusa.

«Fosse dipeso da me», aveva detto il vigile, «ti avrei chiamato subito e in qualche modo avremmo fatto per recuperare 'ste scarpe.»

Ma tempo un quarto d'ora lì alla foce del fiume c'era già tanta di quella gente che sembrava il giorno dell'apertura alla trota. Proprio tali e quali, chi con in mano le canne da pesca chi con in mano un ramo bello lungo chi anche con il quadrato per pescare gli agoni.

«Solo che pescavano le tue scarpe», aveva sorriso l'Oltramonti adombrandosi subito al vedere l'espressione del Riffa.

Incazzati anche, perché tiravano a riva solo scarpe destre, visto che le sinistre erano tutte chiuse nel famoso sacco.

«Non dici niente?» aveva chiesto alla fine del racconto il vigile.

«È un disastro», aveva commentato il Riffa.

Quello lo sapeva anche lui, era stato il pensiero del vigile, non bisognava essere delle aquile per immaginarlo.

Tuttavia nemmeno a lui sfuggiva che quella faccenda di scarpe destre da una parte e sinistre dall'altra fosse alquanto strana.

69.

L'amore è strano.

«Fa commettere follie», sentenziò il maresciallo Alborati. Cosa non si faceva per una donna, eh?

Il Dubbio si strinse nelle spalle, non sapeva cosa rispondere alle uscite del maresciallo che peraltro dimostrò presto di non avere finito.

Perché tuttavia, continuò, per quanto comprendesse gli slanci di un cuore giovane e innamorato...

«Anch'io ho fatto le mie ai miei tempi!»

... tuttavia non poteva dimenticare di essere maresciallo dei carabinieri.

Quindi, come gli imponeva il dovere, prima di lasciarlo andare raccomandandogli da amico di essere più accorto in una prossima occasione, avrebbe mandato a chiamare questa ragazza, questa... Tina?...

«Tina, sì», rispose con un miagolio il Dubbio.

... giusto per avere conferma della storia che il giovanotto gli aveva fornito.

Cioè che si conoscevano, anche se tale conoscenza risaliva ad appena la sera precedente, quando in compagnia di un amico, tal Biagio Riffa, e di una di lei amica, Valeria se ricordava bene, erano saliti al crotto del Buco dell'Orso e lui di questa Valeria si era, come dire?, innamorato?... forse innamorato era un po' troppo visto che si trattava di un primo incontro... diciamo... diciamo che si era sentito attratto al punto che la mattina del giorno seguente...

«Cioè oggi», precisò il maresciallo.

... era partito deciso a rintracciarla ma, non avendo recapiti di sorta, aveva ben pensato di chiedere lumi alla suddetta Tina, della quale conosceva, seppur in modo vago, il lavoro che la stessa svolgeva presso un'abitazione privata.

«Giusto?» chiuse il maresciallo Alborati senza attendere risposta e informando il Dubbio che nell'attesa del confronto aveva il permesso di mettersi comodo nella saletta adibita allo scopo.

70.

Dell'accaduto il commenda non aveva avuto alcun sentore.

Avvisata del malore di sua madre, la Tina non aveva avuto il tempo materiale di metterlo in riga come di solito faceva: il che significava obbligarlo a uscire dal letto, aiutandolo a vincere l'apatia che da giorni ormai contraddistingueva ogni sua azione o reazione alle proposte che gli sottoponeva. Temendo anzi che Maria Teresa Supposta volesse rispolverare le sue antiche arti di infermiera dal ferreo codice, s'era raccomandata affinché lasciasse il commenda a letto per quella mattina, preoccupandosi solo di stare lì in casa per accorrere a eventuali richiami. L'uomo aveva accettato ben volentieri l'insperata tregua degli affettuosi assalti della Tina.

«Dormirò ancora un poco», aveva risposto pur sapendo di aver detto una bugia.

Il sonno, quello vero, l'aveva abbandonato da un pezzo. Ne aveva preso il posto un dormiveglia dentro il quale si agitavano stralci del suo passato e figure, persone che ne avevano fatto parte. Soprattutto di notte, quando piombava in quella specie di purgatorio tra la veglia e il sonno, quelle immagini prendevano possesso della sua mente e diventavano piano piano la realtà del momento, strappandogli a volte sorrisi, ma più spesso, come gli accadeva di recente, gettandolo in un baratro di sconforto e apatia, tormentato da rigurgiti di senso di colpa o di amarezza che gli avvelenavano l'ultima stagione della vita.

Che fosse anziano, lo sapeva da sé. E non aveva certo bisogno che gli si facesse presente che, essendo tale, aveva un carico di vita, di ricordi, di cose fatte e persone conosciute alle spalle.

Ma anche di persone che avrebbe voluto non conoscere, cose che avrebbe voluto non aver fatto.

Come quella che la lettera consegnata per sbaglio gli aveva riportato alla memoria con straziante crudeltà, come se fosse successa il giorno prima e non quel giorno lontano.

71.

Quel giorno.

E quel nome.

Quel giorno il Dalamonti era partito da casa nel primo pomeriggio per andare a trovare sua madre, vedova da pochi mesi. Voleva approfittare della visita anche per sistemare la questione di un pezzo di vigna che avevano sempre avuto dalle parti di Marena: nessuno, morto il padre, se ne sarebbe più curato e la madre gli aveva fatto sapere che s'era fatto avanti un compratore. Con lui aveva voluto partire anche la figlia Francesca, che era ormai all'ottavo mese di gravidanza e che dopo un paio di settimane di piccoli malesseri stava finalmente bene, e aveva voglia di aria e di sole. Nonostante la moglie del Dalamonti si fosse detta contraria a quella che a suo giudizio sarebbe stata una strapazzata, padre e figlia le avevano detto di stare tranquilla.

Cosa temeva che potesse accadere?

Il Dalamonti aveva guidato con prudenza, sebbene non avesse potuto evitare le buche della strada. Tuttavia all'arrivo, tranne un filo di nausea imputato alle curve, Francesca dimostrava di aver superato il viaggio senza problemi.

Il guaio era successo più tardi, mentre lui stava scendendo dalla frazione di Marena e, rientrato nella casa paterna, aveva trovato la figlia in evidente stato di sofferenza: avvertiva un profondo senso di freddo, aveva dolori all'addome, aveva dovuto sdraiarsi.

Sola, oltretutto, perché sua madre, che non aveva telefono in casa, era uscita per cercare aiuto. Era rientrata poco dopo, affannata per l'età e lo spavento, dicendo di aver saputo che la levatrice si trovava a villa Finisterra, lungo la strada che conduceva a Breglia. Era lì infatti, festeggiava insieme col D'Argò il compleanno del padrone di casa. Il Dalamonti non l'aveva vista subito. Prima di farlo aveva dovuto convincere due militi che il console impiegava a mo' di scorta e che, per puro esibizionismo, aveva lasciato di guardia al cancello della villa.

Una volta salita sulla sua macchina, altera come suo solito e per l'occasione anche un poco alterata per via di qualche brindisi di troppo, s'era infine presentata.

«Voglio sperare che non mi abbiate disturbato per una sciocchezza.»

«È una cosa grave», aveva risposto il Dalamonti.

«Se lo dite voi...» aveva lasciato cadere lei.

Poi la gravità della situazione s'era svelata in tutta la sua evidenza.

Alla Dominetti era stato sufficiente uno sguardo per comprendere che il feto, per metà espulso, era ormai morto. Dopo una seconda occhiata aveva detto che bisognava assolutamente chiamare il medico, se non si voleva che anche la madre ci lasciasse la pelle.

Senza rinunciare ai suoi modi bruschi, rispondendo scontrosa, la Dominetti non si era mossa da lì fino a sera tarda e per tutto il tempo che Francesca era restata nella casa di Acquaseria era passata ogni giorno a controllarla, seguendo gli ordini del dottore.

Dopo il fatto, il Dalamonti aveva dovuto farsi forza per entrare ancora in quella casa, avvertendo un pesante senso di colpa e di dolore. Scomparsa sua madre, per anni l'aveva trascurata e solo col tempo e con la nascita, qualche anno dopo, di due splendidi nipotini era riuscito a fare la pace con quelle mura e con i pensieri strazianti che sembravano decise a trattenere.

Una cosa, però, non aveva mai potuto dimenticare: ciò che la Dominetti gli aveva detto a un certo punto quella lontana sera.

«Sarebbe stata una bella bambina.»

Strano a dirsi ma, per quanto fosse solo un'ipotesi, lui a quell'idea ci si era affezionato.

72.

Strano un cazzo!

Strano per chi non conosceva i retroscena.

Colpa di quella...

Colpa sua anche, il Riffa lo sapeva bene.

La destra gliel'aveva regalata.

«Scarpettine per andare a ballare», era stata la richiesta.

Era successo due settimane prima al mercato di Tremenico, paese che stava nel fondo della Valvarrone. Il Riffa ci andava una volta al mese, ma aveva piazza in tutti e quattro i paesi della valle, Vestreno, Introzzo, Sueglio e appunto Tremenico.

La conosceva di nome, Amanda, perché qualche volta si era fermata al suo banco, ma sempre di corsa e senza mai far capire se un paio di scarpe le servisse per davvero, tranne quel giorno.

«Scarpettine per andare a ballare», aveva chiesto.

Il Riffa non s'era mica lasciato scappare l'occasione, impressionato dal moto ondoso delle tette della ragazza che si animava a ogni passo. Una volta che se l'era trovata davanti, aveva rifinito l'ispezione giudicando che rispetto alle tarchie che di solito popolavano quei paesi l'Amanda doveva aver subito qualche innesto foraneo, fosse solo per l'altezza, un bel dieci centimetri in più della media locale, e tutti da attribuire alle gambe.

«Ho quello che fa per te», aveva subito risposto.

Di vernice, con un po' di tacco.

«Dovresti provarle», aveva poi consigliato.

Servizievole, le aveva messo a disposizione la sedia pieghevole sulla quale passava ore anziché agitarsi come la maggior parte dei colleghi per richiamare clienti, e da vero commesso s'era offerto di calzarle le scarpettine.

L'Amanda aveva lasciato fare.

Ma poi, aveva fatto apposta oppure non s'era accorta di niente?

Sta di fatto che dopo averle infilato la destra le gambe della ragazza si erano mosse per offrire al Riffa l'altro piede. Il movimento gli aveva svelato una visione d'interni che, se aveva visto bene, pareva del tutto priva di tendaggi.

Le scarpe le calzavano che era una meraviglia!, aveva esclamato l'Amanda dopo aver fatto qualche passo.

Il Riffa allora le aveva detto che forse avevano un difettino, doveva controllare. Una bugia per chiederle di tornare a sedersi e sfilarle la sinistra.

«Quella tienila pure», le aveva detto indicando la destra.

«Questa invece», aveva aggiunto con la sinistra in mano, «te la regalo domani sera se vieni a fare un giro con me.»

L'Amanda l'aveva guardato aggrottando la fronte. Non aveva aperto bocca. S'era sfilata la scarpa, l'aveva lasciata cadere a terra e se n'era andata a piedi nudi, le scarpe di proprietà in mano.

Chiaro il messaggio?

73.

«Strano un cazzo», disse il Riffa.

«Perché, per te è tutto chiaro?» chiese l'Oltramonti.

Il Biagio fece un mezzo sorriso, sospirò, scosse la testa.

«Colpa mia», rispose.

D'altronde...

D'altronde quando una te la metteva sotto il naso come quella lì!

«Quella lì, chi?» s'incuriosì il vigile.

«Ma, una, su, di Tremenico, una certa Amanda...»

«Ostia, la conosco!» sbottò l'Oltramonti. «L'hai trombata?»

Il Riffa lo guardò di traverso.

Erano domande da fare a uno come lui?

«No perché», si giustificò il vigile, «dicono che ce l'abbia di traverso, nel senso che...»

«Ho capito, va là», fece il Riffa.

«Ma come hai fatto?»

«Eh, lascia perdere», rispose il Riffa cominciando a raccontare. Agganciata al mercato, solita tecnica.

Aveva bisogno di scarpettine per andare a ballare?

Prego si accomodi che gliele calzo io.

Provi a fare due passi.

Vanno bene?

Faccia vedere, provi ancora, due passi, ancora due...

Però, però...

Forse ne ho un paio ancora migliori lì dentro nel camioncino...

È che dovrei cercarle e adesso, con tutta la gente in giro non avrei proprio il tempo, ma...

Potremmo fare così. Io le cerco, intanto lei va a fare i suoi mestieri poi, se vuole, potrebbe fare una scappata qui verso mezzogiorno quando comincia a non esserci in giro nessuno e sistemiamo le cose.

«E lei?» chiese l'Oltramonti.

Che domande?

«Lei, trac!, a mezzogiorno spaccato era lì, davanti a me!»

E poi sotto, rise il Riffa, e poi...

«Orca puttana!» sbalordì il vigile sudando pura ammirazione.

«Ecco spiegato il tutto», sospirò il Riffa guardando l'orizzonte di lago verso il quale parecchie delle sue scarpe erano sfuggite alla pesca selvaggia.

«D'altra parte, toccargli le loro donne a quelli di quei paesi lì», commentò il vigile dando invece un colpo con la testa alle montagne che stavano alle spalle.

«L'avessi solo toccata», rincarò la dose il Riffa.

«Ormai è fatta», fece l'Oltramonti.

E si permise di consigliare che a suo giudizio era meglio se il Riffa avesse lasciato perdere il mercato di Tremenico, forse anche quelli degli altri paesi della valle.

Anche perché, cosa ci andava a vendere visto che ormai non aveva altre scarpe oltre a quelle che portava ai piedi e che gli servivano per tornare a casa, visto che il Viatico, ligio alla parola, non vedendolo comparire era ripartito?

Il Riffa rise amaro.

«Te comunque», disse poi al vigile, «di tutta questa storia acqua in bocca eh!»

Sì, certo, come no!

Riguardo all'acqua, poteva stare tranquillo.

Quando più tardi nel pomeriggio, una volta smessa la divisa, il vigile Oltramonti entrò all'osteria del Pincia, si ritrovò sommerso dalle domande circa il mistero delle scarpe nel fiume.

Per un paio di bicchieri, offerti affinché parlasse, resistette.

Cioè, fece capire che sapeva tutto ma che per parlare gli serviva qualche altro incentivo.

Che arrivò, puntuale e abbondante.

Alla fine del resoconto strascicava un po' la lingua e dovette allenarla prima di emettere la raccomandazione d'uso.

«Mi raccomando però, acqua in bocca.»

Sì, come no!

74.

Il rigido codice cui Maria Teresa Supposta aveva sempre obbedito durante gli anni in cui aveva fatto l'infermiera prevedeva che le cose andassero dette senza ricorrere a giri di parole.

Se i dottori non avevano il coraggio di dire a uno che per colpa di un'infezione bisognava tagliare il piede, ci pensava lei. Se c'era un bambino che sembrava indemoniato all'idea di dover fare un'iniezione, Maria Teresa Supposta risolveva il problema in quattro e quattr'otto, bloccando lo scalmanato, insensibile alle sue urla.

Così, seduta sulla poltrona del salotto sulla quale di solito il commenda passava gran parte dei pomeriggi, la Supposta attendeva il ritorno della Tina per riferirle senza fronzoli l'accaduto e l'ordine ricevuto dal carabiniere Firrìa: controllare se in casa mancasse qualcosa, soldi, preziosi, quadri, tappeti, argenteria, insomma roba di valore.

Addosso il Dubbio non aveva niente, aveva riferito lo stesso carabiniere all'Alborati non appena questi era rientrato dall'ospedale.

Ma poteva darsi che non avesse agito da solo.

Magari aveva un socio cui aveva lanciato la refurtiva dalla finestra.

«Ha dei precedenti?» chiese il maresciallo una volta messo a bagnomaria il Dubbio.

Il Firrìa allargò le braccia.

Come poteva saperlo?

«Come potevi saperlo?» cantilenò a sua volta il maresciallo.

Magari, ironizzò, chiedendolo allo stesso fermato il quale sarebbe stato più che felice di confessare di aver fatto fuori una decina di persone o di aver partecipato a una rapina alla Banca d'Italia.

«Firrìa», disse poi con tutta calma, «non ti è venuto in mente di fare una telefonata ai colleghi di Bellano per farti dare qualche informazione?»

Il carabiniere si strinse nelle spalle.

«Veramente», rispose, «lei maresciallo aveva detto di tenerlo senza far niente fino al suo ritorno...»

«E quando uno dice niente, eh...» sorrise il maresciallo.

75.

«Sicura?» chiese Maria Teresa Supposta.

Un po' per l'età, un po' perché il ladro l'aveva beccato lei, un po' perché aveva parlato coi carabinieri ricevendo precise istruzioni, si sentiva responsabile della situazione e aveva voluto essere certa che la Tina avesse guardato per bene dappertutto, assicurandosi che non mancasse davvero niente.

Sulle prime la ragazza era rimasta stordita, non aveva capito un accidente di quello che era successo perché la Supposta l'aveva subito investita: «Il commendatore sta bene, ho controllato, dormicchia, con tutta probabilità non si è accorto di niente. I carabinieri però vogliono sapere se manca qualcosa».

Con calma!

Di cosa non s'era accorto il commenda?

E i carabinieri?

Cosa c'entravano?

Perché sarebbe dovuto mancare qualcosa?

«Ma cos'è successo?» aveva infine chiesto la Tina.

Maria Teresa Supposta allora si era predisposta a raccontare per bene i fatti come se stesse ripassando una parte.

«Io ero lì in bagno, stavo finendo di asciugarmi i capelli quando do un'occhiata fuori e ti vedo uno che...»

Il monologo dell'ex infermiera era durato un bel quarto d'ora al termine del quale la Tina aveva voluto verificare di persona le condizioni del commenda.

Dormiva adesso, e lo aveva svegliato.
Poi aveva controllato che in casa non mancasse niente.
«Sicura?» chiese Maria Teresa Supposta.
«Sì, certo», rispose la ragazza.
Dalla casa non era sparito niente.

76.

Nemmeno il Dubbio era sparito.

«Non si è annegato e nemmeno l'hanno rapito gli extraterrestri», comunicò il maresciallo Pezzati.

Trattenuto dai colleghi di Menaggio piuttosto.

«E come mai?» chiese il carabiniere Fantarini.

Sorpreso in atteggiamento sospetto in casa di tal commendatore Dalamonti.

«Stava rubando?» sbottò il Fantarini.

«Situazione ancora in fase di accertamento», rispose il maresciallo che ogni tanto aveva il vezzo di parlare come un telegramma. «Il soggetto nega», aggiunse.

Affermava di essere lì per altri motivi.

«Dice che può dimostrarlo», proseguì il Pezzati.

Il maresciallo Alborati, in attesa di metterlo a confronto con un testimone chiamato in causa dallo stesso Dubbio e che a suo dire avrebbe potuto scagionarlo, gli aveva telefonato per avere notizie sul soggetto.

«E lei come gliel'ha descritto?» si permise di chiedere il Fantarini.

Sul viso del maresciallo comparve un mezzo sorriso. Cosa poteva dirgli?

«Che è un balordo, un idiota!»

Non poteva tacere che aveva in ballo un procedimento penale, una storiaccia dentro la quale a suo giudizio era finito proprio perché era un fesso. Ma gli aveva fatto presente che lo riteneva incapace di commettere atti criminosi proprio a causa dei suoi limiti...

«Insomma, gli ho detto che non è stupido ma non ha certo l'intelligenza e la determinazione che un vero criminale dovrebbe avere.»

Il Fantarini approvò con un inconsapevole cenno del capo.

«Sarà meglio avvisare la Finanza che non c'è nessun disperso nel lago allora», disse poi.

«Porcaccio giuda!» sbottò il Pezzati.

Non aveva detto niente al collega della *Canterina*, così da avvisare il Dubbio che la sua barchetta era già tornata a casa.

Va be', l'avrebbe fatto più tardi: l'Alborati gli aveva promesso che, una volta effettuati confronti e riscontri, l'avrebbe informato dei risultati. Poi, prima di chiudere la telefonata, sempre il maresciallo di Menaggio gli aveva chiesto particolari sulla storia di un eventuale disperso la cui segnalazione era partita proprio dalla caserma di Bellano.

«Forse è una bufala», aveva risposto il Pezzati.

Allo stato non c'era traccia di dispersi, nemmeno a cercarli col lanternino.

77.

La *Canterina* era nel molo.

L'altra Canterina s'era assopita.

Il dottor Lonati dovette bussare più volte per svegliarla.

Sua moglie non aveva mollato.

Tipico.

Gli aveva lasciato bere in pace il caffè e poi era tornata alla carica, aveva ripreso il discorso.

Una sciocchezza quella che gli aveva appena sentito dire.

Per sapere ciò che era successo sarebbe stato necessario essere sulla barca quella notte insieme con l'Ernesto!

Era un ragionare quello?

Ragionare era un'altra cosa.

Ragionare era partire dal dato di fatto che qualcosa era successo e non perdere tempo in ipotesi, ma cercare la verità, quale che fosse.

Ragionare era capire se quello che il Dubbio aveva raccontato fosse possibile.

Per esempio, era verosimile che avesse incrociato il corpo di una donna che sembrava morta da poco?

«Non è del tutto impossibile», aveva risposto il Lonati.

«Ti ricordo che fai il medico e non l'azzeccagarbugli», l'aveva stuzzicato lei.

«E io ti ricordo che non sono un medico legale», aveva ribattuto lui.

Per quello che poteva ricordare dei suoi studi, sì, non era del tutto impossibile.

«Metti che...» aveva detto.

Gli era scappato un sorrisetto.

«Metti che abbia intenzione di farti fuori», aveva proseguito.

«Sentiamo», aveva detto lei.

Immaginasse che se la portava a fare un giretto in barca, di sera, allontanandosi un po', un bel po', dalla riva, così che nessuno potesse vedere, e poi...

«E poi?» aveva interloquito Vittoria Lonati.

E poi... boh, poi, con la scusa della luna piena e delle stelle fingesse di volerla abbracciare, baciare e invece le mettesse le mani intorno al collo.

«Così», aveva simulato il Lonati stringendo il proprio.

«Vorrei vederti!» aveva sorriso la moglie.

«Stringo, stringo, stringo fino a che sono sicuro di averti fatto fuori», aveva continuato il dottore, «poi ti butto giù dalla barca, nel lago.»

«E il Dubbio passa e mi incrocia», aveva concluso Vittoria Lonati.

«Oppure...» aveva proseguito l'uomo come se non avesse sentito.

Poteva anche essere che lei non fosse morta ma solo svenuta, una sincope, e che grazie al contatto con l'acqua, mentre affondava, rinvenisse. In quel caso, per il terrore e nel tentativo di riconquistare la superficie, cominciava a ingurgitare acqua e allora affogava in senso proprio.

«E passa ancora il Dubbio che mi incrocia e mi porta a riva», aveva concluso la donna che si era portata le mani attorno al collo senza accorgersene.

«Non lo si può escludere», aveva detto il Lonati.

Infine ci pensavano il vento e le onde. Il lago si riprendeva il corpo e lo inghiottiva per sempre.

«D'accordo», aveva concluso Vittoria Lonati. «Ma, a parte gli scherzi...»

Lui cosa aveva intenzione di fare?

«Niente», aveva risposto il Lonati.

«Contento tu», aveva ribattuto lei avvicinandosi alla finestra della sala e guardando in direzione del molo.

Ma era chiaro che non finiva lì.

Infatti...

«Se sei contento così», aveva ripreso, «vuol dire che ti piace passare per visionario o per stupido.»

Il Lonati l'aveva guardata senza parlare, dandosi il tempo di accendere l'ennesima sigaretta.

«Cioè?» aveva infine chiesto lui dopo una lunga boccata.

La donna aveva aperto la finestra per dare aria al locale.

«Visionario o comunque si possa dire, col signor maresciallo», aveva spiegato levando l'indice della mano destra.

Lui stesso aveva detto che il Pezzati l'aveva lasciato con l'amaro in bocca, dandogli l'impressione di non credergli fino in fondo. E il fatto di non aver trovato alcun cadavere sulla riva non poteva che confermare l'idea, per quanto folle!, che lui si fosse sognato tutto.

«Sennò stupido», aveva proseguito la donna levando anche l'anulare della mano destra.

Due dita, perché c'erano due possibili spiegazioni.

Stupido perché era caduto in uno scherzo di gusto davvero pessimo, macabro addirittura.

O stupido perché si era prestato a una misteriosa manovra, a un imperscrutabile disegno il cui fine era difficile immaginare.

«Allora, visionario o stupido?» aveva chiesto la signora Lonati.

Il dottore aveva reagito con uno sbuffo con il quale aveva soffiato anche l'ultimo tiro della sigaretta.

«Non sono né l'uno né l'altro», aveva detto il dottor Lonati. «E tu lo sai bene.»

«Bisogna che nessuno nemmeno si sogni di pensarlo e tocca a te fare in modo di evitare che qualcuno si senta autorizzato a farlo», aveva ribattuto lei.

Poi gli aveva chiesto di raggiungerla alla finestra, di

guardare verso il molo, se quello che vedeva era proprio ciò che pensava.

«Cosa?» aveva chiesto lui avviandosi.

Marito e moglie si erano guardati negli occhi.

«Bisogna che mi dia da fare», aveva detto lui dopo qualche secondo.

«Era ora», aveva risposto lei.

E non gli aveva chiesto dove stava andando poiché lo aveva già capito.

78.

«Cosa c'è?» chiese la Canterina.

Stupita per quella visita inaspettata?

Oppure spaventata, incredula?

Il suo viso non diceva quasi niente.

Ma non era il momento di approfondire in che stato d'animo fosse.

«Ho bisogno di parlare con l'Ernesto», spiegò il Lonati.

«Non c'è», rispose la padrona di casa.

Era uscito quella mattina, spiegò, andato via con la barca dicendo di avere un servizio da fare, e non era ancora tornato.

«Ma se la barca è nel molo!» fece osservare il dottor Lonati.

L'aveva vista dalla finestra di casa sua dieci minuti prima.

«E lui?» scappò alla Canterina, la voce fredda, un'eco quasi, come se a parlare fossero stati quei muri di contrada.

79.

Ancora seduto nella sala d'attesa della caserma dei carabinieri di Menaggio.

Ecco dov'era.

Sorrideva beato, la libertà a un tiro di schioppo, almeno così pensava.

D'altronde, la Tina aveva appena confermato di conoscerlo. Dopodiché il maresciallo Alborati, arrancando per via del gambone, aveva detto alla ragazza di seguirlo nel suo ufficio.

Prima di inviare il Firrìa a prendere la Tina per effettuare il confronto tra i due, il maresciallo aveva voluto riflettere su come impostarlo, tenendo presenti le parole che il collega bellanese aveva usato per descrivergli il Dubbio.

Un balordo, aveva detto, un idiota, tutt'altro che un criminale.

La razza peggiore quindi, aveva concluso l'Alborati, quella dei sedicenti furbi.

Be', se voleva fare il furbo con lui, aveva sbagliato i conti.

Se, tanto per cominciare, aveva mentito sul fatto di conoscere quella ragazza, avrebbe rimpianto la sua furbizia.

Aveva fatto ritornare il Dubbio nel suo ufficio.

«Giovanotto.»

Che aprisse bene le orecchie e si tappasse la bocca da quel momento sino a nuovo ordine, nemmeno una parola.

«Capito?»
Il Dubbio s'era fermato in tempo.
Un cenno del capo, sì.
«Bene.»
Di lì a poco, aveva spiegato il maresciallo, sarebbe arrivata in caserma la ragazza che lui aveva dichiarato di conoscere. L'avrebbe messa a confronto con lui, sui due piedi, nella saletta d'attesa.
«Parlerò io solo.»
Una sola domanda, rivolta a lei.
«Conosce questo giovanotto?»
La Tina aveva risposto sì.
Il Dubbio aveva sorriso.
L'Alborati aveva incassato.
«Non abbiamo ancora finito», aveva poi detto chiedendo alla ragazza di seguirlo nel suo ufficio.

80.

«Sì, lo conosco», confermò la Tina.

Anche se solo da poco, dalla sera prima.

Però...

«Però?» fece l'Alborati.

Dicesse pure, si sentisse libera.

La Tina non s'era mai trovata dentro una caserma dei carabinieri. L'ansia che aveva provato nel tragitto percorso per raggiungerla s'era piano piano smorzata quando, una volta dentro, non aveva sentito lo stridere di cardini rugginosi e le grida di prigionieri torturati. Ma soprattutto quando aveva notato il gambone del maresciallo, particolare che ai suoi occhi l'aveva reso una volta per tutte umano nonostante la divisa.

Quindi all'invito dell'Alborati aderì pur con un'iniziale timidezza perché...

Insomma, non sapeva come dirlo, era difficile...

Era una sciocchezza anche se in fondo non lo era.

Però, nonostante le poche ore trascorse insieme, lei s'era fatta l'idea che quel giovanotto fosse uno buono, uno incapace di fare del male.

«Non so se mi spiego», disse la Tina.

Avevano mangiato, avevano parlato, erano scesi assieme, a piedi, dal crotto fino in paese.

La vie en rose, stava pensando il maresciallo Alborati mentre il dolore del gambone (forse quei maledetti dottori avevano stretto troppo il gesso?) stava riprendendo vigore.

«Però è entrato in casa sua», interloquì.
«Del commendatore», corresse la Tina.
«Sì, va be', fa lo stesso.»
«Ma non ha rubato niente», osservò la ragazza.
Aveva controllato lei di persona, che ormai conosceva ogni angolo della villetta. Tra l'altro, fece notare, non che ci fossero poi 'ste gran cose da rubare. I soldi stavano in banca, gioielli non ce n'erano.
I quadri?
Tutte stampe.
Ed erano ancora al loro posto.
«D'accordo», fece il maresciallo.
Il giovanotto non aveva rubato niente.
«Ieri sera», chiese allora, «su al crotto, eravate solo voi due?»
La Tina restò per un attimo interdetta.
Che senso aveva quella domanda?
Forse il maresciallo pensava che gli avesse raccontato delle balle?
«Perché?» chiese.

81.

Bella storia, pensò il Lonati.

Avrebbe voluto vedere sua moglie adesso, lì, al suo posto.

L'Ernesto non c'era, la Canterina sì.

E gli aveva già chiesto più volte come mai, cosa c'è, cos'è successo, dov'è l'Ernesto e via col ritornello.

«Con calma», aveva detto lui.

Se, intanto, lo faceva entrare.

Magari sedere.

Sedesse anche lei.

Pallida, un po' sudata, l'occhio sgranato, il Lonati aveva temuto che la Canterina gli svenisse ai piedi. Una volta in cucina le servì di sua iniziativa un bicchiere d'acqua.

«Al momento non so dove sia», cominciò a dire.

Da qualche parte doveva iniziare.

Peraltro, proseguì, era certo che non fosse successo niente di che.

Una negazione che suonava proprio come il suo contrario.

La Canterina colse la bugia.

«Come?»

«Porti pazienza», la frenò lui.

«L'Ernesto...» riprese.

Poi si grattò la nuca.

«Volevo dire, in questi anni...»

Quella parola, anni, turbò per primo lui stesso.

Fu come se prendesse forma e sostanza.

Il Lonati notò solo allora il volto squadrato della donna che gli stava di fronte, il grembiale di casa che indossava e si sentì greve del silenzio dell'ora che stava vivendo, e di tutte le ore come quella, fredde d'inverno, calde nei giorni più afosi d'estate, le ore che avevano segnato gli anni passati tra quelle mura mentre il Dubbio cresceva senza padre e sua madre si dannava per sé e per lui.

«Ecco», riprese cercando di contenere il turbamento. In quegli anni, negli ultimi tempi soprattutto, era mai successo che l'Ernesto le avesse dato materia per preoccuparsi ancora com'era successo quando era più giovane con quelle storie su suo padre...

«Quando andava a cercarlo, quando aveva affermato di averlo visto scambiandolo con il pretore...»

... o comunque che le fosse sembrato strano, avesse comportamenti inspiegabili?

La Canterina era prossima alle lacrime.

Il Lonati comprese di avere imboccato la strada sbagliata. Sua moglie forse sarebbe andata più spedita al nocciolo della questione.

D'accordo allora, fece tra sé.

«Questa notte è successa una cosa», disse.

Il viso della Canterina entrò in allarme. Chissà quante volte in quegli anni aveva contratto così i masseteri per contrastare un pericolo imminente, obbligare l'Ernesto all'obbedienza fino a che le era riuscito...

«Cosa?» chiese lei.

Non c'era più alcuna tentazione di pianto negli occhi della donna.

Scegliendo con cura le parole, o almeno credendo di farlo, il Lonati raccontò.

«Forse», affermò alla fine del resoconto, «si tratta solo di un grosso equivoco.»

La Canterina lo guardò in silenzio per qualche istante.

«Come può essere?» chiese poi.

Come poteva trattarsi di un grosso equivoco se c'era di

mezzo un cadavere che suo figlio aveva affermato di aver trascinato a riva? Lo si poteva soltanto sognare un fatto del genere? Era possibile?

E comunque, se la barca era nel molo, dov'era adesso l'Ernesto?

82.

All'inferno!

Lui e tutti gli uomini del mondo, compresi quelli che dovevano ancora nascere.

Ma prima di tutti, lui e in compagnia del postino col ciuffo!

Dio, se lo avesse avuto tra le mani sarebbe stata capace di strozzarlo.

Mica perché non le credeva il maresciallo Alborati le aveva chiesto se la sera precedente erano soli oppure in compagnia.

Macché!

Piuttosto era stato per verificare se il giovanotto gli aveva raccontato la verità, e cioè che la sera precedente con loro c'era anche una sua amica, bionda, Valeria se non ricordava male, il cui fascino l'aveva colpito all'istante; non sapendo come fare per rintracciarla, aveva cercato lei per avere indicazioni visto che, per le informazioni che s'erano scambiati chiacchierando, aveva capito dove abitasse o comunque prestasse servizio.

«È così?» aveva domandato il maresciallo.

C'era davvero con loro questa Valeria?

La Tina avrebbe voluto rispondere no, sono tutte balle, e così vendicarsi dell'urente delusione che le parole del maresciallo le avevano provocato.

Ma poco prima gli aveva detto che sì!, erano stati in compagnia la sera prima e proprio con la Valeria.

Non le era rimasto altro da fare che spingere la rabbia

in fondo allo stomaco mentre il maresciallo Alborati le prospettava la situazione.

«In termini di reato c'è poco di che.»

Certo, c'era una violazione di proprietà privata. Non c'era scasso però, visto che cancelletto e porta di casa erano aperti, non c'erano stati danneggiamenti di qualche tipo o furti.

«Una bella denuncia comunque la si può sempre fare.»

Toccava però al proprietario di casa, bisognava metterlo in mezzo.

«Il commendatore?» aveva chiesto la Tina.

«E chi, se no?» aveva risposto il maresciallo.

Ne valeva la pena?

Il gioco valeva la candela?

Se non s'era accorto di niente, conveniva turbarlo informandolo, creandogli pensieri, nella situazione in cui era?

«Me lo dica lei», aveva detto il maresciallo.

La Tina, alla domanda dell'Alborati, aveva dato l'impressione di voler riflettere prima di rispondere.

In realtà, mentre ascoltava le parole del carabiniere, non aveva potuto fare a meno di pensare alle coincidenze tra quanto era appena accaduto e quanto invece era successo il giorno in cui era arrivata quella lettera che aveva tanto colpito il commendatore.

Anche quella volta lei non era presente, pronta a proteggerlo, pur essendo in casa. Ma era martedì, giorno del bagno.

83.

Nonostante glielo avesse detto più volte, il commenda non aveva mai ceduto su quella faccenda: alla sua igiene pensava da solo lavandosi a pezzi tutti i giorni e facendo un bagno completo due volte alla settimana, il martedì e il sabato.

In quei giorni la Tina gli preparava l'acqua, sciogliendovi sali da bagno di colore azzurro chc mandavano un profumo da sogno. Poi lo accompagnava, lui con già indosso l'accappatoio, fino a che non era entrato con entrambi i piedi nella vasca. A bagno avvenuto, avvisata da un campanello, lo andava a riprendere: se lo ritrovava davanti sempre in piedi dentro la vasca e con addosso l'accappatoio.

Quel martedì stava preparando l'acqua del bagno.

Forse era stato per colpa dell'acqua che scrosciava.

Quando lei era uscita dal bagno, il commenda le aveva detto di aver sentito suonare alla porta. Lei aveva subito pensato al postino, aveva dato un'occhiata.

Piovigginava.

Al cancelletto non c'era più nessuno.

Il «Corriere della Sera» era appoggiato al muretto di lato, già fradicio.

Lei era uscita di corsa per prenderlo, poi l'aveva appoggiato su un calorifero e aveva accompagnato il commenda in bagno.

Della lettera lei non s'era accorta, infilata tra una pagina e l'altra del quotidiano.

L'aveva trovata il commenda dopo pranzo quando, in attesa che lei finisse di rassettare la cucina per poi andare a leggergli il giornale, lui l'aveva aperto per scrutarne i titoli più grossi.

Se l'era ritrovata tra le dita, gli era scivolata a terra, l'aveva raccolta, guardandola con una infantile meraviglia.

Una lettera!

Da quanto tempo qualcuno non gli scriveva?

84.

Meglio, molto meglio scrivere, stava riflettendo il carabiniere Fantarini approfittando dell'ora oziosa.

Meglio scrivere, anche se per il momento non aveva alcuna penna in mano e nemmeno carta pronta all'uso.

Per il momento gli era sufficiente aver preso la decisione.

Scrivere.

Da quando, un mesetto prima, aveva preso visione del nutrito programma estivo della Pro Loco, non aveva fatto altro che pensarci.

L'occasione era ghiotta.

Anzi, irrinunciabile.

Ovvio che, per poterlo fare, doveva dirlo al maresciallo Pezzati, ottenerne il permesso. Se formale o meno, non avrebbe saputo dirlo, in ogni caso per quel giorno avrebbe dovuto ottenere di essere esentato dal servizio.

Comunque guardasse la faccenda, non gli sembrava un problema.

Se mai, considerato il carattere del comandante, come definirlo?, bizzarro?, umorale forse?, aveva a lungo dibattuto tra sé su cosa fosse meglio fare.

Chiederlo a voce o per iscritto?

A voce era più diretto.

Ma anche più rischioso.

Beccavi il momento sbagliato e quello ti rispondeva no. Poi, una volta negato il permesso, sarebbe stato difficile che tornasse sulla sua decisione.

Per iscritto c'era il rischio di dare alla richiesta un'aura troppo ufficiale, come se si trattasse di chissà che. Però, scripta eccetera eccetera, c'era il vantaggio che il signor maresciallo potesse leggere con comodo e con altrettanto comodo ragionarci su e capire che si trattava di cosa innocentissima.

Quindi, a ragion veduta e ponderati i pro e i contro, il carabiniere semplice Fantarini decise che sarebbe stato meglio, molto meglio scrivere.

85.

Scripta eccetera eccetera.

Verba volant, e certe parole più rapidamente di altre.

Quelle dell'Oltramonti per esempio.

Quello stesso pomeriggio raggiunsero la casa dell'Amanda e le orecchie di suo padre.

Bernardo, settantotto anni, sulle mani calli che sembravano biglie.

L'ambasciatore, tal Freguzzi, lavorava alla cartiera di Dervio ma abitava a Tremenico, e aveva riferito davanti alla famiglia schierata.

Oltre al Bernardo, i due figli, Ozio e Birmino, due larici, la stessa Amanda e la madre Giustina, che non temeva nemmeno il toro quando giungeva in paese per la monta.

«Sentito cosa va in giro a dire quel somaro?» disse il Bernardo alla fine del resoconto del Freguzzi.

«Io glielo taglio via!» proruppe l'Amanda.

E sarebbe stata capace di farlo.

«Sta' buona lì», fece il fratello Ozio.

«Ci pensiamo noi a battezzarlo», completò il Birmino.

Giusto il tempo di organizzare la cerimonia.

86.

«Mi perdoni se glielo chiedo dottore, ma per quanto tempo ancora aveva intenzione di non dirmi niente?» chiese il maresciallo Pezzati.

Il Lonati fece per rispondere.

Il Pezzati agitò una mano per aria.

«Lasci perdere, ormai è fatta», disse.

«Quindi ora come intende procedere?» fece il Lonati.

Il Pezzati lo guardò quasi sorridendo.

Un'espressione, fu il pensiero del dottore, tutt'altro che acconcia al momento, alla situazione, ai motivi che lo avevano spinto fino in caserma.

Una volta messa al corrente la Canterina di quanto era accaduto durante la notte, le aveva anche detto che non se la sentiva più di tenere per sé quello che sapeva, a maggior ragione con l'Ernesto sparito dalla circolazione, finito chissà dove.

«Bisogna che lo dica al maresciallo.»

La donna aveva reagito chiudendo gli occhi e senza parlare per un paio di minuti.

Si stava realizzando il suo peggior pensiero, talmente spaventoso che non era mai riuscito a diventare sogno o incubo ma solo e sempre pensiero: carabinieri, un'aula di pretura, il carcere di Pescarenico.

E poi, quando lei non ci fosse stata più?

Il Lonati aveva dovuto richiamarla.

«Capisce, vero, che non posso fare altrimenti?» aveva detto.

In ogni caso lui aveva deciso di confessare la cosa al Pezzati.

«È anche per il bene dell'Ernesto», le aveva detto, assicurandole che le avrebbe dato tutto l'aiuto, il sostegno possibile.

«Ma dove sarà?» aveva chiesto la Canterina.

Uscendo dalla casa del Dubbio per dirigersi verso la caserma, il dottor Lonati aveva incrociato il Riffa.

Sudato da fare schifo, i capelli appiattiti, uno sguardo di fuoco.

Nessuna merda di macchina si era fermata ai suoi segni, aveva consumato tutto il calendario smadonnando passo dopo passo lungo i sei chilometri che dividevano Corenno Plinio da Bellano e pure le scarpe, vera marca Biagio Trùfa Riffa, avevano assai patito la camminata.

Una volta entrato in paese con l'unico desiderio di buttarsi in acqua anche vestito così com'era, chi aveva incontrato per primo?

Il dottor Lonati che gli chiedeva se avesse notizie del Dubbio.

Porca troia, fosse stato chiunque altro avrebbe risposto: «Che cazzo ne so!».

S'era trattenuto per rispetto invece.

«È da stamattina che non lo vedo», aveva risposto.

Una risposta che aveva lasciato di stucco il dottor Lonati.

L'Ernesto, si era chiesto per l'ennesima volta, che fine aveva fatto?

E s'era confermato nella decisione che la cosa migliore da fare fosse dire al maresciallo Pezzati quello che sapeva.

Chi, se non lui, avrebbe saputo come procedere?

«Come procedere?» chiese il Pezzati senza smettere il sorriso.

Facendo al Dubbio domande precise e pretendendo analoghe risposte.

«O no?»

Al dottor Lonati venne subito un sospetto.
«Mi sta dicendo che lei sa dov'è?» chiese.
Più o meno, rispose il Pezzati agitando la mano.
«Credo che sia circa a metà lago», disse poi.
Sul battello, aggiunse indicando la finestra che dava sull'imbarcadero, che stava navigando in quel momento in direzione di Bellano.
«Abbiamo preparato il comitato di accoglienza», sorrise.
Nella persona del carabiniere semplice Fantarini che, ritto, le mani dietro la schiena, stava amabilmente chiacchierando col battellotto in attesa di Livera Ernesto detto Dubbio.

87.

«Il Dubbio non c'è.»

Fu il battellotto a comunicarlo al Fantarini.

Ce n'erano tre lì pronti a scendere, una di Plesio che un giorno sì e uno no veniva di qua in battello per andare a trovare suo marito in ospedale, il secondo era un ferroviere che lavorava sulla Milano-Sondrio, bellanese ma che s'era sposato a Menaggio e abitava lì, la terza persona non sapeva chi fosse ma, anche solo per il fatto di essere una donna, non poteva essere il Dubbio.

Il Fantarini reagì come se se lo fosse fatto scappare tra le mani.

«E io come faccio adesso, cosa dico al signor maresciallo?»

La logica del battellotto gli venne in soccorso.

«Se al gh'è minga...»

«Ma ci doveva essere», ribatté il Fantarini.

Il battellotto allora scrollò le spalle.

«Se le dìs lù...»

E si allontanò insieme con il comandante del battello *Innominato* per andare a smorzare quel po' di sete che veniva sempre dopo una traversata del lago e che solo un bel bicchiere di vino bianco fresco, dopo tutta quell'acqua, riusciva a sedare.

Il maresciallo Pezzati si avvicinò alla finestra e l'aprì.

Vide il battello che dondolava placido, il suo carabiniere che guardava verso il lago.

«Fantarini!» gridò.

Il giovanotto se l'aspettava.
Si girò, allargò le braccia.
Il maresciallo comprese al volo.
Si girò rivolgendosi al Lonati.
«Non c'è», disse.
Eppure ci doveva essere.

88.

«Chiudiamola qui», aveva detto il maresciallo Alborati.

«Grazie», aveva risposto il Dubbio.

«C'è poco da ringraziare», gli aveva fatto osservare il carabiniere. Piuttosto, aveva proseguito, che riflettesse sul fatto che si era comportato come un bambino di dieci anni e solo per un pelo non era finito in un guaio che di certo non l'avrebbe aiutato a risolvere quell'altra faccenda.

«Non so se mi spiego...»

Era stato fortunato ad avere incontrato persone di senno, non scriteriate come lui, gente che aveva chiuso gli occhi sulla sua idiozia.

Come quella ragazza, per esempio, quella Tina.

Molto più matura di lui!

Aveva deciso di agire nell'interesse del commendatore, evitandogli il trambusto di una denuncia e tutte le sue complicazioni.

Se mai, era lei che doveva ringraziare.

«Lo farò», aveva promesso il Dubbio.

«Nemmeno per idea», era sbottato l'Alborati, «toglitelo dalla testa!»

Perché, prima di riconvocarlo nel suo ufficio per metterlo al corrente della decisione presa, aveva telefonato al collega bellanese e l'aveva informato.

«Bene», aveva risposto il Pezzati. «Adesso lo saluti e gli dici di prendere il battello diretto alla sponda di qua. Ci penso io ad aspettarlo. Però questo non dirglielo, voglio fargli una bella sorpresa.»

«Come credi», aveva approvato l'Alborati.

Quindi, lasciasse in pace quella ragazza.

«Ti prendi il tuo bel battello e te ne torni da dove sei venuto. E guai a te se ti vedo ancora in giro da queste parti.»

Il Dubbio non aveva osato obiettare.

Nemmeno chiedere, ma perché il battello?

89.

Certi delinquenti!

«Bisognerebbe chiuderli in galera e buttare via la chiave», disse Maria Teresa Supposta, indignata dopo aver saputo dalla Tina che tutto era finito in niente: all'intruso della mattina proprio in quel momento il signor maresciallo stava facendo una bella predica con tanto di avviso a non farsi mai più rivedere da quelle parti.

«Tutto lì?» era sbottata.

Fosse dipeso da lei...

Fosse entrato in casa sua...

«E anche quel maresciallo lì...»

Forse non c'erano più i carabinieri di una volta?

La Supposta aveva accettato, di nuovo e di buon grado, di sostituirsi alla Tina nella cura del commendatore mentre lei aveva seguito il carabiniere Firrìa in caserma. E, al ritorno della ragazza, s'era sentita in diritto di sottoporla a un interrogatorio che il maresciallo se lo sognava.

Alle risposte della ragazza s'era via via indignata.

La Tina aveva sopportato con cristiana rassegnazione i suoi inevitabili commenti circa l'accaduto, i tempi insicuri, la paura che attanagliava soprattutto loro anziani, soli in casa e in balia del primo lazzarone di passaggio.

Ai tempi suoi invece... aveva sospirato l'ex infermiera, dando alla ragazza l'illusione che la Supposta fosse giunta al termine della sua perorazione e si predisponesse a lasciarla per ritornare a casa.

Invece no.

L'ex infermiera aveva in canna un'ultima domanda, una curiosità cui aveva deciso fosse venuto il momento di dare soddisfazione.

Perché, d'accordo sul diabete, ma...

«In fin dei conti, cos'ha quell'uomo?» riferendosi al commendatore.

Rispetto ad altre occasioni in cui le era capitato di sostituire la Tina, l'aveva trovato davvero molto cambiato.

E in peggio.

La mattina ancora ancora, infatti gli aveva fatto compagnia per modo di dire: una volta accertato che non si era accorto di niente, l'aveva lasciato a letto a dormicchiare e morta lì.

Nel pomeriggio invece se l'era ritrovato in salotto e lei aveva tentato di avviare più di una conversazione.

«Vuole che accenda la radio, vuole che le legga il giornale, gradisce qualcosa di fresco oppure un caffè?»

Come da raccomandazione, s'era ben guardata dall'accennare a ciò che era successo nel corso della mattina.

Ma, niente.

Non le aveva risposto che poche parole.

No, grazie, non si disturbi.

«Il dottore dice che è un po' per l'età e un po' per il diabete», aveva spiegato la Tina mentre le due avevano finalmente raggiunto la porta di casa.

«Davvero tutto lì?» aveva ribattuto la Supposta.

Perché lei non era scema.

L'età era la stessa di sei mesi prima e il diabete, a giudicare dalla terapia, non era cambiato.

Era cambiato il commenda, invece, tutta un'altra persona.

«Così dice il dottore», aveva ribadito la Tina.

E al sospiro con cui l'ex infermiera l'aveva salutata era stata tentata di rivelarle il suo pensiero. Forse lei avrebbe potuto capirla, capire che non era solo una sua fantasia attribuire il brusco viraggio del commenda al momento in cui era arrivata quella lettera. Quando, insieme, s'erano accorti che sulla busta c'era un altro indirizzo.

Di già sulla soglia di casa, la Tina aveva tentato un primo, timido passo.

«Lei», aveva chiesto alla Supposta, «conosce per caso o ha conosciuto una certa dottoressa Maria Dominetti?»

Per tutta risposta il viso dell'ex infermiera s'era contratto in una smorfia.

«Che cosa?» aveva ringhiato, tanto che la Tina s'era chiesta cosa avesse detto di tanto sbagliato.

90.

Un errore.

Quell'idiota del postino col ciuffo.

Gentile dottoressa.

La Tina aveva subito notato l'indirizzo, la lettera non era per il commendatore.

«Come?» aveva chiesto lui.

Il tono era già cambiato, nel giro di pochi minuti.

Dal momento in cui, dal salotto, il commendatore l'aveva chiamata per gridarle che aveva ricevuto una lettera a quello in cui lei aveva dovuto dirgli che la lettera non era per lui.

Gentile dottoressa.

Dottoressa Maria Dominetti, via alle Betulle, Acquaseria.

Alla Tina era sembrato che il commenda fosse rimasto deluso, forse aveva sperato che qualcuno gli avesse scritto. Un amico d'infanzia magari, una vecchia morosa, chiunque che anche col solo ricordo di lui gli dicesse che il suo tempo durava ancora e lo traesse da una solitudine che non aveva niente a che vedere con la cura che aveva di lui o con le visite che i suoi due figli gli facevano di tanto in tanto? Era ben lontana dall'immaginare lo squarcio che s'era aperto nella memoria, tra i ricordi del Dalamonti.

Aveva detto una cosa il commenda, più che altro l'aveva mormorata a sé stesso, qualcosa che aveva a che fare con la cecità che non solo aveva davanti a sé ma anche dietro, nel suo passato. E aveva stretto per un po' le mani a pugno, rilasciandole subito dopo.

La Tina era rimasta lì per un po', senza sapere cosa fare. Quando aveva aperto la bocca per dire qualcosa, il commenda l'aveva anticipata.

«Rimettila nella busta e va' a imbucarla.»

Di rimando, a lei era venuta un'idea stravagante.

«Non vuole che gliela legga?»

Lui però non aveva risposto.

Aveva solo girato la testa verso di lei e l'aveva guardata, come per rimproverarla, per chiederle cosa le fosse saltato in testa.

«D'accordo», aveva risposto la Tina, rendendosi conto di aver detto un'idiozia.

«Subito», aveva precisato il commenda.

Subito, aveva ripetuto lei.

Era andata in cucina.

Da lì, ancora con la lettera in mano, aveva guardato verso il salotto, la poltrona da cui spuntava il vertice del capo del commendatore. Si era appoggiato, le braccia cascavano di lato ai braccioli. Pur senza vederlo, avrebbe giurato che aveva gli occhi chiusi. Sembrava in ascolto di voci che solo lui poteva sentire.

Poi aveva imbustato la lettera.

Prima però, sentendosi come se temesse che qualcuno la potesse cogliere sul fatto, saltando da una riga all'altra, l'aveva letta da cima a fondo.

91.

Be', non era la prima volta che, per vendetta, gelosia o invidia, qualche pescatore ti ciulava la barca per nascondertela o addirittura affondarla. Scherzi del cazzo, o avvisi, colpa sua che non aveva pensato a nasconderla per bene. Non era il primo cui capitava e stavolta era toccato a lui, fu l'immediato – e unico – pensiero del Dubbio davanti alla riva dove aveva tirato la *Canterina.*

Non c'era più, sparita.

E adesso?, si chiese guardando il lago che il vento pareva non aver più voglia di sbattere. Le sue scuffie sembravano più carezze, come uno che lisciava il pelo a un gatto per chiedere scusa dopo avergli dato un calcio in culo. Tutto congiurava contro di lui. Ma era in momenti come quelli, ragionò, che bisognava prendere delle decisioni anche a costo di correre qualche rischio.

«Perché sono venuto qui?» disse.

Parlare ad alta voce rendeva più chiare le cose.

Per andare fino in fondo alla faccenda di quella notte.

«Bon», si rispose.

L'avrebbe fatto. Si guardò intorno casomai qualche occhio di spia lo stesse curando anche solo per godere della sorpresaccia che gli aveva fatto e cominciò ad allontanarsi dalla riva. Dire che avesse un piano in testa era esagerato. In un modo o nell'altro però doveva trovare quella Tina che, se non fosse scappata dalla caserma come se avesse avuto il diavolo alle calcagna, sarebbe già riuscito a beccare.

92.

Ritardo per ritardo, il dottor Lonati pensò che non poteva, prima di tornare in ambulatorio per l'apertura pomeridiana, non ripassare dalla Canterina per aggiornarla sulle novità.

Innanzitutto, non temesse disgrazie, all'Ernesto non era successo niente, era vivo e vegeto.

«Ma la barca...» interloquì la donna.

«Non so spiegarle come mai la barca è nel molo e lui...»

«E lui?» si inserì la Canterina.

«E lui è di là.»

«Di là, dove?» chiese la Canterina.

Dalle parti di Acquaseria, fu la risposta del Lonati.

Più preciso di così non poteva essere.

Poteva accontentarsi di tanta vaghezza la Canterina?

No.

«Ma a fare cosa?» chiese infatti.

93.

«Ancora qui?» era sbottato il maresciallo Alborati quando il collega bellanese l'aveva avvisato che dal battello il Dubbio non era sbarcato. «A fare cosa?»

«Non lo so», aveva risposto il Pezzati.

Ma, a meno che non si fosse buttato nel lago, ce l'aveva ancora tra i piedi.

L'Alborati aveva ringhiato nella cornetta, pulsare del gambone e giramento di coglioni insieme.

«Se lo becco te lo rimando lì a nuoto», aveva detto.

«Dovresti proprio farlo», aveva confermato il maresciallo Pezzati, tralasciando il tono scherzoso.

Perché intendeva beccarlo e assicurarsi che salisse per davvero su un battello.

«Non pretendo che me lo porti di persona, ma mi servirebbe proprio scambiarci quattro chiacchiere.»

All'Alborati s'era accesa una lampadina.

«C'è sotto qualcosa?» aveva chiesto.

«Guarda, collega», aveva risposto il bellanese, «non voglio scatenare allarmi inutili. Tu fammici parlare e poi ti dirò, se sarà il caso.»

La telefonata si era svolta presente il dottor Lonati.

Il quale, quando il maresciallo aveva deposto la cornetta, aveva chiesto lumi.

Il Pezzati glieli aveva dati.

«Posso tranquillizzare la madre allora?» aveva chiesto il dottore.

«A patto che ci informi subito se sa qualcosa che non

ha voluto dire nemmeno a lei, caro dottore. Oppure di qualunque altra cosa venga a sapere se il Dubbio si farà vivo con lei.»

«D'accordo», fece il Lonati. «Ma credo che non sappia niente di più di quello che mi ha detto, cioè proprio niente.»

«Può essere», rispose il Pezzati.

Ma, aggiunse, si sa come sono le madri, no?

94.

Reticenti, evasive.

Anche furbe, sottili.

Non tutte, certo.

Alcune.

La madre della Tina, per esempio.

Per quanto l'avesse letta di fretta stante la lunghezza, certi passaggi della lettera erano rimasti ben impressi nella mente della ragazza.

L'accenno a un incidente stradale avvenuto circa sei mesi prima dalle parti di Zurigo e la morte, a due mesi di distanza l'una dall'altro, di sua madre prima e di suo padre poi.

I genitori di colei che aveva scritto quella lettera insomma.

«Non voglio dilungarmi.»

Quell'espressione aveva colpito la Tina.

Né, aveva scritto la mittente (non c'era indirizzo sul retro della busta ma la firma in calce allo scritto, benché vergata di fretta, lasciava intuire che la scrivente si chiamasse Astrid o qualcosa di simile) riusciva a trovare le parole per esprimere lo sconcerto provocato da ciò che suo padre, l'uomo che sino a poco prima di chiudere gli occhi per sempre aveva considerato tale, le aveva raccontato.

Ma voleva sapere di una sorella, dei suoi genitori, quelli veri.

«Dobbiamo parlarne», aveva scritto.

Sua madre, a una precisa domanda della Tina, aveva risposto di non conoscere nessuna dottoressa Maria Dominetti.

Anche se...

Insomma, aveva avuto la tentazione di chiedere cosa diavolo le fosse venuto in mente, come mai le aveva chiesto della Dominetti, chi le aveva parlato di lei, perché se ne interessava.

Aveva preferito tenere la curiosità per sé.

Certe chiacchiere, vere o false che fossero, appartenevano al passato e non avrebbero modificato il presente.

E poi, alla domanda della figlia lei aveva risposto correttamente, la Maria Dominetti infatti non era dottoressa.

95.

Gentile maresciallo...
Gentile?, si stava chiedendo il carabiniere Fantarini.
Non tanto perché non lo fosse.
Lo era, quando voleva.
Ma era la parola in sé che non lo convinceva.
Troppo confidenziale, quasi sdolcinata.
Gentile, rifletté, non andava bene.
Spettabile maresciallo...

96.

Cara la mia ragazza... aveva detto Maria Teresa Supposta. E, anziché fare un passo in fuori, cosa che avrebbe permesso alla Tina di chiudere la porta di casa su quella giornata convulsa e tornare a occuparsi del commenda, l'ex infermiera ne aveva fatto uno ideale in dentro e uno vero indietro, afferrando così la maniglia e chiudendo la porta.

Perché certe cose proprio non le sopportava, certe falsità non le andavano giù, era più forte di lei.

«Macché dottoressa dei miei stivali», disse.

Una levatrice!

Una banale, semplice levatrice!

Anche se, ai tempi suoi, sin da quando era arrivata, non sapeva dire perché, avevano cominciato a chiamarla così, dottoressa! E lei, figuriamoci!, non aveva mai fatto niente per impedirlo.

Mentre la Supposta parlava, alla Tina parve che si alzasse, spinta in alto dall'energia che stava mettendo per riferirle quelle cose. Le labbra avevano preso una piega di disprezzo rivolta a una persona che, non poteva essere più chiaro di così, non le era stata di certo simpatica. Che ci fosse di mezzo un po' di gelosia professionale?

Non era comunque cosa che la Tina aveva intenzione di approfondire. In ogni caso, anche se avesse voluto farlo, le sarebbe mancato il tempo.

Terminata la sua filippica contro la presunta dottoressa infatti, la Supposta era passata da una postura di altero disprezzo a quella di una salina immobilità.

Colpa di un pensiero che l'aveva sorpresa mentre stava parlando e che subito sottopose alla Tina.

«Ma è ancora viva?»

Perché se lo era doveva anche lei avere una certa età.

E poi a seguire un altro pensiero, un'altra domanda ancora più urgente, più intrigante.

«Come mai mi hai chiesto di lei?»

La conosceva?

«No», rispose la Tina.

L'aveva mai vista?

Nemmeno.

E allora...

A quel punto la Tina, senza troppo rivelare dei suoi pensieri, disse all'ex infermiera della lettera recapitata per sbaglio.

«Nemmeno chi l'ha scritta», disse allora l'ex infermiera, «deve conoscerla troppo bene.»

Da tempo ormai la «dottoressa Dominetti» non abitava più ad Acquaseria. Dopo gli anni passati in una casetta abbastanza isolata che, non si sa perché, chiamavano la Villa, per quanto ne sapeva lei si era trasferita dalle parti del lago di Piano.

Sul volto della Tina comparve un sorriso di circostanza a titolo di ringraziamento per le spiegazioni. E approfittò del momento di silenzio che seguì per riaprire, fatto un mezzo giro attorno alla sua ospite, la porta di casa.

Gesto inequivocabile.

Che bloccò all'improvviso tutta una serie di domande e curiosità che si stavano infilando una dietro l'altra sulla lingua dell'ex infermiera.

Se era così che si trattava una persona che si era sempre dimostrata disponibile...

Il viso della Supposta assunse il colore della dignità offesa, rosa antico a chiazze.

Poi si girò con un dietro front quasi militare e prese la via di casa.

97.

Nemmeno spettabile.

Spettabile maresciallo... sillabò il Fantarini.

Ma va'!

Aveva un sapore commerciale, come se si stesse rivolgendo a una ditta e non al suo comandante.

Sicuro come la morte che il Pezzati si sarebbe messo a ridere qualora avesse ricevuto uno scritto che partiva così.

Spettabile non andava bene.

Egregio, allora.

Egregio maresciallo...

98.

Il vento aveva ripreso forza, come spesso capita quando si avvicina la fine della giornata. Una giornata di merda per Biagio Trùfa Riffa, che di merda avrebbe dovuto spalarne ancora un bel po'.

Il Ciba Pompista, presso la cui officina il Viatico aveva scaricato il camioncino, gli aveva dato pessime notizie.

«A parte le quattro gomme che sono già una bella spesa», aveva detto. A parte quelle, mentre lo aspettava, s'era permesso di dare un'occhiata anche al motore, capire perché non era più ripartito.

«C'è la distribuzione da rifare», aveva detto.

«Come, la distribuzione?» era esploso il Riffa.

«La distribuzione», aveva confermato il Pompista, «lo sai cos'è no?»

«Lo so, cristo!» aveva confermato il Riffa.

Era una spesa della madonna!

«Appunto», aveva a sua volta concordato il Pompista. Quindi considerate le gomme, la distribuzione, lo stato della carrozzeria del camioncino, gli conveniva darlo dentro a uno sfasciacarrozze e pensare a comperarne uno nuovo.

«Sì, e i soldi me li dai te», aveva risposto il Riffa.

Il Pompista l'aveva guardato sorridendo.

«Poverino...»

«Te scherza», aveva mormorato il Riffa, «ma va' che sono nella merda fino a qui», e aveva alzato la mano fino a toccarsi il mento.

99.

Più su, secondo il maresciallo Pezzati.

«Fin sopra i capelli, se crede di prendermi in giro», aveva specificato parlando con il carabiniere Fantarini dopo averlo messo al corrente dei fatti della notte precedente: non c'erano prove certe, ma era giunto il momento di fare chiarezza.

«Se ti ho informato», disse il Pezzati al Fantarini, «è perché da questo momento in avanti non si gioca più.»

Acqua in bocca con chiunque, soprattutto col Riffa, da andare a prendere al volo invece, riportarlo in caserma e farsi raccontare per filo e per segno quello che lui e l'altro fringuello avevano fatto la sera prima.

Quando se lo trovò davanti, il Pezzati ripeté la frase.

«Vedi di raccontarmela giusta», disse, «se no ti infilo nella merda fin sopra i capelli.»

«Per quello che ne so io...» cominciò a dire il Riffa.

Poi si fermò e riprese.

«Cioè, fino a quando siamo rimasti insieme...»

«Perché, vi siete separati?» aggredì il Pezzati. «Dov'è andato il tuo socio?»

Il Riffa si strinse nelle spalle.

Doveva o no dire quello che gli era venuto in mente?

Si sarebbe incazzato il maresciallo se avesse detto quello che gli era venuto in mente?

D'altronde, se aveva appena dichiarato che si erano separati, come faceva a sapere dove fosse andato a finire il Dubbio?

La cosa più logica non sarebbe stata quella di chiederlo all'interessato?

«Mi scusi, maresciallo», rischiò il Riffa, «ma perché non lo chiede a lui?»

«Tu sai dov'è?»

100.

Nel bosco, come un latitante.

Gli era sembrata la cosa migliore da fare.

Si era allontanato dalla riva e aveva camminato per un po' sulla strada verso Plesio. A un certo punto l'aveva lasciata e s'era buttato nei prati a monte, superate le vigne e s'era inoltrato nel bosco ritornando indietro sino a quando s'era trovato sopra l'abitato di Acquaseria. Una volta lì, s'era seduto, appoggiato a una quercia perché ormai non doveva fare altro che aspettare. Aspettare che passasse un po' di tempo, calasse un po' di buio.

Dopodiché avrebbe attuato il suo piano.

Un piano tutt'altro che perfetto, sulla cui riuscita lui stesso non avrebbe scommesso. Ma non aveva altra scelta o almeno così gli pareva e quindi non poteva fare altrimenti.

Solo una volta raggiunto il comodo rifugio del bosco, il Dubbio lasciò piena libertà a un altro pensiero che sino ad allora aveva ricacciato: sua madre.

Chissà!

Chissà come stava, cosa faceva, cosa stava pensando.

Se avesse potuto, in quell'istante, col pensiero di sua madre che aveva preso il sopravvento, il Dubbio avrebbe dato qualunque cosa pur di averle dato ascolto quando gli consigliava di prendersi un lavoro normale purchessia, fosse al cotonificio o altrove.

«Hai bisogno di qualcuno che ti stia vicino», gli aveva spesso detto.

Per lavorare in proprio bisognava essere furbi e fortunati.

E lui forse non lo era?

Le aveva sempre risposto così.

Ma adesso, nascosto dentro un bosco verso le cinque di un pomeriggio di luglio, ad aspettare che venisse un po' buio per scendere in paese e mettere in atto il suo piano, più che processare la sua furbizia, temeva di non essere abbastanza fortunato.

Certo, perché, se non fosse riuscito a beccare quella Tina?

Oppure, se si fosse spaventata e si fosse messa a gridare?

Era un rischio, una puntata secca, rosso o nero.

Un rischio, ma lo doveva correre.

101.

Con egregio – Egregio maresciallo virgola a capo – al Fantarini parve di aver risolto il problema, sentì che non avrebbe corso rischi di sorta.

Tanto per sentirsi confermato nella decisione presa, volle consultare il pressoché intonso vocabolario della lingua italiana dono, com'era scritto in esergo a caratteri simil gotici, del maestro Fiorentino Crispini a certo maresciallo Ernesto Maccadò.

Egregio, egregio, egregio...

«Che esce dall'ordinario, che è singolare, eccellente...»

Perfetto, ragionò il carabiniere Fantarini.

L'occhio però gli cadde sopra i sinonimi.

Distinto, esimio.

Mica male neanche quelli.

Egregio maresciallo?

Esimio maresciallo?

Distinto maresciallo?

102.

Per quanto fosse in casa da sola e nessuno la potesse vedere, Maria Teresa Supposta non modificò di una virgola la mimica dell'offesa.

Offesa davvero.

Usata.

Da quella ragazzetta che sino a poco prima le era sempre sembrata tanto diversa dalla maggior parte degli abitanti di quel paese e invece le aveva appena dimostrato di essere gretta tale e quale.

E anche un po' falsuccia, se la vogliamo dire tutta.

In fin dei conti lei era pur sempre la figlia del professor Amedeo Modesto Supposta, che aveva tanto di targa nell'atrio dell'ospedale Sant'Anna di Como, uomo di specchiate virtù e sconfinata generosità, e nessuno poteva trattarla come se fosse una sciacquetta, un'impicciona, un gazzettino padano. Ecco, stava pensando la ex infermiera, mentre, per calmare il nervoso, passava in rassegna i locali della villetta, scorrendo con gli occhi le pareti che grondavano di glorie passate, attestati di benemerenza, fotografie, alcune lettere autografe: anche lei, come suo padre, aveva peccato di ge-ne-ro-si-tà!

Non era forse vero che, ogniqualvolta quella l'aveva chiamata, lei aveva sempre risposto presente?

Come quella mattina, come quel pomeriggio.

Ed ecco la paga.

Liquidata come una serva, come una che orecchia i discorsi dei padroni.

Be', ragionò tra sé la Supposta, forse era venuto il momento di mettere a posto le cose, ristabilire le distanze. In sostanza dare una lezioncina a quella presuntuosetta.

Alla prima occasione: «Mi spiace cara, non posso».

Ripeté la frase ad alta voce mentre era in cucina. Una cucina intonsa, senza nessun profumo particolare nell'aria.

Per forza, per andare incontro alle richieste della Tina aveva saltato il pranzo, neanche un bicchiere d'acqua aveva bevuto. E, nonostante ciò, forse per via della rabbia, non avvertiva un filo di fame.

Si avvicinò all'acquaio e aprì il rubinetto.

Quante volte l'aveva sentito ripetere da suo padre a lei e alle sue pazienti e quante volte di conseguenza l'aveva detto anche lei.

«Siamo esseri fatti perlopiù d'acqua!»

Pazienza se per qualche giorno non si mangiava, ma bere acqua sempre, comunquc, anche se non si avvertiva la sete...

L'acqua correva rumorosa, un dito sotto il getto l'ex infermiera attendeva che raggiungesse il giusto grado di freschezza, ripetendo mentalmente la frase della sua vendetta.

«Invece no!» sbottò all'improvviso, portandosi l'indice alle labbra.

Così, no!

Ciò che avrebbe risposto alla Tina non doveva nemmeno per sbaglio sembrare una vendetta, così facendo avrebbe giustificato il sospetto che lei voleva ficcare il naso negli affari suoi e del commenda.

Che era tutto sommato vero, ma non si doveva capire.

Doveva invece negarsi, ma con signorilità.

Una buona, inattaccabile scusa ci voleva. In modo che la ragazza non potesse sospettare che lei se la fosse presa e si trovasse comunque nella situazione di doversi arrangiare da sola.

Così avrebbe capito.

La Supposta, assorta nel pensiero, richiuse il rubinetto senza bere.

Bastava un mal di testa oppure un mal di pancia...

Qualcosa di non troppo grave, ovvio, perché si sapeva, anche se la scienza non riusciva a spiegarne il perché, che a chiamarle certe malattie rispondevano: «Presenti!».

Una cistite anche.

E infatti...

Sul far della sera la sentì arrivare.

L'aveva solo pensata, mai nominata, eppure...

Non era una novità per lei, d'estate soprattutto.

Dimenticava il consiglio del padre professore, beveva poco o niente, e tac, bruciore e vai col tango!

Erano ormai le otto della sera quando l'ex infermiera raggiunse il bagno per la prima volta prevedendo di avere alle viste una notte tribolata.

Una volta che si fu accomodata sulla tazza però, Maria Teresa Supposta, lo sguardo rivolto fuori, rifletté che non tutti i mali venivano per nuocere: la finestruola del suo cesso dava proprio sulla strada, verso la casa del commenda.

Così lo vide.

Senza possibilità di errore, lui.

Ancora lì!

Che fare?

Carabinieri...

Carabinieri, oppure...

No, un momento.

Un momento, perché...

103.

La Tina s'era fatta sulla porta dopo aver sentito suonare, il giovanotto aveva subito gridato qualcosa.

Avesse aperto appena appena la finestrella anche l'ex infermiera in posizione avrebbe sentito qualcosa. Poi, superato il cancelletto, lui era andato verso la ragazza che poi... poi l'aveva addirittura fatto entrare in casa.

Quindi la porta s'era chiusa, fine del cinema.

Carabinieri, pensò allora Maria Teresa Supposta.

Adesso carabinieri.

E partì di volata dimenticando per un istante che aveva le mutande a mezza gamba. Le ridotte dimensioni del suo bagno le impedirono di finire in terra lunga quant'era, se la cavò con una zuccata contro lo stipite della porta. Ma nelle condizioni in cui era non avvertì dolore e se mai bruciava ancora la cistite, prima di ogni altra cosa veniva il suo dovere di cittadina. Il telefono l'avrebbe trovato anche a occhi chiusi, pure il numero della caserma sarebbe riuscita a comporre senza guardare dove infilava l'indice.

«Non so se vi interessa ma quel giovane, quello di stamattina, è ancora qui», disse al telefono riferendo a un carabiniere, Firrìa o chi per esso. Non solo. Al momento si trovava in compagnia di quell'innocentina della ragazza. No, non aveva forzato porte o finestre. L'aveva fatto entrare lei, sua sponte, come fosse un amico, un conoscente.

«Se mi capisce.»

Non sembrava strano?

104.

Il carabiniere Fantarini aveva deciso.

Né esimio, distinto o egregio, niente del genere.

Maresciallo, virgola e a capo.

Attacco maschio, senza fronzoli, degno dell'Arma.

Pacificato circa l'incipit della richiesta che avrebbe inoltrato al Pezzati cominciò a ripassare il canto primaverile del Turdus iliacus, altrimenti noto come tordo sassello.

Era quello su cui si sentiva meno sicuro. Su merlo e tordo bottaccio non temeva rivali. Sul sassello invece...

Il telefono lo interruppe, quasi a volersi mettere in gara.

«Carabinieri Bellano.»

«Adesso ve lo venite a prendere», disse il maresciallo Alborati dopo essersi presentato e aver telegrafato il motivo della chiamata, «se no lo tolgo dalle spese con le mie stesse mani.»

«Intende subito, maresciallo?» chiese il Fantarini.

«Intendo anche prima di subito», rispose quello.

«Vado immediatamente ad avvisare il signor maresciallo», comunicò il Fantarini.

E salendo verso l'appartamento del superiore riprese il canto del tordo sassello interrompendosi sulla porta di casa e preparandosi a rispondere alla domanda che il Pezzati gli avrebbe sicuramente fatto, considerata l'ora quasi notturna.

«Novità?»

«Il Dubbio è in gabbia», rispose il Fantarini, ancora suggestionato dal canto primaverile del Turdus iliacus.

105.

Al sentir suonare il campanello una seconda volta nel giro di mezz'ora, la Tina aveva pensato alla Maria Teresa Supposta.

Un po' se l'aspettava.

Aveva capito che quella se n'era andata con la cappella in piedi, come si diceva.

Offesa, insomma.

In parte era stata colpa sua, con l'accenno alla lettera indirizzata alla Dominetti doveva aver innescato l'inquisizione, evocato cose che avevano fatto la punta alla curiosità della sua vicina.

Nella situazione in cui era però, oltre a non avere intenzione di ritornare sull'argomento, non poteva nemmeno permetterle di entrare in casa.

Le spiaceva doverla trattare così, ma non poteva fare altro: aprire appena appena la porta e, alla richiesta della Supposta che, ne era certa, approfittando degli eventi della giornata era tornata lì per chiedere se le necessitasse qualcosa per affrontare la notte, rispondere grazie no, e mentire dicendo che il commenda era un po' agitato e quindi non aveva il tempo di darle retta.

«Carabinieri, aprite», era stata invece la risposta quando aveva chiesto chi fosse.

Carabinieri, e proprio alla porta di casa, perché il Dubbio una volta che lei gli aveva aperto il cancelletto non l'aveva richiuso.

Il commenda, meno male, era già di sopra a riposare.

Per una volta la Tina aveva seguito il consiglio del dottore e gli aveva somministrato certe goccine che l'aiutavano a dormire.

Il Dubbio, al sentire che c'erano i carabinieri, aveva fatto una mossa.

«Guai a te se ti muovi», l'aveva fulminato la ragazza.

Poi aveva aperto.

Prima un'occhiata ai due militari, il già noto Firrìa e il maresciallo Alborati che nonostante l'ingessatura, ma con l'aiuto di un bastone, non aveva voluto mancare alla sorpresa. Una seconda, rapida, verso la casa dell'ex infermiera, giusto in tempo per vedere oscurarsi la finestrella del bagno.

«Accomodatevi», li aveva poi invitati la Tina.

E, prima ancora che potessero aprire la bocca per dire qualcosa: «Qualunque cosa pensate non è quella», aveva aggiunto.

106.

Adesso o mai più!, s'era detto per l'ennesima volta il Dubbio prima di suonare al cancelletto di casa del commenda.

Poi aveva sparato il colpo.

Di rimando la Tina s'era chiesta cosa diavolo avesse gridato quello.

Le era sembrato di capire.

Forse aveva anche capito bene.

Ma era una cosa che non stava né in cielo né in terra.

La sua amica era morta?

In effetti era proprio quello che il Dubbio aveva gridato.

«La tua amica è morta.»

O la va o la spacca.

O la Tina si sarebbe messa a gridare che c'era un folle alla porta di casa oppure sarebbe rimasta talmente sciocccata dalla sua uscita da permettergli di spiegarsi meglio.

«Giuro che l'ho vista», aveva aggiunto il Dubbio, gridando un po' meno ma comunque facendosi sentire.

Ed era stato grazie a quell'aggiunta che la Tina aveva intuito la stranezza della situazione.

Di più, la stranezza di quel momento.

L'assurdità di ciò che il giovanotto aveva gridato.

Intuizione, come per la faccenda della lettera.

Lei sola sapeva, era certa, che il commenda aveva cominciato a chiudersi in sé dopo aver ricevuto quella lettera.

Così in quel momento aveva intuito che quel giovanotto era una specie di postino: aveva un messaggio da consegnare e la mattina aveva considerato che il maresciallo Alborati non ne fosse il destinatario corretto.

Certo, quello che il giovanotto aveva gridato e che le sue orecchie avevano udito era una follia vera e propria.

Però aveva lasciato che facesse qualche passo verso di lei, le era sembrato calmo, non aveva niente del pazzo scatenato, anzi, le aveva dato l'idea che fosse addirittura impaurito.

«Fermati lì», gli aveva detto quando era stato a portata di voce normale.

Aveva già visto la finestrella del cesso della sua dirimpettaia illuminata, sapeva di avere in lei un'alleata pronta all'azione, le sarebbe bastato gridare.

«Ma cosa stai dicendo?» aveva chiesto.

Il Dubbio si era sentito quasi mancare. Tutti gli eventi della giornata si erano accumulati nelle gambe, la testa si era svuotata, tra l'altro non aveva mangiato niente.

La Tina ne aveva colto il malessere, anche un filo di disperazione.

«Non lo so», aveva risposto lui, «ma mi devi aiutare.»

Si erano guardati.

La finestrella del cesso dell'ex infermiera era sempre illuminata.

«Vieni dentro», aveva infine deciso la Tina.

Quando l'Alborati aveva bussato alla porta, il Dubbio aveva tra le mani una fotografia della Valeria insieme con la Tina, lo sfondo di sassi e di lago.

Stava per dire che era proprio lei quella che aveva trovato la notte passata e poi trainato sulla riva di Morcate.

Gli era toccato dirlo ai carabinieri.

107.

Di andare a rompere i coglioni a quell'ora di notte al Vergonese per chiedergli conferma che sua figlia, la figlia che lui in persona aveva accompagnato all'aeroporto, la figlia che quella mattina s'era anche fermata una decina di minuti fuori da quella stessa casa per salutare la lì presente Tina, fosse viva e vegeta, il maresciallo Alborati non aveva nessuna voglia.

«Di barzellette sui carabinieri ce ne sono fin troppe», aveva dichiarato.

«La barzelletta è quella lì», aveva affermato il Pezzati accennando al Dubbio.

L'Ernesto era pallido.

Era impallidito quando aveva visto entrare i carabinieri. Aveva deposto la fotografia su un tavolino e s'era alzato in piedi anche se nessuno glielo aveva ordinato.

La Tina invece era bella rossa in viso, si sentiva calda.

S'era scaldata via via mentre, balbettando un po', aveva detto ai due marescialli che la Valeria l'aveva vista quella mattina, quando s'era fermata a salutarla prima di ripartire con suo padre.

Quindi...

«Quindi niente», l'aveva chiusa il maresciallo Pezzati.

Era ora di togliere le tende e tornare a casa.

«Nel frattempo», aveva proseguito rivolgendosi al Dubbio, «visto che grazie a te abbiamo da fare un po' di strada assieme ti spiego cosa significa beccarsi una bella denuncia per procurato allarme.»

Cosa che, aveva aggiunto con malizia, non avrebbe certo fatto una bella impressione a chi lo doveva giudicare per la faccenda del quadro.

All'uscita del maresciallo, l'Ernesto era impallidito ancora di più, per quanto sembrasse impossibile.

O forse era sembrato così solo alla Tina alla quale il Dubbio si era rivolto con un'occhiata prima di uscire.

Per chiederle scusa del trambusto che le aveva procurato, del disagio di quella lunga giornata?

108.

Più dell'onor poté il digiuno.

Di notizie.

Nonostante quanto l'immancabile malalingua dicesse, Maria Teresa Supposta non era una pettegola per il solo fatto di non avere e non avere avuto un marito. Nemmeno la scalfivano certi sguardi tra l'ironico e il pietoso.

Viveva sola e stava bene così.

E conosceva i suoi diritti.

Tra i tanti, quello alla tranquillità.

Quindi se la sera prima aveva spento la luce del cesso ma era rimasta al buio a controllare quello che succedeva fuori e, avesse potuto, magari anche dentro la casa del commenda, non era certo perché fosse una spiona. Piuttosto perché tutto l'andirivieni di carabinieri e facce estranee l'aveva agitata, predisponendola a un sonno fitto di incubi e, in sostanza, minando quella tranquillità alla quale sentiva di avere diritto.

E da tale certezza discendeva un altro diritto, quello di informarsi per capire.

Quindi la mattina seguente, mettendo da parte l'onore offeso dai modi sbrigativi che la Tina aveva usato con lei, decise di far visita alla ragazza, forte delle sue buone ragioni.

109.

La frizione della camionetta grattava, quasi a ogni cambio di marcia.

Era ora di cambiarla.

Non era invece l'ora, il momento di farlo presente al maresciallo Pezzati. Il Fantarini infatti non aveva detto niente la sera prima pur se aveva temuto che un viaggio così lungo, da Bellano a Menaggio e ritorno, potesse risultare fatale.

Completata l'andata con successo, aveva affrontato con molta cautela il ritorno in un certo senso adeguandosi all'ordine che il maresciallo aveva dato al Dubbio dopo averlo preso in consegna e alla modalità con la quale l'Ernesto aveva ubbidito.

L'ordine: dirgli tutto, passo dopo passo, minuto dopo minuto, non dimenticare niente, neanche una virgola, nemmeno un sospiro di ciò che aveva fatto il giorno prima.

«Voglio scendere da questa cazzo di camionetta sapendo ogni cosa!»

Il Dubbio aveva obbedito, raccontando a spizzichi e bocconi, per la necessità di non dimenticare proprio niente, tant'è che aveva riferito perfino il totale del conto pagato su al crotto.

Giunti a Bellano, per la soddisfazione il Fantarini aveva ripreso a fischiettare in sordina e s'era fermato, senza spegnere il motore, in piazza Grossi, attendendo ordini.

Il maresciallo stava riflettendo circa il da fare.

Cosa fare del Dubbio soprattutto, quando quest'ultimo se n'era uscito con una bella frase che era calata come una fucilata all'interno dell'abitacolo, tant'è che il carabiniere Fantarini aveva smesso di fischiettare, proprio come se il fringuello che stava imitando fosse stato colpito e abbattuto.

«Però potrei anche essermi sbagliato.»

C'era stato un istante ancora di silenzio durante il quale il maresciallo Pezzati s'era rimesso il cappello che sino ad allora aveva tenuto sulle ginocchia.

Poi l'eruzione dalla sua gola.

«Sbagliato?»

Al Fantarini era sembrato che le pareti della camionetta rispondessero con un'eco.

Ma su cosa?

Cosa voleva dire con «essermi sbagliato»?

Intendeva che non era un cadavere quello che aveva dichiarato di aver trainato a riva?

Oppure adesso era incerto sull'identità dello stesso?

«Allora?»

Allora, niente.

Il Dubbio aveva mormorato un «Non lo so» che anche al papa avrebbe fatto perdere la pazienza.

«Va bene», aveva deciso infine il Pezzati.

Il Dubbio in caserma anziché a casa come era stato vicino a decidere.

E loro due a prendere un'altra volta il Riffa.

«Vediamo un po' se insieme riuscite a convincermi che non siete da manicomio.»

«Subito?» aveva chiesto il carabiniere Fantarini rendendosi conto all'istante che avrebbe fatto meglio a tacere.

«Ma no», aveva risposto infatti il maresciallo, «con tutto comodo, domani, anche dopo...»

110.

Il Riffa abitava con una zia, Infantina, sorella della madre naturale.

L'Infantina, zitella, se l'era preso in casa da quando il padre Sturzio Riffa, emigrato in Francia per lavoro, da un certo momento in avanti non aveva fatto più avere notizie di sé e men che meno spedito soldi alla famiglia, cosa che aveva fatto ammalare di malinconia la moglie Pennica al punto che si era reso necessario ricoverarla per periodi sempre più lunghi presso il manicomio di Como, dove ormai era una residente fissa.

«Non lo si può svegliare», aveva detto l'Infantina ai due quando se li era trovati davanti.

«Ha il sonno così duro?» aveva chiesto il Pezzati che, a dispetto del sorrisetto, era nervoso come una biscia.

«No», aveva ribattuto l'Infantina.

Forse si era spiegata male.

Il fatto era che quando il Biagetto...

Maresciallo e carabiniere si scambiarono uno sguardo.

Biagetto?

«Sì», aveva confermato la donna.

Lo chiamava così sin da quando se la faceva ancora addosso e non aveva mai smesso, anche se a lui adesso dava un po' fastidio.

Però, tornando al punto, il fatto era che quando il Biagetto beveva come aveva fatto quel pomeriggio, poi piombava in un sonno che non si riusciva a interrompere. Era successo così anche quel giorno, al punto che s'era addormentato sulle scale di casa e sarebbe stato ancora lì se, cara grazia!, i vicini non le avessero dato una mano a portarlo dentro.

«Ma non fa così tutti i giorni», aveva aggiunto l'Infantina.

Si comportava in quella maniera solo quando gli capitava qualche guaio, ma di quelli grossi, o qualche dispiacere.

«Presempio», aveva continuato l'Infantina.

Era successo quando un disgraziato gli aveva detto che non era vero che sua mamma era in un ospedale lontano per curarsi il cuore ma era in un posto dove la tenevano chiusa a chiave perché era matta da legare.

E pensare che aveva solo quindici anni, e quella volta era finito in ospedale perché nemmeno il dottore aveva capito che era ubriaco marcio.

O sennò era capitato anche quando si era fatto prestare la moto da un suo amico e l'aveva sfasciata andando a finire contro un muro. Lui non s'era fatto quasi niente ma il suo amico gli aveva promesso che l'avrebbe conciato come la moto, che era da buttare via, se non gliel'avesse ricomprata.

E un'altra volta, quando faceva la naja. Aveva perso il treno e non era riuscito a rientrare in caserma per tempo. S'era così spaventato, poveretto!, diceva che l'avrebbero messo sotto processo e poi in galera.

«Per fortuna, il maresciallo», aveva spiegato l'Infantina, «quello prima di voi...»

L'altro maresciallo insomma, il cui nome le scappava, era stato buono e aveva convinto il dottore a fare un certificato di malattia, così non era successo niente.

«Sennò...» era sembrata decisa a proseguire la donna quando finalmente qualcosa l'aveva bloccata.

Un'intuizione folgorante, la constatazione che in quel momento aveva sotto gli occhi un altro maresciallo con addirittura un carabiniere al seguito.

«Ma ha fatto qualcosa?» aveva allora chiesto.

Il Pezzati aveva lasciato passare qualche secondo prima di aprire la bocca.

«Diglielo tu», aveva poi detto al Fantarini.

«È come il canto della beccaccia», aveva risposto questi.

Né il Pezzati né l'Infantina avevano capito l'allusione.

Ma era semplice, era stata la spiegazione del carabiniere: nessuno lo conosceva, nessuno l'aveva mai sentito.

Un mistero quindi, no?

111.

«Siamo svegli Biagetto?» chiese il maresciallo Pezzati.

«Non ti avrò svegliata?» fece eco, sull'altra sponda del lago, Maria Teresa Supposta.

«Svegliati, Ernesto», concluse la Canterina.

112.

Sveglio il Riffa?

Sì, nel senso che non stava dormendo.

Ma era ancora rintronato da tutto ciò che gli era capitato di vedere prima, e poi da tutto il bere del pomeriggio precedente.

«Bene», proseguì il maresciallo accontentandosi di un cenno del capo quale risposta, «perché così mi saprai spiegare che razza di giochetto avevate in mente tu e il tuo socio Ernesto Livera detto Dubbio.»

Il Riffa eresse il capo.

Quale giochetto?

Poi piegò la testa di lato.

Non è che il maresciallo fosse andato a pensare che con la storia del camioncino e delle scarpe c'entrasse lui?

Il Pezzati intese pur senza che quello avesse detto una parola.

«Lascia perdere il camioncino, Biagetto. Per questa volta sono convinto che tu non c'entri. Intendevo l'altra faccenda.»

La fronte del Riffa si corrugò.

Quale?

«Pensaci bene.»

Il Riffa strinse le palpebre.

«Veramente...» fu la sua prima parola.

«Proprio non ti viene in mente?»

La meraviglia calò sul viso del Riffa.

Che ieri sera, mentre era in bambola come fosse su un

calcinculo, avesse fatto qualcosa di cui ora non ricordava una cippa?

«No», fece il maresciallo.

Nel pomeriggio di venerdì, la gita al crotto...

«Non saprei...» borbottò il Riffa.

«Non sai proprio niente di un cadavere che il tuo amico avrebbe trovato in mezzo al lago e poi trascinato a riva? Cadavere di cui non c'è traccia alcuna e che apparterrebbe a una persona che è stata in tua compagnia sino a tarda ora e che tu saresti stato l'ultimo a vedere?»

«Cadavere?» fu appena in grado di mormorare il Riffa.

Bon, abboccato, fu il pensiero del Pezzati vedendo planare sul viso del giovanotto l'espressione attonita di certe foto segnaletiche.

113.

Svegliata?

Ma se era dalle cinque, forse anche prima, che era in piedi!

La Tina avrebbe volentieri risposto alla ex infermiera usando il tono con cui il pensiero era nato. Ma sua madre stava ancora così così, l'aveva vista una mezz'oretta scappando via da casa del commenda e ritornando sul fare dell'alba, non poteva giocarsi l'aiuto della Supposta.

Così aveva dovuto stendere la cera sulla lingua.

Alla domanda: «Ti disturbo?».

«No.»

Alla domanda: «Posso parlarti un minuto?».

«Certo», rispose, cassando il «No» che premeva per uscirle di bocca.

Quindi: «Venga, si accomodi».

Però, che non si illudesse di tornare sui fatti del giorno prima.

Si accomodasse pure lì in salotto che intanto andava a prepararle un bel caffè.

Che la Supposta lo volesse o meno il bel caffè, la Tina non stette nemmeno a sentire la risposta, era già in cucina a mettere su la caffettiera. Intanto pensava alle chiacchiere con le quali avrebbe potuto intrattenere l'ospite. Chiacchiere fatue che la tenessero lontana dalle curiosità che di sicuro l'avevano spinta lì e facessero trascorrere quel quarto d'ora di cortesia dopo di che avrebbe potuto salutarla senza, sperava, offenderla.

Vassoio in mano, su cui fumavano due tazzine colme di caffè, rientrò in salotto, pronta a sostenere eventuali schermaglie verbali.

E giudicò un colpo di fortuna quello che vide, Maria Teresa Supposta con in mano la fotografia che il Dubbio s'era fatto mostrare la sera prima e che lei aveva dimenticato sul divanetto.

Alla Tina l'occasione parve d'oro, la colse al volo.

«È di soli tre anni fa ma sembra che sia passato un sacco di tempo», disse riferendosi alla fotografia.

Parlare del tempo con una persona che come l'ex infermiera aveva già le sue belle primavere era un sistema rodato per spingerla a rievocare gioventù e imprese del passato, standо alla larga dalle tristezze del presente: era ciò che la Tina voleva.

Banale, la Tina non si fermò: «Volano gli anni!».

Poi, senza attendere commenti, spiegò.

A quel tempo lei non lavorava ancora in casa del commenda e la Valeria, che sino a quel momento aveva sempre portato i capelli a caschetto, aveva deciso di lasciarseli crescere.

«Proprio dopo essersi vista in quella foto», aggiunse la Tina.

La Supposta si chinò verso il tavolino per zuccherare il caffè.

Due cucchiaini.

Anzi, tre.

Poi bevve un sorso di caffè, tacque, gli occhi fissi alla fotografia.

Guardava i volti.

Più quello della Tina, che sembrava ancora una bambina. Nei tratti francamente ingenui del suo viso, che i colori un po' smunti della foto accentuavano e allontanavano ancora di più nel tempo, la Supposta vedeva una sorta di predestinazione: la bella, la Valeria, da una parte già pronta a spiccare il volo, la bruttina dall'altra, pronta per una vita di sacrifici come in effetti stava accadendo. Una madre vedova e non del tutto in salute, un commenda bisognoso di assistenza quotidiana. In mezzo la gioventù della Tina che si consumava.

O bella, non era successo così anche a lei?

Ai suoi tempi si era resa conto che la scelta, se proprio lo era stata, di dedicarsi al genitore l'avrebbe condannata a una vecchiaia solitaria?

E la Tina, immaginava che forse aveva imboccato quella stessa strada?

La ragazza, preoccupata dal silenzio della Supposta che forse preludeva a una domanda precisa e alla quale non avrebbe potuto sfuggire, tornò a parlare della fotografia.

«Se la ricorda quando aveva il caschetto?»

L'ex infermiera trattenne un sospiro e prese un secondo sorso di caffè.

«Non credo», rispose svelando una certa dolcezza.

Usciva poco di casa, giusto il minimo necessario.

«E poi voi giovani crescete, cambiate così in fretta...»

La Tina sorrise.

«E magari lei è stata la prima ad averla tra le mani», disse.

«Cioè?» chiese l'ex infermiera.

La Tina temette di aver detto qualcosa di offensivo.

«Intendevo... col mestiere che ha fatto...»

Glielo aveva detto la Valeria, più di una volta, che era nata in ospedale.

Proprio al Sant'Anna di Como.

«Dove lei e il professore lavoravate.»

Quindi aveva pensato che magari...

«Ma cosa dici», la interruppe l'ex infermiera mentre un progressivo rossore le saliva in viso.

Tra le due cadde un immediato silenzio carico di imbarazzo.

«Io...» disse la Tina tentando di romperlo.

Ma non sapeva cosa dire, non riusciva a immaginare cos'avesse detto di così grave per aver creato una situazione del genere.

«Tu non lo sai allora?» fece Maria Teresa Supposta.

Cioè, voleva dire, non sapeva niente, non...

«Cosa?» chiese la Tina.

Cosa c'era da sapere?

«E nemmeno la tua amica sa niente?» chiese ancora la ex infermiera.

114.

Niente da fare, la sera prima.

La Canterina aveva dovuto arrendersi.

«Dai mamma, domani», aveva detto il Dubbio ed era filato in camera sua con la precisa intenzione di buttarsi sul letto e dormire. Cosa che gli era riuscita, nonostante tutto.

Forse, addirittura, grazie a quello.

Troppo.

Troppe cose in un solo giorno, compresa la repentina decisione del maresciallo Pezzati di lasciarlo tornare a casa, maturata mentre rientrava in caserma dopo la visita a casa dell'Infantina.

Visto che il Riffa non sembrava ancora in grado di sostenere un confronto immediato, aveva deciso di cedere alla pietà che il dottor Lonati gli aveva raccomandato di usare nei confronti della Canterina, e di riconsegnarle il figlio.

Glielo aveva riportato di persona.

Con una precisa raccomandazione suonata con tono d'ordine.

«Non lo faccia uscire da casa e gli ricordi di tenersi pronto a tornare in caserma non appena lo farò chiamare.»

«Ma cos'ha fatto in fin dei conti?» aveva chiesto la donna.

«Se c'è qualcuno che lo sa è lui», aveva risposto il Pezzati.

«Forse», aveva subito aggiunto.

Mentre i due s'erano scambiati queste brevi battute, il Dubbio era rimasto nel corridoio alle spalle di sua madre, senza battere ciglio.

Chiusa la porta, la Canterina non aveva perso tempo.

«Ma cos'è successo?»

Risposta: «Dai mamma, domani».

Una volta sul letto l'Ernesto si era addormentato nel giro di un amen.

La Canterina invece aveva passato la notte ad aspettare che venisse l'alba per tornare dal figlio a chiedergli se fosse sveglio.

«Sei sveglio Ernesto?»

Un occhio sì e uno no, il Dubbio rispose così.

115.

«Innanzitutto, dove hai passato la notte», sparò secco secco il maresciallo Pezzati.

«A ca...» tentò di imitarlo il Riffa.

«No», lo stoppò il maresciallo.

No.

La mattina precedente l'aveva visto scendere dal battello. Quindi si intendessero da subito.

«O me la racconti giusta oppure ti faccio passare un guaio.»

«Ma io non ho fatto niente», fu il piagnucoloso de profundis del Riffa.

«Ti ho forse mosso qualche accusa?» chiese il Pezzati.

Il Biagio deglutì.

«Ho dormito», rispose intenzionato a dire la verità.

«Riffa!» scattò il maresciallo.

Sul viso dell'ambulante scese un velo di spavento. Anche se non gli era mai piaciuto, avrebbe preferito che il maresciallo continuasse a chiamarlo Biagetto, come se fosse la versione maschile della zia Infantina. Quel passaggio brusco all'uso del cognome segnava brutto tempo in arrivo.

«Non mi prendere per il culo», spiegò infatti il Pezzati, «te lo chiedo per l'ultima volta.»

Dove aveva passato la notte tra venerdì e sabato? Come? Semmai, con chi, tanto per essere sicuro che non gli rifilasse altre balle.

«A casa di una», disse il Riffa con voce tutta nasale. «Ma so solo il nome.»

«E tu comincia a dirmi quello», consigliò il Pezzati.
«Si chiama Tina.»
Come la ragazza presso cui avevano recuperato il Dubbio la sera prima. Coincidenza?, rifletté il maresciallo.
«Di Acquaseria?» chiese quindi.
«Sì.»
«Indirizzo.»
«Non lo so.»
«Sarebbe a dire?»
Il Riffa si strinse nelle spalle.
«Che prima dell'altra sera non la conoscevo e mi ha dato solo da dormire. Neanche in casa sua, in una specie di legnaia. Però...»
«Però?»
Al Riffa scappò un sorriso.
«Ti diverti?» chiese il Pezzati.
«Ma no», rispose il Riffa senza smettere l'espressione giuliva. Era che, anche se non sapeva l'indirizzo... non è che non se lo ricordasse, non lo sapeva proprio...
«Va bene, va' avanti.»
«Ecco, mi ricordo che mi ha fatto entrare al buio e non ha voluto che accendessi la luce per non farsi vedere da una vicina, una che abita di fronte a lei, una curiosa, che però...»
Il Riffa non contenne una risata di gola.
Il Pezzati sospirò e si grattò il collo.
«Ma cosa c'è da ridere?» chiese poi.
«Il cognome di quella», rispose il Riffa.
«Davvero? E lo vuoi dire anche a me, così ridiamo insieme?» fece il maresciallo.
«Supposta», confessò il Riffa.
Il Pezzati socchiuse gli occhi.
«Come?»
«Maresciallo, glielo avevo detto che faceva ridere», si giustificò il Riffa.

116.

Non aveva riso il professor Amedeo Modesto Supposta quella domenica, 19 aprile 1942. Quando, dopo aver pranzato insieme con la figlia Maria Teresa presso il ristorante Alla Ruota che Gira, il Vergonese gli aveva chiesto se poteva dirgli due parole in privato.

Era ormai consuetudine che, nei fine settimana di libertà, padre e figlia si dividessero tra Monza, dove la moglie del professore continuava la propria vita, e gite domenicali sul lago alla scoperta di ristoranti e panorami e l'alberghetto del Vergonese era diventata una delle tappe più frequenti. Il professore diceva che quell'angolo di lago gli piaceva in modo particolare, aveva un qualcosa in più che l'attirava lì rispetto ai tanti altri che aveva veduto e se mai, come poi sarebbe accaduto, avesse deciso di acquistare una casetta da quelle parti, sarebbe stato proprio lì.

Sulle prime il Vergonese aveva scambiato lui per un vecchio trombone che si portava a spasso la giovane amante in barba a chissà quale moglie ignara.

Poi invece l'avevano messo al corrente che, no, macché amante.

Padre e figlia.

E che padre!

Perché, se non lo sapeva, lui era il professor eccetera eccetera primario dell'eccetera eccetera.

Standro così le cose, una di quelle domeniche Alessandro Vergonese si era avvicinato al tavolo dei due e aveva chiesto al professore se, terminato il pranzo, aveva la cortesia di dedicargli qualche minuto in privato. Doveva chiedergli un consiglio, cosa delicata.

Nell'ufficio dell'albergo sulla cui porta campeggiava la scritta DIREZIONE, il Vergonese l'aveva messo al corrente di ciò che angustiava lui e sua moglie: non riuscivano ad avere figli nonostante fossero sposati già da qualche anno.

Poteva fornire loro la sua consulenza?

Il Supposta aveva risposto che ben volentieri si sarebbe occupato del caso. Aveva chiesto di poter vedere la signora, anche lì, adesso, subito.

La Maria Teresa non aveva assistito alla visita, se n'era stata quieta a godersi il sole di aprile in attesa del genitore e del relativo responso.

Che era stato quello di disporre un ricovero immediato.

Prima è meglio è, aveva detto senza mezzi termini il Supposta al Vergonese, incaricando la figlia di passare quella stessa sera dal reparto per avvisare dell'arrivo della nuova paziente.

«Se l'istinto non mi inganna», aveva detto alla figlia lungo la via del ritorno a Como, «la faccenda è seria. In sostanza quei due possono archiviare l'idea di avere dei figli.»

L'istinto non l'aveva ingannato.

Dopo una settimana di degenza in ospedale il professore aveva esposto al Vergonese le conclusioni alle quali era giunto.

Sua moglie, gli aveva detto, aveva quella che si chiamava in termini scientifici sindrome di Asherman. In pratica il suo utero era un groviglio di cicatrici, di aderenze, inadatto a ricevere e permettere lo sviluppo di un ovulo fecondato.

Era una cosa abbastanza rara, aveva spiegato. E più che una malattia era una sindrome, la conseguenza a volte di infezioni ripetute della mucosa uterina, spesso silenti, i cui disturbi le pazienti erano portate il più delle volte ad attribuire a cause tra le più varie. Il risultato però era drammatico per quanto concerneva la fertilità.

«Dopo quei fatti, per un lungo periodo non siamo più andati nel suo albergo», disse Maria Teresa Supposta.

In primo luogo era stato lo stesso professore a non volerci passare, diceva che gli sembrava di mettere in imbarazzo il Vergonese. Ma soprattutto la piega che la guerra aveva preso aveva ridimensionato la voglia di divertimento dei due. Sempre più spesso il professore passava l'intero fine settimana in ospedale mentre la figlia, se non era in servizio, si recava a Monza per far compagnia alla madre cercando inutilmente di convincerla a trasferirsi con loro a Como, città più tranquilla, per il momento almeno risparmiata dai bombardamenti.

«Fu un brutto periodo», disse la ex infermiera. «Se ci penso lo vedo privo di colori», aggiunse ridendo.

Ma, come tutti i momenti brutti, anche quello era passato.

Il sole era tornato a splendere, come si diceva.

E il professor Supposta aveva ritrovato quella voglia di lago che lo aveva infine deciso ad acquistare l'agognata casetta.

«Quindi ci trasferimmo qui finalmente», raccontò Maria Teresa Supposta.

Il giorno in cui erano andati a prendere possesso della casa appena acquistata erano passati anche dall'albergo del Vergonese per riallacciare i fili della conoscenza, il tempo ormai doveva aver medicato come solo lui sapeva fare la delusione dei due mancati genitori.

L'albergo s'era abbellito, la sala ristorante era cambiata, più grande e arredata con molto gusto. Li aveva ricevuti una giovane donna che stava dando gli ultimi tocchi ai tavoli pronti per il pranzo. Alla reception, insieme con lei, s'era presentata anche una bella bambina, bionda, sei, forse sette anni.

«È la figlia del signor Vergonese», aveva risposto la

donna a una domanda del professore su chi fosse quella bella bambina.

«Saluta, Valeria», l'aveva invitata la donna.

«È per quello che so tutto», disse in conclusione Maria Teresa Supposta.

La Tina stava guardando la tazzina del caffè, ormai freddo. E allora la Valeria da dove era arrivata? Chiese, o pensò solamente?

Se c'era qualcuno, rispose comunque la ex infermiera, che poteva sapere da dove fosse piovuta la sua amica, quella era la levatrice che operava in zona all'epoca.

«Maria Dominetti», disse la Tina.

«Sì, la "dottoressa"», confermò la Supposta.

Dottoressa, chissà perché. Forse perché era una bella donna...

«Bella, niente da dire, ma non più di tante altre», commentò la Supposta.

... e aveva un incedere imperioso, stava perlopiù sulle sue, silenziosa, uno sguardo freddo...

«La superbia fatta persona!» sintetizzò l'ex infermiera.

... dando così l'impressione di essere nata per dare ordini, come un dottore appunto, che dice quello che va fatto e chiunque, infermiera o levatrice che sia, obbedisce.

Lei non aveva mai smentito.

«Una strana persona», chiosò ancora Maria Teresa Supposta.

Tra le due scese un istante di silenzio.

Poi aprirono la bocca allo stesso tempo bloccandosi l'un l'altra.

«Dimmi», fece l'ex infermiera.

La Tina aveva ormai deciso di rivelarle quello che ricordava della lettera.

Soprattutto un particolare che non era mai riuscita a dimenticare vista la singolare coincidenza.

In quel momento il telefono suonò.

117.

«Maresciallo.»

Il carabiniere Fantarini si fermò.

Guardò l'unica parola che per il momento aveva scritto.

Spiccava.

E suonava anche bene, se si poteva dire. Nella testa di uno che leggeva aveva un bell'impatto.

«Con questa mia...» proseguì.

Adagio, senza fretta.

Occhio alla grafia.

Avrebbe potuto usare la macchina per scrivere.

Ma aveva rinunciato, questione di stile.

Quella che infine s'era approcciato a scrivere era una comunicazione privata, una richiesta personale.

Niente macchina per scrivere, nemmeno un foglio in dotazione alla caserma. Pure quello doveva essere suo e ne aveva acquistati due, si sapeva mai, nella cartolibreria del paese.

La biro, passi, era quella di servizio.

«... vengo a chiederLe la cortesia di concedermi il permesso di esentarmi dal servizio...»

Ma un grido, «Fantarini!», proveniente dall'ufficio del maresciallo l'aveva bloccato.

118.

Il maresciallo Pezzati aveva considerato con estrema calma ogni cosa, compresa la dichiarazione del Riffa che aveva fatto accomodare nell'ufficio della truppa, davanti al carabiniere Fantarini intento a proseguire nell'opera di stesura della sua richiesta e guardato a vista dall'altro militare in forza, carabiniere semplice Guizzanti.

S'era chiuso nel suo ufficio e aveva deciso che era ora di dire basta, era stato fin troppo a quel gioco, se di gioco si trattava.

Basta!

Ci voleva chiarezza. E prima di tutto doverla farla con sé stesso.

Cioè, col maresciallo che era in lui, valeva a dire con un soggetto logico e coerente, che per dovere era chiamato a perseguire reati e delinquenti e non deficienti, visionari o esaltati.

Era un'indagine quella?, si era chiesto.

No.

Poteva dimostrarlo?

Sì.

Non c'erano prove, denunce, segnalazioni ancorché anonime, non c'era un cazzo di niente che confermasse ciò che il Dubbio aveva detto dapprima al dottor Lonati e questi a lui.

Non solo, c'erano testimonianze che affermavano di aver visto quello stesso cadavere in piena salute la mattina seguente alla sua stessa morte, tanto in salute che era in partenza per Londra dove avrebbe imparato per bene l'inglese.

Al Pezzati era scappato un sorriso all'idea di un cadavere che parlava inglese.

Poi s'era ripreso.

Se una storia del genere fosse uscita da quelle mura, s'era chiesto, aveva un'idea della figura di merda che avrebbe fatto?

Però...

L'esperienza, la sua e quella di altri colleghi, gli aveva insegnato che pararsi le spalle non era mai una cattiva cosa.

Quindi...

119.

«Quindi?» chiese la Tina scombussolata per la richiesta che aveva appena ricevuto.

Il carabiniere Fantarini temette di non essersi espresso nel modo più corretto.

Aveva ancora la testa per metà rivolta alla lettera che stava compilando quando aveva ricevuto l'ordine del maresciallo.

Era arrivato a «... di esentarmi dal servizio...» ma si era bloccato.

Due perplessità.

Esentarmi!

Non era forse un po' troppo forte come verbo?

Non insinuava un che di presuntuoso, come se quello che voleva chiedere fosse un suo diritto irrinunciabile?

E poi.

«Dal servizio» oppure «da ogni servizio»?

Già, perché nel caso le cose fossero andate per il verso giusto, sarebbe stato opportuno tenersi la giornata completamente libera.

A quel punto era arrivato l'ordine del maresciallo Pezzati e lui, mollata la biro ma non il pensiero, aveva eseguito.

Probabilmente male però.

Quindi ripeté alla ragazza ciò che il maresciallo Pezzati gli aveva ordinato di comunicarle per telefono.

Stare a disposizione poiché di lì a breve...

Cioè, di lì a un po'...

Insomma, di lì a un paio d'ore circa, frizione della camionetta permettendo, sarebbe passato a prenderla per portarla presso la caserma dei Carabinieri di Bellano, dalla quale la stava chiamando, affinché rilasciasse una dichiarazione firmata volta a confermarne un'altra rilasciata da eccetera eccetera secondo la quale eccetera eccetera.

Più chiaro di così!

120.

... quindi prepararsi ad affrontare ogni eventualità il futuro avesse potuto presentargli e dimostrare a chiunque di aver agito correttamente.

Il che voleva dire verbalizzare la dichiarazione del Riffa e pure quella della ragazza che l'aveva ospitato per la notte, così da togliersi dai piedi due attori di quella bella impresa.

E guarda un po', a proposito di sorprese, cosa avevano sentito le sue orecchie quando aveva chiamato il collega Alborati per sapere prima di tutto se corrispondesse a verità che in Acquaseria abitava una persona che di nome faceva Supposta (risposta, sì, ed è pure infermiera, quando si dice il destino...), e in secondo luogo se poteva dargli l'indirizzo di una sua vicina di casa, dirimpettaia per l'esattezza, una certa Tina che abitava insieme con un commendatore del quale era una specie di assistente domestica.

«Certo che posso», aveva risposto l'Alborati.

Senza nemmeno bisogno di sfogliare la rubrica del telefono, aveva tutto sott'occhio, visto che era la stessa Tina presso il cui domicilio avevano beccato il suo concittadino.

«Il Dubbio. Lo chiamate così, no?»

E tanti saluti alla coincidenza!, era stato il pensiero del Pezzati.

«Qualcosa non va?» aveva chiesto il collega non udendo risposta.

«Tutto bene», aveva risposto il Pezzati sapendo che era vero solo fino a un certo punto.

121.

I

«Meno male», fu il primo pensiero che venne a Maria Teresa Supposta.

Erano quasi le nove e trenta della sera, la Tina aveva appena suonato alla sua porta, lei era già in vestaglia.

Non era da molto che si era preparata per andare a letto.

Per quella sera, aveva deciso, non avrebbe preso alcun sonnifero, si sentiva già abbastanza stanca, pronta al sonno.

Una stanchezza che l'aveva assalita subito dopo essere rientrata nella propria casa.

Una stanchezza non giustificata, visto che non aveva fatto altro che leggere per l'intero pomeriggio, dare un'occhiata a quell'uomo che sembrava sempre più perso chissà dove, aspettando dentro un'ipnotica malavoglia che le ore calde di quel pomeriggio di luglio passassero.

Poi la Tina era tornata e lei aveva preso la via di casa e la stanchezza l'aveva assalita. L'aveva sentita entrarle dentro dalla pianta dei piedi e risalire lentamente fino a darle una sorta di intontimento non del tutto spiacevole.

Infine, il tempo di cambiarsi ed ecco il campanello.

Di nuovo la Tina.

Dentro di sé Maria Teresa Supposta s'era augurata che la ragazza non avesse ancora bisogno del suo aiuto. Nel qual caso avrebbe declinato una scusa qualsiasi e mentre le parole, una dopo l'altra, si preparavano a uscire dalla sua bocca, aveva ascoltato quello che la Tina stava dicendo.

Era stato in quel momento che il pensiero le si era formato nella mente.

Meno male.

Poco carino, poco cristiano anche.

Meno male però.

Meno male che non fosse capitato mentre lei era lì a sostituire la Tina quando, soltanto poche ore prima, aveva dovuto allontanarsi per salire, destinazione Bellano, su una camionetta dei...

II

Carabinieri.

Poi aveva abbassato la cornetta.

Carabinieri?, aveva chiesto l'ex infermiera.

Carabinieri, aveva confermato la ragazza.

Doveva andare da loro.

Anzi, aveva corretto, sarebbero passati loro a prenderla.

Addirittura?

Sì, perché erano quelli di Bellano.

Addirittura!, aveva esclamato la Supposta insensibile alle ripetizioni.

Proprio.

E perché?

La Tina, bugia, non lo so.

Sapeva eccome.

Ma non lo voleva dire.

Meglio tacere, aveva riflettuto, che dopo essersi fatta beccare in casa col Dubbio aveva anche dato notturna ospitalità al suo socio.

Meglio deviare il discorso, suscitare compassione.

Non sapeva come dirlo quindi, era in imbarazzo ma... insomma poteva badare lei, ancora, per il tempo che sarebbe stata via, al commendatore?

Ma certo cara!, la Supposta, sempre più in credito.

Infatti: «Chissà cosa vogliono da te».

«Non ne ho idea», la Tina.

Glielo avrebbe detto al ritorno, il tempo non le sarebbe mancato, qualcosa avrebbe inventato.

«A lui...»

... il commenda...

«... dirò che mia madre non si sente molto bene.»

«Certo, meglio non agitarlo.»

La Tina aveva fatto un gran teatro di braccia sconsolate che le erano cadute lungo i fianchi.

«Non so come scusarmi per tutto questo disturbo.»

«Ma via cara, quando ci si può dare una mano...»

La Supposta aveva poi detto di darle giusto il tempo di sistemare casa, di scegliersi un libro col quale ingannare le ore visto che il commendatore non era più 'sta gran compagnia.

Poi, mentre si avviava verso casa del commenda, aveva incrociato il carabiniere Fantarini e gli aveva segnalato la meta del suo viaggio.

«È lì.»

Anche se lui non aveva chiesto niente. Aveva sorriso, già sapeva che nei paesi le notizie volano. Carino quel carabiniere, aveva giudicato la Supposta. Allegro anche, fischiettava una melodia strana. Forse musica contemporanea. Giovane poi, ventidue, ventitré anni al massimo.

«Va' tranquilla», aveva raccomandato l'ex infermiera.

«Gliela riporto tutta intera», aveva ribattuto il carabiniere.

Poi, sulla camionetta: «Parente?» aveva chiesto. «Forse zia?»

«No, vicina», aveva risposto la Tina.

«Ah!» era sbottato il Fantarini. «La famosa Supposta!»

E avevano riso. E poi chiacchierato e riso ancora. Nemmeno la frizione della camionetta aveva voluto rovinare l'atmosfera di allegria. Fossero stati tutti così, i carabinieri.

Invece, il maresciallo.

III

Sistemata la parte che riguardava il Riffa, e in attesa di archiviarla per sempre con la dichiarazione di conferma della ragazza, il Pezzati era passato al Dubbio.

Per quello gli ci era voluto il dottor Lonati.

«Dottore.»

«Maresciallo.»

Aveva risposto la signora Vittoria.

Sì, suo marito era in casa, glielo passava subito.

«Mi dica.»

Insomma, e infine, aveva attaccato il Pezzati.

Si mettesse nei suoi panni, panni da carabiniere che fino a quel momento lui per primo aveva fatto finta di dimenticare, solo perché la segnalazione del cadavere fantasma, dell'annegata in contumacia, della morta vivente o come diavolo la si volesse chiamare era arrivata da lui, persona che stimava eccetera eccetera.

«Adesso, però, basta.»

Adesso era ora di mettere le cose in chiaro.

Nero su bianco.

«Cioè?» aveva chiesto il dottore.

«Una denuncia formale.»

Se il Dubbio continuava a sostenere la sua tesi, se era convinto di ciò che aveva detto e visto.

Nero su bianco con tanto di firma.

«In caso contrario?» aveva chiesto il dottore.

In caso contrario gli offriva la possibilità di dimenticare tutto a patto che gli raccontasse la verità, lo scopo di quella fantasia.

«Dopodiché lo affido alle sue cure.»

Perché quel giovanotto aveva davvero nella testa qualcosa che non funzionava a dovere.

Il dottor Lonati aveva risposto con un «Capisco» appena percepibile e deposta la cornetta aveva guardato la moglie senza dire niente.

Vittoria Lonati l'aveva interrogato con lo sguardo.

«È incazzato», aveva risposto lui.

«Ma come parli?» l'aveva redarguito lei.

Il Lonati aveva scosso la testa e aveva compreso che quello era l'unico aggettivo per descrivere lo stato d'animo del Pezzati. Il che veniva a dire, concluse tra sé, che era proprio incazzato.

IV

Infatti.

Duro, incazzato.

Dall'atmosfera ormai rilassata della camionetta la Tina era passata a quella tesa dell'ufficio del Pezzati e s'era trovata faccia a faccia col Riffa.

«Lei lo conosce?» era partito in tromba il maresciallo.

Né buongiorno né buonasera.

E poi ancora: risponde al vero che la sera del... lo ha ospitato per la notte, presso la casa di...

«È informata circa le possibili conseguenze del dichiarare il falso?»

«Conferma di aver visto e salutato la mattina del... la sua amica Valeria Vergonese, nata il 16 aprile 1944?»

Non le aveva dato nemmeno il tempo di respirare tra una domanda e l'altra.

Sì, sì, sì.

Pure il carabiniere Fantarini, che faceva da contrappunto a domande e risposte battendo come un dannato sui tasti della macchina per scrivere, sembrava diventato un'altra persona.

Anche il Riffa.

Gli era sparita dalla faccia ogni traccia di ganasseria, non gli aveva sentito uscire dalle labbra nemmeno mezza parola dopo che, vedendola entrare, l'aveva salutata, ma era un saluto quello?, con un mezzo movimento della testa.

La Tina aveva avuto la sensazione, strana, mai provata prima, di sentirsi in colpa senza capire perché, di sentirsi osservata come se stesse nascondendo qualcosa allo sguardo di quel maresciallo che senza guardarla le aveva poi detto di rileggere bene la sua dichiarazione e, se la confermava, di firmarla dopodiché era libera di andare, poteva farla riaccompagnare oppure prendere il battello, scegliesse lei.

«Però...» le era scappato di bocca.

Il Riffa s'era appena girato verso di lei.

Il Fantarini aveva sospeso il ticchettio della macchina per scrivere.

«Però, cosa?» aveva chiesto il maresciallo Pezzati.

Sembrava che avesse parlato con lo sguardo.

La Tina aveva lasciato passare qualche secondo prima di decidersi a rispondere.

«Niente, mi scusi», aveva poi detto.

Aveva scelto il battello.

Una cosa però c'era.

Una cosa che infine sentiva di dover dire a qualcuno.

L'aveva fatto con l'ex infermiera più tardi quando era ritornata a casa del commenda ben sapendo che non avrebbe potuto sottrarsi alla curiosità della sua vicina di casa.

Circa l'accaduto se l'era cavata con una solida bugia ricamata a dovere mentre stava in prua al battello in beata solitudine.

«Niente di che», aveva detto.

Aveva solo dovuto confermare ciò che era accaduto la notte passata e che lei conosceva alla perfezione.

«Ai carabinieri di Bellano?» aveva obiettato subito la Supposta.

«Sì, certo, perché il ragazzo è di là», aveva ribattuto pronta la Tina.

Poi c'era stata quella cosa, quella che stava per dire al maresciallo. Una cosa che le girava in testa da un po' e che avrebbe detto se quel maresciallo così duro non l'avesse guardata come se volesse fulminarla.

«Cosa?» le aveva chiesto Maria Teresa Supposta.

Forse era una cosa sciocca.

Forse c'entrava, aveva detto la Tina, forse no.

Più sì che no forse.

Ma da quando aveva ricevuto quella lettera non riusciva più a dimenticarla.

«Perché, l'hai letta?» il sorriso sornione della ex infermiera.

La Tina era arrossita.

«La data», aveva poi proseguito evitando una risposta diretta.

Quella di nascita che la ragazza, quella che aveva scritto alla Dominetti, aveva specificato.

Era la stessa della Valeria.

«Il 16 aprile del 1944.»

Era strano, non sembrava anche a lei?

«Ne sei certa?» aveva chiesto Maria Teresa Supposta.

«Certissima», aveva risposto la Tina.

Sul volto della Supposta le stimmate della pura curiosità erano sparite lasciando il posto a una serietà che la Tina aveva colto al volo.

«La cosa è strana davvero», aveva mormorato l'ex infermiera.

Strana perché... perché a quell'epoca Maria Dominetti non faceva più la levatrice. Non solo, era anche sposata e di lì a poco sarebbe diventata vedova.

«Ma c'è dell'altro», aveva aggiunto la ex infermiera.

C'era un'altra cosa, un'altra stranezza in quella data.

Maria Teresa Supposta però aveva subito aggiunto che forse, forse sì, quell'ultima stranezza era una cosa sciocca. E poi non poteva dirsi sicura al cento per cento.

Avrebbe verificato, l'avrebbe tenuta al corrente.

Poi era tornata a casa, la stanchezza l'aveva assalita, s'era preparata per andare a letto, quando il campanello l'aveva richiamata alla porta e mentre la Tina le diceva, tremando e con un filo di voce, che il commendatore era morto a lei era sorto quel pensiero.

Meno male che era successo mentre in casa c'era la Tina e non lei.

122.

Quindi.

Col punto interrogativo.

«Quindi?»

La domanda aleggiava nell'aria del salotto di casa Lonati, invisibile come il profumo di lago che entrava dalla finestra aperta e quello delle Turmac fumate a mitraglia dal dottore.

Fumasse pure anche tutto il pacchetto, sembrava dire lo sguardo della moglie.

Prima di lasciarlo andare a dormire, voleva avere una risposta a quella domanda.

Durante la cena lui l'aveva messa al corrente dell'aut aut del maresciallo Pezzati.

Quindi, aveva chiesto lei, cosa aveva intenzione di fare?

Il dottore aveva risposto alla Dubbio.

«Boh!»

«Non è una risposta», aveva chiosato lei.

«Lo so.»

«Quindi?» aveva ripreso lei.

«Dimmelo tu», aveva risposto lui.

«Pronta», aveva detto Vittoria.

«In che senso?»

Nell'unico possibile.

Nel senso che, visto che glielo aveva chiesto, gli avrebbe dato la risposta.

«E sarebbe?» aveva chiesto il dottor Lonati.

«Sarebbe che si fa come ti ha detto il maresciallo.»

Il Lonati era rimasto titubante.

Forse non aveva capito bene.

«Hai capito benissimo», aveva ribadito lei.

Bisognava fare come aveva detto il maresciallo.

«Ma non mi ha detto proprio niente», aveva sorriso lui.

Cosa voleva fare sua moglie, prenderlo in giro?

«Nemmeno per sogno.»

Mai stata così seria.

Dicendogli le cose che le aveva riferito, il signor maresciallo non aveva fatto altro che lavarsi le mani circa la sorte del Dubbio, tale e quale a una specie di Ponzio Pilato, sempre ammesso che quella storia fosse vera e non piuttosto una leggenda. In ogni caso significava che lasciava a lui la scelta.

O il Dubbio metteva per iscritto ciò che diceva fosse accaduto...

«Così si condanna», sottolineò la donna, «e il maresciallo non può che procedere di conseguenza.»

... oppure ritirava ogni cosa, dicendo di essersi sbagliato, sognato, di aver voluto giocare a qualcuno, a chi?, uno scherzo di pessimo gusto...

«E la cosa finisce lì.»

Il Lonati era rimasto in silenzio. La moglie aveva insistito.

«Prova a metterti nei suoi panni», aveva detto.

In quelli del maresciallo.

Il cosiddetto cadavere in quel momento era a Londra a imparare l'inglese. Non c'era uno straccio di prova, tranne la parola del Dubbio che...

«Secondo te si è inventato tutto?» aveva chiesto il dottore.

«Non lo so», aveva risposto sua moglie.

«E io non so cosa fare», aveva ribattuto lui.

«Io sì», aveva affermato Vittoria.

Per il bene del Dubbio, ovvio.

123.

Il postino aveva già suonato tre volte e smadonnato altrettante.

Che cazzo gli costava alla gente mettere fuori dalla porta una cassetta per le lettere così che gli onesti lavoratori non dovessero perdere tempo per consegnare la posta? Peraltro, in quello specifico frangente, ci fosse anche stata, la cassetta per la posta non sarebbe servita perché aveva da consegnare una raccomandata con ricevuta di ritorno.

Quindi si attaccò al campanello col preciso intento di non mollarlo fino a che qualcuno fosse andato ad aprirgli e dargli retta.

Lo fece il vicino di casa, il Schedina.

Dalla finestra: «Allora?» gli chiese.

Fino a quando doveva andare avanti con quella musica?

«Fino a quando la Canterina non mi apre», rispose il postino.

«Se non ti apre vuol dire che non c'è», fece il vicino.

«E il Dubbio?» chiese il postino.

«Chi lo vede quello.»

Il postino tirò giù l'ennesima madonna.

«Se le devo dire qualcosa quando torna...» si mise a disposizione il Schedina.

«Grazie», accettò il postino.

Passare dalla posta in giornata per ritirare una raccomandata.

«E se poi tra tutti vi metteste delle belle cassettine per

le lettere...» non si trattenne dal suggerire mentre riprendeva il giro.

«Ma se c'è da firmare a cosa ti serve la cassetta?» obiettò il Schedina mentre il postino si allontanava.

«Voi cominciate a metterla 'sta cassetta, che tanto non va mica a male», rispose quello senza nemmeno girarsi.

124.

Con ossequio.

O forse era meglio con stima?

Il carabiniere Fantarini stava toccando con mano quanto fosse difficile, oltre che avviare e poi scrivere una lettera, anche darle una degna chiusura. Con che frase poteva concludere la sua richiesta? Non sarebbe stato meglio, pensò, evitare troppi salamelecchi, stime, ossequi eccetera eccetera che potevano indurre a pensare che dietro la richiesta ci fosse chissà cosa, e invece finirla con una frase semplice e sincera?

Per esempio...

«Ecco!» sbottò. «Sinceramente sperando che la presente richiesta venga da lei...» – Elle maiuscola! – «... da Lei accolta...»

E poi?

E poi niente, basta.

La firma.

Carabiniere Augusto Fantarini.

Firmò e rilesse.

Gli parve tutto a posto, virgole, ortografia eccetera. Adesso doveva solo consegnarla.

La imbustò.

E, senza aspettarselo, un nuovo imbarazzo sorse all'orizzonte.

Cosa scrivere sulla busta?

Mettere l'indirizzo completo come se fosse una lettera oppure...

125.

Non una lettera, una raccomandata!

Per quello, aveva spiegato il Schedina alla Canterina, non l'aveva ritirata lui, perché non poteva firmare al suo posto.

La Canterina aveva appreso la novità con un moto di spavento, il marchio dell'angoscia le era disceso sul volto.

Di ricevere posta non aveva l'abitudine. L'ultima cosa che il postino le aveva consegnato era stata la richiesta di abbonarsi a una rivista di certi missionari che operavano in Africa ed era successo prima di Natale.

In ogni caso sospettava sempre della posta.

Lettere, telegrammi, raccomandate, per lei facevano lo stesso, non portavano altro che pessime notizie. A maggior ragione in quei giorni, con l'Ernesto che forse s'era messo nei guai e che, seguendo il suo consiglio, non aveva risposto al postino, fingendo di non essere in casa.

«Chiunque arrivi», aveva detto la Canterina, «è meglio che ci sia anch'io qui con te.»

Adesso tornava dall'ufficio postale, trovato aperto per un pelo, con la raccomandata stretta al petto e un'espressione lievemente diversa. Un poco di ansia permaneva nella mimica di occhi e zigomi che sembravano tanto pronti a contrarsi nel pianto quanto invece a indirizzarsi in un sorriso di sollievo.

Tutto dipendeva dal contenuto della lettera che aveva sulla busta il marchio della Navigazione Lariana ed era indirizzata all'Egregio Signor Livera Ernesto.

Sulla via del ritorno le era venuta la tentazione di fare un passaggio presso la chiesetta di Santa Marta.

L'aveva però cassata.

Era esagerato, presuntuoso addirittura, pretendere che la sua santa d'elezione potesse influenzare ciò che ormai era scritto, mutare a suo favore una decisione che comunque era già nero su bianco.

Proseguì diritta verso casa quindi e, quando fu in vista dell'ingresso, vide sbucare all'altro capo della contrada il dottor Lonati che, presa in carico la decisione della moglie, si avviava a renderla operativa.

Al vederlo la Canterina si rabbuiò di nuovo.

Lettere, dottori… portavano solo disgrazie.

Le caddero le braccia, e pure la raccomandata.

126.

Non mettendoci niente, ragionava il carabiniere Fantarini, avrebbe avuto l'aspetto di una lettera anonima.

Qualcosa, però, ci andava scritto sulla busta.

La cosa più semplice sarebbe stata: «Maresciallo Massimino Pezzati».

O, meglio: «Egregio maresciallo Massimino Pezzati».

Ma così non assumeva il sapore di una richiesta ufficiale, una cosa che riguardava il servizio e che invece, in fondo, era solo una questione privata?

In sostanza, non era il Fantarini carabiniere che scriveva, ma era il Fantarini Augusto, normale essere umano, che chiedeva una cortesia a un altro normale essere umano che, nella vita lavorativa, era il maresciallo da cui dipendeva.

Forse... pensò il Fantarini fulminato da un'idea che lo costrinse a guardare il vuoto per qualche secondo.

Forse la cosa migliore da fare era proprio quella.

127.

«Forse la cosa migliore da fare sarebbe aprire questa benedetta raccomandata e vedere cosa c'è scritto», consigliò il dottor Lonati.

L'aveva raccolta lui da terra la busta e, dopo aver chiarito alla Canterina che era lì proprio perché aveva bisogno di parlare a lei e all'Ernesto, l'aveva seguita fino in cucina.

Il Dubbio, che aveva atteso il ritorno della madre senza mollare il letto e ogni tanto cadendo in una specie di dormiveglia, era comparso con in viso un'espressione da allocco tanto che il Lonati s'era confermato nella convinzione circa la linea da seguire e che era lì a proporre, quasi imporre, così come sua moglie aveva proposto, quasi imposto, a lui poco prima: fargli ritrattare ogni cosa, approfittare dell'offerta del Pezzati e subire le conseguenze di passare per visionario anziché quelle, penali, di una denuncia per procurato allarme o chissà che altro se avesse insistito nella sua versione.

Una volta in casa il Lonati aveva appoggiato la raccomandata proprio sopra il solito fagiano. Aveva detto di essere lì per un preciso motivo, preciso e importante. E aveva pregato la Canterina di stare calma mentre gli era sembrato meno necessario rivolgere la stessa raccomandazione al Dubbio.

Dopodiché i tre s'erano guardati senza parlare per un po': madre e figlio in attesa, il Lonati alla ricerca delle parole migliori per introdurre il discorso.

Era stato un momento in cui il tempo era sembrato fermarsi dentro o forse grazie al tubare noioso dei numerosi piccioni che abitavano i sottotetti lì in giro, un canto che si armonizzava benissimo alla temperatura delle ore del primo pomeriggio. Un momento di vaghezza quasi poetica, come se le percezioni sfumassero sino a diventare quasi inutili e la vanità dell'agire, del fare e disfare, si rivelasse nella sua sorniona ironia.

Bello lasciarsi andare a simili pensieri.

Ma il Lonati, oltre all'ambulatorio da aprire, aveva a casa anche una moglie che aspettava un solido resoconto della sua missione.

Si riscosse.

Anche perché aveva trovato le parole giuste per avviare il discorso.

Forse la cosa migliore da fare era davvero aprire quella benedetta raccomandata e vedere cosa ci fosse scritto.

128.

Non c'era altro da fare, adesso, che attendere l'occasione propizia, coglierla e quindi agire.

L'occasione giunse ancora prima di quanto se l'aspettasse.

Le tre del pomeriggio più o meno.

Il telefono.

Rispose il maresciallo e subito dopo, senza dire niente, uscì.

Fu allora che il Fantarini scattò, la lettera in mano.

Salì le scale che portavano all'appartamento occupato dal Pezzati e dalla signora Elvira. Bussò e col sorriso migliore che aveva si scusò del disturbo chiedendo poi...

«Visto che suo marito al momento è fuori per servizio...»

... se la signora poteva usargli la cortesia...

Usò quelle precise parole, «usargli la cortesia».

... di consegnare quella busta al marito.

«Così non lo disturbo sul lavoro», aggiunse.

Con un altrettanto simpatico sorriso gli rispose la marescialla.

«Ma certo.»

Che il Fantarini convolasse a nozze e quello fosse un invito?, si chiese Elvira Pezzati non appena chiusa la porta. Suo marito non s'era mai lasciato scappare niente al proposito.

In ogni caso, la busta non era sigillata.

Quindi...

129.

Alla fine la raccomandata l'aveva aperta il dottor Lonati e l'aveva letta in silenzio, sentendosi addosso gli occhi dei due.

Più quelli della Canterina in verità perché quelli del Dubbio s'erano incantati a guardare una coppia di germani che riposavano tra le canne di un laghetto sulla cerata che ricopriva la tavola.

«Hai fatto domanda di assunzione alla Navigazione?» aveva chiesto finalmente parlando.

«Sì.»

A rispondere era stata la Canterina, il Dubbio aveva alzato lo sguardo dalle anatre e l'aveva girato verso sua madre.

«D'accordo», aveva allora chiarito il Lonati, «gli dica che l'hanno assunto.»

130.

Pontilista.

In altre parole, addetto al pontile.

In altre parole ancora, doveva tirare e ritirare le passerelle, controllare il flusso dei viaggiatori che salivano e scendevano dai battelli. Per la precisione aiuto pontilista, con una proposta di assunzione temporanea, tre mesi, ed eventuale conferma definitiva nell'incarico nel momento in cui, di lì appunto a tre mesi, il titolare del posto, Ancorati Eugenio, se ne fosse andato in pensione.

Il dottor Lonati ritenne di dover informare subito il maresciallo della novità. Una volta in ambulatorio lo chiamò al telefono.

«Be', quando si dice il destino», fece il Pezzati.

Stava giusto uscendo per andare da lui.

«Ho anch'io una novità», disse.

Abbastanza grossa.

Anzi, grossa almeno quanto quella che gli aveva appena comunicato lui. Una cosa che cambiava decisamente la situazione e della quale preferiva parlargli a quattr'occhi, lontano da orecchie estranee, visto che, in fondo, a essere coinvolti erano stati principalmente loro due.

Scherzando, gli chiese di non farlo stare ad attendere in sala col rischio di far montare qualche bel pettegolezzo su di lui.

Chi cominciava prima?, chiese il maresciallo quando si trovò seduto davanti al dottore come un comune paziente d'ambulatorio.

Iniziò il Lonati, usando le stesse parole che aveva usato poco prima con la Canterina al fine di spiegare che tipo di lavoro la Navigazione stava offrendo al Dubbio e che razza di fortuna insperata fosse entrata nella loro casa.

Era quello che ci voleva!

«Non crede anche lei?» chiese il Lonati al maresciallo che aveva ascoltato senza fare una picga.

Un posto fisso, uno stipendio sicuro, orari precisi e precisi doveri.

Basta espedienti!

Proprio, ribadì, quello che ci voleva per togliere dalla testa di chiunque ubbìe, fantasie, pensieri strani e anche, parlando in qualità di medico, la medicina ideale affinché certi ricordi smettessero di sanguinare.

«Una doppia fortuna», rispose il Pezzati.

Un colpo che di rado la vita offriva due volte.

Il Lonati non capiva, il Pezzati spiegò.

«Con un procedimento penale in corso, la faccenda del quadro, si ricorda dottore?, nessuna azienda pubblica lo assumerebbe. Nei documenti che il Dubbio dovrà firmare deve dichiarare di non avere carichi pendenti. E se non lo fa s'inguaia, dichiarare il falso è reato.»

«O porc...» mormorò il Lonati.

«Alt», ordinò il Pezzati.

Il doppio colpo di culo stava proprio in quello.

Il primo era l'accettazione della domanda di assunzione.

Il secondo, ed è per quello che aveva voluto andare da lui, era il decreto di archiviazione di quella faccenda per quanto riguardava l'Ernesto.

Notizia di poche ore prima di cui lui aveva preso visione subito dopo pranzo.

Per quanto lo riguardava, il magistrato aveva scagionato l'Ernesto e proprio grazie alla confessione dell'altro, quello che la Finanza aveva beccato insieme con lui sulla barca.

Qualche sera prima infatti, a notte fonda, verso le due,

nei pressi della pizzeria Da Ciccio e Maruzzé, a Vimercate, c'era stata una rissa che aveva richiesto l'intervento dei carabinieri e portato all'arresto del sedicente Ermidio Moscarini di buona memoria e di uno dei partecipanti alla zuffa.

«Mi correggo», disse il Pezzati.

Pestaggio più che zuffa. Che aveva come oggetto lo stesso Moscarini o come altrimenti si chiamava.

Il fatto era che il Moscarini, compromesso con una banda che trafficava con ogni genere di cose, s'era assunto l'onere di prendersi in carico il quadro rubato e di consegnarlo a qualcuno che avrebbe poi provveduto a farlo arrivare oltre confine per rivenderlo a un collezionista straniero di opere d'arte sacra. Il colpo era andato storto come ben si sapeva, ma i compari pretendevano in qualche modo di incassare il mancato guadagno: la ripassata che avevano dato al Moscarini era solo un avvertimento di ciò che gli sarebbe accaduto se non avesse provveduto a farlo di tasca sua. Come, non era affar loro.

Durante l'interrogatorio conseguito all'arresto, minacciato di aggiungere il reato di rissa alla denuncia che aveva già in corso e in attesa di giudizio, il Moscarini aveva ceduto, dichiarandosi vittima e confessando la verità circa il furto del quadro, chiarendo che quello della barca non c'entrava, era solo, aveva detto, un cretinoide di cui s'era servito per farsi trasportare sull'altra sponda del lago, pensando che una traversata sull'acqua non riservasse pericoli di sorta. Ma, come aveva già detto, s'era affidato a un vero imbecille e le cose erano andate come si sapeva.

«Il suo Dubbio può ringraziare il proprio angelo custode», concluse il maresciallo Pezzati. «Non crede, dottore?»

Il Lonati non rispose subito.

Mentre il Pezzati parlava, con gli occhi della mente riviveva la scena che si era appena lasciato alle spalle in casa della Canterina.

«Quanto tempo ho per accettare?» era infatti sbottato il Dubbio quando lui gli aveva chiesto se non fosse entusiasta dell'occasione che gli si presentava.

Lo sguardo della Canterina s'era incrociato col suo.

Chi rispondeva per primo?

Aveva vinto il dottore.

«Ma sei suonato!?»

Non ci doveva pensare nemmeno un attimo.

Non solo perché nella lettera era chiaramente specificato che la direzione della Navigazione Lariana chiedeva una conferma di accettazione nel più breve tempo possibile ma anche, anzi, soprattutto perché se non avesse preso al volo l'occasione lui se ne sarebbe lavato le mani e l'avrebbe lasciato solo a vedersela con il maresciallo.

«Ti faccio da garante, lo capisci?» aveva detto il Lonati.

Ma solo a patto che accettasse quel lavoro.

In caso contrario, visto che era stato tirato in mezzo, non poteva fare altro che mettere per iscritto ciò che era accaduto la famosa notte obbligando lo stesso Pezzati a procedere d'ufficio.

«Prendere o lasciare», aveva concluso il Lonati, «adesso!»

«Prende», aveva risposto la Canterina. «Eccome se prende!»

E il Dubbio, pur se con un po' di broncio, non aveva osato dire niente.

«Bene», mormorò il maresciallo Pezzati picchiettando le dita sul cappello.

Faccenda chiusa quindi, però...

«Ma secondo lei, dottore», chiese sporgendosi un po' in avanti, «è possibile che si sia inventato tutto?»

Il Lonati si appoggiò sulla sedia.

«Difficile dirlo», rispose.

«Intende dire che potrebbe esserci qualcosa di vero?» insisté il Pezzati.

Tenendo conto, aggiunse, che allo stato non c'era nemmeno mezza segnalazione di dispersi, nessuna prova, nemmeno il più piccolo sospetto che in giro per il lago ci fosse il cadavere di una ragazza.

«Ancora più difficile dirlo», sentenziò il dottore. «Vede, maresciallo...»

Se non gli rispondeva con chiarezza non era per cattiva volontà ma perché si rendeva conto dei propri limiti, come medico e come uomo.

Forse la minaccia di lasciarlo alle prese con la responsabilità di ciò che diceva di aver visto e fatto quella notte aveva riportato il Dubbio a un senso di realtà che, per vari motivi, poteva aver perduto, sebbene temporaneamente. Non bisognava dimenticare la sua infanzia difficile e tormentata.

«E nemmeno bisogna dimenticare il fatto che, vero o falso che sia ciò che ha detto, si è comunque rivolto a me in prima persona, un medico», osservò il Lonati.

Come se qualcosa dentro di lui l'avesse spinto a rivolgersi alla persona adatta per aiutarlo.

«Un'allucinazione non è certo materia per carabinieri, non crede maresciallo?» sorrise il dottor Lonati.

«Concordo», fece il Pezzati.

«Ed ecco il mio limite», proseguì il Lonati.

Non aver intuito che, col suo rivolgersi a lui, l'Ernesto forse stava ancora vivendo dentro una specie di fantasia, un incubo...

«Qualcosa di non reale che in quel momento, a lui e solo a lui, sembrava invece tale.»

Non c'era alcuna prova infatti che confermasse ciò che il Dubbio aveva detto di aver visto e fatto quella notte.

«Tuttavia...» fece il Lonati.

Il Pezzati con lo sguardo lo invitò a proseguire.

«Tuttavia anche le mie sono solo ipotesi», concluse il dottore.

«Quindi se ho ben capito», volle riassumere il Pezzati, «il Dubbio potrebbe essersi inventato o sognato che dir si voglia tutto...»

«Considerando anche la precarietà della sua vita sino a oggi», lo interruppe il Lonati.

Al maresciallo Pezzati scappò d'istinto l'indice.

Lo puntò muovendolo in direzione del Lonati. Il dottore fece finta di niente.

«Mi sta dicendo che adesso, con un lavoro fisso che lo terrà impegnato, le... le turbe del Dubbio spariranno?»

Il Lonati allargò le braccia.

«Pretende troppo da un povero medico, maresciallo», rispose.

Poteva però garantirgli che di lì a tre giorni, quando sarebbe entrato in carica quale aiuto pontilista, non se lo sarebbe trovato troppo spesso tra i piedi, visto il paese dove l'avrebbero mandato.

«E dove sarebbe?» chiese il Pezzati.

«Acquaseria», rispose, come se confessasse, il dottor Lonati.

«Ma proprio lì?» sbottò il maresciallo.

Prendere o lasciare, rispose il viso del dottor Lonati.

131.

Il Signore dà, il Signore prende.

La frase era uscita dalle labbra della Supposta quasi senza che lei se ne accorgesse quando si era trovata in casa del Dalamonti e con la Tina tra le braccia scossa da un pianto convulso.

Poche parole pronunciate sottovoce, senza altra intenzione se non il significato, semplice e profondo allo stesso tempo, che volevano avere. E mormorandole si era commossa pure lei per l'intenso dolore che la ragazza stava provando.

«Povera cara», aveva sussurrato ancora.

Tra un singhiozzo e l'altro la Tina le aveva raccontato come il Dalamonti avesse cenato e poi si fosse fatto accompagnare in camera. Quando lei era salita per chiedere se avesse bisogno di qualcosa e augurare la buonanotte l'aveva trovato con la testa reclinata. Sembrava che dormisse, e invece...

Per tutto il tempo in cui la ragazza era stata tra le sue braccia sfogando il dolore, alla Supposta era sembrato di tornare ai tempi in cui ancora lavorava con suo padre, ai momenti in cui si era trovata nella condizione di condividere gli istanti di gioia oppure quelli di dolore, momenti in cui il suo aspetto severo, i modi spicci che facevano dire ad alcuni che avrebbe fatto meglio a nascere maschio, lasciavano spazio a un sentire tutto femminile, a una tenerezza di madre o di figlia, secondo i casi.

Quando la Tina aveva cominciato a emettere solo lunghi sospiri, la Supposta l'aveva convinta a scendere con lei nel salotto, a sedere, a lasciare a lei il compito di fare ciò che si doveva in casi come quello.

Ma, prima di riprendere i toni della donna pratica, quasi a volersi scusare di non poter fare altro poiché qualcuno doveva pur pensare ad avvisare il dottore, le onoranze funebri, i figli, le si era seduta accanto e l'aveva abbracciata, tirandola a sé.

«Vedrai che tutto piano piano si sistemerà», le aveva detto.

Il Signore dava e prendeva, anche il dolore.

132.

Il funerale del commendator Dalamonti era finito da qualche minuto e la poca gente che aveva preso parte alla cerimonia aveva lasciato il cimitero alla spicciolata.

Erano le undici del mattino, l'aria era già calda e umida, il sole, su quella sponda, cominciava a scaldare sin dalle prime ore del giorno. Il becchino e il lavorante che lo aiutava avevano abbandonato i ruoli di semplici spettatori per entrare in azione. Adesso, badile in mano, cominciarono a scandire il ritmo del lavoro.

Oplà!

Una palata di terra lui, una l'altro e la bara del commenda stava scomparendo alla vista.

Nei due giorni che avevano preceduto il funerale, Vittorio e Francesca si erano alternati a vegliare la salma del genitore. Alla Tina avevano dato la libertà di stare a casa ma era stato più il tempo che la ragazza aveva passato con l'uno o con l'altra di quello che aveva trascorso con sua madre. Dopo il primo momento di dolore acuto, la Tina aveva cominciato a percepire la sensazione di essere anche lei, al pari dei due figli del commenda, un'orfana. Anzi, le era sembrato di comprendere in pieno cosa significasse dover fare i conti con un'assenza da quel momento in avanti. E non aveva osato confidarsi con sua madre per il timore di offendere lei e la memoria stinta di un padre che aveva conosciuto molto poco.

Stare ancora, ancora per un po', nella casa dove aveva passato tanto tempo le aveva dato conforto, anche grazie alla fraterna gentilezza con la quale i due figli del defunto l'avevano trattata.

Solo quando il seppellitore finì di riempire la fossa e sollevò verso i presenti il viso congesto e sudato dicendo: «Fatto!» la Tina pensò che era davvero tutto finito.

Fu allora che Vittorio le si avvicinò.

«Io e Francesca andiamo, Tina», la informò.

La ragazza non riuscì a formulare alcuna frase. Avrebbe voluto chiedere: «E adesso?» ma evitò rendendosi conto di quanto potesse sembrare sciocca una domanda del genere.

«Le faremo sapere quanto prima il giorno in cui il notaio aprirà il testamento», disse ancora Vittorio.

Maria Teresa Supposta, che le era stata al fianco per tutta la durata della cerimonia funebre, secondo banco in chiesa, seconda fila del corteo, subito dietro i figli, ebbe un incontenibile momento di curiosità.

Se sfuggì alla Tina, non così fu per il figlio del commendatore.

«So per certo che mio padre non si è dimenticato di lei nelle sue ultime volontà», disse, riferendosi alla Tina ma parlando con la Supposta.

«A presto quindi», salutò congedandosi.

Anche la Tina fece la mossa di andarsene. L'ex infermiera le pose una mano sul braccio.

«Ti dispiace», disse, «visto che già siamo qui?»

Una visita, un saluto anche alla tomba del professore suo padre.

«Si figuri», rispose la Tina.

E s'incamminarono lungo le viuzze del cimitero senza quasi proiettare ombra.

La Tina continuava a ripetersi la domanda che non aveva fatto al figlio del commenda.

L'ex infermiera invece aveva sguinzagliato i cani della curiosità: cosa poteva aver donato il commenda alla ragazza?

133.

Non c'entrava niente con matrimoni alle viste o a venire.

Ma non ci sarebbe stato bisogno di andarsela a leggere per saperlo.

Innanzitutto era impossibile che un carabiniere della caserma arrivasse a quel punto senza che nessuno ne sapesse qualcosa. Inoltre la signora marescialla sapeva che, anche per regolamento, suo marito doveva essere informato in caso di nozze e di conseguenza si sarebbe lasciato sfuggire qualcosa con lei.

C'entrava invece con una cosa strana o comunque una cosa che non era riuscita a capire.

Elvira Pezzati aveva unicamente capito, leggiucchiando la lettera che il carabiniere Fantarini le aveva consegnato, che lo stesso chiedeva per il 16 agosto prossimo venturo di essere esentato da ogni servizio per partecipare a una gara di... di...

S'era ripromessa di chiedere a suo marito la sera stessa cosa diavolo fosse quella cosa di cui faticava a ricordare il nome.

Poi non solo s'era dimenticata l'intenzione e la misteriosa parola ma anche dove aveva appoggiato la lettera del Fantarini.

Be', non si creda che la moglie di un maresciallo non abbia altro da fare che attendere il ritorno del marito per coccolarlo con mangiarini e carezze!

In ogni caso era andata così, e chi può dire come sarebbe finita se un paio di giorni più tardi, mentre era in un negozio di alimentari, non fosse andata quasi a sbattere contro il manifesto che annunciava la tradizionale «Mostra-mercato degli uccelli» in programma il giorno 16 agosto.

Tra le manifestazioni in calendario c'era anche la gara che riguardava quella cosa, quella parola che faticava a ricordare e di cui ignorava il significato.

Quindi era tornata a casa e, recuperata non senza fatica la lettera del Fantarini, l'aveva messa in bella vista sulla tavola apparecchiata, appoggiata al bicchiere di suo marito.

Peccato aver dovuto attendere fino a sera perché quel giorno il maresciallo Pezzati aveva dovuto saltare il pranzo per questioni di servizio.

E peccato anche che pure lui non avesse saputo spiegarle cosa diavolo fosse quella cosa per la quale il carabiniere Augusto Fantarini aveva chiesto una specie di licenza per il giorno 16 agosto prossimo venturo.

134.

Amedeo Modesto Supposta
1875-1952
RIP

Nome, cognome, data di nascita e di morte, un metro di terra, una lapide, una lastra di marmo bianco già parecchio carolata, un vaso di rame.

Niente foto, fiori sempre freschi.

Tale era stata la volontà del professore, il cimitero di Acquaseria, nessun orpello.

Il sole era a picco.

L'ex infermiera, una volta raggiunta l'ultima dimora del genitore, si esibì in un pateravegloria di rara velocità.

Forse era per il caldo che stava cominciando a diventare insopportabile, ipotizzò tra sé la Tina.

«Volevo farti vedere una cosa», disse la Supposta interrompendone il pensiero.

Una cosa che da parecchio tempo aveva notato, visto che a trovare suo padre al cimitero e a rinnovare sempre i fiori sulla sua tomba ci andava almeno tre volte a settimana. Una cosa che fino a pochi giorni prima l'aveva solo commossa per ragioni che erano facili da immaginare, una vita così giovane, così breve ma... ma che, da quando la Tina le aveva raccontato della lettera, aveva assunto...

«Non saprei come dirlo, ma...» si interruppe l'ex infermiera.

Insomma, era certo solo un caso, una coincidenza.

Ma non poteva fare a meno, da allora, di continuare a pensarci. Per quello le aveva chiesto di accompagnarla fino alla tomba di suo padre.

«Per farla vedere anche a te», spiegò infine la Supposta.

«E sarebbe?» chiese la Tina.

«Guarda un po' lì», rispose l'ex infermiera indicando la tomba che stava accanto a quella del professore.

Marmo ingrigito, con qualche chiazza di muffa e umidità. Dalle lettere che componevano il nome e la data di nascita e di morte colava ruggine. C'era una foto, ma sbiadita.

Margherita Sanetti
5.2.1921-16.4.1944
Una prece

135.

«Quindicimarzomillenovecento... tto.»

Detto come se fosse ubriaco.

«Scusami tanto ma non ho capito.»

Il Riffa sbuffò, per la terza, forse quarta volta.

Allora Spinetta Bretella depose la biro e lo guardò.

«Ascoltami bene», disse.

La Bretella aveva il doppio dei suoi anni. Il Riffa non la vedeva dai tempi dell'oratorio, da quando lei insegnava la dottrina e lo riempiva di sberle secche soprattutto sulle orecchie fredde gelate. Era tale e quale ad allora: flaccida, vestita di nero o marrone e con un'aria come se uno dei vangeli l'avesse scritto lei. Il Riffa le avrebbe detto più che volentieri quello che a suo giudizio le mancava, che le era sempre mancato e che le sarebbe sempre mancato. Perché, come usavano dire i cacciatori, gli uccelli andavano presi quando c'erano. L'avesse fatto però si sarebbe giocato la possibilità di trovarsi un posto di lavoro al cotonificio. Così stavano le cose per la disperazione del Riffa che quasi quasi avrebbe preferito farsi qualche mese di galera pur di non dover pensare che doveva provvedere al suo immediato futuro. Di soldi per rimettere in piedi al volo l'attività di ambulante, nisba.

Aveva tentato, in verità, di mettere le grinfie sui risparmi della zia Infantina, sapeva che aveva da parte qualcosa. Ma quella s'era opposta con fierezza: quei soldi erano per pagarsi il funerale che doveva essere di prima classe e nessuno le avrebbe fatto dire quanti erano e dove li conservava per tirarli fuori al momento giusto. Il resto della pensioncina se ne andava con l'affitto della casa, le bollette e il mangiare, spese alle quali il Biagetto aveva sempre contribuito con dei «pagherò» sulla parola che solo in alcune occasioni avevano avuto una diversa declinazione.

Di forza, al Riffa s'era imposta la necessità di trovarsi un lavoro. Anche, anzi meglio, temporaneo, tanto per dare un po' di ossigeno alla situazione e intanto guardarsi in giro per capire come fare a rimettersi in sella e non condividere la fine di molti soci, destinati a morire sotto padrone.

Dopo averci ragionato su un paio di giorni, il Riffa aveva chiara una cosa: la fama di inaffidabilità, indolenza, insofferenza alle regole che lo circondava come un'aura gli avrebbe garantito il rifiuto di gran parte di artigiani o piccoli imprenditori che volevano solo dipendenti garantiti.

L'unica possibilità chc avcva visto cra stata quclla di gettarsi a capofitto nel mare magno del cotonificio, ritenendo che lì avrebbe potuto mimetizzarsi tra i tanti, godendo di uno stipendio fisso senza troppo faticare.

Solo che, la mattina in cui si era presentato per fare domanda di assunzione, si era trovato faccia a faccia la Spinetta Bretella nelle vesti di segretaria della direzione, ufficio personale.

Cazzo!

Dover chiedere un lavoro a quella lumacona che lo aveva riempito di sberle per anni!

Gli era venuto spontaneo assumere un atteggiamento come se fosse lui a fare un piacere all'intero cotonificio: mani in tasca, espressione scocciata, sbuffi a mitraglia dopo ogni domanda della Bretella, come quando al mercato la tiravano in lungo per un paio di ciabatte, il colore di una scarpa o lo sconto.

Così alla fine la Bretella era scoppiata.

«Ascoltami bene!»

136.

«Bene», rispose il Dubbio a sua madre.

Il primo giorno di lavoro quale aiuto pontilista era andato bene.

«Bene», gli fece eco la Canterina, ne era felice.

Però si aspettava qualcosa di più.

«Dai, raccontami.»

L'aveva salutato la mattina quando l'Ernesto era uscito di casa come se partisse per andare in guerra. L'emozione di avere un figlio che finalmente, dopo tutto quello che aveva passato, aveva un avvenire assicurato, non disgiunta dalla suggestione di vederlo come se davvero avesse addosso una divisa, quella della Navigazione, bella, blu, che gli donava, aveva creato in lei una somma di sentimenti difficile da interpretare. E aveva passato l'intera giornata col pensiero alla sponda di là, dove suo figlio dirigeva il traffico dei battelli.

L'Ernesto non poteva cavarsela così, con un semplice «Bene».

«Allora?» lo stimolò ancora.

Il Dubbio scrollò le spalle.

Ma cosa doveva dire di più?

Era un lavoro un po'...

Un po' del cazzo, stava per dire ma si bloccò.

Poca fatica e del gran tempo a disposizione, tirare e ritirare passerelle, al massimo dare una mano a scendere o salire a qualche sderenata per evitare che andasse a finire nel lago.

Fu a quel punto che alla Canterina sarebbe piaciuto non aver chiesto niente. Non tanto per la ritrosia con la quale il Dubbio rispondeva alla sua curiosità. Piuttosto per quell'accenno al gran tempo libero che quel lavoro lasciava a suo figlio.

L'ozio, pensò dentro di sé senza osare dirlo, è il padre dei vizi. E quel padre prese forma e viso di cattivo consigliere, tale e quale a quello di certe compagnie che l'Ernesto aveva frequentato e grazie alle quali aveva rischiato di finire in galera.

Ormai però indietro non poteva tornare.

Avanti allora.

Quindi: «E cosa fai di bello mentre aspetti?» chiese con voce che le tremava un po'.

Qualunque risposta le avesse dato le sarebbe andata bene giusto per ritrovare anche solo un filo della tranquillità appena perduta e che avrebbe voluto riavere a ogni costo.

Qualunque, tranne quella che il Dubbio le diede.

«Niente.»

Anche se non era proprio vero del tutto.

137.

Com'era sua inveterata abitudine, la madre non le chiese niente.

Toccò alla Tina darle quella notizia che aveva dell'incredibile.

Non lo fece subito però, appena rientrata in casa, come l'istinto le avrebbe suggerito di fare, anche se il tenersi dentro quella cosa era come avere una lisca di pesce in gola che non voleva saperne di andare né su né giù.

Tuttavia per quella volta la Tina si permise una piccola cattiveria nei confronti di quella donna. Così, per vendicarsi, senza spargimenti di sangue, della sufficienza con la quale aveva appreso la notizia circa il fatto che il commenda aveva lasciato un testamento in cui anche lei era compresa e poi riguardo a un commento che, contrariamente alle sue abitudini, s'era lasciata sfuggire la sera prima.

Sua madre l'aveva vista un po' eccitata all'idea di dover andare, la mattina seguente, a Bellagio presso lo studio del notaio Baldemar Scheper per assistere all'apertura del testamento.

«Se ti ha lasciato le tazzine per il caffè puoi sempre buttarle nel lago quando ritorni a casa col battello.»

La Tina non aveva reagito allo scetticismo di sua madre, lo conosceva bene, ricordava le rare volte in cui aveva tentato di raccontarle qualcosa di più del commenda e dei pensieri che le confidava e le risposte che aveva ricevuto.

«Siamo tutti bravi e buoni quando abbiamo bisogno degli altri.»

E, a dire il vero, non aveva nemmeno mai immaginato che potesse entrare nel testamento del commenda. Quando Vittorio le aveva comunicato data e ora dell'appuntamento dal notaio, non era stata capace di pensare a cosa potesse ricevere in eredità.

Due righe, ecco.

Tanto le sarebbe bastato, due righe che le riconoscessero la premura con la quale si era occupata di lui nel corso di quei lunghi mesi.

Ma da lì a immaginare che le avesse destinato la casetta di Acquaseria, non ci sarebbe mai arrivata.

La scena aveva avuto un momento di sconcerto comico poiché nel momento in cui il notaio, con il suo italiano impestato di inflessioni tedesche benché risiedesse in Italia da quasi sedici anni, aveva letto il passaggio riguardante la casa, la Tina, dopo qualche istante di incredulità, aveva girato gli occhi verso i due figli del commenda, aspettandosi una reazione.

Violenta per di più.

Sebbene non avesse un'esperienza diretta, per sentito dire, da storie che circolavano in paese, conosceva gli odi, i litigi, le guerre sortite per un pezzo di terreno o una cascina lasciata a questo e non a quello.

Lì c'era di mezzo addirittura una casa fornita di tutti i comfort moderni!

Quindi aveva guardato i due figli aspettandosi una reazione di sdegno, proteste, urla e sedie che cadevano all'indietro...

Invece aveva visto due sorrisi discreti e aveva sentito la voce di Vittorio.

Prima la voce, poi era riuscita a mettere a fuoco la bocca da cui stavano uscendo le parole.

«Siamo contenti se lei la vorrà accettare come segno della riconoscenza nostra e di nostro padre.»

Alla Tina era uscito dalle labbra solo un balbettio.

«Nessuno meglio di lei la merita, per abitarla, se lo vorrà, con la splendida famiglia che siamo certi avrà», aveva aggiunto Francesca, che di quella casa conservava un ricordo doloroso e più di tutti vedeva con favore l'idea di quel lascito.

Poi, mentre la Tina riprendeva contatto con il mondo della realtà, sempre Vittorio le aveva detto che quel passaggio del testamento era già noto sia a lui sia a sua sorella. In una delle visite che regolarmente facevano a loro padre lui aveva voluto informarli circa la sua intenzione riguardo alla casa di Acquaseria e né lui né Francesca avevano avuto il benché minimo dubbio che quella fosse la cosa giusta da fare.

«Per quanto riguarda gli atti del passaggio di proprietà», aveva poi detto il notaio, «le farò sapere quali documenti mi servono e fisseremo un appuntamento.»

Le sue parole avevano riportato la situazione entro i confini di un atto d'ufficio, ma non erano servite a sedare la profonda emozione che aveva preso la Tina.

Nemmeno la solitaria passeggiata dallo studio del notaio fino al molo della Navigazione era riuscita a consumare l'eccitazione di cui si sentiva preda e che le sembrava modificare anche i tratti del viso, dandole un'espressione come se fosse spaventata.

Sul battello aveva ripensato alle parole di sua madre.

Non aveva tazzine da gettare nel lago.

Anzi, aveva sorriso tra sé, tornava a casa a mani vuote.

Meno male, perché così era stata libera di portarsele al viso per coprire i segni della seconda, improvvisa emozione di quella memorabile giornata.

138.

Il maresciallo Pezzati non aveva voluto polemizzare con sua moglie.

Lei gli aveva confessato che erano già un paio di giorni che il suo carabiniere le aveva consegnato la busta con la preghiera di darla a lui.

Lui le aveva chiesto come mai, se l'aveva da un paio di giorni, solo adesso si ricordava di consegnargliela.

La memoria, la memoria... aveva solfeggiato lei.

E poi, uè!, non si creda che la moglie di un maresciallo non avesse altro da fare che preparargli mangiarini e aspettarlo dopo le fatiche del lavoro per profondersi in carezze!

A quel punto il Pezzati aveva compreso che stava per imboccare una cattiva strada lungo la quale uno dei due avrebbe potuto farsi del male e s'era taciuto.

Poi aveva aperto la busta, aveva letto e non aveva capito il senso della richiesta.

«Ma cos'è 'sta roba?» era sbottato.

«Se non lo sai tu...» aveva risposto la moglie.

139.

«Quindi l'Ernesto si è inventato tutto.»

La domanda, ma era una domanda?, era uscita a fine cena dalle labbra di Vittoria Lonati.

All'improvviso?

No.

Il Lonati ne era certo.

Meditata piuttosto.

E da tempo.

Ma era un'affermazione o una domanda?, s'era chiesto il dottore.

Aveva propeso per l'affermazione.

«Se lo dici tu…»

«Ho solo chiesto», aveva invece ribattuto la moglie.

«Non mi sembrava una domanda», aveva osservato lui.

«E invece sì», aveva confermato lei.

Pericolo, aveva pensato il dottore.

Meglio abbassare la testa e spiegare con calma, così come aveva fatto col maresciallo Pezzati, che quella era una domanda cui era difficile, forse impossibile dare una risposta esaustiva.

140.

Pure il Riffa aveva dovuto abbassare il crapone.

Perché, dopo avergli ingiunto di ascoltarlo per bene, Spinetta Bretella era tornata a essere l'insegnante di dottrina che menava per fare male.

«Qui», aveva detto, «assumiamo cani e porci perché il lavoro non manca e se ce ne fosse un po' meno non sarebbe male.»

Comunque, come si diceva, guai lamentarsi di gamba sana!

Venendo a loro e allo specifico della situazione: «Io», aveva proseguito la Spinetta, «per il ruolo che ho sono obbligata a prendere nota di tutte le domande di assunzione che mi vengono sottoposte».

Fosse dipeso da lei però, certi infami che approfittavano della situazione, si facevano assumere e poi, dopo una settimana, cominciavano ad andare in mutua per dei mesi, facendo nel frattempo ogni sorta di lavori e mettendosi in tasca due stipendi, li avrebbe cacciati a calci nel sedere.

Anzi, avesse potuto fare come voleva, non li avrebbe nemmeno fatti entrare nel suo ufficio, perché li annusava, ne sentiva il cattivo odore.

Non poteva farlo.

«Però una cosa la posso fare», aveva aggiunto.

E la faceva.

Eccome se la faceva!

Capitava infatti, grazie a lei, che certe domande di assunzione restassero, chissà come mai?, sempre sul fondo del suo cassetto, senza mai giungere sotto gli occhi del direttore per l'approvazione e la firma.

«Ci siamo capiti, Biagio?» aveva finito di spiegare la Spinetta.

E, capendo di averlo domato, gli aveva risparmiato di chiamarlo Biagetto, perché se era vero che nella vita le era sempre mancata quella cosa là, non le difettava certo la memoria.

141.

Impossibile dimenticarsene.

Ma, soprattutto, cosa ci faceva lì?

Nella testa della Tina, alla domanda aveva subito fatto eco la risposta.

Evidente!

Vestito così e con la corda della passerella in mano non poteva fare altro che una cosa, il pontilista.

Ma proprio lì, ad Acquaseria?

E adesso, s'era subito dopo chiesta, cosa doveva fare?

Fingere di niente, di non vederlo?

Ma per farlo non avrebbe dovuto essere lei l'unica passeggera che stava scendendo dal battello di ritorno da Bellagio e il Dubbio l'unico essere umano presente allo scalo visto che non c'era nessuno in attesa di salire.

Alla fine s'erano salutati, in fondo non costava niente.

Lei seria seria, un ciao che aveva il tenore di un buongiorno.

Il Dubbio le aveva risposto e non aveva richiuso subito la bocca, lasciandola aperta anche dopo, quando la Tina s'era avviata verso casa, come se fosse sorpreso di vederla lì.

Mentre camminava, la ragazza aveva pensato a quella coincidenza e a quella bocca semiaperta.

Un'espressione da bamba, da ciula.

Forse, aveva pensato, quel giovanotto non era del tutto a posto, un malmaturo.

Doveva esserlo per forza se si meravigliava di vederla lì

visto che lì lei ci abitava. Anzi, aveva sorriso tra sé, era anche, da poche ore, proprietaria di una casetta da sogno.

Poi ogni pensiero relativo al Dubbio era svanito quando era entrata in casa e, dopo aver tentennato cercando senza successo di fare la punta alla curiosità della madre, aveva ceduto e sparato la notizia.

Sua madre, imperturbabile come al solito, la incassò commentandola stitica.

«Be', vuol dire che mi sono sbagliata sul conto del commendatore.»

E morta lì.

La Tina non se la prese più di tanto.

Rifletté che le avrebbe dato molta più soddisfazione la Maria Teresa Supposta.

Avesse avuto una madre diversa, si sarebbero fatte delle belle risate insieme una volta che le avesse raccontato di essersi trovata il Dubbio proprio lì, ad Acquaseria, vestito da pontilista.

Ma meglio così, in fin dei conti.

Ormai tutto ciò che era accaduto apparteneva al passato, compreso quel giovanotto con il quale non voleva avere più niente a che fare.

142.

Non era del tutto vero quello che il Dubbio aveva detto a sua madre circa ciò che faceva tra un battello e l'altro.

Il pontilista titolare lo aveva informato che nell'intervallo tra un arrivo e una partenza, aveva la libertà di impiegare il tempo come meglio credeva. L'importante, aveva rimarcato, era non ciccare l'appuntamento, stare a tiro del molo insomma, non creare malumori o disservizi nella clientela.

Siccome era lui il titolare, a lui era toccato il compito di istruire il neofita circa le occupazioni di competenza. Per tre giorni, pedante, aveva spiegato al Dubbio obblighi e mansioni e verificato la corretta applicazione degli stessi. Quindi, sempre poiché era lui il titolare, aveva cominciato a sparire mormorando cose circa una moglie da accompagnare dal dottore, un orto che necessitava delle sue cure oppure svanendo nel nulla senza alcuna scusa plausibile.

Al Dubbio di restare lì al molo da solo non dava per niente fastidio. Anzi, meglio, piuttosto che doversi ciucciare le chiacchiere querule del pontilista titolare oppure le sue domande. Così, obbedendo all'ordine di tener sempre d'occhio il lago e aprire per tempo il botteghino dei biglietti, per ingannare l'attesa aveva cominciato a girellare qua e là, andando soprattutto per rive dove si poteva garantire la solitudine e i suoi pensieri in santa pace.

Se quello era far niente, ecco, aveva risposto bene a sua madre.

Ma era stato proprio grazie a quel fare niente che era successa una cosa.

Una cosa che al Dubbio aveva fatto dire: «Lo sapevo».

Sapeva di avere ragione.

143.

Facile profeta, la Tina ebbe ragione nel pensare che, alla notizia della incredibile novità, Maria Teresa Supposta avrebbe reagito con un entusiasmo tale da compensare quello che era mancato a sua madre.

Quando glielo disse, l'ex infermiera reagì senza contenersi.

Batté le mani come una scolaretta, la abbracciò.

«La vita deve continuare», disse.

Poi invitò la ragazza a entrare nel suo regno per la prima volta da che si conoscevano.

Ma bisognava brindare a un evento del genere, o no?

Vermouth, una bottiglia aperta chissà quando e che aveva un poco di incrostazioni sul tappo a vite.

La Tina avrebbe evitato entrambe le cose, visita e vermouth, ma non se la sentì di rifiutare. Dovette seguire l'ex infermiera e sedere composta nel salottino o mausoleo che fosse, vista la concentrazione di fotografie che ne tappezzavano le pareti, per la maggior parte ritratti del professor Supposta, con e senza camice, in compagnia di questa o quella autorità e pure a bordo del dinghy che gli era stato fatale.

Dopo un primo sorso di vermouth la Supposta partì a razzo con un panegirico sugli uomini di una volta, categoria alla quale aveva appena ammesso il defunto commendatore per via della sua esemplare generosità, caratteristica della quale era stato abbondante dispensatore anche il professore suo padre. Poi, dopo un secondo sorso di vermouthino e senza soluzione di continuità, aveva assunto accenti commossi riferendosi al dispiacere di vedere quella casa disabitata ma passando poi, con una risalita di umore, ae prevedere nel futuro della Tina fidanzati e mariti grazie ai quali la casa del commenda sarebbe tornata a vivere.

Sì, ma, nel frattempo?

Nel frattempo il vermouth della Supposta era finito e forse per quello l'ex infermiera tornò a vedere nero nell'immediato futuro.

Nel frattempo infatti, mentre si aspettava che maturasse un fidanzato pronto a diventare marito della Tina, lei cosa avrebbe fatto?

«In che senso?» chiese la Tina che nel suo bicchierino aveva giusto intinto la punta della lingua.

«Intendo dire che non me la sento di stare qui sola», spiegò la Supposta.

In sostanza, l'idea di avere qualcuno di fronte a sé, qualcuno che nella necessità sarebbe corso a darle una mano, l'aveva fatta stare tranquilla sino ad allora.

Il pensiero che adesso e chissà fino a quando, visto che la Tina era tornata a stare con sua madre...

Insomma, per farla breve, al fine di continuare a dormire sonni tranquilli aveva pensato che sarebbe stata buona cosa cambiare le serrature della porta d'entrata e di quella sul retro, rinforzarle, aggiungere chiavistelli eccetera.

Quindi, poteva essere così gentile la Tina di consigliarle qualcuno di cui fidarsi per un lavoro del genere e magari, se non le era di troppo disturbo, accompagnarlo da lei?

144.

Il soggetto giusto c'era, la Tina lo conosceva, anche se non ne conosceva né il nome né il cognome.

La gente lo chiamava Credindio.

Se ci credesse o meno nessuno glielo aveva mai chiesto. Tuttavia quella era l'espressione che gli usciva di bocca quando qualcuno gli sottoponeva un lavoro particolarmente oneroso oppure una richiesta fuori dal comune, come certe ringhiere arzigogolate o robe di fino.

La risposta, che gli era valsa il soprannome, valeva anche come accettazione dell'impegno che in genere veniva poi portato a compimento con perizia e maestria, per la piena soddisfazione del cliente.

Quei lavori lì, come quello che la Tina gli aveva chiesto per conto della Supposta, il Credindio li faceva nei ritagli di tempo.

Nel «temp del'ora» il più delle volte, cioè tra mezzogiorno e l'una, mentre la maggior parte della gente si concedeva l'agio di digerire con comodo.

Lo stesso arco di tempo in cui anche il Dubbio apriva la schiscetta che la Canterina gli preparava la sera prima e che lui riportava a casa lustra come uno specchio.

Non così quel giorno.

Il Credindio era in casa della Supposta da non più di un quarto d'ora e stava trabattando attorno alla serratura della porta principale. La Tina s'era accomodata nel salotto-mausoleo chiacchierando del più e del meno con l'ex infermiera. A un certo punto quest'ultima le aveva chiesto il permesso di allontanarsi un momento, come se non fosse in casa propria.

Aveva alzato a vu indice e medio.

Cesso.

Ma senza cistite.

Dal cesso però, poco dopo, era uscito un urlo che non solo aveva fatto scattare la Tina ma anche provocato una reazione verbale da parte del Credindio, un «Se ghè?» che aveva interrotto il silenzio che di solito avvolgeva le sue giornate.

145.

«Fantarini!»

All'esplodere del punto esclamativo il carabiniere semplice Augusto Fantarini era già davanti alla scrivania del suo comandante maresciallo Massimino Pezzati.

«Comandi!»

«Comandi un cazzo», aveva risposto il Pezzati.

Piuttosto, gli facesse due cortesie.

«Spiegami in cosa consiste la richiesta che mi hai sottoposto e come mai l'hai consegnata a mia moglie anziché darla a me.»

Con ordine.

«Prima di tutto fammi capire bene cosa diavolo è questa gara del chioccolo.»

Il Fantarini si era schiarito la voce.

«È da sapere che innanzitutto il chioccolo è un'arte», aveva cominciato a spiegare.

Un'arte sviluppata dall'essere umano sin dall'antichità che consisteva nell'imitare, con l'uso della propria voce, il chioccolo appunto, che altro non era che il verso, il canto degli uccelli. Tale arte si era estesa non solo all'imitazione di quegli uccelli, come il merlo o il fringuello, che propriamente chioccolavano ma anche a molte altre specie.

«Se in ogni tempo questa straordinaria capacità dell'essere umano di imitare alla perfezione il canto degli uccelli viene usata a scopo venatorio, vi sono applicazioni della stessa che vanno oltre la caccia vera e propria e che trovano la loro ragion d'essere nelle gare di chioccolo, di solito organizzate all'interno di mostre-mercato degli uccelli e articoli vari legati all'attività venatoria, gare durante le quali i chioccolatori si sfidano in bravura come appunto accadrà il prossimo 16 agosto qui.»

«E tu...»

«E io vi vorrei partecipare, se nulla osta», aveva affermato il Fantarini.

«Perché saresti un... uno di quelli che imitano gli uccelli?»

«Chioccolatore», aveva precisato il Fantarini. «E modestamente, anche abbastanza esperto», aveva aggiunto arrossendo.

Bon, si era detto tra sé il Pezzati, aveva infine capito cosa fischiava di tanto in tanto il suo carabiniere, altro che pezzi d'opera o canzonette!

«Va bene, passiamo alla seconda questione.»

«Ecco», fece il Fantarini.

Se si era permesso di far pervenire a lui maresciallo la richiesta per tramite della moglie, era perché l'aveva ritenuto un gesto di rispetto nei confronti suoi, del suo grado, della divisa...

«Eh!» lo aveva interrotto il maresciallo. «Quanta roba!»

«Insomma, trattandosi di cosa privata...»

Il maresciallo Pezzati a quel punto si era fregato le mani.

«Ho capito», aveva soffiato.

A quel punto la cosa riguardava lui.

Mica sapeva se un carabiniere in servizio permanente poteva partecipare a gare pubbliche o se ci fosse qualche angolo di regolamento che prevedesse una situazione del genere.

«Mi capisci, Fantarini?»

Il permesso glielo avrebbe dato volentieri, ma non voleva metterlo a rischio di qualche provvedimento disciplinare per aver partecipato a una gara di... di...

«Chioccolo», aveva suggerito il carabiniere.

«Ecco, appunto», aveva chiuso il Pezzati.

146.

Il Dubbio aveva appena aperto la schiscetta.

Cotoletta impanata su un letto di peperonata. Entrambe cose buone anche se fredde, anzi, forse di più.

Considerata l'ora secca che aveva a disposizione, il bel sole, la rivetta dove non andava mai nessuno e dalla quale comunque poteva tenere d'occhio il lago, l'Ernesto aveva deciso di non restare a consumare il pranzo dentro il gabbiotto dei biglietti, dove peraltro si condensava un caldo della madonna, ma di andarsene all'aperto, a godere l'arrivo della brevetta e l'ombra delle canne che nascondeva quella riva.

Se in quel momento qualcuno gli avesse chiesto come stesse non avrebbe potuto fare a meno di rispondere che, senza alcun dubbio, stava bene. Si sentiva a posto con addosso quella divisa che l'aveva rivestito come se fosse un'armatura dentro la quale maturava un sentimento simile alla sicurezza. Stava bene perché col tranquillo levarsi della breva sentiva la musicale liquidità dell'acqua, il pacifico andare a finire tra un sasso e l'altro, il perdersi di quelle onde che guardava sin da quando era bambino chiedendosi come facessero a riformarsi sempre e a non essere mai uguali una all'altra. Gli faceva bene pensare che di lì a poco, quando il sudore dovuto alla camminata se ne fosse andato, avrebbe addentato una untissima cotoletta impanata e poi, senza bisogno di posate, usando dei pezzi di pane come fossero una forchetta avrebbe spazzolato anche la peperonata.

Aveva alzato gli occhi a guardare la sponda che aveva di fronte, pensando a quante volte aveva assunto quella posizione, seduto sui sassi di quella riva, a guardare verso il lago, aspettando... aspettando lui sapeva cosa. E a come quel pensiero, benché ne conoscesse l'infondatezza, l'aveva sempre spinto a tornare.

Ma lì dov'era adesso era diverso.

Cambiava la prospettiva, era un'altra sponda. Cambiavano i sassi forse o forse il modo in cui l'acqua andava a perdersi tra uno e l'altro.

Cambiava qualcosa.

Dire cosa era difficile.

Ma era stato guardando, cercando le differenze che, mentre la cotoletta gli penzolava tra le dita in attesa del primo morso, il Dubbio l'aveva visto.

Cazzo, un remo!

E poco dopo, non resistendo alla tentazione, dopo averlo preso dall'acqua della riva, con una sensazione che era quasi simile allo spavento aveva cambiato opinione.

Non un remo qualunque: quel remo, il suo!

La cotoletta, la schiscetta, tutti i pensieri relativi alla sponda di là e a quella di qua, le differenze, paf!, svaniti.

Era partito col remo in mano e chi l'aveva visto non aveva potuto fare altro che prenderlo per matto.

147.

Un urlo e la Tina era subito stata lì.

Meno male che aveva avuto il tempo di tirare su le mutande.

Ma cosa ci faceva lì, ancora, quel giovanotto...

Era lui, poi?

«Sì», confermò la Tina rispondendo alla domanda della padrona di casa.

E allora, cosa ci faceva lì, fuori dalla casa del commenda, e con un remo in mano?

«Vado a vedere», disse la Tina.

«No», impose la Supposta.

«No, perché?» chiese la Tina.

Perché si sapeva mai.

Quel remo!

Cosa voleva dire, perché ce l'aveva in mano?

Non pensava che potesse venir usato come un'arma?

«Ma no...» ribatté la Tina.

«Ma sì, invece», insisté la Supposta.

E tanto per essere sicura che la ragazza non facesse colpi di testa le aveva messo una mano sul braccio continuando a guardare il Dubbio che, il remo stretto nella mano sinistra, continuava a bussare alla porta di casa del commenda.

«Vuoi che ti chiami i carabinieri?» chiese dopo qualche istante l'ex infermiera.

Ancora carabinieri?

«Lasciamo stare», rispose la Tina.

«Qualcosa però dobbiamo fare», ragionò la Supposta mentre il Dubbio s'era girato a guardarsi in giro.

«È evidente che non sa che il commenda è morto e la casa è vuota», commentò la ragazza.

Non riusciva a pensare che quel giovanotto fosse lì con cattive intenzioni. Piuttosto percepiva il ridicolo nel vederlo lì con un remo di barca in mano e, in effetti, più che spaventata, come dava a vedere di esserlo l'ex infermiera, si sentiva in preda a una certa curiosità.

«Se non va via però bisogna fare qualcosa», disse, facendo irruzione nei suoi pensieri, la Supposta.

«Cosa?» chiese la Tina.

In fin dei conti, non c'era un uomo in casa lì con loro?

Un uomo che forse sapeva come affrontare certe situazioni, certi soggetti?

Poteva quindi, per cortesia, andare lui a chiedere a quel giovanotto cosa cercasse, di cosa avesse bisogno?

Il Credindio fu lì per rispondere ma lo anticipò il potente segnale del battello che fu come crepa nel silenzio digestivo del dopo pranzo.

Al sentirlo, il Dubbio, mollato il remo accanto alla porta, partì veloce come un ladro colto sul fatto.

148.

Cazzo, l'avesse fatta anche lui domanda di essere assunto dalla Navigazione!

Magari al posto del Dubbio adesso ci sarebbe stato lui a lumare le turiste e a intorcolarle con le sue belle balle, approfittando di tutto il tempo libero che avevano quelli che lavoravano sui battelli e ancora di più quelli che stavano ad aspettarli ai pontili.

Adesso invece il Riffa non poteva fare altro che darsi dell'asino per non averci pensato.

Ma vallo a sapere che gli sarebbe andata storta fino al punto di perdere tutto, scarpe e camioncino.

Comunque scoprire che il Dubbio s'era sistemato era stato un bel colpo, una sorpresa che l'aveva lasciato secco.

Era successo qualche giorno dopo che la Spinetta Bretella gli aveva fatto lo shampoo, quando ancora l'ultima chiacchierata col maresciallo Pezzati gli risuonava nella zucca.

Il Dubbio sembrava sparito dalla circolazione e lui, curioso come una scimmia di capire in che diavolo di guaio aveva tentato di cacciarsi con quella storia di un cadavere che non era cadavere, s'era deciso ad andarlo a cercare a casa.

S'era trovato faccia a faccia con la Canterina cui mancava solo l'aureola per sembrare davvero una santa.

Beata e sorridente: «Lavora!» gli aveva risposto.

La Navigazione l'aveva assunto.

Non lo sapeva?

E come cazzo faceva a saperlo se da quella sera su al crotto non ci aveva più parlato?

«E tu?» gli aveva chiesto la donna.

«Io?» aveva temporeggiato lui.

Be', anch'io, aveva aggiunto subito dopo, dicendo poi alla Canterina di salutargli l'Ernesto e menando le tolle al volo perché non aveva voglia di confessare che da qualche giorno andava al cotone e ne aveva già pieni i coglioni.

Di tutto.

Del rumore delle macchine, dell'odore di grasso, di quelli che gridavano per farsi sentire e di quelli che lo prendevano per il culo ricordandogli le sue dichiarazioni «Sotto padrone mai!».

Delle sirene, dei cambi turno.

Quelle sirene, porca troia!

Se le sognava anche di notte e si svegliava con l'idea che fosse già ora di cominciare il suo turno.

Nel buio della notte gli veniva quasi da piangere e al sonno poteva dire addio.

149.

Così come il Dubbio, gli disse il pontilista titolare, poteva dire addio al posto fisso se avesse fatto ancora un errore del genere e la direzione ne fosse stata informata.

«Ma, dico, lasciar lì ad aspettare un battello carico di turisti e la fila degli altri davanti al botteghino?»

Dopo una lisciata del genere, l'Ernesto non aveva osato mettere nemmeno il naso fuori dal botteghino dei biglietti per il resto della giornata, macerandosi nel calore del gabbiotto e riflettendo che avrebbe fatto bene a lasciar perdere il remo, la Tina, certi pensieri, se non voleva giocarsi il posto di lavoro. Pensava, ecco, quello sì, che avrebbe dovuto recuperare almeno la schiscetta, lasciata sulla riva del lago. Circa la cotoletta era sicuro che qualche gatto randagio ne avesse fatto scempio mentre la peperonata se la vedeva ricoperta da un nugolo di formiche nevrotiche. Non vedeva l'ora di tornare a casa, lasciarsi alle spalle per qualche ora quella sponda di lago e tutto quello che aveva significato.

L'ultimo battello era alle sei del pomeriggio. Un Acquaseria-Dervio-Bellano-Varenna-Bellagio e poi giù, verso Como. Era quello che il Dubbio prendeva finito il lavoro.

La Tina no.

Eppure, alle sei meno dieci, l'Ernesto vide comparire il suo viso nell'oblò del botteghino.

Non parlò nemmeno, comprese al volo che non era lì per prendere un biglietto.

«Cosa significa quel remo?» chiese infatti.

150.

«L'avesse chiesto a me gliel'avrei spiegato», disse il dottor Lonati.

Al bar dell'Imbarcadero servivano gli aperitivi.

Caffè, nonostante l'ora prossima alla cena, per il dottore.

Per il Pezzati niente.

Il maresciallo era uscito dalla caserma solo perché l'aveva visto entrare al bar e voleva l'ennesima assicurazione che da parte del Dubbio non ci fossero altre novità, colpi di testa, nuove fantasie. Di entrare in argomento così di botto però non se l'era sentita.

L'aveva presa larga invece, raccontando al Lonati della richiesta ricevuta dal suo carabiniere.

«Non avevo mai sentito parlare di una cosa del genere», aveva detto riferendosi al chioccolo.

Così il Lonati gli aveva risposto che se gliel'avesse chiesto, gli avrebbe spiegato lui in cosa consistesse.

«Avevo altro per la testa», disse il Pezzati con una mimica fin troppo allusiva.

E, approfittando del momento: «A tal proposito, posso stare tranquillo?» chiese.

Il Lonati sorrise.

«Può dormire tra due guanciali, come si dice», rispose.

«Sicuro?»

«Non ci pensi più, maresciallo», sussurrò il Lonati inghiottendo l'ultimo sorso di caffè e facendo la mossa di andarsene. «E mi saluti la signora.»

«Faccia così anche lei», rispose il Pezzati.

Speriamo che sia vero, pensò il maresciallo mentre guardava il dottore allontanarsi e cedeva all'offerta di un bicchiere di selz con uno schizzo di Punt e Mes.

151.

«Davvero!?» sbottò il maresciallo Pezzati una volta rientrato in caserma dopo la breve sosta all'Imbarcadero.

«Come no, entusiasta!»

Il Pezzati non credeva alle sue orecchie.

Cioè, ci credeva, perché non metteva in dubbio quello che il collega Maraspini della tenenza di Lecco gli aveva appena detto. Vale a dire che il comandante della stessa tenenza, colonnello Agostino Seneca De Maggiori, era un fanatico del chioccolo oltre che appassionato cacciatore. Di conseguenza, non solo aveva detto di non vedere alcunché di male o di lesivo nei confronti della dignità dell'Arma se uno dei suoi rappresentanti partecipava a una gara di tale specialità. Si augurava anzi che vincesse o comunque si distinguesse in una delle varie categorie e che i giornali locali dessero rilevanza alla notizia e faceva infine sapere al maresciallo Pezzati che avrebbe fatto di tutto per salire a Bellano in forma privata allo scopo di assistere alla gara.

Deposta la cornetta, il Pezzati sorrise tra sé.

«Fantarini!» gridò poi.

Come al solito, il punto esclamativo non s'era ancora deposto del tutto che il carabiniere era già lì.

«Permesso accordato», comunicò.

«Davvero?» fece il Fantarini.

«Lo giuro», confermò il Pezzati simulando un'esagerata serietà.

152.

Anche la Tina aveva giurato, più o meno insomma.

All'ex infermiera aveva comunque assicurato che, una volta finiti i lavori del Credindio e prima che lei tornasse da sua madre, avrebbe provveduto ad avvisare i carabinieri di aver rivisto quel giovanotto ronzare attorno alla casa del commenda.

«Perché se non lo fai tu lo faccio io.»

«Stia tranquilla», aveva risposto la Tina.

Adesso erano ormai le otto della sera.

Maria Teresa Supposta aveva da poco controllato, per la quarta, forse quinta volta, e con visibile soddisfazione, l'ottima riuscita del lavoro del Credindio.

Due serrature «speciali», che non ce n'erano mica tante in giro per il lago di Como.

Oltre a quelle, due chiavistelli del diametro di un dito.

Che per entrare in quella casa adesso ci voleva un ariete, sempre a detta del mutacico fabbro ferraio.

Dopo le porte, le finestre.

Ben chiuse, tutte.

Un peccato.

Sarebbe stato bello lasciar correre dentro casa un po' di quell'aria che andava rinfrescandosi e portava con sé un miscuglio di ineffabili profumi.

Ma la sicurezza prima di tutto, mica voleva dormire con un occhio chiuso e l'altro aperto.

La luce però non invitava a infilarsi sotto le lenzuola.

Era una luce che aveva sempre suggerito all'ex infermiera la fine del mondo. Un'idea che aveva cominciato a coltivare da quando aveva conosciuto il lago e i suoi angoli. Ne aveva parlato una volta con il professore suo padre e lui le aveva risposto solo con un sorriso in cui non c'era traccia di condiscendenza. Per il resto aveva sempre tenuto per sé quei pensieri onde evitare il rischio che la prendessero per suonata.

Però di fatto era così.

Una luce che annunciava la fine del mondo, una fine del mondo buona però, una luce come se fosse una specie di strada da seguire per giungere da un'altra parte. Dietro il monte che le stava alle spalle, per esempio, dove per il momento c'era la Svizzera.

Lo dicevano o no che la Svizzera era un paradiso?

Maria Teresa Supposta sorrise all'idea di averlo così a portata di mano e decise di stare ad ammirare lo spettacolo del crepuscolo sino a quando il grigio che annunciava la notte non avesse suonato l'ora della ritirata.

Prima di lui però suonò il campanello di casa.

153.

Il Dubbio aveva fatto la mossa di uscire dal gabbiotto ma la Tina era stata più svelta di lui e gli aveva bloccato la porta.

«Da lì non esci se non mi prometti che mi spieghi tutto.»

Decisa.

Gli aveva fatto chiudere la porta dall'interno e s'era fatta passare le chiavi.

Aveva riaperto solo dopo che l'Ernesto aveva accettato e promesso ed era uscito dal gabbiotto in un bagno di sudore.

«Giuramelo», aveva chiesto la Tina.

«Te lo giuro», aveva risposto il Dubbio mentre si asciugava la fronte.

Non s'era sognato. Men che meno aveva voluto fare uno scherzo. Quello era proprio il suo remo, quello che aveva perduto nel tentativo di allontanare il cadavere...

«Ma che cadavere, di chi?» l'aveva interrotto la Tina.

Il Dubbio era rimasto a bocca aperta.

«Della Valeria?» aveva insistito lei.

Di una che le aveva scritto una cartolina da Londra con su il Big Ben, datata due giorni dopo la sua presunta morte, con scritto «Qui è una pacchia, roba da restarci a vita!»?

Gli sembrava che un cadavere potesse spedire cartoline da Londra e scrivere cose del genere?

Si poteva sapere cosa s'era messo in testa, dove voleva andare a parare?

L'aveva vista sì e no per un'oretta a farla grossa.
Come faceva a essere così sicuro?
Si ricordava, per esempio, com'era vestita quella sera?
Aveva la gonna oppure i pantaloni?
«No», l'aveva interrotta il Dubbio.
«No, cosa?»
«Non aveva i pantaloni, un vestitino...»
«Ecco, vedi!» l'aveva interrotto la Tina.
La Valeria quella sera indossava un paio di pantaloni.
«Oltre che una camicetta e un golfino giallo», aveva aggiunto la ragazza.
«Sì, ma...» s'era ingarbugliato il Dubbio.
«Cosa c'è ancora?» aveva chiesto la Tina.
C'era che... d'accordo... anche col maresciallo ormai...
«Cosa c'entra il maresciallo, lascia stare i carabinieri per favore!» aveva interloquito la Tina.
«Va bene, però...»
Però la Tina, s'era spiegato il Dubbio, doveva sapere che lui non s'era sognato, non aveva voluto scherzare.
Aveva davvero trovato una ragazza morta nel lago quella notte, anche se nessuno gli voleva credere.
Una che era... sì, lo sapeva che poteva sembrare incredibile...
«Ma che era tale e quale alla tua amica», aveva affermato.
«Quella è in Inghilterra, è più viva che mai, te lo vuoi mettere nella testa?» aveva insistito la Tina. «O secondo te mi avrebbe scritto dall'aldilà?»
«Macché aldilà e aldilà, io...» aveva cercato di reagire il Dubbio.
Ma sul viso della Tina era scesa una nuova espressione.
Tale e quale, aveva detto il giovanotto.
E lei aveva parlato di aldilà.
Le immagini del funerale del commenda le erano tornate in mente.

Il marmo della tomba, quella del professore e quella accanto alla sua.

Quella data.

La Maria Teresa Supposta.

«Vieni con me», aveva ordinato al Dubbio.

«Ma io devo tornare a casa», aveva piagnucolato lui.

La Tina però si era già avviata.

154.

La beatitudine della Canterina svanì di colpo, spenta l'aureola della santità.

Dal battello che, partito da Acquaseria, dopo Dervio attraccava a Bellano, l'Ernesto non era sceso.

Alla gioia di vedere il proprio figlio tornare da una giornata di lavoro si sostituì l'angoscia di immaginare nuovi guai.

Le sere precedenti, s'era appostata allo sbocco della contrada sbirciando verso il molo per godersi lo spettacolo dell'Ernesto che, vestito di quel bel blu che faceva tanto marinaio, scendeva dal battello scambiando quattro chiacchiere da pari a pari col pontilista di Bellano.

Resistette alla tentazione di andare a chiedere al battellotto se fosse successo qualcosa. E allo stesso tempo avvertì una certa resistenza a tornare a casa per ritrovarsi sola, come le era già capitato troppe volte, seduta, in cucina, ad aspettare in compagnia dei fagiani e delle anatroccole della tovaglia, spesso invidiati per l'immobile felicità del disegno dentro il quale passavano la vita.

D'altronde non aveva altra scelta.

Si avviò, lenta, con un peso sul petto e altrettanto alle gambe, come se le avesse gonfie al pari della sua collega cuciniera che però almeno aveva uno scompenso e due figli che lavoravano al cotonificio e non le davano pensieri.

La contrada era silenziosa stante l'ora.

Sì, qualche rumore c'era, voci e suoni smorzati che uscivano dalle finestre aperte per via del caldo. Ma che non inficiavano un silenzio più di sostanza, ben noto alle orecchie della Canterina che dentro quelle viuzze c'era nata e cresciuta. Era quel tipo di silenzio che preludeva a qualcosa. Il più delle volte, e nella bella stagione soprattutto, agli ultimi giochi dei bambini che, numerosi, scendevano nelle corti in attesa dei richiami ad alta voce, quando si faceva l'ora del letto.

Ma era un silenzio che precedeva anche le brutte notizie, le morti, le malattie, le disgrazie. Come una specie di avviso, prepararsi al peggio e nel frattempo godere ancora un po' l'illusione.

Quando, sbucata all'altro capo della contrada, la Canterina vide che il dottor Lonati stava per imboccare la scala che saliva a casa sua, vide solo la bocca del dottore che si apriva.

«No, no!»

Il Lonati, al vederla, aveva compreso al volo.

Il pallore che era comparso in viso alla Canterina non era sfuggito al suo occhio clinico.

«No, no!» gridò quindi volando incontro alla donna, caso mai avesse avuto bisogno di essere sostenuta.

«Non è successo niente», disse.

L'Ernesto però per quella notte restava di là, sarebbe tornato l'indomani, come al solito.

Aveva telefonato a casa sua pregandolo di avvisarla.

Ma in verità era stata la signora Lonati a rispondere.

Una volta compreso chi c'era all'altro capo del telefono, Vittoria aveva evitato di passare la cornetta al marito, nonostante l'Ernesto le avesse chiesto di parlare con lui.

«Meglio se dici a me», aveva obiettato lei.

Qualunque novità portasse quella telefonata, sarebbe stato opportuno che tra i due ci fosse qualcuno a far da cuscinetto, non si sapeva mai.

Infatti moglie e marito avevano rischiato di litigare subito dopo.

«Perché non l'hai passato a me?» aveva chiesto il Lonati.

«Perché no», aveva risposto sua moglie.

«Cosa significa?» aveva rilanciato lui.

Significava, aveva spiegato Vittoria Lonati, che, stante i recenti avvenimenti, non riteneva suo marito abbastanza imparziale per poter giudicare con serenità la richiesta che il Dubbio aveva fatto, cioè...

«Cioè un tubo!» era sbottato lui.

Se lei, aveva inveito, pensava che non fosse lucido per ascoltare la richiesta del Dubbio, allora lui non voleva nemmeno sapere cosa le avesse chiesto.

«Chiaro?»

«Vedi?» aveva però osservato lei mantenendo una calma olimpica. Se reagiva così, stizzoso, gridando, non faceva altro che darle ragione.

«Reagisco come mi pare», aveva risposto il Lonati registrando i toni.

«Anzi», aveva aggiunto poi, «ti do ragione.»

Non era abbastanza lucido, imparziale, sereno nei confronti del Dubbio.

«Quindi non voglio nemmeno sapere quello che...»

«E no, mio caro», l'aveva interrotto la moglie.

Lei, aveva chiarito, la sua parte l'aveva fatta.

Quella che non voleva interpretare invece era la parte della moglie impicciona, che sa tutto di tutti, che si fa raccontare dal marito ogni callo che vede in ambulatorio.

«Cosa significa?» aveva chiesto il Lonati.

«Semplice», aveva risposto la moglie.

Significava che adesso lei gli riferiva quello che l'Ernesto le aveva detto al telefono e lui sarebbe andato dalla Canterina a riferire che non si doveva preoccupare, non era successo niente, suo figlio stava bene eccetera eccetera.

Ma allora, se tutto andava bene, se non era successo niente, perché l'Ernesto non era tornato a casa?, fu la domanda logica della Canterina.

Nemmeno Vittoria Lonati lo sapeva.

L'aveva chiesto, ma l'Ernesto era stato vago.

Vallo a sapere, pensò il dottore.

«Dirai solo che ha perso l'ultimo battello», gli aveva suggerito la moglie.

«Ha solo perso il battello», ripeté il Lonati, certo di mentire per conto terzi o quarti.

«Ma come ha fatto?» chiese ancora la Canterina.

«Stia tranquilla, non si agiti», riuscì solo a dire il Lonati.

La Canterina infine lo guardò e tacque, capendo che poteva insistere fin che voleva ma nemmeno il dottore aveva risposte da offrire alle sue domande.

155.

Tra le tante domande che erano salite alle labbra della Supposta dopo aver aperto e aver visto chi aveva suonato, non una era riuscita ad articolarsi in parole. Tant'è che era stata la Tina la prima a rompere il silenzio.

Con una domanda.

«Possiamo entrare?»

Possiamo, due. Lei, e il Dubbio.

Sul giovanotto si era posato lo sguardo dell'ex infermiera. Interrogativo.

«Dovremmo parlare con lei, chiederle delle cose», aveva proseguito la Tina.

«Venite», s'era decisa a parlare la Supposta.

La Tina era entrata, il Dubbio aveva avuto bisogno di un ulteriore incoraggiamento da parte della ragazza.

«Dai!»

Ordine secco, come se parlasse con un cagnolino.

E in effetti, al pari di un cagnolino il Dubbio le era andato dietro poco prima, quando gli aveva imposto di seguirla, senza nemmeno rispondere al mezzo piagnisteo col quale l'Ernesto le aveva detto che per lui s'era fatta l'ora di tornare a casa.

Niente da fare, doveva seguirla.

«Dove, da chi?» aveva chiesto lui.

Dall'unica persona cui la Tina poteva sottoporre tutti i sospetti che le stavano nascendo in testa per cercare di comporli in un pensiero logico, coerente.

156.

Per quanto poteva ricordare, Maria Teresa Supposta era certa che il campanello di casa sua suonava per la prima volta da che abitava lì a quell'ora di sera, quasi le otto.

Prima di aprire aveva sbirciato dalla finestra della cucina.

Una bella sorpresa, la Tina e quel giovanotto.

Senza remo.

Aveva fatto due conti e poi aveva aperto, la ragazza era una garanzia.

Tric trac, un minuto buono tra la serratura nuova e il chiavistello.

Alt, però!

Era uscita e s'era chiusa la porta alle spalle.

«Dovremmo parlare con lei», aveva detto la Tina.

Il crepuscolo era ormai agli sgoccioli. Il grigiore che spesso vedeva dalla sua camera da letto quando era già sotto le lenzuola stava prendendo il posto della strada di luce che portava al paradiso.

Quella luce, quei due giovani uno accanto all'altra davanti a lei le erano sembrati per un momento la metafora degli anni che aveva sulle spalle.

Aveva cacciato via il pensiero.

Se non ne aveva sentito il peso sino ad allora non era proprio quello il momento di cominciare a farlo.

«Venite», aveva detto.

«Grazie», aveva risposto la Tina.

Una volta dentro casa, e col solo sguardo, Maria Teresa Supposta aveva chiesto il motivo della visita. Solo dopo, a cose chiarite, il giovanotto aveva chiesto la cortesia di fare una telefonata onde poter avvisare sua madre che quella sera non sarebbe tornato a casa.

L'ex infermiera non li aveva fatti accomodare nel mausoleo di famiglia, in cucina piuttosto, pensando che, nel caso, aveva sottomano una via di fuga rapida grazie all'uscita posteriore. Poi, fulminata dal pensiero di come l'avesse fatta rinforzare proprio quello stesso giorno, s'era seduta a capotavola, a portata dell'angolo dove appoggiava scope e spazzolone, ottime armi per la difesa personale in mancanza d'altro.

Quindi aveva dato l'avvio alle danze.

«Allora, cosa succede?»

Aveva parlato rivolgendosi alla Tina ma la ragazza le aveva risposto guardando l'Ernesto.

«Parla», aveva detto.

Era necessario che lei sentisse tutta la storia di quella sera, compresa la spiegazione del motivo per cui quel pomeriggio s'era presentato a casa del commenda con un remo in mano.

Alla fine del racconto il Dubbio era tutto sudato. Via via che raccontava il buio aveva invaso la cucina. Maria Teresa Supposta aveva più volte avuto la tentazione di alzarsi dalla sedia e accendere la luce ma non se l'era sentita di interrompere il monologo del giovanotto, qualcosa l'aveva frenata. Era stato proprio il buio.

Le parole dell'Ernesto, per continuare a uscire dalla sua bocca, avevano avuto bisogno del buio. Nel buio trovavano forma e sostanza perché, l'ex infermiera l'aveva avvertito con più di un brivido, venivano con tutta probabilità da un mondo di buio, un mondo che non stava di là, nell'imprecisato luogo dove portava la strada di luce che aveva sempre immaginato, ma in un posto altrettanto lontano.

E buio, come il fondo del lago, secondo quanto le aveva detto una volta il professore suo padre dopo l'unico tentativo di immersione che aveva fatto.

«Non c'è luce lì sotto anche se sembra così, guardando dalla riva.»

Alla fine da quel buio era emersa la voce della Tina.

«Lei cosa ne pensa?»

Ma la Supposta aveva taciuto.

«Non sembra strano anche a lei che la Valeria e quella ragazza, quella Astrid, abbiano la stessa data di nascita? Che lui», aveva detto facendo un cenno del capo in direzione del Dubbio, «si sia confuso?»

Il pensiero dell'ex infermiera era volato alla tomba accanto a quella di suo padre. L'aveva immaginata in quel momento, nel buio della notte, come se quello stesso buio emanasse da sotto terra e togliesse l'ossigeno che a quegli ospiti non serviva più. Ma era a lei adesso che il respiro si stava accorciando. Avrebbe voluto aprire una finestra.

«Che lei sappia...» aveva continuato a dire la Tina.

Le parole della ragazza erano giunte a fatica nelle sue orecchie. No, voleva rispondere, lei non ne sapeva niente. Non sapeva proprio niente circa un'eventuale sorella gemella della sua amica Valeria.

Era ora di finirla con quella storia.

Era ora di accendere la luce e di aprire una finestra.

Così aveva fatto e aveva ritrovato la tranquillità per rispondere ciò che aveva risposto.

Non ne sapeva niente, poteva solo dire che un parto gemellare non era un evento così raro, oltre essere naturale.

In ogni caso lei non aveva mai fatto la levatrice.

Durante quel periodo lei e suo padre frequentavano poco il lago e della Maria Dominetti, l'unica che potesse sapere qualcosa di preciso circa un'eventuale gemella della Valeria, sempre che fosse ancora viva, aveva un ricordo che già definire vago era troppo.

157.

L'aveva vista, intravista più che altro, qualche volta.

Vista per davvero una volta sola ed era stato quando il Vergonese aveva voluto presentarla a suo padre.

Era stato, più o meno, nel settembre del 1940, quando la guerra sembrava per davvero una cosa lontana, che riguardava pochi, una pratica che si sarebbe chiusa alla svelta.

La Dominetti era arrivata da poco sul lago e per i primi tempi, occhio e croce un paio di mesi, aveva soggiornato proprio Alla Ruota che Gira. La giunta amministrativa non aveva potuto fare altrimenti visto che la casetta che le era stata destinata aveva avuto bisogno di più tempo per porre rimedio a delle infiltrazioni d'acqua che avevano fatto marcire parte della soletta.

Erano stati tempi di mosconi!

Figurarsi, una donna così, bella e sola, nonostante l'età perché aveva già passato i trent'anni da un po'.

Non che lei facesse più di tanto per attirare a sé gli sguardi degli uomini, sposati o no che fossero.

Le bastava essere quello che era.

Però sembrava che intorno a lei gravitasse un campo elettrico che li teneva alla larga.

Forse era un effetto del suo sguardo freddo oppure di un certo atteggiamento, come dire?, da cittadina.

Forse era stato per quello che avevano cominciato a chiamarla dottoressa e il titolo, per quanto non le spettasse, le era rimasto appiccicato.

L'unico che si permetteva di prendere qualche confidenza con lei era il Vergonese.

Forte del fatto di essere proprietario dell'albergo, si toglieva spesso lo sfizio di servirla a tavola, a volte di sedere per scambiare quattro chiacchiere.

Niente che fosse meno che formale.

Buongiorno, buonasera, come sta, cosa desidera.

Un paio di mesi, forse anche qualcosa di più, visto che i lavori della casa andavano a rilento.

Durante quel periodo l'albergo del Vergonese era diventato una specie di succursale del consultorio della levatrice e il Vergonese stesso aveva messo a disposizione della Dominetti il proprio telefono per le chiamate d'emergenza. Lui stesso s'era reso disponibile in qualità di autista, se per caso la «dottoressa» fosse dovuta uscire di notte oppure avesse dovuto raggiungere località che ancora non conosceva bene.

Agli amici più intimi, che si potevano permettere di fare allusioni circa tutta quella disponibilità, il Vergonese si limitava a rispondere con un'alzata di spalle.

Pochi però credevano all'innocenza della sua generosità, i più erano convinti che tra i due ci fosse ormai ben altro.

E le chiacchiere avevano contribuito ad alimentare il mistero.

158.

L'Infantina credeva solo ai misteri gaudiosi, dolorosi, gloriosi e luminosi, visto che li ripeteva tutte le sere quando recitava il santo rosario. Per tutto il resto a suo modo di vedere c'era invece, sempre, una spiegazione.

Erano le nove della mattina quando si avviò alla volta del cotonificio. Il Biagetto aveva appena cominciato una settimana col turno di notte, dalle dieci alle sei del mattino, e non era ancora tornato a casa.

Strano, perché nei due giorni precedenti se l'era visto piombare in casa alle sei e un quarto come se avesse volato dal cotone a casa, l'aveva appena salutata, non aveva nemmeno degnato di uno sguardo la colazione che gli aveva preparato e si era buttato sul letto vestito tale e quale piombando nel giro di pochi secondi in un sonno dal quale si era risvegliato solo verso le quattro del pomeriggio.

Magari era stato trattenuto da un lavoro straordinario, aveva ipotizzato. E siccome doveva fare anche un po' di spesa aveva pensato di andare a chiedere notizie al Limusina, il custode del cotonificio.

Lavori straordinari, no, le rispose quello.

«Non ce ne sono in ballo.»

Però...

Adesso che ci pensava...

«Adesso che ci penso», disse il Limusina, «non l'ho mica visto uscire.»

«Ed entrare?» si informò l'Infantina che conosceva bene la testa dispari di suo nipote.

«Entrare sì», disse il custode.
«E allora?» buttò lì l'Infantina.
«È un mistero», concluse il Limusina.
«Macché mistero delle mie scarpe», ribatté la donna.
Il custode allargò le braccia, non sapeva cosa dire.
L'Infantina sentì nascere in sé dei sospetti.
«Sei sicuro di averlo visto entrare?» chiese al Limusina.

159.

Ecco, Maria Teresa Supposta l'aveva vista durante il periodo in cui la Dominetti aveva soggiornato presso l'albergo del Vergonese, quando il Vergonese l'aveva presentata al professore.

Era una domenica di fine settembre, il mondo del lago sembrava una sinfonia. Padre e figlia non avevano resistito all'idea di passare la giornata continuando a scoprire quel paradiso che da poco si era aperto sotto i loro occhi.

«La nostra nuova levatrice!»

Il professore, da quel gentiluomo d'antico stampo che era, s'era alzato da tavola e aveva omaggiato la Dominetti di un mezzo inchino, tenendole la mano come se volesse baciarla.

Per tutta risposta sul viso della Dominetti era comparsa una smorfia di degnazione, come se la celebrità fosse lei. Alla figlia non aveva regalato nemmeno una ruga di saluto e, per tutta risposta, Maria Teresa Supposta si era comportata come se «la nostra nuova levatrice» non esistesse. Anzi, aveva continuato a mangiare, s'era infilata in bocca di proposito una bella fetta di bresaola dell'antipasto, cosa che suo padre più tardi le aveva rimproverato.

«Ma chi crede di essere quella?» aveva risposto lei.

Il professore si era limitato a sorridere all'uscita della figlia.

Forse aveva pensato che più di una certa, comprensibile gelosia professionale, la figlia fosse disturbata dall'indiscutibile bellezza della Dominetti.

Una bellezza altera, un po' distante contro cui la... la normalità, l'assenza di acuti della Maria Teresa nulla poteva.

Ci poteva stare, anche se la figlia del professore mai e poi mai avrebbe ammesso di invidiare qualcosa in quella donna.

E in una seconda occasione aveva avuto modo di ribadire quanto poco le piacesse «la nostra nuova levatrice». Era accaduto quando, tempo dopo, si erano fermati per cenare Alla Ruota che Gira, tornando da un lungo giro che li aveva portati sino al lago di Novate Mezzola. Con la scusa di andare in bagno la Maria Teresa aveva lasciato il padre a tavola e incrociata una cameriera le aveva chiesto notizie della Dominetti.

Quella le aveva risposto con uno sguardo vacuo.

«Quella bella signora che è stata vostra ospite per un po'», s'cra spicgata la Supposta.

«Ah!» aveva compreso la cameriera. «La dottoressa!»

Dottoressa!

Capito che roba!

Comunque non stava più lì, adesso abitava a casa sua.

Però di solito alla domenica andava sempre da loro a pranzo o a cena.

«Ma arriva più tardi», aveva specificato la cameriera, «in compagnia del signor console.»

160.

Visto entrare, sì, il Limusina era sicuro.

Sicuro perché il Riffa era entrato per ultimo, come sempre.

Anche la settimana prima, quando aveva fatto il turno di giorno, era sempre entrato per ultimo e un pochino tardi.

Mica tanta roba, un paio di minuti.

Comunque in ritardo, che prima o poi dalla direzione l'avrebbero richiamato, perché i timbri sul cartellino non mentivano.

«Però non l'hai visto uscire!» insisté l'Infantina.

Perché, così come il Biagetto entrava sempre per ultimo visto il grande amore che nutriva per quel lavoro, per logica stretta doveva anche essere il primo a uscire.

Impossibile non vederlo quindi.

Totale: se il Limusina quella mattina non l'aveva visto uscire, la conclusione era semplice.

«Cioè?» chiese il custode.

«È ancora dentro», rispose l'Infantina.

«Ma non è possibile!»

«Invece sì.»

161.

Il Dubbio era convinto che quella notte non sarebbe riuscito a chiudere occhio. Non tanto per il fatto di essere lontano da casa, fuori dal suo letto, quanto perché la Tina gli aveva offerto di dormire in casa del commenda. Così aveva scoperto che quella era ormai casa della ragazza perché il commenda era morto.

Ma morto da poco, troppo da poco per non immaginare che il suo fantasma si aggirasse ancora in quelle stanze e volesse sapere chi fosse l'estraneo che si era introdotto in casa sua.

Per evitare di cadere in suggestioni tenebrose, aveva rifiutato di dormire sia in quella che era stata la camera del commenda sia in quella che aveva occupato la Tina quando, sempre più spesso, s'era fermata a dormire lì.

La poltrona, aveva detto, la poltrona del salotto.

«Be'», aveva acconsentito la ragazza, «è comoda anche quella. Il commenda ci passava giornate intere.»

Tanto era bastato al Dubbio per scartare pure quella.

Rimasto solo, per un po' non aveva fatto altro che camminare avanti e indietro per i locali del piano terra, attento a cogliere il più piccolo rumore che suonasse strano o misterioso.

Nonostante tutto non aveva percepito altro che un pacifico silenzio dentro il quale piano piano s'era quietato, lasciandosi vincere dal sonno che aveva poi consumato sdraiato sul tappeto del salotto, la testa appoggiata al braccio.

E s'era anche sognato!
Roba da non credere!
S'era sognato di lui che andava in giro a braccetto con la Tina, proprio come aveva appena detto l'ex infermiera della dottoressa e del signor console, finendo il suo racconto.

162.

Non solo dottoressa, ma viaggiava anche con un signor console!

Alla sua uscita, il professor Supposta aveva sorriso.

Console, aveva commentato, per modo di dire. Non certo come sua figlia l'aveva inteso. Nel caso specifico era uno di quei titoli che la prosopopea dell'epoca aveva assegnato ai suoi ducetti prodotti in serie, i quali se ne facevano vanto, si riempivano la bocca. Il console in oggetto infatti altri non era se non il console della milizia confinaria D'Argò che ormai da tempo abitava in una casa che si era fatto assegnare dalla giunta amministrativa. Era un edificio che la gente chiamava la Villa. Non ne aveva le dimensioni, forse una pretesa architettonica, ma ridotta, riassunta. Era abbastanza isolata, con un discreto giardino davanti, il bosco alle spalle, raggiungibile solo grazie a una mulattiera. Scomoda sotto molti punti di vista. Comoda, invece, per certi traffici che secondo la gente del posto il D'Argò aveva cominciato a dirigere, stante la vicinanza del confine.

«Lo vidi una volta», aveva detto Maria Teresa Supposta.

Brillantina e divisa.

Era stato in occasione dell'ultima gita che lei e suo padre avevano fatto sul lago, a guerra ormai in pieno svolgimento e con una fine non così a portata di mano come la propaganda voleva far intendere.

Di sfuggita, mentre lei e il genitore uscivano dall'albergo del Vergonese e la dottoressa entrava sottobraccio al signor console.

163.

«È entrato di sicuro ed è altrettanto sicuro che non è uscito.»

Spinetta Bretella fu categorica.

Bastava controllare il cartellino che non era stato ritirato, il timbro non mentiva.

Ora d'entrata, sei e otto minuti, ora d'uscita...

«Quindi è ancora qui dentro», affermò.

«Ma dove?» chiese l'Infantina.

«E perché?» aggiunse il direttore del cotonificio Laricetti cui la questione era stata sottoposta.

«Il perché ce lo dirà lui quando lo troviamo», disse, come se stesse facendo un giuramento, Spinetta Bretella.

Prima, però, bisognava trovarlo.

164.

Come la Dominetti.

La Tina non ci aveva dormito tutta la notte.

Se solo avesse letto con più calma quella lettera o la ricordasse meglio o addirittura l'avesse tenuta anziché rimbucarla come le aveva ordinato di fare il Dalamonti!

In ogni caso, già quello che sapeva, la data di nascita di quella Astrid che aveva scritto, il sostenere di avere una gemella, il fatto di essersi rivolta alla Dominetti, che peraltro all'epoca non faceva più la levatrice, scrivendole ciò che aveva saputo delle sue origini...

E quello che la ex infermiera le aveva rivelato, che la Valeria non poteva essere figlia di quella che credeva sua madre...

Ecco, tutte quelle cose messe insieme la facevano sentire a volte dentro una fantasia degna del migliore, o peggiore, fotoromanzo e a volte invece come se avesse la testa stretta dentro un vaso dove pian piano l'ossigeno si stava esaurendo.

Come se le persone che aveva frequentato di più, che credeva di conoscere meglio sino ad allora fossero maschere, i loro visi nascosti, e non solo quelli. Per questo sentiva la necessità di parlare con questa Dominetti.

Certo, prima di parlarci doveva trovarla.

Maria Teresa Supposta non le poteva essere di grande aiuto. Aveva addirittura messo in dubbio che potesse essere ancora viva, e comunque, aveva aggiunto, non ne sapeva nulla da tempo immemore.

Quando infatti, finita la guerra, lei e suo padre avevano ricominciato a frequentare il lago e infine ci avevano preso casa, una delle sue prime curiosità era stata quella di chiedere notizie della levatrice.

«Non c'era già più quando tornammo.»

S'era trasferita dopo la morte di suo marito, del console.

Ah già, il console!, era sbottata la Supposta.

Il... il... come si chiamava?

D'Argò, proprio lui.

Morto, sparito nel maggio del '44, di notte, in montagna, durante un'azione.

Morto di sicuro.

Forse caduto, forse colpito da una pallottola vagante, forse chissà cosa.

E anche sparito, perché il corpo non era mai stato ritrovato.

«Sic transit gloria mundi», aveva commentato il professore apprendendo le novità.

Poi, sempre quel giorno, avevano voluto riallacciare il filo col passato e pranzare Alla Ruota che Gira.

E lì si erano trovati faccia a faccia con un'altra novità, una sorpresa.

Al loro ingresso il Vergonese li aveva salutati da lontano e poi era sparito per un quarto d'ora. S'era presentato più tardi mano nella mano con la bambina bionda che la giovane donna che li aveva ricevuti alla reception aveva detto essere la di lui figlia. Le aveva detto di salutare bene il professore e Maria Teresa.

«Adesso torna dalla mamma, Valeria», le aveva poi ordinato.

Amedeo Supposta e la figlia si erano scambiati giusto un'occhiata.

Il Vergonese aveva abbassato la voce.

«Non sa di essere stata adottata», aveva detto.

Anzi, aveva aggiunto rivolgendosi al professore, se più

tardi, quando aveva terminato di pranzare, avesse potuto parlargli in privato...

Alla fine del pranzo il professore aveva chiesto alla figlia di aspettarlo. Sorridendo le aveva detto che, stante la bella giornata, non le sarebbe dispiaciuto prendersi un po' di sole mentre lui dava retta al Vergonese.

Maria Teresa Supposta aveva anche lei risposto con un sorriso al genitore. Ne conosceva e condivideva la discrezione con la quale trattava certe cose. Era la stessa peraltro con la quale, per lunghi anni, aveva tenuto per sé ciò che poco più tardi, tornando verso casa, aveva appreso dalle parole di suo padre.

165.

Più o meno verso mezzogiorno l'Infantina cominciò a pensare che forse, oltre ai misteri del santo rosario, probabilmente ce n'erano anche altri.

Del Biagetto infatti non c'era ancora traccia.

Di reparto in reparto era stata fatta correre la voce che chiunque ne avesse notizie era pregato di riferire alla Spinetta Bretella.

Voci perlopiù infondate e contraddittorie non avevano portato ad alcun risultato.

L'unica cosa da fare sarebbe stata chiedere ai suoi compagni di linea, quelli che avevano fatto la notte con lui.

«Facciamolo», disse il direttore Laricetti.

«Mica facile», rispose Spinetta Bretella.

Perché tutti quelli che facevano la notte, con l'unica probabile eccezione dello scomparso Biagio Riffa, avevano una ragione ben precisa per fare quel turno: tenersi il giorno per lavorare altrove. Era gente di campagna, che veniva dalle frazioni, e non solo quelle comprese nel territorio del comune di Bellano. Per interrogarli bisognava andarli a cercare uno a uno: un lavoro da cani oltre che una perdita di tempo.

A quel punto sarebbe stato meglio chiedere aiuto ai carabinieri o ai vigili del fuoco.

Udite relazione e conclusioni della Bretella, il direttore del cotonificio sbuffò.

«Aspettiamo almeno un paio d'ore ancora prima di dare un allarme del genere», disse.

«Va bene», acconsentì la Bretella.

«Poi, una volta che lo troviamo», aggiunse il Laricetti, «sempre che non sia morto da qualche parte, con una scusa qualsiasi me lo licenzia.»

«Volentieri», obbedì Spinetta Bretella.

166.

La moglie del Vergonese aveva accettato di buon grado la proposta che il marito le aveva fatto e che in un certo senso aveva soddisfatto il desiderio di avere un figlio.

«Ma se non poteva!» aveva subito esclamato Maria Teresa Supposta.

Prima di raccontare, il professore era rimasto in silenzio per un po', s'era lasciato alle spalle l'albergo come se volesse avere la certezza che nessuno, oltre a sua figlia, ascoltasse quello che il Vergonese gli aveva rivelato.

«Ascolta», le aveva detto in tono paziente.

La Vergonese non aveva avuto molto tempo per decidere, aveva dovuto prendere l'occasione al volo oppure lasciarla andare e macerarsi per il resto della vita nell'idea di non poter essere madre.

Insomma, s'era trattato di dare una casa a una neonata la cui madre era morta di parto. Il Vergonese però sapeva che sua moglie non avrebbe accettato facilmente di tenersi in casa la figlia di chissà chi.

«Il patto fu che doveva passare per figlia loro però!»

«E come?» aveva interloquito Maria Teresa.

«Ha studiato per bene la faccenda», aveva risposto il professore.

Dapprima aveva messo in giro la voce che sua moglie finalmente era rimasta incinta. Aveva fatto anche una festicciola in albergo insieme con il personale, garantendosi così una diffusione immediata della novità. Poi, quando secondo i calcoli la donna entrava nel secondo mese di gravidanza, aveva sparso un'altra voce secondo la quale, a causa di certe complicanze non meglio definite, la moglie avrebbe dovuto essere ricoverata, andare lontano da lì.

«E l'ha spedita dalle parti di Sondalo.»

Un colpo di genio.

Sondalo andava a braccetto con tubercolosi.

Il risultato?

Non avrebbe fatto meraviglia se la donna, come in effetti era accaduto, se ne fosse stata lontana dal paese per mesi e mesi per tornare poi, guarita e con tanto di figlioletta in braccio, a prendersi i complimenti di tutti.

«Come di fatto è successo», aveva concluso il professore.

Maria Teresa Supposta era rimasta in silenzio un paio di minuti, giusto il tempo di fare due conti.

Poi aveva parlato.

«Ma nessuno si è insospettito per una assenza così lunga, ben oltre i tempi di una gravidanza normale? Nessuno si è accorto di niente?»

Il professore aveva approvato con un gesto del capo la prontezza intuitiva della figlia.

«A quanto mi ha detto il Vergonese la madre naturale aveva avuto, lei sì, una gravidanza difficile e la neonata era gracile, sofferente alla nascita, tanto che si era temuto che non ce la potesse fare. La neonata aveva un ritardo di sviluppo che poi, come abbiamo potuto notare poco fa, madre natura ha compensato in maniera egregia.»

«Sarà!» aveva commentato Maria Teresa.

Il professore le aveva lanciato un'occhiata. Percepiva nuove domande solleticare le labbra della figlia.

«Le cose ormai stanno così», aveva sentenziato il professore.

E la figlia, obbediente come era sempre stata, s'era tenuta per sé dubbi e obiezioni.

167.

«Ancora questa storia!»

Era, in sostanza, tutto quello che la Tina riuscì a ottenere da sua madre quella mattina.

Prima di tutto, con la scusa di andare a dare un'occhiata a quella che, nonostante fosse sua, continuava a chiamare la casa del commenda, era andata a dare la sveglia al Dubbio.

L'aveva trovato già in piedi.

Gli aveva fatto un caffè e poi l'aveva spedito al lavoro.

Tornata a casa si era occupata di riordinare e preparare il pranzo mentre sua madre si era dedicata per l'intera mattina all'orto che assorbiva tutte le sue attenzioni.

A pranzo, sedute una di fronte all'altra, la Tina prese di petto l'argomento cercando l'aiuto che le serviva per uscire dal groviglio di pensieri che l'avevano fatta dormire malamente.

La Dominetti, la Valeria, il console...

Sua madre le impedì quasi subito di proseguire.

«La devi smettere», disse la Brigida.

E si doveva ficcare in testa che tutte quelle cose, anche quello che era successo, appartenevano a un passato ormai lontano e non serviva a niente e a nessuno ritirarlo in ballo.

«Allora ammetti che qualcosa è successo», obiettò la Tina.

Sua madre però era un osso duro.

«Se anche fosse, è morto e sepolto», rispose.

Sottoterra o sul fondo del lago.

Dove regnava lo stesso silenzio che scese tra madre e figlia.

Alle due, dopo aver sparecchiato e lavato i piatti, la Tina uscì. La Brigida come d'abitudine riposava in camera sua, un paio d'ore almeno.

Si diresse verso la casa del commenda. Aveva in programma di preparare gli scatoloni con la roba che era stata del Dalamonti e che i figli volevano destinare a una casa di riposo.

La Supposta s'era offerta di darle una mano.

Come forza lavoro non le sarebbe stata di grande aiuto ma, ragionò la Tina mentre camminava sotto un sole feroce, avrebbe trovato in lei una golosa ascoltatrice e poi, chissà...

168.

Chissà cos'era successo, dove era stato, dove aveva passato la notte.

La Canterina s'era tormentata con quei dubbi per tutta la giornata e a patirne di più erano stati il risotto, quasi una colla, e il purè, pieno di grumi, che i bambini dell'asilo avevano comunque mangiato perché «Guai sprecare la roba da mangiare!».

Anche se faceva veramente schifo.

Lei stessa si era resa conto che quella mattina aveva la testa da tutt'altra parte e non poteva farci niente. S'era consolata pensando che una giornata storta poteva capitare a tutti e che in ogni caso nessuno sarebbe morto di fame.

Alla fine, con molta, troppa lentezza, le sette della sera stavano arrivando.

La Canterina si stava chiedendo se andare a spiare l'arrivo del figlio allo sbocco della contrada oppure attenderlo in casa.

Aspettò lì.

Seduta, lo sguardo fisso all'orologio da muro che, mai se n'era accorta, faceva un rumore sordo a ogni movimento della lancetta dei secondi.

Sette e uno, sette e cinque, sette e dieci minuti.

Dell'Ernesto nessuna traccia.

Possibile che fosse successo ancora qualcosa?

Cosa doveva fare adesso?, si chiese la Canterina prossima alle lacrime.

169.

Sette e un quarto e il Dubbio non la finiva più di ridere.

«Non ci posso credere», singhiozzava.

«Se non ci credi chiedi a chi vuoi», gli disse il pontilista di Bellano, Aurelio Riporto.

Tanto ormai lo sapeva tutto il paese quello che era successo al Riffa. Il Dubbio era forse l'unico che non ne fosse al corrente e per quello il Riporto l'aveva fermato alla discesa dal battello con quella frase: «Lo sai cos'è successo al Riffa?».

«No», aveva risposto l'Ernesto.

Beccato nudo come un verme nel reparto torcitura del cotonificio!

«Non ci credo», aveva risposto l'Ernesto.

«Ah no?»

Erano le sette e quattro minuti.

170.

In quattro.

Quando mancavano pochi minuti alla fine del turno di notte avevano circondato il Riffa.

Erano tutti della Valvarrone.

Due di Tremenico, uno di Avano, uno di Vestreno.

Di Tremenico, uno era l'Ozio, fratello dell'Amanda, la ragazza cui il Riffa aveva tentato di vendere col trucco le scarpettine da ballo e che, secondo quanto aveva raccontato all'Oltramonti, s'era poi messo di sopra, di sotto e via dicendo: il Riffa lo conosceva, ma non sapeva che lavorasse anche lui al cotonificio. L'altro era un suo amico, lo chiamavano Spina, secco come un morto di tisi e cattivo come l'aglio. Di Avano era il Rusti, primo cugino dell'Amanda, l'altro, quello di Vestreno, era invece il Bertone, socio di caccia del Birmino, l'altro fratello dell'Amanda.

In quanto alle mani, talisqualis tutti: badili.

Il Riffa non aveva nemmeno avuto il tempo di accorgersene, l'avevano già alzato di peso e portato nel cesso. Un bel po' di scotch da pacchi sulla bocca per non farlo gridare e l'avevano spogliato. Poi gli avevano legato le mani e i piedi.

«Mia sorella ha detto di dirti che quelle scarpette le vanno un po' strette», gli aveva sussurrato l'Ozio.

Quindi l'avevano portato sul tetto del cotonificio.

«Adesso arrangiati per tornare a casa», gli avevano detto.

Poi, come se se ne ricordassero solo in quel momento: «A proposito. Se ti fanno male i piedi usa queste».

E gli avevano lasciato un paio di scarpe da donna.

Nuove. A giudicare dalla qualità, venivano senz'altro dalle scorte del suo camioncino. Gliele avevano legate attorno al collo.

«Ti facevo più furbo», gli aveva sussurrato ancora l'Ozio. «Pensavo ti fosse bastato il messaggio. Le scarpe sinistre di qui, quelle destre di là, come fai tu con le ragazze che non dovresti nemmeno guardare. Invece, niente! Insisti, e spari cazzate ai quattro venti. Vediamo adesso se ti passa la voglia», e scambiando gomitate e risate con i compari se n'era andato.

Il Riffa era rimasto lì un po' cercando di slegarsi le mani per togliersi lo scotch dalla bocca e chiamare aiuto. Non c'era riuscito e aveva aspettato che gli venisse qualche idea. Solo che, mentre aspettava, era sorto il sole e se avesse continuato ad aspettare l'idea buona gli sarebbe venuto il coccolone perché lì sul tetto piano piano aveva cominciato a scaldare e avanti di quel passo il Riffa avrebbe fatto la fine di una costina alla brace.

Verso l'una, dai e dai, era riuscito a liberarsi i piedi e s'era avviato. Aveva imboccato la porta che dava sul tetto, aveva cominciato a scendere e davanti al primo portellone dei reparti con una spallata l'aveva aperto e s'era trovato nel reparto della torcitura, dove c'erano quasi solo donne.

«Hanno detto che le prime che l'hanno visto sono quasi svenute per lo spavento», aveva raccontato il Riporto.

Il Riffa, forse un po' rincoglionito per il sole e il calore, era rimasto lì, fermo impalato mentre il caporeparto era andato a chiamare la Spinetta Bretella.

Nessuno aveva pensato a coprirlo. Era stata lei a ordinare di farlo.

«Coprite quella vergogna!» aveva strillato.

Poi l'aveva fatto portare in infermeria.

«E poi?» aveva chiesto il Dubbio.

«Poi boh, non lo so», aveva risposto il Riporto.

171.

La Canterina udì gli amati passi del figlio che salivano i pochi gradini della scala e poi percorrevano il corridoio verso la cucina quando da poco erano passate le sette e trenta: passi strascicati come sempre, sia che l'Ernesto tornasse a casa da giornate inconcludenti sia che tornasse come quella sera dal lavoro.

Passi inconfondibili.

Ancora più strisciati adesso perché il Dubbio, dopo il divertente intermezzo che gli aveva proposto il Riporto, aveva cominciato a chiedersi quale ottima scusa servire a sua madre per giustificare la notte passata fuori casa.

Capiva da sé che sarebbe stato meglio non ritornare sull'argomento del cadavere che aveva trovato, perché l'aveva trovato!, in mezzo al lago.

Ci voleva però qualcosa di solido, un argomento davanti al quale sua madre avrebbe dovuto ritirarsi senza sollevare obiezioni.

Nemmeno lui avrebbe saputo dire quale santo gli corse in aiuto.

Sta di fatto che quando la Canterina, con tutti i bei modi possibili e prendendola molto alla larga, riuscì infine a porre la domanda che le stava sul gozzo, a lui scappò di bocca la risposta esatta.

«Sono stato a morosa!»

E se sua madre avesse voluto sapere com'era e come non era, avrebbe potuto risponderle punto su punto.

Anche dirle come si chiamava.

172.

Era andata come la Tina aveva previsto.

La Supposta non aveva fatto gran che, il grosso del lavoro se l'era smazzato lei.

Tutta la roba del Dalamonti alla fine era stata suddivisa in tre categorie: roba da buttare, roba – vestiti in ottimo stato perlopiù – da consegnare all'ente comunale di assistenza, e roba – un paio di orologi, qualche documento e alcune fotografie – da restituire ai figli.

Verso le sei del pomeriggio le due s'erano fatte un bel caffè e se l'erano bevuto sedute nel salotto, chiacchierando un po'.

Chiacchiere vane: il tempo, luglio stava mantenendo fede alla tradizione di essere il mese più umido e afoso dell'anno, la casa ereditata, il futuro della Tina adesso che si trovava nella necessità di trovarsi un altro lavoro...

Be', in quanto a quello c'era solo l'imbarazzo della scelta.

Anche il Vergonese era in cerca di personale, c'era un cartello su una delle vetrine del ristorante.

«Lo sapevi?» aveva chiesto la Supposta.

«Domani ci vado a parlare», aveva risposto la Tina.

L'ex infermiera, con la tazzina del caffè vuota ancora in mano, aveva scosso la testa.

«Sei proprio sicura di voler fare la cameriera?» aveva chiesto.

«Per niente», aveva risposto la Tina.

173.

Nessuno.

Non era stato nessuno.

La stessa risposta il Biagio Riffa l'aveva data al direttore del cotonificio Laricetti, al suo caporeparto, alla Spinetta Bretella, al dottor Lonati.

Non era stato nessuno a prenderlo, denudarlo, legarlo e portarlo sul tetto del cotonificio.

«Ci prendi per scemi?» era stata l'obiezione comune.

«Non me ne frega un cazzo», era stata la risposta.

Se non parlava però, se voleva far credere a tutti di aver messo in piedi quella sceneggiata da solo, poteva considerarsi licenziato all'istante.

La risposta del Riffa, idem come sopra.

Li conosceva uno per uno quei quattro, nome e cognome, paesi di provenienza.

Rivelare i nomi?

Col cazzo!

Al contrario, li avrebbe ringraziati per non avergli rotto le ossa, cosa che peraltro gli avevano promesso nel caso gli fosse venuto in mente di fare ancora l'asino con l'Amanda o con una qualunque delle ragazze della valle.

Il messaggio gli era arrivato, forte e chiaro, era andata bene così.

Per quanto riguardava il lavoro, non c'era mica solo il cotonificio a Bellano.

Morto un papa se ne fa un altro, o no?

Nessuno quindi.

Non era stato nessuno, aveva continuato a rispondere il Riffa anche alla zia Infantina la quale, una volta che se l'era ritrovato a casa, aveva cominciato a curarlo (chiare d'uova sbattute sulla pianta dei piedi, sulla coppa e su gran parte della schiena, era così che si curavano le scottature, non aveva mica bisogno dei consigli del dottore) e non aveva smesso di chiedere.

Ma chi era stato?

174.

Ma com'era?

«Com'è chi?» fece finta di non capire il Dubbio.

Se sperava che sua madre, grazie a una notte di sonno, si fosse dimenticata la storia della morosa che le aveva raccontato la sera prima, eccolo servito.

Non che la sera precedente non avesse insistito.

Ma lui: «Ti dico domani, dai».

Era stanco, poveretto!

E quel domani era arrivato.

Era adesso, ore sei e trenta del mattino, trenta minuti alla partenza per Acquaseria.

C'era tutto il tempo perché le raccontasse un po'.

Che rispondesse alla domanda.

«Ma com'è 'sta morosa?»

«Carina.»

Si diceva così, no?, di una ragazza né bella né brutta.

175.

Bella o brutta che potesse sembrare, circa un paio d'ore più tardi la Tina aveva la faccia di chi dovesse scegliere se buttar giù dalla torre la mamma o il papà. Era inquieta, disorientata.

Era uscita in quello stato dalla Ruota che Gira, dopo aver parlato col Vergonese, e aveva chiare due cose in testa: le era necessario, subito, sfogarsi con qualcuno, e per quello non c'era niente di meglio che la Maria Teresa Supposta. Ma anche, nonostante tutto, era indispensabile trovare questa benedetta Maria Dominetti. E parlarci, sempre che fosse ancora viva.

Il Vergonese se ne stava al centro della sala, controllava il traffico delle cameriere che servivano le colazioni. I tavoli erano quasi tutti occupati, giusto due, apparecchiati, attendevano ancora gli ospiti dell'albergo. L'uomo l'aveva vista entrare, sulle prime forse non l'aveva riconosciuta o forse aveva finto di farlo. Poi, visto che lei se ne stava lì, le si era avviato incontro.

Rideva, anche se non sembrava contento.

«Mi porti notizie?» le aveva detto a mo' di saluto.

Notizie della Valeria?

Non le aveva nemmeno dato il tempo di salutare.

«Sì, perché per quanto ne so io è arrivata», aveva detto con un tono vagamente polemico.

Di quello era certo, aveva ricevuto una telefonata, il viaggio era andato bene, ciao ciao.

Poi niente.

«Cioè, niente...»

Si era avviato verso il banco della reception e dal bordo dello specchio aveva sfilato una cartolina, la solita veduta del Big Ben, e gliel'aveva mostrata.

«A Carmen, Teresa e Marisa.»

Le tre cameriere dell'albergo per inciso.

«Gooood bye!»

«Solo che il god bai l'ha dato la Marisa a me due giorni fa», aveva commentato il Vergonese.

In quel momento s'era bloccato, frenato da un pensiero. Vuoi vedere che...

Già, già, il commenda era morto, l'aveva saputo, adesso la Tina era senza lavoro...

Magari era lì per...

«No», aveva detto lei.

Peccato, aveva pensato lui, perché la conosceva per una gran lavoratrice.

«Era solo per chiederle un'informazione», aveva chiarito la Tina.

«Va bene, dimmi», il Vergonese, con uno sguardo rapido verso la sala, giusto per far intendere che l'albergo era pieno e il daffare non gli mancava.

«Volevo solo sapere se lei sa qualcosa della levatrice di una volta, Maria Dominetti...»

E la Tina a quel punto aveva visto, visto chiaramente, non solo il volto, ma tutta la persona del Vergonese cambiare, come se si stesse ritirando in sé, si stesse asciugando. Non era riuscito a controllare lo sguardo che era diventato sospettoso, aveva negato prima che con le parole con un breve movimento del capo.

«La levatrice... la levatrice...» aveva recitato arrampicandosi sulle parole.

Sì, certo, se la ricordava. Non bene, erano passati un sacco di anni. Tuttavia un po' se la ricordava ma...

«Chissà dov'è finita», aveva detto.

Sempre che fosse ancora viva.

176.

Viva, certo.

«Non so quanto vegeta», disse Maria Teresa Supposta vedendo lo sguardo della Tina.

«Scherzo», aggiunse subito.

Però le poteva garantire che era viva.

Non solo.

Poteva anche confermarle che, come le aveva già accennato, si era in effetti trasferita dalle parti del lago di Piano dove tutt'ora risiedeva.

Il merito della scoperta era tutto del professore suo padre.

Fosse andata presso gli uffici comunali come una cittadina qualunque a chiedere il nuovo indirizzo di un'altra qualunque cittadina, difficile che avrebbe avuto l'informazione. Invece c'era andata con un motivo ben preciso e aveva avuto la sorpresa di non essere una cittadina qualunque. L'impiegata infatti, gentilissima, si ricordava ancora del professor Supposta perché aveva operato una sua cuginetta che, grazie all'intervento, era stata in grado di diventare poi madre.

«Si figuri, adesso ne ha sei, di figli!»

Davanti a tanto entusiasmo, l'ex infermiera non aveva più temuto niente e aveva sparato con invidiabile sicurezza la balla che s'era preparata.

«Cioè», disse Maria Teresa Supposta, «che ero venuta a conoscenza per caso che per qualche tempo, in quelle zone, aveva fatto la levatrice una tal Maria Dominetti che era stata allieva di mio padre e che mi sarebbe piaciuto conoscerla.»

«Ma guarda che caso», le aveva risposto l'impiegata.

Perché, dopo uno dei portalettere, «Un cretinetti col ciuffo che crede di essere un attore!», lei era la seconda persona che le chiedeva informazioni su quella Dominetti.

Tanto che non aveva nemmeno avuto bisogno di sfogliare registri o altro per darle la risposta, si ricordava alla perfezione dove era andata a stare da quando s'era trasferita altrove.

177.

Sola.

Senza lavoro.

Senza marito.

Al lavoro la Dominetti aveva detto addio nell'estate del 1941, un mese dopo essersi sposata: il console della milizia confinaria D'Argò non poteva tollerare che sua moglie obbedisse ad altri che non fossero lui, si trattasse del dottore o fossero i doveri che la sua professione di levatrice le imponeva. Giusto il tempo perché arrivasse la sua sostituta e la Dominetti s'era dimessa senza remora alcuna: la vita che le si prospettava era ben più lieta di quella che faceva una levatrice. Aveva accettato di fare la signora con la stessa precisione di calcolo con la quale aveva prima accolto la corte del D'Argò e poi la sua proposta di matrimonio.

L'una e l'altra delle due cose erano avvenute nella cornice del ristorante Alla Ruota che Gira che in principio il D'Argò aveva cominciato a frequentare un po' per curiosità e un po', un po' di più a dire il vero, con il preciso intento di continuare a esercitare il suo autorevole ruolo nei confronti dell'ex milite Vergonese, godendo nel fargli intendere che non lo considerava niente di più che un banale cameriere.

Entrava nel ristorante rigorosamente in divisa, con passo marziale, il cappello sotto al braccio e il naso all'aria. Ai più poteva dare l'idea di uno che annusasse gli odori provenienti dalla cucina per decidere cosa mangiare, nelle sue intenzioni invece doveva esternare il superiore disprezzo verso chiunque non indossasse una divisa purchessia.

Il colpo che gli aveva fatto abbassare il naso così da poter inalare un intenso profumo di violetta l'aveva avuto la sera in cui, entrando, aveva visto per la prima volta la Dominetti, seduta a un tavolo e col Vergonese che, seduto di fronte a lei ma senza piatti davanti, chiacchierava sorridendo. Al vederlo il Vergonese aveva avuto uno scatto e s'era alzato come se avesse sentito un ordine. Non bisognava essere dotati di particolare fantasia per capire che al suo ex comandante era simpatico come una merda di cane e che per il quieto vivere sarebbe stato meglio non avere con lui alcun motivo di contrasto.

Il D'Argò s'era gonfiato.

Con una posticcia educazione di stampo militare s'era avvicinato al tavolo e, sempre presente il Vergonese che sembrava essersi messo sull'attenti, aveva salutato.

«La nostra nuova levatrice», aveva presentato il Vergonese.

«Mi compiaccio», aveva risposto il D'Argò, guardando prima la donna e poi la sedia sulla quale sino a poco prima era seduto l'ex milite.

«Permette che le faccia compagnia?» aveva chiesto poi.

La Dominetti, un battito di ciglia, aveva accettato.

Un mese più tardi erano fidanzati.

178.

Però non sembrava.

«Cosa?» chiese il dottor Lonati.

Alla Canterina era sembrato doveroso, vista la premura che le aveva sempre dimostrato, metterlo al corrente circa il fatto che l'assenza notturna dell'Ernesto era dovuta a una morosa.

Però non sembrava, aveva detto la Canterina.

Cioè, suo figlio non sembrava uno che da poco, pochissimo, avesse trovato la morosa.

Non ne parlava, non le aveva detto come si chiamava, come l'aveva conosciuta e poi non aveva perso né l'appetito e nemmeno un po' di sonno come invece, almeno per quanto lei ricordasse, capitava di solito.

Fosse stata un'altra stagione, l'inverno o l'autunno per esempio, con la sala d'attesa gremita di febbriciattole, mal di gola, otiti, catarri e altre amenità broncologiche, il dottor Lonati avrebbe risposto che non era suo compito prendersi cura degli affari di cuore. Anche se di fronte aveva una persona come la Canterina, che meritava tutta la compassione di cui disponeva.

Ma era luglio, splendeva un sole fin troppo caldo e all'acqua del lago mancava poco per bollire tant'era calda. Anche su di lui incombeva il clima di vacanza, si sentiva rilassato, propenso a chiacchiere che di solito non ammetteva entro i confini dell'ambulatorio.

«Direi che...» fece per rispondere.

Non aveva le idee ben chiare pur sapendo che qualcosa avrebbe finito per dire e che la Canterina avrebbe preso le sue parole per oro colato.

Ma la mamma dell'Ernesto gli troncò la risposta.

«Non è che si è immaginato anche questa?»

Il Lonati sorrise.

Fosse anche stato, era un bel passo avanti passare da un cadavere a una morosa.

Tacque però.

«Diamogli tempo», disse invece.

179.

Tempo sei mesi e le nozze si erano celebrate.

Non erano state vere e proprie nozze di guerra.

Anzi, in un certo senso, avevano sancito una pace, quella tra il D'Argò e il Vergonese. La prova migliore, per coloro che erano al corrente degli attriti che c'erano stati tra i due, era stata il pranzo di nozze consumato presso il ristorante Alla Ruota che Gira, per l'occasione chiuso, riservato alla festa degli sposi novelli.

L'evento era stato, sin dal momento del suo annuncio, sulla bocca di tutti.

Bocche complici dalle quali erano usciti complimenti d'ordinanza, ed erano state quelle della cerchia di intimi del D'Argò, che si erano seduti ai tavoli per festeggiare con lui e la Dominetti.

Da altre bocche, non prone all'obbligo della forma, erano invece uscite parole in libertà, fantasiose appendici che volevano perpetuare le chiacchiere nate intorno alla permanenza della sposina sotto il tetto del Vergonese.

Cosa sarebbe accaduto adesso?

Se la sarebbero divisa in due?

E lei, avrebbe accettato una tale promiscuità?

Le donne soprattutto, pur se fingevano di scansare l'argomento, rispondevano sì.

Sì, perché già da tempo avevano inquadrato il tipo.

Un'arrivista.

Una che di sé aveva rivelato poco o niente, motivo per il quale faceva nascere sospetti.

Una che aveva fatto capire comunque ciò che voleva dalla vita, cioè fare la signora.

La signora della Villa, avevano cominciato a chiamarla, non più dottoressa.

Ed era stato così fino a quella notte di maggio del 1944.

180.

Manco se lo avessero pregato in ginocchio di tornare, cosa che non sarebbe accaduta nemmeno per intercessione diretta di Nostro Signore, il Riffa si sarebbe più fatto vivo al cotonificio.

Con la figura che aveva fatto, uè!, nudo completo sotto gli occhi di una decina di donne, soprattutto quelli della Spinetta Bretella!, si era sputtanato da lì all'eternità e anche oltre.

E non solo all'interno del cotonificio, ma in tutto il paese.

Nonostante il parere contrario della zia Infantina, «Biagetto non sei ancora guarito del tutto», il Riffa volle fare un giro il giorno dopo la sua disavventura: prima o poi doveva affrontare il mondo esterno.

Meglio prima, aveva pensato.

I soli sguardi che s'era attirato sarebbero stati sufficienti a fargli capire di essere diventato una barzelletta.

La consapevolezza però la raggiunse quando, entrato all'osteria del Ponte, uno gli chiese, senza troppo badare al tono della voce, se per caso l'avesse anche preso nel culo, visto che camminava con le gambe un po' larghe per evitare che le cosce, ancora irritate, sfregassero contro la stoffa dei pantaloni.

Il Riffa tentò una risposta di pari livello.

«Perché, nel caso c'avresti invidia?»

Ma le sue parole annegarono tristemente tra le risate provocate dall'uscita dell'altro. Il Riffa allora si ritirò, senza bere e rosso in viso, ustione più vergogna, con la precisa idea che quel paese ormai era diventato troppo stretto per lui.

Una volta rientrato in casa, lo disse alla zia.

«Be', ma non esiste solo questo paese al mondo», rispose lei, che da Bellano non era mai uscita una sola volta da che era nata.

181.

Mai stata, nemmeno con suo padre, le aveva detto Maria Teresa Supposta.

«Nemmeno io», aveva risposto la Tina.

Per quanto potesse sembrare strano per una che come lei era nata e cresciuta lì ad Acquaseria, nemmeno lei era mai stata dalle parti del lago di Piano.

E in tutta sincerità non aveva neanche mai sentito nominare quella località...

«Tavordo», aveva ribadito l'ex infermiera.

Ecco, Tavordo.

La località dove era andata a finire la Maria Dominetti dopo che, una volta morto il console suo marito, aveva lasciato la Villa ed era sparita dalla circolazione.

182.

«Quel giovanotto, quello del quadro», disse con orgoglio il carabiniere Firrìa, «circola ancora nel nostro territorio.»

«Sarebbe a dire?» fece il maresciallo Alborati mentre con un rametto di salice opportunamente sfrangiato in punta si grattava la caviglia ancora ingessata.

Fosse stato più intuitivo il Firrìa avrebbe notato lo scarso entusiasmo con cui il maresciallo aveva reagito a tanta rivelazione. Considerò afa e prurito e si ritenne soddisfatto poiché non sapeva che l'Alborati era già stato informato dal collega bellanese.

«Se te lo ritrovi ancora tra i coglioni», gli aveva detto il Pezzati, «sappi che lavora lì.»

«L'ho visto ben due volte», spiegò di conseguenza il Firrìa.

La prima non era stato ben certo che fosse lui.

La seconda invece l'aveva riconosciuto senza errore.

In entrambe le occasioni passeggiava sfaccendato, le mani in tasca, solo e lontano dal centro abitato, in atteggiamento...

«Sospetto?» lo interruppe il maresciallo.

Il Firrìa si strinse nelle spalle.

«Proprio sospetto no, però...»

«Però cosa?»

Però, considerati i precedenti, si permetteva di chiedere il permesso di poter avvisare la ragazza, quella che aveva messo di mezzo un paio di volte, della presenza del giovane e di non esitare a chiedere aiuto per ogni necessità.

«Sei un cretino», soffiò il maresciallo.

Senza acredine, troppo caldo anche per insultare con convinzione.

«Non hai visto com'era vestito?» chiese poi.

«Sissignore.»

Tutto di blu, scuro, come i ladri quando si vogliono confondere con il buio della notte!

«O come i dipendenti della Navigazione quando sono in attesa tra un battello e l'altro.»

«Ah!» fece il Firrìa, colpito.

«Contento adesso?» chiese l'Alborati.

Contento, ammise tra sé il carabiniere.

E grazie maresciallo, perché, pur scartando la sua richiesta di allertare la ragazza, gli aveva comunque servito un'altra opportunità per avvicinarla.

Senza mettere di mezzo il servizio, poteva andarla a trovare per dirle che, nel caso avesse visto ancora in giro quel giovane, non si sarebbe dovuta preoccupare visto che era lì per lavoro.

Era pur sempre un'ottima scusa e sarebbe riuscito ad attaccare bottone. Poi, fossero state rose, sarebbero, come si diceva, fiorite.

183.

In fondo non era una notizia che richiedeva il segreto professionale anche se l'aveva appresa in ambulatorio.

In virtù di tale considerazione il dottor Lonati informò la moglie circa la novità.

«L'Ernesto avrebbe trovato la morosa.»

Vittoria Lonati lo guardò ben bene prima di parlare.

«Avrebbe?» chiese soltanto.

E il Lonati si pentì di aver aperto bocca.

«Cos'ho detto di male?» chiese, ben sapendolo.

«Avrebbe o ha?» insisté la moglie.

C'era una bella differenza, non credeva?

«Ma che ne so!» fece lui.

«Tu l'hai detto.»

«L'ha detto la Canterina.»

«E lei l'ha vista?»

«No.»

«E allora?!»

«Allora, cosa?» s'indispettì il Lonati.

Doveva anche spiegarglielo?, chiese Vittoria Lonati.

Non lo vedeva il rischio, il pericolo che l'Ernesto fosse passato da una fantasia all'altra?

«E se non fossero fantasie?» obiettò il dottore.

Se non erano fantasie, spiegò la donna, prima o poi dovevano prendere corpo, sostanza.

Passi per un cadavere, perso nel lago.

Ma una morosa doveva essere di carne e ossa, e soprattutto viva.

«Non credi?» chiese Vittoria Lonati.

Credeva, certo, fece il dottore.

Però, allo stato, preferiva sospendere il giudizio, lasciar cadere il discorso.

184.

Caduto in servizio.

Caduto in montagna.

Caduto, o spinto?

Oppure sparato?

In ogni caso era sparito.

Le chiacchiere intorno alla fine del D'Argò s'erano sprecate dopo quella notte del maggio 1944.

Tra le tante, quella che veniva appena mormorata riguardava la inusuale rapidità con la quale le ricerche erano state sospese, come se non si volesse trovarlo. A fronte di questa non erano in pochi ad accreditare un'altra voce, che ipotizzava una fuga oltre confine del console.

Ma, obiettavano altri, lasciando lì la moglie?

Man mano che i giorni erano passati, la novità della scomparsa del D'Argò aveva perso sempre più smalto, sommersa da altri, più sconcertanti eventi che stavano trascinando la guerra verso una fine drammatica. Facce nuove, strane e anche straniere attraversavano quelle contrade. I tempi stavano cambiando con la velocità di certi voltafaccia che lasciavano dietro di sé sconcerto e paura. La Dominetti, tra i tanti, aveva compreso che l'aria intorno a lei non era più quella di prima. A circa un mese dalla scomparsa del marito aveva cominciato a ricevere biglietti anonimi che la mettevano sull'avviso di stare attenta, di badare alla propria incolumità, di chiedersi se fosse il caso di continuare ad abitare da sola, di passare, sola, le notti presso la Villa, indifesa e lontana da tutti.

La cosa che aveva colpito di più la levatrice era stata il tono di quei biglietti, perché non riusciva a coglierví una vera e propria minaccia. Circa la Villa, aveva già deciso di abbandonarla, nonostante il simbolico accordo che il D'Argò aveva sottoscritto con il proprietario le consentisse di abitarla fino alla fine dell'anno.

Ma dove andare?

L'unica persona cui poteva chiedere aiuto e consiglio era il Vergonese e quando ormai la Dominetti s'era decisa a farlo era successa una cosa.

Una mattina, ai primi di settembre di quell'anno, s'era presentato alla Villa un certo Gaetano Palanzini, un soggetto che sino a qualche anno prima aveva lavorato sulla linea ferroviaria che collegava Menaggio a Porlezza e che, da quando la linea era stata soppressa, campava di espedienti.

La prima cosa che aveva detto alla Dominetti era stata che, se voleva salvare la pelle, doveva più che in fretta abbandonare la Villa. Aveva affermato di sapere per certo che un piccolo comando di tedeschi era intenzionato a occuparla e che per impedirlo alcuni amici suoi, come li aveva definiti, erano intenzionati a darle fuoco.

Vero o falso che fosse, la Dominetti non aveva potuto che credere a ciò che il Palanzini le aveva raccontato.

«Ma io dove vado?» aveva detto.

«Posti ce n'è», aveva risposto l'uomo, «e io li so.»

185.

Posti di lavoro?

Ce n'era un'infinità.

La zia Infantina in un solo giorno ne aveva messa insieme una lista lunga come la fame, studiando la cartina geografica della sponda orientale del lago da Lecco sino a Colico.

Il Caleotto, la Fiocchi, la Leuci, la Ratti Catene, la Moto Guzzi, la Carcano, il vellutificio Valsecchi, la Pallardini Stampe, l'ombrellificio Colombre, la cartiera, la Piatti Marmi, la Norda acque minerali, la trafileria Biscotti, il mollificio Anguria, la Biagi etichette, la Bestelli prodotti chimici per uso agricolo, il cantiere navale Zavatti, la Ferri minuterie metalliche, i caseifici Ostico, Primosale e Vecchi, la Lariana Vernici, la Salvalà forniture per alberghi e ospedali e un'altra decina di ditte più o meno grosse cui, avvisò la zia, con una ricerca più accurata avrebbe potuto aggiungerne un'altra ventina.

Tutti posti che erano alla perenne ricerca di mano d'opera come se fosse ossigeno per respirare. Inoltre, se non voleva chiudersi dentro un capannone o stabilimento che fosse, il Biagetto poteva anche tentare di fare domanda come bidello, portantino presso l'ospedale, spazzino presso qualche amministrazione comunale, portalettere presso le poste e telegrafi, manovale per le ferrovie dello stato, custode notturno di una delle tante ditte elencate, portiere di qualche ufficio pubblico, fosse tribunale, questura, pretura, agenzia delle tasse, catasto eccetera.

Il Riffa aveva ascoltato il rosario della zia Infantina sostenuto da due precisi pensieri: per il momento era in tutto e per tutto nelle mani di quella donna, se voleva fumare una sigaretta o bere un bicchiere dipendeva da lei e dalle sue finanze, quindi era sconsigliabile mandarla sul fico e dirle di pensare ai cazzi suoi. Il secondo pensiero, forte al punto da essere una convinzione, era che non voleva finire sotto padrone, obbedire ad altri che non fosse il suo estro, come aveva fatto sino ad allora.

Intanto la zia Infantina era andata avanti.

«Oppure», stava dicendo, «potresti fare come ha fatto il tuo compare.»

«Sarebbe?» chiese il Riffa.

«L'Ernesto», chiarì la donna.

Quello l'aveva capito.

Ma cosa aveva fatto oltre a mettersi in un casino via l'altro?

«Non si è fatto assumere dalla Navigazione?» ribatté la zia.

Il Riffa si illuminò.

«È vero!» esplose.

Sul viso del Biagetto la zia Infantina vide scendere un sorriso angelico.

«Vedi che alla fine il lavoro giusto per te l'abbiamo trovato?» disse.

186.

La gente che lo conosceva continuava a chiamare Gaetano Palanzini «il ferroviere» anche se non saliva più su un treno da oltre cinque anni.

Figlio di, e lui stesso dipendente della SPT, Società Prealpina Trasporti, che, dopo la prima guerra mondiale, aveva avuto in concessione e gestione la linea ferroviaria tra Menaggio e Porlezza, aveva vissuto il periodo di declino di quella stessa linea sino alla sua definitiva soppressione avvenuta nell'ottobre 1939.

Da quel momento in avanti il Palanzini aveva cominciato ad aspettare la chiamata della Società Anonima Gay di Menaggio che con un servizio di corriere avrebbe garantito il collegamento sino ad allora fornito dai treni, ma aveva smesso di dichiararsi fascista convinto visto che la soppressione della linea era stata una diretta conseguenza della politica autarchica del regime: già in asfissia per il singhiozzare delle sovvenzioni statali che a un certo punto erano venute a mancare, il colpo di grazia era arrivato con l'imposizione di alimentare le locomotive a torba anziché a carbone.

Scopo, risparmio.

Non certo però per il bilancio della stessa Menaggio-Porlezza che, a parità di entrate, aveva dovuto fare i conti con un aumento delle uscite. Nel tentativo di rimanere comunque a galla col taglio delle spese si era raggiunto l'obiettivo di peggiorare il servizio, tralasciando soprattutto la manutenzione di mezzi e linea, fatto che aveva creato le condizioni per il verificarsi di parecchi incidenti, alcuni anche gravi.

A quel punto non c'era stato più niente da fare e sulla ferrovia Menaggio-Porlezza era calato definitivamente il sipario.

Per sua fortuna il Palanzini, sempre in attesa di essere assunto dalla società menaggina, era uomo dal multiforme ingegno, sapeva fare un po' di tutto, s'intendeva tanto di motori quanto di tirar su muri, sapeva anche coltivare la vigna e soprattutto conosceva a memoria tutti i sentieri, anche quelli più nascosti e meno battuti, che salivano e scendevano per la montagna.

Se gli chiedevano che mestiere facesse continuava a rispondere: «Il ferroviere», e così s'era guadagnato l'appellativo.

Era la stessa risposta che aveva dato alla Maria Dominetti quando anche lei glielo aveva chiesto.

Poteva fidarsi di uno che mentiva sapendo di farlo?

«Guarda te», le aveva risposto lui.

Ma prima riflettesse bene.

187.

Tordo bottaccio, sì.

Merlo, anche.

Tordo sassello...

Ecco, circa il tordo sassello il carabiniere Fantarini doveva riflettere bene, decidere se valesse la pena iscriversi anche alla gara di canto che riguardava il Turdus iliacus oppure lasciar perdere e dedicarsi solo al merlo e al bottaccio al fine di perfezionare il più possibile la sua tecnica imitativa. Un po' gli dispiaceva l'idea di non prendere parte a tutte e tre le categorie che costituivano l'eccellenza per coloro che praticavano il chioccolo. D'altra parte, da quando il maresciallo Pezzati gli aveva concesso il permesso richiesto e soprattutto da quando gli aveva comunicato che il colonnello Agostino Seneca De Maggiori era fanatico di quella pratica e avrebbe fatto di tutto per essere presente alla gara, desiderava ardentemente fare bella figura.

Cioè, voleva più di ogni altra cosa vincere almeno in una delle categorie. Per farlo non doveva perdere tempo, esercitarsi, affinare la tecnica, fingere di essere lui stesso tordo bottaccio e merlo.

Anche tordo sassello, se le incertezze che avvertiva quando ne imitava il canto non consigliassero la necessità di un esercizio intensivo che però avrebbe rubato tempo agli altri due volatili.

Oddio, tempo ce n'era ancora, ma il tempo, al pari degli uccelli, volava.

Ed era sempre meno quello che gli restava da destinare alla riflessione.

Tordo bottaccio e merlo, quindi, sì.

Tordo sassello…

188.

C'era stato poco da riflettere, prendere o lasciare.

La Dominetti aveva preso al volo l'occasione.

Di certo alcuni argomenti che il Palanzini le aveva offerto in gentile omaggio l'avevano aiutata.

Era la moglie, o vedova, tanto non c'era differenza, di un console della milizia e con l'aria che stava cambiando sempre di più non era certo un titolo di merito. Senza nessuno che le parasse le chiappe non c'era da scommettere su una vecchiaia tranquilla.

Adesso, invece...

Adesso aveva un'età in cui rifarsi una vita non era impresa impossibile. Pochi anni ancora e, sempre che fosse sopravvissuta, non avrebbe più avuto mercato.

La Dominetti aveva sorvolato su quel modo di parlare. In altri tempi si sarebbe indignata ma ormai aveva compreso di non avere più molte possibilità di scelta.

Era arrivato il momento di giocare le carte che aveva in mano oppure di lasciar perdere tutto.

189.

«Io lascerei perdere.»

Maria Teresa Supposta scandì le tre parole del suo parere come se stesse emettendo una sentenza.

E forse per confermare che era la cosa giusta da fare diede un'occhiata alle pareti del mausoleo di famiglia.

Forse voleva fare intendere che, così come quasi tutte le persone ritratte nelle fotografie appese appartenevano al passato e non sarebbero più tornate, anche le storie del passato andavano lasciate dov'erano.

A cosa serviva riesumarle? Cosa sarebbe cambiato?

«Ma la Dominetti è ancora viva», obiettò la Tina.

Delusa, anche se cercò di non darlo a vedere.

Delusa perché aveva deciso che sarebbe andata da quella levatrice per chiedere, per sapere.

E non da sola.

In compagnia, con un'amica, una testimone.

Chi meglio dell'ex infermiera?

Si era infine decisa quel pomeriggio a sottoporle la sua idea. Tra l'altro, con lei al fianco, con una del mestiere si sarebbe sentita ancora più sicura: la Dominetti non avrebbe osato raccontarle fregnacce.

Purtroppo Maria Teresa Supposta, dopo averla ascoltata, se n'era uscita con quei tre colpi di forbice sulle sue intenzioni.

Non che avesse tutti i torti.

Sapere cos'era successo, come fossero andate le cose non avrebbe cambiato niente.

Tuttavia la Tina era intenzionata a sapere, voleva conoscere la verità.

Anche se non avrebbe cambiato la realtà.

D'accordo, la Supposta non sarebbe stata della partita.

Accettava la sua decisione.

Non il consiglio di lasciar perdere.

E circa la compagnia, aveva già in mente un'alternativa. Forse non così valida, ma meglio di niente.

190.

La Villa non era stata bruciata né occupata dai tedeschi o da altri.

Non era successo niente insomma di ciò che il Palanzini aveva paventato.

O, forse, inventato di sana pianta per spingere la Dominetti ad affidarsi a lui, a seguirlo, infine a vivere con lui.

La Villa era rimasta vuota, mentre la Dominetti era finita a Breglia, un paesino sulla strada che portava verso i monti di Treccione, nella casa dove lo stesso Palanzini era nato e cresciuto e dove abitavano ancora i genitori con un altro fratello e una sorella. Sin da subito la Dominetti aveva compreso che sulla sua vita precedente poteva metterci una croce. Poteva, anzi, doveva chiuderla negli archivi della memoria se non voleva passare il resto del tempo nella malinconia più fonda. L'aveva fatto visto che ormai aveva optato per seguire il Palanzini, ma nel giro di poche settimane aveva iniziato a chiedersi se non sarebbe stato meglio restare dov'era, anche correndo i rischi che quello le aveva prospettato.

Il Palanzini infatti aveva ben presto cominciato a usare i toni e i modi del padrone. Con la scusa che per lei era meglio non farsi vedere troppo in giro le aveva ordinato di stare chiusa in casa, insieme con i genitori dai quali, in risposta ai tentativi di avviare un qualsivoglia discorso, riceveva frasi a monosillabi e sguardi che spesso avevano un fondo di paura. Il fratello e la sorella del Palanzini invece la evitavano senza troppo curarsi di palesare quanto desse loro fastidio la sua presenza in casa. Peraltro andavano e venivano a orari strani e irregolari, li vedeva poco e per quel poco tempo se ne stavano in silenzio. Per ironia della sorte il più regolare era proprio il Palanzini, che se ne usciva spesso molto prima del sorgere del sole e rientrava a buio, senza sprecare troppe parole su ciò che lo teneva impegnato fuori casa.

La Dominetti aveva più volte accarezzato l'idea di approfittare delle sue lunghe assenze per andare via.

Se solo avesse saputo dove, non ci avrebbe pensato più di tanto. Un giorno dopo l'altro avvertiva l'inutilità della propria condizione e a volte si insinuava in lei la percezione di un pericolo.

Fino a quando, una sera poco prima del Natale 1944, il Palanzini rientrato a casa le aveva detto che il giorno dopo doveva seguirlo perché c'era una persona che aveva bisogno di lei.

191.

«Che cosa?» fece il Dubbio.

La Tina lo guardò e fece qualche respiro profondo.

Forse, pensò, aveva parlato troppo in fretta, troppe cose una dietro l'altra.

Mentre riprendeva fiato guardò per bene il giovanotto che le stava davanti.

Vestito da battellotto, tutto in blu, faceva la sua marcia figura. Gli donava anche lo sfondo di lago che aveva alle spalle con il culo del battello che si era appena staccato dal molo e si allontanava lentamente.

E forse non aveva capito quello che gli aveva appena detto non perché fosse deficiente ma perché lei aveva, più che esposto, mitragliato l'idea che aveva in testa, maturata dopo il rifiuto della Maria Teresa Supposta e giudicata come l'unica alternativa valida: cioè chiedere all'Ernesto di andare insieme con lei a Tavordo a trovare la Maria Dominetti per cercare di chiarire una storia che interessava anche lui.

«Anzi, una storia che se non ci fossi stato tu di mezzo non sarebbe mai venuta fuori», aveva detto.

Aveva studiato gli orari, c'era una corriera comoda che partiva da Menaggio alle sei e in mezz'ora sarebbero stati sul posto.

Inoltre, se non gli dispiaceva adesso...

«Proprio adesso», aveva sottolineato.

... adesso doveva prenderla sottobraccio e fare due passi con lei come se fossero morosi.

Ma così, per finta!

Era stato a quel punto che il Dubbio aveva aperto la bocca.

«Che cosa?»

192.

Nel giro di due giorni se l'era trovato dietro, davanti, accanto già quattro o cinque volte.

Spuntato da terra come un fungo o disceso come un angelo dall'alto dei cieli.

Alla Tina non c'era voluto molto di più per capire che il carabiniere Firrìa aveva lanciato l'offensiva.

Con modi urbani e frasi ricamate le aveva già fatto più di un invito.

Una passeggiatina, un gelatino, andare con lui a vedere certi fuochi d'artificio a Sant'Abbondio e, se gradiva, un giretto sugli autoscontri che erano appena arrivati in quel di Menaggio per i quali, tra l'altro, in quanto carabiniere aveva a disposizione gettoni gratuiti.

La Tina aveva rintuzzato gli attacchi dicendo che doveva andare da sua madre, era allergica al gelato, i fuochi d'artificio la spaventavano mentre sugli autoscontri le veniva sempre la nausea.

Ma c'era da scommettere che il Firrìa non avrebbe mollato, quindi alla Tina era venuta l'idea di unire l'utile all'utile. Cioè, all'utilità di avere una compagnia per andare dalla Dominetti aggiungere quella di dissuadere il Firrìa con la dimostrazione che lei era già impegnata.

Niente di meglio che farsi vedere a braccetto con qualcuno. Sul fatto che il carabiniere, appena libero dal servizio, si mettesse sulle sue tracce spiandola e cogliendo il momento migliore per trovarla senza difese, la ragazza non aveva dubbi di sorta.

Circa il qualcuno che avrebbe dovuto interpretare la parte del moroso, chiunque sarebbe andato bene, se non fosse che coinvolgendo l'Ernesto avrebbe preso i classici due piccioni con una fava.

E poi, per dirla tutta, una volta che il Dubbio aveva compreso e accettato, la Tina aveva cominciato a pensare che così com'era, tutto in blu e con il cappello da marinaio, quel giovanotto non era male.

193.

«Dove vai Biagetto?» chiese la zia Infantina.

«A prendere le sigarette», fu l'unica cosa che venne in mente di rispondere al Riffa.

Ma la zia Infantina non era stupida.

«Sono le otto di sera», ribatté, «i tabaccai sono chiusi!»

Però almeno era quasi buio.

E nel buio...

Col buio il Riffa poteva muoversi con maggiore libertà, evitare di incontrare qualcuno che gli rompesse ancora i coglioni con la storia del cotonificio. Nel buio, strisciando lungo i muri e tenendo bassa la testa, nessuno l'avrebbe visto e sarebbe riuscito a raggiungere senza impedimenti la casa del Dubbio.

Perché era lì che voleva andare, dall'Ernesto, per esporgli la proposta che aveva affinato dopo ventiquattr'ore di riflessione e che gli avrebbe permesso di ritrovare un lavoro senza padroni sopra la testa.

«È vero», rispose il Riffa all'obiezione della donna. «Allora vorrà dire che smetto di fumare.»

E senza attendere la replica infilò la porta di casa e uscì.

194.

Nonostante la sua insistenza quella sera il Palanzini non aveva voluto spiegare alla Dominetti a cosa gli servisse, perché il giorno dopo avrebbe dovuto seguirlo. Lei l'aveva compreso quindi solo l'indomani, dopo aver seguito l'uomo per circa un'ora in direzione dell'abitato di Carcente. La giornata era grigia, fredda, nuvolosa. Il cielo prometteva altra neve. Il silenzio era pesante. La Dominetti a un certo punto non l'aveva più sopportato. Si era fermata e, con la meraviglia di sentire la sua stessa voce dentro quella specie di lenzuolo che ammantava ogni cosa, aveva detto al Palanzini che non l'avrebbe più seguito se non le avesse detto subito dove stavano andando e perché.

Nonostante il suo tono, il Palanzini era rimasto calmo, nessuna minaccia o ricatto potevano scalfire la sua sicurezza. Era stato con una certa magnanimità che aveva voluto soddisfare la curiosità della Dominetti.

«Una con il tuo mestiere può essere utile in certe situazioni», aveva risposto.

La frase si era stampata sul viso della donna con una smorfia interrogativa.

Aveva tentato, chiesto, per comprendere meglio.

«Basta domande», era stata la replica del Palanzini.

Se non aveva capito da sé, aveva aggiunto, significava che aveva sbagliato nel giudicarne l'intelligenza.

In ogni caso, di lì a poco ogni cosa le sarebbe stata chiara.

Poi aveva ripreso il cammino.

Lei era rimasta lì, a guardare la sua schiena, a contare i passi regolari con i quali si allontanava.

Aveva capito che in quel momento aveva ancora una possibilità di fuga, non tanto da quell'uomo ma da una vita futura che mai come in quel frangente le era apparsa illeggibile.

Ma, se avesse ripreso la marcia per non perdere contatto col Palanzini, si sarebbe dovuta arrendere a tutto ciò che quel futuro incerto le avesse chiesto da quel momento in avanti.

La prima richiesta era già arrivata, seminascosta in ciò che le parole dell'uomo le avevano fatto intendere poco prima, «visto che era del mestiere».

Il Palanzini intanto aveva continuato a camminare, un passo dopo l'altro, senza voltarsi, sicuro che lei lo stesse seguendo.

195.

Non avrebbe dovuto seguirla fin dentro casa.

Non voleva che, qualunque cosa avesse da dire, quella donna pensasse che si fosse portata qualcuno come una specie di testimone delle sue parole o addirittura perché lei temesse qualcosa e avesse bisogno di una guardia del corpo.

Tuttavia, quattro occhi vedono meglio di due, no?

«In questo caso però non si tratta di vedere, ma di ascoltare. Quindi a cosa ti servo?»

«A te non interessa sapere come sono andate davvero le cose?» aveva chiesto la Tina.

L'Ernesto aveva scrollato le spalle.

«Boh», aveva risposto. «Anche il maresciallo mi ha detto di lasciar perdere.»

«Va bene», aveva detto la Tina.

D'accordo, lo ammetteva.

Di andarci da sola proprio non se la sentiva. Aveva bisogno di una compagnia, si sapeva mai...

Ma se lui non ne aveva la voglia, il coraggio...

«No, no», l'aveva interrotta il Dubbio.

Se la metteva così!

Però c'era una cosa allora che non quadrava.

«Va bene andare in pullman. Ma tornare?»

La Tina non aveva saputo rispondere, non ci aveva pensato.

Il Dubbio sì.

Ma aveva aspettato un po' a rispondere perché non gli

dispiaceva affatto andare su e giù per il lungolago con quella sottobraccio, anche se per finta.

«Ti va di andarci in moto?» aveva infine chiesto.

Proprio come due morosi, era stato il pensiero di entrambi.

«Facciamo domani?» aveva proposto la Tina.

196.

«Domani?» fece il Riffa.

Cazzo!

Ma non lo disse.

La Canterina gli aveva appena detto che l'Ernesto non c'era, non era tornato a casa quella sera.

L'avrebbe trovato l'indomani.

Dopodiché i due cominciarono a parlarsi solo con gli occhi.

Quindi voleva dire che non era nemmeno in giro per il paese?

E già!

Proprio adesso che aveva bisogno di lui!

Se voleva lasciar detto qualcosa a lei...

Ma va'! Certi affari andavano trattati solo tra uomini.

Allora, se le cose stavano così, non gli restava che tornare domani.

Bella merda, quando uno aveva bisogno di un amico, quello spariva dalla circolazione.

Ma dove diavolo era finito?

La Canterina sperava che fosse a morosa.

Con quella morosa di cui sapeva ancora solo che era carina... e che il carabiniere Firrìa, giusto un paio d'ore prima, aveva visto partire in sella a una Guzzi modello Stornello guidata niente meno che da Livera Ernesto detto Dubbio.

197.

Basta dubbi, decise finalmente il carabiniere Fantarini.

Niente tordo sassello.

Merlo e tordo bottaccio invece.

D'accordo che mancavano parecchi giorni alla Mostra-mercato degli uccelli e tempo per allenarsi ce ne sarebbe stato.

Ma il Fantarini non se la sentiva di rischiare perché percepiva che il maresciallo Pezzati da qualche giorno a quella parte lo guardava con qualcosa di diverso nello sguardo, sorta di rispettosa deferenza, forse anche ammirazione.

Era successo quando il Pezzati, spinto dalla curiosità di capire cosa diavolo fosse il chioccolo, aveva preteso, anzi, chiesto con una certa gentilezza, che si esibisse davanti a lui, nel suo ufficio, ed era rimasto allibito nel sentire come suoni del genere potessero uscire da una gola umana.

«Tali e quali a quelli che ci svegliano al mattino», aveva raccontato alla moglie riferendosi ai merli che anticipavano l'alba cantando dagli ippocastani di piazza Grossi, proprio di fronte alla caserma.

Così che poi, per soddisfare la curiosità della donna, il Fantarini, invitato dal Pezzati sempre con modi tutt'altro che da comandante, si era dovuto esibire anche davanti alla marescialla, stupendola come e forse più del marito.

Dopo quelle esibizioni, un po' per merito del Pezzati e un po' grazie alla signora, la voce che la caserma dei carabinieri ospitava un simile fenomeno era uscita dai suoi confini.

Ne erano conseguiti due risultati.

Il primo era stato che maresciallo e signora avevano dovuto fare i conti con la notorietà che il chioccolo aveva tra gran parte dei bellanesi, soprattutto di sesso maschile, e quanto fosse apprezzato chi lo interpretava. Il secondo risultato era calato dritto sulle spalle del carabiniere Fantarini, che era stato circondato da improvvisa fama, fermato da questo o da quello, interrogato su dove come quando e perché aveva appreso l'arte e soprattutto investito dei panni di difensore non solo dell'onore dell'Arma ma anche di quello del primato del paese su ogni altro. I meglio informati l'avevano messo al corrente che avrebbe avuto fior di avversari, due su tutti, il bergamasco Estero Bisanciato e il bresciano Oscar Ravanazzi, abituati a fare man bassa di coppe e medaglie.

Da tutto ciò al Fantarini era derivato un senso di profonda responsabilità grazie al quale aveva risolto i dubbi che lo avevano attanagliato per lunghi giorni, arrivando infine alla decisione di eliminare il tordo sassello.

198.

Lo Stornello era di Ancorati Eugenio, il pontilista titolare.

L'aveva detto un giorno al Dubbio.

«Se senti qualcuno che vuole comperare uno Stornello di seconda mano...»

Versione Sport, come nuovo, l'aveva comperato nel 1961, primo modello, non aveva mai fatto altra strada se non quella da casa sua ad Acquaseria e ritorno. Da un paio d'anni, da quando per l'intervento di chissà quale santo aveva evitato per un pelo un frontale da lasciarci le penne, l'aveva chiuso nel garage e ripreso la bicicletta.

«Potrei comprarlo io», gli aveva detto il Dubbio la sera prima.

«Ma ce l'hai la patente?» s'era informato l'Ancorati.

«E certo!» aveva ribattuto l'Ernesto.

L'Ancorati non aveva intuito la bugia.

«Per me», aveva sussurrato, «tu o un altro...»

«Però...» aveva interloquito il Dubbio.

«Però cosa?»

«Insomma», s'era spiegato l'Ernesto.

Moto che aveva già i suoi anni, chiusa in garage da un sacco di tempo.

«L'ho tenuta come se fosse mia figlia», aveva osservato l'Ancorati.

Niente da dire.

Però, prima di spendere soldi, aveva osservato l'Ernesto, gli sarebbe piaciuto provarla.

Non era una richiesta dell'altro mondo, no?

L'Ancorati ci aveva pensato su un po'.

Poi ne aveva convenuto.

«Va bene.»

«Domani sera», gli aveva subito proposto il Dubbio.

«Perché?» aveva voluto sapere l'Ancorati.

Perché proprio la sera dopo?

Per tutta una serie di motivi, aveva risposto il Dubbio.

E come se stesse ingranando le marce della moto, prima, seconda, terza, glieli aveva elencati.

Perché adesso non aveva con sé la patente.

Perché preferiva provare la moto al di fuori dell'orario di lavoro.

Perché di sera c'era meno traffico.

Perché...

199.

Perché l'aveva seguito?

Una domanda che la Dominetti s'era posta più volte nei mesi successivi e che non aveva risposta se non quella di essersi messa nelle mani di quell'uomo con la prospettiva di una vita che tornasse ad avere un po' di dignità.

Per quello aveva seguito il Palanzini e aveva obbedito ai suoi ordini, rendendosi poi conto che così facendo invece aveva dato l'addio a ogni speranza.

Dopo quel giorno in cui «grazie al mestiere che faceva» una ragazza si era liberata da un impiccio, per la Dominetti era stato un susseguirsi di disillusioni che l'avevano precipitata nell'abiezione.

Il Palanzini era diventato sempre più dispotico, padrone dei destini di entrambi.

Per un po' aveva fatto il camionista e durante i suoi viaggi più di una volta alla Dominetti era toccato seguirlo quando, di qua o di là, trovava un «lavoretto», come lui li chiamava, che necessitava della sua competenza.

Dentro di sé la Dominetti diceva no. Nella pratica invece obbediva e col passare del tempo in lei si era insinuata l'indifferenza verso ciò che faceva.

Sul finire del 1946, una sera, tra il Palanzini e i due fratelli era scoppiato un violento litigio.

La Dominetti era già nella sua camera da letto, una stanza che sino al suo arrivo in quella casa era stata della sorella del Palanzini, abbandonata per fare posto al fratello e alla sua compagna. Stante la piccolezza degli ambienti, e anche perché i litiganti non avevano badato a contenere il tono della voce, la Dominetti aveva compreso che il motivo della discussione era la sua presenza tra loro. Non solo il disagio che aveva creato ma soprattutto le voci che erano via via nate su ciò che faceva, in particolar modo quando partiva insieme con lui. La gente guardava alla famiglia come se tutti fossero complici di quelle turpitudini, i due vecchi avevano vergogna a uscire di casa, avevano addirittura smesso di andare in chiesa.

«Non te ne sei accorto?» aveva gridato la sorella.

Bestemmiando il Palanzini aveva chiuso la discussione. Alla Dominetti quella sera non aveva detto niente. Solo il giorno seguente, rientrato dopo un viaggio col camion, le aveva comunicato di tenersi pronta a partire.

«Avremo una casa tutta per noi.»

L'aveva cercata e trovata nel giro di tre giorni.

A Tavordo.

Una casettina di poche pretese, non molto lontana dalla stazione abbandonata della ferrovia Menaggio-Porlezza.

200.

Ancorati Eugenio, pontilista titolare, stava guardando l'orologio che, piantato come una sentinella di lato al gabbiotto dei biglietti, dettava il tempo a turisti e no.

Da che si conoscevano era sempre stato indietro di una decina di minuti. Nessuno, lui per primo, si era mai preoccupato di rimetterlo al passo.

Perché, in fondo, cos'erano dieci minuti a confronto con l'eternità?

Adesso però cominciava a capirne il valore.

Perché, pur tenendo conto dei dieci minuti di cronico ritardo con cui viaggiava l'orologio della Navigazione, il Dubbio era via da oltre mezz'ora e nell'aria lui non sentiva ancora il ben noto rombo dello Stornello sulla via del ritorno.

201.

La nuova casa era piccola, niente a che vedere con gli agi che le aveva offerto la Villa.

Tuttavia alla Dominetti aveva dato l'impressione di aver trovato infine un'isola di serenità. Solo una volta preso possesso di quei tre locali miserelli, sopra i quali poggiava un secondo piano ancora allo stato grezzo, la levatrice si era resa conto di quanto fosse stata greve l'atmosfera dentro la quale aveva vissuto sino a quel momento.

Un miracolo che il litigio tra fratelli non fosse scoppiato molto prima!

Ad accrescere il benessere per la nuova sistemazione era poi arrivata la notizia, che già correva da un po', circa il ripristino della linea Menaggio-Porlezza.

Il Palanzini gliel'aveva data come cosa fatta: si trattava di un progetto che prevedeva l'elettrificazione della linea e grazie al quale lui sarebbe tornato di diritto a fare il suo vecchio lavoro.

A credere alla realizzazione di tale progetto era stato probabilmente il solo Palanzini.

Sulle prime la Dominetti ne aveva giustificate le fantasie, come quella che loro due sarebbero andati ad abitare nella vecchia stazione di Tavordo con, tra l'altro, il vantaggio di non dover più pagare affitti. Era andata avanti ad accettare, con l'indifferenza della quale si era ormai armata, i «lavoretti» che di tanto in tanto l'uomo le imponeva, fiduciosa che avrebbe potuto smettere quandc la situazione familiare, se di famiglia si poteva parlare per quanto concerneva loro due, si fosse stabilizzata. E solo dopo parecchio tempo si era resa conto che il Palanzini aveva cominciato a vivere come se da un momento all'altro gli potessero mettere un cappello in testa e una paletta in mano, come se dalla sera alla mattina la ferrovia potesse rinascere mentre nella realtà veniva smantellata un pezzo alla volta: bulloni, piastre di ferro, traversine in legno sparivano, rubati o rimossi da chiunque ne vedesse un possibile riutilizzo oppure per essere rivenduti.

Nemmeno quei piccoli indizi erano riusciti a convincere il Palanzini che l'elettrificazione della linea non si sarebbe mai realizzata. Preferiva credere a voci che raccoglieva qua e là, spesso infondate, raccolte nelle osterie dentro le quali sempre più di frequente passava le giornate lasciando che la vivace concorrenza gli rubasse il lavoro. Le parole alterate con le quali riferiva le chiacchiere raccolte avevano convinto la Dominetti che le speranze di una vita che fosse appena un po' serena erano infondate, proprio come il progetto di ridare nuova vita alla ferrovia.

Prevedeva disastri ed era stata facile profeta.

Correva l'anno 1950.

202.

Correva lo Stornello.

Prima, seconda, terza.

Un bel rumore oltre al resto, riempiva il silenzio della sera.

Aveva ragione il Riffa, stava pensando il Dubbio: per guidare non serviva la patente ma una macchina, o una moto, come quella che aveva sotto il culo.

Meglio, una moto, con una sgarzolina dietro che, tale e quale alla Tina in quel momento, si teneva stretta stretta a lui.

Un vero peccato che alla meta non mancasse molto perché, nonostante le curve e l'approssimarsi del buio, c'aveva preso su la mano ormai con la moto e, prima seconda terza seconda terza, sarebbe andato fino ai confini della terra, viaggiando come una scheggia, con quella bell'aria che gli soffiava in faccia e la stretta della Tina sull'addome.

«Rallenta!» gridò proprio la ragazza traendolo dai suoi pensieri.

«Hai paura?» chiese l'Ernesto gridando.

Macché paura!

Non lo vedeva il cartello, TAVORDO!

Erano arrivati.

203.

Quella sera il Palanzini era entrato in casa più alterato del solito e alla Dominetti era bastato uno sguardo per capire che la situazione era arrivata a un punto critico.

Come se stesse parlando del tempo che stava mutando mettendosi al brutto o al bello, l'aveva informata di aver venduto il camioncino che usava per i trasporti.

Già da tempo gli affari non andavano al meglio, i lavori che il Palanzini perdeva perché si rendeva irreperibile oppure perché non era in grado di guidare avevano ridotto all'osso le entrate.

E allora d'accordo, aveva detto la donna, con quei soldi avrebbero tirato avanti per un po' di tempo, ma poi?

Ci aveva pensato il destino a rispondere in maniera definitiva, quando era arrivata la notizia che il tanto chiacchierato progetto di elettrificazione della ferrovia era stato messo in archivio per sempre.

Era una spesa troppo ingente a fronte di quello che avrebbe potuto rendere.

Piuttosto si stavano assumendo operai che, organizzati in squadre, avrebbero lavorato per rimuovere le rotaie e tutto il materiale che non era già stato furtivamente asportato.

Era stata la fine dei sogni, delle fantasie del Palanzini.

Anche della sua vita.

Ai primi del 1951 un infarto l'aveva stroncato.

Così l'inarrestabile declino di Maria Dominetti era cominciato.

204.

Mezz'ora e passa, la cosa cominciava a farsi seria.

L'Ancorati era nervoso, passeggiava su e giù sempre gli stessi metri, e non capiva bene.

Non capiva bene se era più preoccupato o più incazzato.

La preoccupazione ci stava.

Quella testa di cazzo dell'Ernesto in quel momento poteva già essersi spiaccicato contro qualche muro, magari in quel momento lo stavano già raccogliendo col cucchiaino, da una parte i suoi pezzi e dall'altra quelli del suo Stornello.

Però poteva decidere anche di essere incazzato al pensiero che quello fosse andato a girare chissà dove, approfittando tra l'altro del fatto che il serbatoio della moto era pieno, raso, da poter fare il giro del lago senza fermarsi neanche una volta.

Non che avesse alternative, a parte capire quale fosse il suo stato d'animo.

Circa il fare qualcosa...

L'Ancorati guardò l'orologio della Navigazione e, parlando con lui, si concesse ancora mezz'ora di tempo – mezz'ora esatta senza considerarne il ritardo cronico – dopodiché avrebbe preso una decisione.

Quale, l'avrebbe comunicata all'orologio allo scadere dell'ultimo dei minuti concordati.

205.

Non fu un odore particolare a colpire la Tina quando entrò nella casa della Dominetti.

Dagli odori che percepiva spesso identificava un ambiente, era un'esperienza che aveva fatto più volte.

Un odore che, anche fosse stata a occhi chiusi, le avrebbe suggerito senza possibilità di errore dove si trovasse in quel momento.

C'era per esempio l'odore dolciastro che aveva spesso sentito in casa del commenda e che il dottore le aveva spiegato essere una caratteristica di molti diabetici, era il loro respiro. C'era quello di verdure, cipolle, prezzemolo, basilico o quello di minestrone che stagnava stabilmente nella cucina di casa sua, il vero, unico regno, con l'appendice dell'orto, di sua madre e delle sue cento conserve. Quello di stalla di alcune case di amiche di famiglia oppure quello di cera misto a un che di antico che forse promanava dalle innumerevoli foto in bianco e nero del mausoleo in casa della Maria Teresa Supposta.

Fu invece un colore a colpire la Tina non appena entrata nella casa della Dominetti.

Una casa piccola, resa ancora più claustrofobica per l'incredibile disordine che vi regnava, un disordine di poche cose, sedie spaiate, strofinacci ovunque, stoviglie ammucchiate e qualche vaso senza fiori, le pareti, il cui unico decoro era qualche macchia di umidità, un lavandino, un rubinetto che perdeva.

Da tutto ciò che occupava la casa parve alla Tina che uscisse quel colore. Un giallo disperato che rivestiva anche la figura della donna. Un colore che si trasmise anche alle prime parole che la Dominetti disse.

«Pensavo che non arrivassi più.»

206.

Le mani in tasca, le orecchie all'erta, il pontilista titolare Ancorati attendeva di risentire l'amato rombo dello Stornello comprendendo infine perché molti turisti gli confessavano di scegliere quelle sponde per le loro vacanze anche grazie all'impagabile silenzio che si generava durante le ore notturne.

Le mani in tasca, gli occhi sempre fissi alle lancette che scandivano gli ormai pochi minuti che mancavano alla scadenza concordata, giocherellava con un manipolo di monetine che abitavano nelle sue tasche da tempo immemore – monetaglia che, messa assieme, non gli avrebbe garantito nemmeno la spesa di un caffè o di un bianchino, pezzi da cinque e dieci lire, qualche centesimo svizzero, forse un paio di pfennig – quando con una delle dita accarezzò una rugosità che sulle prime gli dipinse in viso un punto interrogativo.

Indice e pollice allora afferrarono il pezzo di metallo e lo isolarono dal resto della miseranda compagnia per portarglielo sotto gli occhi.

Al vedere cos'era, la decisione dell'Ancorati maturò.

La preoccupazione smise di contendere il primato all'incazzatura.

Il pontilista concesse all'orologio l'ultimo dei minuti concordati poi, con il gettone telefonico stretto nel palmo della mano, partì alla volta della cabina telefonica che stava circa a metà del lungolago.

207.

Come da accordi l'Ernesto era rimasto fuori ad aspettarla.

Non proprio fuori dalla casa, un po' più lontano, nei pressi della vecchia stazione di Tavordo.

«Sicura che sai dove abita?» aveva chiesto il Dubbio.

«Tranquillo», aveva risposto lei.

Le indicazioni che la Supposta le aveva dato non potevano essere più chiare, indirizzo e numero civico, e poi in effetti non è che ci si potesse perdere in quel posto.

Una volta entrata però, colpita da quel colore che le si era riversato addosso e dalla frase che era uscita dalla bocca della Dominetti, alla ragazza era venuto il pensiero che forse aveva sbagliato a lasciare fuori il giovanotto.

Contribuiva pure la levatrice a quel disordine, a quel colore che alla Tina pareva essere la sostanza dell'aria di casa. Era seduta su una poltrona di vimini posta a un capo del tavolo, le mani aggrappate ai braccioli e pareva, o forse era davvero, vestita di stracci. La poca luce dell'ambiente impediva di vederla bene e la Tina non aveva alcuna intenzione di fare un passo di più oltre a quelli che aveva fatto superando la soglia della porta che aveva trovato aperta.

Non aveva risposto quando lei aveva bussato, e trovando la porta aperta l'aveva vista fare due passi dentro casa sua.

Solo dopo averla guardata per qualche istante le aveva detto quella frase.

«Mi aspettava forse?» chiese allora la Tina.

La risposta la lasciò di stucco.

«Certo, mio angelo.»

Alla Tina sorse una specie di sorriso. Già, il Vergonese. Forse l'aveva avvisata che lei la stava cercando. Poi il sorriso si tramutò in una smorfia di raccapriccio a sentirsi chiamare così. Non le serviva altro per capire di essere entrata in un luogo diverso da ogni altro che conosceva. Che la Dominetti fosse folle, ubriaca o altro ancora che non poteva immaginare le importava ben poco. Anzi, stava giusto pensando di fare un rapido dietro front e tornarsene a casa quando quella le disse: «Siediti».

Sedere, lì?, si chiese la Tina.

Nemmeno per idea, temeva ineffabili contaminazioni.

«Preferirei stare in piedi», rispose.

«Ti stancherai», osservò la Dominetti.

La storia era lunga, se voleva sapere.

«Non sei qui per questo?» chiese ancora la levatrice.

Non era lì perché voleva sapere?

«Mi stava aspettando davvero?» domandò ancora la Tina.

La Dominetti sospirò immettendo nell'aria un alito giallo di disperante malattia. Il disordine della casa scomparve dall'orizzonte visivo della Tina, il suo sguardo vide solo la donna che stava seduta, isolandola dal resto, per rendersi conto della sua pelle quasi bronzina, rugosa e vecchia ben oltre i sessant'anni e passa che doveva avere e che pareva ritirarsi sul viso là dove una volta c'erano le gote che l'avevano resa così bella e invidiabile.

Con un lento movimento, la Dominetti si portò le mani sull'addome che spingeva sotto gli stracci con cui s'era ricoperta.

«Mancavi solo tu per chiudere il cerchio», disse.

208.

«Carabinieri Menaggio!» rispose d'impeto il carabiniere Firrìa.

L'Ancorati restò in silenzio per qualche istante, preso di sorpresa dal tono combattivo della risposta. E anche, in verità, come meravigliato del fatto che, avendo composto il numero di telefono della caserma dei carabinieri, un carabiniere appunto gli aveva risposto.

«Allora?» chiese il Firrìa come se desse un'unghiata.

Era nervoso. L'immagine del Dubbio sullo Stornello con avvinghiata la Tina continuava a passargli davanti agli occhi. E adesso non c'era stato niente di peggio che essere di servizio quella notte per continuare a rivedere quei due sulla Guzzi.

L'Ancorati si decise.

«Mi hanno rubato la moto!» dichiarò.

A lui la fidanzata, fu il pensiero che traversò la mente del carabiniere.

«Mi dispiace», rispose scopertamente ironico.

Ma in genere al telefono si usava prima di tutto declinare le proprie generalità!

«Pontilista Ancorati Eugenio», sparò il battellotto come se fosse tornato ai tempi della naja.

Ce l'aveva presente, lo conosceva di vista insomma.

Ma che gli avessero fregato la moto, mentre a lui avevano fregato una potenziale fidanzata, fregava assai poco.

Il carabiniere Firrìa rispose come da regolamento.

«Venga domattina a presentare regolare denuncia», consigliò.

Non che l'Ancorati si aspettasse un intervento in forze dell'intera caserma ma, sapendo nome e cognome del ladro...

«Come, come?» lo interruppe il Firrìa.

Sapeva chi gliel'aveva rubata?

«Certo», rispose il pontilista specificando l'identità del, a suo dire, ladro.

Al Firrìa non parve vero.

«Ne è certo?» chiese per conferma.

«L'ho visto coi miei occhi.»

«Ottimo», rispose il Firrìa.

Gli dicesse dov'era allora e non si muovesse da lì. Tempo pochi minuti, giusto per organizzarsi e sarebbe arrivato di persona.

Poi, abbassata la cornetta, picchiò un pugno sul tavolo.

La giustizia trionfava sempre alla fine, mormorò, la verità veniva a galla.

209.

Come i cadaveri.

Ne aveva l'aspetto anche la Dominetti.

Una cosa morta che però parlava.

«Cosa ti ha spinto a venire fin qui?» chiese la levatrice.

Ma aveva il tono di una domanda che non pretendeva risposta.

«Se mi aspettava lo sa bene», rispose comunque la Tina.

«Certo, angelo», sussurrò la Dominetti.

«Perché mai mi chiama così?» sbottò la Tina.

Le dava fastidio quell'appellativo, quel tono.

«Una cosa per volta», rispose la levatrice.

Prima la verità.

«Visto che sei venuta per quella.»

«Esatto», confermò la Tina. «E se la sa vorrei conoscerla, senza perdere altro tempo.»

La Dominetti sorrise, ma era un sorriso di denti lunghi, di informe indifferenza.

Il tempo.

Quel tempo che sembrava ormai così lontano, tanto lontano da non credere quasi che fosse esistito.

Quello della Villa, e del D'Argò.

Gli anni migliori della sua vita li avrebbe potuti definire. Quando la chiamavano dottoressa, e poi signora perché aveva sposato un console della milizia.

«Un trofeo», disse la Dominetti.

Ecco cos'era stata.

Era bella, vanitosa, ambiziosa.

Una semplice levatrice che all'epoca del suo arrivo aveva già rifiutato sciami di pretendenti, morti di fame al pari di lei.

«Il Vergonese?» fece la Dominetti.

Avrebbe potuto sposarlo, diventare direttrice d'albergo, se lui non fosse già stato sposato con quella che non poteva dargli figli.

«Quella donna muta, grigia, che se ne stava sempre sola da qualche parte...»

La levatrice si passò una mano scarna sul viso come se volesse pulirselo da quel giallo che ne scuriva la pelle.

«Hai detto che vuoi conoscere la verità senza perdere tempo», disse poi.

Nemmeno lei aveva intenzione di perderne allora.

Voleva lasciare quanto prima quel mestiere che non le era mai piaciuto, nel quale s'era imbattuta per caso e che per caso aveva, ma sempre malvolentieri, praticato.

«Il console D'Argò è stata la soluzione.»

La Villa, fare la signora...

«Peccato che fosse un imbecille», affermò la Dominetti.

Un trafficone, un maneggione, un corrotto. Uno che s'era accorto in fretta che con il confine così vicino poteva combinare affari di ogni tipo e che aveva addosso la divisa giusta per dirigerli senza correre troppi pericoli.

Anche un porco.

Soprattutto, però, un presuntuoso imbecille.

«Non crederò mai che quella notte in cui sparì per sempre sia caduto da qualche parte senza alcuna possibilità di recuperarne il corpo. Qualcuno piuttosto gli ha fatto pagare il conto di certi affari poco chiari e credo che in pochi abbiano pianto la sua fine. Io...»

«Questo è successo dopo», interloquì interrompendola la Tina.

La Dominetti sospirò un alito acidulo.

«Soltanto qualche mese dopo», specificò la Dominetti.

210.

Solo poco dopo, passato il primo momento di spaesante euforia, il carabiniere Firrìa ragionò.

Gli stava bene cogliere con le mani nel sacco il Livera Ernesto e metterlo di fronte alle sue responsabilità penali.

Meno bene, anzi, per niente bene del tutto gli andava l'idea di beccarlo insieme con la Tina, a rischio di far passare lei per complice con tutto ciò che ne sarebbe seguito.

Quindi, data per scontata l'innocenza della ragazza, doveva fare in modo di incastrare lui solo per poi mettere lei davanti all'evidenza di aver a che fare con un soggetto inaffidabile, candidato a essere prima o poi ospite delle patrie galere.

Al collega Dangolo, che stava dormendo come un angioletto, disse, approfittando del disorientamento dovuto alla sveglia improvvisa, che in virtù di un'urgenza di cui dopo, poi, più tardi gli avrebbe spiegato l'entità, doveva uscire all'istante e necessitava di un cambio nel ruolo di piantone notturno.

Poi uscì, senza divisa per meglio calarsi nell'azione che lo attendeva, per andare a incontrare l'Ancorati che lo aspettava di lato all'orologio della Navigazione Lariana, chiedendosi come mai nessuno, nemmeno il battellotto, avesse mai pensato di regolarlo.

211.

Quella sera il D'Argò era uscito per l'ultima volta dalla Villa.

Sembrava una delle tante, non era nervoso, era uscito senza dire dove andava e quando sarebbe tornato.

«Non che mi mancasse l'intelligenza, l'intuito per capire da me che non fosse solo il suo dovere a farlo muovere di notte.»

Le era bastato fare i conti con l'animo dell'uomo che aveva sposato e che poi aveva imparato a conoscere.

La divisa, glielo aveva già detto, era stata un'opportunità, la frontiera così vicina, e coi tempi che erano cambiati così in fretta, un'altra, ancora più golosa. Il benessere di cui si godeva non era certo solo frutto del soldo mensile.

«Mi capisci?» chiese la Dominetti.

La capiva, rispose la Tina con un cenno del capo.

Ma quello che lei voleva sapere era accaduto prima, prima che il D'Argò sparisse senza più essere ritrovato.

«Sì, certo», acconsentì la Dominetti.

Un mese prima, occhio e croce.

«Forse il 16 aprile?» suggerì la Tina.

La Dominetti si riscosse come se avesse avuto un brivido di freddo.

«Quando aiutai a partorire quella ragazza», disse.

«Come si chiamava, chi era?»

«Pretendi troppo dalla mia memoria», rispose la levatrice.

C'era troppa gente in quella casa.
Ed erano successe troppe cose.
Soprattutto nessuno, nemmeno lei, si aspettava che la ragazza ne avesse due nella pancia.

212.

Una con il suo mestiere avrebbe sempre avuto qualcosa da fare.

Quella frase che si sarebbe sentita ripetere un'infinità di volte negli anni a venire, la Dominetti l'aveva sentita uscire per la prima volta dalla bocca del D'Argò.

«Eravamo sposati da un paio di anni», disse la Dominetti.

Una sera erano partiti in macchina loro due soli, il D'Argò non aveva detto una parola lungo tutto il tragitto. Solo quando, tra Grotto e Carlazzo, avevano imboccato una stradina laterale e poi s'erano fermati davanti a una casa con la stalla a lato, le aveva detto che erano arrivati.

«Scendi, vieni con me.»

Erano entrati in una cucina dove pesava un caldo odore di chiuso, sotto gli occhi di un uomo e una donna ai quali il D'Argò s'era rivolto soltanto chiedendo: «Di sopra?» cui i due avevano risposto con un cenno del capo.

Lui davanti, lei dietro.

«La ragazza avrà avuto diciotto, diciannove anni», disse la Dominetti.

Non aveva risposto al suo saluto. Il D'Argò era rimasto nella camera pochi istanti. Vedi di sistemare le cose, le aveva poi detto prima di uscire.

«L'aveva già fatto altre volte?» chiese la Tina.

La Dominetti chiuse gli occhi, sospirò, lasciando cadere le spalle come se fosse stanchissima.

«Sapevo», rispose, «so come si fa.»

Ma quella volta non c'era stato niente da fare.

Una volta uscito il D'Argò la ragazza aveva aperto la bocca per parlare.

«La gravidanza era troppo avanti.»

Ormai al terzo mese.

Aveva taciuto fino ad allora, confessando il suo stato quando aveva capito che non aveva altra scelta.

Ma adesso era troppo tardi per intervenire, troppo il rischio.

La Dominetti non se l'era sentita. Era scesa nella cucina dove i tre aspettavano e li aveva messi di fronte alla realtà.

Era allora che era scoppiato il finimondo.

I due, anche se abbastanza giovani, si erano rivelati i nonni materni della ragazza. La madre già da qualche tempo era ricoverata nel manicomio di Sondrio, il padre era da qualche parte nei Balcani e di lui mancavano notizie da un bel po'. La giovane nonna era scoppiata a piangere. Un pianto isterico dove forse si potevano reperire tracce della follia della figlia. Aveva gridato che non potevano tenere la ragazza in quello stato, che il padre, con cui non avevano alcun rapporto, qualora fosse tornato e l'avesse trovata con un figlio di chissà chi se la sarebbe presa con loro.

«Fu a quel punto che chiesi se si sapeva chi fosse il padre, chi aveva messo incinta la ragazza», disse la Dominetti.

Per tutta risposta il D'Argò le aveva intimato di pensare ai fatti propri.

Basta piagnistei!, aveva detto.

Pensiamo a sistemare questa storia, d'accordo?, aveva concluso guardando il padrone di casa.

«Ma nessuno, nemmeno io che l'ho fatta partorire, immaginavo che quella ragazza avesse due figli nella pancia.»

213.

L'Ancorati… trepilava.

La lancetta dell'orologio che continuava a fissare scandiva il tempo e a ogni minuto che passava nell'attesa dell'annunciato arrivo del carabiniere, il pontilista sentiva scemare sempre di più la rabbia che l'aveva spinto a telefonare. Aumentava invece la consapevolezza di aver fatto una cazzata.

Quando il Firrìa gli comparve davanti ne fu certo del tutto e si predispose a recitare il mea culpa.

Tra l'altro il caramba vestiva borghese, non ispirava tutto il timore che avrebbe dovuto se avesse indossato la divisa.

All'Ancorati venne così più facile, quando il Firrìa, fremente d'azione, gli chiese: «Allora?» rispondere: «Forse ho esagerato».

«In che senso?» ribatté il carabiniere.

E il tono, quello sì!, sembrava che avesse addosso la divisa, cappello compreso.

Nel senso, spiegò l'Ancorati, che non aveva propriamente assistito al furto.

«Ma se mi ha fatto nome e cognome del ladro!» obiettò sconcertato il Firrìa.

Si era forse inventato tutto?

«Quello no», affermò con ritrovata sicurezza il pontilista.

«E allora?»

Allora, in sostanza, attaccò a spiegare il pontilista, la verità vera era che lui la moto al Livera Ernesto l'aveva prestata...

«Come prestata?» interloquì miagolando il Firrìa.

«Prestata per fare un giretto», chiarì l'Ancorati.

Come sempre si usava, aggiunse, quando in una transazione di qualsivoglia oggetto il venditore voleva dimostrare al potenziale acquirente la trasparenza dell'affare.

«Solo che...» singhiozzò l'Ancorati cacciando dalla tasca il fazzoletto per asciugarsi il sudore che la spiegazione gli stava costando.

«Solo che», riprese, «un giretto è un giretto.»

Mentre l'Ernesto ormai era via da più di due ore.

Il Firrìa allungò il muso dando forma a un pensiero volpino che gli era appena sfrecciato nella mente.

Nulla era perduto.

Due ore, e ancora dello Stornello non si udiva il canto nell'aria.

Se era appena tramontata l'ipotesi di furto vero e proprio, quella di un tentato furto era appena sorta.

«Ci penso io», disse all'Ancorati, e partì sparendo in fretta nel buio della notte.

214.

Era la notte del 16 aprile 1944, aveva appena detto la Dominetti.

«Lo immaginavo», disse la Tina.

«Non saresti qui se non avessi letto quella lettera», rispose la levatrice.

La Tina assentì.

«Tu cosa avresti fatto nei miei panni?» chiese la Dominetti con un sorriso storto, senza aspettare risposta. Aveva parlato giusto per prendere un po' di tempo e poi tornare a inoltrarsi nel ricordo di quella notte.

Il D'Argò le aveva detto che avrebbe pensato lui a ogni cosa. Lei aveva dovuto seguire la gravidanza della ragazza, che da quel primo incontro era rimasta sotto chiave in casa dei nonni, e farla partorire.

E il bambino?

Lei l'aveva chiesto più volte a suo marito.

Non te ne devi preoccupare, era sempre stata la risposta.

La sera in cui la ragazza aveva partorito aveva compreso il perché.

«Te l'ho detto che quella sera c'era un sacco di gente in casa.»

Quattro persone che lei non aveva mai visto.

Due erano di lingua tedesca, con qualche innesto di italiano. Svizzeri di Zurigo, ai quali il D'Argò, grazie ai suoi traffici, aveva venduto il bambino. Erano lì per assicurarsi di fare un buon acquisto, volevano un maschio sano, normale.

Quando avevano visto nascere una femmina erano rimasti perplessi. Ne era nata una mezza discussione.

«Questione di prezzo», chiarì la Dominetti.

La femmina valeva meno. Il D'Argò aveva dovuto cedere.

Gli altri due uomini invece avrebbero anche potuto parlare arabo. Non avevano spiccicato mezza parola. All'ordine del D'Argò erano usciti da casa insieme con i due svizzeri e la neonata.

«Di lei non ho saputo più niente fino a quando ho letto quella lettera che conosci», disse la Dominetti.

«Ha scritto di sapere che non era figlia di quei due, di avere una gemella...»

«Certo», interloquì la Dominetti.

Quella che era nata una mezz'ora più tardi.

Piccola, sofferente, quasi in fin di vita. Coperta dal sangue dell'emorragia che nel giro di un'ora aveva causato la morte di sua madre.

Per un quarto d'ora il D'Argò non aveva fatto altro che insultare chiunque.

«Se la prese con me, con la mia incapacità, coi nonni della ragazza, con la ragazza stessa, maledicendola anche se era appena morta.»

Poi, una volta ritrovata un po' di calma, aveva ordinato a tutti di non muoversi, non fare niente.

Di aspettarlo.

Era ritornato un paio d'ore più tardi, e non era solo.

215.

Forse sarebbe stato meglio tenersi addosso la divisa.

Un po' tardi, adesso, per rimediare, rifletté il Firrìa.

Meglio piuttosto individuare il posto ideale dove appostarsi per beccare il Livera.

Fatta quella riflessione si bloccò.

«Merda!» esclamò.

Poi si guardò in giro, casomai qualcuno avesse potuto sentirlo. Ma merda davvero, perché se quello tornava sul luogo del delitto significava che dopo l'ipotesi del furto, già archiviata, anche quella del tentativo di furto sfumava. E lui per cosa lo arrestava?

Merda, quindi.

Possibile che...

Però...

Il carabiniere Firrìa sentì nascere un sorrisetto.

«Etto», perché non era ben sicuro dell'idea che gli era balenata in mente. Avrebbe voluto avere sottomano il manuale del Codice Penale, lettura peraltro mai fatta, per consultarlo ed essere certo.

Poteva fidarsi di cose che sapeva solo per sentito dire?

Però...

Intanto non bisognava perdere altro tempo.

Se le cose stavano come ormai pensava, Livera Ernesto detto Dubbio, tornando sullo Stornello del pontilista Ancorati, avrebbe fatto tappa a casa della ragazza.

Fu quindi verso quella che, in sella al suo Ciao, si diresse e si appostò.

216.

«Quando entrò non capii subito perché era lì», disse la Dominetti.

«Chi?» chiese la Tina.

«Non dirmi che non l'hai capito», ribatté la levatrice.

Non aveva capito che il Vergonese era lì perché era lui il responsabile di quel guaio?

Quella ragazza aveva lavorato nel suo albergo per qualche mese poi era sparita.

Licenziata, o almeno era ciò che il Vergonese aveva voluto che si sapesse.

«Io più di così non posso fare», aveva detto il D'Argò a quel punto.

Toccava a lui farsi venire qualche idea.

«La ragazza?» aveva subito chiesto il Vergonese.

«Ho visto una tomba con quella data al cimitero di Acquaseria», disse la Tina. «È lei?»

La Dominetti chiuse gli occhi.

Risentiva le parole che il D'Argò le aveva rivolto: il medico non avrebbe sollevato obiezioni per compilare un certificato di morte se lui glielo avesse chiesto. Ma bisognava giustificare quella morte in maniera ineccepibile.

«Al dottore dissero che la ragazza era stata trovata già morta in una stalla dei dintorni dove s'era nascosta nel tentativo di liberarsi da sé.»

«Non la visitò?» chiese la Tina.

«Gliela fecero trovare già composta nella bara quando salì in quella casa», rispose la Dominetti.

A quel punto restava solo da sistemare la seconda nata ed era toccato al Vergonese darsi da fare.

«So già come ha fatto», disse la Tina, «come ci è riuscito.»

La Dominetti cercò di fingere, di sorprendersi.

«E allora se lo sai perché mai sei qui, angelo mio?»

La Tina sbuffò.

Le dava fastidio quel nomignolo, le faceva quasi paura sentirlo uscire da quelle labbra secche, volare sino alle sue orecchie su quell'alito giallo.

«È per l'altra che sono venuta qui.»

«Non avresti dovuto leggere quella lettera», disse la Dominetti.

«L'ho letta di fretta», rispose la Tina, notando nel suo stesso tono un lieve tremore.

Le rughe della levatrice sembravano moltiplicate ma era solo perché aveva chinato un poco il capo, la pelle cascava ancora di più.

«Non avresti dovuto e basta.»

«Ormai l'ho fatto», rispose la ragazza.

S'era scrollata di dosso l'inquietudine che il tono della levatrice le aveva suscitato poco prima. In fin dei conti aveva di fronte una donna sfatta che nemmeno volendo le avrebbe potuto fare alcun male.

«Ormai l'ho fatto e sono qui. E voglio sapere come sono andate le cose», disse con decisione.

«Vuoi sapere dell'altra insomma», disse la Dominetti risollevando il viso con una mossa che chissà quante volte aveva fatto quando era bella e si attirava gli sguardi di tutti gli uomini.

«È stata qui», aggiunse.

217.

Un po' qui, un po' lì, un po' su e un po' giù.

Il tempo passava leeento, qualche rumore nell'aria, ma era un cane che abbaiava oppure una macchina lontana lontana: del rombo dello Stornello nemmeno una nota e il carabiniere Firrìa continuava a cambiare posizione per sgranchirsi le gambe e vedere se, grazie al movimento e al sangue che circolava più rapidamente, gli riuscisse di ricordare qualcosa di più circa il reato, scartati furto e tentativo dello stesso, da imputare al Dubbio.

«Appropriazione indebita.»

Due belle parole, secche, precise.

In compagnia l'una dell'altra suonavano bene, non doveva essere simpatico sentirsi accusare di: «Appropriazione indebita», ripeteva ogni tanto il Firrìa.

Ma quale fosse la pena per un tale reato, chi lo sapeva?

Mentre stava un po' qui e un po' lì giurò più volte a sé stesso che, dal giorno seguente, Codice Penale in mano, avrebbe imparato a memoria tutti gli articoli di legge che riguardavano i reati più frequenti con i quali veniva a contatto, in modo da non farsi mai più prendere alla sprovvista da gente come il Livera Ernesto detto Dubbio.

Mentre stava un po' su e un po' giù, si immaginava già di fermare questo o quello e comunicargli senza la minima esitazione che era in arresto per il tal reato e che avrebbe rischiato tot anni di galera o tot lire di multa.

«E, bello mio...» mormorava di tanto in tanto soddisfatto.

Gli sarebbe piaciuto essere già in quella condizione, poter beccare il Dubbio e sparare ad alzo zero.

Purtroppo, per il momento, al di là del ricordo di quelle due parole, non aveva altre munizioni.

Se le sarebbe fatte bastare.

Il carabiniere Firrìa non aveva dubbi circa il fatto che «L'appropriazione indebita!» fosse comunque un reato e comportasse come tale una bella pena.

218.

Ci aveva riflettuto un po' prima di decidere se rispondere a quella lettera oppure bruciarla e fingere di non averla mai ricevuta.

«Poi l'ho bruciata», disse la Dominetti. «Tienine conto, angelo mio.»

L'aveva bruciata, ma non prima di aver risposto.

Aveva giudicato che fosse pieno diritto di quella ragazza conoscere la verità circa la sua origine, soprattutto adesso che ne aveva scoperta una piccola parte grazie alla confessione di quello che sino ad allora aveva creduto essere il suo vero genitore.

«Però...» fece la levatrice.

Poi scosse la testa come se qualcosa l'avesse distratta.

Pensava invece a ciò che stava per dire e ripensava a come aveva agito. Perché non se l'era sentita di prendere da sé una simile decisione.

«Insomma», disse, «non ero io l'unica depositaria della verità. Mi capisci?»

La Tina fece un passo indietro, avvicinandosi alla porta.

Chissà, forse qualcosa di non detto ma presente nell'alito giallo della Dominetti l'aveva messa in allarme.

«Il suo vero padre?» chiese poi.

La Dominetti annuì con un verso di gola.

«Avete preso insieme la decisione di rispondere, di farla venire qui, di rivelarle ogni cosa?» chiese la Tina.

«Non proprio», rispose la Dominetti.

A ciascuno la propria parte di verità, di responsabilità.

«Io le raccontai quello che mi era toccato fare quella notte», spiegò la levatrice.

«Lui era qui?» chiese la Tina.

«Più o meno dove sei tu adesso», osservò la Dominetti.

«E lui?»

Il Vergonese cosa fece?

«Niente», rispose la Dominetti.

Dopo averla ascoltata, l'aveva ringraziata per l'ospitalità, per ciò che aveva detto e che apprendeva anche lui per la prima volta...

«Non è vero!» interruppe la Tina. «Lui sapeva che quella ragazza aveva partorito due gemelle e che la Valeria era la seconda nata, quindi...»

«Di ciò che veniva a conoscenza per la prima volta», si impose la levatrice. «Così disse.»

La Tina tacque sopraffatta dalla veemenza della Dominetti che di tanto in tanto sembrava ritrovare una forza insospettabile.

«È uscito da qui con lei, dicendo che avrebbe pensato a sistemare ogni cosa, che le avrebbe dato una nuova vita.»

«Certo, come no», fece la Tina.

Le poteva dire come aveva pensato di aggiustare la faccenda?

Era in grado di dirle dov'era finita la ragazza, la gemella della sua amica Valeria?

«Non lo so», rispose la Dominetti.

Conciata com'era, non la vedeva?, come poteva muoversi, brigare, avere contatti con qualcuno a parte le rare persone pietose che le davano una mano per tirare avanti?

«Forse allora lo so io», disse la Tina.

«Davvero?» sorrise la Dominetti.

«Rida pure», disse la Tina, «ma se davvero voleva anche lei che nessuno sapesse avrebbe dovuto evitare di dirmi ciò che ha detto. Dovrà ridire le stesse cose a qualcun altro.»

«Ne sei certa, angelo mio?» chiese la levatrice.

«E la smetta di chiamarmi co…»

Ma la frase morì sulle labbra della Tina.

Con un gesto rapido la Dominetti aveva preso da sotto il sedere una pistola e gliela puntava contro.

«Forse sei entrata nella casa di una povera donna ammalata per rubare, magari anche solo una vecchia storia. Chi potrà dire cosa volevi veramente, oltre a me?» chiese.

219.

In casa della Tina le finestre finalmente si oscurarono, segno che la Brigida s'era decisa ad andare a letto.

Era ora, commentò tra sé il carabiniere Firrìa.

Dopo essere stato un po' qui e un po' lì, un po' su e un po' giù alla ricerca del posto migliore per portare a termine con successo l'appostamento, prese la decisione.

Dietro l'abitazione della Tina c'era un ampio rettangolo di terra adibito a orto, il regno della madre.

Lì, nascosto tra le verzure, avrebbe potuto comodamente avvertire il rombo dello Stornello e quindi saltar fuori dal buio come un folletto sorprendendo i due.

Cioè, si corresse, il Dubbio.

Se non l'aveva fatto sino a ora era solo perché, vedendo le finestre illuminate, non voleva correre il rischio di essere sorpreso dalla padrona di casa. Sapeva bene infatti che quando gli orti erano al massimo del loro splendore, gli ortari non avevano altro pensiero che la salute delle verdure e non tenevano conto di orari o altro: ogni ora del giorno e anche della sera era buona per uscire a controllare zucchine, melanzane e quant'altro.

Si appostò quindi, facendo un giro largo e passando in mezzo ai coltivi, addossandosi al muro posteriore della casa, circonfuso dal profumo che emanava da una fila di pomodori schierata sotto i suoi occhi, l'orecchio all'erta, l'occhio a cercare gli aerei che passavano nel cielo terso o, se avesse avuto fortuna, qualche stella cadente.

220.

«È l'unica cosa che mi è rimasta di quell'imbecille di mio marito, il console!» esclamò la Dominetti muovendo appena un po' l'arma.

«Che intenzioni ha?» chiese la Tina spostando appena la gamba destra all'indietro.

«Ah, ah!» fece la levatrice. «Sta' ferma dove sei.» Voleva sapere che intenzioni aveva con quella pistola in mano?

«Usarla», spiegò.

Le pareva così strano? Perché, secondo lei, l'aveva tirata fuori?

«Solo per spaventarti, angelo mio?»

Nessuno doveva sapere allora.

«Nessuno dovrà sapere adesso», disse ancora.

Questi erano i patti.

«Nemmeno se le dicessi che l'altra ragazza, la prima che lei ha fatto nascere, è morta e che c'è solo una persona al mondo che ci può dire cosa le è successo?»

La Dominetti sbuffò, come se fosse stanca.

«L'hai vista tu?» chiese.

«Qualcuno che conosco l'ha vista. Morta. Nel lago.»

La levatrice abbassò impercettibilmente la pistola.

«C'è un corpo?» chiese.

«Non è ancora stato trovato», rispose la Tina.

«Lo sarà mai?» chiese la Dominetti.

La Tina respirò a fondo.

«Ti prenderanno per un'esaltata se andrai a raccontare una storia simile senza alcuna prova, angelo mio.»

Il braccio della levatrice scendeva sempre di più.
«Lei però sa ogni cosa, potrebbe...»
Il braccio della Dominetti tornò a sollevarsi, la Tina vide nettamente la sua mano stringere il calcio dell'arma.
«No, angelo mio», disse la levatrice.
Era per quello che l'aspettava, per quello aveva temuto che non andasse più da lei.
«Il mio angelo della morte», sorrise stanca.
Finalmente aveva una buona ragione per fare ciò che da tempo meditava.
Poi in un lampo s'infilò la canna della pistola in bocca e tirò il grilletto.

221.

«Via, via!» o «Vai, vai!», una delle due cose.

L'Ernesto non aveva capito bene cosa stesse gridando la Tina quando l'aveva vista ritornare di corsa verso di lui, gridando una di quelle due frasi, saltando sulla moto che era ancora spenta e continuando a gridare e a dargli pacche sulla spalla.

Aveva giusto fatto in tempo a chiedere cosa fosse successo quando la ragazza gli aveva risposto con un cazzotto tra le scapole e non gli era restato altro da fare che avviare lo Stornello e partire.

Poi erano state parole al vento.

Nel vero senso della parola.

Lui aveva continuato a chiedere, girando appena un po' la testa per non perdere d'occhio la strada e la Tina aveva risposto, ma mentre gli stava attaccata, stringendolo forte con le braccia, la testa appiccicata contro la schiena, parlando a spizzichi e bocconi con ogni tanto dei brevi sussulti come se, almeno così era sembrato al Dubbio, avesse il singhiozzo oppure stesse piangendo.

Probabilmente era singhiozzo. Forse la ragazza s'era un po' spaventata per la velocità con la quale lui si mangiava le curve oppure per come sgasava sui rettilinei.

A un certo punto aveva smesso di chiedere fingendo di aver compreso anche se non aveva capito una mazza e pure la Tina s'era quietata rassicurata che con lui alla guida non c'era niente da temere.

Tra l'altro ad Acquaseria non mancava molto ormai,

c'era solo l'ultimo tratto da affrontare, in discesa e ricco di curve, un tratto dove aveva sentito dire che alcuni motociclisti addirittura si sfidavano, facevano gare per dimostrare la reciproca abilità. Un tratto lungo il quale non mancava qualche croce alla memoria.

Concentrato, le aveva infilate una dopo l'altra fino a raggiungere la casa della Tina dove, a motore spento, avrebbe capito infine cosa diavolo era successo in casa della levatrice.

Ma...

222.

Annunciato da un sentore di foglie di piante di pomodoro, spinto in avanti dalla sua stessa foga, il carabiniere Firrìa sbucò da dietro la casa della Tina enunciando un «Altolà!» che sembrò per un momento bloccare il moto stesso dell'universo.

Il Dubbio era ancora in sella.

La Tina aveva una gamba giù e una su.

Avevano entrambi i capelli scomposti e per un istante si guardarono come se non capissero bene cosa stesse succedendo e cosa ci facesse lì quell'uomo.

«Sorpresa!» disse il Firrìa.

In effetti...

Poi il carabiniere si rivolse al solo Ernesto.

«Se vuole seguirmi...» disse.

«Io?» riuscì a spiccicare il Dubbio.

«Vede altri qui in giro?» chiese il Firrìa.

Lo sguardo dell'Ernesto cercò quello della Tina.

Il Firrìa intese.

«Solo lei», specificò.

«E perché?»

Fu la ragazza a parlare.

«Le dice niente il reato di appropriazione indebita?» rispose il carabiniere.

Aveva dato alla voce un tono grave, come se fosse ancora in vigore la pena di morte.

«A me no», rispose la ragazza.

Nemmeno al Firrìa in verità diceva più di tanto. Era solo un asso che sperava di avere nella manica e che ormai stava giocando.

«Glielo spiegherò un'altra volta», rispose lui, cercando di far intendere alla Tina che l'avrebbe fatto più che volentieri. «Per intanto devo occuparmi di questo giovanotto. Se vuole seguirmi, quindi...» concluse tornando a rivolgersi all'Ernesto.

«Ma dove?» insisté la Tina mentre l'Ernesto guardava un po' l'uno e un po' l'altra.

«In caserma. Dove se no!» chiarì il Firrìa.

La Tina aveva ancora la gamba su.

«Vengo anch'io», disse.

Il Firrìa ebbe un momento di disorientamento. Non era prevista la presenza della ragazza.

«Ma lei non c'entra», obiettò.

La Tina diede un colpetto alla schiena dell'Ernesto. Forse lui no, lei però non solo l'aveva mangiata ma già stava cominciando a digerire la foglia.

«Può forse impedirmi di accompagnare il mio fidanzato?» chiese.

Meno male che era buio. Il Firrìa cambiò colore almeno tre volte.

«No, non posso», masticò.

«Bene», fece la Tina. «Allora ci si vede là.»

E, dato un altro colpo alla schiena del Dubbio che questa volta intese, si rimise a sedere sulla moto dopodiché i due partirono mentre il Firrìa, recuperato il Ciao, pedalò per un centinaio di metri smoccolando fino a che il motorino non si accese.

223.

«Va' adagio», disse la Tina.

Seconda, al minimo.

Un bep-bep del motore che al Dubbio ricordava vagamente quello della *Canterina.*

Adagio, perché solo così la Tina se la sentiva di dire al Dubbio cos'era successo, quello che aveva visto.

«Quella donna si è sparata sotto i miei occhi.»

E: «Non fermarti», aggiunse subito, capendo che l'Ernesto stava per farlo.

«Ma come?» disse lui, perché qualcosa doveva dire ma non sapeva cosa.

Sparata e basta, dopo averle raccontato tutto.

Di quella notte del 1944, del console suo marito, del Vergonese che era il vero padre della Valeria ma anche di quell'altra...

«L'altra sarebbe...»

La Tina diede una testata alla schiena dell'Ernesto.

«La gemella della Valeria. Nessuno lo doveva sapere allora e nessuno lo saprà adesso, lo capisci?» disse.

L'Ernesto accennò di sì guardando la strada.

«Lui? Il...»

«Sì.»

Lui ormai era il solo che sapeva tutto, anche quello che la Dominetti non poteva conoscere.

Lui solo avrebbe potuto dire cosa aveva fatto, cos'era accaduto dopo che insieme con l'altra sua figlia era uscito dalla casa della levatrice per andare chissà dove e «aggiustare le cose».

«Allora l'ho vista davvero», disse l'Ernesto, «avevo ragione.»

La Tina ebbe un singulto, forse un mezzo sorriso.

«Se il lago se l'è ripresa quella notte difficile che qualcuno ti possa credere.»

«E se saltasse fuori di nuovo da qualche parte, su qualche altra riva?» chiese il Dubbio.

«Se», disse sommessamente la Tina mentre si profilava la caserma dei carabinieri.

Se...

224.

Era quasi mezzanotte e i volti di tutti i presenti mostravano segni di stanchezza ed emozioni di natura diversa.

L'Ernesto e la Tina avevano gli occhi arrossati e una testa di capelli dentro la quale sembrava avesse soffiato il phon: l'aria della corsa in moto, ma non solo.

Sul volto del carabiniere Firrìa erano comparse molte più rughe del solito, la forza di gravità lo stava aiutando a modellare la maschera per la delusione provata quando aveva sentito come la ragazza aveva definito il Dubbio. Assonnato invece il viso del carabiniere Dangolo, svegliato per la seconda volta. Il pontilista Ancorati infine, che aveva ingannato l'attesa della chiamata del Firrìa facendo compagnia al fornaio Stramulo e al fiasco di vino bianco con cui questi reintegrava le perdite idriche, aveva un'espressione ebete.

Fu il Dangolo a rompere il silenzio dell'insolita riunione notturna.

«Cosa succede?» chiese banalmente.

«L'avrei arrestato», rispose il collega indicando il Dubbio.

E gli altri due allora?

«Sarebbero testimoni.»

Avrei, sarebbero…

Il Dangolo percepì odore di vaghezza.

In altre parole, possibili guai col maresciallo.

«Motivo dell'arresto?» chiese.

«Appropriazione indebita», rispose il Firrìa.

Il Dangolo si fermò per tempo, stava per chiedere in cosa consistesse.

«Procedi tu?» disse invece.

Al Firrìa la domanda parve un'accusa.

«È un reato o no?» si difese.

«Così parrebbe», rispose il Dangolo trincerandosi pure lui dietro il condizionale.

Altro da fare non restava, quindi, se non procedere.

«Avanti, allora.»

«Calma», consigliò il Firrìa che non sapeva da che parte cominciare.

Cazzo, se solo avesse potuto mettere le mani sul Codice Penale e dargli un'occhiata.

«Calma», ripeté, «non c'è nessuna fretta.»

«Ah no?»

Fu la Tina a interloquire.

Gli sguardi di tutti si concentrarono su di lei.

«Io un po' di fretta invece l'avrei», disse. «E vorrei capire il prima possibile perché mi trovo qui in caserma in compagnia del mio fidanzato.»

E dai!, morse lo stomaco del Firrìa.

«Non sarebbe meglio per tutti chiamare il signor maresciallo?» chiese.

Il Dangolo accennò subito sì.

Il Firrìa attese qualche secondo in più, questione di orgoglio.

Poi accettò.

«Solo perché me lo chiede lei», concesse.

Ma era la soluzione ideale per uscire da quell'imbuto.

225.

Il sangue giallo della levatrice s'era scavato un piccolo sentiero che era andato a finire sotto la cucina economica.

Ormai non colava più, quello a terra era quasi coagulato. La pistola era ben stretta nella sua mano.

Era lì, in attesa di farsi trovare.

L'avrebbe fatto, di lì a poche ore, la donna che con la sua famiglia abitava nella vecchia stazione di Tavordo e che quasi tutte le mattine passava da lei per vedere come stesse e di cosa avesse bisogno.

Sempre con lo stesso pensiero in testa, la solita macabra previsione, che non si tratteneva di ripetere sin troppo spesso in casa anche al cospetto dei figli piccoli che la guardavano con spavento e al marito che le diceva di finirla con quella lagna.

«Ma vedrai», rispondeva lei.

Vedrai, diceva, che un giorno o l'altro me la troverò davanti bella e morta.

226.

«Che cazzo c'è, chi è morto?» esordì il maresciallo Alborati entrando in ufficio e completando il mosaico di visi sconvolti.

Quel giorno aveva tolto il gesso ma zoppicava ancora un po'. Indossava la giacca da maresciallo ma sotto si intuiva una canottiera e i pantaloni erano quelli da casa, un vellutino beige ormai vittima di troppi lavaggi.

Gli occhi di tutti si puntarono sul Firrìa ma fu il Dangolo a parlare.

«Un arresto», disse.

Il maresciallo fece la mossa di togliersi la foschia del sonno dagli occhi. Forse poco prima, entrando con l'impeto dell'incazzato, non l'aveva notato.

Adesso sì però.

«Ancora lui?» fece puntando il Dubbio.

Non aspettò risposta.

«Cos'ha fatto?»

Toccava al Firrìa adesso.

Un bel respiro e una preghiera affinché il Codice Penale gli desse ragione.

«Appropriazione indebita», comunicò.

Sulla fronte dell'Alborati comparvero rughe come righe sulle quali si andavano evidenziando le parole del Codice relative al reato comunicato.

«Cioè cioè?» chiese.

Il Firrìa, e usando l'imperfetto come gli sembrava d'obbligo, riassunse la situazione.

«Da cui l'arresto», concluse.

L'Alborati, mentre quello parlava, s'era seduto, sistemata la giacca, chiusa fino al collo che comunque, restando privo di camicia, rimaneva nudo e strano al vedersi, e si era dato qualche grattatina alla caviglia.

«Cioè tu mi stai dicendo», esordì, «che quello...»

E indicò il pontilista Ancorati che con gli occhi a mezz'asta sembrava ormai prossimo a crollare.

«... ha prestato la motocicletta a quell'altro...»

E indicò il Dubbio che se ne stava a testa china e mani dietro la schiena, già pronto a essere preso in consegna.

«... e tu l'hai arrestato per appropriazione indebita.»

Il Firrìa non osò parlare. Ritirò la testa tra le spalle, mica poteva negare l'evidenza.

«Appropriazione indebita», annunciò il maresciallo sillabando.

«Chiunque, per procurare a sé o ad altri un ingiusto profitto, si appropria del denaro o della cosa mobile di cui abbia, a qualsiasi titolo, il possesso, è punito a querela della persona offesa con la reclusione fino a tre anni e con la multa fino a lire ottocentomila.»

«È chiaro?» disse poi asciugandosi il sudore.

Dov'era la querela della persona offesa?

Era vero, secondo quanto lui stesso aveva appena riferito, che la persona che avrebbe dovuto ritenersi offesa aveva prestato spontaneamente la moto al giovanotto?

Ed era vero che il suddetto giovanotto era ritornato nello stesso luogo da cui era partito con l'evidente intento di restituire il mezzo?

«Quindi chiedo, dove cazzo è il reato?» gridò il maresciallo.

«Ma sono stati via un sacco di tempo», osò osservare il Firrìa.

«E allora?» rincarò l'Alborati.

Poi schioccò le dita alla volta della persona offesa, richiamandola alla realtà.

«Lei ha forse posto un limite temporale alla prova della motocicletta?» chiese.

L'Ancorati sgranò gli occhi e rispose che, no, aveva concesso un giro di prova e basta.

«Ma non immaginavo che fosse andato lo sa il Signore dove.»

«Se è per quello», interloquì il Dubbio, «siamo andati fino a Ta...»

Ma un calcetto della Tina nello stinco gli tranciò la parola.

«Tavernola e ritorno», completò.

«Mi avete fatto fuori un serbatoio», piagnucolò l'Ancorati.

«Te lo ripago», assicurò il Dubbio.

«Non sono affari miei», troncò il maresciallo.

Piuttosto gli sarebbe piaciuto sapere cosa ci facesse lì la signorina, cosa c'entrasse.

«Sono la sua fidanzata, il giro in moto l'abbiamo fatto assieme», rispose prontamente la Tina.

Il carabiniere Firrìa chiuse gli occhi, quella era una dichiarazione pubblica, poteva dire addio anche alle speranze residue.

«Auguri e figli maschi», disse il maresciallo, «la seduta è tolta.»

Si alzò e puntò l'indice sul carabiniere.

«Il Codice Penale», disse, «prima di applicarlo va conosciuto.»

Poi senza dire altro, e zoppicando un po', uscì.

227.

Lo Stornello?

Sì, ci avrebbe pensato, gli avrebbe fatto sapere.

«La benzina però...» insisté l'Ancorati.

La benzina, d'accordo, domani stesso gli avrebbe dato i soldi. Però adesso che lo lasciasse andare, disse il Dubbio all'Ancorati dopo aver percorso una cinquantina di metri fuori dalla caserma.

Il pontilista s'era appiccicato ai due mentre la Tina s'era letteralmente appesa all'Ernesto, l'aveva arpionato appena uscita, trasmettendogli una specie di tremore, il silenzioso invito ad allontanarsi da lì, a restare soli, cosa che l'Ancorati non sospettava nemmeno, continuando a insistere circa il destino dello Stornello e il pieno del serbatoio.

«Domani ho detto!» sbottò l'Ernesto, subito guardandosi in giro perché era notte piena e aveva alzato il tono della voce.

Ma soprattutto aveva sentito il corpo della ragazza stringersi contro il suo fianco e sul braccio, quello cui lei si teneva appesa, aveva avvertito un umidore di lacrime.

«Va bene, domani, non è mica il caso di gridare», fece il pontilista girando sui tacchi e sparendo senza salutare.

Allora la Tina si fermò e pianse.

Così come fino a pochi secondi prima aveva desiderato che il pontilista si togliesse di torno adesso l'Ernesto desiderò che fosse ancora lì per dargli una mano, perlomeno non lasciarlo solo con la ragazza che piangeva senza freni.

Non sapeva cosa fare né cosa dire e infine se ne uscì con una frase che avrebbe fatto meglio a trattenere.

«Cosa c'è?» chiese, anche se, pur in maniera imprecisa, immaginava quello che stava accadendo alla Tina: finalmente libera di farlo, stava scaricando la tensione che aveva accumulato dopo aver visto ciò che gli aveva raccontato e pure quella per l'inaspettato sipárietto in caserma, di fronte al maresciallo.

Certo, anche quello c'entrava.

Ma la ragazza avrebbe voluto rispondere che stava piangendo perché si sentiva dentro una nostalgia per qualcosa che non riusciva a definire. Le mancavano le parole per comunicare la malinconia che avvertiva, una sorta di pena che la avvolgeva e comprendeva anche l'Ernesto, sua madre, l'ex infermiera, un sentimento colorato di giallo come il colore che aveva visto nella casa della levatrice, nei suoi occhi, in quelli della giovane che affondava sempre di più nell'acqua del lago e che vedeva aperti come volesse chiedere ragione dell'essere stata trattata così dopo che era stata venduta. Avrebbe voluto parlare della tomba della sua vera madre, chiedere se almeno una volta ogni tanto il Vergonese le avesse portato un fiore, dire della Valeria, la Valeria adesso, la sua amica d'infanzia, parlare delle chiacchiere che aveva sempre condiviso con lei sola senza sapere che un'altra con loro avrebbe potuto ascoltarle e poi giocare, fare progetti, ridere, scherzare, diventare donne. Avrebbe voluto dire che vedeva intorno a sé non il buio della notte ma quello spaventoso del fondo del lago, così difficile da immaginare guardando la sua superficie luminosa soprattutto nelle belle mattine d'estate come quella che sarebbe arrivata di lì a qualche ora. Ma non trovava le parole per dire niente di tutto ciò.

«Certo, capisco», disse d'impeto l'Ernesto rispondendo infine al suo silenzio mentre la ragazza, svelando quei pensieri a sé stessa senza la possibilità di raccontarli ad altri, si era un poco calmata.

«Siamo di fronte a qualcosa che somiglia al niente», disse.

Il Dubbio pensò che si riferisse al fatto che non avevano niente in mano per dimostrare quanto era successo.

La Tina si riferiva a tutto ciò che non riusciva a dire.

Ma andava bene anche così.

228.

Un grido che poco aveva di umano trasse la Tina dal dormiveglia dentro il quale era finalmente piombata un paio d'ore prima. Non aveva idea di che ora fosse quando aveva raggiunto il letto, forse l'una del mattino, adesso intuì che l'alba non era ancora completamente sorta. Più che dormire aveva convissuto con immagini che, a differenza di ciò che le capitava con i sogni, la popolavano ancora. La Valeria soprattutto, che le veniva incontro sorridente, uscendo dall'albergo, camminando lentamente come stesse facendo una sfilata e mentre la salutava con una mano, con l'altra si toglieva dalla faccia una maschera sotto la quale mostrava di avere lo stesso viso, quello che lei conosceva da sempre. Le si avvicinava continuando a dire: «Sono io», rimettendo e togliendo la maschera, accompagnando quel gesto con un rumore che era d'acqua, di onda. Senza rendersene conto la Tina, nonostante l'aria della sua camera fosse calda, le finestre chiuse, s'era tirata le lenzuola fin sopra la testa perché la Valeria che aveva sognato aveva spostato verso di lei una corrente di aria fredda e buia e di bocche di pesci golosi.

Non era ancora l'alba piena quando quel grido la svegliò.

Era l'ora in cui si innaffiano gli orti, il grido era uscito dalla bocca della Brigida quando, poco prima, aveva scoperto che Attila o chi per esso era passato dal suo orto senza fare prigionieri.

Sette piante di pomodori giacevano al suolo ferite a morte.

Il metro quadrato del prezzemolo, seminato ben tre volte prima di ottenere qualcosa, calpestato con scientifica crudeltà.

Tre melanzane, ormai pronte per il consumo, erano cadute al suolo come bombe a mano inesplose, ed erano già preda di quelle schifose lumache senza guscio.

Per non parlare dei peperoni...

Dopo l'urlo di dolore, la donna era rimasta un momento a riflettere, fotografando i danni procurati dall'anonimo barbaro.

La Tina la trovò che, contrariamente alle abitudini dell'ora e del giorno, si stava vestendo di tutto punto come quando faceva in vista di un'uscita importante, funerale, messa, processione del Corpus Domini.

«Dove vai?» chiese.

«Dai carabinieri», rispose la Brigida.

Si stava pettinando, non si girò nemmeno, vedeva sua figlia nello specchio sopra il comò. Aveva usato un tono come se quella che si apprestava a fare fosse la cosa più logica del mondo, come se tutti, nessuno escluso, sapessero del proditorio attacco cui era stato sottoposto il suo orto.

Alla Tina venne il sospetto, tanto fugace quanto infondato, che la risposta di sua madre fosse in qualche modo collegata a ciò che le era capitato la notte appena vissuta, a quello che ormai sapeva.

Che le fosse sfuggito qualcosa durante quella specie di sonno durato poche ore?

Fu la stessa madre a fugarne i dubbi, prendendola per un braccio e, a piedi nudi perché ancora non aveva calzato le scarpe, portandola con sé.

«Vieni a vedere.»

Presa visione del disastro, la Tina si sentì sollevata al punto di chiedere cosa c'entrassero i carabinieri, pur sapendo che c'entravano eccome!

«Faccio denuncia», chiarì sua madre.

Era un po' presto però, il maresciallo probabilmente non era ancora in servizio.

«Aspetterò», rispose con decisione la madre.

Voleva essere la prima.

Una volta rimasta sola la Tina si trovò a chiedersi cosa fare adesso.

La risposta venne da sé.

La cosa più semplice.

La mormorò giusto per sentirla.

«Riposati.»

Tornò nella sua camera, aprì le finestre lasciando le persiane accostate, si sdraiò.

Di dormire non ci sarebbe stato verso ma non aveva senso, stanca e stravolta com'era, stare a pensare all'immediato futuro rimanendo in piedi.

Sdraiata, a occhi chiusi, lasciandosi invadere da quel denso profumo di aria d'estate che percorreva invisibili sentieri, deviando anche dentro la sua stanza, da una finestra all'altra. Era il profumo saporito dell'infanzia, dei giochi, del bagno nel lago come facevano lei e la Valeria, spingendosi fin quando riuscivano ancora a vedersi i piedi e mai oltre, dove cominciava il buio.

Quello dell'acqua fonda.

Quello degli occhi chiusi dietro i quali infine la Tina, senza accorgersene, piombò nel sonno.

229.

Ci pensò la Brigida a svegliarla e ormai era mezzogiorno passato.

«Passato?» si meravigliò la Tina.

Passato, sì, confermò sua madre.

Passato, oltre che per andare e tornare da Menaggio, ad aspettare che il signor maresciallo trovasse il tempo per occuparsi di lei e delle sue verdure.

Sfortuna, spiegò la donna.

Sfortuna perché era capitata in caserma in un momento di turbolenza.

Il maresciallo?, aveva chiesto lei.

Era occupato, le aveva risposto un carabiniere piccolo, dall'accento strano e dalla faccia triste triste.

Va bene, aspetterò, aveva risposto lei.

Potrebbe volerci qualche ora, l'aveva informata quello.

«Ho tempo», aveva risposto la Brigida, sentendo crescere anche un po' di curiosità perché l'agitazione nella caserma era palpabile.

«Se intanto vuole dire a me», aveva proposto sempre quel carabiniere.

Ma la madre della Tina aveva declinato l'offerta.

«Preferirei parlare col signor maresciallo.»

Roba da non credere, ma sulla faccia di quello la tristezza le era sembrata aumentare. Come se la sua risposta l'avesse offeso, cosa che non era nelle sue intenzioni, oppure avesse aggravato una pena che si portava dentro già da prima.

Comunque fosse era stato gentile e l'aveva fatta accomodare di sopra, al piano degli uffici, quasi vicino a quello del maresciallo che aveva la porta chiusa.

«Sentivo la voce però», continuò a raccontare la donna.

Era al telefono.

Faceva domande, rispondeva.

Capiva poco, quasi niente.

Una volta rimasta sola, s'era anche avvicinata un po' alla porta dell'ufficio.

Niente da fare, fatica sprecata.

Fatica sprecata anche perché, verso le undici, quando la calma era ritornata e il maresciallo l'aveva ricevuta, lui in persona, ma che gentile che era stato!, s'era scusato per la lunga attesa spiegandole – dicendo più di quanto avrebbe dovuto – che purtroppo avevano per le mani il caso fresco fresco di un presunto suicidio, cioè suicidio vero e proprio in realtà, tuttavia in situazioni come quella c'erano sempre delle cose da fare, accertamenti da effettuare, particolari da chiarire... presunto suicidio insomma di una donna, una ex levatrice, malata eh!, malata di un male brutto, che però per qualche anno aveva abitato da quelle parti e insomma il maresciallo di Porlezza, sbarbatello al primo comando di stazione, gli aveva chiesto per cortesia se poteva dargli una mano a capire bene come muoversi per non fare del fatto un casus belli.

Dopodiché le aveva chiesto cosa potesse fare per lei e una volta che lei gli aveva raccontato il perché e il percome fosse lì, da quello che lui aveva detto in risposta, sempre gentile neh!, aveva capito che non le restava altro da fare che salvare il salvabile e mettere una bella pietra sopra l'idea di beccare il delinquente che le aveva massacrato l'orto.

«Non mi resta altro da fare se non voglio che mi venga l'ulcera», disse la donna. «È meglio che non ci pensi più.»

«Credo proprio di sì», rispose la Tina.

Ma si riferiva a ben altro.

230.

L'Ernesto aveva dormito nella taverna del commenda.

Dormito, anche lui, per modo di dire.

Dormicchiato, a causa della confusione dei pensieri che l'atteggiamento della Tina non aveva certo contribuito a migliorare.

Prima di lasciarlo la ragazza gli aveva raccomandato di non dire niente, non fare niente, non...

Un sacco di parole, di cose, anche confuse, che, appunto, l'avevano lasciato confuso oltre che inquieto.

Poi era sparita e beato chi l'aveva più vista.

Chissà dov'era finita!

Ci aveva pensato il pontilista Ancorati a occupargli la mente con altri pensieri.

Prima di tutto, prima ancora di salutarlo, i soldi della benza che aveva consumato.

E che cazzo, glieli avrebbe dati, cosa poteva farci se non li aveva in tasca!

Non poteva stamparli, non era la zecca e non sarebbe cascato il mondo se glieli avesse portati l'indomani.

Poi, lo Stornello.

Lo prendeva o no?

«Non lo so, ci devo pensare», aveva risposto l'Ernesto.

«Ancora?» s'era incazzato l'Ancorati.

Dopo che ci aveva fatto sopra mezzo giro del lago, aveva ancora bisogno di pensarci su?

Una menata che era andata avanti tutta la mattina e che s'era quietata solo dopo mezzogiorno.

L'Ancorati infatti, forse perché non aveva ancora smaltito del tutto la notte parzialmente insonne appena trascorsa, alla ripresa del lavoro, e con la pancia piena, s'era addormentato come un somaro dentro il gabbiotto dei biglietti, steso su una panchina che stava contro la parete di fondo, incurante del caldo e delle sirene dei battelli. E il Dubbio s'era ben volentieri caricato di tutto il lavoro pur di non svegliarlo e sentirlo ricominciare con la solfa del mattino.

Lo svegliò solo quando mancava mezz'ora all'ultimo battello, quello che avrebbe preso lui per tornare a casa.

Il pontilista titolare fece per dire qualcosa. Prima però l'occhio gli scappò sull'orologio.

«Ostia!» commentò.

Il Dubbio capì il senso dell'esclamazione, scrollò le spalle per dire che andava tutto bene.

Bene soprattutto perché non aveva altra voglia che saltare sul battello, non sentire, non vedere nessuno per un po', raggiungere la pace della sua cameretta e chiudersi dentro fino al giorno dopo cercando di cacciare dalla testa ogni pensiero.

Invece...

231.

«Faccio due passi», disse la Tina.

Aveva rimandato per troppe ore.

«Adesso che è quasi l'ora della cena?» borbottò sua madre.

Avevano mangiato giusto un boccone quando era quasi l'una. La Brigida senza appetito per la gran rabbia che aveva nello stomaco, la Tina senza appetito e basta. Poi la donna s'era fiondata nell'orto nonostante il sole a picco per dare avvio alla ricostruzione, la Tina era rimasta in casa a cincischiare, rinviando quel momento, tentata a tratti di rivelare almeno il nome di uno dei due colpevoli, del barbaro assassino che aveva sconvolto l'orto materno.

Carabiniere Qualcosa Firrìa!

E dal pensiero aveva ricavato un sorriso amaro, fino a che, avvicinandosi il crepuscolo, aveva capito che non avrebbe più potuto rinviare oltre, anche se ormai si avvicinava l'ora della cena.

«Ritorno subito», rispose e uscì.

La notizia l'avrà già raggiunta?, pensava mentre si avvicinava alla meta.

Forse, senza che lo capisse davvero, quel cincischiare con il quale aveva trascorso il pomeriggio aveva avuto l'obiettivo di far sì che la notizia di quel suicidio volasse di bocca in bocca anche e soprattutto grazie a chi ricordava ancora chi fosse e fosse stata la Dominetti.

Così che non dovesse parlare, spiegare più di tanto.

Così che all'ex infermiera Maria Teresa Supposta dovesse porre solo quella domanda.

E adesso?

Cosa doveva fare?

Cosa doveva dire alla Valeria soprattutto?

La Supposta la vide arrivare dalla finestra del salotto.

Sapeva già.

L'aveva aspettata per tutto il pomeriggio ma senza fretta, certa che sarebbe arrivata.

L'anticipò di un paio di minuti, mettendosi sulla soglia della porta di casa e guardando la stanchezza che emanava dal corpo della ragazza, dal suo procedere con pesante lentezza.

Parlarono così, una davanti all'altra, quasi in silenzio, come due personaggi di un film muto.

Ma tanto lì intorno non c'era nessuno, nessuno poteva sentirle.

«Così come nessuno doveva sapere», disse l'ex infermiera.

La Tina, per tutta risposta, socchiuse gli occhi.

232.

Il Dubbio invece li aprì bene.

Li sgranò, anzi.

Li sgranò per cercare di individuare meglio la figura che, dalla passerella del molo, si sbracciava in direzione del battello. Più che evidente la sua intenzione di farsi notare da qualcuno che viaggiava sul battello e soprattutto che sarebbe sceso a Bellano. Il Dubbio concluse facilmente che, essendo l'unico viaggiatore diretto lì, il Riffa stava aspettando lui. Avesse potuto l'avrebbe evitato.

Non era cattiveria.

Piuttosto la necessità di rimanere per qualche ora ancora, sino all'indomani perlomeno, dentro il silenzio che l'aveva avvolto non appena salito sul battello allontanandosi, sia fisicamente sia mentalmente, dalla sera precedente, da tutto ciò che era accaduto e da come l'avventura, cominciata l'infausta notte in cui aveva incrociato il cadavere di quella ragazza, s'era conclusa.

In niente appunto, nel silenzio di chi non c'era più e di chi, pur essendoci ancora, per una ragione o per l'altra non poteva o non doveva squarciare quel silenzio.

Fosse stato su un treno, l'Ernesto sarebbe sceso da una portiera diversa e avrebbe seminato il Riffa. Ma il battello aveva una sola uscita, non c'era via di scampo.

Il saluto che il Riffa gli rivolse: «Ma dove cazzo eri finito?» fece temere al Dubbio che quello volesse sapere ciò che lui non aveva invece alcuna intenzione di raccontargli.

Rifletté che doveva inventarsi subito una balla che stesse in piedi.

Ecco, il resoconto di una notte passata a pastrugnarsi la Tina nella casa del commenda avrebbe soddisfatto alla grande l'appetito del socio.

Ma quello: «Ti devo chiedere una cosa e non puoi dirmi no», gli disse quando ancora non erano usciti da sotto la pensilina del molo.

No, eh!, fu allora il pensiero dell'Ernesto.

Se il Riffa aveva messo in piedi un altro ghetto come quello del crotto con la Valeria e la Tina poteva andare a cercarsi qualche altro pistola da portarsi appresso.

Lui ne aveva abbastanza di quello che era successo, non aveva bisogno di finire in qualche altro guaio, di conoscere altri marescialli, fossero della Finanza o dei caramba.

All'altezza del bar dell'Imbarcadero il Riffa gli propose di entrare a bere qualcosa.

Il Dubbio trovò le parole per dirgli che era stanco e voleva andare a riposare.

Se doveva dirgli qualcosa, gliela dicesse lì, subito, mentre lui si preparava a rispondere no, qualunque cosa stesse per uscire dalla sua bocca.

«Va bene», accettò il Riffa.

Poi fece un colpetto di tosse.

Quindi parlò.

«Non è che mi presteresti per un po' di tempo la *Canterina*?»

233.

Mezz'ora più tardi, con la Canterina, sua madre, che ronzava irrequieta per casa, l'Ernesto era disteso nel suo letto ma non proprio così come aveva desiderato.

Aveva sperato di tornare a casa e chiudersi la porta alle spalle. Chiuderla non solo sulla giornata appena finita ma su tutto quello che era accaduto, sui pensieri, tutti, nessuno escluso.

Invece, una volta sdraiato sul letto, se n'erano aggiunti altri due.

Prestare al Riffa la sua barca, permettendogli di fare quello che aveva bene o male fatto lui sino a poco tempo prima, compreso fornire sigarette di contrabbando ai suoi clienti, dottor Lonati in testa?

E l'altro pensiero, l'altra domanda.

Pure per rispondere a quella s'era preso tempo.

Gliel'aveva fatta la Canterina, sua madre, dopo avergli concesso giusto il tempo di succhiare la minestra.

«Non è ora», aveva detto, «di farmi conoscere questa morosa?»

Troppe cose nella testa.

Bisognava affrontarle una alla volta.

Il primo a dirgli che se voleva fare le cose per bene doveva prenderle una alla volta era stato suo padre.

Certo, negli anni a seguire non era stato l'unico.

Sua madre glielo aveva spesso ripetuto.

Ma anche il dottor Lonati, pure il maresciallo Pezzati quando l'aveva interrogato, forse addirittura la stessa Tina.

Una cosa alla volta, rifletté l'Ernesto mentre cominciava ad addormentarsi.

Una cosa alla volta, a cominciare dalla più urgente.

234.

La Tina gli aveva detto sì.

Capiva, e gli restituiva il favore. Visto che lui s'era prestato a fare la parte del fidanzato per smorzare le *avances* del carabiniere Firrìa, era giusto che lei ricambiasse e non si negasse alla richiesta che l'Ernesto le aveva fatto.

«Però domenica», aveva detto.

La prima di agosto.

«Va bene», aveva risposto l'Ernesto.

Domenica o lunedì, per lui faceva lo stesso.

Non così per la ragazza.

Prima di concedersi a interpretare la parte della fidanzatina, la Tina doveva fare una cosa che le avrebbe alleggerito l'animo. Le sembrava di doversi togliere una specie di ragnatela da davanti agli occhi che per il momento le impediva di avere le idee sul futuro, e anche la vista, chiare.

In poche parole doveva vedere in faccia la Valeria.

Guardarla.

Capire cosa avrebbe provato nel rivedersela davanti, dopo aver saputo tutto ciò che aveva scoperto, sentire cosa le avrebbe detto il cuore: se fosse meglio tacere davvero oppure, contro una certa logica, quella che animava il consiglio dell'ex infermiera per esempio, rivelarle ogni cosa e poi subirne le conseguenze.

Del Vergonese non aveva il minimo timore, qualunque cosa fosse accaduta nel rivederlo, era certa che se la sarebbe cavata: se, dalla sera dell'incontro con la Dominetti, era rimasta alla larga dall'albergo era perché non voleva vedere altri che la Valeria. Stava quindi aspettando con calma che arrivasse la fine del mese, quel 30 di luglio destinato al ritorno sul lago dell'amica, quando la sera del 29 il telefono di casa squillò e la Brigida, com'era solita fare quando c'era anche la figlia, disse: «Rispondi tu e vedi chi è».

Il che significava che la Tina doveva effettuare una cernita tra le persone, poche in verità e quasi sempre donne, con le quali sua madre parlava volentieri e altre alle quali preferiva negarsi.

La telefonata fu breve. La madre della Tina immaginò che all'altro capo del filo ci fosse stata una della sua lista nera.

«Cosa le hai detto?» chiese alla figlia.

Che scusa s'era inventata per non passargliela?

Era fondamentale saperlo per essere preparata all'evenienza di incontrarla, magari il giorno seguente.

«La Valeria», rispose la Tina ancora turbata.

La donna guardò sua figlia con un'espressione corrucciata come se faticasse a capire chi fosse quella tal Valeria.

«Ah», fece subito dopo, «la tua amica.»

Che aveva parlato piena di eccitazione, mangiandosi le frasi e trasmettendo una vivacità da fare invidia. Stava così bene a Londra che non le pareva di essere mai stata tanto viva, viva più che mai! Ma non era potuta stare troppo al telefono. Voleva solo avvisare lei prima di ogni altra persona. Non sarebbe tornata a casa, avrebbe prolungato il soggiorno a Londra di un altro mese.

Udite, udite!, aveva detto, con un colpo di fortuna le avevano offerto un posto di lavoro alla reception di un albergo a Chelsea. Provvisorio, un mese, ma c'erano delle prospettive per il futuro.

«Quindi...» aveva interloquito la Tina.

«Quindi niente», l'aveva interrotta la Valeria, «per adesso sto a vedere, ti terrò informata.»

Doveva salutarla adesso, aveva fretta. Dopo di lei, doveva informare suo padre della novità.

«Puoi immaginare come sarà contento», aveva detto ridendo francamente.

Diventerà una bestia, aveva aggiunto.

«Cos'ha detto di bello?» chiese sua madre, davvero stranamente poiché non era solita fare domande.

«Niente», rispose la Tina, «ci saluta.»

E non intendeva soltanto loro due.

235.

La prima domenica d'agosto il tempo si mise al brutto sin dal mattino. Nuvolaglia dalla bergamasca e dal basso lago stavano gareggiando a chi arrivasse prima per scaricare acqua a secchi. A meno di scontrarsi proprio sopra il centro lago e scatenare un'iradiddio.

La Tina, come da promessa, salì sul battello delle tredici e quaranta, arrivo alle quattordici e cinque a Bellano, giusto in tempo per beccarsi due ventacci uno contro l'altro che si baloccarono col battello e le misero lo stomaco sottosopra.

L'Ernesto l'aspettava al molo. I patti li conosceva bene, chiari. La Tina gli aveva concesso due orette per il teatrino previsto per la giornata. Due orette in totale che dovevano comprendere una toccata e fuga dalla Canterina, un gelato e l'immancabile visita all'Orrido che la ragazza non aveva mai visto.

Non appena scesa dal battello gli si appese al braccio.

Non fu tanto la necessità di entrare subito nel ruolo quanto la paura, tant'era sbattuta dal su e giù del viaggio, di aver smarrito il senso dell'equilibrio.

Due minuti di sosta per riprendere contatto con la terraferma, poi s'erano avviati.

«Mi raccomando eh!» lo avvisò lei con il primo fiato utile a veicolare parole.

Intendeva, rispettiamo i patti.

Poiché in fondo le spiaceva dover ingannare la madre dell'Ernesto.

«Tranquilla», la rassicurò lui senza immaginare ciò che attendeva entrambi.

La Canterina infatti si era organizzata di nascosto.

Uè, mica poteva passare in segreto il fatto che suo figlio avesse una morosa!

Era una soddisfazione e anche, per dirla tutta, il modo di consumare qualche piccola vendetta.

La soddisfazione era stata invitare a una festicciola domestica, architettata per ricevere degnamente la morosa del figlio, la direttrice dell'asilo Tommaso Grossi, suor Giuntina, e l'aiuto cuciniera Fedina Cagli che aveva portato due crostate fatte con la marmellata di sambuco sfruttando, all'insaputa della stessa suora, la dispensa e il forno dell'asilo. Di suo la Canterina aveva messo a disposizione due bottiglie di spumantino Gancia che si sarebbero rivelate d'annata, passate là in sostanza e dal sapore marsalato. Infine, dopo averci ben pensato, aveva deciso di estendere l'invito anche al dottor Lonati.

A lui e signora naturalmente.

Il Lonati aveva accolto graziosamente il pensiero. Forte dell'essere in ambulatorio, quindi lontano da orecchie domestiche, aveva risposto che purtroppo un impegno l'avrebbe tenuto lontano dal paese proprio la domenica a venire.

In ogni caso lo dirò a mia moglie, aveva assicurato.

«Che bugia ti sei inventato per non partecipare?» aveva chiesto Vittoria Lonati che del marito conosceva vizi e virtù.

«Niente di che», aveva risposto lui.

Però aveva lasciato intendere alla Canterina che forse anche lei non avrebbe potuto esserci così, se voleva saltare sul carro della sua stessa bugia...

«Sei gentile», aveva sorriso la moglie.

Ma lei un'occhiatina alla festicciola la voleva dare.

«Sono proprio curiosa di vederla in faccia la morosa dell'Ernesto.»

Per vendetta invece la padrona di casa aveva invitato i vicini, gli Schedina, così detti per l'abitudine che moglie e marito avevano di giocare ogni sabato alla Sisal: era il momento infatti, dopo aver subito per anni consigli, rimproveri e velate minacce a causa dell'Ernesto, di dimostrare che suo figlio aveva infine imboccato la via giusta, non solo il lavoro alla Navigazione ma anche la morosa, e di fuori paese.

Nessuno degli invitati aveva osato dire no alla Canterina, così che all'ingresso in casa dei due presunti fidanzati, se da una parte si levò un applauso avviato dalla Canterina, dall'altra ci fu una sorta di paralisi, spontanea anche per quanto riguardò il Dubbio.

La Tina, superata la sorpresa e valutata la situazione, reagì per prima.

«Non dovevate disturbarvi», disse.

In fondo, aggiunse con tutta la chiarezza che le riuscì, non poteva che fermarsi pochi minuti.

«Vero, Ernesto?»

Il Dubbio confermò senza aprire bocca.

Però almeno il tempo per mangiare una fetta di torta ce l'aveva, vero?, si preoccupò la Canterina.

Lo stomaco della ragazza non era ancora del tutto in asse. Fu merito della crostata con la marmellata di sambuco se la Tina dovette chiedere soccorso.

L'aiuto cuciniera dell'asilo infatti usava burro come se glielo regalassero, a maggior ragione quando non lo pagava lei. Il risultato fu che la Tina si trovò in bocca un impasto quasi colloso dal dittatoriale sapore di burro. Il tentativo di mandar giù le scatenò la nausea e, a seguire, la necessità di vomitare il tutto.

Dovette chiedere licenza di raggiungere il luogo comodo, mentre il Schedina, guardando di sottecchi la moglie, cercava di farle intendere che forse la ragazza era già incinta.

Le fece perlomeno gioco, subito dopo, la radicata convinzione che a chi dà di stomaco giova, pari a una medicina, fare due passi e respirare un poco di aria fresca: lasciando gli ospiti, in parte delusi in parte indifferenti per la cattiva riuscita della festicciola, l'Ernesto e la Tina uscirono di casa a tirar l'ora che mancava al battello del ritorno.

Passeggiarono, non più sottobraccio l'uno all'altra, e perlopiù in silenzio.

Solo poco prima dell'imbarco la ragazza volle sottoporre una questione all'Ernesto.

«Ma cosa s'è messa in testa tua madre?»

«Boh», rispose il Dubbio secondo consuetudine.

236.

Boh!

Mica era un'esclusiva del Dubbio uscirsene con quella risposta che tutto poteva essere tranne che, appunto, una risposta.

«Boh», disse quindi Vittoria Lonati.

La donna, prima di uscire per recarsi dalla Canterina, aveva augurato a suo marito buon riposo.

Il dottore era già stravaccato in poltrona, le gambe allungate, la finestra della sala aperta sulla vista del lago e delle vele che lo stavano percorrendo.

«Farò del mio meglio», aveva risposto lui prevedendo di addormentarsi prima ancora che sua moglie raggiungesse la meta.

Era andata proprio così.

Non aveva previsto di dormire tanto però.

Si svegliò infatti quando Vittoria Lonati rientrò. Non finse nemmeno di aver fatto dell'altro nel frattempo.

«Com'è andata?» chiese in mezzo a uno sbadiglio.

«Così», rispose la donna.

Aveva la fetta di torta sullo stomaco, la testa intronata dalle chiacchiere degli altri ospiti alle quali aveva dovuto contribuire.

«E la morosa dell'Ernesto com'è?»

«Boh», rispose la donna.

«Come, boh?» fece il marito.

«Boh», ribadì la moglie.

Boh era boh, nient'altro.

Boh voleva dire che non era né bella né brutta.

Ma, boh!, voleva anche dire, per quello che aveva notato, intuito, che non avrebbe messo la mano sul fuoco né scommesso una cicca sul fatto che quella ragazza fosse la morosa del Dubbio.

«Se non è la morosa cos'è allora?» chiese il Lonati alzandosi dalla poltrona.

La risposta era già pronta.

«Boh», Vittoria Lonati, per la terza volta.

237.

Da quando il commenda era morto e la Tina era tornata a casa con sua madre, l'ex infermiera Maria Teresa Supposta non aveva smesso un minuto di pensare a due cose, due destini: quello della casa che aveva di fronte e quello della Tina.

Temeva che avrebbero fatto la stessa fine.

La casa, secondo quanto la stessa ragazza le aveva detto, venduta, poiché secondo sua madre era inutile tenersela, un debito, meglio farci moneta. E pure la Tina venduta, non certo per farne moneta, ma arresa a una filosofia di vita che troppo spesso l'ex infermiera aveva notato intorno a sé: come se il futuro fosse già segnato, niente si potesse cambiare, i figli dovessero ripercorrere le orme dei genitori. Un invecchiamento precoce più mentale che fisico, una morte lenta, un'asfissia.

Ne aveva conosciute e ne conosceva di persone che avevano accettato il proprio destino con una scrollata di spalle, come se non potessero fare niente per modificarlo. E molte di costoro pensavano che anche lei fosse di quella pasta, non immaginavano che lei avesse SCELTO di dedicarsi al lavoro e a suo padre, SCELTO di restare zitella.

SCELTO anche di tenersi quel cognome condividendo la SCELTA che a suo tempo aveva fatto il professore quando qualcuno gli aveva fatto presente che, seguendo una certa via burocratica, sarebbe stato possibile cambiarlo.

«Utrum nomina essentialia concreta possint supponere pro persona», aveva risposto il Supposta citando la

Somma Teologica di Tommaso D'Aquino e poi spiegando che in sostanza un nome era solo una piccola cosa, spettava a chi lo portava dargli dignità, quale che fosse.

Quindi, dopo aver guardato per giorni e giorni le persiane chiuse della casa che aveva di fronte e aver ragionato su quanta compagnia le avesse fatto negli anni passati aver visto quelle finestre illuminate, segno che non era proprio così sola al mondo, l'ex infermiera decise di passare all'azione.

DECISE che quella casa meritava un ben diverso destino e che la Tina lo avrebbe condiviso.

In fin dei conti in quel paese mancavano un sacco di cose e, tra le tante, le era sempre sembrato assurdo che una qualunque casalinga per comperarsi un banale strofinaccio o quattro bicchieri da tavola dovesse imbarcarsi in un viaggio verso Menaggio oppure aspettare il mercato, sempre che non piovesse troppo o soffiasse vento.

Un bel negozietto di casalinghi, ecco quello che ci voleva. E magari con un settore dedicato a secchiellini, palette, ciabatte da spiaggia da esporre nel giardinetto durante la stagione estiva.

Piano terra negozio, primo piano casa d'abitazione.

Perché prima o poi la Tina un fidanzato da trasformare in marito l'avrebbe trovato, sempre che non ci fosse già.

238.

Alle diciotto e quindici del 12 agosto il casellante Miagoletti, rendendosi conto all'istante della situazione e non sapendo cos'altro fare, agì senza perdere tempo e dimostrando un criterio che gli sarebbe valso nei giorni a seguire una menzione sul quotidiano locale con tanto di foto: il meccanismo del passaggio a livello infatti non funzionava, sia quello elettrico sia quello manuale non rispondevano. Essendo in arrivo il diretto delle diciotto e trenta da Sondrio, innanzitutto reclutò moglie e figlio e, dotatili di una bandierina rossa, li pose ai due estremi del passaggio onde bloccare il traffico. Solo dopo avvisò del guaio il capostazione il quale mise al corrente la direzione del compartimento, i vigili del fuoco e la caserma dei carabinieri.

Il tempestivo intervento del Miagoletti evitò tragedie. Fu altrettanto tempestivo l'intervento di una pattuglia di tecnici che peraltro dovette lavorare non poco per comprendere dove si nascondesse l'accidente che aveva messo fuori uso entrambi i meccanismi del passaggio a livello, che riprese a funzionare perfettamente la mattina della vigilia di Ferragosto, lasciandosi alle spalle solo un ferito grave nella persona del carabiniere Fantarini.

Mentre i tecnici lavoravano infatti era stato necessario creare una catena di sicurezza che bloccasse il traffico a ogni passaggio di treno. Anche di notte poiché, a orari variabili, passavano treni merci o vagoni passeggeri completamente vuoti in trasferimento. All'operazione erano stati comandati, oltre che lo stesso casellante, i vigili del fuoco, molti dei quali peraltro volontari e quindi con una disponibilità limitata, uomini della polizia ferroviaria e gli stessi carabinieri della caserma bellanese.

Al carabiniere Fantarini, ormai lanciato verso la gara del chioccolo, era toccato un solo turno di guardia, quattro ore a cominciare dalla mezzanotte del 13 agosto. Notte chiara, che s'era però rabbuiata e caricata di umidità. Verso le due e trenta, segnalato dal passaggio di un merci, s'era scatenato un maltempo che aveva scaricato quasi cinquanta millimetri di pioggia e poi se n'era andato altrove spinto da un'aria fresca che aveva intirizzito il Fantarini dentro la divisa fradicia.

Il primo a rendersi conto del risultato era stato il maresciallo Pezzati verso le otto della mattina seguente quando, chiedendo al Fantarini se fosse andato tutto bene, si era reso conto che al giovanotto restava solo il linguaggio dei segni per rispondere poiché la laringe era andata a farsi benedire.

E adesso?, s'era chiesto.

Alle otto e trenta il dottor Lonati era già lì a valutare il malato. Non gli ci era voluto più di un minuto per emettere la diagnosi e consigliare la terapia.

Laringite acuta da una parte, riposo funzionale e cortisone dall'altra: in poche parole il Fantarini doveva stare zitto più che poteva, far riposare le sue corde vocali, il resto l'avrebbe fatto il cortisone.

«Gliene dia tanto», aveva quasi pregato il Pezzati.

«Di cosa?» aveva chiesto il Lonati. «Di cortisone?»

«Proprio.»

«Gli darò la dose massima che si può dare a un essere umano.»

«Non potrebbe fare un po' di più?» aveva insistito il maresciallo.

Era un momento delicato, doveva capirlo.

Il Lonati l'aveva solo guardato, senza far intuire se intendesse cedere o meno all'insolita richiesta.

239.

La Tina si era infiammata all'idea, la Brigida gliel'aveva smorzata, l'aveva spenta con foga, come quando bagnava l'orto dopo tre giorni di arsura.

Un negozio di casalinghi?

Bella idea!

E i soldi necessari a ristrutturare il piano terra, quelli per l'arredamento, quelli per le forniture dove andava a prenderli?

Voleva forse provare a seminare una moneta e poi vedere se crescesse la pianta?

«Con le giuste garanzie, forse potrei avere un prestito», aveva osservato la Tina.

«Mai fatti debiti nella nostra famiglia», era stata la risposta della Brigida.

Coi debiti non sapevi mai come andava a finire.

I passi andavano fatti secondo la gamba.

«Meglio se ti togli dalla testa certe idee», aveva concluso la donna. «Cercati un lavoro piuttosto, qualcuno che alla fine del mese ti paghi e ti permetta di dormire sonni tranquilli.»

«Tua madre ha ragione.»

Fu l'ex infermiera Maria Teresa Supposta a uscirsene con questa affermazione dopo che la Tina la mise al corrente del bel risultato ottenuto dal colloquio con sua madre.

Era la metà pomeriggio del 14 agosto, già le prime foglie di alcune piante di pomodori e zucchine erano ingiallite, l'aria della sera cominciava a profumare di fine estate.

«Ma come?» esplose la Tina.

Se era stata proprio lei a ficcarle in testa quell'idea, a convincerla che poteva essere un'ottima soluzione per il suo futuro?

La Supposta sorrise.

«Ecco come siete voi giovani, così trancianti!»

Se aveva dato ragione a sua madre, spiegò, non voleva dire che dava torto a lei.

«Tua madre ha ragione, dal suo punto di vista. Ma tu, dal tuo, non hai torto.»

Lei, continuò, al pari di sua madre, aveva una vita ormai alle spalle ed entrambe giudicavano secondo l'esperienza che avevano avuto.

«Non giudico quella di tua madre», disse la Maria Teresa.

Per quanto la riguardava, grazie al tempo solitario che aveva avuto per pensare a ciò che aveva fatto nella vita, poteva ritenersi soddisfatta. Checché se ne potesse pensare, aveva liberamente scelto di seguire il genitore, di condividerne la vita e di stare con lui fino alla fine.

«Anche se non me la sento di affermare che sia stata la scelta migliore.»

Avrebbe potuto fare una scelta diversa, darsi un'altra vita, farsi una famiglia eccetera.

«Voglio soltanto dirti che la padrona del tuo destino sei tu. Se pensi che tua madre abbia ragione, nessuno può dire il contrario. Ma se pieghi la testa solo per un sentimento di sciocca obbedienza, allora avrai modo di pentirtene fino a che campi.»

«Ho capito», disse la Tina. «Ma...»

C'era un ma.

Quelle dell'ex infermiera erano belle parole che, come al solito, non andavano d'accordo con la pratica.

I soldi, i debiti...

«Su quello do ragione a tua madre.»
A far debiti non si sapeva mai dove si andava a parare.
«Quindi...» fece per obiettare la Tina.
Ma la Supposta la frenò con un gesto della mano.
«È ovvio che tutto dipende dalla persona con la quale li contrai.»
«Vale a dire?» chiese la ragazza.
«Siediti», la invitò l'ex infermiera, «che ti spiego.»

240.

La mattina del 16 agosto il maresciallo Pezzati salì in caserma dopo aver parcheggiato l'850 di proprietà poco oltre.

Era uscito da casa un quarto d'ora prima per prendere la macchina, dicendo alla moglie, che si stava preparando, che l'avrebbe attesa in strada per poi partire alla volta dell'Isola Comacina, visita che per una ragione o per l'altra era stata rinviata a data da destinare almeno una decina di volte e che quel giorno finalmente sembrava concretizzarsi, stante anche il fatto che il colonnello De Maggiori aveva dovuto rinunciare ad assistere alla gara di chioccolo in programma quel giorno, liberando il maresciallo dall'obbligo di presenza e permettendogli così di assolvere all'impegno preso con la moglie.

Ma le donne, si sa!

Forse la signora stava dando ancora gli ultimi ritocchi al trucco oppure, guardandosi allo specchio per l'ennesima volta, aveva deciso che la camicetta non andava bene oppure... Comunque fosse, vista l'assenza della moglie, aveva parcheggiato ed era salito in caserma il cui comando per quel giorno passava all'appuntato Scevola, al momento assente. Gli aprì il portone il carabiniere Guizzanti e fatti due passi all'interno avvertì calare dall'alto, come una pioggia dorata, i virtuosismi vocali del Fantarini.

Il Guizzanti, anche approfittando del fatto che il comandante era in borghese, né giacca né cravatta, si permise di esprimere un parere succinto.

«Che due coglioni!»
Dalle cinque del mattino il collega non aveva smesso che per qualche minuto.
Inoltre durante la notte non aveva fatto altro che entrare e uscire dalla branda, andare su e giù per le scale della caserma, bere un bicchiere d'acqua dopo l'altro, pisciare ogni mezz'ora e poi tirare lo sciacquone, aprire e chiudere la finestra per guardare fuori...
«Sembra matto», asserì il carabiniere.
«È la tensione prima della gara», lo rassicurò il Pezzati.
«Sarà», fece il carabiniere.
Certo però che se andava avanti così tutto il giorno...
Il maresciallo fece per aprire la bocca e chiamare il Fantarini, spinto dall'idea di consigliargli un po' di cautela onde non rovinarsi la voce.
Lo fermò il campanello del portone cui seguì lo scatto del Guizzanti.
Sulla soglia c'era la moglie del Pezzati.
«Ah, sei qui!»
Il tono era chiaramente da rimprovero.
Il Pezzati, di nuovo, fece per dire qualcosa.
«Vogliamo andare o aspettiamo che sia l'Isola Comacina a venire da noi?» riprese la donna.
Il Pezzati guardò il carabiniere.
«Fa' i miei auguri al Fantarini», disse mentre si avviava.
«Lasci fare, maresciallo», rispose il Guizzanti riflettendo che, stante il tono che aveva avvertito nelle parole della marescialla, un po' di auguri non avrebbero fatto male pure al Pezzati.

241.

«Mio padre ripeteva spesso una cosa», aveva detto l'ex infermiera dopo che la Tina aveva accettato di sedersi e ascoltarla.

Forse era la cosa che, più di ogni altra, le aveva impedito di avere una vita propria, un marito, una famiglia, per dedicarsi a lui.

«Cosa della quale non mi pento, sia ben chiaro, sebbene la maggior parte della gente sia convinta del contrario.»

Diceva che bisogna vivere anche per sé stessi, ma non solo.

«E adesso per me è venuto il momento di mettere in pratica quelle parole, proprio come ha fatto lui per tanti anni», confessò Maria Teresa Supposta.

La maggior parte della sua vita ormai le stava alle spalle.

La Tina aveva avuto una mezza reazione, l'ex infermiera l'aveva fermata.

«No, per favore, evita di dire le sciocchezze che chiunque potrebbe pronunciare in occasioni come questa.»

Anche lei, aveva aggiunto, si augurava di campare il più a lungo possibile ma c'era pure un limite oltre il quale non si poteva andare. E a quel limite lei voleva arrivare sapendo di aver vissuto come doveva e voleva.

Per farlo doveva sistemare solo un paio di cosette.

«Questa villetta, per esempio.»

Una volta morta, visto che non aveva parenti vicini o lontani cui lasciarla…

«E la cosa non mi dispiace affatto.»

... aveva già predisposto che finisse all'amministrazione pubblica in modo da poterla trasformare in una scuola, un asilo, una biblioteca e magari, qualunque fosse il suo destino, dedicata alla memoria del professore suo padre.

«Ma, i soldi?» aveva poi subito chiesto l'ex infermiera.

Lo sapeva la Tina che fine facevano?

Quelli che restavano nascosti, chiusi nei conti correnti, negli investimenti, nelle misteriose azioni e via dicendo quando il loro legittimo proprietario moriva senza avere eredi?

La Tina aveva scrollato le spalle.

Conti correnti, azioni eccetera erano, tanto per lei quanto per sua madre, entità astratte: sapevano che esistevano ma non avevano mai avuto il piacere di conoscersi.

«Te lo dico io. Se nessuno se li prende, se li tiene la banca che non ha certo bisogno di simili regali. Tuttavia è così. In ogni caso la sottoscritta Maria Teresa Supposta non ha intenzione di diventare benefattrice di chi già naviga nell'oro.»

La Tina aveva intuito dove l'ex infermiera stava andando a parare e aveva tentato un'obiezione.

«Aspetta», l'aveva di nuovo zittita.

«Io ho dei soldi in banca», aveva detto.

Non sapeva dire se fossero tanti o pochi, se la si potesse definire ricca o solo benestante. Non era una questione di termini ma di essersi resa conto che, per quanto tempo le restasse ancora da vivere, non sarebbe riuscita a spenderli tutti, a meno di darsi alla pazza vita.

«Cosa che non ho intenzione di fare», aveva aggiunto.

Viveva bene, non le mancava niente e non si faceva mancare niente, eppure quel capitale che aveva in banca grazie a suo padre e a lei, ai risparmi di entrambi, non faceva che aumentare.

Non le restava altro da dire se non giungere alla conclusione di quel discorso.

«I soldi che ti servono per sistemare la casetta del commenda te li do io. Pagherò io le spese di tutto. Me li restituirai poco alla volta, quando potrai.»

La Tina l'aveva guardata senza parlare.

«Non ti fidi di questa vecchia zitella?» aveva chiesto l'ex infermiera.

«No», aveva risposto la Tina.

Non era quello.

Temeva piuttosto che sua madre non avrebbe mai accettato quell'offerta.

Per paura, per orgoglio...

«Ma non l'ho fatta a tua madre l'offerta», aveva ribattuto Maria Teresa Supposta. «L'ho fatta a te.»

La vita era sua, il futuro era suo.

Lei, e lei sola, doveva decidere se accettare o meno.

242.

La sera del 16 agosto, al rientro dalla gita presso l'Isola Comacina, il maresciallo Pezzati trovò ad attenderlo sia l'appuntato Scevola, che per logica d'orario doveva ormai essere fuori servizio, sia il carabiniere Guizzanti.

Era curioso anche lui di sapere come fosse andata la giornata, soprattutto se il Fantarini si fosse distinto nella gara di quella cosa il cui nome continuava a sfuggirgli, ma, come disse: «Non era il caso di formarc un comitato di accoglienza!».

Era il caso invece, si permise di rispondere l'appuntato.

La gara era andata bene, benissimo, il Fantarini aveva vinto.

Anzi, stravinto.

Aveva stracciato tutti, compresi il bergamasco e il bresciano che, obtorto collo, avevano dovuto ammettere che un chioccolatore siffatto e così giovane era un vero fenomeno. Finita la gara, il Fantarini era rimasto per un paio d'ore nello spazio della fiera, godendosi i complimenti degli spettatori, esibendosi a richiesta fino a quando lo stesso Guizzanti, giudicando che fosse il caso di intervenire, l'aveva convinto a smettere e a tornare in caserma.

Seppur lontano dal campo di gara e dai curiosi, però, il Fantarini non aveva cambiato atteggiamento. Agitato, continuava a parlottare, rosso in viso come un gallo, chiedeva da bere e da mangiare ogni dieci minuti.

«Non era il solito», riassunse il Guizzanti.

A un certo punto, non sapendo cosa fare, l'aveva convinto a sdraiarsi per riposare un po' e poi l'aveva chiuso nella camera.

A chiave.

«A chiave?» sbottò il Pezzati.

«A chiave», confermò l'appuntato Scevola.

Dopo averlo chiuso infatti il carabiniere Guizzanti l'aveva chiamato mettendolo al corrente della situazione e chiedendo consiglio.

L'appuntato aveva confermato la necessità della misura cautelare non prima di averla giudicata eccessiva.

«Una volta giunto», spiegò al maresciallo, «ho voluto rimetterlo in libertà.»

Non appena libero però il Fantarini aveva dichiarato di voler uscire per recarsi in piazza Grossi onde proseguire le sue esibizioni canore per attirare a sé merli e fringuelli. Allora anche lo Scevola si era adeguato a una misura di custodia preventiva, al fine di non mettere in ridicolo, prima ancora del Fantarini, l'Arma che rappresentava.

«Ma è impazzito?» chiese il Pezzati.

«È brutto da dire, ma sembra proprio così», fece il Guizzanti.

«Cosa volete che faccia io?» chiese il Pezzati.

Se le cose stavano così, non restava altro che chiamare il dottore.

243.

Giusto tre giorni prima il Lonati era rimasto a corto di sigarette, le adorate Turmac.

Mai successo da quando il Dubbio s'era assunto l'impegno di fornirlo a scadenze regolari, senza necessità di richiesta, conoscendo l'entità del consumo.

Ma, adesso?

Di adeguarsi, di abituare il palato a un altro tipo di tabacco non era nemmeno il caso di parlare.

«Provare a smettere?» aveva proposto la moglie.

La risposta era stata un grugnito.

Per intanto aveva cominciato a centellinare la scorta e un paio di volte era andato ad aspettare il Dubbio di ritorno da Acquaseria.

«E allora?» gli aveva chiesto.

L'Ernesto aveva sempre risposto allargando le braccia e scusandosi a nome del Riffa.

Perché ormai era diventato lui il fornitore ufficiale del dottor Lonati e degli altri clienti che erano stati fedeli al Dubbio.

«Deve ancora prenderci su l'abitudine, calcolare bene i tempi», l'aveva giustificato il Dubbio.

In fin dei conti era da appena un paio di settimane che gli aveva concesso, col permesso della madre, la *Canterina* affinché sbarcasse il lunario, in attesa che al suo orizzonte sorgessero tempi migliori.

Quando, la sera del 16 agosto, il dottor Lonati uscì da casa per rispondere alla chiamata del maresciallo Pezzati, aveva da poco intaccato l'ultimo pacchetto di sigarette e apposta, per risparmiarlo, l'aveva lasciato a casa anziché portarlo con sé com'era solito fare.

Sulla porta della caserma, in attesa che gli venisse aperto, con gesto automatico si infilò una mano in tasca cercando senza trovarlo il contatto con il cartone del pacchetto.

Fu il carabiniere Guizzanti ad aprirgli.

«Buonasera», salutò il Lonati.

«Lei fuma?» chiese dopo che il militare ebbe risposto al saluto.

Sì, il Guizzanti sfumacchiava un po', mica tanto, soprattutto dopo pranzo o dopo aver bevuto un caffè, però...

«Va bene, va bene, ne parliamo dopo», troncò il Lonati. «Adesso andiamo a vedere il malato.»

Il Fantarini non era più sotto chiave, lo teneva d'occhio il Pezzati però, nella stanza dove dormiva con il Guizzanti.

Pure il maresciallo, benché quello non fosse il suo mestiere, una volta entrato nel locale e datagli un'occhiata, aveva intuito che qualcosa non andava per davvero nel Fantarini.

Al Lonati, una volta entrato, e proprio perché quello era il suo mestiere, bastò invece una sola occhiata non solo per capire che avevano fatto bene a chiamarlo ma anche per intuire la ragione di quello stato.

«Qual è il comodino del ragazzo?» chiese, prima ancora di visitare il Fantarini.

Il Pezzati glielo indicò e lo osservò mentre ne perquisiva, sotto lo sguardo del Fantarini che dall'ingresso del Lonati s'era zittito, il contenuto, mostrandogli infine con soddisfazione ciò che aveva trovato.

«Eccolo qua il colpevole», disse lanciando la scatoletta che aveva in mano al maresciallo Pezzati, che la prese al volo, e uno sguardo in tralice al sempre più muto Fantarini.

«Cortiplus», disse il dottore.

Cortisone in pratica, spiegò.

L'aveva dato al Fantarini per decongestionare in fretta le corde vocali e prepararlo alla gara.

«Una compressa al mattino e una nel tardo pomeriggio», spiegò.

Quelle erano state le sue indicazioni.

Nella confezione però c'erano ancora, solo!, tre pastiglie, segno che il Fantarini aveva fatto di testa sua e s'era almeno triplicato la dose.

«Da cui tutto quello che gli è accaduto.»

Aumento della sete e della fame, agitazione, irritabilità, pensieri stravaganti.

«Anche una bella pressione alta», disse dopo che l'ebbe visitato.

«E adesso?» chiese il Pezzati.

«Tranquillo», disse il dottore.

L'Arma non avrebbe avuto perdite. Sempre che, per rimediare al danno, venissero seguite le indicazioni che avrebbe dato senza ulteriori aggiunte personali.

«Garantisco io», fece il Pezzati.

«Mi fido», sorrise il dottor Lonati.

Poi, prima di andare, chiese del carabiniere Guizzanti.

«È malato anche lui?» si informò il maresciallo.

«No. Però so che fuma», rispose il dottore.

E non gli avrebbe certo negato il regalo di una sigaretta, quale che fosse.

244.

Alla fine di agosto la Valeria tornò a casa giusto per litigare con suo padre.

Cioè, litigare non era la priorità ma dovendogli comunicare ciò che aveva in animo di fare, sapeva che non avrebbe potuto finire altrimenti.

Perciò litigò, ma lo fece solo dopo tre giorni dal suo ritorno ad Acquaseria e dopo aver visto e parlato, prima che con altri, con la Tina.

Lo fece il giorno stesso del suo ritorno.

La Tina sapeva che si sarebbero viste e, nonostante fosse già immersa nel progetto di trasformare il piano terra della casa ereditata in negozio, assistita da un consigliere di eccezione nella persona di Maria Teresa Supposta che per conto suo valutava progetti e soppesava preventivi di spesa, per quel giorno riuscì a tralasciare ogni altra cosa, tant'era l'emozione di rivedere l'amica, e conscia di ciò che sapeva.

Era insomma giunto il momento che aveva temuto e atteso, quello di rivelare ciò che aveva scoperto oppure tenerlo per sempre dentro di sé: si immaginava di avere un sasso in mano.

L'avrebbe scagliato contro la Valeria o l'avrebbe buttato nel lago, lasciandolo andare a fondo, come…

Il pensiero di quel corpo, di quel viso tale e quale a quello dell'amica che vagava nell'acqua buia da qualche parte, si nascose dietro quello vero, vivo e vegeto, quando la Valeria, prima ancora di salutarla, la strinse in un abbraccio e poi, con la voce dell'emozione, le disse che c'era una cosa che voleva lei sapesse prima di ogni altra persona.

«Me ne vado da qui.»

La Tina chiuse gli occhi. Le sfrecciò nella mente il pensiero che qualcosa di lei sarebbe comunque rimasto, non avrebbe mai potuto andarsene.

Pensava a quell'immagine, sorrideva e ascoltava la Valeria che raccontava la meraviglia della vita che aveva condotto in quei due mesi, il lavoro che aveva trovato, le possibilità che le venivano offerte.

«Non voglio morire in questo posto.»

Come sua madre, aggiunse, che benché viva sembrava morta da un pezzo.

La Tina pensò che qualcosa di lei era già morto.

Disse invece: «Ma tuo padre?» immaginando che non sarebbe stato d'accordo.

«La vita è mia», fu la risposta della Valeria.

«Preparati alla guerra», ribatté la Tina.

E guerra fu.

Persa in partenza, questo il Vergonese lo capì all'istante.

Sua figlia non era tornata per chiedere permessi ma per comunicare una decisione già presa. A Londra la aspettavano un lavoro, una casa, forse anche un fidanzato figlio di quella terra.

In sostanza un'altra vita.

La Valeria aveva già in tasca il biglietto aereo per il ritorno in Inghilterra.

«E questo albergo, tutto questo, che fine farà?» aveva gridato il Vergonese.

«Forse la fine che si merita», aveva risposto la Valeria con un po' di veleno sulla lingua.

In ogni caso andare avanti a discutere era inutile.

Decidesse lui, gli aveva detto la figlia, se, di lì a tre giorni, quando sarebbe ripartita, voleva dirle arrivederci o addio.

«Arrangiati!» era stata l'indispettita risposta che il padre le aveva dato al momento.

La Valeria già aveva immaginato che avrebbe dovuto arrangiarsi per conto proprio, non desiderava altro in fondo se non prendere in mano le redini della propria vita, e così fece il giorno della partenza.

Alla corriera per raggiungere Como e poi da lì Milano preferì il battello, un congedo più consono alla vita che aveva condotto sino a pochi mesi prima, al paesaggio dentro il quale era cresciuta.

Acquaseria-Bellano-Varenna, poi il diretto per Milano Centrale.

L'accompagnò la Tina, il Dubbio era lì, fresco di divisa che la Canterina aveva lavato e poi stirato la sera prima.

Salutò lui per primo, le due risposero.

Poi la Valeria prese sottobraccio l'amica e abbassò la voce.

«Ma quello non è...»

«Sì, sì, è lui», rispose la Tina troncandole la domanda.

245.

«È lui?» chiese il colonnello De Maggiori squadrando il Fantarini dal basso della sua sedia.

«Sì, è lui», confermò il maresciallo Pezzati.

Era una delle ultime mattine d'agosto e dopo più di un rinvio il colonnello della tenenza di Lecco aveva fatto sapere di essere desideroso di ricevere e conoscere il fenomeno.

«Bravo», disse, alzandosi in piedi.

Poi strinse le mani dietro la schiena.

«Se questioni di cui non fa conto parlare mi hanno impedito di assistere di persona alla tua splendida gara, di cui peraltro ho letto le cronache relative, sono comunque felice che il momento della reciproca conoscenza sia finalmente giunto.»

Col pensiero il maresciallo Pezzati sbuffò. Il De Maggiori s'era preparato un discorso, manco dovesse dare una medaglia al Fantarini.

«Io», stava intanto continuando il colonnello, «sono particolarmente orgoglioso di te, l'Arma lo è. Eccellere nelle cose belle e buone della vita fa parte di quelle qualità che di un carabiniere fanno un ottimo carabiniere. E pur se l'arte che tu pratichi è da pochi conosciuta e da ancora meno apprezzata, ciò non significa che sia minore. Dico bene?»

La domanda, rifletté il Pezzati, era retorica. Del tipo, cioè, che non voleva risposta. Il colonnello però aveva fatto una pausa. Onde evitare imbarazzi il Pezzati fece per rispondere: «Certo!» ma il De Maggiori lo bruciò sul tempo.

«Bene infatti», riprese, «è mantenere in vita, tramandare, evitare che si disperda un patrimonio che fa dell'essere umano una creatura superiore a tutte le altre viventi sulla terra.»

Un quarto d'ora ormai era passato e l'enfasi del colonnello non faceva ben sperare per una rapida fine del pistolotto che s'era preparato e che stava esponendo con evidente soddisfazione oratoria.

Il Pezzati decise di isolarsi in attesa che quello, prima o poi, giungesse alla conclusione e desse spazio al Fantarini e alla sua esibizione.

Perché per quello erano lì.

O, perlomeno, per quello sia il Pezzati sia il Fantarini avevano raggiunto Lecco e stavano adesso in piedi di fronte al comandante di entrambi.

Pure il Fantarini s'era isolato col pensiero, ripassando mentalmente i canti dell'avifauna grazie ai quali il giornalista del quotidiano locale l'aveva definito un «usignolo in divisa».

Il De Maggiori intanto era andato avanti imperterrito.

Aveva citato antenati e tradizioni, l'uomo delle caverne per il quale la caccia era stata fonte di sopravvivenza e l'uomo moderno dentro il quale l'istinto permaneva a dispetto di ogni progresso.

Con un deciso colpo di tosse, che aveva riportato al presente sia il Pezzati sia il Fantarini e che soprattutto annunciava la fine del discorso, chiarì il motivo per cui aveva chiesto di poter incontrare il Fantarini.

Oltre che per conoscerlo, oltre che per elogiarlo, oltre che per incoraggiarlo a non deflettere dalla sua passione, andare avanti invece e sempre più migliorarsi!

Il Pezzati corrugò la fronte, temendo un colpo a sorpresa.

Il Fantarini, pure lui intuendo che qualcosa non stava

andando come previsto, girò appena il viso verso il suo maresciallo.

A quel punto il De Maggiori sparò.

Gli chiedeva di unirsi a lui nelle uscite mattutine della stagione di caccia che stava per cominciare.

A lui, e alla muta di uccelli da richiamo dei quali sarebbe diventato una sorta di trascinatore.

«Il loro comandante!» esplose ridendo il De Maggiori.

Naturalmente non poteva, non voleva essere un ordine.

«Mi rimetto alla tua passione, alla tua buona volontà», concluse il colonnello.

Ed era certo, disse con un luminoso sorriso, che non avrebbe detto no.

246.

La luce della croce di Camaggiore.

Più sotto quella del campanile di Noceno.

Più sotto ancora quella del santuario della...

Madonna santa che fatica si faceva a remare!

Il Riffa non l'avrebbe mai immaginato.

Gli avrebbe fatto comodo un bel motorino, anche quel tre cavalli del cazzo, vecchio come il cucco, che il Dubbio gli aveva dato insieme con la barca.

Purtroppo si era fuso.

Cioè, a dirla tutta, lui l'aveva fuso.

Non aveva voluto tener conto delle raccomandazioni del socio, non spingerlo più di tanto, e dopo due giorni quello aveva detto addio al mondo dei motori.

Non gli erano restati che i remi per andare su e giù per il lago.

Per attraversarlo soprattutto, come stava facendo adesso, a notte fonda, sotto un cielo di fine agosto un po' torbido, con un mezzo carico di sigarette, Turmac, Astor, Muratti eccetera, un po' di vento al traverso che prometteva un bel temporale che avrebbe spazzato via l'estate e tutto quello che era suc...

I pensieri del Riffa, sudato marcio mentre continuava a spingere sui remi, si interruppero bruscamente quando la *Canterina* andò a sbattere contro qualcosa.

Il Riffa si fece di sale, immobile, come in un fermo immagine.

E freddo, nonostante la temperatura fosse ancora gradevole, mentre cercava di immaginare contro cosa la barca fosse andata a sbattere.

Per saperlo non doveva fare altro che ritirare i remi in barca, prendere la torcia, accenderla e dare un'occhiata.

Esatto.

Proprio per quello cassò all'istante l'idea di illuminare il buio dell'acqua lì intorno e, trovando in sé inimmaginabili energie, riprese a remare con vigore.

Qualunque cosa fosse, lasciava ad altri il piacere di scoprirlo.

Perché lui non era il Dubbio, ma Biagio Trùfa Riffa, uno che si faceva i cazzi suoi.

I personaggi di *Viva più che mai*

Alborati – maresciallo dei carabinieri di Menaggio

Amanda – bella ragazza di Tremenico, cliente mancata del Riffa

Ancorati Eugenio – pontilista titolare del molo di Acquaseria

Astrid – ragazza straniera, scrive una lettera

Bellani Giacomo – pittore del Settecento

Bellematti – guardia notturna di Bellano

Bernacchi – proprietario dell'omonima osteria di Dervio

Bernardo – di Tremenico, padre di Amanda, sulle mani ha calli come biglie

Bertazza Mistico – mandriano che mangia le noci col guscio e tutto

Bertone – di Vestreno, operaio al cotonificio di Bellano

Birmino – di Tremenico, fratello di Amanda

Bisanciato Estero – bergamasco, campione di chioccolo

Bologna Biagina – raccoglitrice di oggetti vari sulle rive di Dervio

Bombola – fornitore di cherosene di Bellano

Borrazza Stefano – ex ambulante di Bellano

Bretella Spinetta – segretaria di direzione del cotonificio di Bellano, già catechista del Riffa

Brigida – madre della Tina

Buzzini – medico di Menaggio

Cagli Fedina – aiuto cuciniera dell'asilo di Bellano

Càmola – straccivendolo di Bellano

Carmen – cameriera dell'albergo Alla Ruota che Gira di Acquaseria

Circina – battellotto di Bellano

Colletti Inusina – paziente bellanese del dottor Lonati

Coloniali – droghiere di Bellano

Credindio – mutacico fabbro di Acquaseria

Crispini Fiorentino – maestro di scuola di Bellano negli anni Trenta

D'Argò Virgilio – Primo Seniore,

comandante del presidio della milizia confinaria, un duce in miniatura

Dalamonti Alessio – commendatore a riposo originario di Acquaseria, assistito dalla Tina

Dalamonti Francesca – figlia di Alessio Dalamonti

Dalamonti Vittorio – figlio di Alessio Dalamonti

Dangolo – carabiniere scelto di Menaggio

De Maggiori Agostino Seneca – colonnello dei carabinieri di Lecco

Degregoli – sagrestano di Taceno

Delpasso Mirmino – pretore di Bellano

Dominetti Maria – levatrice consorziale e moglie di Virgilio D'Argò

Eugenio – nuovo postino di Acquaseria: bello, simpatico, gentile, premuroso, ha il ciuffo e fa un po' il cretinetti

Fantarini Augusto – carabiniere di Bellano e chioccolatore esperto

Farfatti – rileva la falegnameria del padre del Dubbio

Finali Guerino, detto Ciurcill – annunciatore seriale di sue (prossime) traversate a nuoto del lago

Firrìa – carabiniere semplice di Menaggio

Fisichetti – ragioniere di banca di Bellano

Franciscia – contrabbandiere caposquadra e magazziniere

Freguzzi – di Tremenico, ambasciatore delle ganassate del Riffa

Girgetta – custode del molo di Bellano

Giubbiani Severino – pensionato di Dervio, pescatore, ha preso l'ultima trota diciotto mesi fa

Giubbiani Vivarina – moglie di Severino

Giuntina – suora direttrice dell'asilo di Bellano

Giustina – di Tremenico, madre di Amanda

Gormetti – barcaiolo di Varenna

Guerriera – superiora delle suore dell'asilo di Bellano

Guizzanti – carabiniere semplice di Bellano

Infantina – zia del Riffa

Inverighi – carabiniere di Menaggio

Laricetti – direttore del cotonificio di Bellano

Limusina – custode del cotonificio di Bellano

Livera Ernesto detto Dubbio – orfano del padre a tredici anni, improbabile contrabbandiere di sigarette e poi... boh!

Lonati – medico di Bellano

Lonati Vittoria – moglie del dottor Lonati

Maccadò Ernesto – maresciallo dei carabinieri di Bellano negli anni Trenta

Maraspini – maresciallo dei carabinieri di Lecco

Marinai – maggiore dei carabinieri di Lecco

Marisa – cameriera dell'albergo Alla Ruota che Gira di Acquaseria

Mellito – brigadiere dei carabinieri di Bellano

Mezzi don Olindo – prevosto di Taceno

Miagoletti – casellante della stazione di Bellano

Moscarini Ermidio – identità usurpata da un ladro di presunte opere d'arte

Nano Gaspare – assicuratore, con una certa aria di superiorità

Oltramonti – vigile urbano di Dervio

Ozio – di Tremenico, fratello di Amanda

Palanzati Wermer – aiuto chirurgo all'ospedale Sant'Anna di Como, metà svizzero tedesco e metà varesotto

Palanzini Gaetano – ex ferroviere della linea Menaggio-Porlezza, vive di espedienti

Pezzati Elvira – moglie del maresciallo Massimino Pezzati

Pezzati Massimino – maresciallo dei carabinieri di Bellano

Pinza Giordano – bagnino tuttofare del lido di Bellagio

Pompista Ciba – meccanico e gommista di Bellano

Pontida Severo – comandante del battello *Nibbio*

Prestoni – taciturno proprietario del caffè dell'Imbarcadero di Bellano

Ravanazzi Oscar – bresciano, campione di chioccolo

Remègola – pescatore di Bellano

Riffa Biagio detto Trùfa o Biagetto – commerciante di scarpe scadenti e gran cacciatore di prede femminili

Riffa Pennica – madre di Biagio, da tempo ricoverata al manicomio di Como

Riffa Sturzio – padre di Biagio, emigrato in Francia per lavoro e poi svanito nel nulla

Riporto Aurelio – pontilista del molo di Bellano

Rispola – cameriera varicosa dell'osteria del Ponte di Bellano

Romanò – vescovo di Como

Rusti – di Avano, operaio al cotonificio di Bellano, cugino di Amanda

Saliva Ivano – pescatore di Bellagio

Sanetti Margherita – ragazza madre

Sbaffi Canterina – madre di Ernesto Livera e cuciniera dell'asilo di Bellano

Scaccola – fratelli fornai di Bellano

Scamozzi Agordo e signora, detti Schedina – vicini di casa di Ernesto Livera, cosiddetti in quanto accaniti giocatori della Sisal

Scevola – appuntato dei carabinieri di Bellano

Scheper Baldemar – notaio di Bellagio

Sciusciòt – barcaiolo di Dervio

Sparagna – brigadiere dei carabinieri di Menaggio

Spaventa – colonnello dei carabinieri del comando provinciale

Speranza – figlia del gestore del crotto dell'Orso: capelli neri e occhi da matta

Spina – di Tremenico, operaio al cotonificio di Bellano, secco come un tisico e cattivo come l'aglio

Stramulo – fornaio di Acquaseria dedito al vino bianco

Supposta Amedeo Modesto – primario ostetrico-ginecologico dell'ospedale Sant'Anna di Como, padre di Maria Teresa

Supposta Maria Teresa – ex infermiera e dirimpettaia del Dalamonti

Tedeschetti Assirto – console, comandante del presidio fascista di Menaggio

Teresa – cameriera dell'albergo Alla Ruota che Gira di Acquaseria

Tina – assistente presso il commendator Dalamonti

Vergonese Alessandro – padre di Valeria, gestore dell'albergo Alla Ruota che Gira di Acquaseria, ex membro della milizia confinaria

Vergonese Valeria – bionda, bella, figlia di Alessandro Vergonese

Viatico – addetto al soccorso stradale di Dervio

Visignola Gerlina – moglie del Vergonese

Visignola Gino – titolare della omonima ditta di cappelli, padre di Gerlina

Visignola Verdella – moglie di Gino e madre di Gerlina

Andrea Vitali

UNA FINESTRA VISTALAGO

Di Arrigoni Giuseppe ce ne sono tanti a Bellano, un paese del lago di Como. Impossibile conoscerli tutti. Anche nella vita di Eraldo Bonomi, operaio tessile del locale cotonificio, ce ne sono troppi. E sarà proprio un Arrigoni Giuseppe a segnare il suo destino, dove brillano l'amore per la bella Elena e la militanza politica nel PSIUP. Il colpo di fulmine per Elena fa del Bonomi un uomo pericoloso, che sfiora segreti, scopre altarini, esuma scheletri sapientemente nascosti negli armadi di una provincia che sembra monotona, in quei paesi dove l'omonimia può essere fonte di equivoci ma anche, a volte, il viatico verso la libertà.

Andrea Vitali

LA SIGNORINA TECLA MANZI

Siamo negli anni Trenta, all'epoca del fascismo più placido e trionfante. Nella stazione dei Carabinieri di Bellano, sotto gli occhi del carabiniere Locatelli (bergamasco), rivaleggiano il brigadiere Mannu (sardo) e l'appuntato Misfatti (siciliano). Un'anziana signora, «piccola, vestita con un cappotto grigio color topo, una borsetta tenuta con due mani all'altezza dello stomaco», vuole a tutti i costi parlare con il maresciallo Maccadò. La donna – anzi, la signorina Tecla Manzi – è venuta a denunciare un furto improbabile: il quadretto con il Sacro Cuore di Gesù che teneva appeso sopra la testata del letto. Inizia così una strana indagine alla ricerca di un oggetto senza valore, che porta alla luce una trama di fratelli scomparsi e ricomparsi, bancari e usurai, gerarchi fascisti e belle donne, preti e contrabbandieri.

Andrea Vitali

LA FIGLIA DEL PODESTÀ

Bellano è in gran subbuglio. Con apposita delibera, Agostino Meccia, l'autorevole podestà della cittadina affacciata sul lago, ha deciso di perseguire un progetto assai moderno e ambizioso: una linea di idrovolanti che collegherà Como, Bellano e Lugano, e darà lustro alla sua amministrazione, attirerà frotte di turisti e farà schiattare d'invidia i comuni limitrofi. Tutto sembra filare liscio, in quel placido e fascistissimo 1931. Anche se c'è un problema: per le casse di un piccolo comune l'investimento sarà enorme, e oltretutto l'idrovolante dovrà essere debitamente collaudato. E poi Renata, la figlia del podestà: fino a ieri era solo una bambina, ora è diventata così strana, non avrà mica qualche nuovo capriccio?

Andrea Vitali

OLIVE COMPRESE

Quattro ragazzi di paese, una banda di «imbecilli», stanno mettendo a soqquadro l'intera Bellano. Naturalmente finiscono subito nel mirino del maresciallo Ernesto Maccadò, che avverte le famiglie gettandole nel panico. A far da controcanto, la sorella di uno di loro: la piccola, pallida, tenera Filzina, segretaria perfetta che nel tempo libero si dedica alle opere di carità: ma anche lei, come altre eroine di Vitali, finirà per stupirci.
Tutto intorno si muove come un coro l'intera cittadina: il prevosto e i carabinieri, il podestà e la sua stranita consorte, la filanda con i suoi dirigenti e gli operai. E la Luigina Piovati, meglio nota come l'Uselànda (ovvero l'ornitologa...); Eufrasia Sofistrà, in grado di leggere il destino suo e quello degli altri; e una vecchina svanita come una nuvoletta, che suona al pianoforte l'*Internazionale* mentre il Duce conquista il suo Impero africano...

Andrea Vitali

LA MODISTA

Nella notte hanno tentato un furto in comune, ma la guardia Firmato Bicicli non ha visto nulla. Invece, quando al gruppetto dei curiosi accorsi davanti al municipio s'avvicina Anna Montani, il maresciallo Accadi la vede, eccome: un vestito di cotonina leggera e lì sotto pienezze e avvallamenti da far venire l'acquolina in bocca. Da quel giorno Bicicli avrà un solo pensiero: acciuffare i ladri che l'hanno messo in ridicolo e che continuano a colpire indisturbati. Anche il maresciallo Accadi, da poco comandante della locale stazione dei carabinieri, da quel momento ha un'idea fissa. Ma intorno alla bella modista e al suo segreto ronzano altri mosconi: per primo Romeo Gargassa, che ha fatto i soldi con il mercato nero durante la guerra e ora continua i suoi loschi traffici; e anche il giovane Eugenio Pochezza, erede della benestante signora Eutrice nonché corrispondente locale della «Provincia».

Andrea Vitali

ALMENO IL CAPPELLO

Ad accogliere i viaggiatori che d'estate sbarcano sul molo di Bellano dal traghetto *Savoia*, c'è solo la scalcagnata fanfara guidata dal maestro Zaccaria Vergottini, prima cornetta e direttore. Un organico di otto elementi che fa sfigurare l'intero paese, anche se nel gruppetto svetta il virtuoso del bombardino, Lindo Nasazzi, fresco vedovo alle prese con la giovane e robusta seconda moglie Noemi. Per dare alla città una banda come si deve ci vuole un uomo di polso, un visionario che sappia però districarsi nelle trame e nelle inerzie della politica e della burocrazia. Un insieme di imprevedibili circostanze può forse portare verso Bellano il ragionier Onorato Geminazzi, che vive sull'altra sponda del lago, a Menaggio, e con lui la speranza di fondare finalmente il Corpo Musicale Bellanese.

Andrea Vitali

GALEOTTO FU IL COLLIER

Lidio Cerevelli è figlio unico di madre vedova. Un bravo ragazzo, finché alla festa organizzata al Circolo della Vela non arriva Helga: bella, disinibita e abbastanza ubriaca. Prima che finisca la cena, sono in riva al lago: una notte indimenticabile. Lirica, la severa madre di Lidio, abile e ricca imprenditrice dell'edilizia, ha vedute molto diverse. Suo figlio deve trovare una moglie «made in Italy», una ragazza come si deve. Ma forse Lidio ha trovato il modo per uscire dalla trappola e realizzare tutti i suoi sogni: durante un sopralluogo per un lavoro di ristrutturazione, in un muro maestro scova un gruzzolo di monete d'oro, nascosto chissà da chi e chissà quando. Sono l'assicurazione per un futuro radioso o l'inizio di un mare di guai?

Andrea Vitali

UN BEL SOGNO D'AMORE

Bellano, febbraio 1973: gira voce che presso il cinema della Casa del Popolo verrà proiettato *Ultimo tango a Parigi*. In paese si scatena una guerra senza frontiere tra gli impazienti che fantasticano sulle vertiginose scene di nudo che ci si aspetta di vedere sullo schermo e coloro che pretendono di evitare una simile depravazione, e snocciolano rosari a raffica. I tempi però sono cambiati e nulla può fermare il «progresso», né intralciare gli affari di Idolo Geppi, gestore del cinema, che ha già provveduto a maggiorare i prezzi dei biglietti. Anche Adelaide, giovane e volitiva operaia del cotonificio, vuole approfittare dell'occasione. Mette con le spalle al muro Alfredo, il fidanzato eternamente indeciso: o la porterà al cinema o lei ci andrà lo stesso, magari con Ernesto, che le ha già messo gli occhi addosso e che a lei non dispiace neanche un po', per quanto sia una testa matta e finirà presto per mettersi nei guai.

Andrea Vitali

QUATTRO SBERLE BENEDETTE

In quel fine ottobre del 1929, a Bellano non succede nulla di che. Ma se potessero, tra le contrade volerebbero sberle, eccome. Se le sventolerebbero a vicenda il brigadiere Efisio Mannu, sardo, e l'appuntato Misfatti, siciliano, che non si possono sopportare e studiano notte e giorno il modo di rovinarsi la vita l'un l'altro. E forse c'è chi, pur col dovuto rispetto, ne mollerebbe almeno una al giovane don Sisto Secchia, il malmostoso coadiutore del parroco arrivato in paese l'anno prima e che sembra un pesce di mare aperto costretto a boccheggiare nell'acqua chiusa e insipida del lago. E poi ci sono sberle più metaforiche, ma non meno sonore, che arrivano in caserma nero su bianco. Sono quelle che qualcuno ha deciso di mettere in rima e spedire in forma anonima ai carabinieri, forse per spingerli a indagare sul fatto che a frequentare ragazze di facili costumi, in quel di Lecco, è persona che a rigore non dovrebbe. D'accordo, ma quale sarebbe il reato? E chi è l'anonimo autore delle missive? Ma, soprattutto, con chi ce l'ha?

Andrea Vitali

BIGLIETTO, SIGNORINA

Alla stazione ferroviaria di Varenna c'è trambusto. È stata beccata una passeggera senza biglietto. E senza un quattrino per pagare la multa. Ma non parla bene l'italiano, e capire cosa vuole è un bel busillis. Ora il capostazione si trova lì, nel suo ufficetto, con davanti Marta Bisovich. Bella, scura di carnagione, capelli corvini, dentatura perfetta, origini forse triestine, esotica e selvatica da togliere il fiato. Siamo nel giugno del 1949, e sul lago di Como, in quel di Bellano, tira un'aria effervescente di novità. Ci sono in ballo le elezioni del nuovo sindaco, e le varie fazioni si stanno organizzando per la sfida nelle urne. Su tutte, la Dc, fresca dei clamorosi successi alle politiche del '48, attraversata ora da lotte intestine orchestrate dall'attuale vicesindaco Amedeo Torelli, che aspira alla massima carica. La bella e conturbante Marta, invece, ha altre aspirazioni. Le basterebbe trovare un posto dove vivere, e questo è il motivo per cui ha deciso di puntare le sue ultime chance sulla ruota di Bellano, dove certe conoscenze non sono nelle condizioni di negarle un aiuto.

Andrea Vitali e Massimo Picozzi

LA RUGA DEL CRETINO

Birce è nata storta. Ha una macchia sulla guancia sinistra e ogni tanto si perde via e dice e fa cose strane. Chi la vuole una così? È l'agosto del 1893 e per lei forse è arrivata l'occasione giusta. Perché una devota, Giuditta Carvasana, è intenzionata a fare del bene, per esempio aiutare una giovane senza futuro. Per Birce non sarebbe cosa da poco, perché la vita non pare riservarle un destino felice. Come a quella povera fioraia di Torino massacrata per strada. Che, a dire il vero, non è la prima vittima.
I corpi sono a disposizione della sala anatomica dell'università torinese, dove il dottor Ottolenghi, assistente del noto alienista Cesare Lombroso, li analizza, convinto che dalla medicina possa venire un aiuto alle indagini. Dalle tasche delle sventurate salta fuori un biglietto con segni matematici. Indicano un collegamento tra quelle morti? E nel mirino dell'omicida può essere finito lo stesso Lombroso, che già aveva ricevuto un analogo foglietto anonimo? Trovare la soluzione non è cosa per cui possa bastare il rigore della scienza.
Forse, fantastica il Lombroso,
lo spiritismo potrebbe dare un contributo.

Andrea Vitali

LE BELLE CECE

Maggio 1936. Con la fine della guerra d'Etiopia nasce l'impero fascista. E Fulvio Semola, segretario bellanese del Partito, non ha intenzione di lasciarsi scappare l'occasione per celebrare degnamente l'evento: un concerto di campane che coinvolge tutti i campanili di chiese e chiesette del comune. Ma l'euforia bellica e l'orgoglio imperiale si stemperano presto in questioni ben più urgenti per le sorti del suo mandato politico. In casa del potente e temutissimo ispettore di produzione del cotonificio locale, Eudilio Malversati, si sta consumando una tragedia. Dopo un'aggressione notturna ai danni dell'ispettore medesimo, spariscono in modo del tutto incomprensibile alcune paia di mutande della signora. Uno è già stato rinvenuto nella tasca della giacca del Malversati. Domanda: chi ce l'ha messo? E perché? Il problema vero, però, è dove potrebbero saltar fuori le altre mettendo in ridicolo i Malversati? Non essendo il caso di coinvolgere i carabinieri, il Semola viene incaricato di risolvere l'enigma. Ma alla svelta, o le campane, questa volta, le suonerà il Malversati, con le sue mani, e saranno rintocchi poco allegri per la carriera del segretario.

Dal catalogo

Garzanti

Andrea Vitali

LA VERITÀ DELLA SUORA STORTA

Sisto Santo ha la manualità e la fantasia giuste del meccanico di rango. Da ragazzo ha riparato perfino una Peugeot 403 senza fare una piega, lasciando a bocca aperta il Scatòn, il suo capo officina, che i diesel manco li conosceva. Però adesso fa il tassista. Si è comprato un Millenove e aspetta i clienti alla stazione ferroviaria di Bellano. Pochi. Arrivano da Sondrio o da Lecco e Milano, e vanno in visita all'ospedale o su al cimitero. Oggi gli è capitato un fattaccio. Una donna arrivata dopopranzo, poco prima che dalla radiolina che tiene in macchina partisse la sigla di *Tutto il calcio minuto per minuto.* Non che fosse importante: ultima giornata; campionato 1970 già bell'e andato al Cagliari, però... Gli ha chiesto di essere portata al cimitero, che non sa nemmeno dov'è. Ma poi, arrivati là, il Sisto si è accorto che la donna era morta. Proprio lì, sul sedile posteriore del Millenove, macchiandolo pure di urina. Un guaio mica da ridere. Da tirare in ballo il maresciallo Riversi. Anche perché la donna è senza borsetta e non si riesce a capire chi sia, né chi stesse cercando al cimitero di Bellano in quel pomeriggio di fine aprile.

Andrea Vitali

LE MELE DI KAFKA

Abramo Ferrascini, quello della ferramenta di Bellano, è un giocatore di bocce imbattibile. È stato tirato su a puntino dal gestore del Circolo dei Lavoratori, Mario Stimolo, e ora ha tutte le carte in regola per vincere le semifinali del Campionato provinciale in programma a Cermenate domenica prossima. Ma c'è un intoppo. Suo cognato, l'Eraldo, quello che vive a Lucerna, sta male. Quarantotto ore gli hanno dato i medici di là, svizzeri, precisi. E adesso la moglie di Abramo, Rosalba, vuole a tutti i costi raggiungere la sorella, ma soprattutto dare all'Eraldo un ultimo saluto, magari un ultimo bacio. Ma ce la faranno ad andare e a tornare in tempo per le semifinali? Dipende. Se l'Eraldo muore entro martedì, mercoledì al massimo, si può fare. Bon, via allora. Un'occhiata al 1100, olio freni gomme; carta d'identità rinnovata all'ultimo minuto; prima tappa il passo del San Bernardino, poi giù dritti fino a Lucerna: basta seguire i cartelli, anche se sono in tedesco, perché il nome di quella città lì si capisce lo stesso.

Finito di stampare nel mese di novembre 2016
presso ELCOGRAF S.p.A. Stabilimento di Cles (TN)